Neagoe Basarab – Princeps Christianus

Studies in Eastern Orthodoxy

Series Editors

René Gothóni

and

Graham Speake

PETER LANG

Oxford · Bern · Berlin · Bruxelles · New York · Wien

Neagoe Basarab – Princeps Christianus

The Semantics of *Christianitas* in Comparison with Erasmus, Luther and Machiavelli (1513–1523)

MIHAI-D. GRIGORE

PETER LANG

Oxford · Bern · Berlin · Bruxelles · New York · Wien

Bibliographic information published by Die Deutsche Nationalbibliothek.

Die Deutsche Nationalbibliothek lists this publication in the Deutsche National-bibliografie; detailed bibliographic data is available on the Internet at http://dnb.d-nb.de.

A catalogue record for this book is available from the British Library.

Library of Congress Cataloging-in-Publication Data

Names: Grigore, Mihai-D., author. | Grigore, Mihai-D. Neagoe Basarab -- Princeps Christianus.

Title: Neagoe Basarab -- Princeps Christianus : the semantics of Christianitas in comparison with Erasmus, Luther and Machiavelli (1513-1523) / Mihai-D. Grigore.

Other titles: Neagoe Basarab -- Princeps Christianus. English

Description: Oxford ; New York : Peter Lang, 2021. | Series: Studies in Eastern Orthodoxy, 2235-1930 ; vol. 6 | Includes bibliographical references and index.

Identifiers: LCCN 2020038374 (print) | LCCN 2020038375 (ebook) | ISBN 9781800790605 (paperback) | ISBN 9781800790612 (ebook) | ISBN 9781800790629 (epub) | ISBN 9781800790636 (mobi)

Subjects: LCSH: Orthodox Eastern Church--Doctrines--History--16th century. | Europe--Church history--16th century. | Neagoe Basarab, Voivode of Wallachia, 1482?-1521. Slova nakazatel'nyia voevody valashskago Ioanna Niegoia k synu Feodosiiu. | Erasmus, Desiderius, -1536.t Institutio principis Christiani. | Luther, Martin, 1483-1546. Von weltlicher Obrigkeit. | Machiavelli, Niccolò, 1469-1527. Principe.

Classification: LCC BX323 .G75 2021 (print) | LCC BX323 (ebook) | DDC 261.709/031--dc23

LC record available at https://lccn.loc.gov/2020038374

LC ebook record available at https://lccn.loc.gov/2020038375

ISBN 978-1-80079-060-5 (print) • ISBN 978-1-80079-061-2 (ePDF)
ISBN 978-1-80079-063-6 (ePub) • ISBN 978-1-80079-062-9 (mobi)

The translation of this work was funded by Geisteswissenschaften International - Translation Funding for Work in the Humanities and Social Sciences from Germany, a joint initiative of the Fritz Thyssen Foundation, the German Federal Foreign Office, the collecting society VG WORT and the Börsenverein des Deutschen Buchhandels (German Publishers & Booksellers Association).

© Peter Lang Group AG 2021

Published by Peter Lang Ltd, International Academic Publishers,
52 St Giles, Oxford, OX1 3LU, United Kingdom
oxford@peterlang.com, www.peterlang.com

Mihai-D. Grigore has asserted his right under the Copyright, Designs and Patents Act, 1988, to be identified as Author of this Work.

This publication has been peer reviewed

To Birgit, my wife, and Sofia, my daughter, with love and gratitude

Contents

Preface

The following study was accepted as a *Habilitation* thesis by the University of Erfurt in 2013. As is always the case with a project of this scope, this book owes a great deal to a number of individuals and institutions to whom I would like to take this opportunity to express my gratitude.

I wish to thank Berndt Hamm, my doctoral adviser at the University of Erlangen, who was the first to believe in this idea. I wish also to thank Vasilios N. Makrides for the energy, skill and dynamism with which he accompanied me throughout the *Habilitation* process, and for accepting this book into the series in which it was originally published, the *Erfurter Studien zur Kulturgeschichte des Orthodoxen Christentums*. Thanks are due to the readers of this second dissertation, Alexander Thumfart and Wolfgang Dahmen. I am grateful to Wolfgang Reinhard, Hans Joas, Hans Kippenberg and Michael Borgolte, with whom I spent two inspiring years at the *Max-Weber-Kolleg* – two years that exerted a decisive influence on my research project. I would like to thank Hans G. Ulrich of the University of Erlangen for enriching conversations on political ethics. Nor should I forget the crucial part played by Nikos Panou of Stony Brook University in developing the chapter on Neagoe Basarab. Thanks are due to Patrick J. Geary of the Institute of Advanced Study, Princeton, for his kindness in facilitating contacts with historians of south-eastern Europe.

The generous support I enjoyed was not only personal in nature, but also institutional. Foundations were laid during my time at the Max-Weber-Kolleg in Erfurt, where I benefited from enormously productive exchanges with my colleagues. The University of Erfurt subsequently supported me with a Christoph Martin Wieland Fellowship. I would particularly like to thank the Center for Hellenic Studies at Princeton University, and especially its executive director Dimitri Gondicas, for having placed at my disposal the Center's excellent infrastructure for both research and networking. My time there as Stanley Seeger Visiting Fellow contributed decisively to the completion of this book's key section, that on Neagoe Basarab. Above all, however, I wish to thank the Leibniz Institute of European History in Mainz, and particularly Irene Dingel, the director of the Department of Religious History, for providing such an inspiring environment in which to continue my research on the history of Christianity in south-eastern Europe.

I would not have been able to bring this undertaking to a successful conclusion had it not been for the indispensable and indefatigable efforts of my proofreaders. My deepest gratitude thus goes to my wife, Birgit Grigore, my Erlangen friend of many years, Johannes Frey, and to Saskia Steinbeck of the Leibniz Institute of European History.

Mainz, May 2015
Mihai-D. Grigore

Preface to the English Edition

It is a great pleasure to see one's book appear in English with a major publisher. For this to come to pass has required much hard work on the part of several excellent professionals, whom I would like to take this opportunity to thank.

My thanks are due above all to Hermann Ühlein, my German editor at Peter Lang. Not only did he have a decisive role to play in the publication of this book's original German edition, but he was also instrumental in launching its successful entry for a translation grant from the association of the German book trade – the *Börsenverein des Deutschen Buchhandels* – for whose support I am most grateful. I wish to thank Graham Speake and René Gothóni for kindly accepting this monograph as part of the Studies in Eastern Orthodoxy series. Dr Speake also offered his generous and expert guidance in seeing this translation through its various stages. Lucy Melville, Publishing Director at Peter Lang Oxford, was crucial to this book's successful production. Meanwhile, the Leibniz Institute of European History in Mainz provided me with the infrastructure necessary to complete this project. I am particularly grateful to Irene Dingel, the director of the Institute.

Special credit is due to the efforts of Joe Paul Kroll, who succeeded admirably in translating some extremely difficult – not to say hermetic – theoretical, theological, patristic and philosophical arguments into English while not letting himself be confounded by the complexities of south-east European history. It has been a pleasure working with him, and I am grateful for his kindness, diligence and cooperation as well as his expertise.

I wish to express my warmest thanks to all the above and to many others whom I have not mentioned by name – and to all in the certainty that this important achievement in my academic life would not have been possible without them.

Mihai-D. Grigore
Mainz, October 6, 2020

CHAPTER I

Introduction: Beyond Concepts

This project's hermeneutic contribution consists not in demonstrating how atomised – in a deconstructive sense – are such blanket terms as 'Christianity', '*Christianitas*', 'Protestantism', 'Orthodoxy' and the like. Its challenge rather consists in explaining how manifold plurality in Europe might sometimes nonetheless allow surprising instances of parallelism or simultaneity to emerge or persist. Within the framework of a distinct 'European history of religions' (as opposed to a 'history of religions in Europe'),[1] the present study seeks to examine how differences are formed and emphases overlap within a particular semantic field of European Christianity, and how its particularities and specificities emerge.

On the one hand, Friedrich Wilhelm Graf[2] has already called attention to the fact there are no such things as religions – in an essentialist understanding of that term – or even denominations. What we are faced with are rather local or regional configurations of accents, emphases, peculiarities, influences, hybrids and processes of transfer and communication, which must be considered and understood in their diversity and complexity. Such a diagnosis applies to virtually any religious form found in Europe, irrespective of era or place. On the other hand, we are aware of the presence of concepts that likewise exerted an influence over European cultures across time and space. They still do so, for Europe has always been in possession of a so-called 'political language' by which complex communication and the understanding of historical events were mediated or which even determined them.[3]

1   Rüpke 2009. See also Davie 2002: 2.
2   Graf 2004.
3   Kosuch 2011: 30f.

What I am concerned with above all are those mechanisms which, in terms of the study of religion, can be regarded as forms of the emergence and efficiency of norms in the political theology of the early sixteenth century. An instance of this process can be found in *Christianitas*, the idea of the Christian faith of the European peoples, which conferred something of a shared sense of identity on pre-modern Europe. Notwithstanding all due caution against generalisations, the integrative and normative power of this concept simply cannot be ignored. But what does *Christianitas* actually mean?

Though it is ubiquitous in early modern Europe, the term '*Christianitas*' seems strangely elusive. That discussion surrounding it might be approached from three different angles testifies to the fact that this syntagma is far from being self-explanatory. Attempts to address it out of context soon meet with insurmountable obstacles; further points of reference are needed.

First, *Christianitas* can be considered as a geopolitical dimension, to the extent that Europe is regarded (often from outside)[4] as the one continent that was historically largely Christian.[5] As an idea, 'Europe' was associated with the continent's progressive Christianisation, a process today discussed as the 'making of Europe', in which Christianisation is understood as a form of political consolidation.[6]

> The development of Christendom consisted of more than the spread of a new religion. Numerous scholars have pointed out that the ninth to the eleventh or twelfth centuries was the period of the 'birth of Europe': the political units that took shape then continued with some variations to become Europe as we know it.[7]

Accordingly, *Europa Christiana* was used to denote a unity of faith and largely also of (political) culture[8] whose geographical frontiers, though contested, were fairly well defined.

The Ebstorf Map, a fourteenth-century *mappa mundi*, depicts Europe as a continent whose civilisation is ordered and unified by roads and cities

4   Lepsius 2004: 3.
5   Grigore 2019.
6   Berend 2007: 1f. and 6. See also Mitterauer 2004: 152ff.
7   Berend 2007: 9.
8   Fuchs/Trakulhun 2003: 8f.

and which is situated on the right hand of the risen Christ.[9] *Christianitas* long served the traditions of Europe as a medium of communication founded on shared values; as such, it symbolically and declaratively placed Europe on the world stage as a whole.[10] There was then – as there is now – a discourse of 'European values', of the 'cultural values of Europe', of 'Europe's cultural and intellectual roots'.[11]

Given the absence or indeed impossibility of a 'value-neutral concept of Europe', it seems not at all far-fetched to consider 'Europe' first of all as a 'historical idea'.[12] St Augustine and the entire tradition inaugurated by him considered Europe to be an *oikumene* bounded in the East by the river Don. Contemporaries in the Middle Ages and early modern period saw this boundary as separating not only Europe and Asia, but also the world of Christian faith from that of the infidel or heathen.[13] In the account of his voyage to meet the Mongol khan, the Franciscan Wilhelm von Rubruk (d. 1270) wrote of the Christian world ending at the Tanaïs (Don).

On the other hand, Europeans of the early modern age became increasingly aware of their continent's geographically small stature. Against the background of this realisation, Christian Europe came to think of itself as having an eschatological destiny for the benefit of the wider world. Steadily, we find late medieval authors referring to the mission of the 'Europeans' to Christianise the world.[14]

This reflects an increasing awareness that *Europa Christiana* was no longer as self-evident as it had been at the time of the Crusades. Europe now faced multiple threats, from the Tatars and Ottomans as well as from internecine religious conflict. Multiple levels of perception began to open up. People had to come to terms with the idea that, for instance, Christian cultures persisted under the non-Christian rule of the Ottomans, which meant that the idea of a unified *Europa Christiana* was consigned to the past. Among the conceptions of *Europa Christiana* that sought to

9   Wolter-von dem Knesebeck 2013.
10 Wagner 2006.
11 Reale 2004; Joas/Wiegandt 2005; Seibt 2005.
12 Borgolte 2001: 17.
13 Klueting 2007: 17.
14 Kochanek 2004: 437f. and 442.

accommodate this reality under the impression of the perpetual Ottoman threat was locating the European boundary at the lower Danube, where so-called 'free Christendom' was now said to begin. The notion of the Danubian Principalities as the 'gateway to Christendom' has remained influential in European historiography to this day.[15]

Yet *Christianitas* may also be understood as having – secondly – an anthropological frame of reference in human beings themselves. *Christianitas* thus appears as a horizon for action that is both existential and practical, a way of life that is proposed to and indeed expected of adherents of the Christian faith. At issue is the conformity of individuals, but also of communities, to a canon of virtues and attitudes going back to the person of Christ, the archetype of the Christian 'new man'. The task is to make Christ present among human beings repeatedly and at all times, to instantiate and perpetuate Him in His historicity. Moreover, how else to do so but in the improved humanity of the God-man, the imitation of whom is the task of all human beings? The Christian – to amplify an idea of Martin Luther – is Christ Himself, Christ-like or indeed equal to Christ, a *Christomimetes*, a *Homoousios*.

This second complex of *Christianitas* contains a third, namely its anthropological and political reference with its strong ethical implications, in which the above-mentioned instantiation of Christ is brought to bear specifically in political life. The Christian state conceives of itself as a concentric entity built around the archetype of Christ, who on the one hand is active and effective in a generalised form in each political subject. On the other hand, Christ is imagined as ruling among human beings in intensified presence and guiding their destiny in the shape of the Christian ruler. It is from this third aspect that my study takes its cue.

The present book is structured around the comparison of four well-known 'how-to books' or 'mirrors for princes'[16] published in continental

15 Kührer 2011.
16 'A mirror for princes [*Fürstenspiegel*] is a self-contained work giving as complete a discussion as possible of the right conduct of the ruler in light of his special position. Its purpose is to offer instruction in basic knowledge or to exhort the ruler, to whom the author mostly stands in some kind of personal relationship' (Herbert Hunger apud Blum 1981: 31). Moreover: 'A mirror for princes is a disquisition, composed with parenetic intent, and addressed to a king, prince or regent personally

Europe in the early sixteenth century: *The Teachings of Neagoe Basarab to His Son Theodosius* (c. 1520), Erasmus of Rotterdam's *Institutio Principis Christiani* (*The Education of a Christian Prince*, 1516), Martin Luther's *Von weltlicher Obrigkeit* (*On Secular Authority*, 1523) and finally *Il Principe* (*The Prince*, 1513) by Niccolò Machiavelli. The point of common reference here is the normative concept of the *Princeps Christianus*, that is to say, how each author imagines the ruler to relate to Christ. To be a 'Christian ruler' derives its justification, legitimacy and purpose from the ruler's quality of being able to re-present[17] Christ Himself, time and again to make Him actively present in the state.

The idea of comparing Basarab's mirror for princes with those of Erasmus or Machiavelli is not a new one.[18] Dan Zamfirescu, the Slavist and Basarab scholar, is only one Romanian voice to have expressed such a desideratum, but it has so far remained unfulfilled. Scholarship was caught in endless debates on textual criticism or linguistics, or – worse still – gradually lost interest in Basarab as a character supposedly 'over-studied' in his native Romania. The volume produced to mark the 500th anniversary of Basarab's coronation as ruler of Wallachia,[19] published by the Romanian Orthodox Patriarchate from a sense of somewhat reluctant obligation to the prince it canonised in 2008,[20] had a laughably small print run and

---

or to a (fictitious) dignitary as representative of a social group. It must be written as a freestanding work or as part of a larger conception' (Anton 2006: 3; see also Eberhardt 1977: 280f.). The generic title is taken from the syntagma 'speculum principis' by Godfrey of Viterbo (d. between 1192 and 1202) (Eberhardt 1977: 5). The important criterion of the adviser's personal bond with the advisee leads Herbert Hunger to distinguish between encomia and mirrors of princes, with the former lacking such a tie (see Hunger 1978: 157).

17 Not, I should take this opportunity to stress, in the sense of being His deputy, but of 'reproducing' Christ Himself.

18 In western Europe, too, recent studies have compared Erasmus and Machiavelli in terms of their views on the ruler and rule. One of the most recent of these studies is Lehmkuhl 2008.

19 Câdă 2012.

20 Neaogoe Basarab was canonised by the Holy Synod of the Romanian Orthodox Church at its meeting on 8–9 July 2008; his feast day is celebrated on 26 September. Basarab's canonisation continues a long tradition in the Eastern Church of so-called 'political saints', beginning with Constantine the Great. The term 'political

was not free of clerical and hagiographic bias. A comprehensive analysis of the content of Basarab's work is still outstanding, not to speak of a comparative perspective that would consider Basarab as a participant in a pan-European discourse and debate on normative Christian references in the exercise of power.

Against the background of a general discussion that rightly seeks to prevent the reification of *Europa Christiana* by emphasising the regional, confessional and religious diversity of 'Christendom' past and present, this study attempts a new approach. My inclusion of Basarab assumes that *Christianitas* may nonetheless be sustained as a geopolitical term as long as it is considered in its plurality, its polyvalence, and is understood as a mesh of interrelated phenomena. From this it follows that to speak of *Europa Christiana* would make no sense if the continent's south-eastern, Orthodox[21] part was to be excluded.[22] That part is to be thought of as in no way exotic, new, different, fascinating, special or even peculiar, but rather *is* Europe and ought as a matter of course to be treated as belonging to the European whole.[23]

The example of Basarab's mirror for princes testifies to the fact that the traditions of south-eastern Europe are not so different at all in their history, their religious discourses and the history of their Churches. Basarab

---

saints' refers to rulers or political dignitaries canonised in recognition of services to their respective official churches. The canonised princes of Romanian Orthodoxy are Stephen the Great (1457–1504), Constantin Brâncoveanu (1688–1714), both canonised in 1992, and Neagoe Basarab (1512–1521). On the phenomenology of the 'political saints' in the Eastern Churches see Graupner 2009: 35ff. and 40f.

21   As I use it here, the term 'Orthodoxy' denotes a Church standing in dogmatic, institutional and jurisdictional union with the first seven so-called Ecumenical Councils, held between 325 and 787, and with the Patriarchates of Alexandria, Antioch, Jerusalem, Constantinople and Rome (until the schism of 1054). It is this Church that is known as the 'Eastern' or 'Orthodox' Church, as distinct from the so-called oriental Churches, which do not recognise all of the seven Ecumenical Councils.

22   Since the 1940s, the study of south-eastern Europe has thought of itself as being part of the history of Europe as a whole: what happens in south-eastern Europe happens in Europe (see Clewing/Schmitt 2011: 13).

23   Sutton/van den Bercken 2003.

also shows that Orthodox Christianity was preoccupied with the same theological and political issues as the rest of Europe and participated in and responded to these debates. Far from representing 'the other' Europe, it was every bit as European as, say, its Catholic, Lutheran or Calvinist traditions. To borrow a pointed question from Vasilios N. Makrides: 'Is Orthodox Eastern and South Eastern Europe so different from the Latin West that it needs to be examined on its own, separately?'[24]

Considering 'modernity' not as a historical caesura or epoch within a linear conception of time, but rather in its etymological relationship with the Latin *modus*, opens up an understanding of modernity as a manner of being of one's time. To do so changes the terms of the discussion and helps to realise that every era in the history of the world was somehow and at its time 'modern' itself. Such 'modernity' is to be imagined not as a radical break, but rather as a continuing process of bringing human ways of life up to date.[25]

Bearing this in mind, a study of Prince Basarab offers a twofold approach to Wallachian modernity or, to be more precise, Wallachian proto-modernity. On the one hand, Basarab and his mirror for princes fit squarely into a European trend that uses the form of the *specula principum* to scrutinise the syntagma *Princeps Christianus*. On the other hand, Basarab's reign is when the first signs of a Wallachian 'proto-modernity' – this time indeed understood chronologically – are discernible. The key factors here are a distinct 'internalisation of rule' and the regulatory use of a variety of measures and procedures in the practice of rule. There certainly are peculiarities to this 'modernity', for instance the absence of secularisation,[26] which suggest that we would do well to keep in mind Shmuel N. Eisenstadt's idea of 'multiple modernities'.[27]

Careful readers will have noticed that this comparison is framed as a synchronous look[28] at the 'career' of a normative term in the history of

---

24 Makrides 2010: 193; Kaser 2002: 23 claims that there was no such thing as south-east European history *stricto sensu*, but only 'European history in south-eastern Europe'.

25 Makrides 2011: 16.

26 Grigore 2012d.

27 Eisenstadt 2003.

28 Jörn Rüsen's term 'synchronous comparison' (Rüsen 1998: 59ff.).

European Christianity – the term '*Princeps Christianus*'. The chronology of this account is of secondary importance to the extent that the authors considered here did not know each other, the exception being Erasmus and Luther. This study is conceived as a cross-section through the history of Christian discourses at the European level. For this purpose, I have chosen, as it were, four snapshots – four works of the same genre that were written independently of each other within ten years. They are representative because of their confessional connotations of south-east European Orthodoxy, (humanist) Catholicism and Lutheran Protestantism respectively.

The hermeneutic interest in the comparison lies in the limits against which key concepts run up as well as in the historical determination of religious discourses, as seen from the perspective of the study of religion. What happens to the discourse dynamics when Basarab, Erasmus or Luther speaks of the 'Christian prince', but their meanings diverge to varying degrees? How are analogue conclusions possible under conditions of mutual ignorance? At stake here is the key question of the diffusion of religious ideas throughout history, which from shared sources (Holy Scriptures, the Church Fathers, classical and Hellenistic authors) draw different conclusions, while also displaying some remarkable instances of agreement. Accordingly, the present study also considers the author's historical milieu or the textual history of each particular work.

Another question observant readers might ask is why a comparison should be made with Machiavelli, an author who may well be described as indifferent to Christianity. Yet the answer is already contained in the question: if we are to reach an understanding of the norms and duties imposed by early modern European cultures, it is crucial to observe how the decisive realm of politics becomes uncoupled from Christian theology, how political discourse becomes indifferent to Christianity and how new lines of epistemic and theoretical argumentation come to be articulated. The choice of Machiavelli was guided by the following question: what is it that causes the theoretical potential of Christian political theology to become exhausted and causes the Florentine *segredario* to take a different turn? And why did this occur in the sixteenth century, thoroughly religious as it was?

The crucial part here is played not by the 'rationalisation of Christian theology' of which Rodney Stark has spoken. According to Stark, reason had been thought of as God's most important gift to man, allowing the latter to explore Creation and put it to his own use. This was supposedly the precondition of (technological and economic) progress.[29]

My argument, on the other hand, is that Christian theology, which in spite of the space it gave to reason was still preoccupied with matters transcendent and otherworldly, did not *per se* prepare the ground for the early modern idea of progress. The preconditions of the early modern renewal were rather the sensualisation of religion,[30] the incorporation of human experience and sensory observation and the development of methods for deriving knowledge from immanence and applying that knowledge to the calculation and prediction of the future. In Machiavelli's case, we can observe the attempt to develop a method by which the history of the world and the future of humankind were to be shaped. His example is indispensable to tracing this transition and the concomitant 'scientisation' of political discourse.

Methodologically speaking, the four mirrors for princes discussed here are objects of a 'thick description' in which the texts and their contexts are examined with regard to the semantic dimension of the concept of the *Princeps Christianus*. Of course, this process will also draw upon secondary sources – correspondences, chronicles, accounts or *vitae* – to ensure that the analysis remains 'grounded' in history. It would barely be possible to conceive of a history of ideas that could dispense with a consideration of the intellectual contexts in which ideas live and function. Historical events are reflected in theories, and theories in their turn may make history.[31] Accordingly, this study is not intended solely as a contribution to theory formation and hence does not draw exclusively on theoretical writings.[32] How these authors are rooted in the microhistory of their surroundings is of crucial importance to the analysis of their works.[33]

---

29 Stark 2005: Xff.
30 Boer/Göttler 2013.
31 Kosuch 2011: 28f.
32 Kosuch 2011: 33.
33 On 'microhistory' and 'micropolitics', see Wolfgang Reinhard's writings on the topic, esp. Reinhard 2005 and Reinhard 2009.

I decided on a descriptive, cultural-historical[34] comparison of four contemporaneous works on a single theme, in the expectation that the comparative method would turn out to be fruitful if trans-regional discourses and problems were traced.[35] Although wherever possible I avoid passing judgement on the authors, methods and viewpoints examined here, I do try, in the last chapter, to use the concept of the 'Christian ruler' in order to present the semantics of *Christianitas* as a complex and lively dimension in which to the observe how political, theological, anthropological and biographical aspects are historically interwoven in Europe.

> Every comparison needs an organising parameter. Before looking at the materials in which historical thought manifests itself (texts, oral traditions, images, rituals, monuments, memorials etc.) it is necessary to know what are the facts of the matter that are to be examined in the first place.[36]

In the present study, accordingly, the comparison is structured around the syntagma or even the concept *Princeps Christianus*, as it is used in the literary genre of mirrors for princes in the early sixteenth century or, to be precise, the years 1513 to 1523.[37]

34　I here draw upon Reinhard Blänkner's definition of cultural history as an 'approach that subjects the cultural preconditions and implications of human thought and action to historical examination' (Blänkner 2005: 72; see also ibid. 74, n. 14). A cultural history specifically of the political would 'thus claim to integrate the perspectives of micro- and macrohistory, to mediate between structure and semantics [...]' (Stollberg-Rillinger 2005: 21).

35　Espagne 2013: 37.

36　Rüsen 1998: 40.

37　It is worth pointing out here that this is only one of the many comparisons possible. Basarab's mirror for princes is a fount of ideas that is far from having been fully explored in its variety. They range from diplomacy and the study of legations to military and strategic instructions, from patronage for the arts to broad social welfare, from the selection of officials and advisers to the foundations of political advice itself. It would thus remain for other studies to draw such comparisons, for example, between Machiavelli's *Art of War* (*Dell'Arte della Guerra*) and the corresponding chapters of Basarab's. The *Art of War* was composed in 1519–1520 and thus at the very same time as Basarab's teachings.

If one decides to pursue a comparative approach, one should do so in the awareness that this is a demanding one indeed,[38] and one that comes with certain dangers.[39] The objects of comparison are isolated from the complex context of their development and posited as singular, valid bearers of a general principle.[40] Consciously or unconsciously, the claim to examine entire phenomena in their complex and interwoven totality is abandoned in favour of 'surgical' yet effectively mutilating operations such as 'selection, abstraction, and detachment from context'.[41] Yet this objectification of the points of comparison nonetheless offers an insight into the plausibility of comparison as a method of scholarship in cultural history. For it is indeed the case that

> values, norms and symbols receive their contours only by being situated in the context of social practices, their bearers and the conditions under which the latter act. Comparing them reveals information on the historical reality of particular societies. Historical comparison of cultural interpretations of patterns of action thus virtually challenges us to take seriously culture's dependence on context and to explore the possible connections between cultural and social history.[42]

If we abandon comparison in the mode of the social sciences, which seeks to find confirmation of general principles, in favour of historical comparison – to adopt Patrick Geary's polarity – this choice is in favour of the thick description of a cultural context. At issue here is a comparison within a cultural sphere – 'European *Christianitas*'– and thus an approach to considering closely related and situated occurrences and discourses. We are in the realm of that 'comparison between similar things' which demands that we forgo generalisations:

---

38 Haupt/Kocka 1996: 24.

39 Not to mention that a nationally oriented method of comparison was an instrument of choice for nineteenth-century western European historiography to establish, in an altogether Eurocentric and colonialist manner, a hierarchy of nations, civilisations and cultures (Liakos 2013: 337).

40 Geary 2001: 30f.

41 Haupt/Kocka 1996: 23; Geary 2001: 31.

42 Haupt/Kocka 1996: 39.

> By comparing similar things of recognizably shared origins and by emphasizing their
> subtle differences, we can reach a more refined understanding not only of differ-
> ences and similarities, but also of the historical circumstances that produced them.[43]

Such a comparison helps scholars above all to see the objects of comparison in their nuanced and differentiated complexity and thus to open
their eyes to the potential inherent in complex phenomena. Patrick Geary
aptly distinguishes between the heuristic and open comparison, on the
one hand, and that intended to prove a point or serve as an example, on
the other.[44]

The latter kind of comparison tends to be particularly encouraged by
similar cultural contexts. Jörn Rüsen has warned historians that intercultural
comparisons were in danger of examining 'exotic' cultures only from our
perspective. This means applying our own concepts and meanings to other
cultures, though these ascriptions are alien and only hamper communication.[45] The present analysis has thus set itself the task of focusing on a
Christian, European cultural compass centred on shared cultural reference
points, for instance on the Holy Scriptures, the Church Fathers and the
authors of Greek and Roman antiquity. In this cultural sphere, to produce
advisory literature for rulers in the form of mirrors for princes had already
been customary for centuries during the period studied here.

'Cultures can and should be [however] compared also with regard to
the fundamental ideas that define the form and content of reality and of
human self-understanding.'[46] All the cultures I consider here are European
and part of a common history, and here we find them at the beginning of
the sixteenth century asking urgent questions about the authenticity of the
Christian ruler. This schematic description of the material under consideration here does not preclude difference, specificity and nuance. On the
contrary, observing and describing them are central to this study, which
incorporates them and traces their concurrence in overarching concepts like
Europe, *Christianitas* and *Princeps Christianus*. The theoretical assumption,

---

43   Geary 2001: 33.
44   Geary 2001: 38. See also Espagne 2013: 39.
45   Rüsen 1998: 40ff.
46   Rüsen 1998: 47.

here methodically developed in the sense of a history of entanglement (Verflechtungsgeschichte),[47] is that there are no such things as closed cultures or cultural spheres, but rather dimensions of interdependence, communication, mobility, exchange, transfer, semantics.

I draw support from the fact that the four authors, though they may not have known one another, referred to more or less the same set of events, personages or ideas – for instance wars (of religion), Pope Leo X, the religious status of secular authority, etc. – and interpreted them in ways that sometimes diverge and sometimes overlap. If I may be permitted to appropriate the terminology of Claude Lévi-Strauss and Niklas Luhmann, we are confronted with a manifold *bricolage* of structures and forms that are subjected to semantic processing. Such interrelatedness stands in the way of clear boundaries and identifications. Though borders seem to recede under scrutiny, the sources do speak in terms of 'us' and 'the others', of 'Christians' and 'non-Christians' or indeed 'infidels', and inasmuch as they do so, no serious exegesis can afford to ignore these constructions as they are. As long as the sources give an insight into the history of so-called 'big traditions', those traditions may be said, in a certain sense, *to be*. The final chapter will consider the manner in which history is thus depicted, moulded, symbolised and interpreted.

I have tried to make this book's structure as intuitive as possible. Each one of its four parts examines a single author, and these strands are then tied together in a concluding chapter. Each section is divided broadly into a biographical and historical part, a part concerned with the history of texts and the critique of sources, and finally an analytical part. The main focus of this comparison, however, is on Neagoe Basarab, who is largely unknown, though his importance is considerable. The section devoted to the Prince of Wallachia (1512–1521) opens this study and is approximately three times the length of the sections on Erasmus, Luther or Machiavelli.

The reason for this emphasis is that the only extant research of any note on Basarab is in Romanian, Russian, Bulgarian and modern Greek, and addresses problems and events of which there is little awareness in Western scholarship and which thus require detailed explanation. Moreover,

47 Werner/Zimmermann 2002; Kaelble 2003; Schäbler 2007.

Basarab's mirror for princes is simply far longer than those of his better-known contemporaries. It is also worth remembering that of the four authors who write of the (Christian) prince and how he is to behave and rule, only Basarab was himself a prince. Experience, which Machiavelli extolled as an essential epistemic category, is a quality that Basarab possessed in a form that sheds entirely new light on the Florentine's much-vaunted 'realism' and 'pragmatism'. Seen from that perspective, the present study may be seen as something of an exercise in popularisation,[48] all the more so for having been completed in 2012, the year in which the 500th anniversary of Basarab's accession to the throne was celebrated.

I shall leave it to the conclusion to provide a theoretical underpinning for my analytical instrument, the 'semantics of *Christianitas*', which will follow from the theoretical discussion of the insights gained in the preceding chapters. Some of the central terms used in this study nonetheless warrant a brief definition beforehand.

Politics, the political, public sphere. The concept of the 'political' to which this study refers is founded on the fact of common human existence and the forms of association that it engenders. These forms enable institutionalisation, semanticisation, agency, symbolisation, organisation and, finally, the existence of a public sphere, all of which are dimensions of the political. The political thus appears as the framework of the public sphere that forms human existence. Human existence takes place and is fulfilled as shared public existence[49] – not by individuals, but by persons.

In the Christian cultures of early (as opposed to late) modern Europe, the public sphere as the medium of political discourse was subjected to norms rather than being a free or neutral space in which actions, values,

---

48 'Popularisation', that is, in the sense of 'making familiar', of introducing a historical character to the audience. One of my study's key aims is to reject the notorious 'protochronism' of the Ceauşescu era, a school of Romanian history that sought to portray events in Romanian national history as having prefigured key events in the history of Europe. For instance, the uprising of the Transylvanian peasants under Horea, Cloşca and Crişan (1784) was interpreted as having anticipated the French revolution. By the same token Paul Anghel considers the *Teachings* to be the better political treatise, richer in ideas, than Machiavelli's *Prince* (see Boia 2003:97; I am grateful to Wolfgang Dahmen for pointing this out to me).

49 Leidhold 2000: 437f.

norms, rules and procedures might be negotiated.[50] It was no 'level playing field' in which forces and tensions might be balanced, but rather a space that was centred and organised, a *predetermined* space. We are talking about a cultural and historical dimension that was dependent on the faith in Christ with all its implications. People in pre-modern societies had no notion of a state as distinct from the social system of hopes, desires, symbols and norms. This system turns individuals into political persons: 'Human beings are animals which, by virtue of being embedded from the outset in public networks of social relationships, first develop the competences that make them into persons.'[51]

The 'political' accordingly appears as a semantic field of 'politics' and the 'public sphere', in which communication forms the bond between members of a political community. In the first book of his *Politics*, Aristotle recognised this decisive role played by communication between actors in the field of the political.[52] Politics, the political and the public sphere are made possible, according to Aristotle, by language. It is only by language – that is, by communication – that human beings can form states and thus become 'state-building creatures'.[53] I accordingly find the description of politics as *communicatio politica* by William of Moerbecke, the first translator into Latin of Aristotle's *Politics*, to be very apt indeed.[54]

My notion of the political is situated between, on the one hand, an idealism that treats it as a transcendent idea, a metaphysical '*locus philosophiae*', in Claude Lefort's term,[55] beyond the immanence of human society and the world, and on the other hand the socio-political liberalism of Jürgen Habermas or Niklas Luhmann, in which the political is imagined as a pure process of societal communication.[56] According to this latter

---

50 Calhoun 2012: 193. On the religion in the modern public sphere see Abmeier/ Borchard/Riemenschneider 2013.
51 Habermas 2014 [2005]: 13.
52 Baumann 2003: 19.
53 Meister 1966: 37; Grigore 2010: 110.
54 Skinner 1978: 349.
55 Apud Habermas 212: 30f.
56 Accordingly, I understand the political not as a process that, as Niklas Luhmann would have it, continually renews itself autopoetically, but as a process decisively

conception, the political represents the societal process of a constantly renewed distribution of power between social actors, who are driven by their interests and the institutions regulating them.

The political, as it is understood in the present study, is what Alf Lüdtke has called a 'social practice' encompassing objectified obligations, norms, values and concepts.[57] Society and culture enact the political in a set of normative and ideal obligations whose emergence and interpretation may be culturally specific, but which may take on lives of their own and be generalised across cultures.[58] This, for instance, is the case with such ideas as 'Christian rule' or the *Princeps Christianus* in the period I am examining here.

Recent scholarship in political science distinguishes three levels at which the political unfolds and works:

> First, we find ourselves at the level of the subjectivity of political persons, of 'the people', of 'subjects'. With their attitudes, desires and proclivities, whose political effects can be detected in 'basic attitudes' and 'valuation patterns', they shape the political in a decisive manner.[59]

At the second level, we are faced with the symbolisation of the political as a 'public space of significances'.[60] This means that the world in which we live is signified and symbolically implied through the prism of meaning that is either found or created.[61]

Finally, the political appears as the 'institutional framing' of public communication, of balance, equity and negotiation. Institutions serve as forms to regulate tensions and inequities and to make binding decisions, from which the legitimacy and authority of political power derive.[62]

---

dependent on its environment, institutions, norms (Blänkner 2005: 76). The political is thus determined by structures.

57   Habermas 2012: 29.

58   Which is why a coercive state imposing 'alien' valuations would be either impossible or dictatorial and tyrannical (see Etzioni 2003: 92f.).

59   Gosewinkel/Schuppert 2008: 13f.

60   Charles Taylor apud Gosewinkel/Schuppert 2008: 17.

61   Blänkner 2005: 74.

62   Gosewinkel/Schuppert 2008: 19, 22ff. and 29ff.

Rule. The working use of the term 'rule' (*Herrschaft*) in the present study follows Alf Lüdtke in understanding the complex of rule as a 'force field'. More importantly still, rule presents itself as a complex not fully fathomable by language. It is semantics: 'Rule moreover denotes a social praxis which particularly palpably absorbs such realities as are irreducible to language.'[63] Rule as a force field emerges between actors shaped by and exposed to their historical environment. The interaction that takes shape here forms a sphere of communication, exchange and conflict, between political subjects.[64] The ruler as active factor and subject at the same time shaped in the late medieval and early modern period the rule. This is not to say that the ruler was the absolute subject of rule. He was, as a part of the aforementioned field, in equal measure an object of rule, exposed and subjected to its dynamics.[65]

I am thinking here of the complex phenomenon and process of legitimating rule in the European traditions of the early modern age. Conformity to the traditional canon of valuations, to the normative centrality of certain persons, actions and texts, to the moral presence of the ruler in the field of (religious and political) tension between 'good' and 'evil', to a praxis of rule guided by procedures and institutions. These were not only dimensions of the ruler's credibility, but criteria of legitimate rule *tout court*.[66] The subjects are accorded the part of active observers by the right of protest, which offers them means to combat illegitimate and unjust rule ranging from 'rebellion' and 'treason' to 'tyrannicide'.

This is key to understanding the discussion of the *Princeps Christianus* as a burning issue in the early sixteenth century: there was broad agreement that the consolidation of early modern territorial rule had to come to terms with multiple sets of social and religious problems, while also requiring a

---

63   Lüdtke 1991: 17.

64   Lütdtke prefers to speak of 'actors' to avoid the aura of authority accruing to 'the subject' as an entity intervening in the force field from outside (see Lüdtke 1991: 13). I take this to imply a distancing from Luhmann's system theory, in which the subject figures as the system's 'environment'.

65   Grigore/Dinu/Zivojinovic 2012: 14f.

66   Grigore 2012c.

unified normative canon that would serve to bridge differences and provide orientation to both rulers and their subjects.

The examination of historical concepts ought to bear these considerations in mind, as Quentin Skinner has emphasised:

> [W]e shall do well to concentrate in particular on the concepts we employ to describe and appraise what Hobbes called our artificial world, the world of politics and morality. This in turn means that we shall need to focus on the various terms – the entire normative vocabulary – in which such concepts are habitually expressed. [...] [T]hese terms, the paradigms of which are the names of the virtues and vices, are those which perform evaluative as well as descriptive functions in natural languages.[67]

At the time *Princeps Christianus* or Christian normativity represented a highly effective political instrument indeed and as such provide the modern scholar of religion with ample subject matter for research.

Political Theology. The present study is also conceived as an analysis of discourses of political theology in the early modern era. Despite many claims to the contrary, Christianity and political theology are by no means incompatible.[68]

---

67   Skinner 2009: 175.
68   'The origins of the concept of political theology [...] are to be found in Graeco-Roman antiquity. From a Christian perspective, it denotes the impermissible "theologisation" of existing forms of state and society, their religious transfiguration (or, as the Fathers would have it, their transformation into idols) to the degree that matters of the state and of the divine, of worship and politics, become intertwined. To classical man, such intertwining is altogether self-evident, for he lives in a world in which the State and the gods form a constitutive unity, in which there can be no such thing as a godless state or a stateless deity. To the understanding of antiquity, *polis* and *civitas* are both religious concepts and both endowed with the quality of the divine. It is only Christianity that breaks the bond of theological-political immanence by its world-transcending idea of God, and accordingly it is in the Christian era that we encounter a critique of political theology' (Maier 1970: 17). This diagnosis, however, has applied only since St Augustine's *De civitate Dei* and only to those traditions of scriptural interpretation that have followed his lead. Considering, however, the biblical statements in Matt. 22.15–21, 1 Pet. 2.17 and Rom. 13 as well as the arguments of the Christian apologists of the second and third centuries, one can only conclude that, like all people of late antiquity, the early Christians, too, thought of the political order as expressing the will of God and as a means of God's intervention in the world.

The concept of 'political theology' that informs the present analysis has little to do with that of Carl Schmitt, the well-known proponent of political theology as theological justification of anti-secular political orders.[69] Moreover, I take it to mean neither a theological vindication of politics nor the task of social and political criticism that the Churches sometimes take upon themselves[70] – nor, indeed, is it a demand for such political activity on their part.[71] By no means should it be mistaken for a *theologia negativa*, the critique by Christians and Churches of what they perceived to be un-Christian about society and politics exemplified by Johann Baptist Metz.[72] Such views would be too simple to do justice to a complicated phenomenon. Nor would I consider political theology to be a mere aspect of *any* engagement with theology. As I understand it, Christian theology itself possesses political valences and takes on political forms, be they institutional, symbolic or subjective.[73]

By its very claim to universality, Christianity encourages and facilitates the emergence and ordering of human communities. From the beginning, Christian instances saw themselves as instances of the citizens, and their theology represented the civil dimension of religious existence in the manner of a θεολογία πολιτική (*theologia civilis*). 'The Christian religion was [from the outset] a process of communication by media, both written and spoken [...].'[74] A 'global communication event' took shape by, and around, media as a communicational environment itself. By its very nature, therefore, Christianity was and is political.[75]

Christianity and *Christianitas* are to be considered as dogmatic, practical and institutional entities that, by virtue of their founder, their shared body of scripture, their common institutional framework and their claim to 'one truth', certainly aim at universality. Yet as assertions such religious claims have often existed in tension with historical reality, as exemplified

69 See the diagnosis in Manemann 2002: 164ff.; Ottmann 2004a: 74.
70 Maier 1969: 3.
71 Maier 1969: 1.
72 Maier 1969: 15.
73 See the three aspects of the political discussed above.
74 Karrer 2009: 80.
75 Karrer 2009: 81.

by the relationship between *Christianitas* (as an ideal) and one form or another of *theologia civilis* (as the concrete historical discursive form taken on by a metaphysical idea).

It is at this intersection that the following comparative analysis begins: though claimed by all, *Christianitas* is theologically specified by different contexts of rule. This theological formation of difference and discourse inevitably permeates each particular form of Christian politics. A *Princeps Christianus* is thus a ruler of a specifically theological hue. Yet for all that he remains a *Christianus Princeps*. To show what a complex semantic pattern is imposed on the conceptual meta-level of 'the Christian' or *Christianitas* by various Christian-theological political references is the challenge confronting this study.

My understanding of political theology is founded on the observation that Christianity not only comes with certain 'political tasks'[76] by which it contributes to social and political coexistence and which furnish it with 'value competences'. To put it bluntly, Christianity *is* political at every level.[77] Based, then, on the selected material, my study attempts to show to what extent Christianity discloses its meaning by gathering human beings, forming them into a community and ultimately allowing them to live in accordance with their nature as 'state-building creatures' endowed with political reason. Because of the manner in which religious convictions are enacted in political existence, the language – or *theologia* – of such a religion is necessarily a political language.

At least in the pre-modern and not yet individualised Christian traditions of Europe, before the claim that 'religion is a private matter' could even have been understood and in which no genuine separation between 'religion' and 'politics' obtained,[78] Christian theology also supplied politics with its foundational arguments. In modernity, religion or religiosity are considered the private business of individuals and their associations, including the Churches. Franz X. Kaufmann has accordingly spoken of Christianity as having become *verkirchlicht*, that is, reduced or limited to the Church.[79] The Christianity of pre- and early modern Europe, on the

---

76   Dingel/Tietz 2011: 9.
77   Seeber 1969: 27; Burkard 2011: 145f.
78   Bogner 2001; Burkard 2011: 144.
79   Apud Karrer 2009: 79.

other hand, tended rather to be socially embedded, with religion governing the existence both of the state and of political subjects. In the early modern era, the political order itself was religious, while religion in turn regarded itself as ordered and as a dimension of control, influence, power and rule.

Following Manfred Walther's definition, I use the term 'political theology' here to denote the '[relations] between religion and politics, Church(es) and state, which derive from a theological interpretation and permeation of a religion or of its basic heuristics – rules, that is, in which *religion is the controlling force* and which hence as a rule are laid down by theologians'.[80] To this definition, I have to add only that in the 'political theologies' (note the plural) of the early modern era, which was a religious age, theology and political philosophy did not represent separate spheres. Religion was indeed the 'controlling force' inasmuch as any consideration of political questions was inevitably tied to questions of salvation and indeed accorded them priority. Political theory in the sixteenth century is political theology.[81]

Accordingly, the point of departure for political theology are the political aspects of the Christian religion. Political theology, on the one hand, informs the language of human plurality in relation to the creator (God), if we are to maintain Hannah Arendt's distinction between man (singular) as God's Creation and human beings (plural) as a socio-political product on earth.[82] On the other hand, political theology means enacting this plurality in religious life – with all the expectations, excuses, fears, convictions, justifications, reasons, attitudes, actions and concepts that entails. The language that describes this reality – the reality, that is, of Christianity itself being political – thus informs political theology, which is open to study in its historical, practical and religious aspects.

South-eastern Europe. To attempt a definition of 'south-eastern Europe' is apt to be an awkward undertaking – so much so that the second edition of Karl Kaser's *Südosteuropäische Geschichte und Geschichtswissenschaft* (unlike the first) dispenses with a definition of the term altogether.[83] Yet

---

80 Walther 2004: 106.
81 Schorn-Schütte 2004b: 227f. and 232; Kobusch 2006: 26ff.
82 Arendt 2006: 77ff; Blänkner 2005: 78.
83 Kaser 2002: 19.

though some scholars describe it only as a 'thematically limited device',[84] the term 'south-eastern Europe' nonetheless has found its way into the names of numerous institutions and (cultural) media organisations. It is hence possessed of a quality of its own that requires explanation.

To treat south-eastern Europe as a discrete entity with fixed borders and consisting of a clearly defined set of 'nations', as an element apart from 'Europe' or even its opposite (taking, i.e., 'western Europe' to be the 'real' Europe), would not only be inaccurate, but a misrepresentation of the historical record. Many books have been written in an attempt to localise such concepts as 'the Balkans' or 'south-eastern Europe', and a particularly illuminating effort was made by the Bulgarian historian Maria Todorova in her book *Imagining the Balkans*.[85] Over the years, 'south-eastern Europe' has proved a highly flexible term. For instance, Byzantine historians of the sixth century already considered the area between the Adriatic and the Black Sea, between the Danube and Constantinople, to form a coherent entity.[86]

However, the term 'south-eastern Europe' seems itself to be a Eurocentric construct – centred, that is, on western Europe. 'It is important to record that since the early modern age, the key special concepts pertaining to this region were developed *outside* south-eastern Europe and that the discussion was for a long time carried on without the involvement of anyone from that region.'[87]

Like other areas of the continent, south-eastern Europe has always been part of the political agenda of newly formed nations in the process of negotiating power, spheres of influence and claims to entitlement.[88] The term 'south-eastern Europe' first appeared in 1813, in the work of the Austrian Slavist Bartholomäus Kopitar, who launched the syntagma on a career that would culminate in the foundation of an Institute for South-East European Studies in Bucharest one hundred years later.[89]

---

84   Bak 2010–2011: 395.

85   Maria Todorova, *Imagining the Balkans*, Oxford et al. 1997.

86   Clewing/Schmitt 2011: 8.

87   Clewing/Schmitt 2011: 8; emphasis added.

88   Mishkova/Stråth/Trencsényi 2013: 258f., 266ff.

89   The *Institutul de studii sud-est europene* continues within the Romanian Academy of sciences (URL: <http://www.acadsudest.ro> – last accessed 07.09.2019) (see

In modern scholarship, however, the trend is rather an overcoming of such seemingly fixed terminologies in favour of an understanding of south-eastern Europe as a European space characterised by complex inter-relations, networks and processes. If, in this book, I continue to use the term 'south-eastern Europe', then I do so in the sense of a *Geschehenseinheit*, of an entity, that is formed and bound together by certain historical events occurring within it.[90]

Recent historiography has taken the regions constituting south-eastern Europe to include the territories of modern-day Greece, the European part of Turkey, Bulgaria, Macedonia, Kosovo, Albania, Montenegro, Serbia, Bosnia and Hercegovina, Romania and Hungary (the latter chiefly on account of its so-called 'Ottoman past' after 1526). At the beginning of the sixteenth century, this space was largely dominated by religious Orthodoxy in the form of a Graeco-Byzantine Church that still benefited from structures established in the former Byzantine Empire.[91] This history is reflected in such terms as the 'Orthodox Balkan area' or 'Balkan Orthodoxy'.[92]

It is this very complexity that imparts to south-eastern Europe its individuality as a *Geschehenseinheit* of the coexistence of several cultures, traditions and societies, which are held together in a lively process of exchange, mobility and transfer.[93] Yet this process inevitably involved them in broader European history.

Clewing/Schmitt 2011: 10). The institute was founded by the historian Nicolae Iorga and the archaeologist Vasile Pârvan.

90 The term is found in Clewing/Schmitt 2011: 3 and was developed under the influence of Holm Sundhaussen (Clewing/Schmitt 2011: 14).

91 Oikonomou/Stassinopoulou/Zelepos 2011.

92 Zelepos 2011: 112ff.

93 Brunnbauer 2011; Grigore/Dinu/Zivojinovic 2012: 15.

Neagoe Basarab: A Christian Prince in the Early Sixteenth Century

For glory and honour proceed from the New Commandment, when you make Christ your head, when you partake of his body in the Lord's Supper, when you are a brother and an heir to him, and resemble him in all respects.

Neagoe Basarab

Because each seer is a new priest, a new mediator, a new organ.

Friedrich Schleiermacher

Historical Background

A Note on the Sources

Letters and documents aside, unfortunately only a single contemporary source is preserved that casts light on the life and works of Neagoe Basarab, ruler of (Greater) Wallachia[1] between 1512 and 1521. The source in question is the *Life of Saint Niphon. Patriarch of Constantinople*, a hagiographic work by Gabriel Protos, elder monk (πρῶτος) of the monastic

---

1   As distinct from Moldavia or 'Lesser Wallachia', referred to thus (*Cleine Walachey*) by Johann Schiltberger (d. c. 1427). A similar name is used by Ghillebert von Lannoy (d. 1462), a Flemish diplomat and Knight of the Golden Fleece, who refers to Moldavia as 'Wallachie la petite' (see Holban, I, 1968: 50, n. 8). On the History of Moldavia see Nouzille 2005.

community on Mount Athos.² The *Life* was written in 1517 or 1519, at
or immediately after the time when Protos visited Wallachia at Basarab's
invitation.³

Notwithstanding the panegyric and hagiographic tone surrounding
the protagonist, Ecumenical Patriarch Niphon II (1486–1488, 1497–1498,
1502), this work, several versions of which in Greek and Old Romanian
are preserved,⁴ affords valuable insights into the actions of Prince Neagoe
Basarab, who was the patriarch's protégé. Attention is paid primarily to the
ruler's symbolic and religiously inspired actions, his works as a benefactor
and his princely presence, which is portrayed as having been endowed with
cosmological responsibility. Though one must be wary of exaggeration, as
indeed with any account of a saintly life, this work nonetheless contains
valuable detail on Basarab, including precise and technical descriptions of
the size, location, and other aspects of his donations and foundations. The
list is long and was maintained in a painstaking, almost actuarial fashion.
It is impossible that the author would really have felt able grossly to distort such bald facts – all the more so because the activities recorded were
public in nature and could thus be easily denied or verified by a significant
number of people. This holds true in spite of the fact that the generosity
of rulers was prone to literary exaggeration.⁵ The symbolic meaning of a
ruler's actions is the field I shall seek to analyse, and, for this, Gabriel Protos
offers a wealth of material.

We can further look to two preserved Ottoman letters dating from
the early sixteenth century to provide us with important information regarding Neagoe Basarab, the dynastic questions surrounding him and his
role in the power struggles within the Ottoman Empire in the last years of
Bayezid II (1481–1512). One of these letters was written in circles hostile to
the Craioveşti⁶ family and sent to the Sublime Porte with slanderous intent.

---

2   On accounts of Mount Athos from the fifteenth and sixteenth centuries, see
     Mureşan 2007.
3   Grecu 1944: 6, 7, 8, 22.
4   Grecu 1944: 5.
5   Some Marxist historians take the *Vita* to be political propaganda in favour of the
     Craioveşti (see Stănescu 1961: IX).
6   The boyar family from which Neagoe Basarab was descended.

The other letter is addressed to the young Sultan Selim I (1512–1520) and is from the pen of a young Ottoman dignitary, Hassan, beylerbey of Rumelia.[7]

I have also drawn upon Wallachian chronicles written on the cusp of the eighteenth century, the so-called *Cantacuzène Letopiset*[8] (c. 1690) composed by an anonymous figure close to the Cantacuzène family[9] and the *Letopiset of Radu Popescu Vornicul*[10] (composed in three stages: 1686–1690, 1719–1723 and 1723–1729),[11] also known as the *Letopiset of the Băleni*.[12] Both of these were written long after Neagoe Basarab in Old Romanian and using the Cyrillic alphabet. Scholarship classifies them as belonging to

---

7 Mehmet 1968.

8 Originally *Istoriia Țării Rumânești de când au descălecat pravoslavnicii creștini* (History of Wallachia since the descent of the true-believing Christians). The verb *a descăleca* means 'to dismount a horse' or 'to descend' and denotes, among other things, the symbolic gesture of founding, claiming or taking possession of a territory by the fact of the ruler's dismounting. Hence *descălecători* (dismounters) is the name given to the princes who established Moldavia and Wallachia as independent political entities: the mythic Negru-Vodă (dates unknown) for Wallachia and Dragoș-Vodă (c. 1347-c. 1354) für Moldavia (on this see Xenopol 1889: 16ff., 28f.; Huber 1973; Giurescu 1980; Durandin 1995; Kahl/Metzeltin/Ungureanu 2006; Schar/ Gräf 2008: 145, 193).

9 Grecescu/Simonescu 1960: XIVf. and XVII. Though several attempts have been made to identify the author, the question remains unanswered, which is why he is often referred to as the 'Cantacuzène Anonymous' (see the discussion in Stănescu 1961: VIIff.). On the time of writing see Stănescu 1961: VIIIf. The literary historian Nicolae Cartojan claims to have identified the author as Stoica Ludescu (see Cartojan 1980: 424 and 433).

10 Originally *Istoriile Domnilor Țărâi Rumânești* (Histories of the Lords of Wallachia). In the Wallachian hierarchy of offices, a *vornic* is more or less equivalent to the Western medieval *palatinus*, the Merovingian and Carolingian *major domus* or *rector palatii*, or the *Pflazgraf* (count palatine) of the German-speaking lands (see Brezoianu 1882; Giurescu 1926; Gerstner 1941; Kuchenbuch 1991; Becher 2009: 28, 90; Spieß 2009). On the offices in Wallachia in the age of Basarab see Sacerdoțeanu 1964. On Radu Popescu Vornicul see Cartojan 1980: 436ff.

11 Stănescu 1961: XV.

12 Stănescu 1961: VI. *Băleni* is the Romanian plural of the name *Băleanu*. Radu Popescu (d. 1729) was a member of this family through his mother and through his wife. His chronicle in many respects is written as a family chronicle, hence the name *Letopiset of the Băleni* (see Georgescu 1960; Stănescu 1961: XIff.).

so-called 'Boyar historiography', which denotes a kind of history writing
that overemphasises the fundamental role of the aristocracy in the political existence of the Wallachian Principalities. It must be read through the
prism of the political and economic interests of the aristocratic families
from whose circles these chronicles emanated.[13]

As for the Basarab's reign, both texts draw upon Gabriel Protos, who
is often appropriated verbatim. Yet here and there they also incorporate
information from older sources that have since been lost to posterity. Not
drawn from Gabriel Protos, for instance, are Radu Popescu's highly critical remarks on Basarab's rough treatment of certain grand boyars of his
day, which was part of the voivode's efforts to curb centrifugal tendencies among the nobility. What is 'good' about this approach is that Radu
Popescu strips the original account by Gabriel Protos of its apologetic
elements concerning Neagoe Basarab.[14] Of the chronicles I drew upon, it
is also worth mentioning the *Chronicle of Macarius* written in the sixteenth
century, not long after Basarab's death.[15]

A final important source for Basarab's reign are the sixteenth-century
epitaphs or founder's inscriptions that are to be found in Wallachian
churches, as well as deeds of endowment issued by the voivode's chancellery, which both testify to Neagoe Basarab's beneficent activities and
describe the political circumstances of his reign.

Voivode and Lord of Wallachia

Legend has it that the Principality of Wallachia was founded by one
(Radu) Negru-Vodă,[16] a mysterious character belonging to myth rather
than history. He figures in all the seventeenth- and eighteenth-century
chronicles, but in none that date to his purported lifetime:

13   Stănescu 1963: XVII.
14   Cartojan 1980: 442.
15   Macarius.
16   Chihaia 1976: 15f. *Negru* = black; *Vodă* = short for *Voevod* or voivode.

And as in the course of the time was marked the Year of Adam 6798, there was in the Hungarian Land [i.e. Transylvania] a voivode by the name of Radu Negrul the Voivode, Grand Duke of Almaş and Făgăraş, who thence with all his house and with countless populations: Romanians, Papists, Saxons, and all manner of people arose and – riding downstream along the River Dâmboviţa – began to found a new land.[17]

Negru-Vodă may be encountered in many a legend and ballad of Old Romanian popular epic, which Romanian historians take as a licence to treat him as a historical figure. Though there may be no mention of any Negru-Vodă in the chronicles, they argue that his ubiquity in popular literature is such that he could hardly be an entirely fictional character.

According to legend, Negru-Vodă was a native of the Duchy of Făgăraş, situated in the south of Transylvania between Sibiu (Hermannstadt) and Braşov (Kronstadt). In the thirteenth century he is supposed to have crossed the Carpathian Mountains and founded an autonomous political entity with Câmpulung[18] as its capital. Hungarian documents of the late thirteenth century do indeed report increasing pressure by the Hungarian crown on ethnic Wallachians and their noble houses in Transylvania, which may have led some local noblemen of Wallachian origin and Catholic or Orthodox faith to emigrate.[19] (Up to Nicolae Alexandru [1352–1364], the voivodes of Wallachia were from time to time drawn to the Latin Church,[20] though the local population was largely Orthodox.)

17 'Iar când au fost la cursul anilor de la Adam 6798, fiind în Ţara Ungurească un voevod ce l-au chemat Radul Negrul voevod, mare herţeg pre Almaş şi Făgăraş, rădicatu-s-au de acolo cu toată casa lui şi cu mulţime de noroade: rumâni, papistaşi, saşi, de tot feliul de oameni, pogorându-se pre apa Dâmboviţii, început-au a face ţară noao' (Cantacuzène Anonymous A: 1–2; all translations from the Old Romanian chronicles are my own). I would like to take this opportunity to explain the Byzantine chronology, in which the years are counted since the world's Creation on 1 September 5509 BC. To obtain the more familiar *anno Domini* year for that given above, it is necessary to subtract 5509 from 6798, thus arriving at AD 1289 (Brincken 2000: 93ff.; Bryer 2008: 33). In my translations, I have tried to preserve something of the unusual flavour of Old Romanian syntax, which accounts for the possibly unidiomatic style of some of these translations.

18 Some forty kilometres north of the Romanian town of Piteşti, south of the Carpathian Mountains.

19 Xenopol 1889: 12f.; Neagoe 1971: 22f.

20 Which Cazacu/Mureşan 2013: 204ff. deny.

The first ruler of the Basarab dynasty for whom documentary evidence exists is Basarab I the Founder (c. 1310–1352),[21] son of Tihomir (*Thochomerius*; d. c. 1310).[22] The sources give no explanation for the passing of power from Negru-Vodă, who appears not to have been a Basarab, to Tihomir/Thochomerius and thence to Basarab I. Such was his mythical aura that some Romanian historians of the early twentieth century claimed that Basarab was in fact Negru-Vodă himself,[23] though modern scholarship roundly rejects any such notion. Yet a recent study by Neagu Djuvara tries to prove that Negru-Vodă was in fact none other than Tihomir/Thochomerius. To prove his point, the historian adduces the manifestly Cuman roots of the names *Basarab* and *Thochomerius* and uses a combination of physiognomic and etymological evidence[24] in an attempt to prove that Tihomir, the father of Basarab I, was called *Negru-Vodă* by his Wallachian subjects on account of his darker complexion, which was due in turn to his Cuman descent. Nicolae Iorga already discussed the Cuman roots of the first members of the Basarab dynasty in the late nineteenth century.[25] That Tihomir/Thochomerius should be identical to Negru-Vodă, however, remains in the realm of speculation.

The ruler of Wallachia carried the titles *Voevod* (voivode) and *Domn* (lord, Latin *dominus*, Greek δόμνος). These titles were originally distinct from one another, referring to two separate functions. *Voevod* originally denoted a ruler's military role, a military leader (*voj* = army, *vodjti* = to lead), more or less in the sense of a *dux* or *bellidux*, as well as the possession of jurisdictional authority in a particular territory.[26] That a voivode was understood as resembling a German *Herzog* (duke) is evident from

---

21   *Basarab* is of Cuman origin (Iorga 1894: 9ff.; Donat 1934; Conea 1935: 3, 10ff., 16f., 21).

22   Oţetea 1972: 567.

23   Kogălniceanu 1908.

24   Djuvara 2000.

25   Iorga 1984. Yet critical objections to Djuvara's theory are still raised, for example, by Matei Cazacu in his most recent publication on the subject, Cazacu/Mureşan 2013: 25ff.

26   Bogdan 1902: 13ff.; Ştefănescu 1965: 16. The voivodes were originally elected; only later did the office become heritable (Platon 1992: 49).

the travelogue of Johann Schiltberger (d. c. 1427), in which the Wallachian ruler Mircea-Voivode is referred to as *Mercer waywod* and *Hertzog von der Walachey*.[27] The word *voivode* is of Slavic origin, its cognates including *vojevoda* (Bulgarian), *woewoeda* (Russian), *wojewoda* (Polish), *wojwoda* (Czech) and *vojevoda* (Serbo-Croatian).[28] Hungarian sources refer to Basarab I of Wallachia, for instance, as *vayvoda transalpina*.[29]

The title *Domn*, on the other hand, points to the ruler's administrative and political tasks and was a marker of autocracy, of dominion that was autonomous or independent.[30] Semantically, *Domn* more or less corresponds to the Slavonic *samoderžecŭ*, the Latin *dominus* (as mentioned above) or the Greek αὐτοκράτωρ.[31] Both titles, *Voevod* and *Domn*, later came to be used synonymously and were invariably held by a single ruler; whether it was ever otherwise is uncertain. The Cantacuzène Anonymous gives the full styles and titles of the Wallachian rulers for the example of Negru-Vodă, which were adopted by all subsequent Wallachian rulers:

27   Hans Schiltberger: 2; Holban, I, 1968: 29. Giovanni Maria Angioletto (d. 1525), notary in Vicenza, who was taken prisoner by the Ottomans and participated in their wars against Stephen the Great of Moldavia (1457–1504), refers to that Moldavian prince by the title of a 'count': 'Conte Stefano, signor della Vallachia [i.e. Moldavia]' (see Holban, I, 1968: 133). On the correct term, 'voevod' or 'voievod', see Cazacu/Mureşan 2013: 41, n. 29.

28   Xenopol 1889: 179. It is interesting to note that *voivode* as a ruler's title, its Slavic roots notwithstanding, is commonly found only in the Danubian Principalities. The Slavic cultures of south-eastern Europe referred to their rulers as *czar, knez, khan* (Bulgaria) or *despot, kralj, banj, zhupanj* (Serbia) (see Bogdan 1902: 1).

29   I. Bogdan 1902: 15, with citation. *Voivoda, vayvoda* and *voyvoda* were the standard terms used by the Hungarian chancellery for the rulers of Moldavia and Wallachia (Veress 1914: passim). In a letter by the Hungarian King Louis II, for instance, Neagoe Basarab is referred to as 'noster Spectabilis et Magnificus Bozorab, waywoda noster Transalpinensis' (Veress 1914: 112). Besides *voivode*, the title *knez* or *knyaz* is occasionally found among Wallachian princes (Bogdan 1904: 113; Platon 1992: 45ff.).

30   Bogdan 1902: 16f.

31   Neagoe 1972: 45; Platon 1992: 61.

In God Christ true-believing and venerable and Christ-loving and alone triumphant, Io[32] Radu-Voivode, by the grace of God Lord of all Greater Wallachia, come from the Hungarian Land and here dismounted, Duke of Almaş and Făgăraş.[33]

Craiovescu or Basarab?

Neagoe Basarab was not a member of the Wallachian dynasty. He was the first ruler of Wallachia to interrupt the dynastic succession that had continued since Basarab I.

Neagoe Basarab was descended from the Craiovescu[34] family of grand boyars from Oltenia, and was born in 1481 or 1482.[35] His grandfather was Neagoe of Craiova, (grand) ban of Oltenia (*Bano Grande* in Italian sources; the second tier of the state hierarchy below the voivode).[36] Neagoe's parents were Pârvu Craiovescu,[37] *Vornic* (*palatinus*) of Oltenia, and Neaga, who – as will be discussed – was said to have had an extra-marital affair with Voivode Basarab the Younger. It is by way of compensation for his

32   The meaning of the particle *Io* in the style of the Wallachian rulers remains unclear to this day. There is some agreement that it might be an abbreviation of the Greek Ἰωάννης (Johannes, John), which derives from the Hebrew for 'God is gracious' or 'graced by God'. This is suggestive of the theocratic notion of authority. The particle Iω̃ or Hω̃ was used in the ninth century by the chancelleries of Bulgarian or Serbian rulers. The Wallachian rulers of Wallachia or Moldavia invariably used *Io* regardless of whether the actual ruler happened to be called John or not (see the exhaustive analysis in Vârtosu 1960: 13, 60, 67–84, 92, 98). On this see also Platon 1992: 79.

33   Cantacuzène Anonymous B: 84. On this see also Platon 1992: 79.

34   The name derives from the fief of Craiova. A table of their ancestry can be found in Filitti 1922a: 224f. On this, see also Nicolescu 1903; Vergatti 2009: 24ff.

35   Ionescu 1971: 658; Vergatti 2009: 35.

36   Holban, III, 1971: 8 n. 7. The rank of ban was roughly equivalent to that of a margrave under the Carolingian system. The office of ban as governor is first recorded among the South Slavs of the tenth century. It was subsequently introduced to the Kingdom of Hungary, from where it was adopted in the Wallachian principalities, where the ban was tasked with defending the frontier provinces (Ştefănescu 1965: 19f.). On the banate of Oltenia see Minea 1934.

37   On whom see Filitti 1922a: 200ff.

wounded honour that Neagoe 'the Elder' is supposed to have been awarded the office of grand ban by the Wallachian ruler.[38]

The Craioveşti first appeared on the political stage in the latter half of the fifteenth century and were involved in power struggles in Wallachia from then on until 1535, when the male line ended.[39] The extraordinary influence of the Craiovescu family was founded above all on their wealth. A report on investigations brought against the Craioveşti by the authorities of Voivode Mihnea Turcitul ('he who became a Turk'; 1577–1583 and 1585–1591) contains an inventory of possessions on a tremendous scale, the foundations of which were probably laid even before the Principality of Wallachia was established in the early fourteenth century. Among the items listed are 182 properties – villages, Roma settlements, plots of land, fiefs and forests.[40] According to the mentality of the proprietary church system (*ecclesia propria*), even the Oltenian monastery of Bistriţa, though built with donations from everywhere, seems to have been considered family property. It was, according to the chronicler, laid to waste in a feud brought by Voivode Mihnea the Wrongdoer (Mihnea cel Rău, 1508–1509) against the Craioveşti along with *other* of the family's possessions.[41]

The first reference to the Craioveşti is dated to 16 March 1494, in a deed of endowment issued by Voivode Vlad the Monk (September-November 1481 and 1482–1495).[42] They are also mentioned in an epitaph on the tomb of Vladislav II (d. 1456), which was erected during the reign of Neagoe Basarab:

> Passed away hath Io Vladislav Voivode in the year 6963, in the month of August, day the 22nd. And was this tombstone donated in the time of Io Neagoe Voivode by Barbu the Ban and Pârvu the Vornic and their brothers, the sons of Neagoe of Craiova, for Vladislav too in his turn did raise them to the office of *vlasteli*.[43]

38 Neagoe 1971: 16.
39 Ştefănescu 1965: 91; Neagoe 1971: 13.
40 DRG V: Nr. 420, S. 403ff.; Neagoe 1971: 19.
41 Gabriel Protos 1944: 127 and Cantacuzène Anonymous B: 94.
42 Filitti 1922a: 194. Also mentioned, albeit with a wrong date, in Ionnescu-Gion 1902: 75.
43 'A răposat Io Vladislav voevod, în anul 6963, luna lui August a 22-a zi. Şi s-a făcut această piatră în zilele lui Io Neagoe voevod: au făcut-o Barbu banul şi Pârvu vornicul şi cu fraţii lor, fiii lui Neagoe de la Craiova, pentru că şi Vladislav i-a ridicat

Several attempts have been made to account for the epithet 'Basarab', as applied to Prince Neagoe, which also respond to questions concerning dynastic succession and the legitimacy of his rule. One explanation holds that the Oltenian Basarab family, from which Basarab was descended, had been a branch of the ruling dynasty. An indication of this is found in the fact that the dynasty's roots lay in Oltenia and Hunedoara (German *Eisenmarkt*).[44] As the chronicler reports:

> First, we shall speak of those Romanians who did separate from the Romans and journeyed to the north. Having crossed the Danube, they dismounted their horses at Turnu Severin. Others did likewise in the Hungarian Land, others by the River Olt, the River Mures or the River Tisza. And those who dismounted at Turnu Severin did spread out at the foot of the hills all the way to River Olt; others travelled towards the Danube. And thus did the land become full of them. They afterwards came close to Nicopolis. Then from among their ranks arose boyars of greater descent. And these men did as *banovetzi* (i.e. grand ban) beget a house by the name of Basarab. Their first seat was at Turnu Severin, the second at Strehaia and the third in Craiova. And so passed a long time in which they ruled and guarded this part of the world. [...] Then did the Basarabi and all the other boyars who had always dwelt beyond the River Olt arise and came before Radu the Voivode, and pledged unto him submission to his rule and that he alone should wield power over all.[45]

---

vlasteli' (IRK: 100; SRD 1905: 325; see I. C. Filitti 1922a: 198). It is difficult to be more precise about the office of *vlastel*, since the title seldom appears in the sources. It may however be that *vlasteli* refers to the boyars of the council (see Beagoe 1971: 14f.).

44 Xenopol 1889: 15.

45 'Însă dintâi izvodindu-se de rumânii carii s-au despărțit de la romani și au pribegit spre miazănoapte. Deci trecând apa Dunării, au descălecat la Turnul Severinului; alții în Țara Ungurească, pre apa Oltului și pre apa Morășului, și pre apa Tisei ajungând și până la Maramurăș. Iar cei ce au descălecat la Turnul Severinului s-au tins pre supt poalele muntelui până în apa Oltului; alții s-au pogorât pre Dunăre în jos. Și așa umplându-se tot locul de ei, au venit până în marginea Necopolei. Atunce s-au ales dintr-înșii boiarii carii au fost de neam mare. Și puseră banoveți un neam ce le zicea Basarabi, să le fie lor cap (adecă mari bani) și-i așezară întâi să le fie scaunul la Turnul Severinului, al doilea scaun s-au pogorât la Strehaia, al treilea scaun s-au pogorât la Craiova. Și așa fiind, multă vréme au trecut tot ei oblăduind acea parte de loc. [...] Atuncea și Băsărăbeștii cu toată boierimea ce era mai înainte peste Olt s-au sculat cu toții de au venit la Radul vodă, închinându-se să fie supt porunca lui și numai el să fie preste toți' (Cantacuzène Anonymous B: 83f.).

'Boyar historiography' would accordingly have us believe that the boyar house of Basarab had preceded the founding figure, Negru Voivode, as lords of those lands, which might be interpreted as a belated attempt to underscore the rank and entitlement of the great nobles of the seventeenth and nineteenth centuries. What is clear, however, is that nobody, not even his rival claimants to the throne, challenged Neagoe's right to the name of 'Basarab'. Yet what this theory fails to explain is the nature of the connection between the Craioveşti and the Basarabi, for Neagoe Basarab was undoubtedly born a Craiovescu.

Another explanation holds that the epithet 'Basarab', as bestowed upon Neagoe, son of Pârvu Craiovescu, was mere flattery on the part of Gabriel Protos. According to this interpretation, portraying him as a member of a glorious ruling dynasty was the Church's way of expressing its gratitude to a generous donor.[46] It has been claimed, moreover, that 'Basarab' was merely a nickname adopted by the Craioveşti to flaunt their power and importance.[47]

A third line of speculation – and the most important – argues that Neagoe Basarab was an illegitimate son of Voivode Basarab IV the Younger (1477–1482, with an interruption from September to November 1481) by an affair with Neaga, wife of Pârvu Craiovescu.[48] In July 1481 Stephen the Great of Moldavia (1457–1504)[49] attacked Wallachia and defeated Basarab IV, forcing him to flee to Craiova, the seat of the powerful Craiovescu family. This is also the moment when the hitherto little-mentioned Craioveşti began to assume a decisive role in the power struggles in the Danubian Principalities. At the court of Craiova, Basarab IV hoped to rally support against Stephen the Great and his protégé on the Wallachian throne, and it was during this stay that he is supposed to have had an affair with Pârvu's wife, Neaga. Yet this seems barely credible, for it would have been extremely unwise of Basarab IV to slight a powerful ally in such a manner.[50]

---

46 Neagoe 1971: 24.
47 Filitti 1922a: 193, 222, 228.
48 Neagoe 1971: 27f.
49 On whom see Binder Iijima/Dumbravă 2005.
50 Filitti 1922a: 218ff.; Oţetea 1972: 137; Neagoe 1971: 17.

However, the chronicle of Radu Popescu Vornicul reports that Voivode
Vlad the Younger (1510–1512), who feared Neagoe Basarab as a rival claimant
to the throne, later demanded that the Craioveşti swear under oath that
on no account was Neagoe the son of Basarab IV. That they were unable
to do so is taken by chroniclers as indirect evidence of Neagoe's princely
paternity.[51] Yet the same chronicle, only a few pages later and perhaps for
want of proof to the contrary, avers that Neagoe Basarab certainly was the
'son of Pârvu Vornicul, nephew of Barbu, the [Grand] Ban of Craiova.'[52]
The report of the investigation from 1589 cited previously likewise considers Pârvu Vornic to have been the biological father of Neagoe Basarab.[53]

It seems that Neagoe was not particularly troubled by rumours concerning his adulterous paternity – on the contrary, for they offered some
justification for an ascent to power that, as we shall see, was somewhat problematic. It was of fundamental importance that the country's ruler should
be of voivode blood, indeed, 'of ruling bone' (de os domnesc).[54] Neagoe
Basarab hence took care himself to mention his 'own' voivodal descent in
the seal of his house[55] or in deeds issued in his name:[56]

> In God Christ true-believing and truly honouring and Christ-loving and alone
> ruling, Io Neagoe, which is called Basarab Voivode and by the mercy of God and
> the grace of God [is] ruling and governing over all Greater Wallachia, even over the
> parts beyond the mountains, duke of Almaş and Făgăraş.[57]

---

51   Radu Popescu Vornicul 1963: 29, l. 6–11.
52   Radu Popescu Vornicul 1963: 33, l. 6.
53   DRG V: Nr. 420, p. 405.
54   Buzescu 1943: 67; Platon 1992: 64; Vergatti 2009: 36. In contrast to the Roman
      Empire, for instance, the Danube Principalities set great store by the ruler's legitim-
      ation by blood, that is to say, by his noble descent, in a manner similar to Germanic
      ius sanguinis (see Piepenbrink 2010: 62).
55   Neagoe's crest displayed a raven upon a shield (vgl. Neagoe 1971: 48; Vergatti
      2009: 51).
56   Xenopol 1889: 475; Sacerdoţeanu 1964: 413; Ionescu 1971: 654f.
57   'Întru Hristos Dumnezeu, binecredinciosul şi binecinstitorul şi de Hristos
      iubitorul şi singur stăpânitorul, Io Neagoe cel numit Basarab voevod şi din mila
      lui Dumnezeu şi cu darul lui Dumnezeu, stăpânind şi domnind peste toată ţara
      Ungrovlahiei încă şi al părţilor de peste munţi, Amlaşului şi Făgăraşului herţeg'
      (DRG I: No. 151, p. 149). See DRG I: passim between nos. 75–171.

Meanwhile his political rivals denounced Neagoe Basrab as having usurped his throne from the rightful dynasty.[58] Indeed, Hassan, beylerbey of Rumelia, in one of the two contemporary Ottoman letters mentioned previously (see *A note on the sources*), refers to Neagoe Basarab as 'haramzade bi-asl', which means something like 'bastard' or 'of unknown paternity', rather than the usual appellation for Neagoe, which was *Pârvu-Oglu* (son of Pârvu).[59] This may, however, have been a conscious provocation or insult. A further, albeit indirect point in favour of the theory of his voivodal descent might be that at the outset of his reign Neagoe was a very young, unimportant and far from one of the most respected members of the Craiovescu family. A dynastic connection would seem to offer a plausible explanation of his rapid ascent.[60]

Therefore, there is no certain answer to this question. For want of any persuasive evidence, historians continue to treat Neagoe Basarab as the son of Pârvu Craiovescu.

A Problematic Accession

The situation described above was in any case awkward with regard to the legitimacy of Neagoe Basarab's rule, for only direct and undoubted descendants of Basarab I could claim the throne. In spite of the rumours to the contrary, which he was able to exploit to his advantage, Neagoe Basarab could hardly claim such august descent. Since he was known in the region only as a simple captain of archers and later as a boyar of the council, contemporaries are likely to have had trouble regarding him as heir to Basarab I the Founder.

We know little of Neagoe Basarab's youth. Documents dating from between 1487 and 1495 make frequent mention of one *Neagul postelnic*, which may denote both a court chamberlain (equivalent to the German *Hofmarschall*) and a secretary of the Craiova banate.[61] Some historians

58 Maxim 1993: 239.
59 Mehmet 1968: 923.
60 Xenopol 1889: 476.
61 Brezoianu 1882: 9; Giurescu 1926: 155ff.; Sacerdoțeanu 1964.

give more precise dates, according to which Neagoe was *(mare) postelnic* from 1501 to 1509 and *mare comis* (master of the stables) from 1510 to 1511.[62] In 1512 Neagoe Basarab would appear to have been captain of the archers (*vătaf de vânători*), for both the Cantacuzène Anonymous and Radu Popescu Vornicul mention this fact without further comment.[63] In that capacity, Neagoe Basarab led a detachment consisting of Ottoman troops and supporters of the Craioveşti against Voivode Mircea III (October 1509–February 1510), deposing him from the throne of Wallachia in favour of Vlad the Younger.[64]

This allows us to form an image of the political abilities of the Craiovescu family. On the one hand, it was able to convince the sultan to dispatch troops against Mihnea the Evil, a voivode hostile to the boyars, and his son Mircea III. On the other hand, they were able to put up troops of their own under Neagoe's command and defeat the voivode's army in battle.[65]

The new ruler, Vlad V the Younger, nephew of the notorious Vlad III (the Impaler, 1448, 1455–1462, 1476),[66] is likely to have been wary of the great power of Craioveşti, in spite of the fact that he had reason to be grateful to them for raising him to the office of voivode.[67] He had even more reason to worry as rumours of Neagoe Basarab's supposed princely descent began to circulate at court.[68] Vlad V was probably aware that his power hung by a thread if Neagoe should turn out to be possessed not only of political power and military strength, but also of a dynastic claim. The voivode hence tried to break the power of the Craioveşti, an attempt that fits into a general political pattern of voivodes taking centralising measures

---

62   Neagoe 1971: 42; Zamfirescu 1973: 91.

63   Cantacuzène Anonymous B: 96 and Radu Popescu Vornicul B: 259 and 260.

64   Cantacuzène Anonymous B: 96f.

65   Gabriel Protos 1944: 127; Cantacuzène Anonymous B: 95f. and Radu Popescu Vornicul B: 259.

66   On Vlad III. Dracula or the Impaler, see Harmening 1983; Treptow 2000; Trow 2003; Kroner 2005.

67   The first deed of Vlad the Younger is dated 1 April 1510 and records a donation to the monastery of Bistriţa, which the Craioveşti regarded as their own (DRG I: no. 50).

68   Cantacuzène Anonymous B: 97; Radu Popescu Vornicul B: 259.

in order to restrict the centrifugal tendencies of the great nobles. Such disputes are not mere family squabbles or political game-playing, though they may have served as triggers or pretexts for far-reaching political processes.

In foreign policy Vlad V participated in the dynastic struggles for the throne of the ailing sultan, Bayezid II. Bayezid had named as his successor his eldest son, Ahmed, much to the chagrin of the Janissaries, who would have preferred Ahmed's brother Selim, thought to be of stronger character and greater military ability.[69] Aided by the Janissaries and with the support of others, including Vlad V of Wallachia, Selim rose against his father, but was defeated in Thrace and forced into exile.[70]

> *Note:* Like his predecessor Mihnea the Evil, Vlad V the Younger tried to uphold the Wallachian rulers' policy of independence vis-à-vis the Sublime Porte. This policy, however, came up against increasing military pressure from the Ottomans, which ultimately cost both voivodes their head. More successful were voivodes like Radu the Great (1495–1508) or Neagoe Basarab (1512–1521), who pursued a more discreet but all the more effective policy of counterbalancing Ottoman influence by means of contacts to Western Christian powers. Yet they too could not prevent Wallachia from falling under Ottoman domination. In spite of the military efforts of Radu of Afumaţi (1522–1529, with interruptions), who put up armed resistance, the voivodes failed. They were hampered by a lack of help from other Christian powers,[71] which had been unable to embark on their planned crusade[72] on account not least of the propagandistic efforts against it by Luther and Erasmus.

In Wallachia, the situation between Vlad the Younger, who was increasingly dissatisfied with growing boyar dominance, and the Craiovescu family became ever more tense.

Vlad clearly let himself be worried by the rumours about Neagoe Basarab and tried to rid himself of the Craioveşti by attacking their fief. The Craioveşti, however, had been warned and fled to Nicopolis, where they requested Ottoman aid against the 'tyrant' Vlad V. Sultan Bayezid II had not forgotten Vlad's previous allegiance with the usurper Selim and soon

---

69 Matuz 1994: 78f.; Majoros/Rill 2004: 208f.
70 Radu Popescu Vornicul B: 260ff.; Anonymus Hanivaldanus 254ff.; M. Neagoe 1971: 50ff.
71 Denize 1995: 176.
72 Poumarède 2004.

took advantage of internal difficulties in Wallachia to expand Ottoman influence in the country. He ordered Mehmed, pasha of Nicopolis and supposedly related to the Craiovești,[73] to 'remove' the recalcitrant Vlad.[74] At Văcărești, close to Bucharest, the Ottoman army under Mehmed and Neagoe Basarab encountered the troops of Vlad V. The voivode was defeated, taken prisoner and on that same day, 23 January 1512, beheaded for having breached the peace.[75]

Reports disagree, however, as to who dealt the fatal blow against the voivode. Gabriel Protos, a writer favourable to Neagoe Basarab, and the chroniclers using him as their source claim that Pasha Mehmed himself, in his character as arbiter and keeper of the peace on the Ottoman frontier, had administered the *coup de grâce* 'beneath a pear tree'.[76] A stronger indication still is found in the letter of Hassan, beylerbey of Rumelia, to Sultan Selim I, in which Mehmed Pasha is likewise named as the man who had beheaded Vlad V.[77] Yet Vlad's tomb in the church of Dealu (adjacent to the then capital Târgoviște) clearly states the man who killed Vlad was none other than Neagoe Basarab.[78] The letter of complaint addressed by the defeated party around Vlad V the Younger to the Sublime Porte also accuses Neagoe of having been Vlad's killer, though this may have been slander. Overall, however, the letter contains much plausible detail, including the names and functions another eleven grand boyars who were put to death at the orders of Neagoe.[79]

If the latter hypothesis were true, it would mean not only that Neagoe had no dynastic claim to the Wallachian throne, but also that he acceded to

73 Ştefănescu 1965: 96, 98. It seems that Mehmed's mother was Wallachian and related to the Craiovescu family (see Mehmet 1968: 923). The Chronicle of Macarius, written in Church Slavonic, claims that Mehmed Pasha was descended 'din neamul lui [Neagoe]', which may mean either that Mehmed was descended from the same Wallachian people or from the same family as Neagoe (see Macarius: 93, line 18).

74 Neagoe 1966: 747.

75 See accounts by Gabriel Protos 135ff.; Cantacuzène Anonymous B: 98; Radu Popescu Vornicul B: 260. On this Bulat n. d.: 13.

76 Cantacuzène Anonymous B: 98; Radu Popescu Vornicul B: 260.

77 Mehmet 1968: 923.

78 IRK: 101; Filitti 1922: 299.

79 Mehmet 1968: 928.

it by murdering the incumbent. The efforts of the Cantacuzène Anonymous to exonerate Neagoe Basarab strike me as suspicious:

> [Vlad the Younger] was seized by the soldiers of Mehmed-Pasha, who brought him in fetters before the pasha in Bucharest. And when pasha saw him, he said angrily: 'O thou perjurer, thou shalt suffer as thou didst thyself swear in thine oath, and my sword shall cut off thy head.' And so it came to pass, for Pasha *himself, by his own hand*, did cut off his head beneath a pear tree in the city of Bucharest; as in days of yore it happened to Absalom – whose hair was caught in oak in the wood of Ephraim – when he was shot in the heart with darts by Joab. And thus were fulfilled the sentence and God's just vengeance.[80]

The chronicler here displays a marked tendency to make things appear in a particular light and ensure that responsibility is clearly ascribed. The biblical motif of Absalom is added as an analogy to justify the killing of a legitimate ruler who has proved rebellious and treacherous. What is more, the Cantacuzène Anonymous depicts Neagoe Basarab's ascent to the throne as a prophetic act by which God elects His servant for a special mission: 'Before I formed thee in the belly I knew thee; and before thou camest forth out of the womb I sanctified thee, and I ordained thee a prophet unto the nations' (Jer. 1.5).[81]

Yet all this does not constitute proof that the chronicler is hiding the truth and that the killer of Vlad V really was Neagoe Basarab. That is suggested above all by the pasha's role as arbiter, whose tasks as the leader of a frontier province included by all means keeping the border peaceful. This is clear, for instance, from the mutual assistance and non-aggression pact that Vlad V made with the Craiovești in 1510, which was agreed upon at Pasha Mehmed's behest and was sealed in his presence.[82] He was thus able

---

80 '[F]u prins de oastea lui Mehmet-pașa și-l duseră în București la pașa legat. Iar deacă-l văzu pașa îi zise cu ocară: "O, călcător de jurământ, iată să-ți fie după cuvântul jurământului tău și să taie sabiia mea capul tău". Cum să și umplu, că însuși pașa cu mâna lui i-au tăiat capul în oraș în București, supt un păr, ca și pre Avesalom când îl săgetă Ioav, fiind el încurcat de păr în ramura unui stejariu, în lunca Efremului. Și să umplu judecata și răscumpărarea lui Dumnezeu, cea dreaptă' (Cantacuzène Anonymous B: 98; emphasis added).

81 Cantacuzène Anonymous B: 98.

82 Gabriel Protos: 129; Cantacuzène Anonymous B: 95.

invoke it at Vlad's execution two years later and execute the voivode for having broken his oath as well as the peace. For his part, Neagoe Basarab is likely to have been aware of the shadow cast by the killing of a voivode of the blood on the legitimacy of his rule and would hence have been relieved to see 'justice' (as the Cantacuzène Anonymous would have it) done in his stead by the pasha. In spite of the clear ascription of guilt on Vlad V's tombstone, where Neagoe Basarab is named as the voivode's killer, recent research has tended to exonerate him.[83]

Accession by Rightful Procedure

The difficult circumstances in which Vlad the Younger was toppled presented a challenge to Neagoe Basarab, who could not point to his own voivode descent in support of his rule's legitimacy. For its part, the Craiovescu family appears to have been determined to avoid any further surprises. From its experiences with hostile princes, they drew the conclusion that only a ruler who was himself a Craiovescu could bring about the kind of peace in which their own economic and political power was likely to flourish. This probably explains why, after the Battle of Văcăreşti, no new ruler from the dynastic house of Basarab was placed on the throne anymore, but rather Neagoe Basarab, son of Parvu Craiovescu.

In terms of domestic politics, it was important for Neagoe Basarab that his accession should be legitimised by due cutumiar procedures, that is, through election by the council of boyars. From the outset, the institution of the voivodes in Wallachia was a form of consensual rule. Although rulers typically inherited the office, they nonetheless required confirmation or, in cases of more justified claimants, election by the nobility. The strength of the boyars' electoral power fluctuated in the course of history. At the time of Neagoe Basarab, it had dwindled to a mere formality of acclamation – not least on account of Ottoman predominance. Yet this elective system

83   Sandu 1938: 7f.

endured in Wallachia into the seventeenth century.[84] It continued to fulfil an important symbolic function, especially in such 'problematic' cases as that of Neagoe Basarab. Shortly after the execution of Vlad the Younger, Neagoe summoned the people of Bucharest – that is, the aldermen and the boyars of the Great Council (*Marele Sfat*) – and had himself proclaimed Lord of Wallachia.

A ceremony was performed on this occasion that is repeatedly found in the history both the Christian West and the Byzantine Empire. As Gabriel Protos reports:

> And thus did the Pasha [i.e. Mehmet] […] ask the boyars present whom they would have as their lord. And all replied that they would have the most faithful Neagoe Basarab. When Neagoe heard this, he cried out with a loud voice: 'Let them choose another, for I am not worthy [ἄξιος]!' Yet the people cried: 'We would have none but thee, Neagoe, most Christian one.' And thus did the pasha at the people's behest vest the power in Neagoe and place him on the ruling throne of all Wallachia.[85]

Neagoe Basarab was thus 'persuaded' to rule, much as Gregory VII (d. 1085) had been persuaded to accept the papacy or, earlier still, Gregory of Nazianzus (d. 390) or John Chrysostom (d. 407) had been persuaded to become patriarchs of Constantinople.[86] In the middle Byzantine era, the crowd gathered in the church for the emperor's coronation was asked three times 'ἄξιος?' (Is he worthy?), to which the crowd each time answered 'ἄξιος!' No such elaborate ceremonial is recorded in Neagoe's case. Yet the manner in which Neagoe humbly protested to the people that he was not worthy of ruling the country suggests that this was essentially

---

84 Buzescu 1943: 66ff. Cases are recorded of voivodes who were unable to take office for lack of recognition by the boyars of the council, which demonstrates that it was not always a mere formality (see Platon 1992: 70f.).

85 Ὁ δὲ πασᾶς […] εἶπεν εἰς τοὺς παρεστῶτας ἄρχοντας ποῖον θέλουν νὰ κάμουν αὐθέντην; καὶ πάντες ἀπεκρίθησαν, ὅτι θέλουν τὸν εὐσεβέστατον Νέαγγον Βασαράβαν. Ὁ δὲ Νέαγγος ἀκούσας ἔλεγε μεγάλῃ τῇ φωνῇ· "Ἄλλον ἂς κάμουν, ὅτι ἐγὼ δὲν εἶμαι ἄξιος." Ὁ δὲ λαὸς ἔκραζον· "Δὲν θέλομεν ἄλλον, μόνον ἐσένα, χριστιανικώτατε Νεάγγουλε." Ὅθεν ὁ πασᾶς κατὰ τὴν ζήτησιν τοῦ λαοῦ ἔδωκε τὴν ἐξουσίαν εἰς τὸν Νέαγγον καὶ ἀνεβίβασαν αὐτὸν εἰς τὸν θρόνον τῆς ἡγεμονίας πάσης Οὑγκροβλαχίας' (Gabriel Protos: 138). See the account of the Cantacuzène Anonymous B: 99.

86 Grigore 2009: 267 n. 275.

the same ritual. It appears to have been an important aspect of the procedures and of the ceremony that the 'candidate' should be seen not to seize power himself, but to be called upon to rule. In symbolic terms, this underscores the contingency of the ruler's person compared with God's omnipotence expressed in the Christian people, the organ of God's will (*vox populi, vox Dei*).

One of the first actions taken by Neagoe Basarb as a ruler was to take revenge on the Moldavian boyar Bogdan, who in c. 1507 had come as a refugee to the Wallachian court of Radu the Great, where he was granted asylum, and became the voivode's secretary (*postelnic*). There, Bogdan contracted what was clearly a polygamous marriage – he was already married in Moldavia – with Radu's sister, causing a rift between the voivode and the Wallachian metropolitan, Niphon, the former patriarch of Constantinople. We shall return to this conflict later on. Bogdan, the Moldavian boyar, was among the favourites at the Wallachian court under both Radu the Great and his brother Radu V the Younger, his brothers-in-law. Hence it was Bogdan who had previously incited Radu the Great against Metropolitan Niphon, the friend of the Craiovești. He had also whispered in Vlad the Younger's ear to beware of Neagoe, the supposedly 'illegitimate son' of Voivode Basarab IV. Bogdan's intriguing thus led Vlad the Younger to embark on his ill-fated feud with the Craiovești.

Neagoe Basarab accordingly had more than one reason to move Bogdan, the Moldavian, out of the way. Given, however, that he had himself not been voivode for long, he was compelled to present what was an act of political vengeance as fulfilling his ruler's duty to do justice. It could be portrayed thus because Bogdan had unlawfully become bother-in-law to Radu the Great and had no less unlawfully urged Vlad the Younger to break his oath of peace. Neagoe Basarab had him arrested on these grounds. As Gabriel Protos records:

> And to the lawbreaking Bogdan he [Neagoe Basarab] said that he must return all property and riches that he had embezzled with the connivance of the lord [Vlad the Younger], and his life would be spared. The villain however refused; and thus it came to pass that he was first severely tortured and finally hanged; and began to rot and was thrown to the dogs to be eaten. Yet they would not even come close, for

the saint [Niphon] had anathemised him. They therefore took him and buried him in the ground, that the misery might be ended.[87]

Some 150 years later, the Cantacuzène Anonymous gives a far more detailed account:

And Bogdan, the anathemised, desired to flee, yet God's judgement prevented him from doing so, on account of his plots against Saint Niphon and of his cunning. He fell into the cunningly laid net and they caught him like a lying beast that walks into the trap with both legs, and Bogdan caught himself in the snare that he had laid for Neagoe. For, as he sought to flee Neagoe as from a lion, he fell into the Danube and, though he escaped the crocodile, was caught by the serpent and brought before Neagoe Voivode. And he said unto him, when he beheld Bogdan in his misery: 'Oh, woe unto thee, scoundrel, how couldst thou weave such a plot, didst thou not fear God, Who sees and knows all that is hidden and unseen? And wherefore must so much blood be shed on account of thy plots? Yet I shall forgive thee all for God's sake. Henceforth thou shalt rue and do penance for thy wrongs, and the voivodal riches, which thou hast unlawfully made thine own, thou shalt return and no harm will come to thee; if not, the sin shall be upon thy head and thy soul.' Yet he said nothing, for the Devil – to whom he was beholden – had darkened his mind and his heart, and he was tormented with manifold tortures, just as Saint Niphon had prophesied, when he foretold that Bogdan would die a violent death. And neither beasts, nor fowl, nor the earth would eat up his corpse, instead it only shrivelled and blackened, to the disgust of all.[88]

87 Ἐις δὲ τὸν παράνομον Μπόγδανον νὰ μαρτυρήσῃ εἶπε τὸν βίον καὶ τὰ ἄσπρα, ὁπου ἐπῆρε τυραννικῶς μὲ τὸν αὐθέντην, καὶ νὰ τοῦ χαρίσῃ τὴν ζωήν του. Ο δὲ μιαρὸς οὐκ ἠθέλησε καὶ ἔτζι τὸν ἐβασάνισε μὲ μεγάλα παιδευτήρια καὶ εἰς τὸν ὕστερον τὸν ἐκρέμασεν καὶ ἐπρήσθη καὶ τὸν ἀνέρριψαν ἔξω κατάβρωμα εἰς τοὺς σκύλους. Ἀλλὰ δὲν τὸν ἔγγιξαν τελείως οἱ σκύλοι ὡς ἀφωρισμένον ὑπὸ τοῦ ἁγίου. Οθεν τὸν ἔχωσαν εἰς τὴν γῆν, διὰ νὰ παύσῃ ἡ καταίσχυνη' (Gabriel Protos: 137f.).

88 'Iar Bogdan cel afurisit vru să fugă, ci judecata lui Dumnezeu nu-l lăsă, pentru mozaviriia ce mozavirise pre Sfântul Nifon şi pentru hicleniia, ci căzu în mreaja cea hicleană şi-l apucară ca pe o hiară înşelătoare care să prinde cu amândouă picioarele în cursă şi să vână el în laţul care vrea să vâneze pre Neagoe. Că fugind de Neagoe-vodă ca de leu, dede în Dunăre şi scăpă de corcodel, iar de şarpe fu apucat şi trimis la Neagoe-vodă. Iar el deacă-l văzu într-atâta pedeapsă, zise-i: "O, vai de tine, ocaanice, dar căzutu-ţi-s-au ţie să faci hiclenie ca aceasta, căci nu te-ai temut de Dumnezeu, cela ce ştie şi véde toate ştiutele şi neştiutele? Dar pentru ce varsă hicleşugul tău cel fărădelege atâta sânge? Iată, de toate te iert, pentru Dumnezeu. Şi de acum înainte să te pocăieşti de răutăţile tale, iar avuţiile céle domneşti care le-ai

The second account's detail may be because the Cantacuzène Anonymous had far more material at his disposal some 150 years after the events. It is more likely, however, that the account was written and must be read as a hagiographic embellishment, for Neagoe Basarab had in the meantime become the idealised example of a Christian, true-believing and great ruler. From his account of Vlad the Younger's death, we know that the Cantacuzène Anonymous had a propensity for finding religious justifications even for questionable actions of Neagoe Basarab. Accordingly, the execution of Bogdan, too, is depicted not as an act of personal revenge, but as one of cosmic justice performed by Neagoe Basarab in his capacity as *ruler*. Bogdan, the criminal, meanwhile is demonised for allegedly being in league with Satan and shunned by all creatures.

The emoluments, fiefs and other property that Bogdan received from Radu the Great or Vlad the Younger in recognition of his loyalty and reliability – the signs, that is, of his service and his honour[89] – were now treated as stolen goods. To the new ruler, they must appear as tokens of an honour no longer valid under the altered circumstances but on the contrary were now signs of treason. Bogdan was accordingly asked to return them, which he quite naturally refused to do, since they constituted his symbolic capital. Though Neagoe pretended to be merciful, the conditions he imposed were such that Bogdan's refusal was only to be expected.

This seems to have been an astute move on the part of Neagoe Basarab, for it allowed both chroniclers to suggest in good faith that Bogdan had only himself to blame for his grisly demise. Yet the accusatory undertone of another chronicler's very sparse account, that of Radu Popescu Vornicul, indicates that not all observers found the case of Bogdan to be altogether

---

luat tu făr de dreptate și le-ai ascuns, să mi le spui și nu vei păți nici o nevoie; iar de nu, păcatul să fie pre capul tău." Iar el nu vru să spuie nimic, că-i întunecase diavolul, cel ce-l iubea pe el, mintea și inima, pentru care lucru multe munci au luat până ce ș-au dat și sufletul, cum au prorocit de aceasta Sfântul Nifon, de au zis că cu rea moarte va să moară Bogdan. Iar trupul lui nici fiarăle, nici pasările, nici pământul nu l-au putu mânca, ci numai ce s-au pârjolit și au negrit întru răutatea tuturor' (Cantacuzène Anonymous B: 99).

89 On the relationship between honour and material wealth in the medieval era, see Grigore 2009: 118ff.

clear-cut. This attitude may be due in part to the fact that Radu Popescu Vornicul was himself a member of a great family of boyars that had also suffered at the hands of the voivodes and their 'arbitrary' ways. Yet it may also be that the events themselves were ethically dubious and that the historians found it safer to skirt the topic rather than incriminate him.[90]

Yet the execution of Bogdan also contributed to underpinning the legitimacy of Neagoe as rightful ruler. Lacking any claim to the throne by descent, he tried to acquire the legitimacy he needed by his actions. Put bluntly, he sought to prove that a true ruler is a ruler not by birth, but one who proves himself by his actions. The sacramental and dynastic logic can be seen gradually to give way to political and ethical line of argument. The ruler came to be measured by his actions to a greater extent than previously. Neagoe Basarab was aware of this and hence took a number of steps to remake his rule, which he had acquired illegitimately, as legitimate.[91]

The first of these steps was the more or less formal *electio* by the council of boyars, coupled with the official acclamation by the people. The second was to fulfil the obligation to justice by punishing Bogdan for conspiracy. Yet Neagoe Basarab also needed recognition from abroad, which is why in 1513 he renewed the tribute arrangement with Selim I, who had been sultan since having pushed aside his brother Ahmed the previous year.

In light of the support rendered by Vlad V the Younger to Selim I in his struggle against his brother Ahmed, the young sultan was not initially inclined to look kindly on Neagoe Basarab, who had, after all, removed a useful ally from his throne. However, the new tribute arrangement and the homage[92] paid to Selim I by Neagoe Basarab in 1513 soon established good relations between the two. Neagoe had negotiated a good deal, keeping

90 Radu Popescu Vornicul B: 267.

91 Grigore 2012c. Nor did Neagoe Basarab ever lack critics or rivals to the throne. His attempts at building legitimacy may thus be considered at most a qualified success (see Zamfirescu 1973: 42).

92 The homage paid by the Wallachian voivodes to the sultan should not be confused with the *homagium* of the West. At Calomeea in 1485, Stephen the Great paid homage to the Polish King Casimir IV (1447–1492) in the Western manner, by bowing his head and lowering his flag. To pay homage to the Ottomans initially meant simply to acknowledge the obligation to pay tribute. Later, the voivode was expected to kiss the sultan's hand, to kneel before him, to kiss his feet, even to lay his

the tribute payment at 12,000 ducats, as in the previous arrangement with Radu the Great.[93] In its provisions, the treaty appears to have confirmed its predecessor.[94] For his part, Selim I must have been pleased to see the empire's northern frontier pacified and hence, as a Hungarian document records,[95] pledged not to interfere in Wallachia's internal affairs as long as the tribute was paid on time. In return for his undertakings, Neagoe Basarab received from the sultan the regal insignia, which confirmed his legitimate rule as *eflak* (Lord) of Wallachia: the *kaftan* or robe, the *sanjak* or banner and the drum.[96]

By these steps Neagoe Basarab inaugurated his reign; a reign which, compared with most of his predecessors on the throne, lasted the relatively long time of nine years. Neagoe Basarab died on 15 September 1521 aged around forty, of unknown causes. His death occurred while the Ottomans under Suleiman the Magnificent (1520–1566), in 1520 and 1521, were preparing their European campaign. In the course of this military attack on Christendom, Belgrade fell in 1521 and the largest part of Hungary was turned into a *sanjak* after 1526.[97] Neagoe's underage son Theodosius succeeded, albeit very briefly, to the throne of Wallachia, with Neagoe's brother, Preda Craiovescu, as regent:

---

head beneath the sultan's feet before being invested by him with the regal insignia (flag and garb) (Costăchel/ Panaitescu 1957: 323; Panaite 1997: 293ff.).

93 Cândea/Giurescu/Maliţu 1966: 108.

94 Neagoe 1966: 749. Wallachia was tied to the Sublime Porte by complex relations of dependency. The voivodes had to be confirmed and invested by the sultan; they were obliged to come to his assistance with troops in the case of war and even to accompany him personally on campaigns. Radu the Great initially paid 8,000 ducats in tribute, but was later forced to accept a raise of 4,000 ducats. He was further compelled to give up the Danube fords and the tax income they yielded to the Ottomans (Cândea/Giurescu/Maliţu 1966: 102).

95 Cândea/Giurescu/Maliţu 1966: 102.

96 Mehmet 1968: 926; Vergatti 2009: 114f. With some differences, these insignia recall those of imperial Rome: the *paludamentum* corresponds to the Wallachian 'kaftan' or the *mappa* to the *sanjak*. The Ottoman tradition adds the drum as regal insignia, though unlike it lacks lance and diadem (Piepenbrink 2010: 63).

97 Macarius 1959: 93; Neagoe 1971: 89.

And after the death of Basarab Voivode did Preda, his brother, ascend to the throne, in order to hold power for his nephew Theodosius. However, the boyars did not agree with this and elected another voivode, Radu Voivode the Monk who came from the region of Buzău. And Radu Voivode came with boyars and troops to do battle with Preda close by Târgoviște, and victory was with Radu Voivode, and Preda was killed [in battle] […]. [A]nd death came to Theodosius in Istanbul.[98]

In fact, however, Theodosius, who in a document of 30 October 1517 was already mentioned as co-regent,[99] ruled for so short a time (September 1521–December 1522, with an interruption) that the chronicle of Macarius, written in Church Slavonic, does not even mention him.[100] Immediately upon the death of Neagoe Basarab, Mehmed, pasha of Nicopolis, seized power in Wallachia and intended to have himself installed as the country's ruler.[101]

It did not come to this because the Wallachian aristocracy saw through the Ottomans' plans. Michael Bocignoli (d. 1534), at the time rector of the Republic of Ragusa, knew Neagoe Basarab personally and was well informed of the situation in Wallachia. He reported that the Ottomans were seeking to take advantage of Theodosius's minority in order to turn the country into a province of their empire. They had understood, continues Bocignoli, that the road through Wallachia was the shortest and safest way to move their troops swiftly against the Western powers. It was for this reason that Suleiman I had given young Theodosius an Ottoman guardian,[102] so 'that Romanians might learn to live under Ottoman rule'. But the Romanians had disagreed and rejected both Theodosius and his

---

98 'Iar după moartea lui Băsărab-Vodă s-au înălțat domn Preda, fratele lui Băsărab-Voevod, ca să ție domnia lui Theodosie, nepotu-său. Iar boiarii nu l-au priimit și au rădicat alt domn, pre nume Radul-Vodă Călugărul, despre partea Buzăului. Și au venit Radu-Vodă cu boiarii și cu oaste, ca să se lovească cu Preda, la Târgoviște, și au fost izbânda Radului-Vodă și au perit Preda. […] [Ș]i pre Theodosie l-au ajuns moartea la Țarigrad.' (Cantacuzène Anonymous B: 113).

99 DRG I: no. 129, p. 127.

100 Macarius: 93.

101 See the 1521 letter of Louis II of Hungary to Sigismund I of Poland (DGR II/3: 264, p. 374); also, Cantacuzène Anonymous B: 113; Radu Popescu Vornicul B: 269f.

102 This apparently refers to 'Mehmet Pasha', who is mentioned by the Cantacuzène Anonymous.

guardian. They impressed upon the sultan that the child was unfit to rule and that the people would in any case not stand for being subjugated by Ottomans, cleaving as they did to their old autonomy.[103]

Majesty and Its Christian Subjects

What particularly distinguished Neagoe's rule was that it inaugurated a new era of the prestige of Wallachian princes, who sought to assert their status as *principes Christiani* no longer by force of arms directed against the 'infidels', but rather by symbolic gestures and intensified cultural activities both within and beyond their frontiers. Such an active presence was facilitated above all by the 'highly interconnected cultural landscape of the Orthodox peoples',[104] which gave the Orthodoxy of south-eastern Europe the appearance of a single 'family'.

In the difficult final decades of the Byzantine Empire, the Wallachian rulers displayed an increasing tendency to take on the Byzantine emperors' function as guardians and sponsors of the Orthodox Churches in south-eastern Europe.[105] One reason for this mounting self-confidence on the rulers' part was their military power, which in the fourteenth and fifteenth centuries had not yet been broken by the Ottomans; another was the economic power they derived from the geopolitically advantageous position of the Danubian Principalities[106] and an astute policy of granting trading privileges.

103   Michael Bocignoli apud Holban, I, 1968: 178. See also Maxim 1993: 111. In the fifteenth and sixteenth centuries, the principalities of Moldavia and Wallachia enjoyed enhanced autonomy *vis-à-vis* the Ottoman Empire, as testified by contemporary Ottoman sources, in which these entities are described as *dâr-ül-kefere* (lands of war, i.e., the countries to be conquered) in contrast to *dâr-ül-Islam* (house of peace), the conquered territories in the Balkans (see Panaite 1997: 278ff.).

104   Grecu 1924: 1.

105   Turdeanu 1939: 146ff.; Moldoveanu 2007: 55; Bojović 2008: 44ff.

106   Situated at the frontier between the Slavic, Latin and Byzantine cultural realms, the Danubian Principalities were a site of cultural transfer as well as facilitating the mobility of people and goods, as well as international communication (Theodorescu 1972: 100).

Although the time of Neagoe Basarab marked the peak of charitable foundations and donations to the other 'Orthodoxies', the trend could already be discerned in such 'soldier princes' as Mircea the Elder (1386–1418), Stephen the Great or Vlad III the Impaler. They gave the monastic communities of Athos or Meteora not only their financial support, but also used their authority to defend their rights with the Sublime Porte.[107] The aforementioned Radu the Great simultaneously supported the monasteries on Mount Athos,[108] the Ecumenical Patriarchate of Constantinople, the Serbian Patriarchate of Peč and Kremikovsky monastery in Bulgaria.

We are faced here with a princely presence on a large scale, large enough indeed for Prince Radu to be acclaimed by the population of Constantinople like a Byzantine autocrat. The Wallachian princes commemorated their commitment to Orthodoxy and their special status as 'true-believing rulers' – following the ideology of Byzantine rulers – resulting from it by having themselves depicted, in frescoes of the churches they built, in the imperial garb of Byzantium and surrounded by such holy persons as the Virgin Mary or John the Baptist.[109] Again, an example is provided by Radu the Great, who had himself depicted on the wall of the cathedral of Curtea de Argeş wearing red shoes, which in Eastern Christianity was usually a mark and the sole privilege of the Byzantine emperor.[110]

This quasi-imperial consciousness of power reached its peak in the Moldavian prince Vasile Lupu (1634–1643, with a brief interruption), who both summoned a pan-Orthodox synod and controlled the election of the Ecumenical Patriarch.[111] According to an account by the Moldavian

---

107   Iorga 1972: 126f., 138.
108   Bojović 2008: 51, 63f.
109   Neagoe 1971: 96; Iorga 1972: 134; Barbu 2001: 197. We are dealing here with the political motif of 'upon thy right hand did stand the queen' (Ps. 45.9) in Moldavian church painting in the time of Stephen the Great. In several of the churches he founded, Stephen is depicted in the august company of the Virgin Mary and John the Baptist, most likely with the intention of representing the earthly kingdom in image of the heavenly one. The rightful and true-believing ruler benefits from the intercession of saints, thus proving his status as willed by God (Chihaia 1976: 186).
110   Nicolescu 1970: 92.
111   Iorga 1972: 167ff.; Bazilescu 1971: 677. All these phenomena led the early twentieth-century Romanian historian Nicolae Iorga to speak of a so-called 'Byzantium after

scholar and voivode Dimitrie Cantemir (1710–1711),[112] Wallachian voivodes were crowned and anointed by the country's patriarch from at least the late seventeenth century onwards. Having been confirmed by the sultan, they were once again anointed, this time by the Ecumenical Patriarch in Istanbul, while the coronation mass of the Byzantine emperors was read.[113]

Even noble families gave support to the Orthodox brother peoples in the Balkans, not merely in financial and material form, but also by means of a far-reaching and tightly woven matrimonial policy including the deposed ruling houses of Serbia, Bulgaria or even Byzantium. An example from the late fifteenth century is the Craiovescu family, whose matrimonial policy in Serbia created the preconditions for the decisive role Neagoe Basarab was later to play in affairs, both spiritual and political, south of the Danube.[114] Neagoe himself was married to Despina, a scion of the ancient Serbian despot dynasty of Branković.[115] This tradition of contracting promising marriages continued in following centuries and came also to include Venetian or Levantine families.[116]

Byzantium' in the Wallachian Principalities (Iorga 1972). This syntagma has since been rejected by more recent Romanian scholars, who find the 'Byzantine-like' presence of the Wallachian princes to be no more than a construct of national historiography that ignores above all the individuality and the proper complexity of early modern politics in the Danubian Principalities. Modern scholarship instead has suggested terms like 'Byzantium against Byzantium', 'Non-Byzantium' (see Barbu 2001: 17) or even 'Byzantium before Byzantium' (Silvestri 2006), the latter to emphasise the cultural role of the Wallachian population in preserving Eastern Roman traditions north of the Danube between the fourth and sixth centuries. On the prerogatives of the Byzantine emperors in ecclesiastical affairs, see the letter written in 1395 by Ecumenical Patriarch Antonios IV to Grand Prince Vasily I of Moscow (apud Barker 1957: 194).

112   In his *Descriptio Moldaviae* (Pars secunda, caput III), written in 1714 at the behest of the Royal Academy of Sciences, Berlin, of which Cantemir was a member. (URL: <http://la.wikisource.org/wiki/Descriptio_Moldaviae> – last accessed 24.03.2014). On Dimitrie Cantemir: Bahner 1974; Luburici 2003; Bîrsan 2004; Bochmann 2008.

113   Buzescu 1943: 74.

114   Neagoe 1971: 39.

115   Filitti 1922b: 312ff.

116   Luca 2008.

The Craioveşti were known as consistent donors to the Orthodox Church of Wallachia. In 1506, for instance, they paid for the building of an entire monastery complex, including a church, outbuildings, cells, a hospice, a library, a calligraphy workshop, etc., in the Oltenian monastery of Bistriţa,[117] 'a cultural oasis in the Wallachian sixteenth century'.[118] The sacred objects with which the church was endowed testify to close commercial and cultural connections with the West. For instance, liturgical silverware and a Gospel binding of precious metal were made in Italian, Dalmatian or German workshops.[119]

Neagoe Basarab continued this policy of protection and responsibility towards the Orthodox Church of his own country and towards the Orthodox Churches of the Balkans.[120] As the first Wallachian ruler with a marked proclivity for learning, having himself enjoyed a thorough education in both the Greek and Church Slavonic traditions,[121] Basarab on the one hand devoted himself to making charitable religious foundations and to monastic culture, as well as supporting the work of Wallachian master printers,[122] while on the other he adopted a typical Renaissance lifestyle, for instance by engaging an Italian physician (Hieronymus Matievič of Ragusa), commissioning luxury items and jewellery from the goldsmiths of Sibiu[123] and cultivating diplomatic relations with Venice and the Roman *Curia*.[124]

---

117 A bell dating from 1496 suggests that the monastery of Bistriţa was built on the site of a previous (wooden) church (Ştefănescu 1981: 121).

118 Sandu 1938: 6; Stoicescu 1970: 21; Ionescu 1971: 663.

119 Costăchel et al. 1957: 247; Ştefănescu 1965: 94; Nicolescu 1968: 136, 171, 200f., 202ff.; Ionescu 1971: 664ff.

120 Bulat n.d.: 19ff.; Bazilescu 1971: 682ff.

121 See Bulat n.d.: 10; Toma 1943: 4f.; Ionaşcu 2005: 10. Neagoe Basarab appears to have spent much of his childhood and youth at the monastery of Bistriţa, the foundation of his family, and been educated by scholarly monks (Toma 1943: 8; Vergatti 2009: 38f.). A note in the hand of Neagoe Basarab can be found to this day in a book in the monastery's library that he had once borrowed (Ionaşcu 2005: 18). As a young man, between 1495 and 1501, Neagoe is supposed to have travelled to Hungary and Istanbul, though there is no documentary evidence for this (Ionescu 1971: 659; Vergatti 2009: 42f.).

122 Toma 1943: 6; Ionescu 1971: 662f.; Ionaşcu 2005: 7.

123 Vătăşianu 1959: 898, 903; Nicolescu 1968: 17.

124 Cândea et al. 1966: 112. A study shows the Wallachian rulers to have imported luxury clothes from Flanders, France, Venice, Florence and Germany, as well as from Brusa (Bursa), Damascus, Aleppo, etc. (Nicolescu 1970: 17ff.).

While the West was gradually beginning to discover the world's immanence and found the Christian ethos to be increasingly dispensable to politics, Orthodox Wallachia under Prince Neagoe Basarab seems instead to display an intensification of religious purpose and sentiment, as well as an increased interest in (hesychastic) mysticism.[125] This may testify not only to a spiritual, but also to a political attitude in the Danubian Principalities, which were still managing to preserve their freedom. To cultivate a mystical, ascetic and monastic form of Christianity may well have been an assertion of a distinct (political) identity against the mounting threat from Islam.

Such attitudes probably also lie at the root of the Christian ruler's self-image, which the Wallachian princes, in the absence of a Christian empire, adopted from the Byzantine emperors. Here was an opportunity to free Wallachian Orthodoxy from its Byzantine 'shackles' and to assume the leadership of Orthodox spirituality oneself – as well as establishing a material infrastructure, both civil and military, within the Ottoman Empire.[126] The Wallachian princes thus formed the first link in the chain connecting the Byzantine political construct of the 'new Rome' with that of the 'third Rome', which the ideology of imperial Russia claimed to embody.

As for the significance of Neagoe Basarab for Wallachian Orthodoxy in the early sixteenth century, the extent of his charitable foundations and endowments seems almost boundless.[127] Of ninety-six deeds issued by the voivodal chancellery under Neagoe Basarab, forty-nine are deeds of endowment for monasteries and churches. Gabriel Protos provides a list of the most important endowments,[128] which accords with the original deeds held by the endowed monasteries themselves.

Basarab's single most important endowment was the cathedral of Curtea de Argeş, an architectural monument of rare magnificence and beauty, decorated with the most intricate masonry, as Radu Popescu Vornicul remarks:

---

125   Bazilescu 1971: 680.
126   Neagoe 1971: 43, 97.
127   Moldoveanu 2007: 56f.; Săsăujan 2012: 72ff.
128   Gabriel Protos 1944: 157ff. For recently edited deeds of donation, see Zahariuc 2010.

[Curtea de Argeş], like which there was nothing in the world – it seems to me – on account of the masterly making of all objects to be seen [in and on the church]. The stone walls on the exterior, indeed the whole church, are decorated with carved stone flowers. And though there are countless such flowers, you will never find any two to resemble one another.[129]

Some commissions for construction and decoration work went to German builders and stonemasons from Sibiu (Hermannstadt) and Braşov (Kronstadt),[130] which suggests that the cathedral was a multi-cultural 'product' of all population groups in the Wallachian Principalities. Money appears to have been no object for Neagoe Basarab in building this church; he 'spared not his own property, spending it for the glory of God [...], when [he] paid for this church at tremendous expense'.[131] It has been claimed that Basarab had taken on the expense of building this magnificent edifice from a sense of guilt, to atone for the killing of Vlad the Younger.[132]

Among the contemporaries present at the consecration of the cathedral on 15 August 1517[133] was Gabriel Protos, who recorded his astonishment at its beauty:

> And he had the archiepiscopal church at Argeş torn to the ground and on its site built another holy church of carven and smoothed and flower-decorated stones only. And he connected the back of each stone, one to another, by a brace, with great mastery, and thereinto he poured lead, so as to fix them strongly in place. And through the centre of the narthex he erected twelve pillars, made only of carven stone and beautifully turned, which represent the twelve apostles. And in the altar above the holy table he did also erect a wonderful work with little cast iron towers. But the

---

129 '[Curtea de Argeş] care potrivă nu avea în toată lumea, mi să pare, în meşteşugul lucrurilor ce să văd, pe denafară de piatră cioplită peste tot şi cu flori săpate peste toate pietrăle şi toată biserica; ce sunt atâtea sute dăblai şi nu să află douǎ flori să să aseamăne una cu alta' (Radu Popescu Vornicul 1963: 33, l. 10–14).

130 Sandu 1938: 11.

131 '[C]ă nu şi-au cruţat avuţiea, ci o au cheltuit întru slava lui Dumnezeu, făcând această mănăstire cu mare cheltuială' (Radu Popescu Vornicul 1963: 33, l. 16–17).

132 Cantacuzène Anonymous A: 205. On this see also Cazacu 1967: 782f.; Ionescu 1971: 653 n. 4.

133 Gabriel Protos 1944: 166; Moldoveanu 2007: 56.

windows of the church and of the altar and also the skylights of the narthex he made all of carven and of broken-through stone, and around the centre he surrounded the church entirely with a stone belt of three braids, decorated with flowers and gilded, the church, the altar, and the narthex, which represent the Holy Trinity. Under the lowest eaves however all around the church he erected a cornice all of white marble with carven flowers, which were very beautifully hewn and wrought. The roof however was all of lead blended with tin; the crosses on the towers were all polished with gold; and the towers too were carven with flowers and some were built twisted; and all around the vaulting were applied coats of arms, which were artfully carven from stone and polished with gold. And in front of the church he erected a small pavilion with four pillars of coloured marble and a wonderful vaulted and painted roof, and the roof too was covered with lead. And the stairs leading up to the church he made likewise of stone with carven flowers and with twelve steps, which represent the twelve tribes of Israel; in the whole church, in the narthex, in the sanctuary, in that little pavilion he made the floor of white marble. And the church he inwardly and outwardly decorated very beautifully and all the cavities of the stones on the exterior walls he painted with blue lapis lazuli and gilded the flowers. *And thus we can say that truly it is not so large and extensive as that Zion, which Solomon built, nor as Hagia Sophia, which the great Emperor Justinian built, yet in its beauty it surpasses them.*[134]

Architecturally, the church generously combines Oriental and Armenian elements with a baroque opulence of decoration that recalls certain monuments of the West.[135] The church's icons form part of the so-called Serbian-Byzantine Renaissance and display some Venetian influences.[136] It seems appropriate to call Curtea de Argeş an architectural synthesis of a number of cultural traditions and in instance of what has been called the 'Wallachian Baroque' of the early modern era.[137]

Neagoe Basarab's patronage crossed borders, indeed reaching as far as the Sinai Peninsula.[138] The intensity and focus of these endowments are remarkable, testifying not only to cultural and religious interests, but also to the construction of a sphere of political influence by subtler means

---

134   Gabriel Protos 1944: 162 (translation by Vasile Grecu; emphasis added). An expert description of the cathedral of Curtea de Argeş can be found in Vătăşianu 1959: 498ff.
135   Ghika-Budeşti 1927: 144ff.; Vătăşianu 1959: 493, 498.
136   Ştefănescu 1981: 124.
137   Giurescu 1926: 130f; Duţu 1984.
138   Sandu 1938: 13ff.; Marinescu 2012.

than armed force. Historians have noted how the cultural and scholarly flourishing of sixteenth-century Moldavia and Wallachia was accompanied by political crisis and military disintegration. A concern for culture and religion offered an alternative means of political assertion. Wallachian 'modernity' begins with religious reforms, with increased mystical intensity, with a new flourishing of the media thanks to the printing press and with widespread support for oppressed Orthodoxies elsewhere.[139] In Neagoe Basarab, the Orthodox Churches in the Ottoman Empire found a patron and a protector, while Wallachia became home to churchmen and scholars fleeing the Ottomans.[140]

Nineteenth-century 'national' historiography in Romania completely misunderstood both the extent and the opulence of Neagoe Basarab's spending and endowments for the preservation of an 'Orthodox infrastructure' in the Ottoman Empire. One of that era's most important historians, Alexandru D. Xenopol (d. 1920), was unsparing in his judgement:

> The outcome of Neagoe Basarab's reign was fatal to Wallachia. Excessive spending on ecclesiastical matters impoverished the people, whilst politically, the country subsisted in unspeakable degradation [...]. In ignoble servitude to the Turks, in vassalage to the Hungarians, true to the ecclesiastical principle so staunchly upheld by the most pious Neagoe: 'The sword will spare the bowed head'.[141]

And indeed all chroniclers confirm the exorbitance of Neagoe Basarab's material and spiritual commitment to the Orthodox lands under Ottoman rule.

Neagoe Basarab's endowments continue where his predecessor, Radu the Great, had left off at the time of his death: on Mount Athos.[142] He paid for the completion of Koutloumousiou monastery, which had been begun by Radu and was surrounded by a stone wall. Basarab also built the church of St Nicholas, which was provided with towers, cells for the monks, a refectory, cellars, a bakery and kitchen, gardens, a gatehouse, a hospice and

---

139 Stănescu 1963: XI; Grigore 2012d.
140 Panou 2006 and 2007.
141 Xenopol 1889: 482 (my translation).
142 Sandu 1938: 8; Bazilescu 1971: 682ff.

storerooms. To Dionysiou monastery, which he refurbished, he donated a reliquary for the remains of St Niphon, a chest made 'of pure silver and [...] decorated with fine pearls and other precious gemstones and with enamel'.[143] On the shore, he built a small port by the name of Askalon, which he equipped with a perimeter wall, towers, an arsenal, cannons, and a large and a small ship. The lavra of St Athanasios received a new lead roof, gold and silver vessels for liturgical purposes, and an endowment of 90,000 thalers. The lavras of Iviron and Chilandar were granted an annual stipend of 5,000 thalers[144] as well as aqueducts providing them with water from a considerable distance.[145] Many other communities on Mount Athos likewise enjoyed the support of the Wallachian prince:

> Why make more words by naming all the monasteries one by one? For all monasteries on the Holy Mount Athos did he enrich with money and manorial villages, also he gave them cattle and raised many a *wall*. And he became grand *Ktetor* [κτήτωρ] of all Sfetagora [Sveta Gora].[146]

Mount Athos can thus be seen to be turning into a forward post of Orthodoxy, not only in a spiritual, but also in a strategic sense, being fortified with walls, towers, a port and an arsenal, and being defended by cannon and (possibly) ships.

Athos was not the sole beneficiary of Neagoe Basarab's munificence. Gabriel Protos continues: the Ecumenical Patriarchate in Constantinople received a new lead roof, was able to refurbish all monks' cells and received a generous amount of money as well as many objects. The Sinai monastery received, among other things, an annual stipend from Basarab, nor did he ignore the churches in Jerusalem and throughout the Holy Land. Basarab's

---

143   Gabriel Protos 1944: 155.
144   See the deed issued by Basarab in 1517 (Doc. no. 12, apud Bojcović 2008: 160ff.).
145   Gabriel Protos 1944: 157ff.; DRG I: nos. 75, 87 and 126; Nicolaescu 1924; Nicolaescu 1933; Iorga 1972: 129ff.; Ionaşcu 2005: 7. For an inventory of the items made of precious metal and given by Basarab to the monasteries of Mount Athos, see Vătăşianu 1959: 898ff. On this, see also Giurescu 1926: 125, 126ff.; Panou 2007: 70ff.
146   Gabriel Protos 1944: 158f. (according to the German translation by Vasile Grecu; emphasis added).

generosity also extended to the monasteries of Meteora in Greece, Kuznica in Macedonia and Treskavec in Pelagonia. Gabriel Protos concludes:

> To what purpose should we enumerate these things individually and the monasteries on which he bestowed gifts? Let us recount them at once: all, those in Evrota, in Thrace, in Hellas, in Achaia, in Illyricum, in Campania, in Hellespont, in Mysia, in Macedonia, in Thettalia, in Sirmium, in Lugdonia, in Pelagonia, in Dalmatia and in all lands from sunrise to sunset, from midday to midnight did he preserve all holy churches and everywhere made many gifts. And particularly did he with no austerity care for the maintenance of those as had retreated to deserts and caves and hermitages. And he was good not only to Christians but also to the heathen, and he was a *gracious father*, in that he resembled the heavenly Lord, who lets his sun shine and his rain fall on the good as on the bad, as the Holy Gospels show.[147]

Though we should not allow ourselves to be deceived by Gabriel Protos's sometimes unbridled enthusiasm for his subject, it does seem clear that by means of a wide-ranging policy of 'investment', Neagoe Basarab provided for the preservation of Orthodox Christian identity and autonomy (even material independence).[148]

By his endowments and donations, Neagoe Basarab established a symbolic presence that gave him such authority and credibility among the Christians of south-eastern Europe in their 'Babylonian captivity' that he was honoured with epithets of the Byzantine emperors of old. In an epigram, the poet Maximos the Greek (d. 1556) referred to Basarab as 'the divine' (Νάγγοε θεῖος), while Manuel of Corinth, rhetor of the Great Church in Constantinople from 1483 to 1484, addresses the Wallachian prince as *basileus* and *autokrator*.[149]

Like the former Byzantine emperors, under Ottoman rule the new *advocati* of Orthodoxy, the Wallachian voivodes, were received on their visits to Istanbul by the Ecumenical Patriarch and acclaimed by the city's Christian population. A fresco in the cathedral of Curtea de Argeş depicts

---

147 Gabriel Protos 1944: 160 (according to the German translation by Vasile Grecu, emphasis added). On this, see also Cândea 1966: 111. For a comparison, see Eusebius-Vita Constantini: I, 43, 3, p. 203.

148 Tiţa 2009.

149 Ševčenko 1997: 67; Tanaşoca 2011: 6/7, l. 1–2. See comments in Chihaia 1995b: 175; Ionescu 1971: 672; Mureşan 2008: 127.

Basarab in imperial garb (including the double-headed eagle) alongside his family.[150] Like the former Byzantine autocrats, he took care to be regarded as a generous φιλάνθρωπος (loving mankind), φιλόδωρος (one who gladly gives), μεγαλόδωρος (large-scale donor) and finally θεραπευτής (caregiver) to all Orthodox subjects both within and beyond his own country's frontiers. In this capacity, he was able to mediate disputes over jurisdiction on Mount Athos, choose the metropolitan of Wallachia and call regional synods.[151]

With symbolic extravagance, Neagoe Basarab presented himself not only as *pater patriae*, but also as a *paterfamilias* – the father, that is, of the 'Orthodox family'. In his conduct, he reaffirmed the cosmological responsibility of a Christian ruler for the flourishing of faith and the Church on the earth, and in so doing recalls Christ Himself, faithful and caring, and is seen to strive for *homoiosis* or likeness to God.[152] By building individual churches, the generous ruler contributes to building the universal Church of God. According to this logic, his function is apostolic. The Wallachian prince, like the Byzantine emperors before him, thus revealed himself as an ἰσαπόστολος, one equal to the apostles.[153]

Basarab was well aware of his role as a true-believing Christian ruler and tried to restore the Byzantine tradition of symphonic rule.[154] He set about the symbolic reconciliation of the late Prince Radu the Great and the likewise deceased metropolitan of Wallachia, the aforementioned Niphon (who, as Niphon II, had been patriarch of Constantinople), whose remains were interred on Mount Athos. Niphon and Radu had been at odds over the implementation of ecclesiastical and moral reforms in the principality,[155] a dispute that had ended with Niphon's banishment.[156]

Neagoe had Niphon's mortal remains returned to Wallachia in a grandly staged procession and placed his coffin over Radu's tomb in the church of Dealu (near Târgoviște).[157] In a state of ecstasy (ἔκστασις), Neagoe

---

150   Nicolescu 1970: 94; Văetiși 2012: 186ff.
151   Neagoe 1971: 101f.; Anca 2010: 113ff.
152   On this term, see Grigore 2010: 146.
153   Albu 2008: 137.
154   Carabă 2012.
155   See Panou 2007: 64ff.
156   Gabriel Protos 1944: 87f.
157   Cantacuzène Anonymous B: 92.

Basarab claimed to have had a vision vindicating his efforts to create harmony and his attitude of cosmological responsibility.[158] This gesture of reconciliation gave Gabriel Protos cause to compare Neagoe with another peacemaker, the Byzantine Emperor Theodosios II (408–450), who likewise had brought the remains of the Patriarch John Chrysostom (d. 407) back from the place his death in exile to Constantinople.[159] The cosmological responsibility of the Christian ruler thus extends beyond death, though such powers are usually the preserve of God.[160]

What to Alexandru D. Xenopol, writing in the nineteenth century, appeared as Basarab's supine attitude before foreign political and ecclesiastical power appears in a new light today. We now recognise that Basarab's endowments not only aimed at geographical breadth, but also opened up new strategic and even – and why not? – military opportunities. In this context, it might be said that he was building cultural hegemony,[161] though I do not mean to argue that Basarab's regal generosity in the religious and ecclesiastical sphere had only political and immanent purpose in subverting the structures of the Ottoman state and was devoid of any religious meaning – on the contrary.

The personal religious preoccupation with salvation of the soul through donations, endowments, philanthropy and almsgiving inevitably contributed to fostering coherent communities in which were gathered Orthodox subjects of the Ottoman Empire dependent on support from Wallachia. Such support was reliably forthcoming during the reign of Neagoe Basarab.

The purely religious Christian practice of giving thus had political implications. In the Christians of the Ottoman Empire, it inspired hopes that Constantinople might one day be reconquered for Christendom and the Orthodox *oikumene* restored.[162] The logic of philanthropy thus to

---

158   Gabriel Protos 1944: 151f.; cf. Constantinescu 1921.
159   Gabriel Protos 1944: 143; Ionaşcu 2005: 18f. On John Chrysostom and his condemnation of the immoral lifestyle of Empress Eudoxia, which led to his banishment, see Perthes 1853; Baur 1930; Verosta 1960; Brändle 1999; Tiersch 2002.
160   Grigore 2012c: 87ff.
161   Sandu 1938: 8.
162   Lăzărescu 1967: 192.

some extent blurred with that of the *Reconquista* and the Crusades.[163] However, the association by religion – most south-eastern Europeans were Orthodox – also imparted structures from which could grow a sense of political solidarity and resistance able to profit from the religious liberties granted by the Ottoman Empire.

Neagoe Basarab himself was aware of his mission in Christ's name, as the iconographic programme of the cathedral of Curtea de Argeş, described above, makes amply clear. In a study from the 1960s, Emil Lăzărescu proved that the church's *pronaos* was originally decorated with a highly symbolic and programmatic set of icons.

The *pronaos* provided space for the graves of voivodes, for whom the cathedral was intended as a necropolis. A wall of icons separated the tombs from the rest of the room. Facing the tombs were icons of the Church Fathers (sainted bishops, ascetics and teachers of the Church), facing inwards were icons of 'military' saints, for instance of Saints George or Demetrios. This was surely no accident, and scholarship has found a political message here: the tension between dynamic and meditative motifs indicated that the Christian princes had died in the true faith and doctrine, as good sons of the Church, while also recalling their other duties as (armed) guardians of Orthodoxy and upholders of Orthodox identity. Like St George, depicted as a dragon-slayer, the most Christian voivodes, too, saw themselves as fighters against the Ottoman 'beast' or indeed the Antichrist.[164]

Moreover, the militant clues in the decorative programme at Curtea de Argeş did not end in the narthex of the Church. A panel on the bell-tower features a billy-goat impaling a dragon on his horns. The billy-goat was originally coloured red, the colour of the Byzantine Empire and the soldier saints, whereas the dragon was green – like the Ottoman flag.[165] The political messages encoded in the architectural details throughout the cathedral precincts are as numerous as they are subtle.

---

163   Iorga 1972: 144.
164   Lăzărescu 1967; Hering 1989. A political programme has also been detected in the design of the pavilion in front of the cathedral of Curtea de Argeş (cf. Chihaia 1995a: 91f.). On the Ottomans as the Antichrist, see Schnapp 2010.
165   Chihaia 1964.

Diplomatic Relations with the Christian Powers

In the early sixteenth century Wallachia was in a twofold relationship of vassalage – with regard to the Hungarian crown, on the one hand, and with the Sublime Porte on the other – with the influence of the latter continually growing. Princes like Mihnea the Evil or Vlad V the Younger tried to reverse this tendency at the expense of their crown and their life. Radu the Great, on the other hand, tried to contain the increasing influence of the Ottomans by a policy of compromise and by playing off the great powers against each other.[166]

Neagoe Basarab, too, was to pursue this policy. On the one hand, he maintained diplomatic relations with Pope Leo X as well as the Venetians, Poles and Hungarians – that is, with the potential sponsors of the new crusade – while on the other hand underscoring his willingness to pay obeisance and tribute to the Sublime Porte, to which end he travelled to Istanbul in September 1515.[167] We can observe here something of Machiavelli's well-known dictum, according to which a prince should combine the cunning of the fox with the strength of the lion. The complaint to the Sublime Porte (cited above) of certain Wallachian boyars opposed to the Craioveşti exposed this two-track policy,[168] though with no consequences for Basarab, who was able to continue it unimpeded.

Already in the first years of his reign, Basarab ensured good neighbourly relations by sealing a non-aggression pact with the Hungarian crown. Moreover, Basarab delivered regular reports of Ottoman plans and movements to Buda, as is evident from a letter written in 1513 by King Vladislaus II of Hungary (1490–1516) to Basarab.[169] For their part, the Hungarians tried to mediate in the conflict between Neagoe Basarab and the voivode of Moldavia, Bogdan III (the Blind, 1504–1517).[170]

---

166 Denize 1995: 176.
167 Tappe 1964: 20f.; Neagoe 1966: 747; Cândea 1966: 108f.; Ionescu 1971: 669f.;
     Neagoe 1971: 39, 56f.; Vergatti 2009: 116.
168 Mehmet 1968: 925, where Basarab is said to have forged an anti-Ottoman front in
     agreement with the Transylvanian prince, Johannes Zapolya (1510–1526).
169 Veress 1914: Letter 81, p. 105f.
170 DGR II/3: no. 57, p. 50; on this, see also Neagoe 1966: 754; Ionescu 1971: 669;
     Ciobanu 1985: 120. A letter from King Sigismund I (the Elder, 1506–1548) of

Neagoe Basarab was well aware of his principality's geostrategic position, for the roads connecting Istanbul with Hungary and Poland passed through Wallachia. As a result, the Wallachian authorities were in a position to compel any mission passing between these powers to account for its activities.[171] This occurred, for instance, in the case of Georg Krupski, the Polish emissary, who had been Basarab's guest in 1512 on his way to Istanbul. It would appear that Târgovişte, Basarab's capital, was something like an assembly point for Christian legations on their way to the Sublime Porte, an opportunity to discuss common policies towards the Sultan.[172] Yet the Wallachian prince was not merely a stop-off, but a frequent destination in its own right of Polish (1514) or Hungarian legations, for instance in 1520, when the Hungarian Marm Horwath informed Basarab of his king's plans for an attack on the Ottomans.[173]

On 1 February 1518 Basarab's emissary, Hieronymus Matievič,[174] arrived in Venice to discuss the possibility of a common front of Christendom against the Ottomans, whose conquest of Syria and Egypt had been injurious not least to Venetian interests in the eastern Mediterranean. The emissary presented a gift from Neagoe Basarab, a cup of gilded silver, and was in return knighted by the doge (*per il Serenissimo Principe nostro fato cavalier*) and received a robe worth 100 ducats (*una vesta di panno d'oro, in la qual non si spendi più di ducati 100*).[175] He remained in the city for some two months.[176] The same emissary was dispatched to the Republic of Ragusa in December 1518.[177]

In January 1519 Antonio Paikalas, another emissary, visited Pope Leo X in Rome at the behest of Neagoe Basarab. Yet Paikalas spoke in the name not only of Wallachia, but also of Moldavia, thus testifying to the joint foreign policy of the Danubian Principalities.[178] The emissary delivered a clear

_____

          Poland remarks on tensions between the two voivodes in 1512, DGR II/3: no. 55,
          p. 47. See also DGR II/3: no. 65, p. 61.
171   DGR II/3: no. 83, p. 79 and no. 136, p. 147.
172   DGR II/3: no. 139, p. 151 and no. 140, p. 152.
173   Ionescu 1971: 670; Şerban 1972: 56f.
174   Matievič was Basarab's personal physician.
175   Haşdeu 1865: 284.
176   Neagoe 1966: 758 and Neagoe 1971: 82; Denize 1995: 185f.; Vergatti 2009: 125.
177   Iorga 1989.
178   Lăzărescu/Stoicescu 1972: 97ff.; Denize 1995: 186.

message from Neagoe Basarab: in the event of a crusade, Wallachia would offer the Christian powers assistance, in return for which it expected a share of the reconquered territories.[179] This same Paikalas was to be encountered in Venice on 24 June 1519, where one of his tasks was to find a physician for Basarab, who was gravely ill.[180]

Neagoe Basarab was apparently quick to respond to Leo X's plans, who in 1517 redoubled his attempts to organise a crusade.[181] This seems altogether understandable in light of the fact that Selim II and his army were occupying Egypt at the time[182] and testifies to the hope on the part of the south-eastern European states for a strong response to the Ottoman offensive and indeed to their dream of a *Reconquista*. It also proves that the traditional idea of a joint struggle of Christendom – as defined in the letters of the Venetian Marino Sanudo the Elder (d. after 1334)[183] – against the Tatar and later the Ottoman threat had not yet been forgotten.[184]

179 DGR II/3: no. 224, p. 307ff.
180 Neagoe 1971: 83f.; Şerban 1972: 55; Vergatti 2009: 127f.
181 Pope Leo X had already begun to organise a crusade in 1513 and charged the archbishop of Strigonium/Esztergom, Thomas (1498–1521), with preaching crusading sermons in Poland, Hungary and Wallachia (see DGR II/3: no. 119, p. 113; Neagoe 1966: 757).
182 Neagoe 1971: 65f.; Engel 1994: 280ff.; Matuz 1994: 82f.; Rohlmann 2002: 263f.; Schreiner 2004: 27.
183 Kunstmann 1855: 812: 'Hence there is much reason to fear that all Christendom is in grave peril if the Turks were to conquer the lands of the western Romania, as they have already conquered the lands of the eastern Romania, which were largely conquered in recent times, then [the Turks] will join with the Tatars of the north to make clear their firm purpose.' (Ideo timendum est valde, quia si Turchi acquirerent terras Romaniae occidentis – sicut acquiviserunt terras Romaniae orientis, cujus acquisitio – nis et major pars fuit in eo tempore – sociando se cum Tartaris semptentrionalibus, ut effective in voluntate ostendunt, tota christianitas est in maximo periculo constituta.)
184 See the letter of Vlad II Dracul (1436–1442 and 1443–1447) to the aldermen of Kronstadt, in which he asks for assistance in arming the fortress of Giurgiu on the Danube, which was of great relevance as a site for the defence of 'all Christians' (apud Chihaia 1976: 190). In 1343, for instance, a series of military successes on the part of the Christian coalition (Poland, Moldavia, Hungary, the Teutonic Knights)

On the other hand, Moldavia and Wallachia played a key part in the
Roman Curia's crusading strategy: Pope Leo X 'granted' Neagoe Basarab a
number of territories, with the qualification, of course, that they had yet to
be wrested from the Ottomans.[185] Their importance is further confirmed
by King Louis II of Hungary (1516–1526) warning in 1516 that Moldavia
and Wallachia must under no circumstance allowed to fall into Ottoman
hands if the planned crusade was not to lose one of its most important sta-
ging posts.[186] In April 1520 Basarab informed the aldermen of Kronstadt
that he was ready to mobilise a force of 40,000 men in case of a crusade.[187]

Basarab's Times in Historiographical Interpretation

Romanian historical scholarship interprets the period of Wallachian
history following the death in 1504 of Stephen the Great, the last of
the Danubian Principalities' important 'soldier princes', in accordance
with two paradigms. It is striking that the military significance of the
Wallachian rulers diminished in the early sixteenth century while activities in the cultural sphere intensified, as expressed in diplomatic relations, literary production, economic growth, scholarly exchange, cultural transfer, endowments and the printing press.[188] At the international
level, the political importance of the Danubian Principalities remained
unchanged till the death of Neagoe Basarab. However, it was barely any

---

under the leadership of the Wallachian voivode Nicolae Alexandru (1352–1364)
forced the Tatars of the Golden Horde to surrender control over the lower Danube
(See Papacostea 2008: 521f.). Such examples show that the rulers of Wallachia had
always been actively involved in the common struggle of 'Christendom' against the
'Infidel' (Denize 1995: 14).

185 See Tappe 1964: VI, p. 20f.; Prunduş 2001: 17; Vergatti 2009: 127. The pope had
already assigned roles to the Christian powers: the Holy Roman Emperor, alongside the Poles, Hungarians and Wallachians, was to attack the Balkans, the French,
Italians and Venetians were to move through Epirus to threaten Istanbul, while the
Spanish and English were to attack the city directly (Iorga 1972: 30f.).

186 DGR II/3: no. 193, p. 246; Ciobanu 1985: 124.

187 BbFb: 181; Ionescu 1971: 670; Prunduş 2001: 18; Vergatti 2009: 129.

188 Lăzărescu 1967: 190.

longer won by force of arms, but rather secured by cultural achievement and political communication. This represents something of a paradox, to which historians responded by developing two patterns of interpretation, one Marxist and the other historical-aesthetic.

In two studies on the so-called 'Romanian Baroque' published in 1977,[189] Edgar Papu took up an established tradition in Romanian historiography that sought to understand the caesura of the early sixteenth century as the transition from military to cultural forms of resistance. This resistance, which was said to have sprung from a 'defensive attitude to life',[190] had been concerned with preserving south-eastern European Orthodoxy and bolstering its identity once its ideological, spiritual and political infrastructure had been destroyed. Religious consciousness was thus held to have been a vehicle for revisionist political hope for the reconquest of Constantinople. After 100 years of struggle, the Wallachian rulers found themselves compelled by the force of Ottoman arms to reconsider their policy.[191]

The portraits of the voivodes painted in churches evince a change of register, from the soldier-rulers of the fourteenth and fifteenth centuries (Mircea the Elder, Vladislav I, Radu I) to the 'hieratic' princes. Whereas the former are depicted in the knightly garb of the Latin West, equipped with lance, armour helmet and shield, the latter are shown wearing imperial Byzantine finery in the company of holy persons, thus underscoring the sacred aspect of their rule, willed by God.[192] They can thus be seen to have resorted to a form of 'spiritual imperialism', giving cultural, but also infrastructural succour to subjugated Orthodoxies in the Balkans or trying to persuade Western Christendom to launch a crusade.[193] Artistic expressions of this 'baroque' attitude in the time of Basarab could be found, according to Edgar Papu, in the extravagantly rich decoration of the cathedral of

---

189   Papu 1977: 250f. and 1977b: 20ff.
190   Papu 1977: 258.
191   Maxim 1993: 111ff.; Denize 1995.
192   Cândea/Giurescu/Malițu 1966: 111; Nicolescu 1970: 11, 83ff.; Chihaia 1995: 172, 180, 187, 189.
193   Papu 1977: 260.

Curtea de Argeş as well as in the finely wrought and flowery prose style of Basarab's own mirror for princes.

The ideal of the Romanian Baroque had thus been to survive by architecture and literature rather than by martial glory.[194] As several scholars have emphasised, the Wallachian rulers tried their best to maintain the vanished tradition of Byzantine theocracy while not being averse to dreams of *renovatio imperii*.[195] The Romanian Baroque is thus read as a form of political survival that relied on intellectual, religious and artistic forms, but also used economic and diplomatic means.

The other paradigm conforms to a Marxist ideological framework dominant in Romanian scholarship until 1989. It was developed by Eugen Stănescu and based on remarks in the 1882 correspondence between Karl Marx and Friedrich Engels,[196] according to which all territories east of the River Elbe had experienced a seizure of power on the part of the grand nobles. Applied to the Danubian Principalities, this had meant a 'second edition of serfdom'.[197] An initial period of feudal fragmentation in the fourteenth century had been succeeded by one of centralisation under the leadership of the voivodes, the so-called 'centralised voivodal-feudal state'. This period had begun under Vlad the Impaler in Wallachia and Stephen the Great in Moldavia and reached its peak in the mid-sixteenth century. In the late sixteenth century there followed the period of the foundation of a so-called 'centralised aristocratic-feudal state', in which power is held by the great families of the nobility who succeed in using the state's centralised power structures to further their family interests.

This pattern of interpretation takes a particular historic configuration and reads it according to the trans-historical principle of the class struggle. Tested against the actual historical situation in the Danubian Principalities of the fifteenth and sixteenth centuries, this interpretive paradigm looks rather shaky. For one thing, it relies on an ideologically charged terminology that conflicts with scrupulous historical scholarship. To conflate such terms as 'feudal', 'centralised', 'state', 'aristocratic-feudal', 'voivodal-feudal',

---

194   Papu 1977: 269.
195   Sandu 1938: 14.
196   Stănescu 1961: XXVn2.
197   Friedrich Engels to Karl Marx, 16 December 1882. Marx/Engels 1982 vol. 19: 130f.

'ruler as president of an aristocratic republic', etc., scarcely does justice to the complex realities of medieval and early modern Wallachia.[198] Nor is the theory borne out by the facts of the matter, as can be seen by examining the case of Neagoe Basarab as a typical example of a power grab by noble families in the early sixteenth century. That Neagoe broke the dynastic line of voivodes does not prove the consolidation of voivodal power, as the theoretical construct would have it, but on the contrary indicates its waning. It should be remembered that Basarab's predecessors likewise fell victim to the intrigues and centrifugal tendencies of the grand boyars.

Since it is far from self-evident that we can speak of 'Romania' or 'Romanians' in the late medieval and early modern eras, it is easy to lapse into somewhat anachronistic terminology. That caveat aside, the first approach discussed, the historical-aesthetic interpretation of the 'Romanian Baroque', represents an attempt at overcoming the one-sided and mechanistic accounts advanced by some Romanian scholars in the materialist and Marxist tradition and restoring nuance to the study of this period. By situating historical phenomena in broad, *intertwined* cultural history of interdisciplinary relevance rather than in the narrow paradigms of class struggle and social and economic history, I would contend that we obtain not only a deeper analysis, but also use a more versatile tool. Such a methodological approach seems more appropriate to examining the content of Basarab's highly significant mirror for princes, the *Teachings to his Son Theodosius*.

The *Teachings to Theodosius*: Their Textual History

The Teachings of Neagoe Basarab to his Son Theodosius (*Teachings* for short) belong to the literary genre of the mirrors for princes and constitute a masterpiece of theological, political, military and diplomatic scholarship. The book consists of two parts. While the first part (a single chapter with twenty-one subheadings) addresses theological and theoretical questions – politics, the cosmic order, the God-likeness of the Christian

198 Stănescu 1961: XXIVff.

prince, the ruler's enlightenment in the hesychast manner and the political seen as the doxological community of worshippers – the slightly larger second part (thirteen chapters) forms the work's practical section. The argument here concerns such matters as the selection of counsellors, servants and officials or receiving and dispatching envoys. Diplomatic relations, military strategy, social and philanthropic efforts or protocol at the princely court are among the other topics touched upon.

Yet to researchers, the *Teachings* provide questions rather than certainties. What is the work's manuscript tradition, and what does it have to say about its reception in the south-eastern European *oikumene*? Who was the book's actual author – was it really the Wallachian voivode or merely a later, anonymous writer? In what language – Church Slavonic, Greek, Old Romanian[199] – was it originally written? What are the stylistic or rhetorical devices used by the author? In what tradition does he situate himself and what are the sources he makes use of in his work? Are the *Teachings* just a chaotic compilation of material and disordered quotations? Finally, what point has scholarship reached in studying this text, what do think we know and what remains to be done?

To all these questions the present chapter hopes to give, if not definitive answers, then at least such indications as the state of knowledge the text allows.

Manuscript Traditions, Editions and Impact of the Teachings

In 1838 the Romanian Vasile Popp became the first modern scholar to draw attention to the *Teachings*, in his *Disertaţie despre tipografiile româneşti din Transilvania şi învecinatele ţări, de la începutul lor până în vremurile noastre* (Dissertation on the Romanian printing presses in Transylvania and the neighbouring countries from the beginnings to the present).[200]

---

199   Once the Cyrillic letters are transliterated into Latin, Old Romanian is not that
        different from modern Romanian. To the averagely educated contemporary
        Romanian, it is likely to look like the language of Shakespeare does to English
        speakers. The greatest differences are in vocabulary (see Mihăilă 1974).

200   Teodor 1962: 229; Mihăilă 1996: XLVIII.

The work's manuscript tradition gives it no title – neither its Church Slavonic nor in its Old Romanian or Greek versions – which is why scholars had to find one. The first to call this mirror for princes the *Teachings of Neagoe Basarab* was the Romanian editor Ioan Eclesiarhul in his *editio princeps* of 1843 (Figure 3).[201] Since the Church Slavonic original had lost its title page, it was necessary to resort to the Old Romanian version, in the corpus of which the words *învăţătură* (singular) or *învăţături* (plural) frequently occur. The sixteenth-century Greek version likewise uses *logoi* (λόγοι διδακτικοί), that is, 'words of teaching', 'speeches', 'instructions', 'teachings'. The editors of the Church Slavonic fragments, Piotr A. Lavrov and, later, Gheorghe Mihăilă, use the Slavonic *slova*, which also means 'words' or 'speeches'.[202] I thus find it more appropriate to use the word 'teachings' rather than 'admonitions' (*Mahnreden*), as the Slavist Stojan Romanski did in his Leipzig dissertation of 1908.[203] German specialists in Romanian literary history have suggested 'advice' as a translation,[204] which is as far from the Old Romanian term as it from the Greek or Church Slavonic.

The work came to international attention in a notice published by the Russian philologist and Slavicist Piotr A. Lavrov in the journal *Chteniya* in 1896, in which he announced the discovery of the Church Slavonic manuscript if the *Teachings*[205] in the SS. Cyril and Methodius National Library (CMNL) in Sofia and drew attention to the particular language, later known as 'Romanian Church Slavonic', which he took first to have

---

201 *Învăţăturile bunului şi credinciosului Domn al Ţării Româneşti Neagoe Basarab VVd. către fiul său Teodosie VVd., Bucureşti în tipografia colegiului Sfântul Sava 1843* (The teachings of the good and faithful Lord of Wallachia, Neagoe Basarab Voivode, to his son Theodosius Voivode. Bucharest at the Printing Press of St Sava College]. On this Romanski 1908: 139. A good synthetic overview on manuscript tradition, versions, editions and translations can be found, for example, in Piru 1961: 40 or Chiţimia 1963: 317ff.

202 Neagoe Basarab 1996: 267, Romanski 1908: 141. See below for more on Lavrov's edition.

203 Romanski 1908.

204 Bochmann/Stiehler 2010: 70.

205 The article reproduces a lecture delivered to the Imperial Russian Historical and Archaeological Society. The Church Slavonic version had been discovered in the previous year, 1895 (see Romanski 1908: 136).

developed with this work. Neither Neagoe Basarab nor later Romanian copyists, he argued, had themselves been native speakers of a Slavic language and thus had added manifold Romanian forms to it.[206] In 1904 the same Piotr A. Lavrov published the fragments hitherto discovered under the title *Slova nakažatelnьija voevodьj Valaškago Ioanna Njagoia k sьnu Feodosjiu* (*Teachings of the Wallachian voivode John Neagoe to his son Theodosius*).[207] The previous study and this critical edition draw the attention of Slavists to this long-lost treasure of south-eastern European political culture, and they were followed by a string of Slavist studies and philological analyses by scholars such as A. J. Iacimirski or Polihron Sîrcu.[208]

Most specialists hold the Church Slavonic version of the *Teachings* to be the original. The manuscript consists of fragments, a shorter section of the first part and several of the second. The manuscript is catalogued as MS 313 at the CMNL. The odyssey of these fragments begins with the eight pages that were catalogued by the same library as MS 83 in the nineteenth century. In 1891 the library acquired another ninety pages, which it had bought from the photographer Ivan Karastoianov and were initially catalogued separately from the first eight pages as MS 123.[209] In 1910 the two fragments (MSS 83 and 123 CMNL) were merged into a new manuscript and given the catalogue number 313. To this were added in 1921 the last thirteen pages, which though the CMNL had for some time held them first as MS 369, then as MS 784, were not recognised as part of the Church Slavonic version of the *Teachings* by anybody until 1921.[210] A total of 111 pages have thus been preserved, and specialists express little hope of finding any more.[211]

206   Bărbulescu 1928; Mihăilă 1996: LIf. Most studies on Romanian Church Slavonic were published in the journal *Romanoslavica*.

207   Published in St Petersburg. On this, see Ciobanu 1989: 41; Mitescu 1993: If.

208   'Valaškii Merk Aurelij i ego poucenija', in: *Izvestija otdelenija russkogo iazíka; slovesnosti akademii nauk*, vol. X, 4, 1905, pp. 339–374 and *K voprosu o podlinnike Poučenij valaşkogo gospodaria Ioanna Neagoe*, St Petersburg 1901. See the remark in Zamfirescu 1973: 19.

209   Panaitescu 1959: 214; Olteanu 1975: 385f.

210   Bogdan 1968.

211   Mihăilă 1973: 327 and 1996: LII.

The manuscript's elaborate decoration, with initials in gold and carefully executed half-uncial letters in purple or blue on glossy Italian paper, led scholars to conclude that MS 313 CMNL might even be the official copy for the use of Theodosius, the heir to the throne, for outwardly it is a small-format book, a typical 'pocket-sized' reading copy of the time. The paper used was only produced between 1518 and 1538, which makes it at least possible that the copy was produced during the lifetime of Neagoe Basarab and at his court.[212] The paper's watermarks (types 446, *anchor* and 3471, *cardinal's hat*)[213] further restrict the production span to 1519–1529.[214] As far as we know, no further copies of this version are preserved. It was translated fairly early into Greek (mid-sixteenth century) and later (mid-seventeenth century) into Old Romanian, which suggests a certain reputation for the text within the Orthodox sphere.[215]

The first mention we have of the Greek version is in the catalogue of the *Greek Manuscripts on Mount Athos* published in 1895 by Spyridon Lambros, where it is listed as Ἰωάννου Νάγγοε βοεβόδα καὶ αὐτοκράτορος Οὐγγροβλαχίας λόγοι. At the time it was catalogued, the manuscript was numbered MS 3755.[216] It was and remains in the possession of the library of Dionysiou monastery on Mount Athos, where it is today catalogued as MS 221. Its measurements are 20 by 14 centimetres.[217] The manuscript consists of 164 sheets and reproduces only the second part of the *Teachings*. The first, theological part would appear not to have been important enough to the monks, who were already well acquainted with ascetic and mystic subjects, and hence not translated. Also missing is part two, chapter 6, on the selection of councillors and other officials.[218]

---

212   Mihăilă 1973: 328f.; Zamfirescu 1973: 208; Cazacu 1989: 111f.

213   Briquet 1968: 35–37, 222–223.

214   Mihăilă 1973: 328f.; Olteanu 1975: 385.

215   Mihăilă 1996: LIV.

216   Lampros 1895: 367.

217   Cazacu 1989: 112.

218   'Învăţătură iar a lui Neagoe Voevod cătră coconii săi şi cătră alţi de Dumnezeu aleşi domni. Cum vor pune boiarii şi slugile lor la boerie şi la cinste şi cum îi vor scoate dintr-acéstea, pentru lucrurile lor. Cuvântu 13' (Teaching of the same Neagoe Voivode to his sons and other princes chosen by God. How they should install

Leandros Vranoussis, in a paper delivered at the second Congress of South-East European Studies in 1970, showed that this manuscript is an autograph by Manuel of Corinth (d. 1530), grand rhetor of Hagia Sophia and from 1480 to 1539 teacher at the patriarchal school at Constantinople/Istanbul.[219] Manuel was hence the translator, rather than Matthew of Myra (d. 1624), as had long been assumed.[220] This was an important discovery, since the consensus even in the early twentieth century had been that the Dionysiou manuscript was of seventeenth-century origin.[221] Considering that the original was written around 1519–1520, the *Teachings* were translated into Greek fairly early, no later than 1530.[222] Manuel of Corinth appears to have translated from the Church Slavonic, since the titles of the Greek version are equivalent to those of the original, whereas the titles are altered in the Old Romanian version.[223] From MS 221 Dionysiou, the late sixteenth-century MS 610 Dionysiou also adopted a fragment from the *Teachings* on the love of God under the heading 'Τοῦ ἐκλαμπροτάτου καὶ εὐσεβεστάτου αὐθέντου Ἰωάννου Νάγγοε μεγάλου βοεβόδα καὶ αὐτοκράτορος μεγάλης Οὑγγροβλαχίας λόγος διδακτικὸς περὶ ἀγάπης Θεοῦ.'[224] The translation testifies to the considerable impression the *Teachings* appear to have made in the Greek Orthodox circles of the Ecumenical Patriarchate and of Mount Athos.

---

their boyars and servants in office and how to dismiss them, according to their merit. Word 13) (Neagoe Basarab 1984: 151ff.). On this, see Zamfirescu 1973: 212; Mihăilă 1996: LXXVIII.

219   Zamfirescu 1973: 208.

220   Ciobanu 1942.

221   Romanski 1908: 138f.

222   Zamfirescu 1973: 212.

223   Romanski 1908: 146. In a 1959 study, the Romanian Slavicist Petre P. Panaitescu affirms that the Greek translation had been based on a Romanian original (see Panaitescu 1959: 216).

224   'The teaching of the most noble and most pious Lord John Neagoe, grand voivode and lone ruler [*autokrator*] of Great Wallachia, on loving God.' The author of this manuscript would appear to have been Georgios of Enos in the second half of the sixteenth century, who did not simply adopt the Greek version of MS 221 Dionysiou, but rather adapted it (see Grecu 1943: 296ff., 300, 303).

The complete text of the *Teachings* is preserved only in the Old Romanian version dating from the seventeenth century, while only fragments amounting to less than one third of the work remain of the older Church Slavonic manuscript, as indicated above[225] – 111 of originally about 390 pages. Of these 111 pages, 95 contain passages from the second part of the work.[226] The Old Romanian manuscripts all use the Cyrillic alphabet.

Three copies of the Old Romanian version are preserved today. The oldest and most valuable can be traced to the private library of the Wallachian prince, Ștefan Cantacuzino (1714–1716). Each sheet bears the prince's stamp, allowing the manuscript to be dated to before 1716. It is today catalogued as MS 109 at the Cluj-Napoca branch of the Romanian Academy Library (RALC). MS 109 RALC consists of 273 sheets measuring 20 x 16 centimetres. It reproduces both the *Teachings* as well as Gabriel Protos's life of St Niphon, of which the end is missing as well as six further sheets from the *Teachings*. The copyist is stated to have been one '*Mâinea, cântăreț de la Mitropolie*' (Mâinea, cantor at the Metropolitan Church).[227] This manuscript undoubtedly represents a translation of the Church Slavonic version, a translation produced during the reign of the Wallachian voivode, Matei Basarab (1632–1654). This periodisation is suggested by the currency mentioned (*srebrьnikь/costandă, medь* or *cet/mangâr*), which only circulated in Wallachia between 1600 and 1650.[228] Moreover, the time around 1635 seems particularly likely for the translation, since we know that demand for Romanian-language books saw a marked increase around that time.[229] Though the translator is unknown, he is likely to have been an educated court official, perhaps even, as historians suppose, the grand boyar and scholar Udriște Năsturel (1596–1659).[230]

---

225   Panaitescu 1959: 216; Zamfirescu 1996: XVIIIf.
226   Mihăilă 1996: XLVI.
227   'Ispisach az Mîinę pebec ot Mitropolie', apud Zamfirescu 1973: 361.
228   Iliescu 1967. In the early twentieth century, the Old Romanian translation was still dated to 1654 (Romanski 1908: 134).
229   Teodor 1962: 231; Zamfirescu 1973: 362.
230   Cazacu 1989: 112; Mihăilă 1996: XLVII.

MS 109 RALC may have been used to produce a Polish copy or translation, for several pages display marginal notes like 'do tyd', 'tyd pisano', 'do
tyd pisano', which in Polish mean roughly 'up to here' or 'written up to
here'.[231] Its very preservation is remarkable. After Ştefan Cantacuzino it
passed through the hands of several owners before Antonie Sion gave it to
St Sava College, Bucharest, in 1841. It was subsequently in the possession of
the city library of Bucharest, from where it went missing around 1879, only
to reappear in the library of the town of Blaj in Transylvania as MS 115.[232]
    Another, slightly abridged, copy of the Old Romanian translation
was prepared in 1727 for Phanariot Nicholaos Mavrocordatos, prince of
Wallachia (January–November 1716 and 1719–1730) by Radu Logofeţel de
Divan.[233] The copy performs something of a 'secularisation' on the original
text by omitting a number of sections dealing with religion, theology and
morality. This copy is preserved as MS 1062 in the Romanian Academy
Library (RAL) and was given to the Romanian state by the Jewish scholar
Moses Gaster (1856–1939).[234] The third copy dates from the early eighteenth
century and is also to be found in the RAL, in this instance as MS 3488.
It likewise contains the *Teachings* and the life of Niphon, though the end
is missing from both texts. This copy, which was given to Romanian state
by Petre Gârboviceanu in 1909, is valuable chiefly for containing the pages
missing from MS 109 RALC and could thus be used to reconstruct the Old
Romanian translation in its entirety.[235] Combining MSS 1062 and 3488
RAL produced new, hybrid versions, the nineteenth-century MSS 3402,
2714 and 1069 RAL.[236] Marginal notes in MS 3488 give instructions for the
making of further copies. MS 2714 is the oldest of the three hybrid copies
and was prepared according to the instructions contained in MS 3488. It

231   Zamfirescu 1973: Anm. 8, S. 377.
232   Grecu 1939: 1865; Crăciun/Ilieş 1963: 147; Romanski 1908: 134; Zamfirescu
       1973: 363f.
233   A kind of secretary, who arranged, presided over and recorded meetings of the
       Grand Council.
234   The manuscript was registered as MS 1 in the Gaster library. On this, see Zamfirescu
       1973: 367ff.
235   Zamfirescu 1973: 364.
236   Russo 1939: 563.

forms the basis for MSS 1069 and 3402 RAL.[237] Other manuscripts – MSS 464, 3672[238] and 3580[239] RAL – reproduce only parts of the *Teachings*. Among these is a collection of texts discovered in the Astra Library at Sibiu in 1970, which contains a small proportion of the *Teachings*.[240]

A side-by-side comparison of the Church Slavonic fragments and the Romanian version contained in MS 190 RALC enabled a fairly precise identification of the missing sections. It was further possible to calculate that a page of twenty-one lines in the Church Slavonic original corresponded to a page of twenty-four lines in the Old Romanian translation. The most recent translation of the Church Slavonic fragments, by Gheorghe Mihăilă in 1996, was given a more compact design, allowing the twenty-one lines of a Church Slavonic page to be rendered in a twenty-one-line page of translation.[241] Furthermore, the Old Romanian translation (MS 109 RALC) is generally faithful to the original with any minimal difference resulting from the few interpolations, some efforts to bring certain terms up to date and some minor liberties taken by the translator. It should not, after all, be forgotten that some 115 years separate the two redactions.[242] The sequence of ideas and statements, and of sentences and chapters, is however identical. 'There can […] no longer be any doubt that the seventeenth-century Romanian and the Church Slavonic versions are identical in structure, extent and contents.'[243]

At least three copies of the Church Slavonic version have existed. The first was an accurate copy in the chancellery of the Wallachian princes, on which the Old Romanian translation MS 109 RALC was based. A second copy – today's MS 313 CMNL – displays a gap in the text found neither in the Greek MS 221 Dionysiou nor in the Romanian version. The third

---

237 MS 1069 RAL was MS 8 in the Gaster library. It contains only six chapters of the *Teachings* (Romanski 1908: 136).

238 Copied in 1781 by Sava Popovici of Rășinari. The manuscript is part of a collection of texts entitled *Albina* ('The Bee', see Zamfirescu 1973: 366).

239 Copied in 1809 by Daniel Popovici, son of Sava Popovici, also from Rășinari.

240 Avram 1970: 39f.; Zamfirescu 1973: 360f.; Mihăilă 1996: XLVII.

241 Mihăilă 1996: LV.

242 Mihăilă 1973: 346.

243 Zamfirescu 1973: 211.

copy was held in Constantinople and was the basis for the Greek translation, MS 221 Dionysiou, as is evident from two gaps in the text that can
also be found in MS 313 CMNL, but not in the Old Romanian MS 109
RALC.[244] It seems that the history of the writing and the translation into
Greek of the *Teachings* was completed in 1530, the year in which their
Greek translator, Manuel of Corinth, died. They have since undergone
no significant change.[245]

The Greek MS 221 Dionysiou is not the only one of its kind. In
1988 Santo Luca drew attention to a Greek manuscript in the Biblioteca
Vallicelliana in Rome containing the instructions in Greek of a Russian
monk by the name of Barlaam to his son John or Ivan.[246] Said Balaam was
in fact Grand Prince Vasily III (Ivanovič) of Moscow (1479–1533), father
of the infamous Ivan IV (the Terrible, 1533–1584), and hence it is to this
czar that these instructions are addressed. This work of Barlaam's was presented to the Ecumenical Patriarch in 1557 with the aim of conciliating him
and of persuading him to bestow the title of czar upon young Ivan. The
manuscript mentions Theodore Mamalachos, the grand prince's envoy to
the Ecumenical Patriarchate, who was tasked, it would seem, with securing
the recognition of Ivan's claim to the title of czar. To this end, he carried a
number of manuscripts that were intended to prove the learning, linguistic
ability, reading, piety and conformity to the true faith (i.e., Orthodoxy) of
the young czar – his suitability, that is, as a Christian prince.

Yet this work is in fact 'stolen property' or rather an instance of plagiarism, as Santo Luca was the first to recognise and as was proved by Ion
Dumitriu-Snagov, the first scholar to make a careful study of the manuscript. The section headings simply replace the name Neagoe with that of
Barlaam and that of Theodosius with that of John or Ivan. Yet whoever
copied the original omitted to make such changes in the body text, where
references remain to Neagoe's mother, Neaga. The Romanian scholar also
found that chapter three of the second part, in which Neagoe's sons John,
Peter and his daughter Angeline are discussed, was reproduced verbatim
in the Greek version from Moscow – except for mention of Angeline.

244   Zamfirescu 1973: 212.
245   Zamfirescu 1973: 213.
246   Luca 1988; Pippidi 2001: 155; Dumitriu-Snagov 1996: 90; Cândea 1998: 208f.

Macarius, the metropolitan of Wallachia, also makes an appearance.[247] Comparing the Greek manuscript of the Barlaam text from the Vallicelliana Library with that from Dionysiou, Dan Zamfirescu and Ion Dumitriu-Snagov were able to show that, with the exception of the partly altered names, the two Greek texts are identical. The Barlaam manuscript is thus a copy of the Dionysiou manuscript and as such represents nothing less than an act of wilful plagiarism.[248] Yet this manuscript also testifies to the great authority enjoyed by the *Teachings* in the Orthodox world, from Constantinople to Moscow, as well as to their theoretical achievement in underpinning Christian rule in the Orthodox tradition. There is no other explanation for such brazen plagiarism.[249]

In passing, it is worth noting that the Romanian historian Nicolae Iorga claimed to have identified a German translation of part two, chapter seven, on table manners and court protocol.[250] Iorga spoke of a manuscript supposedly found in the estate of Prince Petru Şchiopul of Moldavia (1574–1577, 1578–1579, 1583–1591), who died in exile in Tyrol. The manuscript was recorded in the library of Archduke Ferdinand II (d. 1595) as *Maniera wie man die grossen Potentaten traktieren soll. Ain Buch in Quart mit gelbem Leder überzogen* (How to play host to great potentates. A quarto volume covered in yellow leather) and was acquired after the death of its Wallachian owner.[251] The hypothesis according to which this was a German translation from the *Teachings of Neagoe Basarab* has not yet been confirmed.

In summary of this overview of the manuscript tradition, we can conclude that three principal versions, each of which exists in several copies, have survived to this day. Only a single manuscript, MS 313 CMNL, exists of the original Church Slavonic version. The Greek version, produced

---

247 Dumitriu-Snagov 1996: 92.
248 Mihăilă 1996: XCVIII.
249 Dumitriu-Snagov 1996: 93; Mihăilă 1996: XCIX.
250 'Iar a lui Neagoe voevodul învăţătură cătră fie-său Theodosie şi cătră alţi domni, cătră toţi. Cum să cade domnilor să şază la masă şi cum vor mânca şi vor bea. Slovo 14' (Another lesson of Neagoe Voivode to his son Theodosius and to other lords, to all. How it is mannerly to sit at table, how they should eat and drink. Word 14).
251 DGR IX/1: 555; N. Iorga 1925: 59; Zamfirescu 1973: 66f. n111; Mihăilă 1996: CXIIIn76.

shortly afterwards, is most likely a translation of the Slavonic original and is preserved in MS 221 Dionysiou and in the plagiarised manuscript in the Biblioteca Vallicelliana in Rome. The Old Romanian translation from the early seventeenth century has come down to us in MS 109 RALC, which forms the basis of all subsequent (Old) Romanian copies.

The text's editions present a less complicated picture than its manuscripts. Whereas several editions were produced of the Church Slavonic and Romanian versions, there is only one of the Greek. No edition has yet been produced of the plagiarised Vallicelliana manuscript.

The first printing of the *Teachings to Theodosius* was the aforementioned one by Ioan Eclesiarhul, published in 1843.[252] It was printed at the press of St Sava College in Bucharest and is essentially a publication of the Old Romanian MS 109 RALC, which at the time was in the college's library, without yet having been able to consult the other Old Romanian manuscripts, which were still unknown to scholarship. The book is printed in the transitional alphabet, consisting of both Latin and Cyrillic characters, that is typical for Romanian in the first half of the nineteenth century. The editorial quality is poor, and the edition is of value largely as a historical document. Its editor, Ioan Eclesiarhul, omitted numerous passages and appears not to have understood and hence mistranscribed a great many words. He also took liberties with the text to the point of 'improving' – that is, modifying – it.[253] We are left with an unprofessional, imprecise, partly corrupted and frequently incomprehensible reproduction of the Old Romanian version that is of scant use to scholarship.[254]

Later incomplete editions of the nineteenth century are in effect adaptations of that of Ioan Eclesiarhul – those of Iosif Naniescu and Constantin Erbiceanu (1888) and Theodor Codrescu (1895).[255] The only professional, critical edition produced by a specialist in the nineteenth century is that of the philologist Bogdan Petriceicu Haşdeu (1838–1907), whose work is

252   Romanski 1908: 134; Ciobanu 1989: 41.
253   Zamfirescu 1973: 372.
254   Mihăilă 1996: XLVIII.
255   Published in the journal *Uricariul* 24/1895, pp. 212–214. See Zamfirescu 1973: 65.

completely independent of the 1843 edition, of which he appears not to have been aware.[256] Unfortunately, however, Haşdeu's edition is incomplete. It consists first of three chapters (V, VII, X) from the second part that were published in *Arhiva istorică a României* (Historical Archive of Romania; vol. 1/2, Bucharest 1865, pp. 111–116 and 120–132) and then part two, chapter VIII in *Buletinul instrucţiunii publice* (Bulletin of Public Education; 1/1865–1866, pp. 76–80).[257] This edition, too, was based entirely on MS 109 RALC; it is highly accurate and printed in Latin characters. The Eclesiarhul edition was also reprinted in Latin characters in 1910, by Nicolae Iorga under his own imprint, Vălenii-de-Munte.[258] It is a fairly poor edition, divided into seemingly arbitrary chapters and was produced without consulting the manuscripts. It nonetheless remained the standard edition in Old Romanian of the *Teachings* till 1970.[259] Four chapters (I, V, VI, VIII) from part two were published in 1938 by Dumitru Ciurezu in a rather obscure series called *Albina* (The Bee).[260] The best and only complete edition of the *Teachings* appeared in 1970 in the Bucharest publishing house of Minerva.[261] This edition was produced using the Old Romanian manuscripts as well as the Church Slavonic original. Its editors were the philologists Florica Moisil and Dan Zamfirescu and it was entitled *Învăţăturile lui Neagoe Basarab către fiul său Theodosie* (*The Teachings of Neagoe Basarab to His Son Theodosius*).[262] Established as the standard edition, it was republished in 2010 under the editorship of Dan Zamfirescu with expanded commentary and references to biblical and patristic authors quoted in the text. The new edition appeared as *Învăţăturile lui Neagoe Basarab către fiul său Theodosie. Versiunea românească de la Curtea de Argeş*

---

256 Russo 1910: 20. See Haşdeu 1865–1866: 76f.
257 Zamfirescu 1973: 67 n. 15, 373; Mihăilă 1996: L.
258 Mihăilă 1996: XLVIII.
259 Zamfirescu 1973: 375; Ciobanu 1989: 41.
260 Zamfirescu 1973: 375; Mihăilă 1996: XLIX.
261 A second edition appeared as early as 1971 (see Zamfirescu 1973: 65 n. 8).
262 Neagoe Basarab 1984. On this, see Mihăilă 1996: LI. This standard edition was preceded by the publication by Dan Zamfirescu, in 1969, of pt. 1, ch. III and pt. 2, chs. VII (in part) and VIII (Mihăilă/Zamfirescu 1969: 117–154; Zamfirescu 1973: 375).

(*The Teachings of Neagoe Basarab to His Son Theodosius*. The Old Romanian Version of Curtea de Argeș).[263]

The Church Slavonic fragments were edited later than the Old Romanian ones, being first published posthumously in St Petersburg in 1904 by the Russian Slavicist Piotr A. Lavrov (1823–1900). At the time, not all fragments had yet been discovered; thirteen more pages have since come to light.[264] Yet the edition is useless for another reason. It is quite disordered; the manuscript's sheets are reproduced in no particular order and Lavrov appears to have made no attempt to reconstruct anything like the original sequence of the chapters.[265] That work was undertaken by the Romanian historian and Slavist P. P. Panaitescu (1900–1967) and by the Slavist Gheorghe Mihăilă (1930–2011) in 1959[266] and 1967[267] respectively. Whereas Panaitescu, who did not yet have all the fragments at his disposal, still rendered the chapter sequence inaccurately, Mihăilă produced a critical edition of all Church Slavonic fragments along with photographic negatives of each page and with Romanian translations.[268] This edition formed the basis for that of Gheorghe Mihăilăs, published in 1996 with Roza Vânturilor of Bucharest, which contains a facsimile of MS 313 CMNL, a Romanian translation and an extensive introduction (Figure 2).[269]

The Greek version of MS 221 Dionysiou was published by the Byzantinist Vasile Grecu with Monitorul Oficial și Imprimeria Statului in 1942.[270] The Greek text is accompanied by a Romanian translation. In 1941 Grecu had already published the Greek fragment of MS 610 Dionysiou.[271]

---

263 Neagoe Basarab 2010.
264 Piru 1961: 40; Mihăilă 1996: LXIV.
265 Romanski 1908: 137.
266 Neagoe Basarab 1959.
267 Mihăilă 1967.
268 Mihăilă 1973: 331ff. Gheorghe Mihăilă added the thirteen missing pages to his edition and prepared a comprehensive critical edition during a research stay in Sofia from October to December 1971 (Mihăilă 1973: 328), but this edition was not to appear till 1996. For a precise listing and the sequence of the Church Slavonic chapters, see Mihăilă 1996: LVff.
269 Neagoe Basarab 1996.
270 Neagoe Basarab 1942.
271 Grecu 1943 and 1943a. On this, see Zamfirescu 1973: 57.

The only translation into another language is that of the Panaitescu edition of 1959 into Italian. The translation by Adriana Mitescu is based not on the Church Slavonic fragments, but on the Romanian translation included in that bilingual edition.[272] I understand that the Romanian scholar Adriana Mihaela Sapovici is currently working on a translation of the *Teachings* into modern Greek. At the time of writing, Alice Isabella Sullivan is working on a translation into English.

As is clear from the above discussion of the manuscript tradition, Basarab's *Teachings* enjoyed a broad and early reception in Orthodox cultural circles.[273] Preserved are not only three copies of the sixteenth-century Church Slavonic original, but also the Greek translation by Manuel of Corinth, MS 610 Dionysiou and the plagiarised version of Theodore Mamalachos. The teachings were well known in Wallachia too, as indicated by frescos in the church of Călui (c. 1585), in which, for instance, the portrait of Voivode Petru Cercel (Earring) is framed by passages from the *Teachings*.[274]

The seventeenth, eighteenth and nineteenth centuries saw the diffusion of the Old Romanian translation in numerous copies. We now know that the *Teachings* were very popular with the Phanariot rulers of Wallachia. MSS 109 RALC and 1062 RAL were both commissioned by a Phanariot, Ștefan Cantacuzino and Nicholas Mavrocordatos, respectively. Remarkably, Nicholas Mavrocordatos not only read the *Teachings*, but felt inspired by them to make his contribution to the genre, in the form of a mirror for princes written in Greek for the benefit of his son Constantine.[275]

Also preserved is another manual, addressed by Matthew of Myra to Prince Alexandru Iliaș (1616–1618).[276] In 1715, under the influence of the *Teachings*, Antim Ivireanul (d. 1716), metropolitan of Wallachia, composed an instruction in Christian politics for Ștefan Cantacuzino, the proud owner of the first translation of Basarab's mirror for princes into Old Romanian (MS 109 RALC). It was entitled Ἀουθεσίαι χριστιανικο-π

---

272 Mitescu 1993.
273 Iorga 1985: 50; Völkl 1979: 296f.
274 Chihaia 1972: 166ff.; Joantă 1992: 89.
275 Dapontès 1880: 337ff.; Duțu 1968: 466.
276 Camarino-Cioran 1979: 131f.

ολιτικαί.[277] Ştefan Cantacuzino was clearly an avid reader of mirrors for princes, as is clear from his ambition to own a nearly 100-year-old manuscript of the *Teachings*, to each sheet of which he went on to apply his personal stamp. We also have the example of Prince Mihail Racoviţă (in Moldavia: 1703–1705, 1707–1709, 1716–1726; in Wallachia: 1730–1731 and 1741–1744), who commissioned a political manual for his sons from a Greek scholar, Asarios Cigalas.[278] Also worth mentioning in this context are the parenetic writings and translations of Sebastos Kyminetes (d. 1703), the head of the Princely Academy of Bucharest, who made crucial contributions to the popularisation of such authors as Synesios of Cyrene, Agapetus and Theophylact of Ohrid.[279]

A Pseudepigraphical Work?

Since Basarab's mirror for princes was first 'discovered', in the early nineteenth century, in its Old Romanian version, most Romanian scholars – who felt national pride at the existence of such a cultural monument in the Romanian language – tended uncritically to ascribe the *Teachings* to Neagoe Basarab, voivode of Wallachia. The few dissenting opinions that held that Prince Basarab might after all not be the author were either ignored or bludgeoned with the weight of mainstream argument. Yet it took the historian Alexandru D. Xenopol's questioning of the *Teachings'* intellectual value and his assessment of them as a statement of deference to the Church and as a compilation of pious writings for Romanian scholars to begin seriously to subject the *Teachings* to technical and scholarly scrutiny. Not to be outdone, Xenopol added that the *Teachings* had in fact been written in Greek. The notion thus began to take hold that the work as it was known was merely the Old Romanian translation of an original written in another language and that the author was certainly not Neagoe Basarab.

---

277   Bianu/N. Hodoş 1903: 498f.; Duţu 1968: 449; Camarino-Cioran 1979: 132.
278   Russo 1982: 59.
279   Kyminitis 1967; Muthu 1976: 53; Karanasios 2001.

Theodor Codrescu, in an analysis from 1895 of the Old Romanian version,[280] tried to prove that the *Teachings* must have been written after 1648, since they quoted from the Old Romanian translation, by Udrişte Năsturel, of the popular novel *Barlaam and Josaphat*, which had appeared in 1648. Codrescu further doubted that Basarab, the Wallachian prince, could have been possessed of such a broad theological education. It rather seemed self-evident to him that the author had been a learned monk of the seventeenth century: 'The long ecclesiastical sentence structure, the flawless knowledge of the Holy Scriptures, the theological and Christian style indicate that the author wore a mitre rather than a crown.'[281]

Codrescu's doubts were shared by other scholars, such as Moses Gaster or Alexandru Philippide, who found themselves unable to imagine Basarab as the author of the *Teachings*.[282] In the absence of much secure knowledge of the manuscript tradition, the German Wilhelm Rudow too, in his *Geschichte des rumänischen Schrifttums* (History of Romanian Literature, 1892), stated his opinion that the *Teachings* were a seventeenth-century translation from the Greek.[283] Such 'blasphemous' claims, which challenged national pride and self-esteem, were opposed by philologists like Bogdan Petriceicu Haşdeu, who proposed a comprehensive critical edition of the only manuscript version known at the time. Haşdeu was convinced that the *Teachings* had originally been written in Romanian by a Romanian, and that that Romanian was Neagoe Basarab. Indeed, most scholars who studied the *Teachings* in the nineteenth century expressed reservations, if any, regarding the original language of the work, but not the author, who they continued to believe was Neagoe Basarab.

Until the Church Slavonic fragments from Sofia were discovered and published, however, the doubts of some scholars seemed very justified indeed. How could a text of such political and theological erudition have been written in *Romanian* in the early sixteenth century, a time when the language of culture and officialdom in the Danubian Principalities was

---

280   In *Uricariul* 24/1895, pp. 212–214.
281   My own translation from Theodor Codrescu (apud Zamfirescu 1973: 14f.). On this, see Zamfirescu 1963: 73; Panaitescu 1971d: 164; Mihăilă 1996: LXXIII.
282   Zamfirescu 1963: 72.
283   Rudow 1892: 20.

Church Slavonic? After the discovery of the Church Slavonic original
and the unmasking of the Old Romanian version as a translation from the
Church Slavonic, that case seemed altogether implausible.[284]

The role of 'devil's advocate'[285] in this matter fell to the Byzantinist
Demostene Russo,[286] who was born in Greece, had studied in Athens, Berlin
and Leipzig, and came to Romania in 1894 to teach at the University of
Bucharest. Russo was particularly interested in cultural transfer between
Greece and Romania in the medieval and modern eras, and the *Teachings*
were thus of key importance to him. Himself the owner of an extensive
and excellently appointed library, Russo was also an avid collector of old
manuscripts, in pursuit of which he travelled throughout south-eastern
Europe. In the course of his travels, he came upon MS 221 Dionysiou on
Mount Athos and was permitted to transcribe it. He dated it not to the
sixteenth century, but 100 years later. His careful study of the manuscript
confirmed, to his mind, Alexandru D. Xenopol's opinion that the *Teachings*
had originally been composed in Greek. Russo held the newly discovered
manuscript to be the original, of which the Old Romanian and Church
Slavonic versions were translations.[287] In support of his argument, in 1906[288]
he invoked Theodor Codrescu's 1895 thesis that held the author of this
mirror for princes to be an anonymous learned monk of the seventeenth
century and added arguments and reasons of his own.[289] And thus began

284   Zamfirescu 1973: 14.
285   Scholarship in general remained convinced of the *Teachings'* authenticity (Piru
       1961: 40; Popovici 1945: 4f.; Turdeanu 1947: 107).
286   Zamfirescu 1967: 73.
287   Mihăilă 1996: LXXIVf.
288   First published in 1906 in the journal *Biserica Ortodoxă Română*, the studies were
       reprinted the following year in Russo's collected essays, which appeared as *Studii
       bizantino-române* (Byzantine-Romanian Studies, Bucharest 1907). See Zamfirescu
       1973: 16, 65 n. 9.
289   'In the early seventeenth century, a monk who was grateful to Neagoe Basarab
       for his unbounded generosity towards the clergy, wrote the *Teachings* in Church
       Slavonic. Their form and extent were originally more or less those of the Greek
       version to be found today on Mount Athos [i.e. MS 221 Dionysiou]. Shortly
       afterwards, the *Teachings* were translated into Greek. Other imitators expanded
       the Church Slavonic text, modified it and probably added the first part of the
       Teachings. This expanded text is preserved in the Church Slavonic manuscript at

the 'Homeric question'[290] of Old Romanian literature: who *did* write the *Teachings to Theodosius*?

To bolster his thesis, Demostene Russo devised a complex argument analysing both passages from the text itself and its historical context. In 1907 the Byzantinist reversed his opinion on the original language. Not being himself an expert in Church Slavonic, he asked a Bulgarian doctoral student as well as the Romanian Slavist Ioan Bogdan to help him examine the Church Slavonic manuscript. Upon thorough analysis, Russo concluded that the Greek version must itself be a translation from the Church Slavonic.[291] Yet to his death in 1938 he maintained that the author of the *Teachings* must be an anonymous seventeenth-century monk.[292]

What led Demostene Russo to this opinion was above all the highly theological tone of the *Teachings*, in which the Bible, the Church Fathers and Eastern monastic devotional literature are extensively quoted. Russo was the first to succeed in proving that the author of the *Teachings* had – as Russo put it – 'plagiarised'[293] entire sections from Ephrem the Syrian or the *Grief for Sin* (Κατάνυξις) of Symeon Monachos, a tenth-century Byzantine author.[294]

Russo objected that a prince – a man of the world, preoccupied with all manner of difficulties – would have had neither the time nor the requisite theological and monastic education to write such a compendious tract.[295] Nor would a sixteenth-century prince, in Russo's estimation, have been sufficiently well versed in Church Slavonic to be able to quote so many sources in that language freely and apparently by heart.[296] The *Teachings* were full of hesychast doctrines; they were concerned with monkish asceticism rather

---

Sofia [MS 313 CMNL], and it is upon such an expanded text that all Romanian versions [note the plural!] are based.' (Demostene Russo apud Zamfirescu 1973: 32; my own translation from the Romanian).

290   This term, which has since become established in Romanian literary history, was coined by Demostene Russo himself (D. Russo 1910: 1).

291   Russo 1939: 226 n. 2; Mihăilă 1996: LXXV.

292   Russo 1939: 208; Ciobanu 1989: 42.

293   Russo 1910: 3, 26; Bulat n.d.: 33.

294   Zamfirescu 2009: 9.

295   Russo 1939: 226 n. 2.

296   Zamfirescu 1973: 36.

than being a mirror for a temporal prince. They testified to a high level of speculation and flawless command of Orthodox systematic theology. The author was well read and demonstrated remarkable competence in moving freely between authors, theories and concepts. In fact, the text was most likely the work of several authors, a learned but somewhat chaotic compendium of quotations from sermons and theological tracts, of heterogeneous sources, of tangential arguments and subsequent interpolations.[297]

Yet the previous chapter on Neagoe Basarab's historical background showed that the Wallachian ruler indeed was educated and spoke several languages. That Basarab should have known Old Slavonic sources by heart is merely speculation on Russo's part; he may very well have looked them up in books.

Russo further thought that the *Teachings* revealed inconsistencies with regard to Basarab's family. Writing in the seventeenth century, the author was clearly not sure which of Basarab's children were still alive at the time of the book's purported writing. Neagoe Basarab had three sons and three daughters: Theodosius, Peter and John, as well as Angeline, Ruxandra and Stana.[298] The *Teachings* are sometimes addressed to Theodosius alone and sometimes to Theodosius and Peter, though the latter died in 1520.[299] The last chapter of the *Teachings* – part II, chapter 13[300] – was supposedly

---

297   Zamfirescu 1973: 33f.

298   The entire family – Neagoe, his wife Despina and all his children – is depicted in an *epitrachelion* (ἐπιτραχήλιον) given to Xenophontos monastery at some point prior to the death of John (Millet 1947: Fig. LXXVI).

299   Dan Zamfirescu has shown that Peter is likely to have died after 20 April 1520, before which date he is occasionally mentioned in deeds of endowment and letters (and even in a letter from Pope Leo X to Neagoe Basarab). His tombstone gives 15 June 1520 as the date of his death.

300   'Rugăciunea lui Ioan Neagoe voevod, care au făcut la eşirea sufletului său cătră Domnul nostru Iisus Hristos. Şi ertarea carea s-au ertat de cătră coconii săi şi de cătră cocoane şi de cătră boiarii săi cei mari şi cei mici şi de cătră alte slugi ale sale, de cătră toate. Cu cuvinte de umilinţă. Slovo 29' (The prayer of Neagoe Basarab voivode to Our Lord Jesus Christ upon the parting of his soul. And the forgiveness which he received from his sons and his daughters, from his greater and lesser boyars, and from several of his servants, from all. With a profession of humility. Word 29) (Neagoe Basarab 1984: 237ff.).

written in 1520 but nonetheless addresses both, 'my sons Theodosius and Peter'. Sometimes, the author writes 'look, my son' (*fătul mieu*); elsewhere, however, the exhortation is 'listen, my sons' (*feții miei*).[301] To alternate thus between son and sons, singular and plural, was surely proof, to Russo's mind, that the seventeenth-century author had got his facts muddled.

Yet Russo seems not to have noticed the difference in context of the writing, the issue at stake being the dispatch of ambassadors: 'Then you must privily instruct your servant, whom you have chosen as your envoy; softly say to him the following: "My son [*fătul mieu*] and my dear servant …".'[302] This indicates that the author does not always use 'my son' or 'my sons' to address his physical children, but used the phrase – as it has also been used in English or German – to refer to favourites and to trusted servants, officials, subjects. The phrase 'my son' (*fătul mieu*) then as now signals fatherly love, wisdom and solicitude; in Wallachia it might be used by a village elder, by the clergy to their flock or by the prince in his capacity as *pater patriae* when it came to offering advice and instruction or simply as a form of address. The author even used the semantically more restricted *coconii miei* (my progeny) to people with whom he was not even related. That the author was aware of this difficulty arising from *coconi* normally being applied only to physical sons is evident from the explanation he felt compelled to add: he addressed the subjects he instructed as *coconi* because he regarded them as sons born to him through the Holy Spirit.[303]

At no point in his *Teachings*, continues Russo, did 'Pseudo-Neagoe' refer to Neagoe Basarab's wife, Princess Despina,[304] though he was known

301 Zamfirescu 1973: 34.
302 'Apoi să chemi sluga ta în taină, pre care-l vei fi ales să fie sol şi vorbeşte cu dânsul cuvinte dulci şi zi: "Fătul mieu şi sluga mea" […]' (Neagoe Basarab 1984: 194; Neagoe Basarab 1996: 292/293). See also Neagoe Basarab 1984: 278.
303 Neagoe Basarab 1984: 285f.
304 Princess Despina (d. 1544) was a descendant of the famed Serbian ruling family of Brancovič. She was the daughter of John Brancovič and sister of Helena, who married the Moldavian Prince Petru Rareş (1527–1538; 1941–1946) (see Filitti 1931). On her life after the deaths of Neagoe Basarab and Theodosius, when she became a nun under the name of Platonida, see Neamţiu 1945: 373ff. The princess was entered under both names into the memorial scroll (Church Slavonic *pomelnik*, French *obituaire*, English 'obituary') of Curtea de Argeş monastery: '*gospodja*

to have been devoted to her and to have owed her a great deal. A contemporary (early sixteenth-century) fresco in Neagoe Basarab's foundation, the cathedral of Curtea de Argeş, depicts Despina alongside her husband and all six children (Figure 1). In the *Teachings*, by contrast, she is completely ignored.[305]

Russo also argues that there is a contradiction with regard to Neaga, Neagoe Basarab's mother. On the second burial – customary in the Balkan Orthodox tradition – in Curtea de Argeş,[306] which he was unable to attend personally, Basarab wrote an *oratio* (ἠθοποιΐαι) in the form of a letter to his deceased mother, in which he excused himself, saying that at least he was sending his sons and daughters.[307] This *oratio*, according to Russo, not only lacked any historical foundation, but was in fact merely a piece of plagiarism and historical game play.[308] It was a sign, Russo argued, that the anonymous author was no longer aware that, at the time of Neaga's second burial, only Theodosius remained alive of the three sons of Neagoe Basarab. Yet all this

---

     Despina' (p. 1, col. 1) and '*Gospodja monahja Platonita*' (Sacerdoţeanu 1965: 304, 306; Turdeanu 1985: 112).

305 Russo 1910: 6; Zamfirescu 1973: 34.

306 Zamfirescu 1973: 135.

307 See Russo 1939: 208. See part II, ch. 3: 'Cartea lui Neagoe voevod cătră chir vlădica Macarie şi cătră alţi egumeni şi ieromonahi şi preoţi şi cătră tot clirosul, cându au îngropat a doao oară, în mănăstire la Argeş, oasele mume-sei, doamnei Neagăi, şi ale coconilor lui Petru voevod şi Ioan voevod, şi a doamnei Anghelinii. Cu cuvinte şi învăţături de umilinţă. Cuvântul al şaselea' (The letter of Neagoe Basarab voivode to Lord Bishop Macarius and to other abbots and hieromonks and to all the clergy on burying for a second time the remains of his mother, the Princess Neaga, and of his sons, Peter voivode and John voivode, and of Lady Angeline in the monastery of Argeş. With a confession and and teachings of humility. Sixth word) (Neagoe Basarab 1984: 123ff.).

308 Ion C. Chiţimia 'unmasked' Russo's problematic method of proving that the *oratio* to Neaga was 'plagiarised', to which end Russo had created a synopsis in which the text of the *Teachings* was contrasted with a speech of John Chrysostom, from which the author of the *Teachings* made certain vague – by no means verbatim – borrowings. Yet the quotation adduced by Russo turned out not even to be from the *oratio* to Neagoe's mother Neaga but rather from an altogether different chapter of the *Teachings* that is in no way related to the supposedly incriminating funeral address (Chiţimia 1963: 310f., reprinted: Chiţimia 1972).

was nothing but wilful distortion of the text on the part of Demostene Russo,[309] as the relevant passage in the *Teachings* proves: 'I was unable to attend the reinterment of your bones on account of my many sins; in order to quench my sorrowful longing for you, I sent my beloved son Theodosius and my dear daughters Stana and Ruxandra [...].'[310]

As we can see, the author clearly speaks of sending only his one remaining living son, Theodosius, and only his two living daughters, Stana and Ruxandra – Angeline had already died at this time. All this proves that the author was very well aware of the facts of the matter.

Yet Russo also complains that it was unclear where Neaga was even second-buried. In the *oratio* to Basarab's mother, the author rhetorically invokes Peter, who died around 1519, brother of Theodosius: 'Arise, my seed, arise, for to you shall come the bones of your grandmother, who is mother to you as to me, and with you shall they find their deserved rest.'[311] According to Russo, this was contradicted by the graves at Curtea de Argeş, among which there certainly was one of Peter, but no trace of Neaga's tomb.[312] If Neagoe had indeed been the author of the work attributed to him, he would surely have known where his beloved mother was buried, over whom he had grieved so eloquently in the *oratio*.[313] However, Demostene Russo appears not to have understood the above passage from the *Teachings*, which makes it amply clear that the bones of Neaga were to be interred next to those of Peter *in the same grave*, which is borne out not only by the *Teachings*, but by anthropological evidence of practices in

309   In developing this argument, Russo does not even quote from the *Teachings*, but rather contents himself with paraphrases.

310   'Iar la aducerea oaselor tale, eu, pentru păcatele mele, iar nu putui veni la tine, ca să mă satur de dorul tău, ci am trimis în locul mieu pre iubitul mieu fiiu pre Theodosie şi pre dragile mele cocoane, pre Stana şi pre Ruxandra' (Neagoe Basarab 1984: 133f.).

311   'Scoală, fătul mieu, scoală, că au venit şi oasele moaşă-ta la tine, şi-ţi iaste şi ţie mumă, ca şi mie, ca să aibă şi iale odihnă lângă tine' (Neagoe Basarab 1984: 135).

312   Russo 1939: 211.

313   Zamfirescu 1973: 35.

wide circles of European cultures from the Stone Age to this day.[314] Peter's
grave – which does indeed exist – hence can be found to contain the remains of two persons, those of Peter and of his grandmother Neaga.

Demostene Russo's claims were examined and criticised by the philologist Sextil Pușcariu (1877–1948),[315] in the Leipzig doctoral thesis of the
Slavist Stojan Romanski (1882–1959) and particularly by the Romanian
historian and politician[316] Nicolae Iorga (1871–1940).[317] A heated debate
between Russo and Iorga unfolded in the 1920s.[318] For his part, Iorga never
doubted that the *Teachings* were written by Neagoe Basarab, prince of
Wallachia. He systematically refuted each of Russo's arguments and aroused
such hostility to him that Russo eventually gave up publishing his studies
on the *Teachings* altogether. Only after his death did Russo's followers publish them in a volume containing a collection of the Byzantinist's studies,
essays and articles.[319]

Above all, Iorga saw no reason to consider Neagoe Basarab a plagiarist,
even if he had lifted certain passages from the *Grief* of Symeon Monachos
(c. tenth century)[320] without acknowledging their source. This was not
plagiarism, Iorga maintained, because the appropriated passages fulfilled
a completely new purpose in the context of the *Teachings*. Their purpose
was no longer spiritual edification, as it had originally been, but rather to
serve as the political advice of a secular ruler.[321] Moreover, it was possible
to prove that the author of the *Teachings* drew far less from the *Grief* than
Demostene Russo supposed, though it was indeed curious that the first
part, which deals with theology, mysticism and asceticism, did not quote

---

314   The second burial, an archaic funerary practice in which the remains of family
       members are placed in a common grave over generations might be ranked among
       what Kuckenburg has called 'splatter events' (Kuckenburg 2007: 20ff.).
315   Pușcariu 1921: 32, 34f.
316   Member of the Roman political parties *Partidul Național Democrat* (National
       Democratic Party) and *Partidul Naționalist al Poporului* (Nationalist People's
       Party).
317   Iorga 1904: 7ff.
318   Cartojan 1980: 75ff.; Mitescu 1993: IIIff.
319   Russo 1939.
320   Symeon Monachos 2009.
321   Mihăilă 1996: LXXXVIf.

from it at all.[322] Moreover, Iorga remarked that a seventeenth-century author was highly improbable, since the tendency at that time had been rather to replace Church Slavonic with Romanian literature, making a Church Slavonic text of the length of the *Teachings* quite unusual. Besides, Neagoe Basarab was little remembered in the seventeenth century. Why would anyone write a book under *his* name? Another argument in favour of Basarab's authorship was that monastic culture in seventeenth-century Wallachia experienced a crisis and was unlikely to produce a work of such a strongly ascetic, mystic and monkish bent.[323] Iorga also showed in what accurate detail Neagoe's family connections were described in the *Teachings* and how genuine the father's pain at the death of his sons sounded in the *oratio* to Neaga.[324]

The debate between Iorga and Russo was kept alive by Vasile Grecu, the editor of the critical edition of MS 221 Dionysiou, and by P. P. Panaitescu.[325] Panaitescu, who continued to uphold Russo's claims in the 1940s and 1950s,[326] emerged as the most important opponent of the *Teachings'* authenticity.[327] As early as 1944, Panaitescu wrote a little study[328] in which he restated Russo's principal claims, though he did beg to differ with the master on one point: the handwriting of the *Teachings* as well as the paper and its watermarks suggested that they were set down not in the seventeenth, but in the late sixteenth century.[329] Panaitescu was later to retract this claim and concur with Russo that the work was of early seventeenth-century

---

322   Zamfirescu 1973: 37f.
323   Iorga 1985: 51f. For further arguments based on the social and political situation in sixteenth- and seventeenth-century Wallachia, see Balotă 1969.
324   Iorga 1985: 55.
325   A heated debate between the two was printed in the reviews section of the literary journal *Convorbiri literare* 77/1944. The trigger was a 1939 essay by Vasile Grecu (Grecu 1939; Chiţimia 1963: 312 n. 2).
326   Zamfirescu 1973: 70 n. 46.
327   Panaitescu was not the only scholar to support the claim that the *Teachings* were pseudepigraphical. For instance, the Polish scholar Stefan Glixelli published two studies in which he defended Russo's theory (Glixelli 1933: 328 and 1937: 113f.).
328   Reprinted in Panaitescu 1971.
329   Panaitescu 1971: 161.

origin.[330] He was particularly convinced by Russo's argument concerning the *Teachings'* peculiar structure:

> The teachings ascribed to Neagoe are a pseudepigraphical work composed not by a ruler, but by a monk. Only thus can be explained the fundamental contradiction in their structure, that is, the ascetic attitude of turning away from the world (by which I do not just mean the religious attitude normal for the time) in a book supposed to describe secular rule.[331]

What Panaitescu fails to consider here, however, is that it is barely possible to speak of Christian rule in the world without first establishing the semantics of what 'Christian' means conceptually, in discourse and practice.

With regard to the structure of works in this genre, it was customary to begin with theologically grounded claims that could then be applied to specific cases. The arguments of the *Teachings* are structured as follows: (1) theory, (2) example and (3) conclusion with application. This structure applies not just to the work as a whole, but to each individual chapter. It should further be stressed that the second, practical part proves that it, at any rate, could not have been written by a monk, since the author is evidently actively involved in political events at the highest level. For instance, the *Teachings* contain unique strategic instructions that could only have been given by somebody with military background – an officer or politician involved in frequent campaigns, something unlikely in a monk, particularly in the seventeenth century.[332] In the Danubian Principalities, at least, the seventeenth century was notably peaceful and without major conflicts.[333] What is more, the *Teachings* do not adopt any of the stock phrases of monkish philanthropy and poor relief, but rather state that the ruler should above all ensure that his own retinue was suitably provided for. The poor, they argue, were looked after by all, whereas only the prince could take care of his own court.[334] As for the religious and theological

---

330   Panaitescu 1959: 217 and 1971d: 229.
331   Panaitescu 1971c: 422.
332   Iorga 1985: 52.
333   Zamfirescu 1973: 24, 48ff.
334   'Căci că săracului, de nu-l vei afla să-i dai milă într-un loc, iar într-altul tu-l vei afla, si-i vei da. Sau de nu-l vei milui tu, alţii îl vor milui, şi tot va fi miluit. Iar sluga ta

first part, it would in fact be quite normal for a sixteenth-century layman to make a detailed study of Christian doctrine.[335] The next subsection will examine the revealing and intuitive structure of the *Teachings* in more detail.

Panaitescu developed a new argument that is not to be found in Russo and according to which their favourable stance towards the boyars proved that the *Teachings* could not have been written any earlier than the second half of the sixteenth century. The late sixteenth century, according to Panaitescu, was marked by strong centrifugal tendencies among the Wallachian nobility. Neagoe, himself the scion of a boyar family, had not written a word of criticism of the nobility in his mirror for princes and indeed displayed a slight tendency to look favourably on such dangerous activities. A prince, argues Panaitescu, could not have treated them so casually.[336] In the following subsection, however, which addresses Basarab's notion of the monarchy, I will show this is far from being the case.

P. P. Panaitescu's claims were refuted in the 1960s and 1970s by Gheorghe Mihăilă and Dan Zamfirescu. The latter summarised his objections to the arguments of Panaitescu and Russo in the first two chapters of his doctoral thesis, which was published in 1973 and in which, working with the utmost attention to detail and surgical precision, he virtually buried the opponents of the *Teachings*' authenticity in counter-arguments.[337] Zamfirescu's principal claims are that Neagoe Basarab wrote the *Teachings*

---

nu mai aşteaptă altă milă de la nimeni, fără numai de la tine. Că ei de-ar vrea să şi cée, le iaste ruşine, că să cheamă slugi domneşti. Pentr-acéia, deaca nu-ţi vei milui slugile tale cu mîinile tale, altă nădéjde ei nu mai au la nimeni să-i miluiască' (For, though the pauper may not now be with you, in order that you may take care of him, you will sooner or later find him and be able to give to him anyhow. Even though you may not give to him, others will take pity and he will not go uncared for. But your servants can expect to be looked after by no one but you. Their shame forbids them even to ask for such a thing, for they are the courtiers of a prince. Hence they have no other hope of being looked after if you omit to do so yourself without delay) (Neagoe Basarab 1984: 190).

335 Zamfirescu 1973: 48ff.
336 Panaitescu 1971c: 271ff.
337 Zamfirescu 1973: 13ff., 81ff. Zamfirescu published these arguments in condensed form in the journal *Romanoslavica*; they were originally made in a lecture delivered in 1961 (Zamfirescu 1963).

in Church Slavonic. They were addressed to Basarab's son Theodosius, but
they were written not, as it were, in one go, as a single text, but rather suc-
cessively, as a series of individual writings and letters, beginning in 1517 and
ending in 1520. This would explain such apparent inconsistencies as two sons
being addressed, even though, by 1520, only Theodosius was still alive.[338]
The changes made by subsequent copyists had added to the confusion.[339]

Zamfirescu also addressed the argument of the exclusion of Princess
Despina from the *Teachings*. It was indeed impossible to know why Neagoe
had not mentioned his wife in his mirror for princes. Yet this is less a reason
to doubt his authorship than an argument in its support, for Neagoe had
also failed to mention his wife in the text of the epitaph tablets at Curtea de
Argeş,[340] which he undoubtedly had written. To Zamfirescu, this underscored
Neagoe's consistently held belief that politics was no business for women. That
the *oratio* to his mother Neaga should mention all the children but not their
mother might, according to Zamfirescu, prove that Despina did not attend
the second burial. The Wallachian prince has asked his son Theodosius to
deputise for him on that occasion.[341]

Following the critical edition of Vasile Grecu's Greek version (1942) and
that of the Old Romanian one by Florica Moisil and Dan Zamfirescu (1970),
and in light of the detailed studies in which Gheorghe Mihăilă refuted the
claims of P. P. Panaitescu, the authorship of Neagoe Basarab and hence the
authenticity of the *Teachings* seemed to have been confirmed. This was not,
however, the case.

In 1970 Leandros Vranoussis, the director of the Centre for Medieval
and Modern Greek Studies in Athens, delivered two lectures[342] to the

338   Zamfirescu 1973: 50ff.
339   Zamfirescu 1973: 61ff.
340   Năsturel 1960; Olteanu 1967: 353ff. It is in any case a strong argument in favour of
      the *Teachings'* authenticity that the epitaph tablets appear unchanged in the text
      of the *Teachings*. It may, however, be objected that they would have been accessible
      to anybody in the seventeenth century, and particularly to the monks of Curtea de
      Argeş. They could easily have been transcribed.
341   Zamfirescu 1973: 55f.
342   Vranoussis 1972 and 1978. Vranoussis's lecture in Bucharest was entitled 'Texte
      şi documente privind Ţara Românească scoase din manuscrisele si arhivele de
      la Meteore şi din alte mănăstiri din Grecia' ('Texts and documents concerning

second Congress of South-East European Studies in Athens (and later to the fourteenth Congress for Byzantine Studies in Bucharest). In these lectures, he announced a revolutionary discovery: his research in the library of Dionysiou monastery on Mount Athos had revealed that MS 221 was undoubtedly the work of the Greek scholar and grand rhetor of Hagia Sophia, Manuel of Corinth (d. 1530). He reached this conclusion by comparing MS 221 Dionysiou with other manuscripts in the library of which Manuel was known to have been the author. From this, Vranoussis went so far as to conclude that Manuel was not just the *Teachings*' copyist or translator, but their actual author.[343] Neagoe Basarab, with whom Manuel of Corinth had already collaborated and who had commissioned the clergyman to produce a tract on the dogmatic differences between the Latin and Orthodox Churches,[344] had probably also charged him with committing to paper the *Teachings*. Basarab was at most their 'moral author', while the text itself was the fruit of Manuel's extensive learning in theology and patristics.[345]

Yet Vranoussis's claims are simply preposterous and show him to have been unfamiliar with the various versions and manuscripts of the *Teachings*. Nor, apparently, had he kept abreast of the rich body of research literature that had already grown up around the *Teachings*, or else he would have known that Demostene Russo – himself well acquainted with the Greek

---

Wallachia from Meteora and other monasteries in Greece) (Zamfirescu 1973: 222). In the appendix to his dissertation, Dan Zamfirescu gives a transcript of the discussion following Vranoussis's lecture, in which such participants as Ion C. Chiţimia or Dan Zamfirescu himself express enthusiasm for the new and uncontroversial dating of MS 221 Dionysiou to the sixteenth century, but express considerable reservations regarding the idea that Manuel of Corinth was the *Teachings*' author (Zamfirescu 1973: 220, 386ff.).

343 This 'discovery' led Vranoussis proudly to proclaim that the 'Homeric question' had finally been resolved (question homérique de la littérature slavoroumaine enfin résolue) (see Mihăilă 1996: XCV). The Romanian Gheorghe Mihăilă was aghast at ascriptions of the *Teachings* to the Greek Manuel of Corinth, describing it as an attempt 'to dispossess Romanian literature of its first great work' (Mihăilă 1996: XCV).

344 Tanaşoca 2011 and 2012.

345 Vranoussis 1972: 8.

MS 221 Dionysiou – had proved beyond doubt that the *Teachings* had been originally composed in Church Slavonic. Had he been more thorough in his work, Vranoussis would surely have noticed that the Greek author of MS 221 Dionysiou did not even use the Greek Bible or the Greek original of the *Grief*, but rather retranslated into Greek the Church Slavonic translations of both. In fact, it seems quite clear that the Greek translator of the *Teachings* did not realise that he was dealing with quotations and thus simply translated them as he did the remaining text. This process of double translation – from Greek into Church Slavonic and back into Greek – produced a number of glaring errors and distortions of meaning with regard to the Greek Bible and the *Grief*.[346] It is inconceivable that a scholar like Manuel of Corinth, in writing an important dogmatic work in Greek (as Vranoussis believed), should not have used original Greek versions of his sources. He had done so in the aforementioned study on the dogmatic differences between Latin and Orthodox Churches commissioned by Neagoe Basarab. Why then should he not do the same in the far more important *Teachings to Theodosius*?

Gheorghe Mihăilă developed a different counter-argument to the claims of Leandros Vranoussis by showing that the Greek version (MS 221 Dionysiou) lacks the very important section detailing the selection and installation of officials and boyar councillors at court. The Romanian Slavicist explained this lacuna by the lack of interest on the part of the monks of Mount Athos, for whom the Greek translation had been prepared, in matters concerning temporal rule and court administration of a foreign prince.[347] Yet none of these arguments brought against Vranoussis prevented the emergence of a national myth that went unquestioned in

346 'Neither the Greek nor the Romanian translator knew that many of the textual fragments they were studying in Church Slavonic were actually translations from Greek sources; if at least the Greek translator had been aware of this, he would probably not have made so many translation errors, but instead would simply have taken the quotations from the [Greek] originals of Ephrem the Syrian, of the *Barlaam and Josaphat* legend and of Symeon Monachos' (Demostene Russo apud Zamfirescu 1973: 228; my own translation from the Romanian). On this see Mihăilă 1973: 359ff.

347 Mihăilă 1973: 352. The argument loses force somewhat, however, when one begins to ask what interest the monks of Mount Athos might have had in listening to

Greece and according to which the *Teachings* were the work of Manuel of Corinth and thus an achievement of the Greek mind. This axiomatic 'truth' continues to be taught at universities. Not only is it not subjected to critical scrutiny, but also it barely seems to require justification, to the great dismay of Romanian national historians.[348]

Ion C. Chiţimia proposed a conciliatory settlement to the debate.[349] He recognised Neagoe Basarab as the author of the first version of the *Teachings*, but argued that this had been expanded with significant interpolations over the years by the text's copyists, to the point at which it was barely any longer possible to discern that Basarab's original version had been far less extensive. There may have been a seventeenth-century monk who made numerous additions to Basarab's text in order to adapt it to the tastes of his time.[350] Basarab's authorship would thus have been diminished by the substantial interpolations of subsequent editors. Yet Gheorghe Mihăilă and Dan Zamfirescu, drawing on extensive passages from the Church Slavonic, Greek and Old Romanian texts, were able to prove that this was not the case. They proved the Old Romanian version from the seventeenth century to represent a faithful rendering of the original and the copyist's input hence to be negligible.[351] Pavel Chihaia was able to show that 'the work [i.e. the *Teachings*] was completed after 15 June 1520 [and before the death of Basarab in September 1521] in the form in which we know it today', which is to say that the text underwent no significant alterations subsequently.[352] If indeed there was any trend to be observed among the later Old Romanian manuscripts in relation to MS 109 RALC, it was that they tended to condense rather than expand the original.[353]

In the years after 1980 Petre Ş. Năsturel (1923–2012) and his student Dan Ioan Mureşan cut a new path between these two rival paradigms. They

---

disquisitions on military tactics. It seems unlikely, for instance, that they were planning an armed uprising against the Ottoman Empire.

348 Mihăilă 1996: XCVII.
349 Zamfirescu 1973: 201.
350 Chiţimia 1963: 318f. and 1972: 138.
351 Piru 1961: 41; Ciobanu 1989: 50.
352 Chihaia 1971: 3.
353 Zamfirescu 1973: 209, 360.

seem not to have wanted to place themselves in outright opposition to the
mainstream of Romanian opinion while, as Byzantinists and students of
Leandros Vranoussis, having a strong affection for Greek culture. In consequence, they argued that Manuel of Corinth had not been the author of
the *Teachings*, but rather their 'editor'.[354] According to this theory, MS 221
Dionysiou was a first rudimentary draft of the text and hence the original.[355]
This draft was then sent to Wallachia to be examined by Neagoe, in whose
chancellery scribes completed the first, theological part and translated the
whole into Church Slavonic. For the Greek sketch, Manuel of Corinth
had used the sources in their (Old) Church Slavonic translations, which
he then translated back into Greek, because these Church Slavonic translations had been the only versions in use at the Wallachian court. Manuel of
Corinth had produced the Greek draft at the request of Neagoe Basarab for
the benefit of Theodosius,[356] who had been held hostage at the Byzantine
court and whose education had been entrusted to Manuel of Corinth. This
Greek 'sketch', which largely consists of the second part of the *Teachings*,
was to be considered something of a textbook for Theodosius. Altogether,
this thesis is highly speculative and ultimately does little more than bring
Vranoussis's claims up to date by stating that Neagoe Basarab had been
the *Teachings*' author only 'in a moral sense' (*l'auteur morale*).[357] Dan Ioan
Mureşan refers to a '*rédaction en parallele*'[358] between Basarab and Manuel.

Nevertheless, consider the following. First, this account does not state
how familiar Manuel of Corinth was with Church Slavonic. The number
of (Old) Church Slavonic translations of theological writers held at Mount
Athos or Constantinople was fairly small – so how was Manuel to find

354   Mureşan/Năsturel 2011: 255.

355   Mureşan/Năsturel 2011: 253.

356   Andrei Pippidi has proposed a further variant in this scenario, according to which
       Basarab had commissioned Gabriel Protos (!) to write the *Teachings*, and it was
       the resulting text that had then been corrected by Manuel of Corinth (Pippidi
       2001: 159f.). The sources provide no support for this purely imaginative take on
       history, which resembles a Dan Brown novel rather than scholarship worthy of
       the name.

357   Năsturel 1971: 256f., 267; Mihăilă 1973: 348; Zamfirescu 1973: 7; Cazacu
       1989: 115ff.; Mitescu 1993: VIf., XV.

358   Mureşan 2003: 320.

the (Old) Church Slavonic sources from which he is supposed to have quoted? Why should a Greek theologian, who wrote in Greek and used Greek sources, even use (Old) Church Slavonic translations that he barely understood, as the grave errors in their retranslation into Greek shows? Second, it makes no sense for a thoroughly educated theologian who had already written a theological tract for Basarab to handle not the theological, but rather the practical part of the *Teachings*. After all, Manuel of Corinth, an able theologian who had spent all his adult life as a monk, knew little of military and diplomatic affairs, of table manners, musicians, servants, officials and court administration.

While Petre Ş. Năsturel made little effort to support this bold theory, Dan Ioan Mureşan tried to provide the scholarly underpinnings for his teacher's ideas. He succeeded in making a case – by no means uncontested – that Theodosius *may* have been held hostage in Constantinople.[359] We are dealing here with an argument that rests on a single piece of reliable information, which is that Manuel of Corinth wrote a theological work for Neagoe Basarab, the aforesaid tract on the differences between Orthodox and Latins.[360] Yet the sources remain utterly silent on such claims as 'textbook', 'editor', 'redaction' of the *Teachings* and the like, all the while providing no clear proof of Neagoe writing them, either. There is accordingly much scope for speculation.

In sum, it would seem that the 'Homeric question' of Old Romanian literature is destined to remain 'Homeric' – that is, inconclusive. The debate continues. What the comparison of the two paradigms of interpretation I presented above shows is that the scholars arguing in favour of the *Teachings'* authenticity have, on the whole, invested more effort and detective work as well as more philological skill in their cause, producing more relevant and convincing arguments. While the opponents of the authenticity of the *Teachings* tended to be content with poorly supported claims, those seeking to prove it produced a rich body of research literature, editions, translations and monographs. It is unlikely to be altogether a coincidence that all the editors of the preserved versions – the scholars,

359 Mureşan 2003: 306ff.
360 The manuscript is in the possession of the University of Illinois at Urbana-Champaign (Năsturel 1971: 252).

that is, who have studied the text the closest – come out in favour of its authenticity. I also hope that this chapter provides Western scholars with an insight into an acute problem that is of great relevance for political education, national consciousness, prestige, literary culture and the social and political dynamic of south-eastern Europe.

Though it may never be possible to state with absolute certainty who wrote the *Teachings to Theodosius* and in what language, I can only conclude from the historical material that the available evidence seems to *favour* the authorship of Neagoe Basarab, prince of Wallachia, and Church Slavonic as their original language.[361]

Church Slavonic as the Original Language of the Teachings

As we have seen, the question of the *Teachings'* author is closely bound up with that of their original language. Various opinions have been expressed amid the polemics surrounding the work from the nineteenth century to this day. In the nineteenth century, before the discovery of MS 313 CMNL, the general opinion was that the work had been written in Old Romanian. Among the scholars supporting this opinion were Bogdan Petriceicu Hașdeu, the first critical editor of MS 109 RALC, and Aron Densușianu (d. 1900).[362]

By contrast, the Romanian historian Alexandru D. Xenopol, also writing in the nineteenth century, believed the mirror for princes originally to have been written in Greek,[363] an opinion briefly shared by Demostene Russo.[364] The argument for the Greek original continues to be made today by such scholars as Dan Ioan Mureșan and Andrei Pippidi.

Most scholars, however, were of the opinion that the *Teaching* had first been written in Church Slavonic, were soon afterwards translated into

---

361   Rosetti 1964: 278.
362   Hașdeu 1865: 112; Mihăilă 1996: LXXIII.
363   Xenopol 1953: 219; Romanski 1908: 136; Ciobanu 1989: 41.
364   Zamfirescu 1973: 29. Russo changed his mind in 1907, henceforth defending the
       opinion that the Church Slavonic version was indeed the original one (Russo
       1939: 226 n. 2; Zamfirescu 1973: 198f.; Mihăilă 1996: LXXV).

Greek by Manuel of Corinth and only later, in the seventeenth century, into Romanian by an anonymous translator. The first to recognise that the *Teachings* had first been written in Church Slavonic was the Jewish scholar Moses Gaster, though he was unaware of the Church Slavonic fragments at Sofia. Gaster propounded this theory in his history of Romanian vernacular literature, published in 1883.[365] He was also the first to date the Old Romanian translation of the *Teachings* to the mid-seventeenth century. Only much later was the Russian Slavist Piotr A. Lavrov able to confirm this theory, as mentioned above.[366] Analysing the sources used in the *Teachings*, Stojan Romanski was able to support Lavrov's thesis and show that the work's author had used and quoted from (Old) Church Slavonic sources exclusively.[367] P. P. Panaitescu found that the Church Slavonic version had been written in Middle Bulgarian,[368] with some phonetic and lexical influences from the Serbian.[369]

More recent Slavist scholarship has called the Church Slavonian of the *Teachings* 'Romanian Church Slavonic' (*slavona românească*),[370] a language supposedly common to all Church Slavonic documents from the Danubian Principalities. Besides the Serbian influence already mentioned, Romanian Church Slavonic is held to contain many Romanian terms and phrases as well as distinctly Romanian morphological and syntactical features. It is thus to be considered a discrete branch of Church Slavonic.[371] Romanian Church Slavonic is thus a hybrid form, adapted to Romanian, the living vernacular of the Danubian Principalities. As experts have noted,

---

365 Gaster 1883: 35 and 1891: XLVIII. On this, see Zamfirescu 1973: 13.

366 Romanski 1908: 137; Iorga 1925: 142f.; Zamfirescu 1973: 14.

367 Romanski 1908: 152.

368 On the differences between Middle Bulgarian and Paleo-Slavic, see Olteanu 1975: 253ff.

369 Panaitescu 1959: 217 and 1971b. Examples are the Romanian terms 'spatare' ('spătar'), 'kourtanьj' ('curteni') and 'kredinčare' ('credincer'), which entered Romanian from the Latin 'spatha', 'cohortem' and 'credentia' (see Mihăilă 1973: 355).

370 Djomo-Diaconiţă 1965: 105; Zamfirescu 1973: 330. The Slavist V. V. Vinogradov, apud Mihăilă 1996: C, coined the term.

371 Olteanu 1975: 16.

people may have written in Church Slavonic, but they were thinking in
Romanian while doing so.[372]

Church Slavonic was the lingua franca of the medieval Orthodox
Balkans, with the obvious exception of the Greek regions. It was less an
ethnic marker than the cultural language of Orthodoxy, and it flourished
on the geopolitical foundations first laid by the Byzantine Empire, which
for centuries provided the infrastructure for exchange, mobility and cultural
transfer between the peoples of the Balkans. These structures were further
developed by the Serbian Despotate and Old Great Bulgaria, with Church
Slavonic culture becoming an emblem of so-called 'Balkan solidarity'.[373] In
the Wallachian Principalities north of the Danube, Church Slavonic was
the official administrative, ecclesiastical and literary language,[374] though
it would be wrong to claim that it had also been the vernacular of the
elites in these territories.[375] Romanian was spoken at all levels of society,
while Church Slavonic was inaccessible and incomprehensible to most
people. Even in the Middle Ages, moreover, Romanians were well aware
of their Romanianness.[376] Old Church Slavonic,[377] to which some lin-
guists refer as 'Old Bulgarian', originated in a Bulgarian dialect spoken in
southern Macedonia in the ninth century.[378] Yet even Slavists sometimes
seem unable to agree just what is to be considered 'Old Church Slavonic'.
A common definition holds it to be 'the language of a group of texts originating from translations by Constantine (Cyril) and Methodius, the
teachers of the Slavs, in the course of their mission work'.[379] 'Old Church

---

372   Olteanu 1975: 289ff.; Djamo-Diaconiță 1977.
373   Turdeanu 1985: 13; Tapkova-Zaimova 2010b.
374   Romanski 1908: 113; Ciobanu 1989: 22; Bochmann/Stiehler 2010: 69f.
375   Romanski 1908: 115.
376   Papacostea 1965. This is not to say that medieval Romanians were aware of speaking
       a Romance language and having a cultural connection with Rome and the Roman
       Empire. The sources to not permit such a conclusion. What is at stake here is a
       sense not of *Romanity*, but of *Romanianness*: Medieval Romanians referred to
       themselves as Romanians, testifying to a sense of linguistic and ethnic community.
       They were called Wallachians only by other ethnic groups.
377   Miklosich 1862–1865.
378   Olteanu 1975: 15.
379   Hock 2003: 35. I am grateful to Wolfgang Dahmen for bringing this to my
       attention.

Slavonic' thus refers exclusively to a clearly delineated corpus of tenth- and eleventh-century sources. All subsequent Slavic literature is hence considered 'Church Slavonic', a literary language barely used in everyday life, even by the Slavic populations south of the Danube. As early as the twelfth or thirteenth century, Church Slavonic lost contact with spoken Slavic dialects and became a 'dead language'.[380]

Yet their relatively strong autonomy in relation to the Ottomans paradoxically allowed the Danubian Principalities also to serve as a cultural laboratory for the preservation of Church Slavonic. Significant literary production virtually ceased in Bulgaria and Serbia once they were conquered and shifted to Wallachia and Moldavia. A symptomatic case is that of the Bulgarian Patriarch, Euthymius of Tarnovo (1375–1393), whose works are today edited following manuscripts produced in the Danubian Principalities.[381] The *Teachings* have tellingly been called 'the best that Slavic [*sic*] literature of that era has to offer'.[382]

Already in the thirteenth century[383] we find in Wallachia and in Transylvania a Middle Bulgarian form of Church Slavonic, which in the course of the fifteenth century was subject to influence from Serbian in Wallachia and Transylvania, and from Ukrainian in Moldavia.[384] Yet the Church Slavonic used in the Danubian Principalities testifies most strongly to Romanian influences. The earliest Slavic inscriptions north of the Danube, in Cyrillic characters, were found near the town of Ploieşti in modern Romania and date from the tenth century.[385] Church Slavonic in the Danubian Principalities reached its peak in the fifteenth and early sixteenth centuries, during which liturgical books in particular were copied

---

380 Rosetti 1964: 236.
381 Mihăilă 1996: LXXXIII. The only Middle Bulgarian copy of the *Vita Euthymii* was made by his student Gregorios Camblak in fifteenth-century Moldavia. The Church Slavonic manuscripts produced in the Wallachian Principalities contain peculiar letter-types and ornaments found in no other Slavonic manuscripts (Rosetti 1964: 241).
382 Romanski 1908: 121.
383 It has been claimed that Church Slavonic entered the regions north of the Danube as early as the eleventh century (Piscupescu 1939: 19; Nandriş 1946: 168ff.).
384 Rosetti 1964: 236.
385 Rosetti 1964: 235; Olteanu 1975: 15.

and printed.[386] The first Slavonic–Old Romanian dictionary was published towards the end of the sixteenth century.[387] The first half of the seventeenth century, when the *Teachings* were translated into Old Romanian, is described by scholars as already witnessing the 'death throes' of Church Slavonic in the Wallachian Principalities.[388]

The Time of Writing of the Teachings to Theodosius

Neagoe Basarab (c. 1482–1521) wrote the *Teachings* to his son Theodosius in the last years of his life.[389] He seems to have done so, moreover, in a considerable hurry, under the shadow of his own untimely death. The prince was suffering from an incurable disease – probably tuberculosis[390] – and tried to set down his advice to his underage son Theodosius. He had good reason to do so, for Basarab was aware that Theodosius would be considered the son of a usurper and have rival claimants to the throne and general adversity to contend with.[391]

The sources for Basarab's reign make no mention of the *Teachings*. Scholars once believed they had found an allusion to the work in the chronicle of the Cantacuzène Anonymous, which states that Neagoe Basarab had written a book recording all his donations and endowments.[392] This, however, represents a later interpolation, which is not to be found in all versions of the Cantacuzène Anonymous (writing some 150 years after Basarab's death), but only in MS 91 RAL, which recounts that Neagoe Basarab had

> built many churches and monasteries both in our country and in other countries and did many other good works in the world, which are all recorded in detail in

---

386   Iorga 1904: 7ff.; Romanski 1908: 119.
387   Mardarie Cozianul 1900.
388   'L'agonie des lettres slavonnes en Valachie' (Cândea 1968: 246, 266, 274).
389   Piru 1961: 40. The reign of Neagoe Basarab lasted from 23 January 1512 to 15 September 1521.
390   Cazacu 1989: 111.
391   Zamfirescu 1996: V.
392   Ştefănescu 1964: 123 n. 32.

a book that he wrote about his foundations and which he entrusted to the Holy Metropolitan See for safekeeping.[393]

The book referred to here is in fact the *Life of St Niphon* by Gabriel Protos, which indeed resembles an inventory of Basarab's foundations, whereas the *Teachings* only once mention his endowment of Curtea de Argeş, but do not give an entire list.[394] It should be noted, however, that historians of the seventeenth and early eighteenth centuries were indeed aware that Neagoe Basarab had written a book, though they confused the contents of the *Teachings* with those of the *Vita Niphonis*.

The *Teachings* were not written all at once, but are rather the result of the successive redaction and collation of a number of different letters, speeches and textual passages, most likely compiled by Neagoe Basarab himself. Pavel Chihaia conjectures that a scribe in the chancellery might have assembled the various redactions and Basarab's own writings without the prince, who died soon after, having had the opportunity to correct the text and rid it completely of inconsistencies.[395] It was established above that the *Teachings* as we know them today were written after 15 June 1520, that is, after the death of Peter, Basarab's second son. In the *oratio* to his mother Neaga, Basarab refers to Peter as already having died, while other chapters address two sons, Peter and Theodosius. Peter was last referred to as alive in a letter to Basarab from Pope Leo X and in a *phelonion* (φαιλόνιον) dating from 1519 that Peter's mother Despina donated to the monastery of Krušedol in Serbia.[396] The epitaph of Peter gives the date of his death as either 15 March or 15 June 1520 (the readings differ). The *Teachings* would thus appear to have been written between c. 1519 (when Peter was still alive) and late 1520 (by which time he had died).[397]

393   'Făcut-au şi beserici şi mănăstiri multe şi aicea şi în ţară şi în alte ţări şi alte multe bunătăţi au făcut în lume, care sunt scrise mai pă largu la o carte ce o au facut de toate jitiile lui şi s-au dat să fie stătătoare la Sfânta Mitropolie' (Cantacuzène Anonymous A: 205).

394   Rudow 1892: 25f.; Romanski 1908: 135.

395   Chihaia 1971: 3.

396   Millet 1947: 32.

397   Romanski 1908: 149.

The Style of the Teachings to Theodosius

No less than in virtually any other aspect of the work, scholarly opinion is divided on the style of the *Teachings*. Demostene Russo held them to be a somewhat trite compilation, a ragbag of biblical quotations, pious texts, theological excerpts and hackneyed wisdom (see above).[398] The *Teachings* simply plagiarised earlier writers. Long passages from other texts, for example, Euthymius of Tarnovo's panegyric on Constantine the Great or the *Grief for Sin* of Symeon Monachos, had been taken unchanged into the text of the *Teachings*. They were an unstructured work lacking any kind of common theme.[399] Stojan Romanski accused the author of the *Teachings* of having 'used his sources unscrupulously by simply copying entire passages'.[400]

It would, however, be anachronistic to expect a sixteenth-century author – writing at a time when originality meant not novelty, but taking one's place in a tradition[401] – to adhere scrupulously to modern rules of citation. The lodestars were the great figures of the Christian past – notably Athanasius of Alexandria (d. 373), Basil of Caesarea (d. 379) and John Chrysostom (d. 407) – while more recent authors, demoted to the rank of *scriptores minores*, were simply appropriated. The ethics of citation as we know them today were far from being developed in the sixteenth century. Simply to copy or paraphrase other authors without even naming them was considered neither unusual nor dishonourable, provided that they were not in the first rank of the great immortals. The practice was no different in the Western Middle Ages or the early modern era and can frequently be observed in Erasmus or Machiavelli.[402] Moreover, a comparison of passages

---

398   Mihăilă 1996: LXXX.
399   Russo 1910: 9f.
400   Romanski 1908: 166f.
401   In order to create the impression of metahistorical, context-independent and objective truth (Noica 1991: 14).
402   Unlike the humanists, the author of the *Teachings* demonstrates no particular interest in approaching his sources with an attitude of textual criticism, nor does he worry about distinguishing the authentic writings of the authors used from their pseudepigraphical ones.

appropriated with those attributed to the author himself reveals that, of the 216 pages of the complete Old Romanian version, only sixty-six consist of quotations (fifty in the first part, sixteen in the second).[403] There can be no doubt that Basarab treated Patristics and wisdom literature as a quarry from which he might help himself to such building blocks as he required. Yet this does not make him a plagiarist or even a copyist, for he used the material to develop ideas of his own. The originality of the whole resides in the particular manner in which the parts are arranged.[404]

This mosaic of quotations from the Bible and the Church Fathers (who are cited by name) is one of the beauties of this mirror for princes. No other work in this genre testifies to such familiarity with Scripture and Christian authors, and none takes such pleasure in quotation.[405] A wealth of quotations is skilfully interwoven with the author's own reflections to form a quasi-impressionistic image.[406] The writing is nearly baroque in style, with entire passages, extending over pages, appearing as masterpieces of the aesthetic concatenation of words. In fact, this style was a characteristically Byzantine device and was known in South Slavic literature as *slovapletenie* (word-mesh).[407]

Neagoe Basarab interweaves biblical quotations in order to underpin his own ideas and opinion. The Bible is put to such intense use that it sometimes comes close to a *petitio principii*:[408]

> For we who are powerful have the duty to help the weak and to raise them up in all matters, and to be guided not by our own will, but by the will of our neighbour and of the poor and powerless, as long as the great [apostle] Paul would have us do so. And the apostle James, also called the brother of God, says: 'Let the brother of low degree rejoice in that he is exalted: But the rich, in that he is made low: because as the flower of the grass he shall pass away. For the sun is no sooner risen with a burning heat, but it withereth the grass, and the flower thereof falleth, and the grace of the fashion of it perisheth: so also shall the rich man fade away in his ways' [Jas. 1:9–11].

403 Zamfirescu 1973: 211.
404 Anghel 1972: 77f.
405 I refer to 'quotations' under the conditions previously discussed.
406 Chihaia 1971: 3; Zamfirescu 1996: XV; Mihăilă 1996: LXXVII.
407 Murko 1971: 142.
408 Mihăilă 1996: LXXVI.

And again he says: 'Go to now, ye rich men, weep and howl for your miseries that shall come upon you. Your riches are corrupted, and your garments are motheaten. Your gold and silver is cankered; and the rust of them shall be a witness against you, and shall eat your flesh as it were fire. Ye have heaped treasure together for the last days' [Jas. 5:1–3]. And Christ for his part proclaimed: 'And again I say unto you, It is easier for a camel to go through the eye of a needle, than for a rich man to enter into the kingdom of God' [Matt. 19:24; Mark 10:25; Luke 18:25]. The apostle Peter, moreover, said that that everyone, before being visited by death, should bedeck himself with righteous judgement, with charitable deeds, with purity, with sound mind and other good works, with these all [paraphrase of 1 Pet. 2:11–12]. For 'it is a fearful thing to fall into the hands of the living God' [Heb. 10:31]. And he who labours in charity, prayer and other works of goodness shall be cleansed of the multitude of sins. For once more Christ says in the Gospel: 'Lay not up for yourselves treasures upon earth, where moth and rust doth corrupt, and where thieves break through and steal: But lay up for yourselves treasures in heaven, where neither moth nor rust doth corrupt, and where thieves do not break through nor steal: For where your treasure is, there will your heart be also' [Matt. 6:19–21].[409]

409   'Iată că suntem datori, noi ceşti putérnici, să ajutăm celor slabi şi să-i îndreptăm, şi să nu facem atâta în voia noastră, cât în voia vecinului şi săracului şi a neputernicului, că aşa zice marele Pavel. Iar Iacov apostol, care să cheamă fratele lui Dumnezeu, zice: "Fratele cel smerit să să laude întru mărirea sa, iar cel bogat întru smerenia sa. Că, cum răsare soaréle cu căldură şi să veştejescu buruenile, şi florile lor să scutură, aşa şi bogaţii care nu să bogăţescu întru Dumnezeu, să vor veşteji întru umbletele lor". Şi iar mai zice: "Ni, acum bogaţilor, plângeţi, văetându-vă de întristăciunile ce vin asupra voastră, că bogăţiia voastră au putrezit, hainile voastre le-au mâncat moliile, aurul şi argintul vostru au ruginit şi rugina lor fi-va voao mărturie şi va topi trupurile voastre ca focul, că i-aţi strânsu avuţie în zilele céle de apoi". Iar Hristos au zis: "Mai lesne va intra funea corăbiei prin urechile acului, decât bogatul întru împărăţiia ceriului". Petru apostol încă au zis: "Tot omul mai nainte de moarte să să împodobească cu judecată, cu milostenie, cu curăţie, cu mintea cea întreagă şi cu alte fapte bune, cu toate". Că "înfricoşat lucru iaste a cădea în mâinile Dumnezeului celui viu". Iar cel ce să va nevoi cu milostenie, cu rugă şi cu alte bunătăţi, acelui i să vor curăţi mulţimea păcatelor. Şi iar mai zice Hristos la Evanghelie: "Nu îngropareţi avuţiia voastră în pământu, unde o strică viermii şi o putréjeşte putréjunea şi o sapă furii şi o fură, ci strângeţi avuţiia voastră în ceriu, unde nici viermii nu o strică, nici putréjunea o putréjeşte şi unde furii nu o sapă, nici o fură. Că unde iaste avuţia voastră acolo iaste şi inima voastra"' (Neagoe Basarab 1984: 16f.). Biblical references added.

We can see how the author of the *Teachings* makes a broad call for social justice and for the obligations of the powerful towards the weak and poor, though in the Middle Ages this did not necessarily mean the poor in a material sense.[410] Yet in a skilful act of semantic appropriation, the author supports his claims with quotations and paraphrases from the Bible that seem only and specifically to refer to material wealth.

A close reading of the *Teachings* reveals that, rather than imitating any other work, they embody a distinct stylistic approach of their own, quite aside from the substance of their argument. Though the author may deliberately copy substantial passages from other authors, he does so with an original purpose of his own. The 'quotations' end up fulfilling a purpose quite distinct from their function in the source work. Without ever stooping to oversimplification, the *Teachings* touch on all major topics in Orthodox theology, from its account of the Creation and anthropology to Christology, soteriology, mysticism and social theology.[411] Theological matters are discussed at a consistently high level and there is a logical continuum between the chapters and parts of the work. If transitions occasionally seem quite sudden, this is due to the manner in which the book was written, as discussed above: in segments and over the course of two years.[412] The author was nonetheless quite successful in smoothing out these transitions. The false impression of a disjointed text, of which so much was made by Demostene Russo and others, is due not least to the dilettantism of Ioan Eclesiarhul's edition of 1843. A comparison of the Old Romanian manuscripts reveals quite a clear logical and argumentative line, which is sadly missing from the *editio princeps*.[413]

The *Teachings*, as has already been pointed out, constitute not just a theological and political treatise, but also a 'reader' containing texts and passages that were canonical in contemporary Wallachia. It was addressed, it would seem, both to the country's intellectual elite and to a broader readership – assuming that it was able to read Church Slavonic – for only thus can

---

410 Grigore 2009: 368ff.
411 Zamfirescu 1996: VI.
412 Zamfirescu 1971 and 1973: 52. Zamfirescu considers that the second part of the *Teachings* was written before the first (see Zamfirescu 1973: 75 n. 90).
413 Zamfirescu 1973: 39ff.

the presence in the *Teachings* of passages from *Barlaam and Josaphat* or the *Alexander Romance* be explained, both very popular works of literature in sixteenth-century Wallachia.[414] The author provides extensive commentary on the individual quotations, which are often used as *exempla*, to prove a point. Over long passages, the style of commentary follows the pattern of questions and answers, as is typical, for instance, of the *Summa Theologica* of Thomas Aquinas.[415] The author of the teachings usually begins with an assertion concerning the nature of the Christian ruler, which is followed by a long list of *exempla* drawn from the Old Testament, with each *exemplum* being briefly explained. The 'moral' of the story is underscored by several biblical quotations; the conclusion deals with its concrete application and is introduced by such phrases as 'Hence' (*pentru aceia*), 'Accordingly' (*dreptu aceia*), 'See' (*vezi*) or 'Understand' (*ia aminte*).[416]

A striking feature of the *Teachings*, in their original Old Romanian version, is the range and suppleness of the metaphors, the clarity of structure and description and the variety of its poetic forms. Neagoe Basarab – if he was indeed the author of the *Teachings* – produced a masterpiece of rhetoric and as such a pioneering work of Romanian literature.

The Tradition of Political Writing in South-Eastern Europe

The tradition of political parenesis was carefully cultivated in late antiquity and the Byzantine era.[417] It took the form of mirrors for princes as well as of homilies or eulogies and played a defining role both in political and in religious discourse. Yet the mirrors for princes (*specula principum*) are surely the most important part of this parenetic literature. Numerous authors of political treatises, and of mirrors for princes in particular, are recorded from late antiquity and the Byzantine world. Agapetus, Theophylact of Ohrid, Thomas Magister or Emperor Constantine VII Porphyrogennetos not only defined the sub-genre of the Christian

414   Mihăilă 1996: LXXVII.
415   Neagoe Basarab 1984: 13f. On this, see Plămădeală 1969: 248; Zamfirescu 1973: 335.
416   Neagoe Basarab 1984: 26ff.
417   Hunger 1978: 157,159.

mirror for princes,[418] but were also widely read in the Eastern Church and in the various cultural traditions ranging from the Balkans to the Russia of the czars. After the Bulgars settled south of the Danube and adopted Christianity, the region saw the growth of a lively culture and literary production in Church Slavonic, of which parenetic writings were an integral part. We are thus faced with a fairly long Christian tradition reaching from Synesios of Cyrene and Deacon Agapetus to Emperor Manuel II Palaiologos and from Bulgaria to Russia, comprising the eleventh-century *Poučenia* (Instruction) of Vladimir II Monomakh and the political correspondence between Ivan the Terrible and the *knez* Kurbsky in the sixteenth century.[419]

Synesios of Cyrene (d. c. 413) was the author of a highly influential treatise on the rule of the emperor ('Περὶ βασιλείας'), which he appears to have read to Emperor Arcadius (395–408) in his capacity as the envoy of the city of Cyrene (in modern-day Libya).[420] Synesios mentions a number of key Christian behaviours demanded of a ruler, motives that can be found throughout the history of the mirror for princes all the way to Erasmus of Rotterdam, Neagoe Basarab or Martin Luther: 'reliance on God alone', for instance, or the emperor's role as 'donor of the good'.[421] This work was particularly influential in the Danubian Principalities. The library of the

---

418 Christian mirrors for princes are entirely in the tradition of their classical or Hellenistic predecessors, whose structure and core ideas they adopt and dress in more or less explicitly Christian terms. Authors like Isocrates (fourth century AD) or Hellenistic neo-Pythagoreans like Ecphanthus [who he?] were widely received and applied in Christian late antiquity.

419 Piru 1961: 41; Camarino-Cioran 1979: 118; Zamfirescu 1996: VII. The great political and parenetic tradition of the West, on the other hand, appears to have been largely ignored by the East. Neagoe Basarab, too, writing around the same time as Erasmus, Luther and Machiavelli, wax ignorant of Latin, Italian or German and knew nothing of his eminent Western counterparts (Zamfirescu 1996: IX). Comparable non-Christian literature in the Hindu or Islamic and Persian traditions, for example, the *Panchatantra* or the writings of Al-Ghazali, fall outside the scope of this study (on these see Benfey 1859; Hertel 1908; Edgerton 1924: 3; Ghazali 1964; Bagley 1964: ixff., xvi).

420 Krabinger 1850; Lacombrade 1951.

421 Blum 1981: 32.

Romanian Academy alone today owns twelve manuscript versions, all of which, however, were produced after the time of Neagoe Basarab.[422]

Around 530[423] Deacon Agapetus, of whose life we know quite little,[424] wrote – supposedly as teacher to the emperor[425] – a mirror for Justinian I (527–565) entitled Ἔκθεσις (*Ekthesis*).[426] The first letters of its seventy-two chapters form an acrostic, spelling out the words Τῷ Θειοτάτῳ καὶ εὐσεβεστάτῳ βασιλεῖ ἡμῶν Ἰουστινιανῷ Ἀγαπητὸς ὁ ἐλάχιστος διάκονος' (Deacon Agapetus, the lowest of all, to our most divine and pious Emperor Justinian).[427]The text adopts much of *Ad Nicoclem*, Isocrates' mirror for princes.[428] Among the key ideas developed by Agapetus in his mirror is *homoiosis*, the Christian ruler's resemblance or likeness to God. Agapetus further holds the ruler, by virtue of works of philanthropy, to be God's creditor, though the emperor was ultimately only a man and as such accountable to God. The emperor carried out his office with the help of God, to whom the ruler prayed for the state's welfare and flourishing – an old Christian idea derived from second-century apologetic literature.[429] Even Emperor Justinian I himself referred to the power of prayer in upholding the political order in the 133rd of his *Novellae* (539).[430] Besides *homoiosis*, Agapetus' most important idea – which can also be found among his successors, including Basarab – is that the Christian emperor is God's co-regent in heaven.[431]

On account less of its scope than its wealth of ideas, the mirror for princes of Agapetus went on to become the most influential of its kind in

---

422   Camarino-Cioran 1979: 120.
423   Henry III 1967: 282f.; Bell 2009: 18f.
424   Praechter 1908; Bell 2009: 8f.
425   This information is not uncontroversial (Krumbacher 1897: 456).
426   Text in PG 86/1, 1163–1186. On this, see Krumbacher 1897: 456. Also preserved from the time of Justinian is an anonymous political treatise, the so-called *Dialogue on Political Science*, which, however, never attained the celebrity of the Agapetus' *Ecthesis*. See also O'Meara 2002.
427   Blum 1981: 80 n. 1.
428   Bellomo 1906: 62ff.
429   Grigore 2010: 126.
430   Henry III 1967: 298 n. 50.
431   Agapetus 1981: ch. LXXII.

the Byzantine Empire and the wider Christian world, being used even as a school textbook. The *Ekthesis* was translated into Russian in the twelfth century and influenced the political discussion carried in the correspondence between the *knez* Andrey Kurbsky (1528–1583) and Ivan IV (the Terrible).[432] Louis XIII of France (1610–1643) translated Agapetus into French after the Byzantine author had become known in the West through two translations into English and several more into German and Latin.[433] Wilhelm Blum was able to identify twenty sixteenth-century editions.[434] In a Church Slavonic translation, the work of Agapetus was introduced to the Danubian Principalities in the sixteenth century and translated into Romanian in the seventeenth.[435] The *Ekthesis* was also much appreciated at the court of Wallachia's humanist prince, Constantin Brâncoveanu (1688–1714).[436]

The author of the work known today as *Parenetic Chapters of Emperor Basil I* (Βασιλείου κεφάλαια παραινετικά)[437] is unknown. Evidently, the anonymous author made liberal use of the similar works of Isocrates or Agapetus.[438] It is not altogether impossible that the work might have been written by Photios, patriarch of Constantinople (858–867; 878–886), a well-known theologian and man of letters. What is certain is that Emperor Basil I (867–886) himself cannot have been the author, for he was most likely illiterate.[439] This mirror, too, contains an acrostic like that in Agapetus.[440]

The next noteworthy Byzantine mirror for princes is the eleventh-century *Strategikon* of Kekaumenos, commander of the Theme (province) of Paristrion.[441] Kekaumenos strongly emphasises the emperor's role as a normative centre and as an example of the highest Christian virtues,[442] an idea central – as we shall see – to Neagoe Basarab.

432 Šěvčenko 1954: 147, 164ff.
433 Blum 1981: 35f.
434 Blum 1981: 38 n. 121.
435 Camarino-Cioran 1979: 123; Blum 1981: 39 n. 130.
436 Grecu 1950: passim, esp. 234f.
437 Chiţimia 1963: 316. Text in PG 107, XXI–LVI.
438 Emminger 1913: 23.
439 Blum 1981: 39.
440 Blum 1981: 41 n. 147.
441 Kekaumenos 1956.
442 Blum 1981: 42. English translation in Barker 1957: 120–129.

As important to the tradition of parenetic literature as Agapetus is
the work of Theophylact (d. c. 1120–1126), bishop (since c. 1092) of Ohrid.
Theophylact was a student of the Byzantine scholar Michael Psellos and
had studied in Athens and Constantinople, where for a while he held
the office of deacon of the Grand Church. Theophylact was also tutor to
Constantine, son of Emperor Michael VII Doukas (1067–1078).[443] It was
to Constantine that Theophylact addressed his mirror for princes, entitled
'Παιδεία βασιλική' (*The Science of Government*) and composed in 1088.[444]
The work of Theophylact was much admired in the South Slavic realms,
where its impact was considerable.[445] In its Church Slavonic translations,
the mirror for princes is likely also to have found readers north of the
Danube. Among the key ideas likewise addressed by Neagoe Basarab are
the importance to the young prince of chastity and abstinence, the detailed
discussion (influenced by Aristotle) of the opposition between tyranny
and (Christian) monarchy, as well as the important etymology of the title
Basileus as applied to the Christian emperor: βασιλεὺς βάσις τοῦ λαοῦ ('the
emperor is the foundation of the people').[446] This notion of the emperor
as foundation, 'catalyst' and centre of the political community is of crucial
significance to Neagoe Basarab in developing his theology of the political.

Among the other Byzantine mirrors for princes that deserve a mention
here[447] are, first, the *Muses* of Emperor Alexios I Komnenos (1081–1118)
to his son, the future Emperor John II Komnenos (1118–1143)[448]; second,
the mirror addressed by Nikephoros Blemmydes (d. 1272) to Emperor
Theodore II Laskaris (1254–1258);[449] and third, that of Thomas Magistros
(d. c. 1325), who was tutor to the emperor's son Constantine. Among the

443   Blum 1981: 43; Podskalsky 2000: 233.
444   Text in PG 126, 253–265.
445   Podskalsky 2000: 210.
446   Blum 1981: 45f.
447   Missing from this selection is the well-known text *De administrando imperio*,
       addressed by Emperor Constantine VII Porphyrogennetos (913–959) to his son
       Romanos. It is, however, less a mirror for princes than an account of the Byzantine
       Empire's geopolitical position.
448   'Μοῦσαι Ἀλεξιάδες κομνηνιάδες' (see Maas 1913; Blum 1981: 46). Text in PG 142:
       657–674.
449   Blum 1981: 48 and 48 n. 183.

important themes in the latter text are the imitation of God by the Christian ruler (μιμητής Θεοῦ), a commonplace of Hellenistic political literature; the idea of concord, implanted in human nature, as the foundation of peace in the Empire – an idea likewise central to Erasmus of Rotterdam; and the idea of the political as a contract between ruler and ruled, as it is discussed in the first book of Plato's *Republic*.[450] Another highly important instance for the idea of the ruler as servant, following the pattern of the kenotic Christ – as it was later also maintained by Luther – is the mirror for princes of Emperor Manuel II Palaiologos (1391–1425) to his son John, composed in 1417.[451]

Slavic languages and traditions (South and East Slavic) also produced a considerable body of parenetic literature, which was in circulation throughout the Orthodox sphere.

Soon after his baptism, Czar Boris-Mihail of Bulgaria received, in 865, a solemn letter from the Ecumenical Patriarch, Photios, who had supported the czar's baptism.[452] This letter or treatise is divided into two parts, the first being a history of the Christian creed and the seven ecumenical councils, the second an account of the Christian ruler's rights and obligations, with an emphasis on good works and virtuous actions.[453] The letter was translated from Greek into Church Slavonic[454] in the fourteenth or fifteenth century and spread across Europe in Latin, French and Russian versions.[455] A similar instructional letter was addressed in 1393 by Patriarch Antonios IV of Constantinople (1389–1390; 1391–1397) to the Grand Prince of Moscow, Vasily I (1389–1425).[456] Geographical as well as ideological proximity suggest that the 'mirror for princes' of Photios may have been known in the Wallachia of Neagoe Basarab.

---

450 Blum 1981: 51ff.

451 Chiţimia 1963: 316; Blum 1981: 54f. Text in PG 156, 320–384.

452 Keipert 1988: 89.

453 Herenröther 1867: 594ff., 604ff.; partly translated into English by Barker1957: 112–115.

454 Two Church Slavonic manuscripts from the sixteenth century are preserved. The translation from the Greek seems to have been made not in Bulgaria, but in Russia (see Keipert 1988: 90, 104, 112).

455 Podskalsky 2000: 53f.

456 Mureşan/Năsturel 2011: 10. English translation by Barker 1957: 194f.

Another political work connected with Bulgaria and from which
Neagoe Basarab adopted passages verbatim in the *Teachings*[457] is the panegyric of Patriarch Euthymius of Tarnovo[458] on Constantine the Great
and his mother Helena, which in turn was strongly influenced by Eusebius
of Caesarea and the Byzantine Church historian Nikephoros Kallistos
Xanthopoulos (d. c. 1328).[459] The panegyric of Euthymius enjoyed considerable popularity in the Wallachian Principalities; for instance, the
Moldavian Prince Stephen the Great (1457–1504) is known to have commissioned several richly illuminated manuscripts of this particular work.[460]

What is in effect the political testament of Vladimir II Monomakh,
grand prince of Kievan Rus' (1113–1125), is perhaps the best-known product
of the interest in this literary genre in the Slavic world. His *Instruction*
(*Poučenie*)[461] to his sons has come down to us as an appendix to the (so-
called) *Chronicle of Nestor* (c. 1110).[462] Much as Neagoe Basarab would
later do in the second part of his *Teachings* (chapter VIII),[463] Vladimir
Monomakh gives instructions for receiving guests and strangers at the
princely court. Like Basarab, Vladimir Monomakh was inspired by the
monastic ideal of *ora et labora* and proclaimed the importance of manual
work and perpetual prayer to the Christian ruler.[464] Both Monomakh and
Basarab used their work to address the experience of their sons' premature
death, Oleg in the case of Vladimir Monomakh, Peter in that of Neagoe

---

457   Turdeanu 1947: 105f.
458   See the brief *Vitae* of Euthymius in Kaluzniacki 1901: XIIIff.; Turdeanu 1947: 67ff.;
      Podskalsky 2000: 253.
459   Euthymius of Bulgarien 1901: 103–146. For an edition of the Church Slavonic
      Original and an Old Romanian tranlation see Mihăilă 1979: 281–332, 333–379. On
      this, see Mihăilă 1979: 231; Podskalsky 2000: 317f.
460   Mihăilă 1979: 274.
461   Chițimia 1963: 316; Ciobanu 1989: 48. For a critical edition, see Tschiżewskij 1969.
462   Popa-Lisseanu 1935: 10, 97, 204–218; Blum 1981: 23.
463   'Învățătură a lui Neagoe voevod cătră fie-său Theodosie voevod și cătră alți domni,
      cătră toți, pentru solii și pentru războaie' (A teaching of Neagoe Voivode to his
      son Theodosius and other lords, to all, concerning envoys and warfare) (Neagoe
      Basarab 1984: 161ff.).
464   Blum 1981: 25.

Basarab.[465] Both mirrors for princes are structured similarly, beginning with a theological and ending with a practical part, both displaying the same baroque technique of quotation.[466] A political panegyric meriting at least a passing mention is the elegy to Vladimir the Great (St Vladimir), delivered by Bishop Hilarion around 1050. It follows the tradition of Synesios of Kyrene and may have influenced the panegyrics of the Bulgarian Patriarch Euthymius of Tarnovo, since both he and Hilarion discuss the missionary and 'civilisational' role of the Christian ruler.[467]

Of great importance for Slavic political literature is the correspondence between *knez* Andrey Mihailovic Kurbsky, who had been exiled to Lithuania, and Czar Ivan IV the Terrible from the mid-sixteenth century.[468] Though it does not form part of the mirror for princes as a genre, it is of relevance for the diffusion of theological and political ideas in the cultures of post-Byzantine Orthodoxy, being to a large extant an adaptation and application of Agapetus.[469] Another example of a Slavic work are the counsels for Christian politics of Joseph of Volokolamsk (d. 1515).[470]

The Sources of the Teachings to Theodosius

Influences on the *Teachings* are numerous and hard to identify. The absence of anything like a deontology of citation has already been alluded to.[471] Moreover, the author of this mirror for princes appears unconcerned

---

465 Unlike Peter, Oleg suffered a violent death. The sight of his young son's bloddied corpse drove Vladimir to introduce a radical ban on capital punishment in his principality: 'Put to death neither a just man nor a wrongdoer, do not suffer anybody to be killed' (Vladimir Monomakh apud Blum 19181: 25). Such a progressive position on the part of a prince is unique in eleventh-century Europe (Ciobanu 1989: 49).

466 Trautmann 1931: XXIf.

467 Leger 1884; Sčepkin 1897; Trautmann 1931; Müller 1962: 23; Blum 1981: 26. A German translation: Nestor 2001, the lesson is on pp. 340ff.

468 Fennell 1955: IX.

469 Blum 1981: 27.

470 Blum 1981: 27.

471 Although he draws extensive passages from the *Grief for Sin* of Symeon Monachos, the author of the *Teachings* never so much as refers to him.

whether the sources he draws upon are authentic or pseudepigraphical. Textual criticism is alien to him; priority is given to the content of the works used. The author is clearly a well-read man. Besides the Bible – the historical books of the Old Testament, the Gospels and the epistles of St Paul being his preferred sources[472] – he is also familiar with Church Fathers such as John Chrysostom (referred to by Basarab as *Zlatoust*), Ephrem the Syrian or John Climacus.[473]

Painstaking study of detail has allowed scholars surely to identify several direct sources that are either mentioned or adopted verbatim from Church Slavonic translations. All the sources that the author of the *Teachings* found to be of interest and which he incorporated into his text – John Chrysostom, Basil of Caesarea (Basil the Great),[474] Ephrem the Syrian and John Climacus as well as *Barlaam and Josaphat* – were translated into Church Slavonic between the tenth and twelfth centuries. From the thirteenth to the fourteenth century, numerous Church Slavonic manuscripts were introduced from Bulgaria into Wallachia and Moldavia, and a lively local production of manuscripts in Church Slavonic began in the Wallachian Principalities in the fifteenth century, after the South Slavic political entities had been conquered by the Ottomans. It lasted to the end of the sixteenth century[475] and comprised not only missals and other texts for liturgical use, but also dogmatic, ascetic and hagiographical writings both from the Patristic tradition and from the more recent theological literature of Eastern Christianity.[476]

Most of these sources, however, had only an indirect impact on the *Teachings*, their ideas reaching the text in roundabout ways, which makes it difficult for links of interdependence to be reconstructed. The author drew from something of a shared pool of Orthodox Christian theology. In this pool, ideas took on an existence independent of individual thinkers and circulated widely, in part orally, to be freely used by other authors. One of

---

472   Mihăilă 1996: IX.
473   Olteanu 1967: 341; Mihăilă 1996: LVIf., LXII.
474   Among the Patristic sources of the *Teachings* is the famous address to Christian youth of Basil the Great on dealing with pagan literature any mythology, a detailed examination of which will be found in the next chapters.
475   Piscupescu 1939: 129ff.; Grecu 1950: 234f.; Ciobanu 1989: 25, 27f., 33.
476   Romanski 1908: 119.

the challenges confronting this study is thus to trace the often subliminal diffusion of political philosophy into the work of Neagoe Basarab. These indirect sources, many of which I was able to identify, will be discussed in the next section.

In order to do justice to their complexity, I shall discuss the sources on which Neagoe Basarab drew either knowingly or subconsciously as falling into one of two categories: the authority works of the Church Fathers and other ecclesiastical authors, on the one hand, and those of vernacular literature, on the other.[477] The direct sources are largely those that scholars of Neagoe Basarab have previously identified.[478]

Besides the Bible, the homilies of *John Chrysostom* (d. 407) were the *Teachings'* most important source. A direct source upon which Basarab drew and which I was able to identify are John's homilies on Genesis, especially the third homily, which Basarab paraphrases liberally. It was on this third homily that Basarab founded his anthropological account of the Fall and its consequences,[479] as I shall explain in due course. Besides the commentary on the eighth psalm, which discusses man as the crown of Creation,[480] other direct sources have been found in John's sixty-ninth homily on the Gospel of St Matthew,[481] his sermon on patience and his catechetical sermon on the resurrection.[482] Neagoe Basarab is known to have possessed a Church Slavonic manuscript of John Chrysostom's homilies, which he later donated to the monastery of Krušedol.[483]

The *Sermon on the Transfiguration of Christ* by Ephrem the Syrian (d. c. 373),[484] preserved in Greek and Armenian translations,[485] provided the

477 Russo 1910: 8; Zamfirescu 1973: 100; Ciobanu 1989: 50.
478 Romanski 1908: 166; Piru 1961: 41f.; Rosetti 1964: 281; Olteanu 1967: 341; Cazacu 1989: 113.
479 John Chrysostom, Homilien über die Genesis, Homilie 3: 20f.
480 Johannes Chrysostomus-Psalms, 1998; Anghel 1972: 817f.
481 Johannes Chrysostomus, Kommentar zu Matthäus, 1916. See also Mureşan 2003: 307.
482 Zamfirescu 1973: 100.
483 Balotă 1969: 279.
484 On Ephrem, see Biesen 2002, though it is doubtful whether Ephrem truly was the author of this sermon (Cazacu 1989: 114).
485 'Preobraženie' in Church Slavonic. URL: <http://unifr.ch/bkv/kapitel2451.htm> (accessed 22.02.2020). On this, see Zingerle 1870: 231.

author of the *Teachings* with a *model précis* of the doctrine of the two natures of Christ against the Nestorians and Monophysites. The author of the
Teachings adopts several pages of the sermon's Church Slavonic translation.
Neagoe Basarab is likely also to have taken additional arguments from a
so-called *sbornik*, a collection of counter-heretical arguments in Church
Slavonic.[486] Ephrem was well known in the Danubian Principalities, and
at least five Church Slavonic manuscripts produced between the fifteenth
and seventeenth centuries and containing his hymns and sermons have survived.[487] From Ephrem, Basarab is likely to have adopted the theory of the
heavenly tollgates that the souls of the dead had to pass en route to their
individual judgment.[488] The first sections of the *Teachings*, in which man's
prelapsarian state in paradise is discussed, also seem to have been inspired
by Ephrem's hymns on the subject.[489]

From the *Grief for Sin* (Κατάνυξις)[490] of Symeon Monachos, Neagoe
Basarab adopted, as Dan Zamfirescu has shown,[491] the eleventh word (on
drunkenness) and incorporated it into part II, chapter 7 of the *Teachings*,
dealing with the Christian ruler's table manners.[492] The fourteenth word
of the *Grief* (on charity and mercy) resurfaces in part II, chapter 9 of the
Teachings (on jurisdiction[493]), while the twenty-fourth word ('That evil
should not be repaid with evil') was incorporated into part II, chapter 2
('That no grudge should be held').[494] Finally, the twenty-ninth word on the
Last Judgment and on *Parousia* reappears in part II, chapter 10, which deals

---

486   A number of such works circulated in the Danubian Principalities in the fifteenth
        and sixteenth centuries (Rosetti 1964: 242).
487   Olteanu 1967: 348.
488   Russo 1910: 22.
489   Ephräm d. Syrer, Hymnes, 1951. On this, see El-Khoury 1976: 39, 60.
490   Originally entitled 'Λόγοι διάφοροι περιέχοντες τὰς τῶν παθῶν παντῶν κατηγ
        ορίας'. The work received the title 'Κατάνυξις' from its Greek editor, Paisios
        Hieromonachos, in the Athens edition of 1873. There has so far not been a critical
        edition of the text (Zamfirescu 2009: 8).
491   Zamfirescu 1973: 253 and 2009: 15.
492   Symeon Monachos 2009: 117ff.; Neagoe Basarab 1984: 157ff.
493   Symeon Monachos 2009: 147ff.; Neagoe Basarab 1984: 183ff.
494   Symeon Monachos 2009: 295ff.; Neagoe Basarab 1984: 209ff.

with generosity towards the servants at court.[495] At the time of the *Teachings'* composition, the *Grief* was considered the work of John Chrysostom,[496] which is why these quotations are frequently accompanied by the slavicised version of that name, *Zlatoust* or 'Gold-Mouth'. Besides, Basarab used only a Church Slavonic selection from the *Grief*, which retained only nine of the original Greek's thirty-two chapters. This working copy is now preserved as MS 312 in the Library of the Romanian Academy.[497] The eulogy of part II, chapter 3 of the *Teachings* is loosely reminiscent of a similar encomium by Emperor Leo VI the Philosopher to his father, Basil I (867–886).[498] The *Grief* was widely read in the so-called 'Orthodox commonwealth': seven manuscript versions are preserved in the National Library in Athens, nine on Mount Athos, one in Jerusalem and another in Genoa, besides a number of fragments.[499]

That the *Teachings* contain a large part of the panegyric of Euthymius of Tarnovo to Constantine the Great and his mother, Helena, was first noticed by the Slavicist Piotr A. Lavrov.[500] From the panegyric, which was composed at the behest of the last Bulgarian czar, Ivan Sišman (1371–1395),[501] the *Teachings* adopt the entire account of Constantine's life from the vision of the cross to his death.[502] Another important source for the *Teachings* is the *Ladder* (Κλῖμαξ) of John Climacus (d. 649), which particularly influenced the sections on stillness, on *apatheia* and on the Jesus prayer.[503]

It is debated whether the chapter on the departure of the soul from the body (part II, chapter 13) might have been influenced by the treatise Ἱερὶ

---

495 Symeon Monachos 2009: 343ff.; Neagoe Basarab 1984: 190ff.
496 This confusion was only resolved by Demostene Russo, who succeeded in proving that the *Grief* was not the work of Chrysostom. Even a usually well-informed scholar like Stojan Romanski laboured under this misapprehension (Romanski 1908: 184ff.).
497 Zamfirescu 1973: 102 n. 51, 181; Mihăilă 1996: LXXXIV.
498 Vogt/Hausherr 1932; Adonz 1933; Zamfirescu 1973: 330.
499 Zamfirescu 2009: 7f.
500 Mihăilă 1996: LV.
501 Tapkova-Zaimova 2010: 473.
502 Neagoe Basarab 1984: 59ff.; Romanski 1908: 176.
503 Zamfirescu 1973: 47.

ἐξόδου ψυχῆς’ of Cyril of Alexandria (d. 444) or whether the similarity of the title is a mere coincidence. A possible indirect transmission may have occurred via the eleventh-century *Dioptra* of Philip Monotropos, a popularising collection of earlier Patristic text paraphrases,[504] which is known to have influenced the *Teachings* decisively.[505] The *Dioptra* have variously been dated to the years 1096–1097 or c. 1105[506] and consist of two parts: verses of lament addressed at the author's own soul and a dialogue between body and soul[507] – subject matters, that is, close to the chapter on the departure of the soul. Immediately on their publication, the *Dioptra* attained immense success in Byzantine intellectual circles and more generally within mediaeval and early modern Orthodox cultures. *Dioptra's* broad manuscript tradition extends into the nineteenth century,[508] and their Church Slavonic version was well known in the Danubian Principalities.[509]

Among the works of pious vernacular literature, the key sources for the *Teachings* are to be found in the legend of *Barlaam and Josaphat* and in the Byzantine and Church Slavic versions of the *Alexander Romance*. *Barlaam and Josaphat* was, if anything, even better known in the Middle Ages than the *Alexander Romance*, its range extending from India to Iceland and Russia. Some authorities have ascribed this Christian adaptation of the story of the Buddha[510] to the celebrated theologian, John of Damascus (d. 754), while others suppose it to have emerged from the Christian and Manichean milieu of the Persian Empire and others still claim the novel to be the work of a Georgian monk.[511] Scholars have been troubled by the fact that *Barlaam and Josaphat* has several passages and ideas in common with the *Ecthesis* of Agapetus, leading to various theories on who was borrowing from whom.[512] In any case, the legend found its way, in a Church

504   Afentoulidou-Leitgeb 2007: 9; Miklas 2008: 55ff.
505   Romanski 1908: 192.
506   Grumel 1951.
507   Afentoulidou-Leitgeb 2007: 19.
508   Miklas 1975: v.
509   Murko 1971: 150.
510   McQueen 2011.
511   Krumbacher 1897: 457ff., 887; Dölger 1953; Chiţimia 1963: 289; Lang 1983: ixff., xvff., xxff.; Mazilu 2002: 392.
512   Praechter 1893; Barker 1957: 81; Henry 1967: 294ff.

Slavonic version, from Bulgaria and Serbia to the Danubian Principalities, where numerous copies appear to have circulated.[513] The oldest manuscript in Wallachia dates from 1518.[514] An Old Romanian translation of *Barlaam and Josaphat* was produced in 1648 by the scholar Udriște Năsturel.[515]

As Moses Gaster was the first to show, the author of the *Teachings* drew two parables from this novel:[516] that of the sumptuous caskets inwardly full of dead man's putrefaction and pestilence, and that of the nightingale.[517] The many similarities between *Barlaam and Josaphat* on the one hand and the *Ecthesis* of Agapetus – and the fact that the former was so well known to the author of the *Teachings* – may serve to explain the many discourses, ideas and themes common to both the *Teachings* and the *Ecthesis*. Though he did not himself know the latter, or at least not well, his intimate knowledge of *Barlaam and Josaphat* familiarised the author of the *Teachings* with many of Agapetus's ideas. One example is the strong emphasis, both in Agapetus and in Basarab, on the idea of the 'apathetic' ruler – a prince, that is, subject neither to vices nor to passions.[518] Another is the so-called 'chain of mimesis', the idea that the Christian ruler should serve as an example *to* and indeed *is* the normative core of his people, the focal point of people's piety. From the subjects' tendency to imitate the ruler's every action stems the ruler's major responsibility for forming his subjects as pious and Christian people. As long as the ruler imitates Christ and the people in their turn imitate the ruler, the people will be a Christian people and follow Christ. The community of the people is the mirror image of the ruler, as the Christian prince is himself the image of God on earth.[519]

513   Turdeanu 1947: 51f. It was translated in Church Slavonic in the second half of the twelfth century (Mazilu 1981: 58).

514   Gaster 1883: 33.

515   Chițimia 1963: 290; Cândea 1968: 22f.; Cartojan 1974: 291ff.; Turdeanu 1985b; Mazilu 2002: 393.

516   Mazilu 2002: 393. 517 Gaster 1883: 39, 42, 44; Romanski 1908: 179; Iorga 1925: 142f.; Turdeanu 1947: 54.

517   Neagoe Basarab 1984: 91ff., 94ff. See on this, Grigore 2019b: 182ff.

518   Praechter 1893: 446.

519   Barker 1957: 82 n. 2.

The *Alexander Romance*[520] was something of a 'best seller' in the Latin West as well as in the Orthodox East.[521] In the Slavic regions south of the Danube, it had been translated into Church Slavonic as early as the fourteenth century, circulating among educated readers in Wallachia and Moldavia in its so-called 'Serbian' version.[522] Yet the version upon which the *Teachings* draw is that in Middle Bulgarian, whereas the late sixteenth-century Romanian translation used the shorter Serbian version.[523] The *Teachings* borrow from the *Alexander Romance* chiefly in the chapter on mercy (part II, chapter 10).[524] Neagoe Basarab also followed the list of the ruler's virtues from the *Alexander Romance* without transcribing it verbatim:

> And furthermore Alexander said: 'I took with me four helpers. The first was the sweet and gentle word, the second the outstretched hand, the third the rightful judgment and the last the forgiveness of trespasses, by which means I was able to conquer the world, and all rulers should act thus.'[525]

A further source to be mentioned is the *Physiologus* of the second or third century,[526] which was very well known in Basarab's time and from

---

520   On this, see Pfister 1978; Lienert 2001: 26ff.

521   On the spread of the *Alexander Romance*, see Zacher 2009: 13f. The so-called *Alexandria* reached the Danubian Principalities rather later than the West, though it became highly popular as soon as it was translated. On this, see Kristophson 2013. I am grateful to Wolfgang Dahmen for bringing this to my attention.

522   Gaster 1883: 11; Kristophson 2013: 74.

523   Haşdeu 1984: 25ff. The Greek version of the *Alexander Romance* (Pseudo-Kalisthenes) was translated into Latin as early as the tenth century; this Latin version was then translated into Serbo-Croatian. At least one copy is certain to have circulated in the Danubian Principalities and is recorded as having been at the Moldavian monastery of Neamţ in 1592. The first Old Romanian Translation was produced some time before 1600, though the only preserved copy dates from 1620 (Simonescu 1963: 6f.). On this, see Cartojan 1922 and 1974: 269ff.

524   Rosetti 1964: 246.

525   'Alexandru mai zise: avut-am patru ajutori cu mine, unul cuvântul dulce, altul mâna întinsă, altul judecata dreaptă şi altul ertarea la greşiţi, cu acestea am luat toată lumea, aşa trebuie să fie tot omul împărat' (apud Gaster 1883: 25). The virtues referred to here are diplomatic tact, peaceability, righteousness and mercy.

526   Pitra 1855. 'Physiologus is the title given to a work written in Greek and which originally comprised 48 chapters. These chapters initially contain short accounts

which the author of the *Teachings* borrowed three parables, as Moses Gaster has shown: those of the snake, of the dove and of the ostrich (στρουθοκάμηλος).[527] This last parable, in the form it was adopted in the *Teachings*, is to be found only in the Church Slavonic and Old Romanian versions of the *Physiologus* and is quite different from its Greek original or Latin translation,[528] thus providing further proof that Basarab wrote the *Teachings* in Church Slavonic.[529] Though it is preserved only in Old Russian manuscripts, the Church Slavonic translation of the *Physiologus* is of thirteenth-century Bulgarian origin.[530] This version is likely to have circulated in south-eastern Europe and was also known in the Danubian Principalities. Among the other fragments of popular apocryphal literature to resurface in the *Teachings* either directly or indirectly are *Mary's Descent into Hell*, *The Wood of the Cross* and *The Story of King Asa*.[531]

On the Structure of the Teachings to Theodosius. A New Approach

Though scholars have been aware of the *Teachings* since 1838, their study has been marked by periods of one-sidedness and stagnation.[532] A perpetual concern with technical questions of authorship, original language, time of writing, etc., has in many cases stood in the way of a closer engagement with the argument of this remarkable work of literature. Such is the imbalance in the existing scholarship that philological and linguistic

---

of the peculiarities of animals, plants and rocks. [...] This "scientific" part is followed by a second, of Christian interpretation supported by numerous biblical quotations.' (Treu 1998: 111). On this, see also Gaster 1886–1888; Krumbacher 1891: 455ff.; Karnejev 1894; Cartojan 1974: 236ff.; Henkel 1976; Depietri 2010.

527   Gaster 1883: 139; Romanski 1908: 181; Russo 1910: 8,23ff.

528   Reinsch 1892: 158, 172f.; Polívka 1896: 539f.; Goldstaub 1905: 186.

529   Grigore 2019b: 176f.

530   Polívka 1892: 381.

531   Daničić 1872: 75ff.; Zamfirescu 1973: 342. The *Story of Asa* from Serbian apocryphal literature refers to Asa, son of Abijam and king of Israel (1 Kings 15 and 22), though it actually represents a Christian rewriting of a story about the Emperor Jovian from the *Gesta Romanorum* (c. 14th c.) (Murko 1908: 154).

532   Romanski 1908: 153.

studies have been produced to an almost inflationary degree, at the expense of the history of ideas. An intellectual-historical analysis that considers the historical context of the early sixteenth century, the strands of cultural tradition, the process of transfer and exchange of ideas has not yet been attempted. The same is true of a comparative perspective that would situate the *Teachings* in the context of similar European discourses and locate them, both synchronically and diachronically, in the development of political theory.[533]

Key to understanding the argument of the *Teachings* is, I would argue, their very deliberate structure. The work begins with a theological section, profoundly and subtly argued, and concludes with considerations on practical questions.[534] The first part develops an elaborate theological anthropology of the political: the foundation of the political in human nature, the conditions of political life and the theomimetic or homoiotic relationship of the Christian ruler to God. This is followed by the practical application in the second part, which is also full of theological explanations and accounts of the religious purpose in political life.[535] It is no coincidence that the second part begins with a thorough explication of the Orthodox dogma of the seven ecumenical councils, thus depicting true faith as a criterion of Christian rule and of the political community's cohesion.[536] A superficial reading would place the first part in a serious logical contradiction to the second. Indeed, its very richness in theology and political theory has led scholars, whose interest in the text was more philological in nature, to avoid the first part. Most interpretations of the text have preferred to focus on the concrete and tangible statements made in the second part.

Yet a careful reading will quite soon reveal the coherent structure of the *Teachings*, which is fundamentally quite typical of the genre of mirrors for princes as a whole.[537] The *Poučenie* of Vladimir Monomakh follow the same pattern.[538] We are faced with two levels of argument that are hierarchically

533   Plămădeală: 1969: 246; Zamfirescu 1973: 7, 20.
534   Neagoe Basarab 1984: 416ff.; Romanski 1908: 140.
535   Romanski 1908: 167ff.; Cartojan 1980: 72.
536   It may even have been intended as a challenge to Lutheranism, which was beginning to make inroads in Transylvania (Chihaia 1971: 5).
537   Hunger 1978: 157ff.
538   Ciobanu 1989: 49.

structured: the meta-history of man's paradisiacal existence as the crown of Creation, on the one hand, and the historical, that is, contingent, level of earthly power and glory, on the other. Confronting the two levels reveals the former as the ideal state of being in the paradisiacal homeland of innocence, a state to be regained only by acetic purification, spiritual progress and mindfulness. The second sphere, that of man caught *in* the historical circle of becoming, represents a necessary but temporary state on the way to heaven. The ruler's own personal ascetic and mystic experience is to serve the public not only as an example, but also as a means of public sphere formation as doxological community of the Christian people.[539]

Far from being a 'monkish' inventory of homespun wisdom and formulaic statements of conformity to Church and faith, the first part addresses the possibility of rule from the perspective of Christian anthropology and cosmology. Without this detailed first part, the *Teachings* as a whole would make little sense. They are intended not as a guide for just any ruler – which is what Machiavelli's *Prince* aspires to – but instead lay out a manifesto for an *Orthodox Christian* ruler. The divine, heavenly origin of the political and of rule: *that* is the golden thread running through the *Teachings*.

The first part of the *Teachings* hence gives an account of God's history with man in general[540] and the God-beloved ruler in particular. Archetypal case studies depict both tyrants as well as God-beloved rulers, from the Old Testament and from Christian history alike. Together, they constitute a complex and detailed response to the ontological question of human nature and to the existential problems like injustice, death and anguish. While the first part constitutes a meditation on human beings in their trans-historical essence, the second part considers humanity in history.[541]

To distinguish between a 'theological' and a 'practical' part of the *Teachings* is justified only as an analytical device, for they constitute a continuum between the religious and the secular (*saeculum* = world).[542] The existence, the very being of man as God's partner in Creation, is irreconcilable with a Manichean separation between spirit and matter, soul and

539   Noica 1991: 15f.
540   Ulrich 2007: 87ff.
541   Zamfirescu 1973: 327.
542   Muthu 1976: 33.

body, heaven and earth; it would indeed undermine the whole purpose of human community. That is the message of the first part of the *Teachings*, on which any further analysis of their ideas must be founded.

Christomimesis, Theomimesis and Homoiosis in Neagoe Basarab: On the Political Significance of Mysticism

To no less a degree than the general structure of the *Teachings to Theodosius* offers the key to understanding the work as a whole does it also offer the hermeneutic key to the work's first, explicitly theological part. In its analysis and interpretation of the *Teachings*, scholarship has hitherto concentrated on the second part and the concrete instructions it contains. But I shall argue in the following section that the theological first part, with its wealth of mystical, systematic and political-theological thought, rewards closer examination. The first part of the *Teachings* is impressive not only for its sheer abundance of ideas, but especially for the original and innovative manner of their presentation, making this work singular both among mirrors for princes as a genre of European and within Orthodox theology. They represent an eminent example of the reformulation of Byzantine theology in the new context of sixteenth-century Wallachia.[543]

The following analysis begins with some remarks on the structure of the first (religious-theological) part of the *Teachings* as a means of underlining its four principal thematic concerns, which to the author are inseparable from the exercise of power. They are: (1) the political as the doxological[544] community of Christians; (2) the mystic, hesychastic *illuminatio* and its influence on rule; (3) the canon of the Christian ruler's virtues; and, finally, (4) the metaphorics of rule in the *Teachings*. The chapter's conclusion will address the question of *theomimesis* in Neagoe Basarab.

543   Plămădeală 1969: 247; Muthu 1976: 29.
544   From the Greek δόξα, meaning 'glory' or 'glorification'. In Orthodox liturgy, the doxology is equivalent to the *Gloria* of the Latin rite. The Slavic term is 'slava'.

The First Part of the Teachings to Theodosius

The structure of the *Teachings* represents a theological elaboration, in various argumentative stages, with the purpose of validating the political and Christian rule as logical consequences of nature and of inherited human inclinations. Hence, the first part begins with a description of man as doxological being, created to glorify God and to praise and exalt Him communally. As long as man fulfils his given nature, he is God's 'co-regent', 'friend' and 'heir', a lord over the angels of heaven. Because man is a doxological being, he is an organ of God's will on earth, too. Man recognises the Creator's reasons in His Creation.[545] This organ must be transparent in order to allow God's light to pass through into the world, necessitating ascetic purification and mystical illumination in order to liberate man from vice, sin and incontinence and to raise him to the rank of a God-like being.[546] Ahead of all other human beings and Christians, the ruler finds himself in an intensified relationship with God, in a position 'to see the face of God'[547] and thus to enact the will of God in the midst of the doxological community.[548] Rulers stand and fall with their ability to make God present and effective in the world, which is why the first part of the *Teachings* so often refers to the necessity of the Christian ruler's conforming to God's will (*voia lui Dumnezeu*).

Yet the *Teachings* also testify to an awareness of the gulf separating ideal and reality[549] in a manner similar to the *Institutio Principis Christiani* of Erasmus. Whereas the work begins by emphasising man's privileged status as a political being, with the body political constituted as doxological

545 'Similar to the integral harmony of paradisiacal man, the will of the flesh and the will of the spirit, love of creatures and love of God are no longer in conflict, but are united to form one love and one will. Yet this is possible only because the body, by mastery over the passions and control of the physical instincts associated with them, was involved in preparing this unification' (Podskalsky 1966: 211f.).

546 Neagoe Basarab 1984: 17f.

547 Neagoe Basarab 1984: 19.

548 The asceticism referred to here is not of the private kind mentioned in Matt. 6:5–6 and 17–18, but rather a publicly enacted show of exemplary asceticism on the part of the ruler (see Noica 1991: 15f.).

549 Plămădeală 1969: 246.

community and with the ruler as its catalyst, subsequent discussions address the deviations from this ideal that occur when rulers and human beings in general abuse their special natural endowments. Basarab thus feels compelled to speak, in the work's closing chapters, of humility, and to confess how far the individual 'Neagoe Basarab' himself, prince of Wallachia, is from this Christian ideal: 'God has bestowed rich gifts upon us and endowed us with the powers of speech, reason and sound judgment. And yet we are worse than animals and beasts.'[550] The power over their fellow men given to rulers was justified, according to the author of the *Teachings*, by the Aristotelian principle of proportionality:[551]

> He [i.e. God] has given us triumph and victory, that we might protect the week and deliver them from peril, and yet we torment and oppress the innocent. [...] He has given us power and riches, that we might share them with the powerless, and instead of doing so we mock and humiliate them.[552]

Hence, I would argue that no interpretation can do justice to the *Teachings* if it fails to take account of the first part. The *Teachings* form a coherent whole. Basarab structures his work in a highly theological manner that serves as an expression of the cyclical nature of his anthropology: it begins with an account of man's pre-eminent position in the universe, which results from the natural homoiotic theomimesis of man as a doxological being. No less than Gregory of Nyssa in the fourth century, Basarab considers man to have been created as a structurally homoiotic and God-like being – a being conceived to resemble the deity whose image he carries within him (ὁμοίωσις πρὸς τὸ Θεῖον, ὁμοίωσις τοῦ Θεοῦ).[553] In an awareness

---

550 'Iar pe noi ne-au dăruit Dumnezeu şi ne-au cinstit cu graiu şi cu cuvântu şi cu judecată dreaptă. Iar noi suntem mai răi decât hierăle, şi decât dobitoacele' (Neagoe Basarab 1984: 90).

551 Aristoteles 1985: book V, chs. 6 and 7.

552 'Biruinţă ne-au dat în mâinile noastre, ca cu dânsa să păzim şi să răscumpărăm pe cei slabi, iar noi muncim pe cei nevinovaţi şi le facem nevoe. [...] Datu-ne-au putere şi bogăţie, ca să dăm noi celor neputernici, iar noi în locul acestora ne batem joc şi ne râdem de dânşii' (Neagoe Basarab 1984: 108).

553 Merki 1952: 94ff.; Hunger 1964: 58ff. The term 'ἰσόθεος' (God-like one), found in a second or third-century papyrus, means much the same thing.

of the aforementioned gulf between ideal and reality, this first part of the *Teachings* leads to the second, in which are shown the ways of the ruler responsible for the Christian people. Christians are able to return to their homoiotic state, yet not in the monastic isolation of a cell, but rather by being brought together in the shared life of the earthly *politeia*.[554]

Doxology and Rule

My beloved son, above all it is meet and right to honour and to praise God the great, the good, the merciful, our wise Creator, without ceasing [1 Thess. 5:17], day and night, at every hour and in every place. And it is likewise meet and right to glorify and exalt Him with full voice and unceasing song, for He created us and led us from non-being into being. [...] In His great mercy, God dwelt among us, men, and revealed Himself to us. He was God in Heaven and man upon earth, perfect in both. And He made man His dearly beloved son and the heir to His kingdom.[555] [...] And from nothingness He called us forth into existence and created all the incorporeal powers. But to what end? Only to praise the name of Him who created us, the Lord of lords and the God of gods. He created us, that we might bear witness to His name and praise it, that the angels too in their heavens high [might see it and in their wonder] praise Him.[556]

---

554 Merki 1952: 105ff.
555 Ps. 100.
556 'Iubitu mieu fiiu, mai nainte de toate să cade să cinsteşti şi să lauzi neîncetat pre Dumnezeu cel mare şi bun şi milostiv şi ziditoriul nostru cel înţelept, şi zioa şi noaptea şi în tot ceasul şi în tot locul. Şi să foarte cuvine să-l slăveşti şi să-l măreşti neîncetat, cu glas necurmat şi cu cântări nepărăsite, ca pre cela ce ne-au făcut şi ne-au scos din-tunérec la lumină şi den nefiinţă în fiinţă. [...] Dumnezeu, pentru mila sa cea multă, lăcui întru noi oamenii şi să arătă noao. Dumnezeu fu în ceriu şi om pre pământu şi într-amândoao desăvârşit. Şi pre om şi-l făcu fiiu iubit şi moştean împărăţii sale. [...] Şi den nimic ne-au făcut de suntem şi făcu toate puterile céle făr de trupuri. Dar pentru ce? Numai ca să lăudăm numele lui, cel ce ne-au făcut, Domnul domnilor şi Dumnezeul dumnezeilor. Adusu-ne-au în arătarea şi în slava numelui său cel sfânt, ca să-l proslăvească îngerii în ceriurile céle de sus' (Neagoe Basarab 1984: 5f.). Emphasis added.

This programmatic statement, placed at the beginning of the *Teachings*,[557] contains the core element of Basarab's idea of man and his place in the cosmos. We exist only to praise God, for in us He has glorified Himself. To be human is to act according to our 'design' – that is, according to our natural constitution – and continually to cultivate and expand it. By nature, we are designed to contemplate, desire and praise God.[558] Man's naturalness means that he *is* a living, breathing doxology of God.

Human beings are works of art created by God; in the hierarchy of Creation they are placed even above the angels.[559] According to the Platonic trichotomy, we are endowed by God with reason, soul and body.[560] The parts of the body, too – mouth, ears, legs, eyes, hands – each have a doxological purpose to fulfil. Hands are extended towards God in praise, eyes raised up to Him. Accordingly, they are not to be sullied by misdeeds. For each of the organs mentioned, Basarab takes the time to give a detailed account of its functioning within the scheme of the generally doxological nature of human beings.[561] It can thus be seen how the author of the *Teachings* regards man as living testimony to God's power and perfection. Our natural predisposition to give praise is both structural and purposeful: such was the paradisiacal state before the Fall, and such is the path by which lost Eden may be regained.[562] With the whole of Creation, of which human beings

557   A similar approach, based on the exalted position of man as crown of the universe, can be found in Vladimir Monomakh (Popa-Lisseanu 1935: 207). The possibility that Monomakh's *Instruction* may have influenced the author of the *Teachings* can, at any rate, not be excluded.

558   Johnson 2010: 23.

559   Neagoe Basarab 1984: 7, 12f. A similar opinion is shared by the Italian, Giovanni Pico della Mirandola (d. 1494) (Mirandola 1990: 7).

560   Neagoe Basarab 1984: 22; Joantă 1992: 93.

561   Neagoe Basarab 1984: 6f.

562   Johnson 2010: 16. It is important, however, to correct a grave terminological error on the part of Johnson, who on page 16 refers to a 'rediscovery of our own likeness (homousis) [*sic*] to God'. This is wrong both orthographically – the word is 'homoousis' (of identical nature, of the same substance) – and dogmatically, for only the Son and the Holy Spirit are 'homoousioi' (of identical nature, of the same substance) to God the Father.

represent the crown, we thus exist in – and are ourselves deified by – a state of *communio* with Christ and the cosmos.[563]

According to this logic, the only 'natural' human beings are those who pray and give praise, thus acting according to their nature – in an entirely natural manner rather than from a sense of duty imposed from outside. Moreover, this is nothing less than the first step towards becoming a Christian ruler: first to be a Christian like any other (which, as we shall see, is also Luther's argument) and then to epitomise that state in an exemplary fashion: 'And how do the rulers fall from God, their lord? Some by their faith, the others by their works. [...] Yet such men who are subject to others die unto their earthly lords and kings with their bodies; unto God they die with their souls.'[564]

By his presence in the midst of the political community, the Christian monarch plays a *centring* part in that community: 'And all draw upon him for wisdom and instruction; not only his subjects and his people, but likewise men from other lands, who long to receive his instruction and advice.'[565]

The ruler enjoys a privileged position among doxological beings, a form of 'concentrated' humanity allowing him to enter into a special and intensified relationship with his maker.[566] God created him not just to exalt him, like all other human beings, but also entrusted him with rule over them, and particularly with the responsibility for their souls. It is striking that Basarab ascribes this responsibility to the ruler rather than to the Church or clergy. By virtue of his own illumination, the God-beloved ruler has a special insight into God's unexplored ways and can thus act as a centre around which to gather the community of Christians. Eusebius of Caesarea had already explained this in his sermon at the *tricennalia* of Constantine the Great

---

563 Johnson 2010: 23.

564 'Iar domnii în ce chip cad de la Domnul şi Dumnezeul lor? Cad unii din credinţă, iară alţii din fapte. [...] Că oamenii care suntu supt stăpâni, cu trupurile mor domnilor şi împăraţilor pământeşti, iară cu sufletele ei mor lui Dumnezeu' (Neagoe Basarab 1984: 8).

565 'Şi toţi iau învăţătură şi înţelepciune de la dânsul şi încă nu numai slugile şi oamenii den ţara lui, ci şi alţii dintr-alte ţări poftescu să ia învăţătură şi sfat de la dânsul' (Neagoe Basarab 1984: 222).

566 Eberhardt 1977: 413f.

(335).[567] The Christian ruler, to Neagoe Basarab, is among the 'children of the light' (John 12:36; 1 Thess. 5:5) and as such shows God's other children the way, leading them, too, to the light. The author of the *Teachings* shares this opinion with Symeon the New Theologian (d. 1022).[568] This provides the key to understanding the Stoic topos[569] of Orthodox political theology, which led Nikephoros Blemmydes and Theophylact of Ohrid in deriving the etymology of the Byzantine *basileus* from the syntagma ʽἔστι βασιλεὺς βάσις λαοῦʼ (the king is the foundation of the people).[570] Accordingly, the prince is the core and the basis of the harmonic (ἁρμονία) doxological community (κοινωνία);[571] his remit includes the realisation of the doxological nature of humanity, and not even the clergy are meant to surpass him in piety and fear of God.[572] The subjects gaze up at their ruler, and he in turn resembles and reflects his subjects.[573]

As Luther would later agree, rule represented to Neagoe Basarab a vocation, a calling to a particular estate. The ruler performed administrative

---

567   Dvornik II, 1966: 617, plus citation. Dan Zamfirescu accordingly speaks of a 'contract' between God and his earthly deputy (see Zamfirescu 1973: 291), which, however, is inaccurate with regard to Basarab's theology. His attitude is rather Aristotelian, concerned with man's potential and the manner in which its is bred, cultivated and actualised. Basarab makes it quite clear that no contract can obtain where the ruler is determined by contingency and the pure will of God, beyond any justification by merit. The ruler is of course an organ of God's will, installed by God without having 'earned' his dignity or office by his own *merita*. Neagoe here seems to approach Luther's position. The ruler's active participation begins only upon being elected by God; only then is it incumbent upon him to maintain his status as an organ of God by ascetic exercises and mystical contemplation, by prayer, fasting and liturgy.

568   Symeon the New Theologian 2009: 150–151.

569   The old Stoic doctrine holds that the ruler bears the cosmological responsibility for the maintenance of the natural order of Creation (Seidler 1960: 20).

570   Theophylact of Ohrid, ch. VI, pp. 83, 97 n. 7.

571   This is the old neo-Pythagorean doctrine that subsequently influenced Christian thought. It was first expressed by Ekphantos (Martens 2003: 60f.).

572   Theophylact of Ohrid, ch. XII, p. 87.

573   Thomas Magister: 99. This argument, which appears to be something of a *locus communis* in Western mirrors for princes, was also frequently invoked by Erasmus (Anton 1968: 75).

duties (*tocmitor*) towards the community of Christians. But for these works, the ruler would stand empty-handed before God's judgement; only by performing these duties well was he justified before God ('*căci nici nu ai adus nimic cu tine în această lume, nici vei să iai nimic*'). Like any Christian, the ruler was able to find salvation in the fulfilment of his estate. By means of his earthly rule, conscientiously exercised, the ruler would obtain heavenly rule and be crowned by God Himself (*și cu împărățiile lumii acestii trecătoare au dobândit împărățiia cea netrecătoare a ceriului și au luat cununa bunătăților din mâinile lui Dumnezeu*). Each Christian had a calling and an office or duty (*slujbă*) to fulfil, among which to rule was simply a special case.[574] A similar attitude can be found in Luther.

Basarab adheres to the Christian cyclical view of history. The course of history is revealed in the structure of the *Teachings*, which has the beginning and the end coincide: the narrative leads from the ontology of man through the prelapsarian paradisiacal state of humanity to the gulf separating it from the reality of the present before describing the mystical and ascetic path back to former glories. Basarab thus places himself in the tradition of the Cappadocians, of Basil the Great and his brother, Gregory of Nyssa (d. 394), who in turn are likely to have drawn on the Platonic notion of cyclicity. Only with regard to sin is history linear. In the meta-history of God and man there is neither linear nor teleological chronology. Our earthly pilgrimage offers the chance of return to the heavenly home.[575]

This whole theoretical edifice of the political as a doxological community is founded on the optimistic anthropology developed by Basarab, to whom human beings are not simply victims racked by fear and guilt,

574 Neagoe Basarab 1984: 11.
575 Callahan 1958: 38; Escribano-Alberca 1972: 43, 47; Otis 1976; Louth 1981: 1. It is a common misconception to think of the Christian idea of time as being simply teleological, oriented towards an *eschaton*. This is true enough with regard to the *Parousia*, but wrong in the existential sense of Christian life and God's ways to men. As the liturgical cycles of each individual day and of the Church year make amply clear, Christians are each day and each year involved in a story of salvation that is lived individually and collectively and which brings to mind the state of innocence, the Fall, the age of the Old Testament, and the passion, resurrection, and ascension of Christ as well as the Pentecost. Christians are thus not merely spectators, but intimately involved in this perpetual shared history with God.

but rather the crown of the cosmos, the goal to which the Creation was geared:[576]

> Yet behold God's mercy, behold the love with which He has loved us! Behold the gift with which He has favoured us! O, how immeasurable is the number of Thy gifts, o Lord! For He has raised our human nature above all powers of heaven. God ascended and sat upon the august throne of His glory. And all the creatures that wander below the heavens and all the things [from the hand] of God, all are destined and ordained according to our needs and for our service: the sun, the moon, the stars, the ether, the wind, the rain, the earth and the sea, and all [the creatures] within it. And God created man as king and as the [crowning] triumph of all the deeds He ever performed in heaven and on earth. And not only that: He made man His associate and His heir and His beloved son, and by His blessing destined him to be God and co-ruler of His divine kingdom, as it is written: 'Be ye holy; for I am holy [1 Pet. 1:16]; ye shall be gods, for I am God' […].[577]

In contrast to John Chrysostom or Augustine, the author of the *Teachings* does not take temporal rule to be a consequence of the Fall:

> And know how much God cared for men, for the prophet says: 'Thou didst make him for a little while lower than the angels' [Heb. 2:7, cf. Ps. 8:5]. Here the prophet says that this slight diminution compared to the angels had occurred as a consequence

576 'The universe does not exist for its own sake but for the sake of man and the destiny he must work out for himself by life in the universe. The universe must therefore be explained in terms of man, and if the universe exists in succession, that is, in time, this feature of the universe's reality must be related to the pilgrimage of man on earth' (Callahan 1958: 57).

577 'Vezi mila lui Dumnezeu, vezi dragostea lui cu carea au iubit pre noi! Vezi darul lui cu care ne-au dăruit! Cât iaste de multă mulțimea milelor tale, Doamne! Că au urcat firea noastră cea omenească mai deasupra decât toate puterile céle cerești. Dumnezeu s-au înălțat și au șezut pre scaunul mărirei puterilor sale. Iar alte făpturi câte suntu supt ceriu și lucrurile ale lui Dumnezeu, toate suntu tocmite și rânduite în treaba și în slujba neamului omenescu: soarile, luna, stélile, văzduhul, vântul, ploile, pământul și marea și toate câte suntu într-însa. Iar pre omul făcu-l viețuitoriu și împărat și biruitor tuturor faptelor sale câte suntu supt cer, și încă nu numai atâta; ci-l făcu soț și moștean și iubit fiiu și-l dărui de fu Dumnezeu și biruitor împărățiiei sale celei cerești, cum iaste scris și zice: "Fiți sfinți, cum suntu și eu sfânt, fiți dumnezei, cum suntu și eu Dumnezeu!" ' (Neagoe Basarab 1984: 7f.).

of the Fall and the past infraction of our forefather Adam in paradise. But in what respect does man find himself diminished with regard to angels? Surely by death![578]

By ruling over Creation, man is God's fellow and co-regent. As a micro-cosm, man is the epitome of all Creation, a privileged ontological status that man did not lose even in the Fall. Death is and remains an *existential* rather than an *ontological* consequence (as it is, e.g., to Luther). Even after the Fall, man, to Basarab, carries within him the indestructible image of God, an argument previously made by Nicholas Kabasilas (d. 1392), who defined death as 'ἕξις' in the Aristotelian fashion, that is, as ethical and ex-istential, not ontological and essential.[579] The Devil's rule in the postlap-sarian world, harsh though it may be, is merely an *accident* (in the philo-sophical sense) rather than a *datum*.[580] By the Fall, man incurred only a slight curtailment of his rule over Creation, not its forfeiture. The 'good' and useful domestic beasts continue to be at man's service and help him to survive the struggles of everyday life, as Basarab argues in a paraphrase of the third of John Chrysostom's homilies on Genesis:

> Here we see the ineffable love that God has for humankind. For although man con-fessed to his guilt and his sin, God left him the crown of honour and of his original glory, and his stature was not diminished; and if his rule was in fact slightly curtailed, then it was for his own sake. For, before the Fall, man also ruled over the fearsome

578 'Deci, ia aminte, să ştii câtă grijă are Dumnezeu pentru oameni, că zice prorocul: "Cu puţintel oarece l-ai mai micşorat decât îngerii?" Aici zice prorocul şi grăiaşte această micşorare, pentru că cu puţintel oarece au mai micşoratu Dumnezeu pre omu decât pre îngerii, pentru greşala şi călcarea ce greşi dentâi strămoşul nostru Adam în rai. Dar cu ce l-au micşorat puţintel decât pre îngeri? Micşoratu-l-au cu moartea!' (Neagoe Basarab 1984: 12).

579 Plămădeală 1969: 255; Muthu 1976: 39; Joantă 1992: 92f.; Spiteris 2002: 364.

580 In the second part of the *Teachings*, Neagoe Basarab certainly does mention the dreadful consequences of the Fall, stating, for example, that God had turned away from us and driven us from the Garden of Eden. In postlapsarian history, human beings had had to forget the sight of God's 'sweet' countenance and instead been made to behold the 'fearful and sinister' face of Satan. These claims to not contra-dict the Biblical account. The sense of heightened drama is intended to emphasise the gulf between the original idea and the harsh stat of the world. The advent of Christ, according to Basarab, had put an abrupt end to the rule of the Devil (see Neagoe Basarab 1984: 109f. and passim).

and untamed beasts, whereas after the Fall, this untrammelled rule was slightly curtailed. Yet, even after the Fall, man continues to rule over the wild beasts, though
now with greater effort, with fear and with the utmost caution, for his honour has
neither fully vanished nor remained entirely undiminished. All that had been to
his use and need remained at his service. Only the wild beasts did God allow to
leave his rule, in order that he might recognise this and remember that this happened on account of the Fall of Adam, his forefather. Thus is he made to know why
not all creatures are subject to us, which in turn redounds to our benefit: For what
use would it be to us if we were to bend to our will the lion or the panther – even
if they were tame? What use would rule over these and suchlike wild beasts be to
us, except [that it would encourage us to] pride and empty glory?! For this reason,
God left these beasts to be unruly and unbowed, whereas such animals as are useful
to us are docile and obedient and to our bidding: oxen, that we might plough with
them; sheep, that we might cover our nakedness; [and] other animals to help us in
other needs and to feed us.[581]

581   'Aici arată dragostea cea nespusă, care o are Dumnezeu cătră neamul omenescu.
      Că omul, deși cunoscu el însuși păcatul și vina sa, iar Dumnezeu tot îl lăsă să fie
      încorunat cu cinstea și cu slava cea dentâi, și mărirea lui nu o strică; iar de-i și luo
      ceva puținel de suptu putérea lui, și aceasta pentru folosul lui fu: că, mai nainte
      de greșală, și fierăle céle zvăpăiate și cumplite le stăpânea omul, iar după greșală
      puținel de acestă biruință-l opri. Însă și acum tot biruiaște și stăpânéște și pre acélea,
      ce cu meșterșug și cu frică și cu pază mare, că nici i-au luat toată biruința, nici i-au
      lăsat-o toată, ci câte i-au fostu de treabă și de slujbă i le-au lăsat, iar câte sântu fiară
      sălbatece i le-au luat, ca pentru aceasta să-și aducă aminte și să cugete tot omul,
      pentru păcatul strămoșului Adam, și să cunoască, că pentru acela nu să pleacă noao
      toate fierile, și iaste și aceasta de mare folos. Dar leul, măcar de s-ar și pleca noao,
      de ce tréabă ne-ar fi noao, sau pardosul, măcar de ar fi și blându. Așijderea și alte
      hieri sălbateci și spurcate, fără numai o trufă și o mărire deșartă. Pentr-acéia lăsă
      Dumnezeu să fie acéstea seméțe și neplecate, iară céle ce ne sunt dă treabă, iale să
      fac plecate și blânde, și le supuse suptu mâinile noastre: boii, ca să arăm cu dânșii,
      oile, ca să îmbrăcăm goliciunea trupurilor noastre, iar alte dobitoace le lăsă ca să
      poarte ce ne va trebui și să ne hrănim cu dânsele' (Neagoe Basarab 1984: 14). See,
      by comparison, John Chrysostom: '[S]o too in the case of the human being: while
      they enjoyed God's trust they were an object of fear even to the animals, but when
      they fell they eventually had to fear even the least of their fellow slaves. [...] If,
      however fear [of animals] came on the scene afterwards, this is also an extraor-
      dinary token of God's loving kindness. I mean, if after the commandment had been
      broken by the human beings the esteem accorded them had remained unimpaired,
      they would not easily have risen from their fall. You see, when obedient and dis-
      obedient people enjoy the same esteem, they are more inclined to evil and don't

Following the Fall, man is not left alone in the world, but continues to rule over the useful part of the cosmos. In this respect, however, Basarab departs from Genesis (3:17–19).

Whereas John Chrysostom claimed that the political, the state, was but a necessity, a philanthropic intervention on the part of God to keep mankind, plunged into chaos by sin, from mutual destruction,[582] Basarab takes a different view. To him, the foundation of the political is ontological, not existential. The political form of a joint association was, in Basarab's opinion, in accordance with the natural constitution of human beings, and the state was self-evidently the earthly preliminary to the Christian doxological community of the kingdom of God. Even had there been no Fall, human beings would comprise a *politeia* in jointly experiencing and enacting God. Basarab maintains that God's punishment for man's disobedience in paradise was really rather slight. Though humans were now mortal, the glory and the greatness bestowed in the act of Creation were undiminished: 'Here we see the ineffable love that God has for humankind. For although man confessed to his guilt and his sin, God left him the crown of honour and of his original glory, and his stature was not diminished.'[583]

Though Chrysostom, too, introduces God's love as a political category, the place of love in Basarab is both loftier and more concerned with

---

quickly recover from evil. [...] So it is out of his providential care for us that he has removed us from our position of control. Consider now, I ask you, dearly beloved, in this instance God's ineffable love as well, how, on the one hand, Adam infringed the whole commandment and completely broke the law, while, on the other hand, God in his loving kindness proved his goodness superior to our transgressions and did not cancel all our esteem nor remove the human being from all control. Instead, he withdrew from their control only those beings that did not have the greatest contribution to make to their livelihood, whereas the most necessary and useful creatures which performed great service to our living he allowed to remain in subjection and servitude. He left at any rate herds of cattle to draw the plough [...]. He left the beasts of burden to assist our efforts in transporting heavy loads; he left the flocks of sheep so that we might have a sufficient supply of garments for clothing; and he left other kinds of animals to supply us with plenty of resources.' (John Chrysostom, *Homilies on Genesis*, ninth homily, 122f.)

582   Grigore 2010: 132; Grigore 2012: 347ff. On the competing paradigms of the political in Plato and Aristotle, see Steinmetz 1969.

583   See above, note 581.

its application. At issue here is not a condescending, charitable, pedagogical and preventative sort of care[584] – in a word, *philanthropic* love – but
rather the unconditional *erotic*, discriminating, sacrificial, unifying, recognising, sympathetic love for a friend, a comrade or a son. The notion of
philanthropia offers a means for the conceptualisation and rationalisation
of a love transcending the very concept of rationality, a love that is feeling,
striving, desire, longing, experience, awareness. The polarity here is that
between *agapé* and *eros*, between socio-political love and the love that is
sympathetic, mystical. overflowing. *Eros* is the foundation of *agapé*, which
is merely a social, political and ethical form of practising the supra-rational
and trans-argumentative *eros*. Even the disobedience that brought about
the Fall was unable to put a stop to erotic love.[585]

On account of this love, according to Basarab, God regards man as
a participant in his power and his glory, as a co-ruler: 'Hence you should
glorify Him who lifted you up from the earth and raised you to be the son
and ruler of heaven, to be the great victor and commander over men and
peoples [...].'[586] That is the promise that in the eyes of Basarab forms the
very purpose of Christian rule on earth: the prospect of ruling in heaven
alongside God.[587] The idea of the co-regency of the Christian ruler with
God in heaven and on earth has a long tradition in Christianity and derives
from Hellenistic discourses. It can be found in Constantine the Great[588]
and more prominently still in Agapetus, and it represents an adaptation of
biblical claims such as those of Baruch 5:2, Matt. 5:3 and 10, 2 Tim. 4:8 and

---

584 Grigore 2012b: 351ff.
585 Neagoe Basarab 1984: 14.
586 'Pentru acéia dă slavă celui ce te-au rădicat din pământu şi te-au făcut lui fiiu şi
      cerurilor împărat, şii noroadelor şi oamenilor biruitoriu mai mare şi poruncitoriu
      [...]' (Neagoe Basarab 1984: 9).
587 Neagoe Basarab 1984: 237.
588 Constantine claims to feel the deity working alongside him in all his doings and
      continues to solicit its direct assistance for the benefit of the state ('Ita mihi summa
      divinitas semper propitia sit et me incolumem praestet, ut cupio, felicissima et
      florente re publica', Cod. Theodosianus I, ed. T. Mommsen, book IX, 1, 4, Sept.
      325) (Ensslin 1975: 55). Eusebius of Caesarea considered the earthly Roman Empire
      to be the image (εἰκών) of the heavenly kingdom (Dvornik, II, 1966: 617, with cit-
      ation; Farina 1966: 107, 109ff., 113ff.).

2:12, or Rev. 2:10. In these passages, the reference is not to the co-regency of the Christian ruler with God, but rather to the co-regency of all the faithful to whom is promised the inheritance of the kingdom of heaven.[589] Agapetus applies this generalised promise of the scriptures to the specific case of the Christian ruler. According to Agapetus, the Byzantine *basileus* is foremost among Christians in embodying the virtues of the Gospel and is thus likewise ahead of all others in gaining rulership in heaven by the virtuous exercise of his rule.[590] Writing in the eleventh century, Theophylact of Ohrid goes further still and makes the following argument concerning 'συμβασιλεία' (co-rule):[591]

> In truth it would appear that he [the pious emperor] alone could be lord of the whole world. For the world is God's, and if by common opinion the ruler is a friend of God, but that friends hold all things in common, then the lord of the world must be the ruler who is to the greatest degree God's friend.[592]

This is the opinion that Basarab adopts: the Christian ruler involved God in his earthly rule and in turn was involved by God in the kingdom of

---

589 The Latin *conregnabimus* (2 Tim. 2:12) 'was frequently adduced in the Middle Ages and in the process acquired a meaning that the Apostle would not have intended. In order to provide a metaphorical illustration of the glories of the life everlasting, he had promised that "we shall also reign with Him", referring to the proven Christians in Heaven and to their coronation; yet the phrase was used to elevate the rulers' (Schramm 1966: 481).

590 Agapetus 1981: ch. LX, p. 76 and ch. LXXII, p. 79f.

591 Carile 2008: 271. First used in a Christian context by Clement of Alexandria (d. 215) and Eusebius of Caesarea (d. 339), the term 'συμβασιλεία' referred to the anticipated joint rule in heaven, after his death, of the true-believing Constantine (Eusebius of Caesarea 2007: IV, 48, pp. 468–469; Schramm 1966, 482 n. 3). This in fact refers to Constantine as a 'common Christian', in which capacity the Gospels promise him the kingdom of Heaven. For the emperor's joint rule with God on earth Eusebius uses such terms as 'ὕπαρχος' (viceroy, governor) or 'σύνθρονος' (joint ruler, co-regent) (Farina 1966: 112f.; Maier 2003: 132). Eusebius describes the joint rule of God with Constantine on earth in the following terms: 'This is also what God Himself, whom Constantine honoured, standing at Constantine's side at the beginning, the middle and the end of his reign, confirmed by his manifest judgement […]' (Eusebius of Caesarea 1999: 69).

592 Theophylact of Ohrid, ch. XII, p. 87.

heaven.[593] To Basarab, the ruler is not God's deputy on earth, as it has often been maintained in the political theology of the West;[594] rather, God's rule extends to earth through, or with, the Christian ruler by synergetic action. The *Teachings* contain no term that corresponds to the Latin *vicarius Christi*.

Like the other authors of mirrors for Princes, Basarab is aware of the unique nature of the relationship between God and ruler. The author of the *Teachings* is clearly in favour of rule by divine right, without intercession by instances like Church, bishops or Patriarch. Basarab repeatedly emphasises that the princes of Wallachia – that is, he and his son, Theodosius – owed their rule to none but God, though in fact Basarab was installed as prince by a Turkish army and with the sultan's approval.[595] This immediacy with which Basarab is preoccupied is manifest in the notion of *co-regency*. It is necessary, moreover, because none but the ruler is called to answer for the fate of God's flock before the tribunal of Christ.[596] God calls a particular Christian to rule over and administer the Christian communion in the world, a call made according to God's hidden and inscrutable judgment and taking account neither of the ruler's merits nor of the Church's preference. Drawing on Romans 13, Basarab speaks of the duty of subjects to obey their monarch, unjustified resistance being, according to Basarab, an affront to God.[597] The divinely ordained Christian ruler was both friend and fellow to God:

> And thus do we speak also of princes and kings among whom God dwells and abides – as long as they are chosen and installed by God and faithfully act according to His will and His commandments. And though all the world might confront them with envy and rise up against them with machinations and the force of arms, yet they have nothing to fear, for the rebels shall incur the wrath of God and bring upon their own heads the unquenchable fire, in this age as that which is yet to come. […] Hence

593   Păun 2001: 212.
594   Anton 2006: 11.
595   Muthu 1976: 36; Mureşan/Năsturel 2011: 272.
596   This immediacy of the relationship between God and ruler is expressed both by Luther himself and by the Lutheran author Thomas Birk (1550–1629). The latter argues in terms similar to Basarab (Görz 1990: 119).
597   See Neagoe Basarab 1984: 75.

none shall dare, incited by the Devil, neither courtier nor peasant,[598] to rise against his prince and master by stratagems, in deed or even in thought. For every one that falls into temptation and raises his hand *unjustly* against his master, while his ruler is gentle and Christ's anointed, that fool will instantly bring the righteous wrath of God down upon his unrighteous head. Then he shall meet with the punishment of the living God. For kingship and the rule of the true-believing and righteous kings and princes is heavenly kingship and heavenly rule.[599]

Leaving aside his marked conformity with Scripture and Patristic theology, it seems fair to see Basarab's own personal interest at work in this relentless defence of divinely appointed rule, for it serves to make God's will and moral accomplishment the criteria of rule in place of considerations of blood, descent and dynasty.[600] Basarab thus takes care to make

598 That he should mention peasants as possible rebels indicates that Basarab was writing under the impression of the bitterly fought Transylvanian peasants' war of 1514, led by Gheorghe Doja (Ştefănescu 1964: 1125ff.).

599 'Aşişderea zice şi de domni şi de împăraţi, că de vor fi ei aleşi şi puşi de Dumnezeu şi de vor face voile şi poruncile lui cu adevărat, deacii şi Dumnezeu de-a pururea şi în tot locul va fi cu dânşii. Şi măcar de le-ar fi toată lumea pizmaşă şi să să scoale cu vrăjmăşii şi cu oşti asupra lor, nimic nu le va strica, ci încă mai mult vor aţâţa mâniia lui Dumnezeu şi vor aprinde focul cel de veci în capetele lor şi în cestu veac şi în cel ce va să fie. [...] Pentru acéia nimini să nu îndrăznească, nici slujitoriu, nici ţăran, nici nimeni să-şi ridice firea şi gândul cu meşteşug hiclean, dintru îndemnarea diavolului, spre împăratul şi spre domnul şi stăpânul lor. Că cel ce să va ispiti a-şi rădica mâna asupra stăpânului său fără dreptate şi asupra domnului său, carile iaste îngăduitoriu şi unsul lui Hristos Dumnezeu, acela cu adevărat de pripă îşi va aduce mâniia lui Dumnezeu cea dreaptă spre nedereptul său cap, şi urgia Dumnezeului celui viu să va pogorî pre dânsul. Că împărăţiia şi domniia a împăraţilor şi domnilor, care iaste pre împăraţii şi domnii cei credincioşi şi drepţi, acéia iaste împărăţie şi domnie cerească' (Neagoe Basarab 1984: 76, 94). My emphasis. Cf. 2 Sam 23:5–7 (RSV): 'Yea, does not my house stand so with God? For he has made with me an everlasting covenant, ordered in all things and secure. For will he not cause to prosper all my help and my desire? But godless men are all like thorns that are thrown away; for they cannot be taken with the hand; but the man who touches them arms himself with iron and the shaft of a spear, and they are utterly consumed with fire.'

600 Păun 2001: 198. We may recall that Basarab was a usurper, who supported his claim to rule by depicting his predecessor as an arbitrary and unjust (!) tyrant, reviled by God. As long as the notion of rule can be kept separate from dynastic logic and instead be made to depend on the virtue and morality of the prince, Basarab

sure his son understands that he owes his rule to no one but God alone
and that there is no human instance able to stand between him and his
maker:

> I think you already know that it is not they [men] by whom you were chosen and
> anointed, but God […], and indeed, that men did not choose you, nor did men
> anoint you to rule, but God alone elected you, He anointed you and it is Him that
> you must please.[601]

This is nothing new, but rather represents the Byzantine opinion according to which the emperor is elected and crowned by God,[602] as it
is stated in the coronation anthem: 'Glorify God the lord. Glorify God,
Who hath crowned thy head. God, Who hath elected thee to be king.
Glorify God, who hath glorified thee.'[603] No mention is made of the
Church or the Patriarch as instances involved in crowning or anointing
the emperor.[604]

---

had reason to hope that his son would find it easier to defend his rule against rival
claimants to the throne.

601 'Crez, ştii, că nu te-au ales, nici te-au unsu ei domn, ci Dumnezeu, ca să fii tuturor
dreptate' or 'Că nu te-au ales, nici te-au unsu oamenii spre domnie, ci Dumnezeu
te-au ales şi te-au unsu şi a acéluia plăcére să faci' (Neagoe Basarab 1984: 151 and
153f.). See also Neagoe Basarab 1984: 195.

602 Constantinus Porphyrogennitus 1995: 67f.; Seidler 1960: 21; Şerban 1971: 302;
Blum 1974: 110; Ensslin 1975: 56. It may have been the evident failure of the dynastic principle that contributed to the notion of the contingency of rule taking
hold in Byzantium. The widespread belief was that it was ultimately God's will to
elevate an emperor to or topple him from the throne, irrespective of such temporal
factors as birth, inheritance, election, proclamation by the army, nomination, co-
regency, etc. (Christou 1971: 282; Angelov 2007: 125ff.). In Byzantium, the right to
political resistance and protest permitted the deposition of an unjust ruler by a 'superior' claimant, in whom dynastic consideratons were treated as at most optional
(Olster 1993; Morris 1994: 205f., 209).

603 'Δόξα Θεῷ τῷ Δεσπότῃ. Δόξα Θεῷ τῷ στέψαντι τὴν κορυφήν σου. Δόξα Θεῷ τῷ ἀν
αδείξαντί σε βασιλέα. Δόξα Θεῷ τῷ δοξάσαντί σε οὕτως' (apud Wellesz 1949: 98f.).
On this, see Angelov 2007: 127.

604 Agapetus, on the other hand, writing under the influence of Plato, maintained
that the emperor was dependent on the consent of his subjects (Agapetos 1981: ch.
XXV, p. 69; Grigore 2010: 109). Theophylact of Ohrid went further still and
claimed the people itself to be the subject of rule: 'It is not by force that he [the

Rule *Dei gratia* is to Basarab not merely an ideological and theological underpinning of the pre-eminence of the monarch over boyars and people at the domestic level, but also marks a claim in foreign policy. With regard to the sultan, it served as a reminder that the lords of Wallachia considered themselves to be autocrats, rulers in their own right, rather than deputies or officials of the Ottoman Empire. As long as they were chosen and installed by God and not the sultan, the latter could have no rights over them – in theory, at any rate. According to this line of thought, the sultan was merely a visible instrument of God's hidden will.[605]

The immediate relationship between the Christian prince and God is not only a heavy responsibility, but above all the precondition for godly rule. The immediacy of the relationship subsists especially in the immediacy of grace with which God, in an act of mystic illumination, douses his favoured ruler, thus deifying him. Thus illumined, the ruler becomes Christlike, a *homoiousios*, and an enlightened one. Neagoe Basarab is one of the few Orthodox political writers to adopt a position of *political hesychasm*.

Illuminatio and Rule

This section considers the *Teachings* in the context of hesychasm, a distinctive feature of Eastern Christianity. Following some introductory remarks on the concept of hesychasm, on the Jesus Prayer or Prayer of the Heart and on illumination, the phenomenon of hesychasm will be approached in historical terms, particularly with a view to so-called 'political hesychasm', which plays a central part. The section ends with a discussion of the theological and doctrinal position of hesychasm in the

---

Emperor] acquires his rule, but rather it is by the consent of the crowd that he is borne and by a grand assembly of the people that he is honoured [...]' (Theophylact of Ohrid: ch. XI, p. 87). Though Neagoe Basarab himself underwent procedures of election and acclamation in being made prince of Wallachia, no mention is made in his mirror for princes of these proto-modern political forms. He seems not to have set much store by them.

605 Georgescu 1971: 328.

Teachings. Here, too, the accent will be on 'political hesychasm', this time its theoretical and dogmatic aspects.

In the form that emerged in the late Byzantine period, the hesychast *praxis* in Orthodox monasticism[606] consisted in the constant inward repetition of the Jesus Prayer (1 Thess. 5:17[607]): 'Lord Jesus Christ, Son of God, have mercy on me, a sinner' or, in an abbreviated form, 'Lord Jesus Christ, Son of God, have mercy upon me'.[608] Besides prayer, hesychast means of attaining illumination are the good works and the sacraments, among which particularly baptism, confession and the eucharist. To the hesychast practitioner, it is with baptism that the mystical ascent towards God begins.[609] In the later hesychasm of the fourteenth century, prayer is combined, in the solitude of a monk's cell, with breathing exercises, meditation and a particular sitting position.[610] It is therefore appropriate to speak of a psychosomatic practice and its concomitant religious and mystical experiences.[611]

606   A selection of texts by hesychast authors can be found, with an introduction, in Rigo 1993. For a classification of hesychasm, see Lilienfeld 1986; 282, where the categories are: (1) a technical hesychasm beginning in the thirteenth century; (2) a traditional hesychasm beginning in the third century; (3) a theological hesychasm synonymous with the theology of Gregory Palamas (d. c. 1358); (4) a political hesychasm beginning in the fourteenth century; (5) a philocalist hesychasm; and finally (6) a new hesychasm or neo-hesychasm. See also the definition of hesychasm in Podskalsky 1967: 15. For an overview on the foundations of hesychasm, see Meyendorff 1974. On philocalism, see Louth 2003. On the term 'hesychasm', see Ivanka 1952; Meyendorff 1983: 451.

607   'ἀδιαλείπτως προσεύχεσθαι', 'pray without ceasing' (KJV). On this, see Siniossoglou 2011: 94.

608   Ware 2000: 75. Kallistos Ware dates the beginning of the devotion around the name of Jesus to the fifth-century Neilos of Ankyra (see Ware 1986: 177). 'There is a special blessing in the invocation of the divine name. To address Jesus Christ in prayer is to address God. The primal energy of the creator and pure love are hidden presences in the name of Jesus Christ' (Dyckhoff 2006: 101). See also Podskalsky 1967: 17f., 22ff., which contains New Testament references for the Jesus Prayer.

609   Ammann 1948: 33; Podskalsky 1966: 209f.

610   Johnson 2010: 18.

611   Gregor Palamas, for instance, builds on the Christian anthropological notion that body and soul in man form a *diarchy* (synthesis) rather than a *dichotomy* (partition) (Tatakis 1985).

The term 'hesychasm' derives from the Greek 'ἡσυχία' and refers to the calm and silence of the hesychast, apathetic and removed from the world, liberated absolutely from the material plurality of the world and immersed in concentrated contemplation of the One.[612] *Hesychia* 'is thus, positively seen, constant engagement with God' and moreover is 'fundamentally not a moral state, but rather an essential state of being'.[613]

The Jesus Prayer is also known as the Prayer of the Heart,[614] a reflection of the idea that by repeated internalisation of the Jesus Prayer, the mind and the thoughts are 'gathered', allowing the individual to attain the privileged state of emphatic awareness (νῆψις, Latin *diligentia*; Matt. 24:42; Luke 12:37; Mark 13:33, 37).[615] In this state, νόος or νοῦς (reason or *ratio*) is united with the heart,[616] by boundless love is cleansed of all passions and all limitations of the human and is guided to the intuitive and ineffable contemplation of God. God is seen and enjoyed, as it were, with an 'understanding heart', hence also the notion of noetic prayer, 'νοερὰ πρ οσευχή'.[617] This is, as Evagrios Pontikos emphasised in the fourth century, a pure form of prayer, wordless and stripped of ideas. The *nous* at prayer in the heart is naked (γυμνός).[618] Ideas are considered as mere media interfering with the immediate relation to God of the individual at prayer.[619] Human beings are thus able to become pure, praying, doxological beings, with unceasing prayer figuring as the restoration of human beings' natural ontological purpose, inasmuch as they were created for praise and exaltation. For notwithstanding its name, the Prayer of the Heart represents the unification and simplification of man's diarchic being – body and soul, heart and mind – in the pure act of prayer.[620]

---

612 Johannes Chrysostomus 1998: 189. On this, see Podskalsky 1967: 15.
613 Ammann 1948: 35f.
614 Johnson 2010: 19.
615 Louth 1981: 108; Coniaris 1998: 88ff.
616 Ware 2002: 5,15f.
617 Meyendorff 1982: 168; Coniaris 1998: 250ff.; Rossi 2002: 107.
618 Johnson 2010: 32.
619 This kind of prayer begins by speaking words, but gives way to wordlessness and pure contemplation.
620 Johnson 2010: 23.

The goal of hesychasm is *illuminatio* (φωτισμός, ἔλλαμψις, Latin *illuminatio*),[621] the mystical bridging of the chasm separating Creation and the uncreated, rational man and ineffable, supra-rational God.[622] At stake is to behold God directly in His divine light, as He appeared in transfigured form to the disciples on Mount Tabor (Matt. 17; Mark 9; Luke 9).[623] Humans prepare for illumination by physical and mental purity, by freeing themselves from suffering and passions, by striving for *apatheia* (ἀπάθεια).[624] By the mystical bond formed in the light, the hesychast (ἡσύχιος, ἥσυχος) attains illumination, the ineffable, inconceivable, immediate and trans-discursive unity with God, and by being bathed in divine energies himself becomes light[625] and becomes God (Ps. 36:10) in an all-transcending act of θέωσις (deification).[626]

Yet hesychasm is by no means a practice specific to the late Byzantine period. The archaeological record shows that related forms and practices of penance, prayer and meditation have always existed in monastic communities and traditions.[627] We encounter them in the fourth-century Egyptian desert, for example, with Evagrios Pontikos (d. 399), in the Gaza desert, in the fifth and sixth centuries, or in the monastery of Sinai, in the seventh

621 Lilienfeld 1986: 283; Siniossoglou 2011: 167.
622 This is fundamentally a Platonic desideratum (Ivanka 1964: 392), though here its fulfilled by Christian means.
623 Ammann 1948: 34; Harmless 2004: 354.
624 Warkotsch 1973: 383. That *apatheia* is a Stoic concept has long been something of a truism. I can only call to mind that Andrew Louth has situated the semantics of *apatheia* in the Platonic myth of the cave: The deceitful material senses keep the intellect from recognising and contemplating the eternal ideas by letting the mind be shackled to the material world (see Louth 1981: 7).
625 The hesychast becomes an organ of light as a complete human being, in body and soul, and not just in spirit, as Gerhard Podskalsky has mistakenly claimed (Podskalsky 1966: 211 and Podskalsky 1967: 20). It should not be forgotten that hesychast praxis and its aim, illumination, are psychosomatic in nature.
626 Coniaris 1998: 131ff.; Bartos 1999; Williams 1999: 131; Rossi 2002: 107.
627 In Kellia, in the Egyptian desert, which was for many years the residence of Evagrios Pontikos, a sixth-century hermit's cell was discovered to contain inscriptions proving that the Jesus Prayer was already firly established as an element of monastic *devotion* (Harmless 2004: 351). On the history of Hesychasm, see Lilienfeld 1986: 183; Ware 1986: 176f.; Johnson 2010: 19.

century.[628] *Hesychia* was already being used as a technical term in the seventh century, when John Climacus devoted a chapter of his *Ladder* to it.[629] However, the sources fall silent on the subject of hesychastic spirituality between the tenth and fourteenth centuries.[630]

Scholars have distinguished two historical forms of hesychastic tradition. The older and less technical form is referred to as 'Sinaitic hesychasm', which is neither centred on a particular prayer nor requires psychosomatic exercises during its unceasing repetition. Sinaitic hesychasm was content with a spiritual invocation of Christ's name (ἐπίκλησις Ἰησοῦ) in which formal variation was permissible.[631] Among the representatives of this form are John Cassian (d. c. 435), Barsanuphius and John of Gaza (sixth century) as well as John Climacus.[632] This form of hesychasm crystallised around the Sinai monastery and its influence extended as far as Constantinople. The eleventh-century *Instruction* of Vladimir Monomakh contains the exhortation unceasingly to repeat the following phrase: 'Lord, have mercy upon me!',[633] which is surely a form of the Prayer of the Heart. In the fourteenth century, the power of Sinaitic hesychasm appears to have diminished.[634]

The other strand to have emerged is known as 'Athonite hesychasm', a highly technical form that insists on the Jesus Prayer and the unchanging sequence of its words as well as prescribing clearly defined breathing exercises and a specific sitting position during meditation. This second form was introduced to Mount Athos by Gregory of Sinai (d. 1346) and gradually came to replace the older, more relaxed tradition throughout Eastern

---

628 Barsanuphius and John of Gaza: Letter 6, p. 60f. and Letter 298, p. 102f.; Hausherr 1978; Meyendorff 1982: 168; Ware 1987: 32; McGuckin 2001: 110; Stewart 2003; Harmless 2004: 350f.

629 John Climacus 1959: ch. XI, 5. On Climacus, see Chrysavgis 2004.

630 Ware 1986: 184.

631 'Do not be over-sophisticated in the words you use when praying [...]. Do not attempt to talk much when you pray, do not let your mind be distracted in searching for words. [...] Loquacity in prayer often distracts the mind and leads to phantasy, whereas brevity makes for concentration.' (John Climacus 1959: ch. XXVIII, 9f.). On this, see Gillet 1997: 53ff.

632 Russell 2004: 310; Dyckhoff 2006: 103, 503ff.

633 Popa-Lisseanu 1935: 208.

634 Ware 1987: 35ff.

Christendom.[635] Nowadays, the Athonite technique of hesychasm is the only one to be practised in Orthodox monasteries.

Hesychasm found widespread fame or indeed notoriety in the four-teenth century, when the theoretician of hesychasm, Gregory Palamas, archbishop of Thessaloniki (d. 1359),[636] and Barlaam of Calabria (d. 1348), a Byzantine scholar and later a Catholic bishop, engaged in the so-called 'hesychastic controversy'.[637] Barlaam was a representative of so-called late 'Byzantine humanism' and as such found himself at odds with Orthodox monasticism.[638] Following the councils in Byzantium that subsequently became known as the 'hesychastic synods', hesychasm – as a practice, a systematic underpinning and an iconographic programme – acquired the status of dogma in the Eastern Church.[639]

Initially, the students of Gregory of Sinai spread hesychasm only in the South Slavic lands: Bulgaria became the hub from which hesychasm

635 Ware 1987: 53f.; Gillet 1997: 53ff.; McGuckin 2001: 118ff.; Tatakis 2003: 217; Dyckhoff 2006: 500f.; Krausmüller 2006: 108ff.; Blum 2009: 325ff.; Payne 2011: 82.

636 Both catholic and protestant scholars (Gerhard Podskalsky, Dorothea Wendenbourg) of hesychasm consider Palamas to be an innovator among Orthodox theologians, whereas most Orthodox theologians hold him in esteem for synthesising the Fathers who worked on the question of the energies, notably the Cappadocians, Pseudo-Dionysius the Areopagite, Maximus the Confessor, John of Damascus and Symeon the New Theologian (Lilienfeld 1986: 285; Barber 2007: 23ff.).

637 Blum 2009: 355ff.

638 Beck 1963; Fryde 2000; Kapriev 2011; Payne 2011: 85; Siniossoglou 2011: 93, 100ff.

639 Lossky 1973: 125. This triumph of hesychasm in fourteenth-century Byzantium is also reflected in iconography of the late Palaeologue period. From about 1340 onwards, there is a remarkable increase in the number of so-called metamor-phosis icons, that is, depictions of the scene on Mount Tabor. The iconographic programme has Christ bathed in light at the mountain's summit, thus displaying the clear intention of having him symbolise the pinnacle of ascetic and mystical endeavours (Andreopoulos 2005: 225). Furthermore, an iconographic style devel-oped under hesychastic influence 'that combines an agitated expressionism with an optical illusionism. The forms of the baroque style were not only tortured and twisted out of recognition in this new phase, but also dissolved, liquefied into an almost impressionist luminarism [...]' (Demus 1975: 154).

spread across the Balkans, the Danubian Principalities, the kingdom of Hungary and, finally, to Rus'.[640] Besides Gregory Palamas in the Greek lands,[641] important figures of the hesychast 'mission' in fourteenth and fifteenth-century south-eastern Europe include Theodosius of Tarnovo (d. 1363) and Euthymius of Tarnovo (d. c. 1403) in Bulgaria and Nicodemus of Tismana (d. c. 1406) in Wallachia. The spread of hesychasm was facilitated by a growth in literary production and, beginning in the fifteenth century, the use of the printing press.[642] Nicodemus of Tismana organised the Church in Wallachia along hesychastic lines and enabled Anthim, himself a hesychast and *dikaiophylax*, some kind of legal adviser, to the hesychastic Patriarch Philotheos Kokkinos (1353–1354 and 1364–1376) of Constantinople, to become the country's metropolitan. The close relationship between the Wallachian and Moldavian Churches with their Athonite, Bulgarian and Serbian counterparts seems certain to have encouraged the early introduction of hesychastic spirituality to the ecclesiastical life of the Danubian Principalities.[643]

The spread of hesychasm in south-eastern Europe was accompanied by the formation of an Orthodox identity under the leadership of the Ecumenical Patriarchate, a tendency known to scholars as 'political hesychasm'.[644] Following the hesychastic synods of Constantinople (the last of which met in 1351) and the definitive victory of the hesychastic party, something of a hesychastic takeover of ecclesiastical positions appears to have occurred: abbeys as well as the metropolitan sees – and that of the Patriarch himself – were filled with adherents of the hesychast party.[645] Since hesychasts found themselves pitted against the Byzantine humanists – who,

---

640   Meyendorff 1974: VIII, S. 62.
641   South Slavic hesychasm was a phenomenon in its own right, unrelated to the activities of Gregory Palamas, who was not even translated into Church Slavonic till the sixteenth century (Bauve Hébert 1992: 425), which is why we speak of a Slavic hesychasm, but not a Slavic Palamism (Bauve Hébert 1992: 429).
642   Lilienfeld 1986: 283; Angelov 1989: 44; Joantă 1992: 44ff.; Papadakis 1994: 272f.; Russell 2004: 309f.; Haberland 2007; Niţulescu 2009; Johnson 2010: 34; Payne 2011: 101.
643   Meyendorff 1974: VIII, S. 62; Joantă 1992: 30, 40ff.
644   Johnson 2010: 17.
645   Tinnefeld 1986: 100f.; Papadakis 1994: 306.

owing to their predilection for Latin or classical mythology, theology and philosophy were unjustly dismissed as *latinophrones* or *latinophiloi*[646] – the hesychastic attitude developed into one of uncompromising Orthodoxy. In order to maintain its distance from the Latins, late Byzantium presented itself under a guise bereft of all Romanism.[647] The Byzantine Empire became a political phantom and its emperors, who were no longer taken seriously by anybody, depended on the authority and influence of the Church in the Orthodox states to bolster their dwindling power.[648]

The spread of Orthodoxy transcended ethnic and regional boundaries. Among its adherents were powerful Bulgarian, Serbian, Wallachian, Ukrainian and Russian rulers, along with their peoples. Following the hesychastic synods, hesychasm came to be understood as synonymous with Orthodoxy, as a purely Orthodox lifestyle and as capable of sustaining an ethos distinct from that of the 'dangerous' Latins. Hesychasm formed the very soul of Orthodoxy, entailing a spiritual reform of the Orthodox Church in Byzantium itself.[649] A number of clergymen now emerged, who by virtue of their spiritual and ascetic pre-eminence assumed the status of 'pillars of

---

646   Guran 2007: 99f. Byzantine distrust of Latin 'barbarism' dated back to the early Crusades, but was irrevocably strengthened after the sack of Constantinople in 1204 (Makrides 2005: 183ff.).

647   Ivanka 1954: 21ff.; Koder 2003: 313ff.; Grigore 2010: 174.

648   See the aforementioned letter of Patriarch Antonios IV to Grand Prince Vasily I of Moscow (Barker 1957: 194; Nicol 1988: 72). In the early and middle Byzantine periods, the Church depended on the Emperors as protectors and hegemons (Carile 2008: 87; Mureşan/Năsturel 2011: 260, 262). Yet the figure of the emperor kept losing political and religious stature. While Constantine was still able to consider himself a bishop, the last Byzantine emperors were placed below the bishops in the hierarchy of the Church. The emperors became symbolic pawns in the politics of the Patriarchs. Debates of a kind previously restricted to Western Christianity, over such matters as the intercessory powers of the Church, for example, in anointing the ruler, underscoring the dependence of temporal on spiritual power, now arose in Byzantium, too (Angelov 2007: 373f., 415; Matschke 2002: 161f.; Kosuch 2011: 292). In the years of the last Palaeologues, the Patriarchs appropriated many of the symbols originally associated with the emperors (Pitsakis 2007: 236f.).

649   Papadakis 1994: 308.

Orthodoxy'.[650] It thus comes as no surprise that, under the leadership of the Patriarchs, the hesychastically minded clergy should have felt committed to the unity of all Orthodox peoples. Before the Byzantine emperors and other Orthodox rulers, the hesychastic clergy advocated peace as well as the rights and security of the faithful.[651] In the last years of the Byzantine Empire and under Ottoman rule, hesychastic dignitaries tried to compensate for the loss of the political unity and the infrastructure of Orthodoxy that the Byzantine Empire had provided for by developing a *hesychasme eschatologique*.[652] This attempt to preserve hesychasm was all the more vital since the last emperors were willing to make dogmatic compromises with the Latins in order to obtain military assistance from the West.[653]

There was thus an attempt, with the active political involvement of the Ecumenical Patriarchs, to make up for the decline and ultimate disappearance of the political infrastructure of Orthodoxy[654] – that is, the Byzantine Empire – by creating a trans-regional Orthodox 'commonwealth'.[655] This took the concrete form of an aggressive policy of centralisation on the part of the Patriarch. But why was this involvement 'political'? There are three reasons for this. First, that the religious convictions of a particular Church party were elevated to the rank of a general and obligatory dogma; second, that key positions were distributed accordingly; and third, because centralising tendencies were supposed to foster the unity of all the Orthodox faithful within Byzantine Europe. Such ambitions were no longer pursued through the structures of the state, but rather through Church and canonical jurisdiction. Accordingly, the autocephaly of the Serbian and Bulgarian Patriarchates was annulled, putting them under the jurisdiction of Constantinople. New metropolises were established in Wallachia and Moldavia. Since these principalities were pursuing policies to distance themselves from Byzantium, already in its death

---

650   Guran 2007: 409f., 415.

651   Tatakis 2003: 221; Guran 2002.

652   For the term, see Guran 2001: 101. See also McGuckin 2001: 130; Payne 2011: 81.

653   Guran 2001b.

654   Meyendorff 1974: VIII, S. 61; Payne 2011: 102.

655   My use of this term follows the coinage 'Byzantine commonwealth' (Obolensky 1971). See to 'Athonite commonwealth', Speake 2018.

throes,[656] such measures were intended to compensate for the resulting difficulties.[657] While the first metropolitans of Wallachia were Greeks emerging from the networks of Athonite and Constantinople hesychasm, the Moldavian voivode, Alexander the Good (1400–1432), fought hard with the Ecumenical Patriarchate to have ethnic Wallachian metropolitans installed in the country.[658]

All this constitutes the first aspect of 'political hesychasm', its practical and historical dimension. The scholars who have studied it are mostly historians who tend not even to make the effort to situate these practices within the broader theological and systematic framework of hesychasm. Yet the fact that an ascetic, mystical and individualistic movement committed to the contemplative solitude of the monastic cell should have involved itself in social and political affairs seems to require an explanation. How to account for this apparent contradiction between mystical unworldliness and political activity? The following analysis considers political hesychasm under its second aspect, the transformation of personal, mystical illumination into a qualification of political and public concern.

Theological and systematic support for the notions of the deification of man, bridging the gap between the finite and the infinite, was provided by a dialectical trick that had already been performed, under the influence of Plato,[659] by the fourth-century Cappadocians: the separation of God's nature (οὐσία) and His energies (ἐνέργειαι).[660] By His nature, God

656   Elian 1967.
657   Arnakis 1963: 129; Runciman 1971: 37f.; Guran 2001: 121.
658   Joantă 1992: 28ff; Grigore 2017: 48.
659   Plato taught that, in order to exist, things must be both *in se* as well as *in relatione* to something (Jenkins 2006: 150f.). In the *Timaeus* Plato argues that the purpose of knowledge cannot be to negate the world. The task of mind or the soul is to see through the world as the manifestation of the eternal forms or ideas, thus attaining direct contemplation of the eternal forms that order the world and usher the cosmos into existence (Louth 1981: 15).
660   Wendenbourg 1980: 11ff.; Siniossoglou 2011: 98. As early as the polemic against Eunomios, Basil the Great (d. 379) and his brother, Gregory of Nyssa (d. c. 394), developed the theory of God's names, which they held to be either negative names or positive descriptions. The negative names they held to be apophatic in nature and to denominate all that God *was not*, since He transcended everything and ultimately eluded description. We may for instance venture a positive description of

is and remains concealed, absolutely transcendent and unattainable. Yet his nature radiates outwards into the world, where it is an active and effective presence, just as a flame radiates light and warmth.[661] Theologians referred to this outward effect either as uncreated and immaterial 'dynamism' (δυνάμεις) or as 'energies'.[662] These Energies *belong* to God's nature without *being* His nature. Though they are distinct (διακρίσεις) from the nature of God, they do not constitute a division of God, since energies represent neither overcoming nor compulsion, but occur by the will of God. God's energies and nature are intimately related, since to express Himself is in God's nature.[663] God's energies and nature form a unity, their separation existing only at the conceptual and terminological level for the sake of better understanding.[664] The energies are God Himself and not some objectified intermediary instrument between God's nature and the world. God makes His presence felt and in His immeasurable love allows

---

God as 'good', there being no room for evil in Him. Yet in fact God was 'not good', for we neither know nor are able to say how or what He is. According to Gregory of Nyssa, the purpose of positive denominations was to describe God's actions, manifestations and works in the visible world. Positive descriptions thus refer to the energies of God, a term first used to describe God's activities within the world by Gregory of Nyssa (Sheldon-Williams 1967: 434f.; Lossky 1973: 71). A masterly synthesis and systematisation of energies theology was provided by Gregory Palamas (Meyendorff 1982: 191ff.; Müller-Schauenburg 2011: 240ff.). On the historic tradition of the discursive separation between God's nature and energies, see the overview in Lossky 1973: 101.

661   The fourth-century dialectics of Ephrem the Syrian already hint at such a notion (Brock 1992: 26f.).

662   Orthodox theology has maintained this separation between 'dynamics' and 'energies' since the fourth century, with the former term tending to describe God's actions in the world and the latter His effects (Demetracopoulos 2011: 268). Basil of Caesarea and Pseudo-Dionysius the Areopagite preferred to speak of 'dynamics' without taking an explicit stance against 'energies'. Such a stark distinction would not be in the spirit of Orthodox theology, which tends to take an integrative attitude towards its terminology, that of the Trinity excepted. Basil's brother, Gregory of Nyssa, used both terms, 'dynamics' and 'energies', in the argument with Eunomius (Sheldon-Williams 1967: 447).

663   Lossky 1973: 127.

664   Demetracoupoulos 2011: 265f., 369.

human beings to partake of Himself. The energies constitute the medium of human participation in the essentiality of God (μετουσία Θεοῦ).[665] The hesychastic *unio mystica* emphasises participation in God as the opposite of identification with God, the latter notion being very close to heresy. For man is at one with God in the light that unites them, in the energies, but by no account by his nature.[666]

That the energies should be perceptible to human beings and able to be seen with the physical (!) eye as the light of God[667] is due, according to Gregory Palamas, to their quality to be the *modus* of God's action *in*, and interaction *with*, the Creation.[668] This immaterial light (φῶς ἄυλον) represents the 'gleam of the absolute essentiality of God in the world'.[669] Consequently, the episode at Mount Tabor is accorded such centrality in the hesychastic tradition, as its late theoretician, Gregory of Sinai, explains repeatedly and in detail in his treatise on the transfiguration.[670] To the practising hesychast, the transfiguration confirms the possibility of his efforts meeting with visible 'success': to behold the radiant countenance of God and to allow the divine to wash over him.[671] 'He who beholds the divine light is permeated by it through and through, so that his body shines with the glory that he contemplates.'[672]

Among the preferred metaphors in which this hesychastic contemplation of light is expressed is the mirror (κάτοπτρον), as exemplified by a hesychast tract from the fifteenth century:

665   Balas 1966.
666   Ware 1996: 125f.
667   Xanthopoulos 1948: 144. Some modern scholars of hesychasm, such as Gerhard Podskalsky, claim that the hesychast masters saw the light only in spirit, in their mind's eye, as it were.
668   See Ware 1996: 117ff.; Schmidt 2008: 129; Johnson 2010: 35; Demetracopoulos 2011: 272ff.
669   Ammann 1948: 22, 31.
670   Gregory of Sinai 1986; Lilienfeld 1986: 283; McGuckin 2001: 125, 128; Ware 2002: 19f.; Andreopoulos 2005: 16.
671   As understood by Gregory of Nyssa (4th c.), Pseudo-Dionysius (6th c.) or Maximus the Confessor (7th c.) (Sheldon-Williams 1967: 453; Ware 1996: 127; Tatakis 2003: 218; Johnson 2010: 36).
672   Ware 1996: 127.

For, just as silver, when exposed to the sun's rays, itself emits rays, not merely by virtue of its own nature, but also on account of the light of the sun, so too does the soul, once cleansed and shining brighter than any silver, reflect a ray of the glory of the spirit.[673]

Yet the metaphor is far older and can already be found in Chrysostom in the fourth century or Agapetus in the sixth. It would appear first to have been used in *De beatitudinibus* (PG 44: 1271–1272 BC) by Gregory of Nyssa and can also be found in Ephrem the Syrian, in his emphasis on the importance of spiritual purification.[674] Agapetus was the first to use the metaphor of the mirror in connection with rule.[675]

To hesychasts, knowledge (γνῶσις) is possible only through illumination by the light of God's operative grace. Knowledge cannot be attained by human efforts; it is a pure gift of God.[676] At the most, humans can prepare for the eventuality of God electing them for illumination. God is understood in His increate light,[677] yet this is a *post-discursive*, *post-textual* and *post-experimental* knowledge of truth, an observant contemplation and the vigilant perception of truth as effect, not essence.[678] This kind of knowledge no longer bears any resemblance to the intellectual, rational, syllogistic and epistemic illumination of Plato, Origen, Evagrios Pontikos,[679] the Neoplatonists,[680] or the mediaeval authors of the

673 Xanthopoulos 1948: 54. Both authors cite the seventh homily of John Chrysostom on the Second Epistle to the Corinthians (PG 61: 448f.) (see 54 n. 1). On the lives of the brothers, Kallistos and Ignatios Xanthopoulos, see Ammann 1948: 14ff.; Dyckhoff 2006: 502f.; Blum 2009: 461ff.

674 Lossky 1973: 70, 72; Brock 1992: 74f.

675 Agapetus 1981: ch. IX, p. 61.

676 A slight influence of Augustine on Gregory Palamas, the theoretician of hesychasm, can be detected here (Payne 2011: 90).

677 Both Basil the Great and Gregory of Nyssa speak of 'created' (!) light (Sheldon-Williams 1967: 435, 448).

678 Ware 1987: 114.

679 See Otto 1974; Louth 1981: 113; Russell 2004: 239.

680 The Platonism under discussion here is the so-called 'intellectual Platonism', according to which human beings attempt to reach knowledge of the One by διανοία, by discursive and deductive thought embracing the many objects of the world, which leads to abstractions and archetypes. These are abstractions and archetypes of the eternal ideas. Yet abstraction would be impossible but for the *a priori* presence of the idea in reason (νοῦς, νοός). These ideas are rooted in human beings

West.[681] Hesychasm is concerned with mystical illumination, with the dei-fying powers of *episteme*[682] – that is why Gregory of Nyssa, in the fourth century, connected this kind of knowledge with light and referred to its highest form as φωτισμός.[683]

Although hesychasm is a largely monastic and ascetic practice, and as such strongly associated with isolation, solitude and eremitism, in its fun-damental tenets it is intended to be accessible to all Christians.[684] Gregory of Sinai sent his followers forth into the world to instruct laypeople in hesychastic principles,[685] for unceasing inward repetition of the Jesus Prayer is possible at any time and in any place.[686] In the Eastern Church, hesychasm was and indeed remains an element of lay devotion. It would be a distortion of hesychasm to see it only as an unworldly form of spirituality, indifferent to the social and political challenges of everyday human existence.[687] To counter this misunderstanding was the aim of Nikolaos Kabasilas, writing in the fourteenth century – and, under his influence, Neagoe Basarab in the sixteenth century.[688]

---

from birth (see 'traducianism'). Ideas 'dwell' in humans. The discursive process of *dianoia* is illuminated by the *nous* (by reason), allowing our mind to attain know-ledge of the eternal ideas. We would know nothing of 'good' things if the idea of the 'good' had not always existed within us, had not been planted in us as λόγος σπερματικός. This line of thought is advanced by Plotinus, Proclus and later by Michael Psellos, Nicephorus Gregoras and the brothers Kydones. Porphyry, on the other hand, propounded a moderately apophatic view of *nous*, which held that reason would eventually reach a boundary in its knowledge of God and depend on illumination further to explore God's secrets (Joannou 1956: 105f., 116f.; Lloyd 1967: 302ff., 312ff.; Markus 1967: 366; Armstrong 1983: 32f.; Bell 2009: 10 n. 40, 61; Siniossoglou 2011: 96).

681　An example here being that of Giovanni Pico della Mirandola (d. 1494), who, influenced by Plato and the Neoplatonists, spoke of an *illuminatio intellecti* (Mirandola 1990: 15).

682　Lossky 1974: 45ff.; Tatakis 2003: 220f.; Frygos 2005: 94ff.; Siniossoglou 2011: 163ff.

683　Lossky 1973: 68f.; Schmidt 2008: 68f.

684　Coniaris 1998: 217f.; Johnson 2010: 15f.; Payne 2011: 99f.

685　Ware 2000: 94ff.

686　Xanthopoulos 1948: 93ff.

687　Ware 2000: 90ff.

688　Joantă 1992: 90.

A closer look at hesychastic theology reveals that illumination constitutes not a passive 'being illuminated', as a stone is illuminated by the sun, but rather an activating, moving act of God. What occurs is not depersonalisation and dissolution in the divine, but rather the consummation and channelling of all consciousness towards the supra-conscious, pure experience of God's immediate presence.[689] This is very much the opposite, as we shall see, of Lutheran passivity. Thus deified, man can become, in the hesychast view, 'God-like'. He is able to act within the world and by his own will to participate in God, on the one hand, and the life of the world, on the other.[690] *Theosis* is a dynamising act.[691] The virtues represent the fruits of illumination and deification, not vice versa. By contrast, Erasmus of Rotterdam seems to argue – this will be expanded on later in the chapter on Erasmus – that the virtues define the Christian ruler and that his 'God-likeness' is the fruit of his virtuous actions. In hesychasm, on the other hand, 'deification is more than the achievement of moral excellence. It is a *supernatural* gift that transforms both mind and body, making divinity visible.'[692] The Gospel, moreover, confirms the possibility of each believer's illumination: 'That was the true Light, which lighteth every man that cometh into the world' (John 1:9). Not only are all Christians able to ascend to good, they are in fact expected to make this ascent – as the *Ladder* of John Climacus, so popular in lay devotion, suggests.[693]

The *Teachings to Theodosius* are fully part of the tradition of lay hesychasm. They apply such general and practical principles as the cleanliness of body and soul, and unceasing prayer, to the life of Christians *in* the world. Far from being only a mirror for princes, the *Teachings* are also a product of the old Byzantine tradition of the religious education of

689   Johnson 2010: 15.

690   Agapetus 1981: ch. III, p. 59f.

691   Papadakis/Meyendorff 1994: 299. Even Plato described illumination as participation in an idea and ultimately as a form of identifying with this idea, though he spoke of an *illuminatio intellecti*. This means, in turn, that the idea becomes and attitude, a praxis and an ethos on the part of the illuminated. Socrates spoke of knowledge as a virtue (Louth 1981: 2).

692   Russell 2004: 306. My emphasis.

693   Gerstel/Talbot 2006: 91 and passim.

laypeople. This rich vein of literature was concerned less with the spiritual and theoretical problems of monasticism than with everyday life, with the religious needs and devotions of ordinary, secular people.[694]

As an ascetic and mystical practice, hesychasm strongly emphasises the close relationship between master and student, between spiritual father and spiritual son.[695] Aside from the dogmatic foundations of *praxis*, there are very few hesychast tracts, for hesychasm insists on the importance, in spiritual matters, of verbal instruction, tuition, tutelage and observation. This is equally true of political hesychasm, and the *Teachings*, with their many instructions for prayer, ascetic exercises and theoretical and technical directions, are part of this tradition. To Basarab, illumination, which is accessible to any Christian of whatever estate, is the foundation on which the Christian prince builds his rule.

Accordingly – illumination being a path on which a companion is needed – one of the guises Basarab adopts in his treatise is that of a hesychastic teacher. The fresco from the Dionysiou monastery church, in which Basarab is depicted alongside his spiritual master, Niphon II (Figure 4), has already been mentioned. It confirms the statements made by Gabriel Protos in his *Life of St Niphon*, according to which that holy man was like a father to Basarab,[696] and this is a sense that Basarab tries to pass on to Theodosius. The institution of the *abba* (*magistros, starets*) is of crucial importance in the Christian east, as the brothers Xanthopoulos are keen to remind the readers of their hesychast tract:

> Diligently endeavour, then, to find a leader and teacher who is free from error (his freedom of error consists in his ability to support his utterances with Holy Writ), a bearer of the spirit whose way of life matches his words, who is august of knowledge, humble of mind [etc.].[697]

The author of the *Teachings* takes these requirements seriously: he quotes extensively from the Bible and tries to show what fruits illumination can bear in human beings. Moreover, he tries to impart to his son Theodosius

---

694   Plămădeală 1968: 258; Krausmüller 2007.
695   Lilienfeld 1986: 283; Barbu 1998: 38.
696   Gavriil Protul: 92/93, 96/97, 124/125, 140/141; Păun 2001: 196f.
697   Xanthopoulos 1948: 62.

something of his own illumined knowledge for the benefit of his future life and reign. That Basarab quotes so extensively from the Bible suggests that he knew the treatise of the brothers Xanthopoulos well and took their counsels to heart.

Using arguments drawn from hesychastic theology, the author of the *Teachings* underpins his own theory of the exemplary nature and centring function of the Christian ruler. Himself an exponent of lay hesychasm, Basarab strongly emphasises the activating function of illumination:

> And we ought fervently to ask our merciful God to do us the honour of *being perfect* in all things and to grant us all that is good wholly and undividedly: that righteous judgement and justice might be upheld; that we might love undistracted reason and purity and have love [in our lives]; that we might face all [people] with justice and gentleness and mercy.[698]

Through prayer and chastity, the Christian ruler hopes to partake in the perfection of God. Prayer brings illumination: 'And be mindful not to let even one hour pass without prayers, for they bring light into the soul.'[699] The ruler's prayers, as an image of relying on God alone, play a key part in the *Teachings*.[700] For every occasion, be it dispatching envoys, before battles or opening sessions of the Great Council, the author gives a suitable prayer.[701] Basarab may have been familiar with the mirror for princes of Thomas Magistros, who calls upon his readers to remember that '[you

---

698 'Iar noi să rugăm pre Dumnezeul cel milostiv să ne învrednicească să fim în toate lucrurile desăvârşiţi şi în toate bunătăţile întregi şi nici într-unile să nu fim lipsiţi. Să păzim judecata şi să facem dreptate. Mintea cea întreagă şi curăţia să iubim, blânzi şi îngăduitori şi răbdători să fim tuturor în toată vremea' (Neagoe Basarab 1984: 16). My emphasis.

699 'Şi te păzeşte să nu treacă vreun ceas făr' de rugă că acéstea aduc lumina în suflet' (Neagoe Basarab 1984: 118). See also Neagoe Basarab 1984: 26.

700 Neagoe Basarab 1984: 95. This theme can also be found in reformed political theology (Görz 1990: 133), albeit in the passive form of the unfree human will in the hand of God, whereas it is tha active and willing attitude that is key for the Wallachian prince.

701 Agapetos 1981: ch. LVIII, p. 75f.: 'A castle that is secured by indestructible walls makes a mockery of all the enemies besieging it. Your God-fearing imperial rule is buttressed by alms to the poor and fortified with towers of prayer.'

can] by your prayers effect that the fate of all human beings might in every respect be wonderful; for only prayer is a true help, without it you are unable to rule.'[702]

Yet the models of Christian rulership in its quest for illumination are the masters of asceticism and mystical performance:

> And if you could but open the doors of your mind to see their [i.e. the great ascetic masters'] sentiments and inner beauty, you would fall to the ground, because you could not withstand the breathtaking beauty of their souls and the light and the splendour of their raiment, for their shine is brighter even than that of lightning.[703]

It requires great purity on the part of the ordinary Christian even to be able to see the light-filled ascetic master and to recognise his illumination. Basarab is at pains to make it clear to Theodosius that only if his own mind is illumined can he hope to understand the exemplary nature and the benefits of the ascetic life and to recognise the achievements of the great ascetic masters, who dwell in light and are themselves translucent and light-filled beings. It is not by chance that the above quotation ends with a paraphrase of the Transfiguration of Christ on Mount Tabor, with the accent on the disciples who sink to the ground, unable to bear the sight of Christ's dazzling, luminescent figure (Matt. 17:1–6; Mark 9:1–6) – a paraphrase that can only be understood in its full meaning against its hesychastic background.[704]

By means of ascetic practices – prayer, abstinence, confinement, fasting, upright *vigilantia*, forgoing sleep[705], and tears of penance and contrition[706] – both ruler and monk can achieve first

---

702 Thomas Magistros 1981: 99.

703 'Şi numai de ţe-ai putea dăşchide uşa minţii să vezi cugetele şi sufletele lor şi împodobirile lor céle dinlăuntru, tu ai cădea jos pre pământu, că n-ai putea răbda să vezi frumuséţea sufletelor lor şi lumina şi strălucirea hainelor, care strălucescu mai luminos decît fulgerul' (Neagoe Basarab 1984: 86).

704 Neagoe Basarab 1984: 93.

705 John Chrysostom emphasised that too much sleep is bad for the prince as it was for the monk, making both sluggish and numb (Johannes Chrysostomus 1988: ch. III, p. 72).

706 This is a frequent theme in the ascetic and mystical literature of the Eastern Church. In political parenetics, however, I have encountered the term only in Vladimir Monomakh (Popa-Lisseanu 1935: 207).

apatheia[707] and then mystic illumination: 'Everybody who is free of temptation and distraction will see God.'[708] Basarab describes the Prayer of the
Heart in the following terms: 'And you shall bring unto your heavenly Lord
Jesus Christ an undistracted mind, by day and by night and at all times.
That the gentle warmth of the Godhead may come upon your mind and
your heart overflow with the Holy Spirit.'[709] The *apatheia* of prayer and
rule marks an important overlap between hesychast mysticism on the one
hand and political mysticism on the other,[710] which may well be part of the
justification for the ruler's political activities. For as both a lay hesychast
and a political subject, the ruler is, as it were, doubly in need of attaining
apatheia. For purposes of noetic prayer, Theodosius is advised to retire to his
chamber, where he will be safe from temptation.[711] The actual word used in
the context by Basarab is *chilie*, referring to a monk's cell. Like many other
recommendations, this too is taken from the hesychastic treatise of the
brothers Xanthopoulos.[712] Overall, the manner in which the secular ruler
is tied to the monastic ideal is representative of a tendency in the Eastern

707 Already in John Chrysostom, Dvornik II, 1966: 695, with reference.
708 'Cel ce n-are îndârjire, acela vede pe Dumnezeu' (Neagoe Basarab 1984: 118). See
     also Neagoe Basarab 1984: 70, 119; Xanthopoulos 1948: 97.
709 '[Ş]i să aveţi minte întreagă către stăpânul cel de sus, Domnul nostru Iisus Hristos,
     ziua şi noaptea şi în toată vrémea. Ca să pogoare şi să vie căldura dumnezeirii lui în
     minţile voastre [...] şi să să umple inimile voastre de Duhul Sfânt' (Neagoe Basarab
     1984: 199). Basarab here quotes the *Ladder* of John Climacus, ch. VII, 9. The em-
     phasis on the monastic ideal as a modelö for the ruler is far from being proof that
     the *Teachings* might after all have been written by a monk rather than by Basarab.
     Given the socio-political hesychasm that required ordinary Christians, too, to
     put the fruits of their individual acts of devotion and asceticism in the service of
     the community and to contribute to it as improved humans, it stands to reason
     that the ruler above all should aspire to that ideal. Socio-political hesychasm was
     a common lifestyle among laypeople from the fourteenth century onwards, at any
     rate among political elites (Johnson 2010: 16).
710 For instance Thomas Magistros: 'Before you rule as emperor over other men,
     you must rule over yourself and be prepared to bridle your passions' (Thomas
     Magistros 1981: 101).
711 Plămădeală 1968: 257.
712 Xanthopoulos 1948: 86.

Church going back at least as far as John Chrysostom and his comparison of kings and monks.[713]

Perfection by illumination is indispensable to a prince, a ruler over men, for such qualities of the godly exercise of rule as justice, charity or mercy and its corollaries. We have seen that to Basarab, illumination was neither the result nor the manifestation of moral performance,[714] but rather a pure gift of God and the source of all princely virtues. The illumined ruler is able to rule only on account of his insight into the ways of God with the world that are hidden to ordinary people. Accordingly, the first part of the *Teachings* is – among other things – a hesychastic treatise on the steps to be taken towards an immediate relation with God, whereas the second part gives practical advice on the effects in social and political life of the fruits of illumination.[715] Governing requires both common sense and a vision of the right conduct, for which God is to be asked in prayer: 'You shall always gladly pray, and your heart will be illumined, that you might behold God.'[716]

The Christian ruler is one with whom dwells God Himself. God rules in partnership with the *Princeps Christianus* – a co-regency distinct from the idea of the king as God's deputy:

713   Johannes Chrysostomus 1988. I consider the interpretation that holds this work of John Chrysostom to argue for the fundamental superiority of the monastic and ascetic lifestyle over that of the ruler to be fundamentally misguided. It is simply not the case that Chrysostom took pains to prove that the monk was 'head and shoulders above' the prince (Groß-Albenhausen 1999: 201). What Chrysostom is actually concerned with is to show how the Christian ruler stands to benefit from the adoption of ascetic and monastic practices in the exercise of his rule.

714   Luther, Erasmus and others likewise stress how important morality is in a Christian ruler (Görz 1990: 119). Whereas for Luther, moral action is a fruit of faith rather than an act of will, and while Erasmus has morality beget the virtues of rule, Basarab makes the virtues dependent on illumination. To him, it is by morality that human beings can prepare themselves for the gift of illumination, though moral actions by no means guarantee illumination.

715   Johnson 2010: 20.

716   'Fie-ți drag a te ruga de-a pururea, și ți să va lumina inima și va vedea pre Dumnezeu' (Neagoe Basarab 1984: 116). See also Neagoe Basarab 1984: 220. On this see Joantă 1992: 94.

For God is He who stands by them [i.e. the rulers] with counsel in all good things, and God Himself creates rule, He installs kings. Therefore all take heed and bow your heads, for God stands by His servants and helps them, and who could match His glory and His power? Hearken even unto the edge of the world that God is with us kings and princes, His mighty servants.[717]

Godly and illumined rulers are powerful; they share in God's power. They do not stand alone, for God is their aid, their support and their strength. Such joint rule comes to be through illumination, which is a delicate business, being not only a pure gift of God devoid of any logic of merit,[718] but also threatened by manifold dangers. The Devil never sleeps and will try to tear the illumined away from 'God's luminous countenance'.[719] According to Neagoe Basarab, the three greatest dangers to one in search of illumination are fornication, injustice and ignorance:[720]

If then, my beloved son, you take care to keep your body undefiled and in purity, wisdom and other good virtues, until such time as you are of age, as it is meet and right to do, then you will dwell in the face of God and will in body as in soul become a temple to the Holy Spirit [...]. And if one loves purity with all one's heart [...], one truly will *see the face of God.* [...] And if you defile God's work [i.e. the body] with many a hateful and repulsive deed, then, on account of your ignorance and folly, God will take rule away from you and give it to another, one who walks in His will and His commandments.[721]

717 'Că Dumnezeu iaste care dă sfat spre toate lucrurile céle bune şi acela face împărăţiile, şi el pune împăraţi. Pentru acéia pricépeţi toţi şi vă plecaţi, că Dumnezeu stă şi ajută robilor săi şi nimeni nu să va putea potrivi slavei lui Dumnezeu. Auziţi până la mariginile pământului, că Dumnezeu iaste cu noi, cu împăraţii şi cu domnii, care suntem robii lui cei putérnici' (Neagoe Basarab 1984: 78). See Isa. 8:9–10.
718 Neagoe Basarab 1984: 84.
719 Neagoe Basarab 1984: 112.
720 Neagoe Basarab 1984: 18f., 112.
721 'Drept acéia iubitul meu fiiu, de te vei nevoi să-ţi păzeşti trupul aşa, până vei ajunge de vârstă, cum se cade, cu curăţie, cu înţelepciune şi cu altă bunătăţire, te vei afla înaintea lui Dumnezeu, tu te vei face de vei fi şi cu trupul şi cu sufletul bisérică Duhului Sfânt [...], şi [de] veţi iubi cu toată inima [...] curăţiia, cu adevărat faţa lui Dumnezeu veţi vedea. [...] [Ş]i vei batjocori lucrurile lui Dumnzeu cu niscai lucrure spurcate şi scârnave, ce vei face, pentru nechibzuiala şi neînţelepciunea ta, să ştii că va lua Dumnezeu domniia de la tine şi o va da altuia, care va face voia şi poruncile lui Dumnezeu.' (Neagoe Basarab 1984: 19). Emphasis added.

Only in a state of purity can the Christian ruler expect to see the light of God, for the faces by which God shows Himself to the world are His luminescent energies.[722] Any unchaste doings might cloud the Christian ruler's translucent diarchic unity of body and soul. He thus runs the risk of never becoming an organ of God's increate light. Basarab's notion of successful rule, as the ability to recognise God's will and intentions with His people, is remarkable indeed. This ability can only be attained by *illuminatio*.

For the most important aspect of 'political hesychasm' is that it conceives of individual mystic experience as an act of Church and community, and as such of concern to all.[723] Christian rule belongs to better human beings, better Christians, who are charged with the great responsibility of governing doxological God-like creatures – human beings, in a word. With his subjects, the ruler shared the illumination experienced in his 'cell'; the good of which he partakes informs his governance.[724] This is the aspect of hesychasm that addresses the public sphere: illumination is understood as being bathed in the light of God, allowing the person thus illumined to become not only a light in his own right, but a source of light, a sun[725] for others. The outlines of this idea can already be found in the Hellenistic writers, for instance in the fourth-century writings of Ekphantos.[726] Such components of the soul as reason, will and feeling are rendered dynamic and active by the light of God, and this in turn is reflected in action. Eusebius records a similar attitude on the part of Constantine the Great:

> Guarding the divine faith, I participate in the light of truth. Led by the light of truth, I recognize the divine faith. [...] I confess that I hold this cult to be the teacher of the knowledge of the most holy God. Having the power of this God as ally, beginning

722   Podskalsky 1966: 209.
723   Louth 1981: 199ff.
724   Neagoe Basarab 1984: 165f.
725   Of Basarab, Gabriel Protos claims that in the manner of a sun, he shone his light upon the good as on the bad (Gabriel Protos: 160). On the sun as a metaphor for rule, see Dölger 1940.
726   Dvornik, I, 1966: 430.

from the shores of Ocean I have raised up the whole world step by step with sure hopes of salvation.[727]

Previously, I referred to the central and centring presence of the Christian ruler in the midst of the doxological community. From this central position, the illumined prince is able to let his own light shine upon others. The ruler's illumination bears many beneficial fruits, among them wisdom, justice, mercy, clemency, philanthropy or compassion.[728] As the energies of God work within the ruler, so the prince becomes their organ and through him allows them to shine forth into the world, for he is a συνεργός τοῦ Θεοῦ.[729] The ruler is not a mediator between God and Christians, but rather himself an effect of God, for he carries God within himself and is at one with Him. The doxological community of subjects, ruler and God is transformed into a commonality and community of light. This is what Basarab means by the political.

This understanding allows the hesychast actively to participate in the *politeia*.[730] To do so is a responsibility resulting from human nature being rendered active and dynamic. God's effects are always directed outwards: from God's own being towards the ruler and thence on into the political subjects. This occurs within an all-encompassing community of light.

Virtues and Metaphorics of Rule

To the author of the *Teachings*, rule is a pure gift of God, who, by installing a particular prince, pursues his own ends, hidden to man. The ruler is in God's hands and is put in his place without recourse to claims

---

727 Eusebius of Caesarea, *Life of Constantine*: IV, 9: 156–157. Justinian I likewise considered his *Novellae* to be the fruit of divine illumination and hence the work of God. For Justinian, the ruler is granted the powers of government and jurisdiction by illumination (Novella 69, 4, 1 apud Blum 1974: 111; see 144 n. 10). On this, see also Antonopoulou 1997: 73.

728 Neagoe Basarab 1984: 170. On this, see the Patrician texts in Leemans/Matz/ Verstraeten 2011.

729 Plămădeală 1969: 259; Balfour 1986: 155.

730 Plămădeală 1969: 251.

of a merely human nature, such as blood or dynastic heredity. From the human perspective, rule is ultimately absolutely contingent. To Basarab's mind, works can provide neither justification nor rewards – in the manner of Catholic theology – and nor can an accumulation of merits serve to justify us before God, as Agapetus, who was in other respects eminently 'Orthodox', had claimed:

> More than Gold and gemstones we shall *gather* as our treasure the wealth of charity. For this wealth brings us joy here on earth in the hope of joys to come in the hereafter, and in the hereafter it will sweeten life in the real experience of bliss once anticipated.[731]

Basarab does, however, speak of good works as works of justice by which the ruler can act in *accordance* with God's will, though he can do nothing to *determine* it. It is in this idea of works as being in accordance with the will of God that the difference between bad tyrannical rulers and good Christian rulers resides:

> Now behold, my beloved son, the Great King who loved us so and raised us to be earthly kings, as He is one Himself, and placed His desire in us that we too should yet be heavenly kings, and such shall we be. As long as we truly strive unceasingly to do right, we shall rule here and in eternity. For the kingdoms and the rule of this world are in His hands and dependent only on His will, and they are granted us in reward of our good efforts.[732]

Yet contrast this with Basarab's claim a few pages on:

> Therefore shall none deceive himself and rest secure in the false hope that he might claim anything as his own wisdom and his own merit. For all these come from God and He alone grants them to men […]. And we owe it to God to repay what He has lent us […]. And none shall deceive himself and be conceited, though he be king,

---

731   Agapetos 1981: ch. XXXVIII, p. 70. Emphasis added.
732   'Vezi iubitul mieu, pre împăratul cel mare, care ne-au iubit și ne-au făcut și pre noi împărați pre pământu, ca și pre sine, și-i iaste voia să fim și în cer; și deaca vom vrea noi vom fi, numai să facem bine și vom fi împărați în véci. Însă împărățiile și domniile céste după pământu suntu în mâna și voia lui Dumnezeu și în nevoințile noastre céle bune se-au dat' (Neagoe Basarab 1984: 9).

prince, boyar, or whatsoever, for it is God who grants all these [titles] and it is for Him to reclaim them.[733]

What we encounter in Basarab is something of a postponed justification by works, albeit one that is able to change God's mind along the pattern of David and the kings of the Old Testament. From John Chrysostom and Agapetus, Basarab adopts the notion that by good works, we are able to make God our debtor (*datornic*).[734] Basarab's anti-meritorian line of thought converges with that of Luther only in the claim that neither earthly works nor merit entitle one to rule, but that such honours are exclusively gifts from God. Basarab would not, however, go so far as (for example) Melanchthon went in the Augsburg Confession in radically uncoupling justification (to Basarab: Christian rule as the bringer of salvation) from the condition of our worthiness (*ex condicione nostrae dignitatis*).[735]

Like Plato, Basarab is of the opinion that rule represents a heavy burden. It is, moreover, both a temptation and a trial in which a man, thus challenged, is given the chance to prove his worth and stand before God:

---

733   'Dreptu acéia nimeni să nu să înşale şi să să amăgească gândidu că doar are cevaşi întru înţelepţiia şi vrédnicia sa. Că toate suntu de la Dumnezeu şi de la Dumnezeu suntu dăruite oamenilor […]. [P]entru că suntem datori să plătim lui Dumnezeu ce ne-au dat. […] [D]reptu acéia nimeni să nu să amăgească şi să să ţie mare, măcar să fie împărat, măcar domnu, măcar boiariu, măcar fieşte ce va fi; că acéstea toate Dumnezeu le dă, Dumnezeu le ia' (Neagoe Basarab 1984: 29, 39).

734   John Chrysostom 1998: 78; Agapetos 1981: ch. L, p. 73 and, finally, Neagoe Basarab 1984: 204: 'O my soul, you should lend to our God upon earth, that you might find repayment in heaven according to your merits. Make God your debtor, for he is an exceptionally good debtor. He is never in arrears or late in paying his dues, but will in fact repay you one hundredfold and moreover [give] you the life everlasting as interest' ('Deci, o suflete, împrumutează pre Dumnezeu pre pământu, ca să iai în cer plată după vrédnicie-ţi şi ţi-l fă să-ţi fie el ţie dator, că bun datornic iaste. Şi nu va prinde tagă, nici va zăbovi cu plata, ci-ţi va plăti cu o sută de ori mai mult, şi încă îţi va da şi dobândă viaţa cea de veci'). The idea of God as debtor can already be found in Tertullian's *De poenitentia* (Hamm 2012: 246 n. 5).

735   Hamm 1986: 11.

See now to what God has called us in this world of deceit, for it is nothing to which
we might claim by right, but rather a temptation, that God might see our efforts and
our striving to protect His herd.[736]

To Basarab – as to the Carolingian, Byzantine or, later, the protestant mirrors for princes – the absolute archetype of the Christian ruler is David.[737]
Whereas King Melchisedek (Gen 14:18) as priest-king symbolised Christ,
the Christian tradition depicted David as the ruler in the hand of God. It
was God who raised him from shepherd boy to king, and as long as God
held His hand over him, David had nothing to fear from such mighty
foes as Goliath, Saul or Absalom. All that could endanger a king in the
Davidian mould was himself, his own weakness and sinfulness. Yet notwithstanding his grievous sin against Uriah (2 Sam. 11), God forgave King
David once he had done penance and succeeded in placating God.[738]

The significance of Old Testament histories for Christian rule is evident
in the long line of biblical *exempla* that Basarab adduces, beginning with
Elijah and ending with the last kings.[739] Paradoxically, the standard image
of the Christian ruler constructed by Basarab – no less than that of the
Carolingian, Byzantine and Protestant *Fürstenspiegel* and their authors – is
founded almost entirely on the Old Testament.[740] Unsurprisingly, the only
figure from the Christian era is Constantine the Great, who was hugely

736   '[V]edeţi ce tocmeală ne-au dat noao Dumnezeu într-această lume înşelătoare şi
       apoi iaste fără nici un temeiu, ce numai ce ne iaste ispitire, ca să vază cum ne vom
       nevoi şi ne vom osteni să păzim turma lui' (Neagoe Basarab 1984: 124).
737   Anton 2006: 11; Angelov 2007: 127ff. The so-called School of Antioch, of which
       Chrysostom was the best-known representative and which was highly influen-
       tial on Byzantine political theology, could look back on a rich tradition of Old
       Testament exegesis. Chrysostom considered David to be the model par excellence
       for royal conduct (John Chrysostom 2003; Mayer/Allen 2000; Hill 2005).
738   Păun 2001: 196.
739   Neagoe Basarab 1984: 22ff. On this, see Plămădeală 1969: 219.
740   While the Carolingian mirrors for princes concentrated largely on David and
       Solomon as prototypes of the *rex et propheta*, Basarab refers to a much longer
       line of Old Testament kings, among which he distinguishes between good and
       bad kings in order to outline, by comparison and contrast, the image of the godly
       ruler (Anton 1968: 108f., 419f.). On the Old Testament in Protestant mirrors for
       princes, see Görz 1990: 119.

popular in the Danubian Principalities. For his portrayal, Basarab drew extensively on Euthymius of Tarnovo's *History of Emperor Constantine*.[741]

Within Orthodox theology, a distinction exists between a theology of virtues and a moral theology of asceticism. Properly considered, asceticism is not a virtue like faith, hope and love, but rather a practical exercise of somewhat lower rank, a means to an end. By means of prayer, abstinence, chastity, fasting, physical labour and foregoing sleep, the ascetic cleanses his soul, develops a sense of apathy towards the distractions of the world and is then transfigured in light, ultimately reaching self-awareness in the contemplation of God. It is only this state that bears true fruit in the form of the great virtues. These virtues are distinct from the lesser ones by being not means to an end, but ends in, and of, themselves. The great Christian virtues that *show* an illumined person to be a *homoiousios* are those specified by Paul – faith, hope and love.[742]

In addition to these general virtues described in the New Testament, Byzantine political theology developed a canon of virtues specific to the Christian ruler, virtues that are derived from the aforementioned three as well as representing instances of their application. These virtues of rulers are *de facto* adopted directly from the Hellenistic canon and hold that a ruler should be of true faith (ὀρθόδοξος πίστις), of sound mind (εὔνοια) and a model of piety (εὐσέβεια); he should love God (θεοφιλία) and strive for justice (δικαιοσύνη, ἐπιείκεια), manly virtue (ἀνδρεία) and wisdom (σοφία). To this list was later added beneficence (εὐεργεσία), the ruler being committed to works of philanthropy and fatherly care for his subjects.[743] On ascending the throne, the Byzantine basileus had to swear an oath, among the provisions of which was to uphold these virtues of good rule.[744]

---

741 Neagoe Basarab 1984: 59ff.; Ştefănescu 1931. Unlike Basarab, the Carolingian *Fürstenspiegel* did not hark back only to Constantine the Great as an example of Christian rule, but rather adduce a broad spectrum of Christian Roman emperors from late antiquity: Theodosius I and II as well as Justinian I (Anton 1968: 437).

742 Louth 1981: 198.

743 Hunger 1964: 137ff.; Dvornik, II, 1966: 619, 713f.; Georgescu 1969: 194, 207, 321; Bell 2009: 60.

744 This oath had already been established in the Roman Empire with Tiberius (14–37). Evidence of the practice can also be found among the Hellenistic rulers and in the Roman Republic (Herrmann 1968: 25f., 50ff., 121). A canon of virtues of Emperor Constantine can be found at Nicol 1988: 52.

Among these virtues, the key part was played by philanthropy (φιλ
ανθρωπία), in which the three great Christian virtues of faith, hope and
love found joint expression. Itself, however, philanthropy was a compo-
nent of pre-Christian – classical and Hellenistic – codes of virtue[745] and
indeed was used, in the declining years of paganism, as a weapon against
Christianity, whose adherents preferred to use their own term, 'agape.'[746]
Yet after the fourth century, to be a 'lover of men' (φιλάνθρωπος) came to
epitomise the (Byzantine) Christian ruler[747] and was of key importance to
Neagoe Basarab, too.[748] In the *Teachings*, Basarab discusses philanthropy
above all in terms of *caritas*, that is, sympathetic love, unconditional duty
and empathy. Basarab's argument for philanthropy is framed in terms much
like that of Erasmus:[749] 'Therefore you shall, my beloved son, be merciful
unto all men and unto all peoples, which God has entrusted to you, for it
is for them that our lord and saviour Himself did shed His holy blood.'[750]
God had sacrificed Himself for us out of love, and the prize obtained by
His blood – human beings – is entrusted to the Christian ruler. By *kenosis*,
Christ for the sake of man had stripped or emptied Himself of all divine
glory and humbly come to serve human beings. This example was – as

745 Dvornik, II, 1966: 619; Georgescu 1969: 187; Daly 1975: 23ff. Philanthropy origin-
     ally referred to the gods' love of men, which is why God was also the most eminent
     philanthropist in Christianity – as Paul describes Him in Titus 3:4 (Constantelos
     1962: 351).

746 '[A]t the same times the pagan writers, as exemplified by Themistios, Libanius
     and the Emperor Julian, begin to try to develop philanthropia as a principle of
     conduct – both public and private – which they can offer as a counterpart of the
     Christian teaching; thus they seek to show that paganism as a way of life can pro-
     vide principles which are as good as those of Christianity' (Downey 1955: 199).

747 Biondi 1951; Hunger 1963 and 1964: 143ff.; Anca 2010: 123. In fourteenth-century
     Byzantium, the emperor publicly committed himself to upholding this virtue
     (Carile 2008: 86).

748 On philanthropy as a legal matter in the Danubian Principalities, see Georgescu
     1969: 215.

749 See the chapter on Erasmus.

750 'Dreptu acéia, iubitul mieu fiiu, să fii milostiv tuturor oamenilor şi tuturor
     gloatelor care ţi le va da Dumnezeu pre mâna ta, pentru care însuşi Domnul
     Dumnezeul nostru şi mântuitorul Iisus Hristos ş-au vărsat sfântul sânge al său'
     (Neagoe Basarab 1984: 8).

Luther, too, would later argue – binding to the Christian ruler:[751] 'And the prophet moreover speaks: "requite it with thy hand: the poor committeth himself unto thee; thou art the helper of the fatherless" [Ps. 10:14]. For the poor Son of God was likewise sent into this world, as it its recorded. And to you has God confided rule in this short-lived world.'[752] Basarab here also takes his cue from biblical arguments in Matt. 20:26–28 and 1 Tim. 5:8.

This notion of *servitium* is not an established figure of Byzantine political philosophy. In the sixth century, Agapetus expressed the opinion that the purpose of the emperor was not to serve men, but to instruct, lead and judge them.[753] This is an instance of the political Platonism shared by John Chrysostom, who considered the Christian emperor's chief function to reside in keeping people from slaughtering each other.[754] That is the classical conception of the ruler's and ultimately God's philanthropy: the social and political regulation of society and the upholding of order, in which penalties and force are fully justified wherever necessary. According to Justinian I, philanthropy represents God's friendship with man, and the emperor is charged with applying philanthropy in order to resemble God.[755] This somewhat condescending and politically profitable view of philanthropy and munificence and generosity – or indeed pedagogy – was key in Byzantium.[756] Basarab or Luther envisaged philanthropy as the ruler's unconditional love and service (or even servitude!), resembling a supra-rational eros rather than the functional nature of socio-political philanthropy, which is quite a rare theme in earlier Christian thought.[757]

---

751 Plămădeală 1969: 236.
752 'Şi iară mai zice proorocul: ,ție iaste lăsat săracul, şi méserului tu îi fii ajutor'. Că şi fiiul lui Dumnezeu săracul fu trimis în lume cum iaste scris. Iar ţie ţi-au dat Dumnezeu împărăţiia într-această lume scurtă' (Neagoe Basarab 1984: 10). See also Neagoe Basarab 1984: 16.
753 Agapetus 1981: ch. I, p. 59 and ch. XXXIVff., p. 69.
754 Dvornik, II, 1966: 713; Blum 1974: 112.
755 Blum 1974: 111.
756 See Emperor Leo VI (the Philosopher; 886–912) apud Antonopoulou 1997: 75; Constantelos 1962.
757 Augustine was no exception, speaking (in *De civitate Dei*) of a socio-economic, domestic form of charity (Augustine, *The City of God*, Book XIX, ch. 14).

Philanthropy entails the obligation, on the ruler's part, to display generosity (φιλοδωρία) and indeed to be lavish to the point of extravagance in favours to subjects or guests and strangers. Neagoe Basarab's many foundations were discussed in the historical section of this chapter. The costlier his gifts, endowments and donations – so the theory went – the more renown the ruler would gain as a μεγαλόδωρος (one who gives liberally) or φιλόδωρος (one who gladly gives). This virtue is far from being a purely Christian[758] one but rather, like nearly all concepts in political ethics, can be traced to Hellenism.[759] Among the kings of the Old Testament, Neagoe Basarab picks out those who meet the description of *megalodoroi*:

> And King Hezekiah was delighted at this and showed the envoys all his riches and all the gold and silver that were his, and all his little treasure, too, and he led them through his houses and there remained nothing of his riches and his stores of food that he did not show these envoys of the Babylonian Emperor.

Basarab includes this potlatch-like display of wealth to servants and envoys at court in his chapter on envoys in the second part of the *Teachings*.[760] When Christian envoys arrive, the ruler ought to ask his courtiers to dress in their finest clothes and to appear mounted on costly horses in exquisite tack. The envoys themselves were to be pampered and enjoy lavish hospitality: 'Take out the silver cups and make an effort to decorate everything so finely that the envoy might marvel at such splendour.'[761] The ruler is to receive his guests dressed in his finery and upon a richly appointed

---

758   This notion of liberality is distinct from the purely Christian τὸ εὐμετάδοτον, as it was used, for example, by Basil of Caesarea – a kind of 'liberality' that is neither showy nor dares others to match it, but rather is the Christian kind, arising from the power of charity (δύναμις ἀγάπης) and sustains the 'polis' of God on earth, that is, the Christian communion. This liberality is of the Ariostotelian kind, which holds, broadly speaking, that the haves should give to the have-nots in order to create a balance (Nikolau 1981: 25ff.).

759   This princely virtue seems to have found its way into Christianity via Hellenism. It was likewise considered one of the highest virtues of a ruler in the Ottoman Empire or in Arabian Islam (Dilger 1967; Faroqhi 2008: 62).

760   Neagoe Basarab 1984: 161ff.

761   'Scoateți pahară de argint frumoase și siliți să așezați toate frumos, ca să să mire și solul de această podoabă' (Neagoe Basarab 1984: 167).

throne, and the grand boyars surrounding the prince were to dress with matching opulence.[762] The author of the *Teachings* well understands the mechanism by which material capital is converted to symbolic capital: 'For the wise ruler has no use in this world for material riches, but only for the good name that is his. [...] For it seems to me that a good reputation is of greater importance than great material wealth.'[763] Basarab seems intuitively to understand the potlatch mentality:

> You must estimate what gift the other ruler's envoy has brought you, and you must through your envoy make gifts to that ruler in equal measure. Indeed you ought to try to ensure that your gift is better and finer than that of the other ruler, that he might marvel and say 'What a grand thing! Never have I seen so fine and beautiful an artefact, and he has given one to me, which means that he must have many!' And when you are thus praised, you will have earned great honour.[764]

Yet this form of hospitality, too, was a Byzantine tradition that demanded that certain guests be impressed with splendour and showered with riches.[765] Basarab's manner of dealing with guests was common practice in Wallachia. Vlad the Impaler was also known to have astonished envoys to his court with its wealth and his own munificence.[766]

---

762 See Neagoe Basarab 1984: 162.

763 'Că domnul carele are minte nu-i trebuiaşte într-această lume altă avuţie, fără numai numele cel bun. [...] [C]ă mie-mi pare să fie mai bun numele cel bun decât avuţiia cea multă' (Neagoe Basarab 1984: 161).

764 '[T]u socotéşte ce daruri ţe-au adus solul celuilaltu domn care au venit la tine. Aşa trebuiaşte şi tu să trimiţi acelui domn cu solul tău. Încă să te nevoeşti să fie darul care i-l vei trimite tu mai bun şi mai frumos decât al domnului celuilalt, care ţi l-au trimis întâi, ca să să mire el când va vedea darul de la tine şi să zică: "Mare lucru! Eu de-abia aş fi văzut un lucru minunat şi frumos ca acesta, iar el iată că mi l-au dăruit mie: dar la dânsul încă câte vor fi rămas?" Şi dacă te va lăuda aşa şi acéia încă iaste cinste mare' (Neagoe Basarab 1984: 170).

765 'The Byzantine Emperor epitomised the figure of the μεγαλόδωρος. [...] Hence the gifts bestowed by the *basileus* were accompanied by stronger epithets in the Byzantine and other sources. Reference is made to 'lavish gifts' (*doris uberioribus*), 'immense gifts' (*imensa munera*) and 'sumptuous gifts' (δωρήμασιν ἄδροις) (Anca 2010: 98). See also Kresten 2000; Anca 2005; Reinsch 2005

766 Şerban 1971: 302.

Yet a virtue of greater importance even than munificence was for the ruler to be a true believer, to display conformity in matters of faith and doctrine:[767]

> Take care then of the following, my son, for the Holy Scriptures command us to forswear heretics, to avoid having any closer dealings with them or even to converse much with them. But it behoves you all the more to avoid the heathen, who know not God and who have no baptism [...]. For they are enemies of the cross of our Lord Jesus Christ and slander His holy name.[768]

Accordingly, the second part of the *Teachings* – following the example of the Byzantine Pseudo-Kodinos (fourteenth century) – begins with a detailed religious disquisition,[769] a doctrinal treatise giving a compact account of the articles of faith of the seven ecumenical councils and addressing all major Christological heresies: Arians, Macedonites, Nestorians, Monophysites, Iconoclasts.[770] Like the Byzantine emperors before him, Basarab was eager to prove the rightness and dogmatic purity

767   The Orthodox faith was as important to the Byzantine basileus or to the Danubian princes as Sunni Islam was to the Ottoman Sultans, who considered themselves its defenders against the Shiites (see Faroqhi 2008: 59).

768   'Iată, ia aminte şi aceasta, fătul mieu, că poruncescu dumnezeieştile scripturi să te lépezi de eritici, să nu faci taină cu dânşii, nici să vorbeşti multu cu ei; dar încă cu cât mai multu să cade să te fereşti de păgâni, de care nu ştiu de iaste Dumnezeu, nici să boteză [...]. Că aceştea suntu vrăjmaşi crucii Domnului nostru Iisus Hristos, şi numele lui Dumnezeu cel sfântu ei îl hulescu' (Neagoe Basarab 1984: 58).

769   Carile 2008: 86.

770   Neagoe Basarab 1984: 115: 'Therefore shall you – you, my son, and you, my brothers and anointed of God – cleave to and believe all this [that I have said]. And the lying and slandering mouths of the heretics shall be stopped [...]' ('Dreptu aceasta, tu, fătul mieu, şi dumneavoastră, iubiţii miei fraţi şi unşii lui Dumnezeu, de acéstea să cade să vă ţineţi şi acestuia să crédeţi. Iar gurile eriticilor céle mincinoase şi bârfitoare să să astupe ...'). The author of the *Teachings* draws entire passages from the sermon of Ephrem the Syrian (see the discussion of the *Teachings*' sources) that argue in support of Christ's two natures, true God and true man (Ephrem the Syrian: chs 12 and 14; Muthu 1976: 37). The veneration of icons is also expressly commended (Neagoe Basarab 1984: 109). The venartion of saints, particularly of the Virgin Mary, is likewise adduced as criterion of the Orthodox Christian ruler. Against the Nestorians, Mary is referred to as *Theotokos* (Neagoe Basarab 1984: 110, 113ff.). His injunction to combat heresy notwithstanding, there is no concrete advice on how to deal with heretics, though Byzantium, Basarab's model

of his faith, since heresy on the part of the ruler would have provided his subjects with just cause for (armed) opposition.[771] Basarab, whose rule had begun under somewhat unconventional circumstances, was anxious to fend off any challenges to his legitimacy.

Yet the fact that the virtue of right faith should make such a relatively late appearance in the *Teachings* (i.e., in their second part) may also testify to a shifting emphasis with regard to princely virtues in Eastern Christendom. In the dogmatic disputes of the early centuries – between Nicaea 325 and Nicaea 787 – the main criterion of godly rule had indeed been the dogmatic purity of faith. After the dogmatic structure had been established, the accent in the mid- to late Byzantine periods as well as in post-Byzantine political ethics shifted to the ruler's virtuous conduct of life. Moral conduct and social and philanthropic accomplishments of the kind demanded of the ruler in the second part of the *Teachings* acquire, to the mind of their author, something of the rank of priestly virtues discussed in John Chrysostom's treatise on the subject.

Drawing on the examples of Solomon and Constantine, Basarab accordingly divides the virtue of true belief into the ruler's responsibility for upholding and strengthening the Orthodox faith (*cura religionis*) on the one hand and the preservation of Christian morality (*cura moralitatis*) on the other.[772] Neagoe Basarab held up as exemplary all that Constantine had done for the Church and the Christian faith: setting faith free and encouraging its spread by proselytism, charitable foundations and the repression, or even suppression, of competing systems of faith.[773] Moreover, the author of the *Teachings* accords a key role to the ruler's liturgical presence, that is to say, his attendance at divine service: 'And likewise shall you, my beloved ones, pray at the holy church and celebrate mass in song and spiritual hymn.'[774]

---

in so many respects, had a fairly precise idea of what was to be done about them (Alexander 1978).

771   See the letter of Antonios IV to Grand Prince Vasily I of Moscow apud Barker 1957: 195. See also Christou 1971: 283; Ensslin 1975: 233, 133 n. 127.

772   Neagoe Basarab 1984: 33.

773   Neagoe Basarab 1984: 61f.

774   'Aşişderea iubiţii miei, deaca intraţi în sfânta biséricǎ, voi vǎ rugaţi şi faceţi slujbǎ cu cântǎri şi cu cântece sufleteşti' (Neagoe Basarab 1984: 111).

Nor was justice to be forgotten among the virtues enumerated in the *Teachings*, particularly in light of the fact that it has always been a central aspect not only of Christian rule, but also of the general ethos of rulers throughout history.[775] As the Byzantine emperor had been – and had to be – a δίκαιος,[776] so Basarab held up the Christian prince as the embodiment of God's justice on earth: 'Thou, o God, didst create justice and entrust it to kings and princes, while it is for all men to be its witnesses.'[777] Though Basarab does not explicitly speak of the prince as *lex animata* or νόμος ἔμψυχος,[778] he does indicate that it is through the prince that God's justice shines into the *politeia*. Basarab maintains the polarity of political life between the rulers on the one hand – the subjects of the application of justice in political life – and the people on the other – the subjects who know justice and decide what constitutes it. Justice, to Basarab, is proportional in character, subsisting in the 'fair' balancing of symbolic and material resources.[779] Justice is not to be interpreted or apportioned according to the social status of those concerned:

> And you shall not disadvantage the rich while by your judgment giving the advantage to the poor, but rather let justice be done to the rich as well as to the poor. For God has chosen you and given you unto men like a wellspring of water; take care, therefore, lest you be sweet to some and bitter to others.[780]

775   Hunger 1964: 114ff.; Martens 2003: 63ff.
776   Dvornik, II, 1966: 619.
777   'Tu, Doamne, ca un Dumnezeu ai gătit direptatea ta şi o ai dat împăraţilor şi domnilor, iar adeverinţa o ai dat tuturor oamenilor' (Neagoe Basarab 1984: 10).
778   This sytagma represents another instance of Hellenistic influence on Christian terminology, though it is problematic from the perspective of systemic theology by its association with the pagan cult of the emperor, thus conflicting with Christian monotheism. The term can be encountered as early as the apocryphal second-century *Kerygmata Petri* (Hunger 1964: 117ff.; Dvornik, II, 1966: 589f.; Aalders 1969: 329).
779   Neagoe Basarab 1984: 108. Agapetus 1981: ch. XVI, p. 64, gives the following précis of the Aristotelian principle of proportionality: 'In order, then, that both groups [i.e. rich and poor] might receive inward and outward health, they must be cured by taking something away from one and giving a little more to the other, thus turning inequality into equality.'
780   'Şi să nu făţărniceşti celui bogat, nici iar să miluieşti cu judecata pre cel sărac, ci să faci judecată dreaptă şi bogaţilor şi săracilor. Că Dumnezeu v-au ales şi v-au pus

Equal access to justice follows the principle of the equality of all human beings in Creation: all are doxological creatures with the same human nature, and God glorifies Himself equally in each of them. It is striking to observe how Basarab avoids the clichés and stock phrases of Christian thought and argues on the basis of his own reflections. The author of the *Teachings* will hear nothing of the idea that the poor deserved some kind of special treatment, for their weakness might be exploited to pander to or to pity them and thus to distort the truth. To conceive of justice as the proportionate distribution of resources accords with the idea of justice inasmuch as such distribution enables justice in the first place. Yet they differ in their application, since a balanced distribution of resources differs from rigid principle of justice, which leaves little scope for interpretation and admits no double standards. This idea, which can be found in identical form in Agapetus,[781] suggests that Basarab was most likely familiar with the deacon's *Ecthesis*.

The ruler's virtue and his concomitant function as a teacher to his people is a further important point and a *locus communis* of Christian political theology. Basarab, however, throws this *topos* into much sharper relief.[782] He may have come across the idea in *The Martyrdom of Polycarp* (d. c. 155), a work popular and well known in the Orthodox world, or in Eusebius of Caesarea, who was likewise popular.[783] Neagoe Basarab does not limit the teaching role to the indirect example set by a wise ruler,[784] a method for educating citizens in virtue that many political thinkers, following Aristotle, had espoused. The idea was that the people would learn virtue by observation.[785] Yet in writing the *Teachings* and composing sermons and letters on pedagogy, Basarab went further.

---

oamenilor ca un izvor de apă; ci să nu cumva să fiți unora dulci și altora amari [...]' (Neagoe Basarab 1984: 184f.).

781   Agapetos 1981: ch. XLI, p. 71.

782   Neagoe Basarab 1984: 238 and passim.

783   Martyrdom of Polycarp 1901: ch. XVIII, p. 8 and ch. XIX, p. 9. On this, see also Buschmann 1998: 17 n. 3, 324; Dvornik, II, 1966: 580; Farina 1966: 126.

784   A capricious ruler not only risks ridicule for his outbursts, he also – as John Chrysostom warned – loses any claim to set an example and to teach (John Chrysostom 1988: ch. 2, p. 70). The same advioce can be found in the letter of Patriarch Photios to the Bulgarian czar Boris Mikhail (apud Barker 1957: 113f.).

785   Voegelin, III, 1957: 298; Antonopoulou 1997: 73, 76.

To Basarab, being his people's teacher did not mean that the ruler was all-knowing and in no need of counsel – on the contrary: a ruler who neither asked for advice nor followed it was not a wise ruler. As we shall see, this idea brings Neagoe into proximity with Machiavelli, who also held that the prince ought to take the advice of experienced statesmen, while Luther and Erasmus came out in favour of the monarch's independent decision. In Basarab's view, to ignore the counsel of the 'elders' and of the experienced boyars would not only be unwise, but indeed un-Christian, for Christ Himself had taken advice and taught us to listen to the advice of others, conscious of our human weakness, fallibility and ignorance.[786] Not to admit that the prince himself was in need of counsel smacked of satanic pride.

> You ought not to be ashamed or to be too proud or to think in your heart: 'Since I am prince, how I shall I ask the boyars for advice, they being my subjects?' For boyars too are servants of Christ, and it may well be that some of them are more open to the inspiration of Christ than you are.[787] For any prince who fails to seek the counsel of his boyars is mistaken. St Paul the apostle himself maintains and testifies: 'We are unable even to hold a candle to our forefathers!' and likewise does Jesus Christ speak in the Gospel: 'O woe unto him that takes his own advice and asks no other!'[788]

Though the ruler's opinion may differ from that of his counsellors, he is nonetheless advised to bow to the majority and follow their guidance.[789]

As a fine stylist, the author of the *Teachings* frames his theology of the virtues of Christian rule in metaphors, which, though they may not

786   Neagoe Basarab 1984: 41ff.
787   Constantine Porphyrogenitus 1995: 67.
788   'Şi să nu-ţi fie ruşine sau să te ţii mare, cugetând sau zicând în inima ta: "Eu fiind domn, cum poate fi de întreb toţi boiarii miei de sfat, şi ei suntu slugi mie?" Că şi ei robi lui Hristos suntu, şi dar de vor fi unii dentr-înşii îngăduind lui Dumnezeu mai bine decât tine? Pentru că tot Domnul care nu-şi va întreba boierii de sfat, acela nu face bine. Că singur Pavel apostol mărturiseşte şi zice: "Niciodată nu vom putea noi ajunge urma moşilor noştri." Şi la Evanghelie încă grăiaşte Domnul nostru Iisus Hristos şi zice: "Amar celuia ce să sfătuiaşte singur şi pe altul nu-l întreabă!"' (Neagoe Basarab 1984: 164).
789   Neagoe Basarab 1984: 166.

be consistently original, are nonetheless applied in an appropriate and differentiated manner,

Neagoe Basarab's preferred metaphor for rule is the shepherd (*păstor*), and he makes heavy use of what might be called the semantics of pastoralism:

> For even though you may be monarch or lord, the judgment is God's alone. You were ultimately installed by His decision and at His behest as the shepherd and administrator of His works [in the world] [...]. You are God's anointed and *Christian monarchs* and the lords whom He chooses, in your hands will He place God's imperial flock.[790]

In the Christian tradition, the semantics of pastoralism were used in contexts both ecclesiastical – to describe the position of bishops – and political – for the secular ruler. It all the more strongly appears as the ultimate metaphor for rule when it denotes a sacerdotal form of rule combining both aspects, in which the ruler is situated not only in the temporal, but also especially in the spiritual sphere.[791] The shepherd metaphor can already be found in pagan, pre-Christian literature, notably in Homer (ποιμὴν λαῶν),[792] not to mention its centrality among the authors of the ancient East, of Hellenism and late antiquity.[793] In early Christian literature – for instance in *The Martyrdom of Polycarp* – the metaphor naturally referred to Christ, Who had described Himself as the 'good shepherd' (John 10:11).[794] Eusebius, under the influence of Hellenism, makes the metaphor the central motif of Christian rule.[795]

---

790 'Că măcară de eşti şi împăratu sau domnnu, iar judecata tot iaste a lui Dumnezeu şi cu porunca lui eşti pus păstor tu şi tocmitor faptelor lui. [...] [S]unteţi unşii lui Dumnezeu şi împăraţi creştineşti şi domni pre carele va alége Dumnezeu şi va da în mâna lui să păzească turma cea împărătească a lui Hristos [...]' (Neagoe Basarab 1984: 11, 123). Emphasis added. See Agapetus 1981: ch. XXX, p. 68.

791 Antonopoulou 1997: 74.

792 Hunger 1964: 101. Thomas Magister also quote this syntagma of Homer with regard to kings (Thomas Magister 1981: 117).

793 Foucault 1999: 136f.

794 Martyrdom of Polycarp: ch. XIX, p. 9; Buschmann 1998: 19, 2b, S. 343; Dvornik, II, 1966: 580.

795 Hunger 1964: 102; Dvornik, II, 1966: 618 (with citation); Maier 2003: 139.

The proper use of the pastoral metaphor requires caution: it can describe *Christian* rule, but can also be used to criticise *all* kinds of rule as hubristic and arrogant supremacy over human beings. A Christian author, Theophylact of Ohrid, wrote in the eleventh century: 'Thus the lord over the sheep is not himself a sheep, but rather a man; and the lord over the cows is not a cow, but *an overseer*, one to whom *is given reason* and who *by his nature stands far higher than his flock*.'[796] In this form, the metaphor underscores the shepherd's rule and pre-eminence over his flock, which in turn is portrayed as consisting of beasts devoid of reason. Though this may indeed be a common image of rule, as a metaphor for Christian rule in the manner intended by Theophylact, I would argue that it misses the mark completely. Both Christ (John 10:11) and Neagoe Basarab stress the shepherd's love for his flock and his preparedness to lay down his life for it. His task is the loving care of noble and unique creatures: 'Therefore you too, when you are chosen by God and installed as shepherds of His flock, shall be gentle with Christ's flock and graze it with humility and reverence […].'[797] Epithets such as 'Christ's imperial flock' make it clear that Neagoe Basarab does not take the word 'flock' to denote a mass of dumb animals.

Michel Foucault distinguished four principal reasons why the pastoral metaphor was so useful in describing Christian rule. First, the freedom to roam on the part of shepherd and flock underscored that Christian rule, as a matter of principle, transcended territorial limitation: like Christianity itself, Christian rule was a medium with a claim to universality. Second, the existence of the herd was dependent on a shepherd to guide it, protect and keep it together (political argument). Third, the shepherd was responsible for preserving or saving his flock, which was entrusted to him by someone wishing to receive it back unharmed. By saving his flock, the shepherd could thus be seen as saving himself; *in extremis*, he would lay his life down for his flock (soteriological argument). The ruler was an example to his people, and his immoral lifestyle might corrupt the Christian people – many Christian authors claimed that the people reflected upon

796   Theophylact of Ohrid 1981: ch. XXVIII, p. 96. Emphasis added.
797   'Pentr-acéia şi pre voi, ori pre care va alége Dumnezeu şi-l va pune să fie păstor turmei sale, să fiţi blânzi spre turma lui Hristos şi cu multă frică şi smerenie să o paşteţi […]' (Neagoe Basarab 1984: 225).

their ruler. And as Christ sacrificed Himself for mankind, so rulers must be prepared to stake their life on the welfare of their subjects. Fourth and last, the flock was the shepherd's duty, his 'job', as it were, and its welfare is his responsibility. Though doing so may be troublesome, the flock must be looked after and tended to (servitial argument).[798]

The prince as *bee* is another important metaphor for the Christian ruler used by Basarab. In the Christian sphere, the metaphor of the bees had been used to describe literary eclecticism by the Alexandrian school and by Basil of Caesarea,[799] but never in a political sense. Basil invoked the bee in his celebrated address to the youth, as a way of describing how young people might approach pagan mythology and literature. Just as bees did not turn all pollen into honey, so young people, too, were to take from non-Christian writers only what was agreeable and useful for the purpose of sweetening their souls.[800] Though Neagoe Basarab adopts this metaphor, he uses is quite differently:

> You should be wise and circumspect, no different from the bees. For behold the bee as she flies from her hive and strikes out on her own to visit the blooms for pollen and food, for all her profit and benefit derives from blooms. But not all blooms, for among all she chooses only the sweetest from which to gather her harvest. Hence her honeycombs are the sweetest. [...] Likewise also the ruler, whom God has chosen and anointed; to him his subjects are as blooms. If he allows all their words and counsels, the good as well as the bad, to work upon his heart, his heart will never enjoy sweetness, just as the bee's honeycombs would never be sweet if they had been gathered from all pollen, the sweet as well as the bitter. For she avoids the bitter blooms and takes only from those that are good and sweet. That is why her honeycombs are so sweet.[801]

798 Foucault 1999: 137f.
799 Hatcher 1999: 25, 28.
800 Basil the Great: 19; Warkotsch 1973: 386; Payne 2011: 86.
801 'Şi să fiţi înţelepţi şi chibzuiţi de nu mai mult, încai ca albinile. Că vedeţi că albina cât iase din uleiul ei şi umblă prin flori de-şi agoniséşte mannă şi hrană cu multă osteneală, că tot câştigul şi agoniseala ei din flori iaste, însă nu din tot féliul de flori. Că de ar fi aduncând manna ei din tot feliul de flori, n-ar fi fagurii ei aşa de dulci; ce den toate florile alége care suntu mai dulci, de adună agoniseala ei dintr-însele. Pentr-acéia şi fagurii ei suntu atât de dulci [...]. Aşijderea şi domnul care iaste ales şi unsu lui Dumnezeu, aceluia-i sunt slugile ca şi florile. Deci, de va priimi domnul toate cuvintele lor, şi céle bune şi céle rele în inima sa, niciodată nu i să va îndulci inima, cum şi fagurii albinii n-ar fi dulci, de ar fi strânsu mannă din toate florile,

The Christian ruler proceeds in a similarly eclectic manner, taking from his subjects only what is good and useful. He enriches himself by what is good in them in order to do good in his turn: a harmonic reciprocity of the political as a *hortum spiritualium deliciarum*.[802] This idea of humanity and of human coexistence would seem to be a positive reinterpretation of the dark and ominous verses of Isaiah 40:6–8: 'All flesh is grass, and all the goodliness thereof is as the flower of the field: The grass withereth, the flower fadeth: because the spirit of the Lord bloweth upon it: surely the people is grass. The grass withereth, the flower fadeth: but the word of our God shall stand for ever.'[803]

From the metaphor of the bee, Basarab moves on to a related metaphor, that of rule as a *garden*:

> For I have, my beloved sons, a garden. And this garden I, with the gifts and help of God and with many efforts and labours, planted and tended well. This garden with its fine plants consists of my great and honourable boyars. And I have fenced them in, as with a wall of stone, lest somebody should dare enter it and harm the fruit of my labours. The garden I laboured to plant and the plants therein I guarded brought forth fair flowers and grew high. And I refreshed myself in their shadows and beneath their flowers, and my eyes delighted in the merry fairness of the blooms in their dew. And not only did they fill and light my heart with joy, they were moreover glad and willing to give their life and blood for me.[804]

şi din céle dulci, şi din céle amară; ci de céle amară ia să fereşte, iar din céle buni şi dulci ia. Pentr-acéia sunt fagurii aşa de dulci' (Neagoe Basarab 1984: 225).

802 See Martens 2003: 86.

803 Suggested in Callahan 1958: 51.

804 'Că eu, feţii miei, am o grădină. Şi această grădină, cu darul şi cu ajutoriul lui Dumnezeu între multele méle osteninţe şi nevoinţe, o am făcut şi o am crescut frumos şi bine. Grădina acéia şi créştirile céle frumoase dentr-însa suntu boiarii miei cei mari şi cinstiţi. Şi i-am îngrădit cu gard ca cu un zid de piiatră şi grădina mea o am apărat, ca nu cumva să îndrăznească cineva să între într-însa şi să strice ceva den ostenélele mele. Deacii acea osteneală a mea şi grădina şi acéle créşteri ce le apăraiu crescură frumoase şi înflorirả. Şi eu tot supt umbra lor şi a florilor lor m-am răcorit, şi ochii miei să răvenea de roaoa şi de veseliia florilor lor. Şi nu numai ce mă veselea cu veselii şi mă bucura, ce încă şi capetele să şi le pue şi sângele să şi-l vérse toţi voia şi era bucuroşi pentru mine' (Neagoe Basarab 1984: 148f.).

Amid his courtiers and subjects, the prince dwells as in a garden. If the gardener tends his garden diligently, rooting out weeds and removing withered branches, the garden is healthy and an oasis of calm and pleasure. Basarab uses the metaphor of the garden in different forms. In another context, the person of the ruler himself is a garden upon a hill[805] and it is the duty of officials, counsellors and boyars to tend to the ruler – his character, attitudes and conduct – like a tree or a garden. As long as dead branches are cut off and the flower beds are weeded and watered, it (and he) will thrive. Should the gardeners be negligent, the garden is destined to fall barren and the ruler turns into a hateful tyrant.[806] A 'well-cultivated' ruler is not only a delight to the eye, but also a benefit to his people, to whom he is both *water-fountain and nourishment*[807] – another metaphor found in the *Teachings*.

Conclusion

The *Teachings to Theodosius* consider the Christian prince as God-like, as a *homoiousios*. Homoiosis is attained by illumination and represents a mystical personal experience on the part of the ruler by which he is transformed into an organ of the will and the knowledge of God on earth. Through the illumined ruler, God loves the world, the cosmos, His Creation. It is around the illumined ruler – and not, it should be noted, around the institution of the Church – that the doxological community is formed as political association of beings who give praise and who fulfil and enact their nature in doxology. It is this doxological naturalness of man, which is centred, intensified and concentrated in the Christian ruler, that Neagoe Basarab places at the centre of the political organism. The Christian ruler forms the core of the community of the

---

805   On the image of the ruler as a castle upon a hill, see Constantine Porphyrogenitus 1971: 14.
806   See Neagoe Basarab 1984: 164f.
807   Neagoe Basarab 1984: 154, 185.

faithful, which is equivalent to the concentric choirs of heavenly angels surrounding Christ.[808] The political entity that is the earthly state is an image of the kingdom of God, an antechamber to heaven and the site of Christian politics.

It would be inaccurate to portray the thought of Neagoe Basarab as the political instrumentalisation of religious ideas. Instead, religion, Orthodox Christianity, is itself political, a means by which identity, community and a shred political life are constituted. In their theological aspects, the *Teachings* are concerned with revealing how much sociability is required for human life to be properly human and why Christian categories that are normally theological – love, illumination or faith – are in fact universal in their orientation and effect, being factors of human togetherness in a polity of Christian perfection.

No more than Luther or Erasmus does Basarab consider the Christian ideal of the state or the ruler to be unattainable. In his prelapsarian state, man had already dwelt in God's immediacy and in His light, and with the aid of Christ man is on his way back to that state. Neagoe Basarab understands the knowledge of God's promise and His will in the world to result from the ruler being united with God in the increate light of Christ transfigured. In the light, the ruler himself is Christ and indeed God, and in this new quality acts upon the world as a Christian, which is to say Christ-like, ruler. His political activity stems only from the logical and theologically provable necessity of individual mystical experience – what has become known in scholarship as *political hesychasm*. The ruler's *unio mystica* (ἕνωσις) with God gives him, not so much rule in God's stead and name, but rather a political presence as a ruler *with* God, a form of co-regency.[809]

It is in the awareness of the Christian ruler's God-likeness that the author of the *Teachings* uses throughout such phrases as 'God-like one' (*întocmai cu Dumnezeu*),[810] 'fellow of God' (*soţ al lui Dumnezeu*), 'heir of God' (*moştean al lui Dumnezeu*),[811] 'image of God' (*chip al lui Dumnezeu*) and 'in God's service' (*în slujba lui Dumnezeu*). By such terms, he helps

---

808   Anca 2010: 71.
809   Lossky 1973: 129f.
810   Probably adopted from Gregory of Nyssa (see Merki 1952: 138f.).
811   Rom. 8:17.

support the meta-term of the 'Christian rulers' (*împărații creștini*) or the 'Christian lords' (*domnii creștini*).[812] In the hereafter, the Christian ruler will sit at table with Christ and dance with him at the heavenly wedding, and that Basarab seems likely to have taken from Ephrem the Syrian, who interpreted Matt. 22:1–14 along these lines.[813]

Already in the classical or Hellenistic era, the *theomimetes* (μιμητὴς Θεοῦ) was held up as the ideal ruler, and the figure can be found, for instance, in the fourth century B C in Archytas,[814] Diotogenes or Ecphantus, or in Plutarch in the first and second century A D, all of whom place the ruler in the immediate proximity of the Godhead.[815] It would be wrong, however, to claim that the Hellenistic authors had thereby theorised the divine ruler. Their aim was rather to emphasise the divine character of the political order and all its institutions. Diotogenes claimed: 'The rule of kings is an institution that imitates the Godhead.'[816] In the context of Christian soteriology, this idea can be found as early as in Origen and the Cappadocians,[817] in political thought, in Eusebius, Theophylact of Ohrid or Thomas Magister.[818] Neagoe Basarab is likely to have been familiar with Agapetus, who found an early reception in the South Slavic traditions, and this would explain how Basarab came to adopt a number of ideas that Agapetus drew from the common pool of neo-Pythagorean and Hellenistic wisdom: the ruler's divine virtue, the king as shepherd to his people and God as the archetype of the ruler.[819]

---

812 Neagoe Basarab 1984: 60, 161 and *passim*.

813 Neagoe Basarab 1984: 89; Dvornik, II, 1966: 85ff.,94f.

814 Archytas speaks simply of *mimesis*, whereas Ecphantus was apparently the first to relate *mimesis* to God and speak of a *mimesis Theou* (Martens 2003: 59).

815 Delatte 1942: 216; Merlan 1967: 58ff., 84ff.; Thesleff 1968; Gundert 1969: 91, 96; Martens 2003: 55f.; Schulte 2001: 136ff., 148ff., 159ff., 227ff.

816 'ὅτι θεόμιμόν ἔστι πρᾶγμα βασιλεία' (Delatte, p. 45, l. 10–11; see Dvornik, I, 1966: 276; Stewart 2003: 19).

817 In their writings, ethical imitation is depicted as the moral and spiritual path by which to ascent to perfection of virtue (Russell 2004: 161f., 233).

818 Theophylact of Ohrid 1981: ch. XXVI, p. 95 and Thomas Magister 1981: 118. On Eusebius, see Meier 2003: 132.

819 Bell 2009: 28f. The first signs of the infuence of Hellenism on Christian authors can be detected around the second and third centuries (see Dvornik, II, 1966: 583, 591ff.).

Basarab's theo- and christomimetic ideas tend rather towards a likeness, that is, a similarity to God (*homoiosis*) than an imitation of God or Christ (*imitatio* or μίμησις Θεοῦ). Those Byzantine authors who were strongly influenced by Hellenistic thought, like Eusebius or Agapetus, envisaged theomimesis as the imitation of divine actions and deeds. As long as the ruler acted *like* Christ, he *was* Christ by imitation.[820] This is, as it were, an idea of *ethical theomimesis*, as it was likewise propounded by Erasmus or Luther. At the core of ethical theomimesis lies the idea of the unity and harmony of Creation: 'The beauty of the cosmic order, says Ecphantus, is revealed straightway, if the one [the king] who imitates [God] in his virtue is beloved at once by Him, whom he is imitating, and by his subjects.'[821] The ruler who thus imitates guards and preserves the cosmic order, restoring it if necessary. The caring and providential actions of Christ Pantocrator epitomise the imitation of God by the Christian ruler.[822]

Homoiotic theomimesis places the emphasis on human nature, which – in the case of the Christian ruler – can by means of illumination ascend to God-likeness. Neagoe Basarab speaks of the Christian ruler as one 'exactly like God' (*întocmai cu dânsul*), an identity arising not by identical action, but by organic unity, as of two limbs of a single body. Basarab emphasises the sacramental restoration of *homoiosis* by the eucharist, which makes of the ruler a *theophoros* (God-bearer) and a God-like one.[823] Human beings bear the image of God by nature and by the act of Creation, in addition to which illumination does not reward the believer with any capabilities that might be super-natural, 'above nature' (*supernaturalia sunt*), but rather activates and intensifies human nature weakened by sin (*natura lapsa*).

820   Hunger 1964: 59; Dvornik, I, 1966: 275; Farina 1966: 108, 123, 125ff.; Bell 2009: 34; Kosuch 2011.
821   Ecphantus apud Martens 2003: 59.
822   Merki 1952: 105ff.; Anton 1968: 74ff., 111.
823   'If you have Christ as your head and if you consume His body in the eucharist, if you are His brother and His heir, if you are just like Him […]' ('[C]ând ai cap pre Hristos, cându din trupul lui te priceştuieşti, cându eşti frate lui şi moştean *şi întocmai cu dânsul* […]') (Neagoe Basarab 1984: 13). Emphasis added.

According to Basarab, the ruler – like Solomon – becomes the site of Godly wisdom, the *locus divinitatis*: '[A]nd they understood that God's wisdom dwelt within him.'[824] God is always in, with and alongside the ruler and, by that transparent organ, God acts in the world, the ruler allowing God's energies to shine out into the world. He is not God's deputy, but He is made present through the ruler in a form of mystical simultaneity that acquires political visibility. To say that God is with the ruler is to say that God is with His people, as one of Basarab's favourite biblical verses, Isa. 8:9–10 states. In homoiotic thought, virtues and good works are merely the fruits and consequences of *homoiosis*, not its precondition.[825] In other words, the theomimetic ruler acts well because he already is God-like and not because he is striving for God-likeness by imitation.[826]

This is not to say that Basarab was not in favour of acting in a moral and virtuous manner. On the contrary, he misses no opportunity to advocate doing so. But he does not think of virtue as an end in itself.[827] Nothing new could be acquired by virtue that was not already a natural possession bestowed by Creation, that is, immediacy to God and the uninterrupted dwelling in His presence, by which man, centred upon God, is flooded in light and made not only a *theophoros*, but indeed a *homoiousios*. Basarab holds human nature in its true and original state to be virtuous, which is one reason why, in the *Teachings*, he so strongly emphasises Orthodox Chalcedonian dyophysitism (the doctrine of the two natures) and speaks of monarchs as rulers in heaven and on earth. Like Justinian I before him, Neagoe Basarab considers the ruler to be Christ-like and to claim two dimensions of presence as a ruler: 'over life in the world and over life above the world'.[828]

---

824 '[Ş]i pricepură că locuiaşte într-însul înţelepciunea lui Dumnezeu' (Neagoe Basarab 1984: 37).

825 Agapetus was of the opinion that it was only by maintaining justice and showing mercy that the ruler became a homoiousios (see Agapetus 1981: ch. XXXVII, p. 70; XLIV, p. 72; XLV, p. 72 and LXIII, p. 77).

826 Müller-Schauenburg 2011: 297.

827 Voegelin 1957: 203; Kaldelis 2011: 130.

828 See Blum 1974: 121, 123f.

The *Teachings to Theodosius* are the only work of its kind to have been
written by a ruler for a ruler. Authors such as Agapetus, Theophylact of
Ohrid, Thomas Magister, Erasmus of Rotterdam, Martin Luther and
Niccolò Machiavelli never themselves ruled. Neagoe Basarab enjoyed nine
years of successful and calm government,[829] a reign that might well have
lasted some time longer had he not succumbed to disease. This fact ought to
make us reconsider the boundaries between idealism and realism, between
utopia and reality. On the one hand, it is surely a compelling thought that
most of the principles expressed in the treatise would have been applied
in reality. Yet it is sobering to recall that Theodosius, for whom the work
was written, managed to hold on to the Wallachian throne only for a few
months. Virtually nothing is known of his reign – including whether he
was inspired to pursue theomimesis himself. It would seem that the semantics of homoiotic theomimesis or christomimesis were as powerless
as those to be discussed in the following sections in guarding against the
contingency of history.

---

829   No fewer than thirty princes reigned in Wallachia between 1521 and 1623. The
      average reign thus can be seen to have lasted less than three and a half years (Oțetea
      1972: 568).

CHAPTER 3

Erasmus of Rotterdam and His *Education of a Christian Prince*: On the Ethical Theomimesis of the Christian Prince

> [The prince] should be constantly absorbing his [Christ's] teachings, gathered together in some convenient form from the original sources themselves, from which the teaching is imbibed not only more purely but also more effectively.
>
> Erasmus of Rotterdam

On few authors has as much been written as on Erasmus of Rotterdam (c. 1469–1536). Besides the critical editions of his works (and their translations) and correspondence,[1] centuries of scholarship have produced a quantity of studies that is virtually impossible to survey. Even scholars attempting to compile bibliographies of the works of Erasmus and of the studies concerned with them have found it impossible to produce a comprehensive overview.[2] It is therefore difficult for those researching on Erasmus to be sure of having come up with something altogether new.

The following chapter concentrates on the ethical theomimesis within the semantics of *Christianitas* as it features in the *Institutio Principis Christiani* (*Education of a Christian Prince* or *Education* for short), a mirror for princes by Erasmus first published in 1516. I shall begin by sketching out the place of Erasmus in the cultural phenomenon that is known as 'humanism', followed by a brief textual history of the *Education*. The key

---

1   On this, see Rummel 1985; L. Voet 1988.
2   Margolin 1963, 1969 and 1977. See also the updated bibliography of Erasmus in Margolin 2007.

concern, however, is Erasmus's argument regarding *Christianitas*, which he presents as an ethical form of the *imitatio* of God or Christ. Understood thus, *Christianitas* is formed according to the divine pattern of Christ in action, whom it makes present in the world or, specifically, in the political organisation of the state. The Christian ruler is, according to Erasmus, Christ actualised, and the *Education* describes this theomimetic relation of practical *Christianitas* in two principal lines of argument: first, the *Christiana humanitas* of both the ruler and his people as arising from education and piety; and second, the concord characteristic of a polity built around the pillar of Christ.

In this chapter, the second line of argument will be examined in three aspects. First, the question arises, in reading Erasmus, to what extent the ruler has an obligation towards his people – the concept of people having, moreover, a socio-political dimension (as *populus*) and a moral and ethical one (as *vulgus*). Second, it is important to consider the idea of monarchy, which offered Erasmus the theoretical framework for the articulation of his theo- or even christomimetism. The third aspect is the question of (world) peace – the peace, that is, of Christendom – as a medium for the realisation of a Christian (world) order.

All these aspects can be understood as belonging to a political theology of the ruler's God-likeness, a political theology which can be clearly discerned in Erasmus, but which scholarship has not hitherto considered in sufficient depth.

At this point, a hermeneutical clarification is in order. It is perhaps somewhat against the intentions of Erasmus to carve up his 'political system' into its various aspects like education, peace or *philosophia Christiana*. Such a classificatory method may be indispensable to modern analysis, but is quite alien to Erasmus and his integrative, holistic thought. For example, his statements regarding the *bonae litterae* may also be understood as contributing to a theology of Scripture; by the same token, his thoughts on education cannot be uncoupled from those on peace and hence on Christocentrism. Yet since many such *topoi* recur throughout his writings, a 'systemic' examination of Erasmus's political thought may nonetheless be attempted.

Erasmus as a Humanist

Though it is conventional and uncontroversial for scholars to refer to Erasmus as a 'humanist', in the letter dedicating the *Education* to Emperor Charles V (d. 1556), he describes himself as a 'theologian' (*theologus*).[3]

Scholarship – both on Erasmus and on humanism more generally – has failed to agree on a universally acceptable definition of 'humanism'. The following chapter hence assumes that there was never any such thing as 'humanism', understood as a coherent system. Humanism – the term was first used in 1808 by Friedrich Immanuel Niethammer (d. 1848)[4] – is rather the sum of various 'humanisms' or humanist approaches. If this chapter nonetheless refers to 'humanism' in the singular, it does so on the assumption that humanism was something of a unitary working method. As such, humanism promoted a philological and critical approach to literary sources from Greek, Hellenistic, Roman and Christian antiquity. Drawing on their reading of these sources, humanists favoured a practical philosophy and a theology of lived piety. Humanism was a methodology, but it was also a theological, philosophical and moral programme that concerned itself less with the objects of knowledge than with the ways and means by which knowledge might be acquired and imparted.[5] This expressed itself in the heterogeneity of 'humanism' and its discursive formation.[6] 'Humanism' can thus be understood as a

---

3 Erasmus-IPC: 134 (*Education* 4), line 58. On Charles V, see Kohler 1990.

4 Friedrich I. Niethammer, *Der Streit des Philanthropismus und Humanismus in der Theorie des Erziehungsunterrichtes unserer Zeit*, Jena 1808 (see Kristeller 1974: 16; Keßler 1998: 2).

5 In contrast to scholastic methods, which made knowledge itself to their subject, the *studia humanitatis* are forms of discussing the media of knowledge. Scholasticism examined the relationship of *res* and *verbum*, whereas humanism was concerned with the *verbum* as such: the emergence, function and quality of the *verbum* as a vehicle for *res*. The humanists worked, as it were, in the philosophy of language (see Münkler 1993: 555). Following Aristotle, the humanists emphasise that humans are distinct from animals only in language, which gives them an identity. Hence it is knowledge which, through education, becomes the exclusive means by which humans are fully formed (see Münkler 1993: 559f.).

6 Münkler 1993: 553ff.; Buck 1996: 1.

method[7] by which 'humanistic ideals' might be attained: a new and better kind of humanity brought into being by instruction, education and – if not in all humanists, then certainly in Erasmus – piety.

In its concern with *studia humanitatis*,[8] scholarship certainly was one aspect of humanism. But not exclusively so, for humanism was also to be understood as humanity (*humanitas*),[9] an attitude fittingly expressed in a letter by the Florentine chancellor Coluccio Salutati (d. 1406): 'For not only that virtue, which we are wont to call goodness, goes by that name [of *humanitas*], but also experience and erudition.'[10]

Erudition, in the humanist approach, connotes work proceeding by compilation and association (sometimes quite tangential) and drawing on a wide variety of sources from a diversity of historical eras and geographical locations. The example of the humanist Erasmus shows how his notion of erudite study tends towards a mosaic of ideas, encompassing multiple sources, approaches, interpretations, clues, allegories and metaphors.[11] In humanism, as represented by Erasmus, scholarship appears as a form of Christian education to virtues and pious action by knowledge and cultivation of its sources – of Scripture, the writings of the Fathers and the literature of Graeco-Roman antiquity.[12] Erasmus understands any

---

7   Μέθοδος (method), deriving from μετά' (towards) and ὁδός (path) might be understood as 'a path towards a particular goal'. On this see Augustijn 1991: 17.

8   Already in the fifteenth century, the canon of the *studia humanitatis* consisted of grammar, rhetoric, history, poetry and morals/ethics (Kristeller 1974: 17).

9   Kristeller 1974: 17f.

10   Apud Kessler 1968: 44. On Salutati, see Kessler 1968: 40.

11   The principal sources of the *Education* are considered to be the *Morals* of Plutach, the *Republic* of Plato, Cicero's *De Officiis* and authors such as Herodotus, Xenophon and Seneca (Herding 1966: 101; Born 1968: 34).

12   Hamm 1990: 158f, 195. Besides Jerome and Augustine, the Church Fathers whom Erasmus cites most frequently are: Pseudo-Dionysius the Areopagite, Origen, Cyprian, Ambrose, Basil of Caesarea and John Chrysostom (Béné 1969: 137ff., 276f.; Godin 1982; Augustijn 1991: 100). Erasmus knew that Pseudo-Dionysius was not St Paul's disciple mentioned in the Bible, but this did not keep him from quoting him frequently and making him one of the principal sources of the *Education* (Ritter 1993: 153f.). On Origen, Erasmus is recorded as saying: 'One page of Origen teaches me more than ten pages of Augustine' (apud Pfeiffer 1955: 186).

education to be 'humanistic' if it aims, in the Aristotelian sense,[13] to bring human nature, which is both social and endowed with reason, to its full flowering. 'Hence even the common people, in the ordinary language of daily conversation, denominate whatever is connected with mutual good-will, humane; so that the word humanity no longer describes man's nature, merely in a physical sense; but signifies humane manners, or a behaviour, worthy [of] the nature of man [...].'[14]

Concord, piety and education are the three media by which human beings, according to Erasmus, become truly human. The human being that Erasmus almost always has in mind is the Christian who by his actions follows and embodies Christ – the one, that is, who for ethical and practical purposes *is Christ*.[15] According to his own humanistic view of the human, Erasmus has a good deal to say about humans and humanity, but hardly anything about human institutions. To humanists in general and Erasmus in particular, human beings themselves are the *locus* of Christian life and hence themselves the *locus Christi*.[16]

The *Education*, which is under consideration here, is full of such associations. It would thus not do justice to Erasmus if one were to deconstruct his thought by laying bare its manifold tributaries. Often without quoting or citing them, Erasmus draws on sources both directly and, in the form of centuries of exegesis surrounding them, indirectly. To confront him with modern notions of originality would itself be somewhat lacking in that quality. Humanistic originality in general, and its Erasmian form in particular, was concerned less with novelty than with returning to the roots of the human mind and of human knowledge (*renovatio*) – roots that humanists located in the golden age[17] of

13   Aristotle, *Nicomachean Ethics*: book 1, ch. 13 and book 2, ch. 2; *Politics*: book 1.

14   'Hinc est, videlicet, quod vulgus, quidquid ad mutuam benevolentiam pertinet, humanum apellat, ut humanitatis vocabulum non iam naturam nobis declaret, sed mores hominis naturae dignos' (Erasmus of Rotterdam: original quoted according Schottenloher 1971: 671). Translation: Erasmus *Complaint*: p. 6.

15   Caspari 1947.

16   Scribner 1970: 4.

17   The notion of the 'golden age' is of course imaginary and originates in Hesiod (Klein 1988: 605ff.). It is culturally conditioned and has been variously applied throughout history. Christian theology fund its own golden age to have been in

antiquity.[18] What most humanists, Erasmus included, meant by 'antiquity' was in fact Christian antiquity,[19] the time, that is, of the Church Fathers, whose writings and ideas, spread and discussed in many new editions and commentaries, really did enjoy a Renaissance from the fifteenth century onwards. The 'fashionable saints'[20] of the humanists were Jerome (*vir trilinguis, divus litterarum princeps*[21]) and Augustine.[22] The preference for Jerome displays some important traits of humanism, particularly its preference for piety in practice, for lived theology and learning, but also for eloquence

---

the fourth century, at the time of the promulgation of the trinitarian dogmas. The Stoics situated the golden age at the dawn of humanity, in *illud tempus*, an age of innocence, purity, freedom from suffering, etc. The Byzantines, by contrast, understood the golden age to refer to the political blossoming of the Christian community within the boundaries of the Byzantine Empire (Podskalsky 1972: 73; Klein 1988: 608).

18   Herding 1974: 106, 119; Augustijn 1991: 18. The differing adoption of ideas by Erasmus can be seen in his treatment of sources: the ancient authors (Plato, Aristotle, Xenophon) are usually quoted or paraphrased, while mediaeval authors (including even Augustine) are mentioned only rarely. Erasmus did not mention the mirror for princes *De regimine principum* of Giles of Rome (Aegidius Romanus; died 1316) at all, though it was well known at the Burgundian court and most likely also to Erasmus himself. Its French translation was published around the time of the *Education*, the manuscript original had long been in the library of the dukes of Burgundy (Herding 1966: 142). It is nonetheless impossible to condemn Erasmus, for he studied the teachings of the Fathers and internalised them to such a degree that he came to consider them as his own and made use of them accordingly (Herding 1974: 120). On the humanists' image of the Middle Ages, see Mertens 1992.

19   The attraction of the humanists to pagan ideas is often over-emphasised and deserving of scrutiny. Their attempts to free themselves from dogmatic and institutional shackles (Münkler 1993: 553) should not be mistaken for a desire to return to paganism, but rather for a *reformatio* of the Christian faith on a practical and ethical basis. Nonetheless, there is no denying the humanists' progressive approach, without which much ancient learning would now be lost (Keßler 1998: 3 n. 2, 6ff.).

20   The term is from Hamm 1990: 157.

21   An epithet bestowed by his biographer, the Knight Hospitaller Laudivio Zacchia, in his *Vita Beati Hieronymi* (1470) (Rice 1988: 102).

22   Fricke 1967: 17; Béné 1969: 88ff.; Olin 1988; Augustijn 1991: 38; Augustijn 1993: 5. Of Augustine's writings, Erasmus drew most heavily on *De doctrina christiana* (Béné 1969: passim).

in the service of faith and for the appropriation of ideas from pagan philosophy for the purposes of Christianity.

Some scholars have described Erasmian humanism as a 'biblical humanism', aiming for a practical theology of renewal based on the Bible and in the tradition of the Fathers.[23] In this context, classical authors such as Plato, Aristotle and Plutarch[24] played the same role for the humanists as they did for the early Christian authors some one thousand years previously: paving the way for Christ (within the *revelatio naturalis*) by a *praeparatio evangelica*.[25]

In its discussion of the *bonae litterae* (or *politiores litterae*[26]) and their use for Christian *pietas*, humanism harks back to the classical aesthetics of *prodesse et delectare*. It 'seeks, in the *studia humanitatis*, to combine the *delectatio* or *voluptas* of the beautiful with the *utilitas* and *necessitas* of what is good and true'.[27] In a work of his youth, *De contemptu mundi*

23   Augustijn 1993: 2ff.; Mühlenberg 1998: 166ff.
24   Especially the *Morals* (Aulotte 1965: 320).
25   Krumbacher 1897: 39; Pfeiffer 1955: 182; Maier/Meister 1966: 44; Schottenloher 1971: 673; Klein 1988: 602; Wirth 1989: 93; Tatakis 2003: 54ff.
26   'Polished literature' (Augustijn 1991: 18).
27   Hamm 1990: 64 n. 97; see Müller 2006: 108ff. A discussion of the intellectual enjoyment of *delectatio* or of intellectual *voluptas* can first be found in Lucian of Samosata (d. c. 180) in the aesthetic context of classical dance (Lucian, *De saltatione*: sec. 6, l. 4 and sec. 71, l. 2). However, the argument is soon extended to the realms of education, philosophy and science. Basil the Great, in his sermons on the Psalms (*Homiliae super Psalmos*, PG 29: 212) writes of this new understanding that these three spheres not only meet the criteria of *necessitas* required for the soul's salvation, but also offered the advantage of pleasure (*delectatio*). Under the influence of Plato, Augustine discussed the useful as the foundation of the political. He expanded and refined Plato's theory by dividing the useful into the two dimensions of *fruitio* (enjoyment) and *utilitas* (necessity): 'Those things which are objects of enjoyment make us happy. Those things which are objects of use assist, and (so to speak) support us in our efforts after happiness, so that we can attain the things that make us happy and rest in them. We ourselves, again, who enjoy and use these things, being placed among both kinds of objects, if we set ourselves to enjoy those which we ought to use, are hindered in our course, and sometimes even led away from it; so that, getting entangled in the love of lower gratifications, we lag behind in, or even altogether turn back from, the pursuit of the real and proper objects of enjoyment' (Augustine, *On Christian Doctrine* [*De doctrina Christiana*], book I, ch. 3). Enjoyment of God (*fruitio Dei*) was the highest form of love and the good.

(date uncertain, but after his entry into Stein monastery in 1487), Erasmus argued in favour of the Epicurean notion of *voluptas* while redefining it as referring to spiritual and pious pleasures and proposing it instead of the Christian notion of *felicitas*. It was in this context that Erasmus described the monastery and the life it offered as a *hortus deliciarum* and *paradisus voluptatis*.[28]

Much has been made of the humanists' aversion to scholastic methods of attaining knowledge, methods that depended heavily on logical and abstract reasoning in order to obtain knowledge of objects (*res*). This supposed disdain has often been overstated, and not all humanists took an explicit stance against scholasticism. Yet the methodical differences are such that it is indeed justified to speak of a humanistic aversion to highly speculative 'scholasticism',[29] as it was taught at the universities of the late Middle Ages. What they found objectionable was above all the absence of life from the lofty spheres of abstraction. To their mind, not enough space was given in their speculation to useful life, suffering and resurrection of Christ. In scholasticism, the text was seen as an image of substance (*substantia*) and concepts as modes of its subsistence. Logical argumentation by way of *quaestiones* and commentary was a means of retracing being, of making it palpable. In humanistic approaches, by contrast, the text is not a keeper of

---

By virtue of His own goodness, God was merciful to us, but we loved our neighbour by virtue of God's goodness: 'He pities us that we may fully enjoy Himself; we pity one another that we may fully enjoy Him' (Augustine, *On Christian Doctrine*, book I, ch. 33). The *fruitio Dei* is accordingly the medium of charity and hence of the social: 'The good use the world that they may enjoy God: the wicked, on the contrary, that they may enjoy the world would fain use God, – those of them, at least, who have attained to the belief that He is and takes an interest in human affairs' (Augustine, *The City of God*, book XV, ch. 7). The *Decretum Gratiani* likewise shows that what is beautiful must also be useful (*utile*) if it is indeed to be good (i.e., profitable) (see *Decretum Gratiani* C II, 135).

28 Bultot 1969: 237; Mestwerdt 1917: 234f.
29 The term 'scholasticism' is far too broad, there never having been a single scholasticism, but rather several approaches to attaining knowledge in a manner that might generally be called 'scholastic'. Among them were Thomist realism (the *via antiqua*) and Ockhamite nominalism (the *via moderna*), as well as a variety of attempts to mediate between these two main currents (Mestwerdt 1917: 100f.; Dolfen 1936: 7ff.).

being, but rather a complex form of expressing the experience of being in a variety of cultural and practical contexts – hence its striving for philological purity and the accuracy of language, sources and expression.[30]

Erasmus first familiarised himself with the scholastic method, and its nominalist variety in particular, during his first stay in Paris (1495–1499). From the very beginning, he seems to have cared little for that kind of theology, considering it to be dry, remote and lifeless.[31] This impression would have been enhanced by the fact that the contemporary exponents of scholastic methods were themselves but epigones of the old masters; they made no contribution to the advancement of their discipline and remained stuck in the axiomatic and stereotypical clichés of 'classical scholasticism'. Erasmus found that style to be particularly irritating, though he had no fundamental objection to the scholastic manner of argument. He admired Thomas Aquinas, Peter Lombard and Duns Scotus, all of whom he quoted on occasion.[32]

Nor did Erasmus remain immune to the influence of Aristotelianism. In the *Education*, he adopted the three levels on which Aristotelian political theory was supposed to operate, as they were translated by the Provençal scholar Magister Arnulf in the thirteenth century. Rule was understood as (1) political, as rule over many; (2) economic, as rule over the family and household; and (3) ethical, as ruler over the self.[33] Yet at heart Erasmus, like all other humanists, held the Platonic view of the true political philosophy as wisdom in direct opposition to the teachings of the Latin Aristotelians:

> [N]ot that philosophy, I mean, which argues about elements and primal matter and motion and the infinite, but that which frees the mind from the false opinions of the multitude and from wrong desires and demonstrates the principles of right government by reference to the example set by the eternal powers.[34]

30   Walter 1991: 95; Keßler 1998: 8; Nitschke 2000: 115.
31   Allen 1914: 104; Augustijn 1993: 1.
32   Mestwerdt 1917: 224; Dolfen 1936: 10ff., 82ff.; Augustijn 1991: 28, 103, 123.
33   Fidora 2007: 28ff. Aristotle was influential for the humanists, too, as he had been for the scholastics of the high Middle Ages, but especially in his writings on practical philosophy: the *Nicomachean Ethics* and the *Politics* (Kristeller 1974: 43).
34   '[P]hilosophiam, inquam, non istam, quae de principiis de prima materia de motu aut infinito disputat, sed quae falsis vulgi opinionibus ac viciosis affectibus animum liberans ad aeterni numinis exemplar recte gubernandi rationem commonstrat'

In opposition to the highly sophisticated academic scholasticism of the late Middle Ages stood a contemporaneous trend known as *devotio moderna*.[35] Erasmus was familiar with it and most probably influenced by it in some form or another.[36] As a boy, Erasmus had attended the chapter school of St Lebuinus in Deventer, which was influenced by *devotio moderna*, though his memories of that time were far from pleasant. The derogatory remarks he made later in life have led many of his biographers to question the extent to which Erasmus really was influenced by *devotio moderna*, a question on which no consensus has yet been reached.[37]

In 1487 Erasmus entered the monastery of Stein, near Gouda, thus joining the order of the Augustinian Canons[38] and encountering 'humanist' scholarship.[39] The canons were keen readers of the pagan authors, practised the art of poetry and maintained a lively correspondence, both amongst themselves and with other scholars beyond the walls of the monastery.[40] Stimulated by this intellectual atmosphere, Erasmus composed the first writings of his own, *De contemptu mundi* and, around 1495, *Antibarbarorum*

(Erasmus-IPC: 133–134, lines 19–24; *Education* 2). See also Erasmus-IPC: 145, l. 265–268, where Erasmus indirectly advocates a return to Christian antiquity by referring to Plato's opinion whereby there was no difference between 'theology' (speaking of God) and 'philosophy'. This stance can also be found in Christian authors of late antiquity, who argued that Christian theology was nothing but the philosophy of the ancients, perfected by Christ (Kobusch 2006: 26ff.).

35   The movement was initiated by Geert Groote (d. 1384) (Augustijn 1991: 15, plus citations). See also Hyma: 1965; Post 1968.

36   Pfeiffer 1955: 177f.; Scribner 1970: 4f.; Münkler 1993: 553.

37   Though this influence should not be overstated, it certainly was real (Mestwerdt 1917: 174; Ijsewijn 1969; Rummel 1985: 4ff.; Levi 1986: xiv; Halkin 1989: 9ff.; Augustijn 1991: 15, 27; Margolin 2007: 43ff.).

38   On this, see Dickinson 1950.

39   Erasmus-*Briefe* 1956; Béné 1969: 28ff.; DeMolen 1987; Halkin 1989: 15ff.; Augustijn 1993: 1f. In fact, Erasmus's first encounter with humanist scholarship seems to have taken place earlier, as a student in Deventer of the Dutch humanist Alander Hegius, through whom Erasmus came to admire and be influenced by the Italian humanist Lorenzo Valla (Mestwerdt 1917: 149ff.; 207ff., 234ff.; Scribner 1970: 6). On Valla, see Mestwerdt 1917: 29ff.; Garin 1947: 50ff.

40   On correspondence as a medium of group dynamics and formation within monasteries, see Müller 2006: 69ff.

Liber.[41] It was at St Lebunius and Stein that Erasmus acquired the ancient languages, Latin and Greek.[42]

In 1493, Erasmus was appointed secretary to Bishop Henry of Cambrai, a scion of the aristocratic van Bergen[43] family, who was close to the emperor. This position allowed Erasmus to make his first contacts at the imperial and Burgundian court.[44] During the emperor's minority, he would later become *conseiller aux honneurs* to Charles V,[45] to whom he dedicated the first edition of the *Education*.[46]

Erasmus was a humanist by education and interests. In thirteenth- and early fourteenth-century Italy – the heartland of the humanist tradition, among whose earliest representatives was Petrarch (d. 1374)[47] – *humanista* was the epithet given to the teachers and university professors who taught the *trivium* of grammar, rhetoric and poetics.[48] The beginnings of humanism

41 Pfeiffer 1936; Matheeussen 1969: 354ff.; Béné 1969: 52ff., 59ff.; Scribner 1970: 7ff.; DeMolen 1987; Augustijn 1991: 22ff.

42 Latin was Erasmus's forte; his style bordered on perfection and received its final polish in his Paris years. His Greek, on the other hand, was much weaker in his youth. He improved it during visits to England (1499–1500) and Italy (1506–1509) (Augustijn 1993: 1; Fabisch 2008: 195,197). From about 1500 onwards, he acquired the works of Plato, at considerable expense, in an attempt to practise his Greek (Augustijn 1991: 37).

43 Walther 1911: 18ff.; Schoeck 1988; Augustijn 1991: 12, 24.

44 Ribhegge 2000: 164ff., 171f.

45 Though the title was honorary, it came with an annual pension of 200 florins, payment of which, however, was somewhat erratic (Walther 1911: 67; Fricke 1967: 18; Augustijn 1991: 71). 'Around the bureaucratic core, to which the oldest court records still refer simply as the *Conseil Privé*, there accrued the *further council* [emphasis added], in which were assembled all who enjoyed the respect and the attention of the prince and his court. They were especially princes of the blood, knights of the Golden Fleece, provincial governors and the highest officials at the court' (Walser 1959: 7). Erasmus was a member of the 'further council'.

46 On the stations in the life of Erasmus, see Hyma 1972; Reventlow 1997: 55ff.

47 Garin 1947: 11; Buck 1996: 3ff.

48 Münkler 1993: 554. In the 'humanist' age beginning in the fifteenth century, these three disciplines formed the core of the *studia humanitatis*. On the important role played by rhetoric in European humanist discourse, see Helmrath 2013: 159ff.

appear to be linked to a revival of Plato in Italy and especially in Florence.[49] Following the Council of Ferrara-Florence (1438–1439), many scholars from the Byzantine Empire found refuge in the cities of Italy, bringing their knowledge of Greek, important manuscripts and a long tradition of *studium* with them. Manuel Chrysoloras, who was active in fourteenth-century Florence, was one of these important Byzantine scholars.[50] From Italy, the new intellectual trend spread northwards across the Alps and soon reached Germany, France, the Low Countries and England.[51]

In the age of Erasmus, however, humanists tended to congregate not so much at universities as around printing presses.[52] Whereas (late) medi-aeval professors and scholars tended also to be members of the clergy and relied on the infrastructure of the Church for financial security, the human-ists instead attached themselves to the dynamic urban middle class.[53] Like many other humanists, Erasmus, during the early stages of his career, was forced to earn his living as tutor to the sons of patricians and merchants.[54] The growth of printing created, in the 'bourgeois' printing workshop, a

49 Where the Platonic academy of Marsilio Ficino grew. Within the context of this re-naissance of Plato, efforts were made to incorporate the neo-Platonic currents that had continued to play a role in Byzantine philosophy (Garin 1947: 154ff.), in order to reconcile Plato and Aristotle and to create the impression of a continuum of development from one to the other (Mestwerdt 1917: 32f.; Garin 1947: 70ff., 96ff.; Kristeller 1974: 32; Kristeller 1976a; Münkler 1993: 555,572).

50 Kristeller 1974: 151f.; Augustijn 1991: 17. Among the other Byzantine scholars who made important contributions to this cultural transfer were Theodorus Gaza (Ferrara), John Argyropoulos (Florence and Rome), Demetrios Chalkokondyles (Padua, Florence, Pavia), Constantine Laskaris (Messina) and Marcus Musurus (Venice and Padua).

51 Kristeller 1976b.

52 Antwerp, for instance, had no university, but a vigorous intellectual life centred on the printing press. In Basel, too, though there was a university, the centres of cul-tural life were the Froben and Auerbach printing workshops (Augustijn 1991: 11f.; Müller 2006: 296ff.). On the relationship between the humanists and the univer-sities, see Hammerstein 1981; Moraw 1993; Buck 1996: 25.

53 Buck 1987: 177ff.

54 Halkin 1989: 31ff.; Augustijn 1991: 1; Buck 1996: 31. During his stay in England, Erasmus was tutor to a nobleman, William Blount, Lord Mountjoy (Augustijn 1991: 32).

virtual agora of controversy, discussion and scholarly exchange that was far more conducive to humanist study and erudition than the seclusion of monastic libraries is likely to have been.

The humanists cultivated this atmosphere of exchange not least in the genre of the mirror for princes, of which *The Education of a Christian Prince* is an example. This attitude was founded on the humanist observation that humans existed in dialogue with the world and with each other, that is, humans stay in a dialogical relation to everything.[55] To Erasmus the humanist, the state is the communicative and practical medium of Christian realisation, with the prince, according to theomimetic criteria, embodying Christ Himself.[56] The central idea of the *Education* is in keeping with the tradition of the *Fürstenspiegel* as a genre:[57] it is an ethical and moral as well as a political treatise, in which political action and the political presence of the ruler are understood as media of Christian salvation.[58]

On the Textual History of *The Education of a Christian Prince*

Erasmus composed the *Education* at the same time as two other works: the second edition of his *Adagia*[59] and the *Annotationes in Novum Testamentum*. The possibility that these works and their ideas may have had some mutual influence cannot therefore be excluded.[60] Furthermore, the *Education* stand in direct relation to Erasmus's *Panegyricus*, which was composed for Charles V's father, Philip, and proclaimed before the assembled estates of Brabant to celebrate Philip's return from Spain. As Erasmus

55 Garin 1947: 12f.; Münkler 1993: 557f., 560f.; Mertens 1997.
56 Herding 1974: 111.
57 Augustijn 1991: 72.
58 Fricke 1967: 21f.
59 *Adagiorum collectanea* are collections, with commentary, of Greek and Latin proverbs, phrases, riddles, etc. The first edition of the *Adages* was published in 1500, the second in 1515. The collections grew in scope as time went on (Fricke 1967: 17; Born 1968: 5; Halkin 1989: 62ff.; Augustijn 1991: 37, 72; Augustijn 1993: 7).
60 Herding 1974: 97.

wrote in a letter to Marten van Doorp in May 1515, the *Panegyricus* anticipates ideas of the *Education* in its veiled praise of the ruler:

> In my book on the education of the prince I openly expound the subjects in which
> a prince should be brought up. In my *Panegyricus*, though under cover of praising a
> prince, I pursue indirectly the same subject that I pursued openly in the earlier [i.e.
> previously mentioned] work.[61]

Moreover, the first edition of the *Education* was printed, in May 1516,
alongside the *Panegyricus*.[62] Among the other writings to be counted
among the political works of Erasmus are *Encomium moriae* (1511) and
Querela Pacis (1517).[63]

In a letter dated 12 May 1516, Erasmus wrote to the Nuremberg humanist Willibald Pirkheimer (d. 1530)[64] that his *Education* was currently
being printed ('*excuditur nunc libellus De Institutione Principis*').[65] This
libellus may have been written – like the later *Querela Pacis*, which deals
with similar ideas – at the suggestion of the Burgundian statesman Jean le

---

61   'In libello De Principis Institutione palam admonemus quibus rebus principem
       oportet esse instructum. In Panegyrico sub laudis praetextu hoc ipsu tamen agimus
       oblique quod illic egimus aperta fronte' (Erasmus-OE: Ep. 337, p. 93; English
       translation in Erasmus *Correspondence*: Letter 337, pp. 114f.). The *Panegyricus* was
       printed the same year by Martens of Antwerp, on which see Fricke 1967: 19; Born
       1968: 5f.; Levi 1986: xiv; Halkin 1989: 70; Augustijn 1991: 35.
62   Fricke 1967: 17; Born 1968: 7, 26f.; Herding 1974: 99, 105. Scholarship was long
       divided over the date of the first edition of the *Education* (Enthoven 1909: 313).
       May, rather than March 1515 is now the widely accepted date.
63   Levi 1986: xiv; Münkler 1993: 592. Otto Herding does not count the *Encomium*
       among the political writings and considers the *Education* in relation to the
       Enchiridion militis christiani and *Querela Pacis*. The *Enchiridion* (first edition
       1503) was designed to accompany the spiritual struggle of Christians against sin,
       temptation and the flesh. The book was strongly influenced by Plato and Augustine,
       and their division between matter and spirit, body and soul; An *enchiridion* is a
       manual or handbook, but also a dagger or short sword. On this, see Auer 1954;
       Herding 1966: 134; Fricke 1967: 17; Béné 1969: 127ff.; Matheeussen 1969: 357f.;
       Scribner 1970: 5f.; Halkin 1989: 73ff.; Augustijn 1991: 43ff., 99; Jardine 1997.
64   On this, see Holzberg 1981; Fuchs 2006.
65   Erasmus-OE: Ep. 407, p. 236.

Sauvage for Charles V, then still a minor of 15 years.[66] A letter records that in May 1515, Erasmus had a long conversation with le Sauvage in Geneva.[67] The *Education* appears to have been begun in 1515 – it is mentioned in a letter from March 1515[68] – and completed the following year.[69]

The treatise enjoyed considerable success. An edition printed by his employer, the Basel publisher Froben,[70] appeared in the same year. While Erasmus was in England, Dirk Martens of Louvain reprinted another edition without the author's knowledge and much to his annoyance (*libellum de Principe, quem furtim excudit interim cum ego abesse in Anglia*).[71] Further editions soon followed: a third with Badius Ascensius of Paris in March 1517, and a fourth, revised in both style and content, again with Froben in 1518. It is to this edition that Erasmus first refers in a letter to the Englishman Cuthert Tunstall of 22 October 1518,[72] and it is this second Froben edition that tends to be considered the canonical version of the text. Unlike the first edition, it was no longer dedicated to Charles V, but to his brother, Ferdinand I of Habsburg (d. 1564).[73] The treatise ran to 33 editions in Latin and 21 translations into various languages.[74]

---

66 Münkler 1993: 592. The *Querela* was written chiefly as a manifesto of peace for the political reconciliation between European monarchs. A particularly important aim was a peace treaty between the Holy Roman Emperor Maximilian I and Francis I of France (Bainton 1951; Fricke 1967: 18; Born 1968: 7f.; Augustijn 1991: 73; Augustijn 1993: 8).

67 Erasmus-OE: Ep. 332 (to Pieter Gillis, 7. Mai 1515); English translation in Erasmus *Correspondence*: Letter 332, p. 84.

68 Enthoven 1909: 312 (with citation).

69 Herding 1968: 535; Herding 1974: 107.

70 On Froben, see Münkler 1993: 558. Erasmus had lived in Basel since 1514, where he acted as editor of works published by Froben (Augustijn 1991: 40; Augustijn 1993: 2).

71 Erasmus-OE: Ep. 732 (to Beatus Rhenanus, 6. Dezember 1517); English translation in Erasmus *Correspondence*:: Letter 732, p. 229.

72 Erasmus-OE: Ep. 886.

73 On Ferdinand I, see Sicken 1990.

74 Vincent 1937; Herding 1974: 101ff., 114f. This success story may be told by the following dates: In Erasmus's lifetime, German translations were produced, both in 1521, by Leo Jud in Zurich and Georg Spalatin in Augsburg. Though they were popular among German readers, the rift between Erasmus and the Reformation prevented further editions from appearing. Other translations were published in

Erasmus composed the *Education* in his capacity as counsellor (*consiliarius*) to Charles V, an office that he had held before beginning work on the treatise.[75] It was planned, it would seem, also to recommend Erasmus as counsellor to Charles's brother, Ferdinand I of Habsburg. It may be that Erasmus dedicated the second edition of the *Education* to Ferdinand in the hope of furthering his career prospects.[76] Such dedications form part of a long tradition. In 1468 Martinus Phileticus, teacher of Greek in Rome, dedicated his translation of Isocrates' *Ad Nicoclem*[77] to Emperor Frederick III (d. 1493). Erasmus drew on this this work in his own *Education*.[78]

The *Education* was well received at the courts of Europe and used in educating future monarchs: it was read by Henry VIII and Edward VI of England as well as by Charles V and Ferdinand.[79] That numerous rulers were familiar with the treatise is not, of course, to say that they applied its precepts. Compared to Machiavelli, his contemporary, Erasmus may have struck some of his readers as idealistic and unrealistic. Guillaume Budé (Budaeus), a scholar of Greek from Paris who knew Erasmus and was likewise author of a mirror for princes (*Institution du Prince*, 1518),[80] accused the *Education* of being 'meagre, unsubstantial talk full of timidity and too many fine subtleties' ('*tenuis loqui, nimirum anxias ac nimirum subtiles argutias*').[81]

Danish (Roskilde, 1534), Italian (Venice, 1539) and two in French (by Jean Leblond, 1546, and Claude Joly, 1665) (Brissaud 1898; Charlier 1912; Herding 1966: 115f.; Herding 1968: 538f. and n. 40a, p. 544; Augustijn 1993: 2, 9f.). For the period 1515–1703, Ludwig Enthoven found twenty-four complete and four abridged editions as well as fifteen translations (Enthoven 1909: 313). Lester K. Born, in 1968, put the figure at sixteen translations (Born 1968: 28).

75   Herding 1974: 107; Münkler 1993: 592.
76   Herding 1974: 102.
77   Isocrates died 338 BC.
78   Erasmus-IC: 134. See Herding 1966: 102f.; Fricke 1967: 19.
79   Herding 1974: 103; Schrader 1990: 184f.
80   Unlike Erasmus, Budé wrote in favour of absolute monarchy. His treatise can be read as an attempt to praise King Francis I (d. 1547) and his policy of centralisation (Triwunatz 1903; Enthoven 1909: 314; Fricke 1967: 24; Born 1968: 28; Marin 1988).
81   Apud Herding 1974: 99.

Attacks on the work came from several sides: Erasmus was accused of pacifism and his royal readers warned against adopting that attitude. The theologians of the Parisian faculty of arts accused Erasmus of heresy and his pacifism as undermining political order and the power of the ruler (*enervat omnem politiam*). So fierce was some of the criticism he encountered that Erasmus felt compelled to issue an apology in 1531, in which he can be seen to modify some of his earlier pacifist opinions, as expressed in the *Education*.[82] The apology was addressed to one of his critics, Alberto Pio.

Both its popularity and the criticism to which it gave rise testify to the *Education*'s status as an early fifteenth-century bestseller. Among its notable strengths was its theological underpinning, from which Erasmus developed, in an aphoristic style, one of the most important models of early modern political theology. Though Erasmus styled himself as a 'theologian' at the outset of the *Education*, is has barely at all been considered as a theological work by scholars, who have preferred to focus on its political, social and even socio-economic aspects. Yet at the centre of the *Education*'s theoretical structure stands Christ, Christ as the *ruler* who forms the *axis mundi*. The central message of the *Education* is the realisation of *Christianitas* through ruler and people, by the prince becoming Christ actualised in his deeds. As such, the Christian prince is at the centre of the state and of the Christian – that is, the pacific – human world order. If nothing else, that is theology.[83]

Education and Politics: On the Political Education of the Christian Prince

The following chapter is intended to show how the Erasmian view of education and learning constitutes an approach to practical theology, in the sense of a pedagogical work on lived piety.[84] It is a theology, moreover,

82   Herding 1974: 108.
83   Becht 2000: 97.
84   Rädle 1989: 216.

that assumes the soteriological and cosmological finality of the Christian order. Only by understanding this theological finality, with the hereafter as its focal point, can the *Education* be understood appropriately. Earthy happiness in the political framework of the community of Christian states is the preliminary to and image of future bliss in the kingdom of God. To Erasmus, education, rather than asceticism and mysticism, is the path by which human beings can hope to be deified: 'Such is the power of education, as Plato has written, that a man who has been correctly brought up emerges as a kind of divine creature [...].'[85] True Christianity, according to Erasmus, could not be considered apart from education. For a political man, to be a Christian prince was a quality rather of education than of his religious affiliation. It was impossible to act rightly – that is, in a Christian manner – unless one had been brought up to do so. The Erasmian ideal of the Christian ruler admits no division between the *negocium honestissimorum studiorum* and the *negocium principis*:[86] it is among the properties of good rule that the prince should be well educated.

Yet according to Erasmus, education and learning were to strengthen not just the power of the intellect, but also of piety. *Eruditio* was of little use if it did not also lead to *pietas*. In praising the benefits of education, Erasmus summons Basil of Caesarea as authority, whose homily *Ad adolescentes*[87] argued for the necessity of education for a truly Christian life.[88] The study

---

85   'Tantam vim habet educatio, vt Plato scripserit hominem recte institutum in diuinum quoddam animal euadere' (Erasmus-IPC: 188, l. 707–708, *Education* 72).

86   Apud Herding 1974: 102.

87   Basil of Caesarea, *Address to Young Men on the Right Use of Greek Literature*. URL: <https://www.ccel.org/ccel/pearse/morefathers/files/basil_litterature01.htm>, accessed 06-05-2020. On this, see Béné 1969: 138.

88   Buck 1987: 39. Whereas many fourth-century Christians were aware of the benefits of a good classical education, there were voices, particularly among monks, who condemned pagan culture as leading Christians astray and of no use for a pious life. In a fourth-century letter, Gregory of Nazianzus encouraged his friend Basil: 'Go ahead, mock and disparage my region. Whether you're playing around or being serious doesn't matter. Simply let yourself smile, take advantage of our education, and enjoy our friendship' (Gregory of Nazianzus, Ep. 4, p. 58f). See also Basil's answer in Basil of Caesarea, Ep. 94, 158f. Basil was in a lively intellectual exchange with the

of the *bonae litterae* (especially of the moral writings of the classics)[89] was a preliminary to the *sacrae litterae* and found its fulfilment in a pious life according to the example of Christ.[90] The Erasmian ideal human is the *homo duplex*.[91] True *humanitas*, in this view, is *humanitas* healed in Christ (*restauratio verae humanitatis*), while true wisdom is *pietas* grown from *eruditio*.[92]

From a theological perspective, the Erasmian concept of *humanitas* and his partiality for pagan authors has been accused of Pelagianism:

> But it does suggest a confidence in the powers of redeemed nature which, spelled out in theological terms, would clearly have been heretical, because it meant both allowing grace to pagans and endowing nature with the power, at any rate, to accept grace, which was 'semi-pelagian'.[93]

What official Christian dogma rejected was not the notion that grace might be present in pagans. Without the grace of God imparted by the *revelatio naturalis* and the divine *pronoia*, the world – be it Christian or pagan – could not exist at all. Even before Christ there were humans who, as official doctrine maintains, were good and carried within them the moral law (Rom. 2:12ff.) and who were able to recognise the good and partake of grace after a fashion. But for such people, Christ's coming into the world and His message would not have been possible. The Erasmian idea that the pagan philosophers had paved the way for Christ and participated in the *revelatio naturalis*[94] did not contradict the teachings of

---

famous pagan rhetorician, Libanios (d. c. 393), whose paganism did not deter Basil from sending him Christian students for training (Stiglmayr 1914: 17ff.).

89   Plutarch and Cicero were of considerable importance to the practical theology of Erasmus (Scribner 1970: 7; Augustijn 1991: 75).

90   Augustijn 1991: 25.

91   Matheeussen 1969: 353, 363, 374.

92   To the mind of Erasmus, an education neither leading to *pietas* nor even aiming for it was mere paganism (Matheeussen 1969: 364; Scribner 1970: 10; Reventlow 1997: 61). 'It was his firm conviction that ignorance of language and literature were the principal cause for the decline [...] of Christian life, not lack of faith' (Pfeiffer 1955: 182).

93   Levi 1986: xxv.

94   Krumbacher 1897: 39; Ueberweg 1928: 17; Wirth 1989: 93.

the Church and thus did not constitute 'semi-Pelagianism' any more than did Erasmus's criticism of the Augustinian dependence of man on grace.[95]

Erasmus saw the path to *Christianitas* as consisting of education and learning – the *Christianitas*, that is, of both the ruler and the (Christian) people. Through education, it was possible to combine secular, political peace within the state, with religious fulfilment.[96] Education led to the edification of *humanitas*, of a true humanity restored in Christ and residing in political harmony.

In the humanist view, human beings are born, not in possession of perfect humanity, but only with the potential for becoming a perfect human being. This might be accomplished by forming matter through education.[97] Consequently, the Erasmian view of the prince's upbringing and education is also a soteriological claim with regard to Christ and His heavenly kingdom. A Christian prince may contribute to the improvement of the world, just as a tyrant to its ruin. Rule thus appears as a responsibility that is both missionary and cosmological.[98] For it is the ruler's *Christianitas* that constitutes the decisive difference in quality between him and pagan rulers. God having become man in Christ, it was by the criteria of His message that good rule should be measured:

> Whenever you think of yourself as a prince, always remember the fact that you are *a Christian prince*! You should be as different from even the noble pagan prince as a Christian is from a pagan.[99]

The *rex philosophus*, in the sense of the Platonic concept of philosophy,[100] is a medium of moral praxis and virtuous action, both of which are

---

95   Burger 1993.

96   Augustijn 1993: 5.

97   Musolff 2003: 29.

98   Münkler 1993: 593.

99   'Quoties venit in mentem te principem esse, pariter succurrat et illud te Christianum esse principem, vt intelligas te a laudatis quoque gentilium principibus tantum oportere abesse, quantum abest ab ethnico Christianus' (Erasmus-IPC: 146, l. 327–329; *Education* 17, emphasis added).

100 Plato, *Republic*: book IV.

grounded in right knowledge.[101] Moreover, rule is an art (*ars bene regnandi*) to be learned, in the sense of the Greek *techné*.[102] To Erasmus, it is not enough for a ruler to be predisposed by birth to rule well, for he may in time become corrupt and perverted. Nobody could be a Christian ruler without education as the way of consolidating and fulfilling this natural aptitude:

> It is a matter for prayer to the gods that the prince may be born of good character; but beyond this it is to some extent within our [i.e. his tutors'] power to prevent degeneration in one who was born good and to improve by training someone who was born none too good.[103]

Even if the child destined to rule was 'born none too good', this was no serious obstacle to Erasmus the pedagogue, for natural character is of lesser importance than its development, that is, education: '[W]hy should he [i.e. the tutor] think that any human spirit is so hopelessly crude that it will not respond to painstaking education?'[104]

To Erasmus, rule accordingly means nothing less than philosophy, and *philosophia* is always *philosophia Christiana* – though that term appears only twice in the *Education*.[105] And *philosophia Christiana* is, to Erasmus, always the philosophy of a God, who is *experienced* rather than conceptualised in the abstract and intellectual manner of the scholastics.[106] The difference is that between *vita (politica) activa* and *vita contemplativa*.[107] By good (i.e.,

---

101 The philological preference of Erasmus is apparent in his epistemology, according to which ideas are described by concepts and can be recognised only by 'good' (i.e., fitting and appropriate) concepts or formulations. Coarse style and raw language are obstacles to knowledge and thus to the process of the formation of true *humanitas* (Scribner 1970: 11).

102 Erasmus-IPC: 139, line 112.

103 'Vt nascatur probae indolis princeps, id votis optandum a superis. Porro ne bene natus degeneret, aut vt parum bene natus educatione reddatur melior, id partim in nobis situm est' (Erasmus-IPC: 137, lines 40–42; *Education* 6).

104 '[C]ur existimet vllum hominis ingenium tam agreste tamque deploratum, quod dilligenti non mitescat institutione?' (Erasmus-IPC: 141, lines 163–165; *Education* 11).

105 Herding 1966: 133.

106 Augustijn 1991: 73.

107 Mestwerdt 1917: 52ff.; Buck 1987: 176.

Christian) education and by right action, the prince can be example to his people. This exemplary function accorded to the ruler shows that the political theology of Erasmus is above all ethical in character. The Christian ruler is the source of morality, but not, like Machiavelli's prince, by force and power, but by his exemplary nature ('vita principis [...] transformat mores'),[108] just as the example of Christ (Matt. 5:13ff.) paved the way for a renewal of morality.

Clarification is required here. All this does not mean that Erasmus was egalitarian. He was aware that not all human beings could be educated and that many were not made for the life of mind, passed in scholarship and moral purity. He was rather – like Plato – an elitist. Erasmus knew that only few could rise to true learning; and to these few, he believed, matters of state were to be entrusted. Indeed, in the Platonic manner, rulers were to be 'persuaded' to rule. Conscientious rulers understood the burden of rule, and nobody would willingly take on that cross: 'According to Plato, only someone who has assumed the office unwillingly and not without persuasion is fit to be a ruler.'[109]

Seen from the perspective of education, Erasmus held monarchy to be the ideal form of government. The reasons for this were not social and political – Erasmus knew that a people might successfully rule itself in a democratic manner – but moral and intellectual. Erasmus thought it unlikely that the mass of people might live up to the ideals of (political) education and that it was, in any case, technically impossible to educate everybody to excellence. Only a few (or indeed just one) were hence fit to rule.[110] Erasmus was no more of a utopian than he was an egalitarian; if anything, he was an idealist who pursued the ideal of Christian *humanitas* through the concrete method of education and learning.[111]

---

108   Apud Herding 1974: 126. See *Education* 21: 'the life of the prince grips and trans-forms the moral attitudes and character of his subjects'.

109   'Nullo imperio gerendo censetur idoneus authore Platone, nisi qui coactus et inuitus suscipit imperium' (Erasmus-IPC: 152, lines 514–515; *Education* 25).

110   Herding 1974: 123f., 125.

111   Born 1968: 4.

Concord and the Order of the State: Political Christocentrism in Erasmus

Within the theoretical framework of the *Education*, the following section will consider the idea of concord as the realisation of *Christianitas* under three aspects. First, I will enquire into the significance of the people or subjects as a factor of the political; second, I will consider the question of the ideal constitution; and third, the dangers that might jeopardise the political principle of concord are discussed.

One fundamental assumption of the *Education* is that rule is a social pact between rulers and ruled. Erasmus harks back to Platonic and Aristotelian ideas that conceive of a polity of whatever kind as regulating the relationship between the people, the basis of power and the ruler, the custodian and representative of power.[112] To Erasmus – and to his

---

112 Plato, in the *Republic*, was the first to argue that politics was at heart nothing less than a twofold necessity. Rule was necessary, on the one hand, to help subjects address and overcome their needs; on the other hand, it also represented a compulsion of sorts for the ruler to put his actions at the service of his subjects, that is, to act – even against his will – for the benefit of others. To govern responsibly meant above all to govern in awareness of this obligation, for the ruler – assuming him not to be a self-seeking tyrant – to be obliged (!) to rule (Plato, *Republic*, book I: 347b-d). Plato describes relations of authority as constituting a pact between social actors, and in Plato's day, the political organism was not distinct – as it is in modern states – from the social (Plato, *Republic*, book IV: 431d-e; Hinsley 1966: 15ff.; Meyer 1976: 68). The polity thus existed by virtue of a compact, in which the ruled consented to being ruled only because they found it to be in the interest of their own wealth (and good). The laws supposed to safeguard 'justice' were, to that extent, no more than constructions aimed at enforcing the compact that is the 'state'. Plato here argues for a functionalist understanding of justice, which is to say that each person has a place and a task to fulfil within the societal whole and contributes both to the greater good. Society consisted of individuals who helped each other because they were mutually dependent. Human weakness and imperfection compelled individuals to form associations because they could not survive otherwise (Plato, *Republic*, book II, 369b-c; book IV, 441c–443b). Hence, laws are forms of compulsion with the purpose of limiting human weakness and the tendency to act unjustly (Plato, *Republic*, book II, 366a–368b).

aforementioned philosophical models – the ruler is dependent on his people because there are two sides involved in the act of ruling.

Consequently, the people, as the socio-political instance of the order of the state, assume a central position in the thought of Erasmus. In the people resides the consensus on which relations of rule are founded and without which they would be unthinkable.[113] Like Aristotle,[114] Erasmus conceives of rule as a consensual agreement, as *administratio* exercised over free individuals, equal in rights: 'At issue here […] is the core idea of the *Education*, which is the reciprocal assignment of the roles of prince and people in the freedom founded by Christ and demonstrated […] by His conduct.'[115]

To Erasmus the theologian, freedom according to the model set by Christ is the benchmark of political consensus:

> For what can He [Christ] mean by 'it shall not be so among you [as among the pagans]', except that a different practice must obtain among Christians, among whom the office of the prince means *orderly control*, not imperial power, and kingship means helpful supervision, not tyranny?[116]

Aristotle developed the views of his mentor by emphasising that the human urge to form political associations was not to be interpreted in utilitarian manner, but rather represented a natural desire. Man was the only creature capable of forming states (ζῷον πολιτικόν = state-forming being) (Aristotle, *Politik* [introduction], 49; Meister 1966: 37). Justice and polities were thus not mere compacts or conventions, but rather virtues by education and reason, founded on the natural predispositions of human nature and its capacity for reason. Laws were hence to be understood not as means of compulsion, but rather as forms of inculcating virtue, as methods to fulfilling human nature's predisposition to virtue (Aristotle, *Nicomachean Ethics*, book I). The rulers as educators and mentors were thus dependent on the ruled, just as teachers were dependent on their pupils: no ruled, no ruler; no good people, no good prince and so on (Aristotle, *Politik* [introduction], 52ff.). The virtuousness of the ruler – statecraft being the highest of virtues to Aristotle – depended on the virtuousness of the citizens: If they were not virtuous beings capable of engaging on politics, the ruler has clearly failed in his task. This was also the case in tyranny (Aristotle, *Politik* [introduction], 53 and *Politics* 1255b).

113   Becht 2000: 102f.

114   Aristotle, *Politics*, 1252a

115   Herding 1974: 111.

116   'Quid est autem quod ait, non sic erit inter vos, nisi non eodem modo fieri conuenit inter Christianos? Inter quos principatus administratio est, non imperium

Always bear in mind that the words 'dominion', 'imperial authority', 'kingdom', 'majesty', and 'power' are pagan terms, not Christian, the *imperial authority' of Christians* is nothing other than administration, benefaction, and guardianship.[117]

Christian rule is thus neither force nor power (*imperium*) understood as the imposition of the ruler's will, but rather a form of communal life under the administration of a ruler. The ruler in turn is not a *potentatus*, acting instead in the service of his people. Though Otto Herding argues that Erasmus had resolved the tension between absolute Christian freedom and consensual compromise in the state by invoking the Augustinian concept of *administratio* over free and equal individuals,[118] this idea can already be found in the *Politics* of Aristotle.[119]

The ruler, according to Erasmus, is the servant of the common good, and it is with reference to this common good that the people were entitled to elect their ruler:

[A] kingdom is best entrusted to someone who is better endowed than the rest with the qualities of a king, namely wisdom, a sense of justice, personal restraint, foresight, and concern for the public well-being. Family trees, gold, and jewels are no more relevant to governing a state than they are pertinent to a sea-captain in steering his ship. The people must look to the same single object in selecting [!] a prince as the prince should in his administration, which is of course the people's well-being regardless of all personal feelings.[120]

---

et regnum beneficium est, non tyrannis' (Erasmus-IPC: 159, lines 702–704; *Education* 32, emphasis added).

117 'Cogitato semper dominium imperium regnum maiestatem potentiam ethnicorum esse vocabula, non Christianorum; Christianum imperium nihil aliud esse quam administrationem quam beneficentiam quam custodiam' (Erasmus-IPC: 164, lines 889–891; *Education* 38, emphasis added).

118 Herding 1974: 127.

119 Aristotle, *Politics*, 1252b–1253a, 1269a.

120 'Ita regnum ei potissimum est committitur clauus, qui regiis dotibus anteit reliquos, nempe sapientia iusticia animi moderatione prouidentia studio commodi publici. Imagines aurum gemmae nihilo plus habent momenti ad ciuitatis administrationem quam eadem nauclero conductura sint ad nauim gubernandam. Quod vnum oportet spectare principem in administrando, id vnum oportet spectare populum in principe deligendo [...]' (Erasmus-IPC: 136, lines 17–23; *Education* 5).

The meaning of the political was thus to be found primarily in political ethics. No less than Aristotle in his *Politics*, Erasmus was aware that any discussion of the state, rule, etc., had to begin with a discussion of the citizens.[121]

Rule and its agent – the ruler – were dependent upon the citizens as the true subjects of that rule, though this is not to mistake Erasmus for a proponent of popular sovereignty in the modern sense. There was no 'ruling' without 'being ruled'.[122] It was thus for the people, the subjects or the citizens to state their views on the (ethical) quality of a regime or of a ruler by exercising their power of consent or by withholding it. 'It is the spirit that is right for a prince: being a father to the state. It is on this understanding that the people have sworn allegiance to him.'[123] This concept of power, of which the political consequences are consensus on the one hand or the right of resistance on the other, raises the people to the actual subject of power – except, that is, where tyranny is concerned. Erasmus adopts this line of thought from Aristotle and applies it to Christian rule. Christian rule can take hold only over Christian people.

The people are the foundation of the state as well as forming the locus in which rule can either be realised in (Christian) virtue or degenerate into tyranny. Accordingly, the terminology used by Erasmus with regard to the people follows the ethical criterion of upbringing → education → virtue → *Christianus*. When Erasmus refers to the 'people' in the socio-political sense as the medium of the political or of political ethics, as the ruler's partner in a political contract, he usually uses the term '*populus*' or 'Christian people' (*universus Christi populus*).[124] The people in the sense of *populus* were an important factor in building a *corpus rei publicae*.[125] Subjects were to be brought up to be citizens fit to make decisions and form a *populus*. Only educated people, practised in piety, were able ethically to fulfil their true

---

121   Aristotle, *Politics*, 1267b.
122   Augustijn 1991: 82.
123   'Nempe animus principe dignus, hoc es in rempublicam paternus. Hac lege populus in tua iurauit verba' (Erasmus-IPC: 146, lines 317–318; *Education* 17).
124   Schottenloher 1970: 300.
125   Herding 1974: 126.

nature as Christians and politically to contribute to a life under law, consensus and the public sphere (*consensus enim Principem facit*).[126]

When, on the other hand, Erasmus refers to the people in the moral and intellectual sense, he uses the term '*vulgus*'. The Erasmian semantics of *vulgus* are very nuanced indeed. For one thing, such terms as '*vulgus*', '*plebs*', etc., set up a contrast with both the *Princeps Christianus* and the *populus Christianus*. By education, virtue and piety, the *populus Christianus* was unlike the crude and ignorant mob, corrupted as it was by questionable opinions (*venena vulgarium opinionum*[127]) and plebeian desires (*voluptates plebejas*[128]). (This is not to say, however, that Erasmus had favoured an 'educational revolution' as a levelling social process.[129]) This moral aspect of the semantics of *vulgus* is emphasised in Leo Jud's German translation of 1521: 'Ich verstand aber hier unter dem gemeinen volk nit allein die leyen und einfeltigen lüt, sunder alle die, die da also verblent sind, hengen nach iren anfechtungen, achten mee das falsch und betrüglich, dann das war und eerlich, sy syen hoch oder nyder.'[130]

Second, Erasmus applies the semantics of *vulgus* to the crudeness, tyranny and injustice of many a ruler existing outside of *Christianitas*, instead persisting in sin and living to the detriment of their people. In such cases, Erasmus speaks of a *vulgus principum* (a rabble of princes) or

---

126   Erasmus-IPC: 167, lines 987–988. Herding 1966: 121ff.

127   Erasmus-IPC: 140, line 153.

128   Erasmus-IPC: 144, line 234.

129   Enthoven 1909: 317. Humanism in general and Erasmus in particular substitute the aristocracy of the mind (*res publica litteraria*, Buck 1996: 31) for the aristocracy of birth. Education and especially *pietas* level the boundaries between estates and contribute to the ethical uniformity of the Christian people (see Münkler 1993: 560, 593). Erasmus was neither a 'democrat', nor a 'populist', nor an 'egalitarian'. His was a spiritual elitism, which he defended against the coarseness of a majority of people. He was consistent in his disapproval of the masses' indifference to intellectual life, and his home, the Netherlands, became unbearable to him on account of their low standard of education and their superficiality (Augustijn 1991: 10).

130   Leo Jud apud Herding 1968: 540. Roughly: 'But here, by the "common people", I meant not merely the laymen and simple folk, but all such as are deluded, in thrall to their passions, and heed rather that which is false and deceitful that that which is true and honest, be they of high estate or low.'

vulgares principes (vulgar princes). This rejection of the *vulgus* emphasises the role accorded by Erasmus to (Christian) education in forming a political elite. Education, on the one hand, served to raise the ruler above the coarse masses by cultivating his ethical and intellectual virtues, while on the other being to the benefit of Christian citizens. As such, Christian citizens in turn would rise above the vulgar rabble, a rabble, which could be composed of nobles and princes as well as the common people.[131] In a purely moral and intellectual sense, *vulgus* is stripped of any connotation of social or class distinction and comes to stand for human crudeness as such: the *vulgus hominum* is the 'human rabble'.[132]

The virtue of both rulers and people, the product of both education and constant cultivation, creates the foundation for a shared *Christianitas* of all Christians, who are all – be they rulers or ruled – redeemed and set free by Christ and His blood. The consensus without which no state organism can expect to endure is thus framed as a *Christian* consensus. The Erasmian *Princeps Christianus* is always aware that he exists by will of the people and owes his status to the public consensus. Accordingly, the concept of *consensus populi* has a key role to play in Erasmus's account of rule and the relations it produces.[133]

Erasmus's political ideal consists in concord and harmony, resting and centred on the pillar of Christ according to the model set down in the 'celestial hierarchy' of Pseudo-Dionysius the Areopagite. The integrative power of monarchical unity, which in turn rests on Christian virtue, is fulfilled by the freedom and consensus of the subjects.[134] All are one

131   Herding 1974: 123.
132   Erasmus-IPC: 144, line 222.
133   Becht 2000: 98.
134   Erasmus used the metaphor of the body, widespread in the mediaeval mirrors for princes, to describe the organism of the state. Yet unlike, for instance, John of Salisbury (bishop of Chartres, died 1180), who, in his political work *Polycraticus* (1159) associated the ruler with the head, Erasmus held the prince to be the heart of the body politic (Erasmus-IPC: 164, line 898). Following the metaphor of the body, the anatomy of the state would consist of several limbs, whose functions were complementary. For one of them to fail would spell disease or even death for the whole. This opinion is maintained by St Paul (1 Cor. 12:12–31). Augustine and later Jonas, bishop of Orléans (d. 843), in his *De institutione laicali* (818–828) and *De institutione regia* (831) adopted this metaphor of the body (Bosl 1988: 177).

in right Christian action and all are one in the Christian ruler, just as all Creation is one in God. All are one, just as the trinitarian God is one: in freedom and concord.[135] Erasmus likes applying the Pseudo-Dionysian model of hierarchies to the political structure. He simplifies the complex hierarchies of the Heavens and the Church into a tripartite structure of the state, organised around prince, clergy and people.[136] The good – which to Pseudo-Dionysius was the light – could thus be seen to emanate from the ruler as water flows from a spring and 'fills' the subjects:[137]

> This was clearly seen by St Denis, who divided the world into three hierarchies: what God is in the ranks of heaven the bishop should be in the church and the prince in the state. He is supreme in goodness, and all his goodness flows from him to other men as from a spring.[138]

Political *Christianitas* proves itself in its dealings with the subjects and in penal law. Contrary to the Aristotelian notion of 'equity' or ἐπιείκεια, which rests solely on the personal wisdom and insight of the one who applies the law,[139] Erasmus can be seen to prefer structural improvements to the law and hence an objective positivism in legislation. A law must

---

In the body political, the function of the king was that of the head, the site of governing reason, leading the whole and working to its benefit (Berges 1938: 44ff.; Nederman 1990: xxi; Anton 2006: 13).

135 Herding 1974: 124.

136 Schottenloher 1970: 299; Augustijn 1993: 4.

137 This element is not drawn from Plotinus, as Otto Herding as erroneously maintained. It is rather a case of neo-Platonic elements whose importance in the works of Pseudo-Dionysius has been overstated. Though Pseudo-Dionysius cloaked in Christian teaching in neo-Platonic terminology, his 'system' differs from that of Plotinus in several key respects: (1) Pseudo-Dionysius spoke of creation, not of emanation. (2) Unlike Plotinus, he saw an essential difference between *creator* and *creatura*. (3) Pseudo-Dionysius made an ontological distinction between God's essence and His *dynameis*, that is, effects, works, among which is also to be counted the divine light of grace.

138 'Perspexisse videtur haec diuus Dionysius, qui treis fecit hierarchias, vt quod Deus est inter coelitum ordines, id episcopus sit in ecclesia, id princeps in republica, illo nihil melius et ab eo velut a fonte manat in alios, quicquid boni possidet' (Erasmus-IPC: 151, lines 470–473; *Education* 23).

139 Aristotle, *Nicomachean Ethics*: book V, ch. 14, pp. 125ff.

favour the weak and poor in its substance and not merely in its interpretation (this includes fiscal policy[140]). It is not merely a matter, as Aristotle
had held it to be, of applying the law in the favour even in the absence of
any such explicit provision:

> But it [the law] should incline more towards helping the weaker elements, because
> the position of humble men exposes them more easily to danger. The law's indul-
> gence [*humanitas legum*] should compensate for the privileges denied them by their
> station in life.[141]

The *Education* holds the correct manner of dealing with subjects to be
informed by pedagogy and an awareness of their *humanitas*. Its preferred
means ought to be not compulsion (*coercitio*) and physical punishment
for crimes committed, but rather prevention through love. Erasmus is
opposed to the principle of *ius gentium*, in which human society is regarded as the medium of relations of authority and inequality.[142] Instead,
he argued:

140   Erasmus maintained that the poor were not to be subject to taxation (Erasmus-
      IPC: 190, lines 752–754: 'Quod si necessitas flagitat, exigi nonnihil a populo, tum
      boni principis est, it his rationibus facere, ut quam minimum incommodorum
      peruniat ad tenues'; *Education* 74: 'So if necessity requires some taxation of the
      people, then it is the good prince's job to do it such a way that the least possible
      hardship falls on the poor.') Accordingly, attempts have been made to portray
      Erasmus as having anticipated socialist, communitarian and anti-feudalistic ideas
      and other Enlightenment ideals (Rudolph 1969). Yet such statements by Erasmus
      have little to do with class struggle in the Marxist sense, but rather with the notion
      of *Christianitas* as applied to care for the poor; its communitarianism is that devel-
      oped by Plato in the *Republic* (see Isnardi-Parente 1988: 42) and reinterpreted in
      Christian terms by Erasmus.
141   'Verum in hanc partem magis propendeant, ut imbecilioribus subueniatur, quod
      humiliorum fortuna magis exposita sit iniuriis. Quod igitur in fortunae preasidiis
      diminutum est, id legum exaequet humanitas' (Erasmus-IPC: 199, lines 3–6;
      Education 85). On this, see Kisch 1960: 63f.
142   The Roman jurist Ulpianus (d. 223) held natural law to be the property of and
      essential to all living things, whereas the *ius gentium* applied to peoples and was
      a typically human product (CIC I: c. 1, p. 29). Where natural law, which encom-
      passed such natural laws as freedom, was general to all creatures, the *ius gentium* was
      specific to human beings and encompassed, for example, servitude and inequality.
      Another Roman Jurist, Florentinus, likewise claimed: 'Servitus est constitutio iuris

Since nature created all men free and slavery was imposed upon nature (a fact which even the laws of the pagans [i.e. the Roman jurists] concede), […] [w]hat a mockery it is to regard as slaves those whom Christ redeemed with the same blood as redeemed you, whom he set free into the same freedom as you.[143]

In the scheme of the Aristotelian economy, the *principatus Christianus* represents rule as a familial, paternal relationship between the ruler and his people, with the latter dependent on the former for love and care:

The good prince must have the same attitude towards his subjects as a good *paterfamilias* has towards his household […]. For he is set above them and yet he is of the same kind: a man ruling men, a free man ruling free men and not wild beasts, as Aristotle rightly put it.[144]

To Erasmus, a society founded by Christ and with His message of love as its normative standard – a Christian society, in short – is the medium of charity in action. In the *lex christiana*, which represents the *lex naturae* of human liberty (*libertas*) restored in Christ,[145] criminal licence (*licentia*) is suppressed by education and piety, that is, by responsible *humanitas*.[146] That subjects should rise up against authority is simply unimaginable in such a society – not because of political obedience, as Plato or even St

---

gentium, qua quis dominio alieno contra natura subicitur' (CIC I: c. 4, p. 35; see also CIC I: c. 64, p. 205). This discussion was directed not least against Aristotle, who had held slavery to be natural, with some people (notably the barbarian peoples) being by nature destined for slavery and subservience (Aristotle, *Politik* [introduction], 51ff.).

143   'Cum natura genuerit omneis [sic!] homines liberos et praeter naturam inducta sit seruitus, quod ethnicorum etiam leges fatentur […]. Quam absurdum est eos pro seruis habere, quos Christus eodem redemptos sanguine in communem asseruit libertatem …' (Erasmus-IPC: 165, lines 930–936; *Education* 40). According to Erasmus, Christian rule corresponded to the *ius naturale* of human nature remade in Christ.

144   'Bonus princeps non alio animo debet esse in duo ciues, quam bonus paterfamilias in suos domesticos. Excellit enim, sed tamen eiusdem est generis, homo hominibus, liber liberis imperans non beluis, ut recte prodidit Aristoteles' (Erasmus-IPC: 160, lines 738–741; *Education* 33f.). See also: Erasmus-IPC: 163, lines 869–870.

145   Hübner 1983.

146   Pfeiffer 1955: 183.

Paul might have imagined it, but because Christian charity would reign supreme (Matt. 5:39ff.).[147]

Rule of a kind unlike the *imperium* founded on compulsion would respect both the traditions of the people and the political and ethical developments in the country. The prince – according to Erasmus and contrary to Machiavelli's conception – is the guardian of tradition. To safeguard peace in the state, he is to eschew arbitrary measures, heavy-handed rule and change for its own sake. Erasmus is particularly wary of novelty:

> The prince should avoid all innovation as far as proves possible: for even if something is changed for the better, a novel situation is still disturbing in itself. Neither the structure of the state, the customary public business of the city, nor long established laws may be changed without upheaval. [...] On the other hand, if something is such that it cannot be tolerated, it will have to be put right – but subtly and gradually.[148]

The prince embodies tradition, custom and law. He creates no new laws that are not based on the ethos of the people. The Erasmian *princeps* is a *viva lex*, a law both living and lived.[149]

In this context, the question arises as to the constitutional form favoured by Erasmus. He leaves no doubt that the people may govern successfully: 'Vast empires have flourished without a prince, such as Rome and Athens under democracy.'[150] Is this to be understood as a statement in favour of a democratic constitution on the part of Erasmus? Erasmus held tyranny to be the greatest danger lurking in the political realm. If tyranny was the worst political form, the best was the *principatus Christianus*. Only the Christian monarchy was capable of preventing tyranny from emerging.

---

147   Padberg 1969: 310; Schottenloher 1969; Schottenloher 1971: 668, 673; Hoffmann 2008: 92ff.

148   'Omnis nouatio, quoad fieri poterit, fugienda principi. Nam etiam si quid in melius commutetur, tamen ipsa nouitas offendit. Nec vnquam sine tumultu commutatus est vel reipublicae status vel publica ciuitatis consuetudo vel leges olim receptae. [...] Rursum si quid erit eius generis, vt tolerandum non sit, id erit corrigendum, sed arte ac paulatim' (Erasmus-IPC: 187, lines 672–678; *Education* 71).

149   Erasmus-IPC: 194, line 855. Erasmus here continues the line of high mediaeval mirrors for princes. In his book *De regimine civitatum* (c. 1228) Giovanni da Viterbo described the ruler as *lex animata* (see Ioannes Viterbiensis: 266).

150   *Education* 89; Herding 1974: 123.

The constitutional model favoured by Erasmus is that of the participative monarchy, in which virtuous citizens can consensually participate in the political process by electing a *bonus vir* as their Christian prince.[151]

The Christian monarch is the result of the political power of Christian citizens. Rather than pure autocracy, what Erasmus is proposing here is a monarchy tempered by political participation. Theoretically, at least, Erasmus might prefer monarchy pure and simple as the ideal form of government, but man is sinful, weak and given to immorality. It may thus be hard to find a *bonus vir* perfect in all respects and thus able alone (!) to fulfil the duties of Christian rule:

> Although there are many kinds of state, it is pretty well agreed among philosophers that the most healthy form is monarchy [...], by analogy with the deity, when the totality of things is in one person's power [...]. If it happens that your prince is complete with all the virtues, then monarchy pure and simple is the thing. But since this would probably never happen, although it is a fine idea to entertain, if no more than an ordinary man is presented (things being what they are), then monarchy should preferably be checked and diluted with a mixture of aristocracy and democracy to prevent it ever breaking out into tyranny; and just as the elements mutually balance each other, so let the state be stabilised with a similar control.[152]

Under these conditions monarchy,[153] though curtailed by democracy and aristocracy, is the only form of government suitable for human beings.[154]

---

151 Herding 1974: 114,121; Augustijn 1993: 9.

152 'Cum multae sint formae rerum publicarum, philosophorum omnium ferme consensus est saluberrimam esse monarchiam nimirum ad exemplar die vt rerum summa penes vnum sit [...]. Si princeps contingat omnibus absolutus virtutibus, optanda sit pura ac simplex monarchia; verum quando id haud scio an vmquam contingat, quin potius magnum et exoptandum, si detur mediocris, vt nunc sunt res hominum, praestiterit monarchiam aristocratiae et democratiae admixtam temperari diluique, ne quando in tyrannidem erumpat, sed quemadmodum elementa vicissim sese librant ...' (Erasmus-IPC: 162f., lines 837–848; *Education* 37).

153 'Erasmian' monarchy can ultimately be traced to the Aristotelian solution of the mixed constitution in his *Politics* (book IV and *passim*).

154 Enthoven 1909: 316; Born 1968: 33; Münkler 1993: 568, 593; Nitschke 2000: 117.

In his idea of the monarchy Erasmus, rather than instituting a separation between the 'two swords' of Church and state,[155] makes a case for their mutual support in a *res publica Christiana*. Such a Christian commonwealth would serve as the political and educational framework within which the *philosophia Christi* might be realised – that is, a life made pious by the right understanding of the word of God.[156] It is in any case astonishing to what degree Erasmus, while developing a semantics of *Christianitas*, scarcely mentions the Church qua institution: 'First, this Christian prince does not go to church, nor do his subjects [...] go to church. Both ruler and subjects are exhorted to all manner of things but this; the church as an institution hardly appears at all [...].'[157] This indicates that the *Christianitas* of Erasmus is to be understood as a practical form of piety lived and experienced, far from the Church and its sacramental-ceremonial and mechanical ritualism. To Erasmus, *Christianitas* becomes possible only once formalism has been left behind.

However, Christian rule built on love, concord and piety was not possible in the world as Erasmus knew it – the world of wars and conflicts that was Europe of his day.[158] To Erasmus peace alone was the medium by which Christian rule and ultimately a peaceful universal order might be brought about.[159] So-called 'Erasmian cosmopolitanism' was the expression of the concord of all Christians and of their unity across all political and social boundaries. In a world of *eruditio* and *pietas*, of true *humanitas*,

---

155   Kristeller 1976b: 136.
156   Schottenloher 1970: 296f.; Augustijn 1993: 3f.
157   Schrader 1990: 192. On this, see Estes 1992: 56.
158   Since Erasmus personally witnessed both the wars between the houses Habsburg and Valois and those in Italy, the advantages of peace were self-evident to him. Moreover, he saw the advantages of political continuity and coherence imparted by a ruler 'of one's own', that is, one drawn from the nation's own nobility. This brought Erasmus into a certain proximity with the Dutch national party of Adolf of Burgundy, lord of Veere, which sought to install a Dutch prince against Habsburg wishes (Tracy 1978: 14f., 16, 125f.). Erasmus demonstrates this preference for continuity in rule in chapter IX of the *Education* and more clearly still in the *Querela Pacis*. On this, see Duchhardt 2000.
159   Enthoven 1909: 327f.; Born 1968: 16ff., 35; Padberg 1969.

there would be no need for parties, conflicts, nations and petty interests.[160]
Since bloodshed was not compatible with the Redeemer's message, the
efforts of all Christian rulers must be directed towards a permanent 'pan-
European' (i.e., western European) peace treaty.[161] Erasmus instead suggests
putting an end to military conflict by setting up an arbitration committee
consisting of learned men:[162]

> If some dispute arises between princes, why do they not take it to arbitration instead?
> There are plenty of bishops, abbots, scholars, plenty of grave magistrates whose ver-
> dict would settle the matter more satisfactorily than all this carnage, pillaging, and
> universal calamity.[163]

Erasmus was sorely disappointed by political conditions as they obtained
in western Europe at the beginning of the sixteenth century: particularly the thirst for power, conquest, riches and earthly glory. He was ap-
palled especially by the warmongering on the part of the ecclesiastical
princes, notably Pope Julius II (d. 1513). The true mission of the Church of
Christ was instead to encourage a 'politics' of love and concord between
people.[164] Erasmus had personally experienced the disturbances caused by
the papal campaigns during his journeys in Italy, when he was constantly
forced to avoid the various warring armies. In 1506 he had witnessed
Julius's triumphant entry into Bologna,[165] and there was little about the

---

160 Thompson 1955. Not even in the animal kingdom did members of the same species
engage in such bloodshed. The harmony and peace of nature were to be restored
in human nature, once it had been 'healed' by Christ. This line of argument was
frequently used by Erasmus, occurring both in the *Education* and in the in *Querela*
(see Erasmus-IPC: 157, lines 645–646; Erasmus-Querela: 362–363).

161 Scribner 1970: 15; Münkler 1993: 592.

162 On the tradition of arbitration in late mediaeval and early modern peace-
brokering, see Kampmann 2001.

163 'Quod si quod dissidium ortum fuerit inter principes, cur non potius ad arbitros
itur? Sunt tot episcopi tot abbates et eruditi viri tot graues magistratus, quorum
sententia rem confici decebat, potius quam tot stragibus tot expilationibus tot
orbis calamitatibus' (Erasmus-IPC: 216, lines 541–544; *Education* 105f.). On this,
see Born 1968: 19; Münkler 1993: 594.

164 Erasmus-IPC: 218, lines 598–605.

165 Schrader 1990: 183; Fabisch 2008: 196.

pope that brought to mind a spiritual man. To the mind of Erasmus, he instead recalled a secular Italian prince.[166]

Following the death of Julius, Erasmus put great hopes for peace in the new pope, Leo X (d. 1521), whom he had already met in Italy in 1504.[167] Erasmus welcomed Leo X as a pope of peace and *litterae* following the reign of the detested Julius II, admiringly describing him as 'supreme indeed in every way' (*Leo Pontifex modis omnibus maximus*).[168] Erasmus kept up a correspondence with Leo X throughout this period.[169]

In international politics, Erasmian hopes for peace were embodied by Philip (the Fair) of Habsburg (d. 1506), duke of Burgundy and father of Charles V, Holy Roman Emperor. Erasmus considered Philip's efforts to broker peace between the major powers of his day to be worthy of emulation[170] – not least by Leo X. In a letter to the abbot Anton von Bergen (the brother of his bishop at the time, Henry of Cambrai), Erasmus opined that only the pope was able to stop the imminent invasion of France by English, Spanish and imperial troops.[171] In the mediaeval and early modern view, the pope's function was that of a political mediator between the powers, and Erasmus hoped that Leo might act as such:[172]

> It is the proper function of the Roman pontiff, of the cardinals, bishops, and abbots, to settle disputes between Christian princes; this is where they should wield their authority and reveal the power they possess by virtue of men's regard for their holy office. Julius, a pope who was by no means universally approved, succeeded in rousing this hurricane of wars. Cannot Leo, who is scholarly, honourable, and devout, succeed in quieting it? Julius's pretext for going to war was a threat to his own safety; but, even though its cause has been removed, the war still goes on.[173]

166   In 1513 Erasmus wrote a polemic against the pope, entitled *Julius exclusus e coelis* (Schrader 1990: 196; Fabisch 2008: 195ff., esp. 202).
167   As Cardinal Giovanni de Medici. See Padberg 1969: 306.
168   Erasmus-OE: Ep. 326, March 1515, p. 58. English translation in Erasmus *Correspondence*: Letter 326, p. 72.
169   Augustijn 1991: 12, 39, 71.
170   Scribner 1970: 18f.
171   Scribner 1970: 21.
172   Kampmann 2001: 31ff. and 36ff.
173   'Hoc est proprium Romani Pontificis, hoc cardinalium, hoc episcoporum, hoc abbatum munus, Christianorum principum dissidia componere; hic autoritatem

Indeed, Erasmus appears to have been of the opinion that there was no 'justified' cause for warfare:

> Some princes deceive themselves as follows: 'Some wars are entirely just, and I have just cause for starting one.' First, I will suspend judgment on whether any war is entirely just [...]. Augustine too approves it somewhere. Again, St Bernard praises some soldiers. [...] In fact, anyone who examines the matter more closely will find that none of them approves the kind of war which is usually fought today.[174]

Here, Erasmus can be seen to oppose, albeit indirectly, the mediaeval theological justification of war, as it was used especially in the propaganda accompanying the Crusades.[175]

In conclusion, I would like to emphasise that Erasmus's entire political discourse with regard to peace is in fact a theology of peace in Christ: 'Érasme a voulu édifier une théologie cohérente de la paix.'[176] The political merely presents him with an occasion for specifying and developing soteriological aspects of *Christianitas*, of Christian life. Peace – no less so than politics – was unthinkable without Christ, whose sacrifice and blood formed the basis of Christian universalism. Treaties and documents (*syngraphis res*), on the other hand, were merely signs of human imperfection and mistrust.[177] This is one more argument in support of the claim

---

suam proferre et quantum pro sua reuerentia valeant ostendere. Iulius, certe non ab omnibus laudatus Pontifex, potuit hanc bellorum tempestatem excitare; Leo, vir doctus integer ac pius, sedare non poterit? Suscipiendi belli praetextus erat Iulius periclitans; sublata est causa belli nec tamen cessat bellum' (Erasmus-OE, Ep. 288, 14 March 1514, p. 553, English translation in Erasmus *Correspondence*: 281f.).

174 'Sic principes quidam imponunt sibi: est omnino bellum aliquod iustum et mihi causa iusta est suscipiendi. Primum an omnino iustum sit bellum, in medio relinquemus. [...] Et Augustinus alicubi probat. Laudat et diuus Bernardus milites quosdam. [...] Postremo si quis rem excutiat diligentius, is reperirt a nemine probatum hoc bellorum genus, quo nunc uulgo conflictamur' (Erasmus-IPC: 214f., lines 506–513; *Education* 104f.).

175 Bernhard of Clairvaux, De laude: II, 2–3, 18–23, p. 274; Taube 1948; Grigore 2009: 383ff.

176 Halkin 1986: 82.

177 If the eternal concord established by Christ fails for not having been internalised by men, then pacts and alliances are powerless to re-establish it (Erasmus-IPC: 206ff.).

that Erasmus's political theory is an aspect of a comprehensive theology of *humanitas* restored in Christ.

Conclusion

As in many of the late mediaeval mirrors for princes, in Erasmus the syntagma *Princeps Christianus* reveals its dependence on Christian, theological discourse[178] in conceiving of rule as *administratio* over and by Christians set free by Christ.

The state is a political medium for concord, love and *humanitas christiana*.[179] Christian principles are projected onto the political and hence onto secular structures, the *saeculum*.[180] Contrary to the term's modern usage, Erasmian 'secularism' – in the sense of a Christian attitude to the *saeculum* – is thus not to be understood as a polar opposite to the religious and specifically Christian ordering of the world. What the world and the political order represent is instead a complement to and a concretisation of theological and existential meanings. This attitude is based on the cosmological principle which holds Creation to form a *totum* and to be connected ethically – that is, in action and practice – to the Creator. Erasmian secularism can thus be understood as an application of theological structures of meaning to the world and its own structures, notably state and society.[181] The *Education* ought therefore to be read as a work of political theology that aims to create a Christian medium (i.e., Christian rule) as the fulfilment of the Christian message.[182]

In articulating his political theory, Erasmus draws on the Gospel, the spirit of which he looks to realise even in opposition to the ceremonies and ritual of the Church.[183] To Erasmus the *Princeps Christianus*, to the

178   Fricke 1967: 21.
179   Newman 1995.
180   Herding 1974: 129.
181   Schorn-Schütte 2006: 9.
182   Scribner 1970: 16.
183   Augustijn 1991: 75.

extent that he acts justly and hence like Christ, is a *Christ actualised* – actualised, that is, time and again in the deeds and practice of the Christian ruler and the Christian people.

Prayer, asceticism, mysticism and the ritualism of divine service have no part to play in the Erasmian *aedificatio* of the ruler's *Christianitas*, which hinges entirely on the ruler's right action as an *imitatio Christi*. *Christianitas*, to Erasmus, means to be Christ in action.[184] Moreover, the ethical, practical, lived piety expected from a Christian in general and a Christian ruler in particular is of course founded on education and habit. It is above all for this reason that Erasmus places such importance on the education of the prince: without it, *Christianitas* – to resemble Christ in action – could not be realised.

Compared to the God-likeness bestowed by the mediaeval sacrament of anointment,[185] which conferred God's grace (*gratia*) upon the ruler, the likeness upheld by Erasmus is of a practical, active nature. In neither idea, of course, does God-likeness imply an identity of essence. According to the doctrine of the sacraments, grace is an effect emanating from God's very essence, an energy or outpouring which human beings formally receive in the sacraments and in which they are hence passive participants. Erasmus, however, remains wary of the formalism and ministry of the Church, though not of its pedagogical function or doctrinal purity.[186] What Erasmus fears are the effects a mechanistic understanding of grace might have on the piety of Christians.[187] For this reason, Erasmus privileges the ethics of action over sacramental conformity and ritualism – for the people as well as the ruler.

---

184   Augustijn 1991: 80.
185   Kantorowicz 1957: 46 (with reference).
186   Hoffmann 1986: 4, 29f. 'Just as Erasmus' interests are more in Christ as teacher and example than as redeemer and more in the priest as teacher, preacher, and example than as administrator of the sacraments, so his interest is not so much in the sacraments as the mainspring of the Christian life as in the *philosophia Christiana* without which the sacraments are useless. However, just as he does not neglect the role of Christ as redeemer and the priest as administrator of the sacraments, so he does not neglect the role of the sacraments in the Christian life' (Payne 1970: 220).
187   Enthoven 1909: 315; Pfeiffer 1955: 185; Augustijn 1969: 139f., 144ff.

Erasmian theomimetism is ethical rather than sacramental.[188] The prince resembles God by willing and acting like God, not by becoming the organ of some 'dubious' (to Erasmus) sacramental effect:

> But [...] do not think that Christ is found in mere ceremonies, that is, in precepts no longer seriously observed, and in the institution of the church. Who is a true Christian? Not just someone who is baptised or confirmed or who goes to mass: rather it is someone who has embraced Christ in the depths of his heart and who expresses this *by acting in a Christian sprit*.[189]

To be a Christian, in Erasmus's view, is to bear a cross. The ruler's cross is to rule over Christians and to ensure that rule is true to its divine archetype:[190] 'A good prince has the obligation of looking to the welfare of his people even at the cost of his own life if need be. But when a prince loses his life in such a cause, he does not really die.'[191] Moreover:

> You too take your cross, or else Christ will not acknowledge you. 'What then is my cross?' you may ask. I will tell you. So long as you follow what is right, do violence to no one, extort from no one, sell no public office, and are corrupted by no bribes [...]. Again, so long as you take pains to consider the interests of the state in every way you will be leading a life of anxiety, depriving your youthful spirit of its pleasures, and wearing yourself down with sleepless nights and work.[192]

188 Reventlow 1997: 13; Nitschke 2000: 113.
189 'At rursum ne putaris Christum situm esse in ceremoniis, hoc est in praeceptis dumtaxat vtcumque seruatis et ecclesiae constitutionibus. Christianus est non qui lotus est, non qui vnctus, non qui sacris adest, sed qui Christum intimis complectitur affectibus ac piis factis exprimit' (Erasmus-IPC: 147, lines 338–341; *Education* 18, emphasis added).
190 Herding 1966: 136f.
191 Boni principi esse munus vel sua morte, si fors ita res tulerit, populi commodis consulere. Nec perire principem, qui huiusmodi immoriatur negocio' (Erasmus-IPC: 144, lines 246–248; *Education* 14). See also Erasmus-IPC: 148, lines 380–383.
192 'Aut tua crux tibi quoque tollenda est, aut non agnoscet te Christus. Quae tandem mea crux? Inquies. Dicam, dum quod rectum est sequeris, dum nemini vim facis, neminem expilas, nullum vendis magistratum, nullo munere corumperis [...]. Ad haec dum modis omnibus reipublicae consulere studes, sollicitam agis vitam, fraudas aetatem ac genium tuum voluptatibus, maceras te vigiliis ac laboribus ...' (Erasmus-IPC: 148, lines 367–374; *Education* 19).

The ruler is to the state as Christ is to the heavenly kingdom: the heart, the centre.[193] In addition, the ruler must be no less willing than Christ to lay down his life for his people:

> Let him frequently call to mind the example of those who have held the well-being of their citizens more precious than their own lives [...] *so that he binds his citizens to him in the same way that God draws all the world together to himself, by deserving well of them.*[194]

This passage shows how the *Christianitas* of the Erasmian image of the prince is to be understood above all as a resemblance to God: it is an ethical *theomimesis*, in which the ruler may resemble God or be 'God-like', but not by sacramental actions or mystical illumination or deification. Instead, what is decisive is action – works of love, charity, generosity, peace-making and compassion. Practice of the divine ideals of *summa potentia*, *summa sapientia* and *summa bonitas* turn a prince into an *imago Dei*.[195] The concepts central to Erasmian theomimetism are *imago Dei*, *Dei simulacrum* and *Dei vicarius*.[196] The *Christianitas* of the prince above all means his identification with the archetype of Christ:

> When you who are a prince, a Christian prince, hear and read that you are the likeness of God and his vicar, do not swell with pride on this account, but rather let the fact make you all the more concerned to live up to that wonderful archetype of yours; and remember that, though following him is hard, not following him is a sin.[197]

---

193 Enthoven 1909: 316.
194 'Frequenter ingerat sibi eorum exempla, quibus ciuim suorum commoditas ipsa vita fuit antiquior [...]. [V]t eadem via sibi adiugat ciues suos, qua Deus sibi conciliat vniuersos, nempe benemerendo' (Erasmus-IPC: 183, lines 544–546 and lines 553–555; *Education* 66, emphasis added).
195 Herding 1966: 124; Schrader 1990: 193.
196 Erasmus-IPC: 150, lines 441, 450; 150, line 451; 174, lines 249–250.
197 'At tu qui Christianus etiam es princeps, cum audis aut legis te Dei simulacrum esse, te Dei vicarium esse, caue ne quid hinc intumescas animo, quin potius ea res te magis sollicitum reddat, vt respondeas archetypo tuo, pulcherrimo quidem illi, sed quod assequi sit difficillimum, non assequi turpissimum' (Erasmus-IPC: 150, lines 450–453; *Education* 22).

The *mimesis* in question here is to be understood not only as *imitatio*, but as God-likeness (*simulacrum Dei*). The ruler is the image of God, his archetype – he is a living icon of God. It is reasonable to ask why the term applied here is not rather 'christomimetism'. Yet Erasmus always takes Christ to signify the incarnation of God, and his statements regarding the redeemer and His exemplary character presuppose the divinity of Christ.[198] To be Christ-like, in this scheme, is to be God-like. The term 'theomimetism' is therefore the more accurate for the present discussion.

198   Becht 2000: 175ff.

CHAPTER 4

On Secular Authority: Martin Luther and the Prince as Servant[1]

> Observe, however, that a preacher, by whom God rebukes the gods, is to 'stand in the congregation.' He is to 'stand', that is, he is to be firm and confident, and deal uprightly and honestly with it; and 'in the congregation', that is, openly and boldly before God and men.
>
> Martin Luther

This chapter addresses one central question, namely: does Martin Luther's (c. 1483–1546) treatise *On Secular Authority* (OSA)[2] represent an instance of what Karl Barth called the 'two kingdoms doctrine',[3] or does it rather depict the Christian prince as a figure situated at the intersection of these two kingdoms, the spiritual and the temporal?[4] Though these semantic spheres are connected, they are by no means identical. Where the *Princeps Christianus* is concerned, he appears as God's *partner* in political life, and one who allows God's will and justice to be

---

1   In this chapter, I use 'servant' in the meaning of 'to minister' (*ministrare, ministerium*) based on Matt. 20:28, as Luther also did.

2   *Von welltlicher Uberkeytt, wie weyt man yhr gehorsam schuldig sey* (1523) (WA 11: 245–281). Quoted here according to the translation in Harro Höpfl (ed.), *Luther and Calvin on secular authority* (Cambridge 1991).

3   Lohse 1981: 172; Junghans 2008: 23. The idea of the two realms or kingdoms (*Regimente*) barely constitutes a 'doctrine' in the dogmatic sense (Bornkamm 1960: 29). Luther himself considered OSA to constitute not so much a teaching as a pastoral guideline: 'In short, I know nothing about what laws to recommend to a prince; I want only to instruct him how to dispose his heart […]' (OSA 35). Original: 'Darumb weyß ich kein recht eym fursten fur zuschreyben sondernn will nur seyn herz unterrichten, wie das soll gesynnet und geschickt seyn […]' (WA 11: 273, 2–3).

4   Brecht 1981–1987, II: 121.

done on earth, as the final section of OSA shows.[5] It has been argued that the Reformation had at no point been a purely religious phenomenon. It addressed important themes of socio-political development in the early sixteenth century and benefited not least from the constitution of the Holy Roman Empire and the power wielded by strong local princes within the empire's overall structure.[6] It is at *these* princes that OSA is addressed and *they* who are exhorted to be 'Christian' in faith and action. Needless to say, OSA was intended to turn a political attitude into a Christian one, in keeping with the spirit of the Reformation.

From the outset, it must be emphasised that Luther, in OSA, used neither the term 'cooperatio' nor that of 'partnership'. The terms he does use are rather 'secular kingdom/kingship and government', 'God's/Christ's kingdom',[7] 'vocation', 'work', 'service', 'benefit', 'love', 'help' and 'justice'.[8] Yet the question remains whether Luther might not be read differently and whether, regardless of the concepts it uses or not, the logic of the treatise might not indeed suggest a partnership between politically active Christians and God. In making such a suggestion, Luther would be far from unusual, but would rather participate in a long-standing Christian

5   WA 11: 278ff.
6   Moeller/Stackmann 1981: 132; Kohler 1990; Seibt 1990; Kaufmann 2006: 45; Ehrenpreis/Heumann 2008: 1. On the reform of the imperial constitution by the Golden Bull of 1356, promulgated by Charles IV (d. 1378) and by Maximilian I (d. 1519) at the 1495 Diet of Worms, see Kaufmann 2009: 42ff.
7   As with many aspects of Luther's thought, scholarship is divided with regard to his terminology of 'kingdoms' or 'realms'. Whereas some scholars maintain that Luther did not use the two terms synonymously, absorbing the concept of the kingdom (*Reich*) in that of government (*Regiment*), others argue that the terms' parallel usage by Luther does suggest that they are at least to some extent synonymous. I agree with the latter view: By prioritising neither one term nor the other, Luther leaves no doubt that he holds them to be more or less equal in meaning. Moreover, he often uses the word 'sword' as a synonym for secular authority or secular government (Raunio 2004: 151 n. 1). Luther is unlikely to have thought of language and concepts in the terms of modern analytic philosophy. On the discussion, see also Leppin 2011: 247f.
8   As far as I am aware, Siegfried Hoyer is alone in having emphasised the centrality of these concepts to OSA (Hoyer 1986: 127, 130).

discourse of rule. And although Luther can be seen to make his personal imprint on this discourse, he harks back to common sources, notably the Bible and the Patristic tradition.[9]

Luther's thinking was guided by context. The Gospels to him were God's presence in the world's contexts: the kingdom of Christ, European Christendom, Christian life in the German territories. Accordingly, Luther is able to imply a logic of partnership in OSA without ever using the word 'partner'. It must be remembered that, historically speaking, the Reformation was accompanied by a 'particularisation of the ecclesiastical landscape'[10] and a 'parcelling of the Church',[11] which meant that the Roman Curia's claim to supremacy in religion and (particularly) in politics was denied. This entailed a shift from the mediaeval idea of rule as sacred and substituting for God to an idea of rule as partnership and an 'appointment' or 'vocation' (*Berufung*) to office.[12] The logic of the ruler's involvement in a partnership comes to replace the earlier logic of intercession.[13]

Regarding the Lutheran political theology of OSA, the argument to be developed here is that the 'two kingdoms doctrine' represents a form of political 'instruction' that is complementary and geared to cooperation. This can be deduced from both the work's structure and the taxonomy of the concepts it employs. The present argument is based on an attempt to localise the key argument in the third part of the treatise, which is concerned with practical matters. I read OSA as an inverted pyramid, concerned less with the formula of the two kingdoms[14] than with the concrete

9   Hoyer 1986: 130.
10 Hamm 2008b: 5. Walter Ziegler made the following observations regarding the structural properties of the Reformation's early (pre–1530) territorial supporters: they were (1) small territories, lacking both (2) an important position within the empire and (3) a longer tradition reaching back far into the Middle Ages. They (4) were late in making the step towards modern statehood, (5) displayed a weak structure of estates, (6) had not founded a university, (7) did not exist in a 'constitutive relationship' with bishops and (8) were situated far from 'larger, modern states and the emperor's lands' (Ziegler 2008: 76; on this, see Kaufmann 2006: 46).
11 Decot 2007: 31; Brady 2009: 71ff.
12 Green 2000; Hamm 2008b: 25.
13 Lohse 1981: 136.
14 See the sketch of the two kingdoms doctrine in Mörke 2005: 13.

form embodied by *Christianitas* in the prince. In support of this argument, I shall take the following steps:

First, I shall consider the figure of Luther, the reformer, beginning with approaches discussing the 'Reformation', in which the polarising figure of Luther emerges with a presence that is impossible to ignore.[15] This presence is that of a prophet – a task to which Luther himself was given to allude – though to a still greater degree it is that of a scholar. Yet this scholarly presence is too often considered as a secondary aspect of Luther: the Luther of the lectures on Genesis, the Psalms and the Epistle to the Romans, the Luther of academic disputations that have endured.[16]

Second, the treatise *On Secular Authority* itself will be considered. Following some general remarks on Lutheran political theology and a brief textual history, attention will turn to the treatise's structure, which holds the key to its entire purpose.

Third, there follows an account of Luther's concept of authority, in which authority is understood as a divine order[17] and a Christian estate called upon (*berufen*) by God.

Fourth, it is on this idea of calling or *Berufung* that a consideration of the Christian prince from the perspective of a 'curatorial' logic (*cura religionis*) is founded. At stake here is the figure of the Christian taking responsibility. By discharging his office, the Christian both serves his neighbour – thereby emulating Christ's service – and by his serving and *cooperative* presence bridges the gap between the spiritual and temporal realms.

In light of the key terms mentioned above, the conclusion seeks to emphasise that the logic on which OSA rests is that of partnership. This last step will take the form of an analysis of Luther's dialectic with regard to the Christian ruler's involvement, as an instrument and a partner, in the political act.

15   Throughout his life, Luther was subject to both enthusiastic applause and vicious slander (Schuder 2004; Leppin 2005c).

16   'Luther's theological understanding was propelled forward and deepened not only by reading in his own study, but also by the attacks of opponents, questions from friends, his own existential and personal struggle and by doubts and severe crises' (Smolinsky 2006: 31).

17   WA 11: 247, 22; *Sermon on the Eighty-Second Psalm* (Eberle 1873: 799f.).

Luther's Reformatory Presence

This section will begin by discussing so-called 'Reformation theories' before turning to Luther's reformatory personality and his scholarly achievement. It will conclude with a brief discussion of Luther's charismatic popularity, with particular reference to the success of his writings.

Historical gaps or *lacunae* tend to emerge where sources are lacking. This in turn can help to account for research approaches diverging or shifting. The example of Martin Luther[18] shows that even times and phenomena for which copious sources are available are not immune to disagreement.[19] Albrecht Ritschl could even go so far as to claim that, however widely his writings had been distributed and read, both his contemporaries and his successors had failed to understand or even actively misunderstood Luther.[20]

I have no desire to use this opportunity to reopen debates that have been the subject of entire monographs. The concept of 'Reformation' that I use here takes into account the observation that it is as difficult to speak of a 'Reformation' in the singular as it is to speak of a similarly homogeneous 'Humanism'. Scholarship leads us to conclude that 'Reformation', if the term is to mean anything, can refer only generically to a number of processes and developments which, in their differentiation and sometimes competition, ought more properly to be thought of as 'reformations'.[21] Accordingly, historical study now extends beyond the Reformation itself to the changing history of Reformation scholarship and its paradigms.[22]

Roughly speaking, we can identify three major currents, each of which displays branches, tributaries, congruences, divergences and ambiguities of

---

18 Countless bibliographies and overviews have been produced on Luther's life and work. To give just a selection: Manns 1982; Bott/Ebeling/Moeller 1983; Germanisches Nationalmuseum Nürnberg 1983; Mullett 2005; Beutel 2006; Kaufmann 2006; Leppin 2006; Kolb/Dingel/Batka 2014.
19 Hagen et al. 1991; Guggisberg/Krodel 1993.
20 Moeller 1995: 11, 23.
21 Rogge 1983: 188.
22 Winterhager 1999: 67ff.

its own. The first considers the Reformation to have been a phenomenon of upheaval, a historical *caesura* and indeed a revolutionary recasting of the 'Early Modern' age and overcoming of the 'archaic' Middle Ages.[23] Marxist scholars have interpreted events as constituting an 'early bourgeois revolution', and Engels himself propounded the 'powder keg' theory.[24] A second line of thought seeks to understand Luther and the 'Reformers' as children of their age who merely articulated tendencies already present or latent in the (late) Middle Ages. Understood thus, Luther appears simply as the product of mediaeval circumstances, as could be seen from his doctrine of grace, supposedly derived from St Augustine. This doctrine had long been upheld by the Augustinian friars (founded in 1256),[25] thus placing the Reformation in a deterministic relationship of continuity or filiation with the Middle Ages.[26]

A third current seeks to mediate between these two positions, using such concepts as 'normative centring' (*normative Zentrierung*), 'emergence of the reformation' (*Emergenz der Reformation*) and 'Lutheran narrowing'

23   First propounded by Leopold von Ranke, the more recent adherents of this line of thought include Gerhard Ritter and Thomas Kaufmann (Ehrenpreis/Heumann 2008: 18ff.).

24   The tensions forming the 'gunpowder' waiting to 'blow up' society were certainly present; what it took was for someone to put a match to the touchpaper – and that someone was Luther (Moeller 1995: 13). On the Marxist interpretation of the Reformation as an early bourgeois revolution, see Wohlfeil 1973; Laube 1984; Schorn-Schütte 1996: 100ff.; Lehmann 2004; Mörke 2005: 108.

25   This case has been argued by Heiko A. Oberman (Oberman 1981: 61, 85, 129f.; on which see Hamm 2008b: 6). According to this line of argument, Luther came into contact with the so-called *via Gregorii* (after Gregory of Rimini, died 1358) in Erfurt (both at the university and in the monastery) and became its partisan in opposition to the *via Thomae* or *via Scoti*. However, it has been objected that Luther had familiarised himself with Augustine through his own reading before entering the monastery – directly and unmediated by Gregory. Another argument goes that Luther's interest in Augustine had developed in contact with the Erfurt humanists (Köpf 2008: 31f.). On the Augustinian friars, see Kunzelmann 1969–1976 (esp. vol. 3 for the friars in Bavaria and vol. 5 for the Observant Hermits); Gindele 1977; Zumkeller 1979; Gutierrez 1975–1988.

26   Among the members of this 'school' are Ernst Troeltsch, Erich Hassinger and Paul O. Kristeller (Ehrenpreis/Heumann 2008: 21ff.).

(*lutherische Engführung*), which are designed to understand the phenomenon both in its continuity with the Middle Ages and in its gradually emerging novelty.[27] Novelty, however, should not be taken to designate a rupture, but rather in the sense of a singular intensification, compression, clarification and amplification of mediaeval tendencies.[28] Notwithstanding certain difficulties that remain to be conclusively settled, I find myself aligned with this current. I think of the Reformation not as a thing in itself, but rather as a process consisting of a complex mesh of factors, circumstances, tendencies and influences which, though rooted in mediaeval traditions, constituted a 'Reformation' only through the decisive influence of Luther.[29]

The Reformation represents a living process, one that never stops – though the much-criticised theory of confessionalisation has claimed otherwise[30] – and which admits diversity and plurality. Reformers stand at the

27 '[And so,] as a Church historian I should like to conclude with a declaration of affection for that simple notion of emergence associated with the pretty metaphor of the hippopotamus emerging from the water. What it demonstrates to us is the gradual nature of historical change, of which we are apt to lose sight if we are too fixated upon leaps and breaks' (Hamm 2008b: 26; see p. 14). See, moreover, Wendenbourg 1995: 50f.; Mörke 2005: 83ff.; Leppin 2008: 45, 66. The term 'Lutheran narrowing' (*lutherische Engführung*) was coined by Bernd Moeller (Moeller 1995: 21f.), that of 'normative centring' (*normative Zentrierung*) by Berndt Hamm (Hamm 1993).

28 Schorn-Schütte 1996: 27f.; Leppin 2005b: 314f.; Klueting 2007: 144f.; Ehrenpreis/ Heumann 2008: 24f.; Hamm 2008b: 4ff.; Köpf 2008: 29ff.

29 Selge 1976: 592, 615.

30 This social-historical approach was proposed by Wolfgang Reinhard and Heinz Schilling in order to describe the realities, both socio-political and ecclesiastical, that led to the European political sphere being divided along 'confessional' lines. Confessionalisation was made possible only by the constitution of the empire, which allowed princes to 'parcel' faith along territorial lines. The theory has been criticised chiefly for ignoring the all-important search for truth. And this social-historical approach indeed ignores the theological and existential centrality of the search for truth in faith by which people in the sixteenth century were preoccupied and which was fundamental and non-negotiable (Schilling 1995: 16; Frieß/Kießling 1999; Mörke 2005: 79f.; Decot 2007: 32f.; Ziegler 2008: 177ff.; Ehrenpreis/Heumann 2008: 63ff.). Yet here, too, the truth lies somewhere between the extremes, for it is certainly possible to speak of confessionalisation as a political and historical phenomenon. Politically, the problems thrown up by the reformation were dealt with by negotiations and compromises that produced a territorial

centre of several 'reformations', and though their opinions may differ,[31] they can be subsumed under the overarching concept of 'Reformation'. After Luther, Zwingli and Calvin, the religious and ecclesiastical landscape of Christian Europe and its actors would never be the same again. This phenomenon of renewal, intensification and emergence requires an analytical term of its own. All that can be said from the perspective of cultural hermeneutics is that the 'Reformation' is so complex a phenomenon that it cannot be grasped as a whole, but only – and this has usually been the case – by shifting emphasis and focus, by foregrounding particular elements and discourses.

Even with reference to Luther himself, it would be wrong to think of the Reformation as a 'reformatory turn' taking place in a particular year.[32] It is much more of a theological and indeed existential development on Luther's part, spanning virtually his entire life: 'I did not learn my theology all at once. I have had to brood and ponder over it more and more deeply; my *tentationes* have brought me to it, for one learns only by experience.'[33]

Attempts have been made to pin down the Reformation not only ideologically, but also socially: to town or country, to the (lower) aristocracy

---

and confessional mosaic. Theologically, however, as understood by Luther, the term 'confessionalisation' makes little sense, since both 'camps', from an ecclesiological perspective, were concerned with the true faith, which admitted no compromise or coexistence of truths. From a theological perspective, there could be no *modus vivendi*, since both 'confessions' claimed exclusive possession of the truth (*theologische Wahrheitsfrage*) and accused each other of being liars, heretics and adherents of the Antichrist. To my mind, this tension between political compromise and theological intransigence is fully evident in the 1530 Diet of Augsburg (on this, see Kaufmann 2006: 46f.; Decot 2007: 36ff.).

31   Luther and Melanchthon were indeed of different opinion on certain matters, for example, on justification and the eucharist (Flogaus 2000: 14).

32   Martin Brecht, for instance, has spoken of a twofold turn on the part of the Reformation: an outward turn against indulgences and an inward discovery of the merciful God (Brecht 1981–1987, I: 173, 187ff., 230).

33   LW 54:50. (Original: 'Ich hab meine theologiam nit auff ein mal gelernt, sonder hab ymmer tieffer und tieffer grubeln mussen, da haben mich meine tentationes hin bracht, quia sine usu non potest disci' WA TR 1: 146, 12–14). Kaufmann 2007: 204; Hamm 2008c: 105.

and gentry[34] or to the confessions. It has thus been classified as an urban event, without considering that – notwithstanding its communal character[35] and the decision of the imperial cities to adopt the Reformation[36] – it was the princes' choice that gave the Reformation the broad territorial basis it needed to succeed. The territorial princes made from Reformation a *politicum*.[37] Yet this should not be taken to mean that the Reformation had served as a political weapon. It was genuinely concerned with addressing people's desire for salvation – particularly of those people who were worried that the Church, in its existing form, was no longer capable of offering salvation.[38]

The different lines of explanation largely agree that Martin Luther was the key figure of the Reformation and that his protest against the Church's

34 An instance of this are the feuds of Franz von Sickingen. From a socio-political perspective, the minor German aristocracy was in poor shape in the early sixteenth century. The resultant frustration and the impact of Luther's writings encouraged one of its representatives, Franz von Sickingen, to think of himself as the armed wing of the Reformation, which he tried to promote by force of arms, leading a revolt against the prince-archbishop of Trier in 1522–1523. Such events led scholars to conclude that the Reformation owed a great deal to the support of the lower aristocracy and in turn had contributed to solidifying its collective identity. The Reformation was thus imagined as having been supported by the 'common man': peasants, the gentry, town dwellers (Decot 2007: 19f.).

35 The theory of communalism holds that local communities and their core valuations formed the central instance of basic decisions of constitutional rank in old Europe (Schorn-Schütte 1996: 104f.; Smolinksy 2006: 61; Decot 2007: 16; Ziegler 2008: 25, 194; Ehrenpreis/Heumann 2008: 41ff.).

36 Among the Reformation's early adherents were the imperial cities of Nuremberg, Strasbourg, Goslar and Regensburg. The Speyer Protestation of 1529 was signed by fourteen imperial cities (Smolinksy 2006: 60; Eberhardt Bate 2007). The name 'protestants' goes back to the *protestatio* of the imperial states supporting the Reformation at the Diet of Speyer against the recess of 1526, in which restrictions had been placed on the freedom of worship (Ehrenpreis/Heumann 2008: 1). To the general semantics of 'protestants' in early modern period, see Witt 2011.

37 Ziegler 2008: 40. The 'territorial princes' implicated in the early Reformation were the Elector of Saxony, the Landgrave of Hesse, the Duke of Brunswick-Lüneburg, the Margrave of Brandenburg-Ansbach and finally the Prince of Anhalt (Ziegler 2008: 35f., 64).

38 Hamm 1995: 58; Vainio 2008: 25f., 42.

sale of indulgences set in motion the train of events.[39] This is not to reduce
the critical moment to one monk's courageous posting of ninety-five theses
to the church door at Wittenberg – an event whose historical veracity, for
all its legendary aura, has repeatedly been questioned.[40] Luther's theses were
not even intended to question the Church's authority, but were directed
only at a pastoral practice which he held to be dogmatically indefensible.[41]
In speaking of Luther the 'Reformer', I refer to his entire life and the development of a man who, as a scholar and a prophet, brought into existence
a new religious reality.

Attempts have been made to explain Luther's life in psychoanalytic
terms, as a revolt against the all too strict authority of his father, Hans Luder
(d. 1530).[42] Other historians have found Luther to have been in thrall to

39   Kaufmann 2009: 151.
40   The claim that the theses had never been posted but were rather the product of
      early Reformation myth-making was first advanced by Erwin Iserloh (see Iserloh
      1966: passim, esp. 65ff.). In fact, Iserloh argues, the ninety-five theses had formed
      the basis for a standard academic *disputatio* and as such had been sent directly to the
      bishops Hieronymus Schulz and Albrecht of Brandenburg. Iserloh's argument rests
      on the silence both of Luther and other sources on this supposed event. Instead, it
      was Melanchthon who, after Luther's death, had been the first to mention Luther's
      'heroic' posting of the theses, thereby creating a myth that only grew in strength
      over the subsequent years. Though more recent historians have qualified Iserloh's
      arguments, the fact remains that no contemporary source refers explicitly to Luther
      posting the theses to the church door. There is, however, no shortage of indirect evi-
      dence, both in Luther's *Table Talk* and in mediaeval academic practice, that might
      be interpreted as supporting the story's veracity. In any case, scholars remain div-
      ided over this question (Volz 1967; Lohse 1981: 56f.; Smolinksy 2006: 37f.; Decot
      2007: 14; Hamm 2008: 29ff.; Ott/Treu 2008; Kaufmann 2009: 182).
41   Wicks 1983: 97f.
42   The debate was rekindled in the 1970s by the American psychologist Erik E. Erikson,
      who diagnosed Luther with a father complex (according to Freudian terminology).
      It was from this father complex that had supposedly emerged Luther's theology of
      a merciful and forgiving God against the reactionary and compulsive structures
      of the Church of his day. Luther's feeble constitution and his torments are both
      understood as resulting from psychosis and extreme fear rooted in this father com-
      plex. Against such claims stand Luther's strong affection for his parents and the
      forms of child-rearing commonplace in the sixteenth century, which were generally
      strict, not just in Luther's case (Erikson 1975: 282ff., 294, passim; Reiter 1937–1941;
      Becke 1970; Lohse 1981: 33, 37ff.; Oberman 1981: 92; Hendrix 1990; Smolinsky

his mother Margarete (née Lindemann, d. 1531),[43] a claim that has found much support among scholars of gender.[44] Intellectually, his theology has been situated in the monastic tradition, with Platonic influences traceable to contacts with the Erfurt humanists.[45] Taken together, these approaches represent efforts to understand Luther's personality in its full complexity.

What is often ignored is that Luther was above all a scholar. His search for truth in faith would have been impossible but for its solid grounding in scholarship – as would his success. Luther's theology and 'Reformation' were the outcome not only of struggle and polemical pamphleteering (*Flugblätter*),[46] but also of his scholarly productivity, by which Luther's credibility and competence were established. His affirmations were founded upon careful reflection, wide reading, academic discussion and many weeks and months labouring at his desk.

The reformer grew up as one of many children[47] of a lower-middle-class family in the town of Mansfeld, seat of the eponymous county. Though it came of peasant stock, the family set great store by education.[48] Hans Luder, who had achieved a degree of material wealth,[49] was able to pay for young Martin's schooling (until about 1498) and his subsequent studies, from which he graduated as *magister artium* in 1505 and *baccalaureus biblicus* in 1509,[50] and received his son's respect and gratitude in return. Though

---

2006: 32). On Luther's medical history, see Schubart 1917; Oberman 1981: 332ff.; Gaude 1979–1983.

43   Oberman 1981: 95.
44   Karant-Nunn 2004.
45   Leppin 2008b: 101.
46   On Luther's pamphleteering, see Kaufmann 2009: 303ff. 'In scholarship, a pamphlet is considered to be a text printed separately, comprising only a few pages or sheets, and which can be printed and distributed rapidly' (Burkhardt 2002: 28).
47   Luther had eight siblings, but only five children survived to adulthood: Martin, his brother Jakob and three sisters (see Kaufmann 2006: 28).
48   Schwarz 2004: 4; Kaufmann 2006: 29.
49   Oberman 1981: 88ff.; Dohle 2007.
50   The bachelor's degree was awarded at the end of the basic course in philosophy, which included grammar, logic and natural philosophy. The master's degree concluded the main course in philosophy, which included mathematics, arithmetic, astronomy, metaphysics and ethics (Kaufmann 2006: 29ff.).

Hans Luder was not entirely satisfied with his son's ecclesiastical, monastic and theological career, the relationship seems to have been positive overall, Martin holding his father in high esteem.[51] And though his father had hoped that his son would take a law degree,[52] Martin Luther entered the monastery of the Hermits of Saint Augustine at Erfurt on 17 June 1505.[53]

Luther's education was as wide-ranging as his academic contacts.[54] To cite just the key points in his intellectual development: his years at the monastery and university of Erfurt, his Wittenberg companions, his predilection for St Augustine and Bernard of Clairvaux, his acquaintance with other Christian and non-Christian authors, his first relevant disputations on the academic stage. Copious marginal notes testify to the works he read most intensely: Augustine and Jerome, Bernard of Clairvaux, Anselm of Canterbury, Peter Lombard, Bonaventure, William of Occam, Johannes Tauler.[55]

Luther had already made the acquaintance of the *Devotio Moderna* in his early youth, joining one of its lay fraternities, the Brethren of the Common Life, in Magdeburg at the age of fourteen.[56] Later, in Wittenberg, Luther testified to his familiarity with that movement's literary output. He held Johannes Gerster in high esteem, referring to him as 'Doctor Comforter' (*Doktor Tröster*).[57] Luther also received a decent education in Latin, which included training in the *ars epistolandi*. His musical ability is

---

51   See Luther's letter to his father dated 15 February 1530, in: Luther-Briefe an Freunde und Familie 1987: 43ff. He was much saddened by Hans Luders's death (Oberman 1981: 322). See also Bornkamm 1975.

52   Luther had indeed registered to study law in 1505, though he did not complete the course (Kaufmann 2006: 32). On Luther's turbulent youth, see Emme 1983: 10ff. It has furthermore been claimed that Luther's entry into the monastery was not brought about by the vow to St Anne made during a storm near Stotternheim (in Thuringia), but rather by Luther having killed a fellow student at Erfurt (Emme 1983: 253).

53   Lohse 2006: 106; Hamm 2008c: 103. On the Augustinian monastery in Erfurt, see Schmelz/Ludscheidt 2005.

54   According to Bernhard Lohse, the traditions that most affected Luther were those established by Occam, Augustine, Staupitz and humanism (Lohse 1995: 35ff.).

55   Köpf 2008: 37.

56   He had previously attended the grammar school in Mansfeld.

57   Oberman 1981: 100ff.

also likely to have been formed in these years,[58] and he often spoke of the great importance of early school years in the life of Christians and men in general.[59]

At Erfurt,[60] Luther stood in close contact to the circle of humanists. Though their influence on him is undeniable, it ought not to be over-estimated.[61] Alongside a monastic tradition focused on experience and a scholastic and critical tradition, humanism influenced the 'early' Luther by encouraging him to pay close attention to the Scriptures and the Fathers, as well as imparting a strong Christological bent to his theology.[62] The fundamental attitude of a *vita activa* in the service of others, which is also apparent in the emphasis placed on service by *On Secular Authority*, may well have been influenced by these contacts. Through his teachers Jodocus Trutfetter[63] and Bartholomaeus Arnoldi of Usingen, Luther became familiar with the moderate *via moderna* of Occamism.[64] Erfurt Occamism[65] was

---

58 Lohse 1981: 33; Emme 1983; Schwarz 2004: 5; Kaufmann 2006: 29.

59 Hammerstein 2003: 18ff.

60 On the University of Erfurt in the Middle Ages, see Kleineidam 1969.

61 'The influence of early humanism on Luther [in his Erfurt years] did not go far beyond familiarity with certain Latin poets and an increased sensitivity for Latin expression' (Kaufmann 2006: 31; see Oberman 1981: 131; Junghans 1985; Moeller 1991: 101, 108).

62 Decot 2007: 15; Leppin 2008b: 98.

63 Theological disagreements notwithstanding, Luther loved his old teacher Jodocus Trutfetter, whom he addressed as *mi suavissime praeceptor* in a letter written in 1518 (Grane 1975: 128; Emme 1983: 51ff.).

64 Also known as terminism or nominalism (Hamel 1934: 14; Oberman1981: 125, 127; Schorn-Schütte 1996: 28; Schwarz 2004: 7; Kaufmann 2006: 31; Smolinsky 2006: 28ff.). In his early years, Luther had referred to Occam as 'my master' (Oberman 1981: 127). On William of Occam, see Leppin 1995; Richter/Leibold 1998; Spade 1999; Kraml/Leibold 2003. The *via moderna* was critical of the (Thomist) *via antiqua*. While the latter was 'realist', that is, upheld the real exist-ence of universals (abstract concepts), the *via moderna* found their reality to reside in human thought alone, which used them to make sense of the cosmos through in-dividual experience. Individual experience contributed to knowledge of the world by experiences being shared and compared with those of other observers and hence generalised (Kaufmann 2006: 93).

65 Erfurt was an outpost of Occamite nominalism (Lohse 1981: 34; Oberman 1981: 123f.). Generally speaking, the connections between Augustinian theologians

strongly influenced by Gabriel Biel (d. 1495), professor of philosophy at Tübingen. It was highly critical of centralism, the practices of the Roman Curia[66] and of Thomistic theology.[67] His first years in the monastery imprinted monastic practices and piety on Luther, and his later theology was rooted in the doubts and existential torments he experienced and overcame there. Yet this theology was the product not only of an existential struggle, but also the fruit of profound studies, which were crowned when Luther received his doctorate at Wittenberg in 1512.[68] His Wittenberg friends – Philip Melanchthon (d. 1560); Georg Spalatin (d. 1545); Nikolaus von Amsdorff (d. 1565) – had no small part to play in the articulation of Lutheran theology.

Melanchthon came to Wittenberg in 1518 brimming with youthful energy[69] and went on to become Luther's closest friend and collaborator. It was Melanchthon's humanist enthusiasm for languages that encouraged Luther to learn Hebrew, using the grammar of Reuchlin (d. 1522), and Melanchthon himself taught Luther to write Greek characters in 1519.[70]

---

and so-called 'Occamism' appear to have been much closer than was long assumed. More recent research has found a radical division between 'Augustinianism' and 'Occamism' to be untenable, especially after about 1340. They refer to both Staupitz and Luther and their common debt to Biel (Courtenay 2008: 23ff., 349ff.).

66   It may be appropriate here to recall the 'proto-reformatory' case of the Erfurt theologian Johannes von Wese who, as preacher at the cathedral of Worms, had fallen foul of the inquisition by speaking in favour of laypeople receiving the chalice, criticising the practice of indulgences and asserting the sole authority of Scripture. He was sentenced to lifelong imprisonment (Oberman 1981: 122).

67   Lohse 1981: 34; Beckmann 1995: 182f. According to Lohse, Luther barely knew Thomas Aquinas (Lohse 1981: 34: 'Luther is likely barely to have read Thomas at all.').

68   On 18/19 October 1512. On this, see Steinlein 1912: 13f. and passim; Smolinsky 2006: 30. Luther was always convinced of the deep significance of his doctorate, which he initially took as a sign of having been called by God to uphold the Word and the teachings of the Church and later, following his break with the Roman Church, Christ's truth (see Kaufmann 2006: 20). On the University of Wittenberg in Luther's day, see Dingel/Wartenberg 2002.

69   Scheible 2010.

70   Raeder 1961: 308; Oberman 1981: 131; Kaufmann 2006: 112f.

Their joint efforts as well as their disagreements[71] laid the foundations for the theology of the Reformation in its Wittenberg form.[72] Melanchthon's arrival at Wittenberg gave a humanistic impetus to its theologians by emphasising the necessity of the critical examination of sources. In his inaugural address, Melanchthon expressed his intention of recasting theological studies in a humanist mould. A key role in this was to fall to the so-called *syncera theologia*, which was centred on Christ's cross.[73]

The scholarship on Luther is unanimous in recognising St Augustine – *Doctor gratiae* – as the reformer's spiritual mentor, especially in his interpretation of the Pauline epistles (*interpres fidelissimus*) and the doctrine of justification that he derived from them.[74] Luther's Augustine is above all the Augustine of the anti-Pelagian writings (*De spiritu et littera*, etc.), which stress God's grace and sole power to grant salvation, and in which man's free will is denied.[75] Yet disagreement persists as to how Luther familiarised himself with Augustine in the first place, whether it was primarily through his order at Erfurt or rather by his own reading while at university.[76] It is uncontroversial, on the other hand, that Luther referred to Augustine throughout his life and not least in his political theology.[77] There can thus be little doubt that Luther's own doctrine of the two kingdoms is a successor to the Augustinian dualism of the two *civitates* that had such a formative

---

71 Although their relationship was not free of tensions – not least in their dispute over the eucharist – it was largely characterised by mutual respect, esteem and affection (see Neuser 1992).

72 Lohse 1983; Peters 2005; Vind 2007: 97.

73 'Wittenberg theology [pursues] the goal of a syncera et nativa theologia [...] which, by studying languages, arrives at a correct interpretation of the Bible [...]. [Luther] here places Christ's cross at the centre of the theologia syncerissiama. Theologia syncerissima is, to him, the kind of theology in which the attempt is made to arrive at a pure interpretation of Christ's word by emphasising his cross' (Kim 2008: 15).

74 Hamel 1934: 34ff.; Grane 1975: 25; Schulze 2001: 573ff.

75 Hamel 1934: 10; Lohse 1995: 87; Schwarz 2004: 133; Kaufmann 2006: 145; Lohse 2006: 112.

76 Hamel 1934: 5; Saak 2002; Wriedt 2007: 36ff.; Leppin 2005b: 46 and 2008c: 17ff.

77 'The role accorded to Augustine by Luther in the years 1516 to 1519 is far greater than that which he finds himself able to grant him retrospectively in 1538 and 1545' (Grane 1975: 26).

influence on the European Middle Ages.[78] Contrary to Augustine, however, Luther seeks to overcome the separation between the *civitas terrena* (*reych der welt*) and the *civitas Dei perennis* (*reych Gottis*)[79] eschatologically, that is, in the concept of Christ's kingdom on earth (*Reich Christi*).

Aside from Augustine, Bernard of Clairvaux – *Doctor mellifluus* – was the only one of the Church Fathers whom Luther continued to honour, as *Pater Bernhardus*, even after his definitive break with the Church: 'Let us take as an example St Bernard, whom I prefer above all other monks. For if ever there has been a pious monk, it must surely have been St Bernard.'[80] Bernard's influence on Luther's theology seems to have been quite strong.[81] Scholars have found in Bernard precedents both for Luther's principle of *sola fide* as well as for the passivity of faith and for justification as being given not on merit, but as a pure gift on the part of the merciful God.[82] As for the aspect of service according to the model of Christ's own servitude – a question of particular relevance to *On Secular Authority* – Bernard had already said this in his *Sermones super Canticum Canticorum*:

> As for me, dear brothers, from the early days of my conversion, conscious of my grave lack of merits, I made sure to gather for myself this little bunch of myrrh and place it between my breasts. It was culled from all the anxious hours and bitter experiences of my Lord; first from the privations of his infancy, then from the hardships he endured in preaching, the fatigues of his journeys, the long watches in prayer, the temptations when he fasted, his tears of compassion, the heckling when he addressed the people, and finally the dangers from traitors in the brotherhood, the insults, the spitting, the blows, the mockery, the scorn, the nails and similar torments that are multiplied in the Gospels, like trees in the forest, and all for the salvation of our race.[83]

78 Brecht 1981–1987, II: 120.
79 WA 11: 249, 25. On Luther's overcoming of Augustine's radical separation, see Duchrow 1981: 181ff.
80 WA 16: 399, 31–33. Köpf 2008: 39.
81 Oberman 1981: 76ff.; Bell 1993: 361; Bell 1999.
82 Drömann 2007: 332; Köpf 2008: 90 n. 4. On the prehistory of anti-meritorian theology as instanced by the late mediaeval Porretaneans, see Hamm 1977: 26ff.
83 Bernard of Clairvaux SS II, 245. 'Et ergo, fratres, ab ineunte mea conversione, pro acervo meritorum quae mihi deesse sciebam, hunc mihi fasciculum colligare et inter ubera mea collocare curavi, collectum ex omnibus anxietatibus et amaritudinibus Domini mei, primum videlicet infantilium illarum necessitatum, deinde laborum quos pertulit in praedicando, fatigationum in discurrendo, vigiliarum in orando,

This reference of Bernard's to Christ's human suffering for our salvation (see 1 Cor. 2:2, Gal. 6:14) is interpreted by Luther as indicative of the Saviour's humanity in service (see Phil. 2). As for the Christian ruler, Luther addresses him as a Christian who must serve and discharge his office.

Only brief incursions can be made here into the long list of authors, both pagan and Christian, whom Luther discussed and to whom he took a wide range of attitudes, from outright condemnation to praise. Reference should at least be made to his sharp criticisms of Aristotle (*rancidus philosophus*), mediaeval Aristotelianism and Thomism,[84] as well as to his 1521 book directed at the Louvain theologian Jacob Latomus (d. 1544), in which Luther drew upon the rhetorician Quintilian (d. AD 96), whom Luther much admired.[85] St Jerome, by contrast, never comes off particularly well in Luther's writings, though he was fond of quoting the Father's statements against the primacy of the popes, all the better to beat the 'papists' at their own game.[86] Nicholas of Cusa (d. 1464), by contrast, was favourably received by Luther, and many instances of his influence are discernible.[87] On the whole, the Church Fathers played a positive – though far from

---

tentationum in ieiunando, lacrimarum in compatiendo, insidiarum in colloquendo, postremo periculorum in falsis fratribus, conviciorum, sputorum, colaphorum, subsannationum, exprobrationum, clavorum horumque similium, quae in salutem nostri generis silva evangelica copiosissime noscitur protulisse' (Bernard of Clairvaux Sermones CC: Sermo 43, c. 3, pp. 42, 18–27).

84   Luther considered himself knowledgeable enough on Aristotle to criticise him. The invectives levelled by Luther at the ancient philosopher are legion and include such insults as *fabulator, artifex verborum, illusor ingeniorum, seductor scholasticorum doctorum, blinder heyde* (blind pagan), *Fürst der Finsternis* (prince of darkness) (Müller 1981: 55, 57; Oberman 1981: 169). Yet in *To the Christian Nobility* (1520), Luther conceded that Aristotle's logic, poetics and rhetoric were in fact useful and hence worthy of being taught at universities. In fact, Luther's critique of Aristotle is aimed not at the entire *Corpus Aristotelicum*, but merely at certain of its aspects (Müller 1981: 58). See also Dieter 2001; Mühlen 2002.

85   Hermann 1961: 104f.; Vind 2007: 96.

86   Hennings 1998: 95ff.; Schulze 2001: 600ff. Luther also quoted Jerome in the Heidelberg Disputation or in the commentary on Galatians, though this by no means outweighs his sharp attacks on Jerome, Erasmus's favourite, in *On the Bondage of the Will* (Augustijn 1992).

87   Weier 1967: 60ff. and *passim*.

authoritative – role to Luther, at least to the extent that he found their interpretations of the Scriptures to be useful. Luther freely admitted the debt his own biblical commentaries owed to those of Saints John Chrysostom, Jerome and Ambrose.[88]

Of particular interest is Luther's ambivalent stance towards that darling of mediaeval theology, Dionysius the Pseudo-Areopagite. Luther often quoted Dionysius in his early lectures at Wittenberg, but grew increasingly critical of him and especially of his mysticism. Luther accused Dionysius's mysticism of grasping for an obscure God, shrouded in darkness, while failing to recognise that God was close at hand in the world itself. Moreover, Luther was never really comfortable with Dionysius's anthropology, influenced as it was by the Aristotelian doctrine of virtue. The idea that the Fall had not completely destroyed human nature, but rather left intact such natural properties as reason, will and affects, thereby enabling man to contribute to his own salvation, must have struck Luther as essentially Pelagian.[89]

Luther, the academic, confronted formidable opponents in pathbreaking disputations, which proved decisive in determining the development of his theology. For instance, the principle of *Sola Scriptura* emerged from the Leipzig disputation (4–14 July 1519) with Johannes Eck (d. 1543), professor at the University of Ingolstadt.[90] This principle

88   Mühlen 1998: 144, 147; Schulze 2001: 613; Leppin 2005: 45.
89   See the *scholia* on Rom. 5:22 (WA 56: 299) or his critique of the anthropology of the Pseudo-Areopagite in WA 42: 45, 35–39. On this, see Weier 1967: 109; Rochler 1973; Brecht 1981–1987, I: 137; Oberman 1986: 54; Rorem 1997: 300f.; Mühlen 2003; Hamm 2007: 245 n. 21 and 272 n. 111; Kim 2008: 65. Often, the target of criticism is clear without Dionysius being mentioned by name. It is, however, uncertain that Luther knew his works at all well. The criticisms mentioned here indicate that Luther misunderstood Dionysius and may thus have received him only indirectly, via other mediaeval authors (Brecht 1981–1987, I: 137; Malysz 2008: 680f.).
90   Eck forced Luther into such a corner that he was compelled to admit, in order not to contradict his own statements on indulgences, that the decisions of councils were not normative and binding. Councils could thus err, and their canons hence required confirmation by Scripture as the only authoritative instance. However, to deny the authority of councils was heretical under canon law as it then applied, allowing Eck to 'prove' that Luther followed in the heretical tradition of Jan Hus. This did not, however, trouble Luther unduly, who was far more concerned with

stresses the sole authority of the Bible as the word of God against that of the councils. The Heidelberg disputation, which had taken place in the previous year (26 April 1518) had compelled Luther to lay the foundations for his doctrine of justification. It was here that he outlined the tenets of his guiding principle, the so-called *theologia crucis* – the sinfulness of man; bound, unfree will; the operation of grace solely in and by faith; the soteriological centrality of Christ's sacrifice – which Luther opposed to the *theologia gloriae* of the scholastics.[91]

These two disputations are relevant to my analysis of *On Secular Authority* not least because the Leipzig disputation emphasises Luther's anti-clerical programme against the papal Church.[92] From here, a line can easily be drawn to the priesthood of all Christians proclaimed by Luther in *To the Christian Nobility of the German Nation* (1520), in which Luther held that every Christian – the prince included – stood in an unmediated relationship with God. Moreover, the Heidelberg disputation provided the foundation for the further development of Luther's theory of justification, which was spelled out in *On the Freedom of a Christian* (1520) and is also clearly at work in OSA.

Luther was a 'prophet' to the extent that he proclaimed a theology rooted in human experience that ran contrary both to scholastic, speculative approaches and to the mainstream of the Church and its hierarchy: his idea was 'clearly a theology that, rather than losing itself in idle speculation, addressed itself to the key existential problem of the troubled conscience and its consolation'.[93] Luther's pastoral competence[94] was founded on his own experience of temptation, doubt and consolation, on his experience of the gentle, merciful and loving God, who is not swayed by human (in)

---

upholding his truth, which held that the Bible was the medium of God's word and law and hence the guiding instance of Christendom (Lohse 1981: 59; Brecht 1981–1987, I: 302; Schwarz 2004: 66ff.; Wallace 2004: 78f.; Kaufmann 2006: 233ff.; Leppin 2008c: 25f.). The theses of the Leipzig disputation are in WA 2: 160, 28–161, 39. On Johannes Eck, see Schulze 1996.

91 Lohse 1981: 57f.; Loewenich 1989: 323, 325, 327; Schwarz 2004: 154; Kaufmann 2006: 216ff.
92 See the contributions in Dykema/Oberman 1993.
93 Hamm 2008c: 111.
94 Moeller 1995: 17.

ability and achievement, but who by his love gives that which alone can offer salvation, the faith in Christ crucified.[95]

Luther's 'prophetic' style can be seen even in his name, which is an allusive combination of his actual surname *Luder* and the humanist name of *Eleutherius* by which he briefly went.[96] The name *Luther* testifies to the consciousness of Luder, the individual, freed from sin and fear and stepping forth into Christian freedom without losing the man he once was. Yet there he stood, a Christian and hence a new man. Liberation, to Luther, was the result not of a personal struggle against sin and the Devil, but rather a gracious liberation, passively received.[97]

Luther is a prophet not in the sense of one offering a radical renewal, but rather in the sense of one looking to restore and bring back to life an authentically Christian ethos. Accordingly, anything Christian and given to the world by Christ was good and worthy of preservation, even if it belonged to the papacy and the Roman Church:

> We for our part confess that there is much that is Christian and good under the papacy; indeed everything that is Christian and good is to be found there and has come to us from this source. For instance we confess that in the papal Church there are the true holy Scriptures, true baptism, the true sacrament of the altar, the true keys to the forgiveness of sins, the true office of the ministry, the true catechism in the form of the Lord's Prayer, the Ten Commandments, and the articles of the Creed.[98]

Far from being a schismatic process, the Reformation was to mark a return to the true Gospel of Christ. As for Luther himself, his was most likely a propheticism of the unselfish, Old Testament variety,[99] as hinted

---

95   Lohse 1981: 35ff.; Hamm 2008c: 117f., 121.
96   Luther first signed a letter (to Johannes Lang) in the humanistic, graecised version of *Martinus Eleutherius* on 11 November 1517 (Kaufmann 2006: 7; Hamm 2008b: 39). The name *Luther* was first used in a letter to Archbishop Albrecht of Mainz dated 31 October 1517 (Kaufmann 2006: 17). On this, see the groundbreaking study by Moeller/Stackmann 1981: esp. 198ff.
97   Stümke 2007: 109f.
98   LW 40: 231f., WA 26: 147, 14–18.
99   'For all his immense literary output, he received not a penny in royalties' (Lohse 1981: 44).

at by Luther himself,[100] directed against the abuses and corruption of the Church of his time. By no means was it a struggle *against* Christ's Church. To Luther, the true Christian ethos was to be found not in human *praxis*, which was apt to be erroneous, but rather in the spiritual life directed by the word of God.[101] The Church of Rome, however, condemned these opinions as heresy and rebellion. Having been threatened with banishment on 15 July 1520, Luther was indeed excommunicated on 3 January 1521, in a papal bull entitled *Decet Romanum Pontificem*.[102] Henceforth, Luther could no longer take freedom for granted and was threatened by the vengeance of the outraged mob if he ventured into Catholic territories.[103]

Luther's success was remarkable above all for the distribution of his works in print, in which respect he surpassed even Erasmus. He was so popular an author that sales could be generated merely by printing his initials on a book's cover or title page.[104]

100 'But God who has opened my mouth and bidden me to speak, stands firmly by me, and without any counsel or effort of mine strengthens and extends my cause all the more, the more they rage, and seems, as the second Psalm says, "to have them in derision." By this alone any one not blinded by prejudice may see that the work is of God; for it exhibits the divine method, according to which God's cause spreads most rapidly when men exert themselves most to oppose and suppress it' (quoted in Painter 1889, p. 174). ('Aber weyl myr Gott den mund auff gethan hatt und mich heyssen reden, dazu so krefftiglich bey myr stehet und meyne sache on meynen rad und thatt so viel stercker macht und weytter ausbreytt, so viel sie mehr toben, und sich gleich stellet als lache und spotte er yhrs tobens, wie der ander psalm sagt: An wilchem alleyne mercken mag wer nicht verstockt ist, das dies sache mus Gottes eygen seyn. Sintemal sich die art Goettlichs worts und wercks hie euget, wilchs allzeyt denn am meysten zunimpt, wenn mans auffs hoehist verfolgt und dempffen will', WA 15: 27, 12–20). To his contemporaries, too, Luther seemed a prophet in the style of Daniel or Elijah, though Luther himself discouraged such comparisons. Luther's 'prophetic' presence and popularity among his contemporaries was reflected not least in the growing circulation of his portrait (Kaufmann 2006: 22f).

101 Leppin 2008c: 30; Lexutt 2008: 164.

102 Brecht 1981–1987, I: 372; Lohse 1981: 59f. The bull threatening his excommunication was entitled *Exsurge Domine*.

103 Kaufmann 2006: 84.

104 Schottenloher 1940: 369ff.; Burkhardt 2002: 28ff.

Printing provided Luther with a vast and ready audience which Hus could not have imagined. Many of Luther's early writings appeared in short, pithy vernacular pamphlets which could be quickly and cheaply produced and widely distributed. Luther became the publishing industry's first best-selling author, whose name on the cover could quickly sell out a press run. Printers pirated his works or inserted his name as the author of other anticlerical writings.[105]

By the end of 1519, there were already forty-five individual works[106] by Luther on sale in 259 editions, with the total number of copies estimated at around 200,000. German writings were far more successful than Latin ones, a fact which allows inferences to be made concerning Luther's readership. By the winter of 1522–1523, 150 titles were on the market in 110 editions, making it impossible even to estimate the number of copies.[107] In Luther's lifetime, 694 works and anthologies were printed in 3,998 editions, among which were 2,990 in German, 174 in Low German, 667 in Latin and 169 translations into other languages.[108]

On Secular Authority falls into Luther's most productive phase as a writer, between 1521 and 1526.[109] This shows that the 'political' question had a key role to play in these troubled years of the Reformation and contradicts the notion that Luther had had no political interests and hence had

---

105   Wallace 2004: 77.
106   In October 1518 Froben published all of Luther's Latin writings to date. This edition was followed by two new printings, one by Schürer of Strasbourg in February 1519 and another by Cratander of Basel in March 1520. It was the latter, too, who in 1520 published the first edition of all Luther's German treatises to have appeared by the end of the previous year (see Wolgast 1970: 9). Though it is worth calling to mind Luther's fundamental aversion to a collected works, the first volumes of such a collection appeared even during his lifetime, with Melanchthon as its driving force (the *Wittenberger Ausgabe* of 1539–1559, with Latin and German divisions) (see Benzing 1965: 17). With few exceptions, the volumes of this edition were edited by the master printer Hans Lufft (d. 1584). *On Secular Authority* was reprinted, with a preface by Melanchthon in Volume 6 (592b–605b), published in early 1553 (see Wolgast 1970: 14ff., 157, 205).
107   Moeller 1995: 15ff. A detailed list of and statistics concerning these publications can be found in Moeller 2001: 39.
108   Moeller 2001b: 43f.
109   Edwards 1988.

developed no political theology.[110] To Luther, political purpose was part of the broader Christian purpose of the nascent Reformation movement. Luther was aware of the secular presence of Christians, and from his own experience with his patron Frederick III (the Wise; d. 1525)[111] realised how powerful a prince's convictions might be and how heavy was the weight upon his shoulders. This weight indeed resembled that borne by Christ Himself: 'But he [the Christian prince] must anticipate a great deal of envy and suffering. As illustrious a man as this will soon feel the cross lying on his neck.'[112]

The Textual History and Structure of *On Secular Authority*

This section opens with the question whether there exists such a thing as a coherent Lutheran 'political theology'. Is it possible to find a thread running through Luther's manifold publications or would it be more appropriate to consider it as a sequence of phases? An attempt at answering these questions is followed by the textual history and an examination of the structure of *On Secular Authority*, which hold, I think, the exegetical key to this treatise.

On Secular Authority is thematically and systematically related to a number of other writings by Luther that are broadly classed as political and sometimes also as mirrors for princes: *To the Christian Nobility* (1520),[113] his later commentaries on Psalms 101[114] (1527) and 82[115] (1530), as well as his

---

110 'To this extent, the reformer did not so much formulate a decidedly political theology as offer a classical theology in new garb [...]' (Nitschke 2000: 19). I am not sure, however, whether that argument is at all valid, for it would imply that none of Luther's predecessors or contemporaries had ever articulated a 'political theology'. On this discussion, see further Gänssler 1983: 1ff., 52ff.

111 On whom see Ludolphy 2006.

112 OSA 41 ('Aber er muß sich viel neyds unnd leyds druober erwegen. Das Creutz wirtt solchem furnehmen gar bald auff dem hals liegen.' WA 11: 278, 25–26).

113 *An den christlichen Adel deutscher Nation von des christlichen Standes Besserung.* On this, see Brecht 1981–1987, I: 352.

114 WA 51.

115 WA 31.

treatises *Whether Soldiers, Too, Can Be Saved* (1526), *On War Against the Turk* (1529) or the so-called '*Stories of Joseph*' in his lectures on Genesis.[116] Yet the key to Luther's political theology is to be found not only in his political writings, but also in the dogmatic works, including *On the Freedom of a Christian* (*Von der Freiheit eines Christenmenschen*, 1520) and *On the Bondage of the Will* (*De servo arbitrio*, 1525).[117] These works discuss what makes a human being a Christian and in doing so lay the foundations for the semantics of *Christianitas* that is likewise applied to the Christian prince.

To return to the fundamental question: does Luther articulate a coherent political theology, or would it be more appropriate to think of him as a purely 'reactive' author, whose writings formulate spontaneous responses to acute problems and topical issues with few considerations of a systematic nature?

At first glance, it would certainly seem as though Luther had gone on to revise the doctrine of the two realms, as it can be found in OSA and other earlier political writings. This revision took the form of the doctrine of the three estates (in the 1528 confession[118] or the lecture on Genesis of 1535[119]), which appear to supersede Luther's earlier views. It was certainly not lost on Luther that his two kingdoms doctrine had left him open to misunderstanding. Although he had not intended a radically dualistic separation between world and spirit, he was frequently understood as arguing just that. His later doctrine of the three estates was hence intended to emphasise the 'horizontal' presence[120] of Christians in the world. It did so with reference to Christ's promise of salvation, to God having become man. The bipolar logic of the two kingdoms was thus expanded to give the political estate, that is, the rulers, a firm place in the overall structure of Christian life.[121]

---

116   Estes 2003: 216ff.; Kolb 2008: 43ff.; Kolb 2009: 137.
117   Wolf 1965: 219.
118   Stümke 2007: 129.
119   Bayer 1995: 117f.; Voigt-Goy 2008.
120   As opposed to vertical in a two-dimensional system.
121   This is not to privilege the doctrine of the three estates over that of the two kingdoms, as Oswald Bayer has done (Bayer 1995: 121). 'There is to my mind no need to prioritise one doctrine over the other. The doctrine of the two kingdoms is not merely a transitional stage on the way to that of the three estates, but rather serves

There is an obvious continuity between the doctrine of the three estates and *To the Christian Nobility* or *On Secular Authority*: the ruler is considered as a simple Christian, as one of many in Christ's kingdom. And just as all are both priests and addressees of the Word, so are they all *potentially* ready to engage in political action at God's call,[122] for political engagement is a Christian attitude.[123] This is also true of the 'economic' and 'spiritual' estates. Luther's classification by estates does not divide the population into segments, as in a corporatist constitution. It is rather an existential categorisation, one that takes account of the 'creaturely' (*geschöpflich*)[124] three-dimensionality of Christian existence, in which everybody participates[125] in a spiritual, economic[126] and political ethos.

The supposed 'inconsistency' between the doctrines of the two kingdoms and the three estates has led some scholars to divide the reformer's career into that of a 'young' and an 'old' Luther. Against this, I would maintain that Luther's political theology, no less so than the entirety of his thought, should be considered as forming part of the continuous development of his thought. Rather than radically changing his opinions, Luther expanded and refined them. Luther himself later referred back to

to emphasise just how loaded the question of the legitimacy of state authority truly is' (Stümke 2007: 213).

122　Ehmann 2008: 238.

123　Schorn-Schütte 2004: 91.

124　I borrow this term from Hans G. Ulrich (Ulrich 2007).

125　Bayer 1995: 120ff.; Bayer 2003: 135; Voigt-Goy 2008: 78. To Luther, the three estates applied not only among Christians, but also among pagans (Ehmann 2008: 237). At issue here, however, is only the Christian community, to which it falls to build Christ's kingdom on earth. Whereas, among pagans, the corporative order is maintained in the form of natural law, among Christians it is confirmed and even amplified (!) by the incarnation. According to Luther, the natural law of Christians is to love one's neighbour (WA 11: 279, 19ff.; see Raunio 2006: 37). For a discussion of the terminology of *estate* and *function*, see Reinhard 2007: 57ff.; Grigore 2009: 21ff.

126　From οἰκονομία: Luther here squarely participates in the Aristotelian tradition that regards the household as the foundation for and model of the economy. Luther's economy considers 'honour and family, commerce, education and scholarship' (Bayer 2003: 129).

OSA with satisfaction.[127] In turn, OSA begins with a look back at *To the Christian Nobility*.[128]

For one thing, such links are far from being a rarity in Luther. Second, he could not be seen simply to recant or revise his earlier statements in later works. And third, he stood firmly in an academic tradition and practice that prevented him from entangling himself in contradictions over a lifetime. Moreover (fourth), his focus on a single source – the Bible – helped his thought to reach the necessary degree of coherence. What we see in Luther are not so much sweeping revisions as changes in emphasis, by which theories are not so much altered as anchored in the reality of life and history.[129]

Even if, then, Luther's writing may be thought of as 'reactive' – in the sense of reacting to something[130] – this signifies neither wilfulness nor arbitrariness, nor even the neglect of logical and systematic rigour. I would prefer to think of being 'reactive' as something positive, as being responsive to and reflecting on the problems of life, society and human beings in general. It was such responsiveness and closeness that made Luther's propositions seem so plausible to many contemporaries. In the specific instance of the three estates doctrine, it should be read not as a recantation of that of the two kingdoms, but rather as its recontextualisation: whereas the two kingdoms doctrine posed the question of the secular ruler's relationship to (the new) faith and implicitly to God, that of the three estates was an attempt at considering the Christian community in its inner structural coherence.[131]

127 Gänssler 1983: 6 (with reference); MacKenzie 2007: 5 n. 5.
128 'Some time ago, I wrote a pamphlet to the German nobility. In it, I set out their tasks and duties as Christians. How much notice they took of it is plain for all to see. And so I must turn my efforts in another direction and write instead about what they ought *not* to do, and *desist* from doing.' (OSA 5.) Original: 'Ich habe vorhynn eyn buechlin an den deutschen Adel geschrieben und angezeygt was seyn Christlich ampt unnd werck sey. Aber wie sie darnach than haben, ist gnuegßam fur augen. Darumb muß ich meyn vleyß wenden und nu schreyben was sie auch lassen unnd nicht thun sollen [...]' (WA 11: 246, 17–21).
129 Junghans 2008: 37.
130 Lohse 1981: 110; Hort 2000.
131 '[It] is usually ignored that the spiritual is not merely inward, but also outward and secular, whereas the secular in its turn is spiritual [...]' (Bayer 1995: 122). On this, see Dülmen 1983: 100.

On Secular Authority itself reacts to a specific historical incident. Duke George of Saxony (d. 1539), an implacable enemy of Luther's ever since the Leipzig disputation, by a decree of 7 November 1522, not only forbade the sale and purchase of Luther's translation of the New Testament, but also ordered all copies in circulation to be confiscated. The Leipzig theological faculty was called upon to issue a *Gutachten* in support of this move.[132] 'In Luther's view, this touched upon the fundamental question of how far a prince was entitled to intervene in matters concerning the welfare of his subjects' souls.'[133]

Yet Luther by no means spontaneously arrived at the idea of weighing in on the important question concerning political and religious competencies. He had already informed the Bamberg alderman Johann von Schwarzenberg (d. 1528) of such an intention in a letter dated 21 September 1522: 'Of the worldly sword, and how it might accord with the Gospel, I wish indeed to treat in a little book [...].'[134] Moreover, Luther had addressed the problem in a number of sermons: one on the Saxon arms (27 July 1522,[135] one on 1 Pet. 2:13–17 (in summer 1522),[136] and finally in two more, delivered on 24 and 25 October 1522, in the chapel of the palace of Weimar, before Frederick the Wise's brother, Duke John,[137] and the latter's son.[138] *On Secular Authority* was developed from these sermons and published with a dedication to Duke John.[139]

The treatise caused a considerable stir on its publication. The first edition, published by Nickel Schyrlentz of Wittenberg, was quickly followed

---

132 Mühlmann 1983: 28; Schwarz 2004: 133; MacKenzie 2007: 13.
133 Smolinsky 2006: 45.
134 WA Br 2: 600, 24–601, 26. On this, see Lohse 1995: 171.
135 WA 10 III: 251–256.
136 WA 12: 327–335.
137 John (Johann) the Steadfast (d. 1532), duke of Saxony. He became elector on the death of Frederick the Wise in 1525.
138 WA 11: 371–393.
139 Brecht 1981–1987, II: 119f.; Dülmen 1983: 99; Mühlmann 1983: 28; Schwarz 2004: 133. Martin Brecht dates the work's publication to December 1522 (Brecht 1981–1987, II: 120), Gert Wendelborn to early November 1522 (Wendelborn 1983: 203). Most scholars and bibliographers, however, assume March 1523 to be the correct date (Benzing 1965: 177).

by ten more and another in Low German.[140] On 21 March 1523 Duke George of Saxony complained to Elector Frederick the Wise about the manner in which Luther had reacted to his aforementioned decree. Luther had written

> that rulers have begun to order people to hand over books and to believe and think as their rulers tell them. They have had the temerity to put themselves in God's place, to make themselves masters of conscience and belief and to undertake to give lessons to the Holy Spirit from what is in their addled brains.[141]

Having received, in the winter of 1522, a pamphlet in which Luther had described him as a fat bubble 'who flaunts his great belly before the heavens, has forsworn the Gospel, and would devour Christ even as a wolf devours a fly',[142] the duke was disinclined to look kindly upon Luther. Above all, he was annoyed at the success of OSA with readers of all classes. Elector John the Steadfast, for instance, adopted certain lines of argument from OSA in a decree to his officials issued on 28 June 1525 concerning the Peasants' War:

> Dear faithful one, Our own and foreign peasantry and their followers having lately caused and enacted a swift, wilful and *unchristian revolt* and uprising […] [against] the venerable and Holy Gospel's and Divine Scripture's commandment to be obedient unto the authorities […]. Hence it is for us, authority having been instituted by God to strike fear into and punish miscreants and the disobedient who would, as stated, rise

---

140 In 1523 four editions were published in Wittenberg (three by Schyrlentz and one by Rhau-Grunenberg), one in Erfurt (by Maler), two in Strasbourg (by Prüß and Köpfel), one in Speyer (by Eckhart), one in Augsburg (by Ulhart) and one in Low German. Another ten editions appeared between 1523 and 1525, plus one in Latin and two in Dutch (published respectively by Herwagen in Strasbourg and at the *Ketzerpresse* in Hamburg) (Benzing 1965: 177f.; VD: L7309–L7321; Dülmen 1983: 100). The VD records another Low German edition to have been published in Erfurt in 1524.

141 OSA 5. Original: '[D]as sie nu angefangen haben, den leutten zuo gepieten, buecher von sich thun, glewben und hallten was sie fur geben; damit sich vermessen auch ynn Gottis stuel zuo setzen und die gewissen und glawben zuo meystern und nach yhrem tollen gehyrn den heyligen geyst zur schuolen fueren' (WA 11: 246, 27–30).

142 Apud Brecht 1981–1987, II: 112.

against us and other authorities and thereby chiefly against God's order, to take serious and punitive measures to quell and suppress such unchristian and wilful actions.[143]

Whereas the peasants' revolt is considered 'unchristian' for supposedly contradicting the ordinances of the Gospels, John draws on Luther's arguments in OSA to justify intervention by the princes. Authority having been instituted by God to punish and curb disobedience, its actions were 'Christian' inasmuch as they served to suppress such 'unchristian' uprisings against the word of God.[144]

The structure of OSA is such that I feel justified in interpreting Luther's bipolar view of the two kingdoms doctrine, which scholarship has been correct in maintaining, not in light of theoretical analyses,[145] but rather by emphasising certain Christian concepts that Luther repeats almost obsessively. These concepts succeed in transposing the treatise's meaning to the level of Christian life, yet scholars have barely used them at all as an aid to systematic analysis. Analysis of OSA has instead tended to revolve around the problem of the two kingdoms. To me, however, the treatise seems to confront theory (a model or *dispositio*) with life, that is, putting it into practice. Theoretically the world can be divided along simple lines: the

---

143   Emphasis added. Original: 'Lieber getrewer, Nach dem kurz verlauffener zeyt von unser, auch fremdder Bawerschaft, sampt andern yren anhengern ein geschwinde, mutwillige und unchristliche empörunge und auffstehen [...] dem heylbarn und heyligen Evangelion und gottlicher geschrifft, der Oberkeydt gehorßsam zu sein, höchlich vermannent, gepietent, [...] erregt und furgenomen, So haben wir uns, dieweil die Oberkeyt von Got den ungehorßamen und myßhendlern zur straff und forcht eyngesetzt, schuldig erkannt, solchen mutwilligen auffrurern und ungehorßamen myßhendlern, die sich uns und anderer Oberkeyt, wie vorberurt, entlegen zusetzen und also furnemlich widder Gottes ordnunge, hoher dieselbige Oberkeyt ist, zu streben und handeln undterstanden, mit straff und ernst zu nydderdruckunge und dempffunge yres unchristlichen und mutwilligen furnemens zu begegnen' (Förstemann 1842: no. 52, p. 285). On the Peasants' War, see, for example, Blickle 2004.

144   WA 11: 257f.

145   Various interpretations have been proposed of the two kingdoms doctrine. It was seen, for instance, as an attempt to resolve the biblical contradiction between the Christian interdiction on vengeance (Matt. 5:39) and the punitive powers granted to the authorities in Rom. 12:19 and 13:1 (Gänssler 1983: 6).

two orders, good and evil, God and the Devil, spiritual and temporal, Church and state. Yet in practice the world forms the kingdom of Christ, which addresses Christians both actual (i.e., believing, 'true' Christians) and virtual ('unchristians'[146] or non-Christians who may, however, receive faith from God and find Christ). Since God's incarnation in Christ, the kingdom of God has dwelt on earth. Christ has already overcome the separation: 'And Christ came in order to begin the kingdom of God and to establish it in this world.'[147]

In the three-part taxonomy of OSA, Luther intends a threefold clarification. First, against the claims of the Roman Church, he stresses the immediate divinity of secular authority as instituted directly by God and certainly not subordinate to the pope or the spiritual estate. He goes on to turn this claim against the apolitical and chiliastic Anabaptist movements. In the second part, Luther argues against secular rulers enjoying despotic or otherwise unlimited power, reminding them that, though they have no human authority above them, they are subordinate to God. In the third part, Luther outlines the image of the *Christian ruler* who follows his calling to serve his fellow human beings in Christ's earthly kingdom.[148]

The sequence of individual systematic building blocks is revealing; it is explained in the first part of the treatise. Luther begins by stating a basic principle: secular authority is divine order, which means that in theory it is owed unconditional obedience (WA 11: 247f.).[149] A second step addresses the accidents of this principle that spring from the reality of a divine order in a Creation estranged from God. Since sin has made its way into the world, there is a coercive (*coerceo, coercitio*) dimension in the postlapsarian order.[150] This provides Luther, in Part Three (WA 11: 249), with an occasion to indicate his practical turn: though once estranged from God, the world had experienced Christ, thereby becoming the kingdom of Christ, which means God's immediacy through Christ.[151] This opens up space for ethics

---

146   Luther's term for those who are baptised but indifferent to faith.
147   OSA 8. Original: 'Und er auch darumb kommen, das er das reych Gottis anfienge und ynn der welt auffrichtet' (WA 11: 248, 28–29).
148   Mühlhaupt 1972: 447f.; Gänssler 1983: 10.
149   Reinhard 1999: 110.
150   Bayer 1995: 120; Voigt-Goy 2008: 77.
151   Wolf 1965: 221f.; Duchrow 1983: 462; Oberman 1984: 34.

and the practical application of this experience or event (WA 11: 253–257). And now the terms begin to emerge that are repeated with increasing frequency: 'service', 'benefit', 'servant', 'help', 'neighbour'.

Luther himself thus makes his gist perfectly plain. He is no utopian. In my reading, the point the treatise is driving at is that, though it is theoretically conceivable that Christians could dispense with secular authority it would not be practical. The world, Luther emphasises, is what it is: weak and sinful. This affects the coordinates of the Christian life. Christians are obliged to carry the fruits of their faith into the world! If they cannot do anything to win merit and justify themselves before God, they must attempt everything *in* the world, following the example of Christ Himself. In this new reality consequent upon the advent of Christ, Luther holds the Christian rule of 'Christian rulers and lords' to be the only legitimate kind:[152] 'In the same way it is right and necessary that all princes should be good Christians. The Sword and power, *as a special service rendered to God, are more suited to Christians* than to anyone else in the world.'[153]

The prince as topos spans the three dimensions of the kingdom of Christ: its breadth in the world, its depth into humans themselves and its height, reaching for God. The perspective hence undergoes a fundamental shift if one understands the third part – the actual *Fürstenspiegel*[154] – as constituting not some vision of remote ideals, but rather the keystone of the whole, as the decisive point. By this, I mean the semantics of *Christianitas*, which serves Luther as matrix in the third part. Christian rule must express itself in a state of tension between the secular and spiritual realms, between God and world, and in such relational terms as 'relying on God', 'service' or being 'called' to an office.[155]

---

152 OSA 34. Original: 'Christliche fursten und herrn' (WA 11: 271, 30).
153 OSA 18 (emphasis added). Original: 'Und auch wol guott und nott were, das alle fursten rechte guotte Christen weren. Denn das schwerd und die gewallt als eyn sonderlicher gottis dienst gepuert den Christen zuo eigen fur allen andern auff erden' (WA 11: 257, 35–258, 3).
154 Scholars have counted this part among the genre of mirrors for princes (Brecht 1981–1987, II: 121; Dülmen 1983: 100; Wendelborn 1983: 126).
155 Schwarz 2004: 158.

Everyday life proceeds not by theoretical or scholastic antinomies, but by acts and attitudes which assume coherence, continuity and consistency. If these categories of Luther's political thought are emphasised, it might seem less strange to regard the ruler, in his capacity as a Christian, as a partner of God, one who collaborates with God in seeing to it that His will be done, and who serves, in imitation of Christ.

Called to Office

The task in the following section will be to examine the semantics of service in *On Secular Authority* and the conceptual network in which it emerges: 'calling/vocation', 'neighbour', 'love', '(divine) service', 'resistance' and 'works' are the central concepts in which that of 'service' is embedded.

> Now, whoever wants to be a Christian prince must abandon any intention of lording it over people and using force. For all life that is lived and sought after for one's own benefit is cursed and damned: damned are all the works that do not come from love. And the works that spring from love are those that are not done for one's own pleasure, benefit, honour, comfort and well-being, but rather those which are aimed wholly at the benefit, honour and well-being of others.[156]

This is the 'definition' of what Luther takes to be a Christian prince: rather than abusing his rule to his own advantage, he regards it as a calling from God to perform works of love for the benefit of his neighbour. The issue here is rule as the cross and duty of authority: 'For everyone must attend to his own calling and work.'[157] By 'authority', Luther means both the

---

156   OSA 34. Original: 'Welcher nu eyn Christlicher furst sein will, der muß warlich die meynung ablegen, das er hirschen und mit gewallt faren wolle. Denn verflucht und verdampt ist alles leben, das yhm selb zuo nutz und zuo guott gelebt und gesucht wirt, verflucht alle werck, die nit ynn der liebe gehen. Denn aber gehen sie ynn der liebe, wenn sie nicht auff eygen lust, nutz, ehre, gemach und heyl, sondern auff andere nutz, ehre und heyl gericht sind von gantzem hertzen' (WA 11: 271, 35–272, 5).

157   WA 11: 258, 30.

princes themselves and their political apparatus, that is, all who act on the prince's orders.[158]

In his use of the term 'calling' (*Berufung* – *vocatio, professio*), Luther transposes an originally monastic concept into the sphere of Christian life in general:

> The idea of the calling of a particular estate, eminent among Christendom by virtue of its spiritual qualification, Luther reformulated as the conviction that all Christians must have their particular vocation, that is to say, be called to the task proper to their particular estate, sex and age.[159]

The Lutheran logic of calling is expressed in such terms as 'following' or 'imitating' (Christ) and being 'bound' or 'commanded': God has commanded us to imitate Christ, and as Christians, as recipients of faith, it is not for us to decide whether or not to answer to this calling. A calling occurs because we have been elected for a purpose, because God *wants* us to do something:

> Notwithstanding the examples and lives of all the saints every person should attend to the work entrusted to him and guard the honor of his calling. [...] Here Christ works and speaks against this very thing. [...] Do you imagine I wish the same from you as from him? No, not so; you attend to your duties. I desire to have many kinds of servants, but not all to be at the same work.[160]

For in the calling is manifested God's providence in selecting and instituting what is needful for the world. Calling human beings to a duty demonstrates God's omnipotence and the inability of man to get by on his own.

---

158   On this, see Emme 1983; Gänssler 1983; Looß 1986; Härle 1987.
159   Köpf 2008: 34.
160   Christmas Postil 159. Original: 'Unangesehen aller heyligen exempell unnd leben soll eyn iglicher wartten, was ihm befohlen ist, unnd warnhemen seynis beruffis. [...] Darüber handellt und redet hie Christus [...]: Meynstu, ich woll eben das von dyr haben, das von yhm? Neyn, nit alßo, wart du des deynen und was ich dyr sage, yhener wirtt seynis auch woll finden. Ich will mancherley diener haben, sollen aber nitt alle eynis werck seyn' (WA 10 I [1]: 306, 17–307, 12).

Concerning the political estate of authority, all this means that its bearers have been called (*berufen*) to a particular function, as indicated by Luther's *Sermon on the Eighty-Second Psalm*:

> Now because this is not a matter of human will or devising, but God Himself appoints and preserves all rulership [...], especially when, beside the institution itself, we have a word or command of God for it, as among the people of Israel, where the priests, princes, and kings were appointed by the oral command and word of God.[161]

Authority, embodied here by the Christian prince, answers to a calling, which is to say, it fulfils a task (*Auftrag*)[162] – just like any other Christian to whom a divine calling is addressed. And just as faith signifies the calling of all Christians, this calling is an act of God, by which He draws people closer to Him and presents them with a gift. From a corporative viewpoint, a calling represents an act of God addressed to all Christians and hence also to the prince.

According both to Luther's anthropology and soteriology, which hold man to be completely reliant on God's mercy and grace,[163] the ruler too must be aware that he relies on God alone.[164] The prince's 'calling' is to devote himself to keeping Christians free of sin. He is the responsible caretaker of the other Christians. Qualitatively speaking, as Luther stresses repeatedly in OSA, the ruler is equal to others as a free Christian. Functionally, however, he is subordinate to them as a 'servant' or 'handmaiden'[165] bearing responsibility on the model of the kenotic Christ.[166] The relationship in which the ruler stands to God is thus no longer sacramental and representative, as it was in the Middle Ages, but rather ministerial (*ministerium*,

---

161   LW 13, 44. Original: 'Weil es nun nicht aus menschlichem Willen oder Vernehmen kommt, sondern Gott selbst alle Obrigkeit setzt und erhält [...], sonderlich, wo über das Einsetzen auch göttlich Wort und Befehl dazu kommt; wie im Volk Israel die Priester, Fürsten, Könige durch mündlichen Befehl und Wort Gottes bestellt wurden' (WA 31 I, 191).

162   The task being, as we shall see, to cooperate with God (Günter 1976: 23).

163   Lohse 2006: 109.

164   WA 11: 275, 12.

165   OSA 18; WA 11: 254, 8–9.

166   Luther refers in this context to the *forma servi* (Hamel 1934: 199).

[be]amtlich)[167] and hence purely functional and curatorial with regard to the community of Christians.[168]

Seen from below, the definition of secular Christian authority ultimately means that any Christian at any time can be 'commanded' to rule.

> Therefore we must close our eyes, not look at our works, whether they be great, small, honorable, contemptible, spiritual, temporal or what kind of an appearance and name they may have upon earth; but look to the command and to the obedience in the works. Do they govern you? Then the work also is truly right and precious, and completely godly, although it springs forth as insignificant as a straw. However, if obedience and God's commandments do not dominate you, then the work is not right, but damnable, surely the devil's own doings, although it were even so great a work as to raise the dead.[169]

What counts for Christians is not so much the works they are tasked with performing as whether God had even asked – called – them to do so. If called, Christians are obliged to obey and act accordingly, and serve God by setting up and administering His works in the world. The foundation of a possible political vocation of *all* Christians resides in the commandment to love and serve one's neighbour.[170] Christian love is thus the foundation not only of obedience to authority, but also of the obligation of Christians to engage in politics and thereby, as it were, themselves to assume the mantle of authority.[171] The Christian needs no authority, for

167 On calling and the notion of *Verbeamtung*, see Günter 1976: 24; Kolb 2008: 45.

168 Luther had already laid the foundations for this curatorial understanding of the rulers' function vis-à-vis religion in *To the Christian Nobility* (Oberman 1981: 25; Kaufmann 2009: 271). To what extent this curatorial obligation on authority's part towards Church and faith might be considered a *subsidium* or subsidiarity is discussed in Ballor 2013.

169 Christmas Postil 168. Original: 'Darumb mussen wyr die augen zuthun, nit die werck ansehen, ob sie groß, kleyn, ehrlich, vorachtlich, geystlich, leyplich, odder was sie auch fur eyn ansehen und namen auff erden haben mugen, ßondern auff den befehl und gehorsam, der drynnen ist; geht derselb, ßo ist das werck auch recht und kostlich, ganz gotlich, obs ßo geringe were, als eyn strohalm auffheben. Geht aber der gehorsam und befehl nit, ßo ist das werck auch nit recht und vordamlich, gewißlich des teuffels eygen, obs gleych ßo groß were als todten auffwecken' (WA 10 [1]: 310, 14–21).

170 Chester 2009: 102.

171 Lienhard 2007: 222ff.; Ehmann 2008: 234.

authority exists not to make Christians, but to take Christ's side against the evil in the world. Authority is directed outwards.[172]

Luther considers a state that meets the criteria of *Christianitas* to be nothing short of a miracle of God[173] who, by virtue of His love, looks after postlapsarian man rather than leaving him to his fate. This view of Luther's overcomes Augustine's demonisation of the earthly *civitas*, instead pursuing a line of argument that I first encountered in the work of John Chrysostom (d. 407).

To Chrysostom, as to Augustine, all relations of inequality can be traced back to the Fall: it is as punishment for the Fall that woman is servant to man; slavery is the consequence of the sin of Ham, who saw the nakedness of his drunken father; and the state itself is the ultimate consequence of the need to keep human wickedness in check.[174] Though Chrysostom, like Augustine, speaks of two types of cities – of *basileiai* on the one hand and *civitates* on the other – he does not think of the earthly *basileia* as evil and an obstacle to salvation, but on the contrary as necessary for salvation. It is a sign both of God's love for humans and of humans' love for one another. Chrysostom thereby turns the Christian, religious concept of love into a political one, and Luther does something very similar.[175] To him, the essential task of authority and (implicitly) the state is to keep 'the wickedness of sinful man'[176] under control and thereby to pave the way for the coming of Christ's kingdom. It is indeed likely that Luther knew Chrysostom's homilies on both Genesis and Romans.

The logic of human action at divine 'command' (rather than by one's own volition) also provided the foundation for the right to passive[177] resistance to authority, for obedience to authority is not unconditional.

---

172   WA 11: 262, 7–10. On this, see Ehmann 2008: 235.
173   Moeller 2000: 237.
174   John Chrysostom, *Homilien über die Genesis*, 4. Homilie: 22ff.
175   Bornkamm 1975: 263.
176   Leppin 2011: 257.
177   Luther was opposed to active, violent resistance: 'For superiors are not to be resisted by force, but only by witnessing to the truth' (OSA 39). Original: '[D]er uberkeyt soll man nicht widderstehen mit gewalt, ßondern nur mit bekentnis der warheyt' (WA 11: 277, 2–4).

Christ having come to earth, not all rule could claim to be in accordance with the divine order in His kingdom,[178] but only the Christian kind. And Christian rule does not put itself in God's stead and urge human beings to works of their own that are of the enemy, satanic, for only the Devil acts in his own interest. In the Christian community, the works performed are not one's own, but God's.[179] It is only *in* such authority or rule that God can recognise Himself and only *by* such authority that He can speak and judge.[180] Subjects are freed from their obligation to obey when a ruler asks them to follow him into injustice:[181] 'But what if a prince is in the wrong? Are people obliged to obey him even then? No, because no one has a duty to act unjustly; we must obey God (who will have justice prevail), rather than men.'[182]

According to Luther, this whole complex relationship of service is built on an exclusively Christological basis. The prince 'is to set Christ before his eyes and tell himself: here is Christ, the greatest of princes, and yet he came to serve me'.[183] Accordingly, the purpose of the Christian prince is to provide 'service or help'.[184] This is a clear reference to Matt. 20:28: 'Even as

---

178 Wolgast 1977: 65.

179 Gelderen 2005: 307. Luther's idea of contrasting one's own works and one's own will with those of God may derive from Bernard of Clairvaux, who in one of his letters had written: 'I should say that someone had made his own law when he puts his own will before the common and eternal law, wickedly wishing to imitate his Creator, so that just as God is a law unto himself, he too wants to rule himself and make his own will law' (Bernard of Clairvaux, *Selected Works*, p. 202). One's own will and the deeds stemming from it are, to Bernard, satanic, the work of the enemy – with direct reference to Job 7:20 (ibid.).

180 *Sermon on the Eighty-Second Psalm* apud Eberle 1873: 801.

181 *Sermon on the Eighty-Second Psalm* apud Eberle 1873: 802, 805.

182 OSA 40. Original: 'Wie? Wenn denn eyn furst unrecht hette, ist ihm seyn volck auch schuldig zuo folgen? Anttwort: Neyn. Denn wider recht gepuert niemant zuo thun, Sondern man muß Gotte (der das recht haben will) mehr gehorchen denn den menschen' (WA 11: 277, 28–31). Gelderen 2005: 308f.

183 OSA 36. Original: 'Und [der Fürst] soll Christum ynn seyn augen bilden und also sagen: "Sihe, Christus der uberst furst, ist komen und hat myr gedienet"' (WA 11: 273, 13–15).

184 LW 13, 69. Original: 'zu dienen odder zu helffen' (WA 31 I: 215, 7). For the passage in context, see WA 31 I: 214, 20–215, 12.

the Son of man came not to be ministered unto, but to minister [*non venit ministrari sed ministrare*], and to give his life a ransom for many.'

'Luther argues in favour of a Christology of God's earthly, historical contingency and abasement. God's omnipotence is not contradicted, but much rather proved, by his incarnation [...].'[185] The concept of 'service' (*ministerium*, *Dienst*) is defined in relation to the neighbour, to one's fellow human beings and their benefit. According to Luther, there is virtually no separation between Christ and Christians, between life *in Christ* and *among Christians*. The kingdom of Christ is situated wherever service is rendered from love and faith, and hence it is necessarily of this world and for this world.[186] 'But because a true Christian, while he is on the earth, lives for and serves his neighbour and not himself, he does things that are of no benefit to himself, but of which his neighbour stands in need.'[187] Service is thus free of any consideration of utility and self-righteousness (to do good for one's own justification or to please God, etc.).

All this serves further to underscore the necessity of political commitment as divine service. The etymology of 'liturgy' brings us back to the notion of public service, and Luther fills this political concept with theological meaning by interpreting (horizontal) *ministerium* to the community as the fulfilment of a religious calling from God. The Christian prince, like all Christians, thus performs a service to God or indeed a divine service.[188]

The two kingdoms doctrine of OSA can thus be seen to describe not only a twofold form of God's presence on earth, but also – politically speaking – a twofold form of human engagement: service in response to being called by God through faith (private reason) and service to God through engagement in a world dependent on help (public reason).[189] Political life emerges from this tension and is the life of this kind of

185   Bayer 2007: 21.
186   Unruh 1975: 340; Gänssler 1983: 88.
187   OSA 13. Original: 'Aber weyl eyn rechter Christen auff erden nicht yhm selbst sondern seynem nehisten lebt und dienet, ßo thutt er von art seyns geystes auch das, des er nichts bedarff, sondern das seynem nehisten nutz und nott ist' (WA 11: 253, 23–26).
188   WA 11: 261, 32–34.
189   Bornkamm 1975: 265; Ehmann 2008: 233.

community, for the ruler – whom Luther considers as a Christian among Christians – lives not only in Christ through his faith, but also among his fellow human beings through love.[190]

In the human sphere, love means the willingness to help, just as God's love for humanity consists in help and the mercy by which He liberates it from the slavery of sin and gives it freedom. The reason for there being a *politia Christi* in the world lies in the *natura homini imbecilis*.[191] The greatest service a Christian ruler can thus render is to protect and ensure this freedom and to abstain from leading his subjects back into sin and servitude[192]

> so that my faith and righteousness ought to be laid down before God as a covering and intercession for the sins of my neighbour, which I am to take on myself, and so labour and endure servitude in them, as if they were my own; for thus has Christ done for us. *This is true love and the genuine truth of Christian life. But only there is it true and genuine, where there is true and genuine faith.*[193]

For freedom consists in love and is manifest in service. No one may steal what God has given:

190   Luther-Freiheitsschrift: 150; Chester 2009: 99.
191   Wolf 1965: 221.
192   Grobien 2009: 226; Kolb 2009: 137. Rule over 'Unchristians' or non-Christians – those who have not been awakened to faith – is possible only by the sword. The principles of the Gospel – love, freedom and service – apply only indirectly, which is why Luther leaves the impression that the Gospel is to be kept out of political affairs altogether (WA 11: 252, 1ff.). The situation is radically different where a Christian ruler rules over a Christian people, that is, the community of those called to God in faith. This fact does not render political life obsolete, but rather reframes it as ministry among fellow Christians and of Christians to their fellow human beings, be they believers or unbelievers, in terms of love. As far as Christians are concerned, Luther by no means opposes political force as such, but rather the futility of the sword as source of power (WA 11: 249, 36ff.).
193   On the Freedom of a Christian, n. p. (emphasis added). Original: 'Und zwar so sehr, dass ich muss auch meinen Glauben und Gerechtigkeit für meinen Nächsten vor Gott hingeben, seine Sünden zu decken auf mich nehmen und nicht anders tun, denn sie wären sie mein eigen, eben wie Christus uns allen getan hat. Sieh, das ist die Natur der Liebe, wo sie wahrhaftig ist. Da ist sie aber wahrhaftig, wo der Glaube wahrhaftig ist' (Luther-Freiheitsschrift: 150).

> While, however, every man is bound on his conscience, in like manner as he uses
> such liberty himself, not to hinder nor forbid it to any one else, we must also take
> care that liberty *be servant to love and to our neighbour*.[194]

To love one's neighbour is the foundation of the political contract between ruler and ruled.[195] It is love that causes human beings to serve their neighbours. And under this rubric also falls participation in a defensive war, in which fire, looting and killing enemies are classified as acts of Christian love by Luther. What this seems to mean is that in so doing, the righteous Christian preserves God's people[196] from destruction: 'And in such a war, *it is a Christian act*, and an act of love, to kill enemies without scruple, to rob and to burn, and to do whatever damages the enemy, according to the usages of war, until he is defeated.'[197] This is the idea of the 'Christian' war that Luther brings to bear – as we shall see – on the war against the Turks.

Luther's notion of service has nothing in common with the self-righteousness of the meritorian logic. Christians render a service to their neighbours in full consciousness of doing so in 'servitude to God',

---

194   The German Mass and Order of Divine Service, n.p (emphasis added).
       Original: 'Wie wol aber eym iglichen das auff seyn gewissen gestellet ist, wie er
       solcher freyheyt brauche, auch niemands die selbigen zu weren odder zu verbieten
       ist, so ist doch darauff zu sehen, das die freyheyt der liebe und des nehisten diener
       ist und seyn sol' (WA 19: 72, 20–23).
195   Brecht 1981–1987, II: 121.
196   To be a Christian, according to Luther, qualifies any form of hierarchy or rather
       recasts the notion of hierarchy associated with the ministry on the new foundation
       of a hierarchy of function, as Christopher Voigt-Goy (Voigt-Goy 2015: 190) has
       shown. Luther does so by revising the ecclesiology of his day under the assumption
       of a generally equal status of all humans before God. All were both sinners and
       priests in equal measure – a form of religious egalitarianism. God's people existed
       in the Church as the community of those hearing and believing in the Word. This
       people and this Church might be found, according to Luther, anywhere in the
       world, under the papacy as well as among the unbelievers (Kaufmann 2006: 101f.).
197   OSA 40 (emphasis added). Original: '[U]nd ynn solchem krieg ist es Christlich
       und eyn werk der liebe, die feynde getrost wuergen, rauben und brennen und alles
       thun, was schedlich ist, biß man sie uberwinde [...]' (WA 11: 277, 18–20). On this,
       see Lienhard 2007: 222f.

in performing a task demanded by God. Luther hence finds no difficulty in tying together 'service' and 'work' in OSA. What may be considered a work before men (*coram homnibus*) is to God (*coram Deo*) simply the fruit borne by the gift of faith. Man possesses nothing in his own right: he is but a beggar (*pettler*). By doing good works for the benefit of their fellow human beings, Christians follow the Word and raise it up on earth.[198] They are thus in the service of God, and all works performed in God's service redound ultimately to God's credit, are of His making.[199] Yet this is not to deny Christian freedom as fulfilled in civic engagement: 'On the contrary, it is [only] by God's liberating action that human, civic action is made possible.'[200]

Cooperatio as a Political Category

This section considers to what extent the Lutheran category of *cooperatio*, which was originally anthropological and soteriological in reference, is capable of application at the socio-political level of Christian community.

In the sphere of Christian rule, which encompasses ruler, subjects and state, the dualism between the world and the kingdom of God no longer applies. Here, Christians rule over Christians, and it is in this community that Christ's kingdom on earth can be found.

On Secular Authority discusses a division of competencies without intending a radical separation.[201] The historical circumstances of the early Reformation impressed on Luther the importance of the political infrastructure where questions of religion were concerned.[202] And since some contemporary readers, like Zwingli,[203] had misunderstood OSA and begun

---

198 An auxiliary task of the prince is to support the Word by facilitating the office of the preacher in proclaiming it (see Heckel 1938: 231; Estes 2003: 219).
199 Stümke 2007: 135.
200 Ocoleanu 2007: 96.
201 MacKenzie 2007: 5.
202 Kunst 1976.
203 Oberman 1994: 151ff.

to doubt the purpose of authority, rule and the political in the Christian world, Luther took the opportunity to amplify the doctrine of OSA in some of his later writings, notably the aforementioned sermons on Psalms 82 and 101. Already in OSA he had argued that it was the task of authority 'to make the people perfect and to teach them in a true Christian manner.'[204]

Though Luther does not use the term *'cooperatio'* in his political writings, he does so in the dogmatic *On the Bondage of the Will* (*De servo arbitrio*, 1525) with regard to the Christian community. What gives the term its political applicability, however, is the fact that Luther addresses the Christian ruler as a Christian among other Christians and thus as somebody standing in a direct relationship of cooperation with God. The Christian/ruler stands not outside the world, but within it and thereby brings *cooperatio* – the means by which God binds humans to Himself – into the world. Already in 1520, in his *Treatise on Good Works*, Luther had proclaimed: 'But if you should say: "Why does not God do it alone and Himself, since He can and knows how to help each one?" Yes, He can do it; but He does not want to do it alone; He wants us to work with Him, and does us the honor to want to work His work with us and through us.'[205]

Inward, heartfelt faith is a gift from the Holy Spirit, who gently draws human beings towards Christ. By being sounded (like bells) from outside, we become God's *cooperatores* and collaborators.[206]

> [The] goodness of God, who creates and preserves us without ourselves, but does not work in us without ourselves seeing we are those whom he hath created and preserved for this very end, that he may work in us, and we may work together with him [...]. Still he does not work in us without ourselves; seeing we are those whom

---

204   OSA 7. Original: 'vollkommen machen, und recht christlich unterweisen' (WA 11: 248, 28–29).

205   *A Treatise on Good Works*, n.p. Original: 'Sprichstu aber "warumb thuts got nit allein und selber, szo er doch wol kan unnd weisz, einem yeden zuhelffen?" Ja er kans wol, er wil es aber nit allein thun, er wil, das wir mit yhm wircken, unnd thut uns die ehre, das er mit uns und durch uns sein werck wil wircken' (WA 6: 22, 29–31).

206   Danz 2006: 159; Stümke 2007: 108.

he hath created anew and doth preserve, to this very end, that he might work in us, and that we might work together with him.[207]

Politically or publicly – in any case, outwardly – *cooperatio* means that the ruler creates and ensures a socio-political framework for the pastoral ministry, by which alone the people can be awakened to the faith. *Cooperatio* is based on reciprocity: not only does God cooperate with humans, but humans also cooperate with God. This does not mean participation in the workings of the redeeming God, which would run counter to Luther's doctrine of justification, but rather with the creative and caring God in preserving the world.[208] In the inner process of faith, *cooperatio* is resonance; in the outward process of the ministry, it is 'working together' with God (*adiuvare*, see 1 Cor. 3:9).[209]

In the second part of OSA, to which the proponents of a radical political dualism in OSA usually refer,[210] Luther indeed speaks of authority

207 *On the Bondage of the Will*, p. 375. Original: '[B]onitatis die nos sine nobis creantis et conservantis, sed non operatur in nobis sine nobis, ut quos ad hoc creavit et servavit, ut in nobis operaretur et nos ei cooperaremur […]. Sed non operatur sine nobis, ut quos in hoc ipsum recreavit et conservat, ut operaretur in nobis et nos ei cooperaremur' (WA 18: 754, 4–15).

208 Duchrow 1983: 517; Stümke 2007: 111f. 'Though the two spheres may not be mixed, they do refer to one another, for the order of salvation is impossible without the order of Creation as the precondition of its efficacy' (Becke 1970: 45; see Mörke 2005: 13).

209 Wolf 1965: 211.

210 Holl 1921: 325; Wolf 1965: 221f.; Manns 1984: 23; Nitschke 2000: 16ff. 'Though Luther may not have intended it, his interpretation of the doctrine of the two kingdoms implies a secular opening for the legitimation of political order. The prince may not allow himself to be guided by considerations other than obedience to Christian norms of order' (Nitschke 2000: 18). This view is highly questionable, revealing as it does a deficient understanding both of Luther himself and of the *Fürstenreformation*. On the one hand Luther is – somewhat bafflingly – charged with not having understood the implications of his statements; on the other hand, Luther argues is that the prince must precisely not be guided by any consideration other than the Christian kind, for the prince, in Luther's view, possesses such competency and authority as he does only by virtue of being a Christian. While Nitschke understands the prince as secular person meant to take care of religion, Luther understood the prince as Christian serving in the world (*Reich*

being outwardly responsible for its subjects' lives and possessions[211] while denying it any say in matters of faith. As ever, it is necessary to read Luther in context, for the second part of OSA is a manifesto for the Reformation and an indirect plea against the decree of George of Saxony. The border that Luther draws runs not between the spiritual estate and secular authority, but rather, by means of an antithesis, between 'Christian' and 'unchristian' authority. The latter was in league with the pope, the bishops and the 'sophists' to prevent the Word from being preached:

> But this is just what our Emperor and our prudent princes are doing: they let the Pope, the bishops and the sophists lead them, the blind leading the blind, commanding their subjects to believe as they see fit, without God's word. And then *they still want to retain the title of 'Christian Princes'*, which God forbid.[212]

The historical circumstances under which the Reformation spread show how much store the princes set by choosing the 'true' confession for their subjects.[213] Luther himself was aware of this supposed politicisation of the Reformation, and its anti-clerical and anti-centralist implications were indeed consonant with the princes' quest to extend their autonomy.[214] Yet it would be wrong to interpret the so-called *Fürstenreformation* as the demagogic instrumentalisation of a religious impetus[215] when it was

---

Christi). 'Christian prince' and 'Christian rule' (and hence also the state), in Luther's thought, form the semantic link between politics and faith. On this, see also Brecht 1981–1987, II: 122.

211   WA 11: 263, 21–25.

212   OSA 25 (emphasis added). Original: 'Noch faren itzt unser Keyßer und kluoge fursten also unnd lassen sich Bapst Bischoff und Sophisten dahyn fueren ein blind den andern das sie yhren unterthanen gepieten zuo glewben on Gottis wortt wie sie es guott dunckt unnd wollen dennoch Christliche fursten heyssen das Gott fur sey' (WA 11: 263, 21–25).

213   'For God's word cannot be without God's people, and nor can God's people be without Gods word [...].' Original: 'Denn Gottes wort kan nicht on Gottes Volck sein, widerumb Gottes Volck kan nicht on Gottes wort sein [...]' (WA 50: 629, 34–35). On this, see Haug-Moritz 2007.

214   Lutz 1974: 68f., 175; Oberman 1981: 23f.; Moeller 2000: 238; Wallace 2004: 71; Kaufmann 2006: 104; Klueting 2007: 182.

215   Reinhard 2001: 316.

genuinely concerned with the search for truth and salvation.[216] The criterion of *Christianitas* was clearly more than a phrase, but rather the decisive measure of political attitude. The fact that the princes themselves took charge of the Reformation in their respective territories[217] ought not to be understood as their arrogation of a role as *vicarius Christi* in the tradition of mediaeval rulers. While it may be argued that the princes were indeed looking to resurrect a proprietary church system (*ecclesia propria*), they sought to found it not on early mediaeval feudal obligations, but rather on territorial, legal, economic and administrative structures.[218]

These new responsibilities are evident in the revival of customs unknown since the days of Constantine the Great and other Byzantine emperors: canonical visitations of churches,[219] influencing the articles of faith, appointing bishops, summoning councils, introducing the German mass,[220] etc. All these practices led Martin Bucer (d. 1551), in his treatise *De regno Christi* (1551), to allude to a renaissance of the Constantinian principle of the ruler as head and steward of the Church, referring to such antecedents as Constantine, Theodosius and Justinian.[221] Luther did likewise in a letter admonishing the successor of George of Saxony, Duke Heinrich of Saxony (d. 1541):

> Even as Duke George did knowingly shield the Devil and curse Christ, so shall Duke Henry instead shield poor Christ and curse the Devil […]. For the princes, as best they can, shall make short work of Baal and all idolatry, as did the kings of Juda and Israel and thereafter Constantine, Theodosius and Gratian. For princes and lords owe service to their God and Christ their lord no less than anyone else.[222]

---

216 Selge 1976: 603; Ludolphy 2006: 337ff., 481f.; Kaufmann 2009: 505.

217 On territorial rule in the late mediaeval and early modern period, see Selge 1976: 602; Lohse 1981: 17f.; Schubert 1996; Lundt 2009: 56.

218 Decot 2007: 22.

219 The right of canonical visitation was not introduced with the Reformation. German princes had already received the right to inspect churches and order reforms in the fifteenth century (Lohse 1981: 18).

220 Dazu Becke 1970: 58f.

221 Dandelet 2007: passim, esp. p. 541ff.

222 WA Br 8: 482, 20–483, 27. Original: '[G]leich wie H. Georg den Teuffel wissentlich geschutzt und Christum verdampt, Also sol H. Heinrich dagegen den armen Christum schutzen und den Teuffel verdamnen […]. Denn Baal und alle abgotterey sollen die fursten, so es vermugen, kurz abthun, wie die vorigen konige

Constantine's self-image as the *epískopos ton ektós* ('bishop over those out-side')[223] found a fairly close (if not exact) counterpart in the Reformation idea of the *Notbischof* ('bishop by necessity').[224] Luther and Melanchthon invested episcopal tasks in the princes because the real bishops had failed. Unlike the episcopacy exercised by the Byzantine emperors, there was no hieratic quality to the authority exercised over the Church by the territorial prince as *Notbischof*.[225] The office was to be understood in purely administrative, curatorial and missionary terms.

It is under the aspect of ensuring that the Word was preached and his subjects protected[226] that the German emperor's task of warding off the Turkish peril[227] must be understood. Though no mention of it is made in OSA, it is not without relevance for Luther's political theology. Though fighting the Turks was to Luther a Christian work, it was so not in the sense

---

Iuda und Israel, Und hernach Constantinus, Theodosius, Gratianus. Denn fursten und herrn sind eben so wol mit yhrem Gott und hernn Christo zu dienen schuldig, als alle ander.'

223   Eusebius records that Emperor Constantine had thought of himself as μεγάλος βασιλεὺς ὕπαρχος or κοινὸς ἐπίσκοπος (Eusebius of Caesarea, *Life of Constantine*: I, c. 44, p. 28). It is in that context that Eusebius records Contantine's controversial claim to be ἐπίσκοπος τῶν ἐκτός. This term is difficult to translate. Either Constantine claimed to be bishop of the pagans outside the Church (although this would have made no sense in the ecclesiological logic of the earliest Christian centuries) or the bishop responsible for matters falling outside the remit of the Church (Eusebius of Caesarea, *Life of Constantine*: IV, c. 24, p. 126). Eusebius was not alone in referring to the emperor as a priest or bishop. Theophylact Simocatta did so in the seventh century, which suggests that Eusebius inaugurated a long-standing tradition (see Bréhier 1975: 86).

224   Spitz 1953; Moeller 2001: 74; Reinhard 2001: 315.

225   Becke 1970: 58.

226   Wolgast 1977: 65.

227   In the days of Luther and Erasmus, humanist circles in western Europe broadly shared the opinion that the Christian powers ought to put aside their internecine squabbles and wars and instead join to take on 'the Turk' (Niederberger 2005: 81f.). This view did not, however, endure past the late sixteenth century, when the Ottoman Empire increasingly came to be seen as an element in the European balance of power and an equal actor on the political stage (Gräf 2005: 37ff.). On this, see Kaufmann 2008; Pippidi 2012.

of the ideology of the Crusades,[228] but rather as a defensive war against the servants of the Devil and enemies of God which he identified the Turks to be.[229]

In concluding this section, I would like to repeat that Luther's so-called two 'kingdoms' may well be understood as complementary in an age of Christian politics.

> By placing the concept of *cooperatio* at the focal point of his doctrine of kingdoms and regimens, Luther now succeeds, on the one hand, in making a sharp distinction between relations *coram Deo* and *coram mundo* as well as between the old and new Creation, while on the other hand also conceiving of them as strictly concurrent.[230]

The key terms here are '*Christianitas*' and 'Christ's kingdom on earth'. Everybody, rulers as well as ruled, belongs in equal measure to the *regnum mundi* and the *regnum Dei*. In Luther's day, before the modern, trans-personal idea of the state was established, the reformer cannot have had a strict mutual isolation of the two realms in mind.[231] In Luther's view, both the Christian ruler and the Christian people were called to political responsibility and to act as God's *cooperatores*. Though a fundamentally

228 On this, see Grigore 2009: 355ff. Luther's objection to a Crusade interfered with the plans not only of the pope, but also of Venice, which had hoped for the pope and the German emperor to be distracted by a war in the east, the better to pursue its political and mercantile interests in the Italian peninsula (Lohse 1981: 13f.; Oberman 1981: 23).

229 Brecht 1981–1987, III: 351; Raeder 2005: 226f., 229. On the one hand, Luther considered the Turks to be God's punishment for the sins of Christians. To fight them thus meant resisting God's judgment, which was absurd (Ehmann 2008: 225; Kritzl 2008: 30). On the other hand, Christendom's defensive war was justified and indeed nothing less than the emperor's duty (Kritzl 2008: 37). Yet Luther denied the pope – the Antichrist – any authority in this matter (Bobzin 1985; Ehmann 2008: 189). In the argument over indulgences, Luther as a result found himself accused not only of heresy, but of endangering Christendom (Ehmann 2008: 225, 233). It should be noted that Luther made a systematic statement on the Turkish question only late (in 1528) (Kritzl 2008: 17), having hitherto only occasionally warned against it (Kaufmann 2006: 85). An index of Luther's writings on the topic can be found in Göllner 1961: 166ff.

230 Duchrow 1983: 520.

231 Bornkamm 1975: 256.

dogmatic and anthropological category, *cooperatio* cannot ignore the semantic implications of the public presence of the Christian believer. In
any case, the historical development of the *Fürstenreformation* shows that
this understanding took hold[232] and, exaggerations notwithstanding, encouraged protestant princes to engage in a form of *cura religionis* that
was politically organised, but by no means secularist in character. The
very logic of any relationship assumes the presence of a partner in that
relationship.

'To rely on God alone': Instrument or Partner?

As I pointed out at the beginning of this chapter, Luther's political theology must be understood in the context of his theology overall. His
doctrine of justification thus acts as a matrix for understanding the
Christianitas of the ruler. This chapter's conclusion addresses the question whether the Christian prince's partnership with God can be reduced to a simple passive instrumentality in the Hand of God. In other
words, how are we to understand the central maxim of Part Three: 'For
we should place our trust in God alone'?[233] To my mind, this notion of
trusting in or relying on God,[234] which recurs throughout Luther's writings,[235] is the true key to Luther's political thought as expressed in *On
Secular Authority*: '[Y]ou do have to take the risk of entrusting people

---

232   Müller 1999: 435f. This statement refers to the claim made by some scholars that
      OSA had not been well received.
233   OSA 37. Original: 'denn Gott soll man trawen alleyn' (WA 11: 275, 12).
234   Berndt Hamm finds the root of this 'unconditional obedience and perfect imita-
      tion of Christ' most probably to lie in the Observant branch of the Franciscans
      (Order of Friars Minor) and their devotional practices (Hamm 2008c: 119f.).
      His own monastic experience had taught Luther that there is no such thing as
      self-righteousness and that a sinful human being can take refuge only in God's
      mercy and does so in the hope of being set free by Christ (Hamm 2008c: 123).
235   Burger 1999: 190.

with offices, but you must not trust them or rely on them, but on God alone.'[236]

The *Christianitas* of authority and of the ruler consists in their unconditional reliance on God. This solid foundation enables Christian authorities to exercise their curatorial function of making the right decisions for the Christian faith. In casting off any trace of voluntarism, activism or utilitarianism, authority and the ruler contribute to the freedom by which God's grace works. The ruler is called upon to ensure that the Word is preached and the Church protected.[237] To this end, he must surrender himself in faith, thereby becoming a partner in the workings of grace. It is by grace that a Christian becomes a 'religiously productive subject'[238] and hence a socio-political actor or agent. The fruits of grace and the freedom in Christ that it imparts find their concretisation in Christian works (*opera*), especially in providing one's neighbours with care and protection.[239] Moreover, the ruler is invested with a responsibility that is not merely political, but also cosmological, involving him in care (*cura*) for Creation. A Christian ruler who is rooted in his faith and trusts in God *cannot* bring disaster upon his people, but instead is guided by grace (note the passive voice!) to peaceability, justice and care.[240]

236   OSA 38. Original: 'Befehlen unnd wagen solltu vertrawen unnd dich drauff verlassen solltu nicht on alleyn auff Gott' (WA 11: 275, 25–26).

237   'It is ordained by God's word that lawful authority owes Christians, honest citizens, subjects but above all the Church protection from unlawful violence and defence against abuses [...] and should especially undertake that the people be duly instructed in the word of God [...]' ('Die ordentliche Obrigkeit ist den Christen, ehrlichen bürgern, und unterthanen vornemlich aber der kirchen iren schutz widder unrechte gewalt nach Gottes wort schueldig unnd soll dem unrecht wehren [...] unnd sich zum hoechsten darauff befleissigen, das die leut in Gottes worte recht unterweyset [...]') (Amsdorff 1550: G iii [III]). On this, see Hamm 2008b: 13.

238   Voigt-Goy 2014: 186.

239   Voigt-Goy 2014: 126f.

240   Müller 1981: 56; Moeller 2000: 228; Bayer 2003: 39. None of this means that there were no clear boundaries to the power of authority. Authority could intervene in the matter of (right) faith, for faith was effected by God alone through the Holy Spirit. The princes were not mediators of right faith and should not, for instance, involve themselves in the persecution of heretics, which was the task of

A brief remark is due on the logic of responsibility. In OSA Luther, with reference to Matt. 5:39, says that a Christian may not seek vengeance and must bear any suffering in humility.[241] For himself, he requires no secular courts and no law, but is called upon to ensure that others receive justice, protection, assistance and indeed retribution. The Christian, having no need of all this 'for himself', in Luther's words, thereby stands in a direct relationship to God the merciful, whose salvation is all-fulfilling and all-sufficient. Earthly dissatisfaction – for instance over injustices suffered – cannot persist before God. Yet the injustice and hardship suffered by fellow human beings must not be accepted, for Christ had selflessly taken suffering upon Himself to expunge the suffering of humanity. To this extent the Christian *is* Christ to his fellow men. Luther takes a clear stance against indifference.

In its political consequences, this 'for himself' does not signify Luther's approval of perfect Christians coming together in an order free of authority – 'this teaching of Christ is not a "counsel for the perfect"'[242] – and forming an elite removed from the people at large. It refers instead to the individual Christian before God. Meanwhile 'others' – as in the claim that Christians 'may seek retribution […] for others'[243] – refers not just to such Christians as fail to lead a Christian life, but to all fellow human beings, including, ultimately, unbelievers. Responsibility for Christians and unchristians alike is hence nothing less than 'a strict injunction to every Christian'.[244] This logic of responsibility unfolds between the three dimensions of the Christian presence in Creation – verticality, horizontality and depth. It is this three-dimensional presence of Christian existence that is at stake here.

---

the spiritual authorities. Authority was, however, responsible for taking external measures to prevent the spread of heresy (Zecherle 2012: 344).

241   WA 11: 259, 10–13.
242   OSA 20. Original: 'diße lere Christi [sey] nicht eyn radt fur die vollkomen' (WA 11: 259, 17–18).
243   OSA 20. Original: 'fur andere […] sol er rache […] suchen' (WA 11: 259, 11–12).
244   OSA 20. Original: 'eyn gemeyn strengs gepott fur alle Christen' (WA 11: 259, 18–19).

The partnership between God and humankind is founded on the ruler's reliance on and placing himself in the hand of God, just as all human beings depend and rely on God's active role: on His incarnation, sacrifice and resurrection *pro me, pro nobis*.[245] Partnership is a form of dialogue between the one who depends on the other and the one who is needed, between human nature mortally wounded by sin and God who will heal it.[246] It is also in the shared hope and the shared faith of a number of individuals that is founded the political community, which is a medium of hope and freedom by virtue of the immediacy of the 'shared good', that is, God in His 'proximate grace'.[247] The Christian ruler is a curator who, within a political framework, ensures the individual's immediate relationship with the merciful God. This too is a form of partnership.

Because the ruler is a Christian, like every Christian he is bidden to do his duty, confident in his faith. Faith means both a gift from God as well as a decision made oneself in full responsibility. Yet to Luther, this decision by no means constitutes an active option in favour of something, in which case it would be a work deserving of merit. It is instead a passive act of confiding in, surrendering, opening and giving oneself to God's mercy and what it can accomplish.[248]

The ruler can thus be understood as an instrument in the hand of God – an instrument in the sense of a cooperative agent.[249] God does not act in the prince's stead, but by His Word and grace decides over the ruler's success or failure. To be a Christian prince means to enter into service and fully to trust in God's efficacy. For his part, the prince is to be understood

---

245 Luther may have adopted this idea from Bernard of Clairvaux (Köpf 2008b: 49). Christ redeems by action, by 'sanative' salvation according to the model of the active intervention of the Good Samaritan (Hamel 1934: 115).

246 Weier 1967: 111ff.; Duchrow 1983: 462.

247 'Proximate grace' (*nahe Gnade*) is a term I borrow from Berndt Hamm.

248 Especially in prayer (WA 11: 272, 34–273, 1). It is no coincidence that the prayer Luther suggests to the young Duke John Frederick of Saxony in his interpretation of the Magnificat (1520–1521) has been read as a *Fürstenspiegel* in authentic sense of the word, for in it, Luther shows how necessary prayer is to any Christian ruler responsible for the souls of his subjects (Burger 1999: 192; Burger 2014: 165ff.). On this, see also Lohse 2006: 113.

249 Gerstenkorn 1956: 172.

as an instrument of God not in the sense that his personality or subjectivity was annulled, but rather in that his person is 'made good'. By this I mean that the ruler's actions cannot be good as such, but only when God is at work within the prince's human actions.[250] 'Good' actions thus derive not from other people but ultimately from God, whose mercy imparts efficacy and goodness to our actions.[251] 'God endows man with the freedom of *cooperatio* without surrendering Himself and His work to human doings; He remains in charge of the joint effort.'[252]

All Christians – and hence also the prince – are instruments, means or media of God's efficacy or goodness. They can accomplish nothing by and of themselves – not even being elected as instruments of God. They are called to it, they are 'sounded'. This suggests a passive relation to God's grace, a kind of inundation by it. By the same token, a cup accrues no merit by being filled with water, yet the cup is indispensable for bringing water to a thirsty person. The cup is an instrument, but it is also, in this instrumental sense, a *cooperator*. As soon as we have chosen the red cup over the blue – completely irrespective of its qualities – and filled it with water to take to somebody thirsting for it, it is no longer absurd to claim that, from that moment on, the red cup is cooperating with and supporting our will. To qualify the mechanistic aspect of that image, we should recall that human beings, unlike cups, have wills of their own – wills that, according to Luther, are subject either to God or the Devil.

> [B]y acting in cooperation with God, man himself acquires the ability to act [...]. In this context, the *vita passiva* might also be understood as the *vita coactiva* [or *cooperativa*], inasmuch as man's yielding himself into the hand of God is a continuation of human action.[253]

To which one might add that indeed he makes it possible in the first place. Lutheran 'partnership' entails initiative on the part neither of the ruler nor the human being, for human nature is corrupted by sin and unable to obtain merit for itself: 'But since no man is by nature a Christian or just,

250   Gänssler 1983: 8.
251   Gerstenkorn 1956: 460.
252   Wolgast 1977: 29.
253   Ocoleanu 2007: 97.

but all are sinners and evil [...].'[254] This partnership is not a form of activism but, according to Luther's vision, rather a form of being involved. It is only thus that it can be reconciled with the idea of *cooperatio*.[255] It is through God's love that 'blind' instrumentalisation is replaced by cooperative instrumentalisation:

> For when you judge in accordance with love, you will distinguish all things easily, without law-books. But if you remove the law of love and nature, you will never hit on what is pleasing to God, even if you had swallowed all the law-books and the lawyers. On the contrary, the more you think about [what you learn from them], the more insane you become.[256]

---

254 OSA 10. Original: 'Nu aber keyn mensch von natur Christen odder frum ist, sondern altzumal sunder und boese sind [...]' (WA 11: 250, 26–27).

255 Hamm 2008c: 129ff.

256 OSA 42. Original: 'Denn wo du der liebe noch urteylest, wirstu gar leycht alle sachen scheyden und entrichten on alle recht buecher. Wo du aber der liebe unnd natur recht auß den augen thust, wirstu es nymmer so treffen, das es Gotte gefalle, wenn du auch alle recht buecher und Juristen gefressen hettist, sondern sie werden dich nur yrrer machen, yhe mehr du yhn nach denckest' (WA 11: 279, 26–30).

Rule and Method: Machiavelli's *Prince* and the Dispensable Semantics of *Christianitas*

> I can see you haven't read Machiavelli, my dear Simplicius. [...] You're still the same old Simplicius who hasn't read his Machiavelli yet.
>
> Olivier in *Simplicissimus* by Johann Jakob Christoffel von Grimmelshausen

The complexity of a modern text – and Machiavelli's *Il Principe* (*The Prince*, 1513) is such a text in many respects[1] – resides not least in admitting contradictory readings. Whereas the *Education* of Erasmus or Luther's *On Secular Authority* can be read as fundamentally straightforward statements and the hermeneutical process is limited to identifying shifts of emphasis, emphasising nuances or pointing to lines of development, this is not the case with *The Prince*. While scholars read Luther and Erasmus in light of set questions and seek to understand them against the backdrop of existing discourses and traditions, Machiavelli stands on a threshold separating a tradition of fixed questions concerning the state on the one hand and that tradition's reshaping on the other. The textual evidence of *The Prince* – quite unlike that of the unambiguous *Discorsi* (*Discourses*) of 1513–1517 – would seem to support even wildly divergent interpretations.[2]

Maurizio Viroli is hence able to argue persuasively that *The Prince* can be read as a moralistic work,[3] while Leo Strauss, in a somewhat Manichean style, succeeds in proving that it represents the textual concretisation of evil.[4] Benedetto Croce takes an intermediate but no less convincing path,

---

1   On 'modernity' and 'modernisation', see Degele/Dries 2005.

2   Vilches 2007: 2; Walsh 2007.

3   Viroli 2008: 27, 29ff.

4   Strauss 1958 (apud Walsh 2007: 285): 'Machiavelli was a teacher of evil.' On this, see Belliotti 2009: 62ff.

concluding that *The Prince* is an ultimately amoral treatise.[5] It likewise lends itself to feminist, psychological discourses: Machiavelli's writings, it has been argued, reflected a drama of the family and indeed of existence in which the central part was played by the author's relationship with the feminine.[6] In view of Machiavelli's mantic proclivities, some scholars have maintained that *The Prince* must be an esoteric work.[7] The contextual paradigm, whose adherents include Quentin Skinner and Maurizio Viroli,[8] tries to situate Machiavelli in his historical, social and cultural context, avoiding metahistorical interpretations as far as possible.[9] Charles Singleton finds Machiavelli's originality to reside in an aesthetic vision of politics based on the Aristotelian idea of *poiesis* and imagining it as a work of art possessed of both beauty and utility.[10] This aesthetic interpretation goes so far as to depict *The Prince* as evidence of Machiavelli's narcissistic 'self-preference'.[11] As a theorist of power, there is a convincing case to be made for reading Machiavelli in terms of a Foucauldian discourse analysis.[12] Other scholars meanwhile have found *The Prince* to constitute a caricature or satire of tyranny, a subversive screed aimed at undermining the legitimacy of autocracy in general and the rule of the Florentine Medici in particular.[13] Both Eric Voegelin and Herfried Münkler read it as a response to the historical crisis of republican Florence and Christendom more broadly in the late Middle Ages; the vehemence of the treatise could thus be seen as reflecting the

---

5   Belliotti 2009: 75ff.

6   Pitkin 1984; Falco 2004; Cavalo 2007. See King 2007: 235: '[A]n intriguing feminist reading [...] sees the work [*Il Principe*] as a "family drama" anxiously pitting masculine enterprises such as law and politics against the dark and volatile feminine agency of Fortune.' On Machiavelli's psychological view of history, see Dilthey 1914: 31; Horkheimer 1930: 27ff.; Belliotti 2009: 81ff.

7   This interpretation is examined and rejected by Belliotti 2009: 66f.

8   Viroli 2008: 1.

9   Walsh 2007: 280.

10 Singleton 1953.

11 Finnis 2008. See also Verspohl 2001: 14f.

12 McCanles 1983; Günsberg 1995.

13 Mattingly 1957–1958: 491; Berlin 1997: 27; Dietz/Langton 1987; Kersting 2006: 94; Belliotti 2009: 83, 87ff.

severity of the situation.[14] This reading clearly echoes Virioli's contextual approach in an amplified form.[15]

Last but not least, scholars such as Ernst Cassirer, Leonard Olschi, Norman Wilde or Gaetano Mosca have sought to understand *The Prince* as a technical book and situated Machiavelli at the beginnings of modern empirical methods[16] and of a scientific approach to historical phenomena.[17] Cassirer suggests a connection between Machiavelli's method and Kant's hypothetical imperatives, showing that Machiavelli proceeds in a manner resembling that of a judge establishing, examining, proving and confirming hypothetical knowledge.[18]

In light of such a plurality of approaches to interpreting *The Prince*,[19] it comes as no surprise to find that the literature on the Florentine *segredario* is almost impossible to survey.[20] This chapter will examine *The Prince* from the perspective of the history of science (understood broadly in the sense of *Wissenschaft*) and attempt to support the argument that Machiavelli's book proposes rule as a method or mode (*modo*)[21] of action and of obtaining knowledge. The prince accordingly is a scientist of sorts, one whose political engagement (if we can indeed think of Machiavelli as concerned with

14 Florentine republicanism was not democratic in nature, put plutocratic and oligarchic (Najemy 2000: 103; Höchli 2005).

15 Voegelin 1951.

16 Berlin 1997: 37.

17 Berlin 1997: 30; Deppe 1987: 290; Ramsay 2002: 25f.; Walsh 2007: 287.

18 Belliotti 2009: 67. 'The examining judge is tasked with reconstructing a series of events that is in the past and in which he was not himself involved. This reconstruction, however, is not arbitrary, for the judge has material to work with, [...] has at his disposal reports, findings and statements [...]' (Oexle 2007: 66). For his part, Kant argued: 'Reason [...] must approach nature with its principles in one hand [...] and in the other hand, the experiments [...] – yet in order to be instructed by nature not like a pupil, who has recited to him whatever the teacher wants him to say, but like an appointed judge who compels witnesses to answer the questions he puts to them' (Kant 1998: B xiii).

19 Cochrane 1961.

20 See the bibliographies on Machiavelli in Villari 1882; Tommasini 1883–1911; Clark 1970; Geerken 1976; Bertelli/Innocenti 1979; Cutinelli-Rèndina 1987 and 1994; Fiore 1990.

21 Machiavelli, Principe: 36–37, 38–39. *Modo* may be translated as 'method', 'means' or 'mode'.

'politics'[22]) represents a methodical process with political success as its aim. Machiavelli himself emphasised that rule was associated with the medium of factual truth,[23] and rule is hence conceived of as an empirical method of gathering data, measurement, observation, evaluation and prognosis.[24] The prince's own experience constitutes a form of contact with reality that as such is quantifiable and falsifiable.[25] This leaves no scope for the semantics of *Christianitas*, which now finds itself an irrelevant and dispensable discourse.

Aware that this reading is only one of many possible readings, I shall seek to substantiate it by the following steps.

First, I shall look at the experience that Machiavelli so often invoked. This experience drew on two sources: one indirect, consisting of historical and political works he studied, and one direct, the personal experiences of his political career.[26] These two kinds of experience are too tightly interwoven in Machiavelli's life and work to permit separate examination.

The second step will be to consider the textual history of *The Prince*, to which its relation to the *Discourses*, which were written around the same time, is of immense importance.

Third, I shall outline Machiavelli's empirical method, consider its finality or otherwise and situate it in a broader context of intellectual history. I shall then examine the epistemic processes which the Machiavellian method of rule assumes before proceeding to emphasise the aspects in which it differs from other methods.

Fourth, I shall attempt to consider Machiavelli's method in parallel to more recent scholarly traditions, particularly that identified with Gerard van der Leeuw. The thirteenth chapter of *The Prince* offers a striking instance of the manner in which the phenomenological steps taken by Machiavelli seem to foreshadow those of van der Leeuw.

22   In Machiavelli's day, the terms 'politics', 'political', etc., carried a negative connotation, suggesting falsity, deception and low cunning. Machiavelli used these terms not once in the *Prince* and a mere four times in the *Discourses* (Sternberger 1974: 35f., 49).

23   Jeremias 2005: 282.

24   Meinecke 1929: 38.

25   Sfez 1998: 280.

26   Raspa 2006: 160, 163.

All this leads me to conclude (fifth) that *The Prince* is a methodological textbook for rulers. Rather than offering solutions, it provides the prince with guidelines for successfully conducting their rule as a scientific procedure. In this methodical approach to rule as a (rational, logical) science, there is no space for the semantics of *Christianitas*.

A Man of Experience

Little is known of Machiavelli's childhood and education.[27] His father,[28] Bernardo Machiavelli, a lawyer born to an ancient family of the minor aristocracy,[29] was of republican convictions. He was only just able to make a living, and his family's existence is likely to have been anything but carefree. All he was therefore able to bequeath to his son Niccolò, born on 3 May 1469, was an appetite for the study of the classics and a well-stocked library to feed it.[30] Like his father, Niccolò Machiavelli was a man of the world, well-read, erudite and urbane.[31] He was largely self-taught, and was especially well versed in the historical works of the ancients.[32]

---

27 Vasoli 2006: 578. Other biographies of Machiavelli include Barincou 1958; Buck 1985; Mittermaier 1990; Viroli 2000.
28 Machiavelli's mother was named Bartolomea and was a member of a noble Florentine family, the Nelli (King 2007: 3).
29 Machiavelli's father was officially known as Bernardo di Niccolò Buoninsegna Machiavelli (Diesner 1993: 9). The family could look back on a long involvement in affairs of state, with several of Niccolò Machiavelli's ancestors having risen to the highest position in the Florentine bureaucracy, that of *Gonfaloniere della Giustizia* or 'standard-bearer of justice', the head of government and bearer of the executive power. To ensure continuity, the office was bestowed for life from 1502 onwards and known as *Gonfaloniere a vita* (Rubinstein 1972: 9; Gil 1994: 30; King 2007: 8, 10, 47; Belliotti 2009: xviii). The first holder of the office under this new rule was Pier Soderini (d. 1522), a friend of Machiavelli's (Bertelli 1975).
30 Gil 1994: 18f.
31 King 2007: 4; Vilches 2007: 5; Viroli 2008: 1.
32 Vilches 2007: 8. Machiavelli had no Greek and hence read the classics in Latin (Zăgrean 2002: 23; Belliotti 2009: xv).

We know, however, that young Niccolò did for a time attend the *Studio Fiorentino* as well as being privately tutored by Maestro Malto and Paolo di Ronciglione.[33]

Machiavelli's political career began at the age of 29, on 28 May of the eventful year of 1498, shortly after the execution of Savonarola, of whom Machiavelli had always disapproved.[34] The council of the eighty (*Gran Consiglio*) appointed him second *segredario* – secretary, that is, of the second chancellery which was in charge of internal affairs. On 14 July 1498, Machiavelli received the additional title of secretary of the *Dieci di Libertà e Pace*, the council of ten which handled the republic's foreign affairs.[35] At 128 florins, his annual salary, however, remained that of a second secretary.[36]

In his capacity as secretary of the *Dieci*, Machiavelli travelled to numerous European courts. Between 1498 and 1512, he undertook some two dozen voyages, as a member of Florentine delegations, throughout Italy and Europe,[37] including to France (1504 and 1510–1511), the court of Maximilian I (d. 1519) in Austria (1508 and 1509),[38] and to Rome (1506), to the court of *papa terribile* Julius II.[39] The pleasures of this diplomatic activity were mixed, to say the least. He often had to beg his superiors for travel funds, shoulder the costs himself or suffer privations. His first mission to France in 1504 ended in disaster, with Louis XII (d. 1515) making no secret of his disdain for the insignificant and indecisive republic of Florence. Machiavelli found himself mocked at the French court as *ser Nihilo*, 'Mr Nothing'.[40]

---

33   Bertelli 1975: 1; Gil 1994: 19; King 2007: 6. *Studio Fiorentino* was a university founded in 1348; it moved to Pisa 1472–1473.

34   Colish 1999: 614.

35   Rubinstein 1972: 6; Bertelli 1975: 1; Buck 1985: 28; Gil 1994: 32; Ottmann 2006: 12.

36   King 2007: 9.

37   Skinner 2008: 17ff.; Belliotti 2009: xviii.

38   Brosch 1903. Machiavelli found Maximilian I to be an incompetent monarch (Buck 1985: 33; King 2007: 95f.). What Machiavelli did admire was German municipal government and 'German liberty', by which he meant the self-government and privileges of the free imperial cities (*Reichsstädte*) (Schröder 2004: 23ff.). His relatively good knowledge of Germany notwithstanding, he seems not to have been aware of the Reformation (Berlin 1997: 48).

39   King 2007: 84.

40   Walsh 2007: 279; King 2007: 30. *Nihilo* was clearly a pun on *Niccolò*.

Machiavelli would return to France as an envoy three more times, in 1505, 1510 and 1511.[41]

Machiavelli was charged not only with foreign affairs, but also with matters of the military. In the course of the fifteenth century, the activities of mercenaries in the Italian peninsula had become more and more of a nuisance. The armies led by the so-called *condottieri* were often guided solely by profit and sold their services to the highest bidder. Treason, mutiny, disobedience and desertion were rife.[42]

The Florentines, too, who for years had been trying to reconquer their former port of Pisa,[43] were betrayed by such a *condottiere*, Polo Vitelli (d. 1499).[44] Although treason was punishable by beheading, this was not enough to bring Pisa back under Florentine rule. Machiavelli's opinion as second secretary was that only a native army would be reliably patriotic and disciplined enough to ensure military success. Both the Prince and the *Discourses* leave no doubt as to Machiavelli's contempt for mercenaries. He praised Cesare Borgia, also known as 'Valentino',[45] for his 'astute' murder of several hostile *condottieri*.[46]

41 Buck 1985: 30f.; King 2007: 66, 111, 117.

42 On this, see Argegni 1936–1937; Trease 1974; Del Treppo 2002; Lang 2009; Förster 2010.

43 Pisa had been under Florentine rule since 1406. The city regained its independence in 1494, when Florence pawned it to Charles VIII (d. 1498), who did not return it (Gil 1994: 21, 24, 41ff.; Belliotti 2009: xvii). On the Italian states in the fourteenth and fifteenth centuries, see Reinhardt 2003: 89ff., 99; Goez 2010: 227ff.

44 Florence had contracted with Paolo Vitelli to reconquer Pisa. Vitelli's artillery broke through the ring wall surrounding the port city, but he inexplicably held his forces back from storming the city at the decisive moment, which the Florentine government considered an act of treachery. It had Vitelli arrested, put on trial and executed (King 2007: 23ff.; Belliotti 2009: xix).

45 The epithet derives from the Duchy of Valentinois on the Rhône, of which Louis XII had created Cesare Borgia duke in 1498. Scholars largely agree on Machiavelli's admiration for Cesare Borgia. On this, see Fusero 1966; Sasso 1966; Bradford 1979; Gil 1994: 39f.; Ottmann 2006: 27; Neumahr 2007. The opposite opinion, according to which Borgia could not have served as an example for *The Prince*, is expressed – stereotypically, as it were – by Mattingly 1957–1958: 490.

46 Cesare Borgia lured four treacherous *condottieri* (Vitellozzo Vitelli, Oliverotto da Fermo, Paolo Orsini and the duke of Gravina) to Senigallia near Ancona under false pretences and had them murdered (Buck 1985: 32).

Machiavelli's insistence on the benefits of a Florentine army – as with so many other things, the example in his mind was that of Cesare Borgia[47] – succeeded in persuading the key decision-makers, and in 1505 he was allowed to assemble a force in the territories of Florence.[48] Of course he did not fulfil his dreams of a force of ten thousand, having to settle for one thousand peasants. Yet so forceful was Machiavelli's strategic vision that he persuaded the government to hire Leonardo da Vinci as an engineer. Leonardo was to divert the river Arno in order to cut Pisa off from vital supplies of food shipped from Venice.[49] Though that scheme failed, Machiavelli did succeed in starving the Pisans into submission by cutting their supply lines with his 'own' little militia. The gates of the recalcitrant city were finally thrown open to the Florentines in 1509, and much of the credit fell to Niccolò di Bernardo Machiavelli.[50]

Yet Machiavelli's political career ended abruptly on 7 November 1512, when Spanish forces toppled the republican government of Florence and reinstalled the Medici, who had been banished in 1494,[51] under the leadership of Lorenzo II de' Medici (d. 1519), grandson of Lorenzo the Magnificent (d. 1492).[52] Machiavelli was even arrested under suspicion of conspiracy to murder and tortured with the *strappado*.[53] On 12 March 1513, he was released under a general amnesty and banished to his small country estate in the village of Sant' Andrea in Percussina, in the commune of San Casciano, where he lived in straitened circumstances with his large family.[54] Only in 1526[55] did Machiavelli succeed in regaining at least the partial confidence

---

47   Borgia had raised a fairly successful militia in the Romagna. It was led by a Spaniard, Miguel da Corella (also known as Don Michelotto), whom Machiavelli later hired as the captain of his 'own' militia (King 2007: 81).

48   On the development of the Florentine territories in Tuscany, see Cohn 1999; Zorzi 2011; Crum/Paoletti 2006.

49   On this, see Masters 1999.

50   King 2007: 97f.

51   On the Medici: Reinhardt 1998; Kent 2000; Reinhardt 2009; Goez 2010: 237ff.

52   Belliotti 2009: 1.

53   King 2007: 130, 134, 139; Belliotti 2009: xx.

54   Machiavelli had five sons and two daughters (King 2007: 143ff.).

55   Machiavelli died on 21 June 1527 and was buried next to his father in the church of Santa Croce, where Michelangelo and Galileo are also interred (Belliotti 2009: xxii).

of the Medici and was charged with fairly minor tasks by Clement VII (d. 1534), the Medici pope.[56]

Niccolò Machiavelli's political experience was not only practical in nature and derived from his own activities in the republic's service.[57] It was also intellectual, fed by his reading of the classical historians. The sources he refers to most often are largely historical works: those of Livy, Plutarch, Polybius, Curtius Rufus, Sallust, Suetonius, Tacitus, Thucydides and Xenophon, to name but a few – though Aristotle and Plato also influenced him in many respects.[58] Machiavelli's preference for history was shared with many of the late Renaissance humanists, including Erasmus.[59] Of the Italian humanist authors who wrote mirrors for princes before Machiavelli, it is worth recalling Egidio Colonna (d. 1316), Poggio Bracciolini (d. 1459), Bartolomeo Platina (d. 1481), Giuniano Majo (d. 1493), Francesco Patrizi (d. 1494), Giovanni Pontano (d. 1503) and Filippo Beroaldo (d. 1505).[60]

56   Cardinal Giulio de' Medici was elected pope on 18 November 1523 and assumed the name of Clement VII. Among the tasks Machiavelli carried out for Clement VII, beginning in 1526, were setting up a militia for the Papal States, improving the fortifications surrounding Florence and reorganising the papal infantry in Lombardy (Diesner 1994: 64; King 2007: 165, 189ff., 216, 220; Belliotti 2009: xxii).

57   Machiavelli's position gave him access to all state information, secret or otherwise. He was always well informed of developments in Italy, Germany, Spain, France and the Ottoman Empire (see Gil 1994: 32).

58   Reinhardt 1962; Diesner 1994: 65, 181; Martelli 1998; Zăgrean 2002: 190ff.; Bausi 2005: 217; Vasoli 2006: 578, 585.

59   Livy, for example, was a model not only to Machiavelli, but also to his predecessors as chroniclers of the city of Florence, Leonardo Bruni (d. 1444) and Poggio Bracciolini (Voegelin 1951: 151f.; Coleman 1995). Machiavelli and Erasmus were not acquainted with one another, but both participate in the long tradition of the mirrors for princes (Gilbert 1939: 4; Ottmann 2006: 14), a fairly homogeneous literary genre that drew on common sources (Aristotle, Isocrates, Xenophon) and reached wide distribution in the sixteenth century among educated circles thanks to the growth of the printing press. This makes it all the more likely that Erasmus and Machiavelli were familiar not only with the same classical authors, but at least some of the same contemporary ones in the field. These latter-day authors, however – to whom Machiavelli by the blanket term '*scrittori*' – were cited neither by Erasmus nor by Machiavelli, it being unusual at the time to credit mere 'epigones' by name (Gilbert 1939: 6f., 11).

60   On these authors and their mirrors for princes, see Gilbert 1939: 461ff.

This heavy reliance on historical works led Machiavelli to develop a highly distinctive method. The equally distinctive vision of history on which this method was based was only beginning to emerge at the time but seems to anticipate certain modern approaches to history that might broadly be referred to as 'phenomenological'. I shall discuss this in the third section.

The Textual History of *The Prince*

Machiavelli's key political works, *The Prince* and the *Discourses*, were written 'within closed chambers and while in exile',[61] but they did not go unnoticed. The two works are closely connected, for in 1513 Machiavelli took a break from his work on the *Discourses* to write a little book on principalities. That book, which was completed in the same year, was originally entitled *De principatibus* and is now known as *Il Principe* (*The Prince*).

No autograph of *The Prince* is preserved,[62] nor is the autograph of the later epistle dedicatory to Lorenzo II de' Medici, which is prefaced to the treatise in all modern editions. In a letter to his younger friend Francesco Vettori (d. 1539)[63] dated 10 December 1513, Machiavelli first mentions having completed a book by the title of *De principatibus*:[64]

> I have jotted down what I have profited from in [the ancients'] conversation and composed a short study, *De principatibus*, in which I delve as deeply as I can into the ideas concerning this topic, discussing the definition of a princedom, the categories of princedoms, how they are acquired how they are retained, and why they are lost. [65]

61 Vilches 2007: 1.
62 Gerber, I, 1912: 82.
63 On Vettori and his friendship with Machiavelli, see King 2007: 140f.; Reinhardt 2007.
64 Bausi 2005: 194. Niccolò Guicciardini (d. 1557), a nephew of Francesco Guicciardini (d. 1540) and one of *The Prince*'s first readers, also knew it as *De principatibus*, as recorded in a letter of 29 July 1517 (see Bausi 2005: 364 n. 3; Gaille-Nikodimov 2007: 23).
65 '[I]o ho notato quello di che per la loro conversazione ho fatto capitale, e composto uno opusculo De principatibus, dove io mi profondo quanto io posso

This means that the treatise was written in exile at San Casciano (see above) shortly after Machiavelli's release from prison.[66] Among its earliest readers were Filippo Casavecchia and the aforementioned Francesco Vettori, to whom Machiavelli promises soon to send the treatise to Rome.[67] The period of writing is not entirely certain, though it is commonly given as summer and autumn 1513. And though it seems reasonably clear that Machiavelli had begun work by August 1513,[68] it would be misguided to try to pin down the date too precisely, for Machiavelli kept returning to the treatise over the years and frequently amended it, a process to which he referred as *ingrassare* and *pulire*.[69] As it has come down to us, *The Prince* was written over a longer period of time, extending from the summer of 1513 to 1518.[70] Machiavelli wrote the epistle dedicatory to Lorenzo II in March 1516 in the hope of winning favour with the new regime. This might smack of opportunism, and *The Prince* has indeed been read as a form of job application.[71] Be that as it may, it is certain that Lorenzo II never read the book.[72]

---

nelle cogitazioni di questo subbietto, disputando che cosa è principato, die quale spezie sono, come e' si aquistono, come e' si mantengono, perché e' si perdono' (Machiavelli, *Lettere*: 296). The English translations of the letters are those of Atkinson and Sices (Atkinson/Sices 1996: letter 224, p. 264).

66 Gaille-Nikodimov 2007: 21.

67 Machiavelli, *Lettere*: 296, 301; Gil 1994: 223f.; Martelli 2006: 24f. Vettori wrote to Machiavelli on 18 January 1514 to report that he had read the book with pleasure (see Machiavelli, Lettere: 308). Filippo Casavecchia (nicknamed 'Casa') was a close friend and confidant of Machiavelli's as well as an associate in the *Signoria*.

68 In a letter to Vettori dated 26 August 1513, Machiavelli used one of his favourite metaphors from *The Prince* (see Machiavelli, Principe: 136–137, 154–155), that of the fox and the lion (Machiavelli, *Lettere*: 287). This may indicate that he was already thinking about the subject matter of *The Prince*. On this, see also Atkinson/Sices 1996: letter 222, p. 257.

69 Gerber, I, 1912: 82, 100.

70 Buck 1985: 59; Bausi 2005: 199; Gaille-Nikodimov 2007: 22.

71 Ottmann 2006: 13.

72 In contrast to Luther or Erasmus, Machiavelli (in chapter 22 of *The Prince*) stresses the need for prince to appoint a competent *ministro* who might even be left in charge of government, though this is largely wishful thinking (Machiavelli, Principe: ch. XXII; Gerber, I, 1912: 82; King 2007: 166ff.; Vacano 2007: 65; Belliotti 2009: 86). Machiavelli seems originally to have wanted to dedicate *The Prince* to Giuliano de'

For some twenty years, *The Prince* circulated in manuscript copies[73] and was fairly well known in diplomatic circles, both in Machiavelli's own Florentine milieu and in Rome.[74] The work was first printed in 1532, with the blessing of Pope Clement VII, by Blado in Rome and soon afterwards by Bernardo di Gunta in Florence.[75] All these editions bear the title *Il Principe*, not *De principatibus*.[76] *Il Principe* was printed eight times between 1532 and 1540[77] and soon began to be translated.[78] In 1559, it was placed – on account of its cynical, amoral tone and anti-ecclesiastical arguments – on

Medici (d. 1516), the uncle of Lorenzo II (Machiavelli, *Lettere*: 296; Gil 1994: 235; Belliotti 2009: 1). The idea that *The Prince*'s true addressee was Vettori, however, verges on the speculative (Najemy 1993).

73 We know of at least seven such manuscript copies, three of which were produced by Biagio Buonarcosi, an associate of Machiavelli's at the *Signoria* (*suo co-adiutore in cancelleria*) (Richardson 1995: 19; Bausi 2005: 199).

74 Anglo 2005: 183; Tarlton 2007: 43. For examples, see Gerber, IV, 1912: facsimiles 1ff. This is not to say that *The Prince* was generally known and had been a commercial success in the manner of Luther's writings (King 2007: 162, 231f.). Allusions to the treatise can often be found in correspondence or in reports on political questions (e.g., by Francesco and Niccolò Guicciardini or Lodovico Alamanni), but also in monographs (in Agostino Niffo's *De regnandi peritia* of 1523 and in Antonio Brucioli's *Dialogi* of 1529) (Richardson 1995: 25ff., 29ff., 33ff.; Bausi 2005: 364). Agostino Niffo takes over so much from *The Prince* that many scholars have seen fit to accuse him of plagiarism (Anglo 2005: 42; Bausi 2005: 199, 366; Keßler 2008: 157ff.).

75 The title page reads: IL PRINCIPE DI NICCHOLO MACHIA-VELLO AL MAGNIFICO LOREN.ZO DI PIERO DE MEDICI [...] Con Gratie, & Privilegi di. N. S. Clemente VII. (Gerber, IV, 1912: facsimile 44).

76 Gaille-Nikodimov 2007: 22.

77 In January 1532 by Antonio Blado (Rome), in May 1532 and in 1540 by Bernardo di Giunta (Florence), in 1537 probably by Pasini & Bindoni (Venice), in 1537 probably by Zanetti (Venice) and finally in 1535 and twice in 1538 probably in Venice (see Gerber, I, 1912: 22ff.).

78 Seven translations were published between 1553 and 1680: three into French (Gaspar d'Auvergne, 1553; Guillaume Cappel, 1553; Jacques Gohory, 1571), one into Latin (Sylvester Tegli, 1560, reprinted six times till 1599), one into English (Edward Dacres, 1640), one into Dutch (van Nievelt, 1615 and 1652–1653) and finally one into Spanish (Juan Vélez de León, 1680), which was nor printed on account of the papal ban on Machiavelli's works (Gerber, III, 1912: passim; Anglo 2005: 182ff., 194f.).

the *Index librorum prohibitorum* by Pope Paul IV (d. 1559), along with Machiavelli's other writings.[79]

The question that long preoccupied Machiavellian scholarship concerns the relationship between *The Prince* and its 'sister' work, the *Discourses* (1513–1514).[80] It seems strange that these two works, which were written more or less in parallel, should find Machiavelli making diametrically opposed arguments. Whereas the former argues in favour of the prince's (despotic and unscrupulous) personal rule, the latter is full of praise for the republican order of ancient Rome.[81]

Several attempts have been made to explain this apparent contradiction. One was to argue that Machiavelli's true opinions were reflected in the *Discourses*,[82] which were first read at Orti Oricellari[83] to intimate friends and confidants. This circle was largely opposed to the despotic rule of the Medici and instead favoured an oligarchic republic of the kind that had governed Florence between 1449 and 1512. The *Discourses* were hence sincere and *The Prince* merely a token of opportunism on the part of an author who had hoped for preferment by flattering the Medici.[84] The 'Machiavellian' character of *The Prince* thus consisted mainly in its author having no compunction in suppressing his true republican convictions for material advantage.

What bridges the gap between these two works is, to my mind, first the 'scientific', technical and neutral method which they both share and second the purpose (*fine*) pursued by their argument. The 'finality' to be attained in each case is a functioning and successful state, be it a despotism or a republic. Several scholars have pursued this line to argue that *The*

---

79 Meinecke 1929: 57f.; Polcar 2002: 11; Ross 2007: 232; Belliotti 2009: xv.

80 Belliotti 2009: xv. On the term '*discorso*' in the late Renaissance and in Machiavelli, see Zwierlein 2006: 194ff.

81 Conaway Bondanella 2007.

82 Vilches 2007: 2f.

83 The palace gardens of the Medici, originally laid out by their friend Bernardo Rucellai (d. 1514). By the time Machiavelli became a regular visitor to the Orti Oricellari, they had already become the gathering place of the anti-Medici faction in Florence, of the *spiritus rector* of which was Cosimo, the nephew of Bernardo Rucellai (Gil 1994: 233f.; King 2007: 169f.; Belliotti 2009: xxi; Benner 2009: 43).

84 Nitschke 2000: 41.

Prince and the *Discourses* might be read as complementary works seeking to promote the political success of Florence regardless of its political structure.[85] Others have found the two works to be united by a vision of history as cyclical or open to repetition.[86] Though these scholars may differ over questions of detail, they agree that there must be a connection between the two works. Since they were written simultaneously, anything else would be hard to imagine.[87]

The Europe-wide reception of *The Prince* set in fairly early, and in its originality and idiosyncrasy the book proved divisive from the very start. Some early readers went so far as to identify Machiavelli with the Devil, for whom English offered the handy byname of 'Old Nick'.[88] A French Huguenot, Innocent Gentillet (d. 1588),[89] published a *Contre-Machiavel* (1576) holding Machiavelli and *The Prince* responsible for the St Bartholomew's Day massacre of 24 August 1572. Cardinal Reginald Pole, the last Roman Catholic archbishop of Canterbury (d. 1558),[90] called the Florentine an 'enemy of the human race' in his *Apologia ad Carolum Quintum* (1539) and blamed him for the anti-clerical policies of Henry VIII. The Devil's own finger, according to Pole, had been at work in the writing of *The Prince*. Elizabethan poets and playwrights[91] attached the name of Machiavelli to scoundrels and evildoers. Yet he also had his defenders, including Paolo Giovio, Giovan Matteo Toscano and Alberico Gentili in the late sixteenth century. What is more, *The Prince* is reputed to have been the favourite book of Charles V. In 1640, the Frenchman Louis Machon even composed an apology of the *segredario*. Francis Bacon held him to be a sober realist; to Spinoza he was a true republican and a genuine patriot to Fichte and Hegel.[92]

85   Black 1986: 993; Fischer 2000: 114ff.; Gaille-Nikodimov 2007: 40f.
86   Münkler 1985: 35.
87   Ramsay 2002: 31.
88   Berlin 1997: 35; Rippel 2007: 225; Vilches 2007: 7.
89   On this, see Meinecke 1929: 63; Rathé 1965.
90   On this, see Anglo 2005: 115.
91   On this, see Roe 2002.
92   Cherel 1935: 47ff.; Berlin 1997: 33; Münkler 1985: 48ff.; Polcar 2002: 11, 16, 45ff.,
       64ff.; Ramsay 2002: 367ff.; Schröder 2004: 121ff.; Jeremias 2005: 239; Ottmann
       2006: 47ff.; King 2007: 232ff.; Zwierlein 2007: 101f.

The Discovery of Facticity

This section begins with a general account of Machiavelli's 'realism' and the manner of its concretisation in the methodical exercise of rule. A method is a means to an end, which is why it is important first of all to understand the end that Machiavelli pursued by this quasi-scientific[93] method. I shall then try to answer the question why Machiavelli decided in favour of 'realism' and what that method's advantages were compared to other methods that would have been available at the time. After situating the 'realist' method in the broader context of late Renaissance intellectual history, I shall analyse Machiavelli's procedure and each step of the epistemic process by which the Florentine hopes to secure efficient knowledge. This section will conclude with the discussion of Machiavelli's method by his friend Francesco Guicciardini and the critique resulting from it.

Machiavelli's method[94] for facilitating successful rule can be expressed, if somewhat crudely, in three general concepts: (first) practical *experience*

93   In the following, I shall continue to use, albeit cautiously, the terms 'science', 'scientific', etc., in the broader sense of *Wissenschaft*, that is, not only the natural sciences. I do so aware that this terminology is not without its difficulties today and even less so with regard to Machiavelli's day. In nonetheless persisting with these terms, I mean them to refer to methodically regulated procedures of scrutinising and reflecting upon 'reality', of the data, that is, that are sought in the world, in history and culture, with the end of obtaining knowledge of a particular kind. What I call 'scientific' in Machiavelli is the manner in which he dispenses with theological, transcendent and revealed truths admitting of no reflection, critique or challenge. His 'scientificity' consists in the immanentisation of his knowledge objectives by focussing on tangible events in the world and in history.

94   I use this term in spite of possible misgivings about the essentialist flavour it might convey. Machiavelli himself devised this method as a coherent whole and used it quite consistently throughout his work. An overview of what I call 'Machiavelli's method' can be found in Coleman 2000: 241ff. It is striking that *The Prince* is distinctly more systematic in approach than the aphoristic style of Erasmus (Rippel 2007: 242). The systematic character of *The Prince* is a function not least of the remarkably consistent use of key concepts: *fortuna, virtù, modo (di governare), necessità, prudenza*, etc. A contrary view is that of Wolin 1960: 211.

of (second) the *factual*, and it is this experience of the factual that finds its concretisation (third) *general rules* of understanding and of action.[95] The path from perceiving events – whether by reading or through one's own perception – to political action is long and passes through several stages. The method suggested by Machiavelli is the concretisation of political action based on the experience and understanding of the factual, of things as they are (*verità effettuale della cosa*[96]), and not – as Machiavelli emphasises – as we might like them to be.[97]

Machiavelli refers to this form of facticity as *verità*, truth. Reading *The Prince* with the hermeneutical method of Gadamer's *Truth and Method* in mind, rule and the act of ruling become intelligible as media of understanding and of enacting factual, immanent and 'real' truth. 'Rule and method' might hence be the heading for this search for truth that is present and actualised politically. Pragmatically speaking, rule is not a given, but a form guided by interests.[98] The effective truth of a thing (*verità effettuale della cosa*) is to Machiavelli the key to successful action and refers to the reality of the 'things' that, once they have been epistemically reflected and internalised, lead to effective concretisation in political action: to 'things' understood being put into practice.[99]

---

95   Gaille-Nikodimov 2007: 25; Vilches 2007b: 1.
96   Machiavelli, Principe: 118–119. English translations variously render *verità effettuale della cosa* as 'what really happens' (*Prince* 4) or 'the truth of the matter' (Gilbert, I 1965: 57; Vilches 2007: 4f.).
97   'For many have imagined republics and principalities that have never been seen or known to exist. However, how men live is so different from how they should live that a ruler who does not do what is generally done, but persists in doing what ought to be done, will undermine his power rather than maintain it' (*Prince* 54). On this, see Gilbert 1991: 37.
98   A certain Occamite influence is discernible here, according to which constitutional change is susceptible to planning. According to Occam, human beings were able to decide what form of rule best served the attainment of their own interests (Miethke 2008: 286).
99   'Thus, it is the duty of a good man to teach others the good you yourself were unable to accomplish due to the malignity of the times or of fortune, so that among the many people capable of such actions, some of the more favoured by heaven may accomplish it' (Machiavelli, *Discourses*: 152). On this, see Deppe 1987: 29; Borelli 2009: 189.

With this in mind, we can understand why Machiavelli's method drew so heavily on historical knowledge: to him, 'understanding' and 'science' came into being only by contact with and contemplation of historical knowledge. Historical knowledge, moreover, provided the premises for both practical and theoretical understanding. It was for these reasons that Machiavelli's method was largely historical:[100] 'I have not found among my belongings anything that I hold more dear or valuable than my knowledge of the conduct of great men, learned through long experience of modern affairs and continual study of ancient history.'[101]

History demonstrates an inner necessity (*necessità*)[102] of the facts. The facts in turn make present effective truth by constituting the effects and causes of other facts.[103] This entire method stems from a historical form of an originally rhetorical mode of the humanists' approach to sources. *Il Principe* is a quasi-scientific *oratio* which is hortatory by design on the one hand while on the other adopting key epistemic procedures from the humanists, notably an emphasis on context, criticism, example and history.[104]

Friedrich Meinecke dubbed Machiavelli's method '*voraussetzungsloser Empirismus*' – an empiricism, that is, without presuppositions.[105] It is worth questioning, however, whether Machiavelli's methodical edifice was truly as self-sufficient as all that, founded as it is on unquestioned axioms like

100 Kocìs 1998: 219ff.; Gaille-Nikodimov 2007: 24ff.; Vilches 2007: 13; Viroli 2008: 48.

101 *Prince* 3, emphasis added. Original: '[N]on ho trovato, intra la mia suppellettile, cosa quale io abbi piú cara o tanto esístimi quanto la cognizione della azioni degli uomini grandi, imparata da me con una longa esperienzia delle cose moderne e una continua legazione delle antique' (Machiavelli, *Principe*: 4–5).

102 On this, see Kluxen 1967.

103 Münkler 1990: 252. That Machiavelli's method emphasises observation of the concrete, of what is self-evident and visible, should not be misconstrued to claim that his 'realism' was tantamount to a politics of appearances ('se laisse réduire à une politique des apparences') (Sfez 1998: 279). To this, Machiavelli would likely reply that this was rather a politics of sustained success along the lines of that which had been successful in the Roman world for a thousand years and was founded on a profound appreciation of the human condition.

104 Zăgrean 2002: 25.

105 Meinecke 1929: 48. Buck 1985: 61, who uses the same term.

of that of the cyclical character of history, the ἀνακύκλωσις (*anacyclosis*) of Polybius.[106] Machiavelli believed nature to display a coherent order, and history presented it itself as no less governed by *causa* and *effectum*, the workings of which could be read in and deduced from history:[107]

> Usually provinces go most of the time, in the changes they make, from order to disorder and then pass again from disorder to order, for worldly things are not allowed by nature to stand still. As soon as they reach their ultimate perfection, having no further to rise, they must descend; and similarly, once they have descended and through their disorders arrived at the ultimate depth, since they cannot descend further, of necessity they must rise.[108]

It is only by virtue of being repeatable – and this may safely be called a presupposition – that history is open to such epistemic processes as analysis, imitation and comparison: only that can be thought which has already existed.[109] The idea of truth in evidence here is based on deduction from experience, of truth as discursive coherence emerging from coherent historical and political action: a coherence of argumentation that provides a discursive translation of political and historical events.[110] Where statecraft (*arte dello stato*)[111] is concerned, Machiavelli takes all this to mean the ability to deal with situations that occurred previously, had similar or identical causes, pursued similar or identical ends and were open to analogous action.

> Men must be studied in their behaviour as well as in their professions. There is no *a priori* route to the knowledge of the human material with which a ruler must deal. There is, no doubt, an unchanging human nature the range of whose responses to

---

106 Polybius, *History*, book VI; Horkheimer 1930: 13f.; Münkler 1990: 39, 103, 121, 261; Diesner 1994: 68.
107 Klein 1984: 80f.; Münkler 1990: 101.
108 Machiavelli, *Florentine Histories* 185; see also Machiavelli, Discorsi (M): I, S. 135.
109 Horkheimer 1930: 11; Gilbert 1991: 49; Borelli 2009: 188.
110 Raspa 2006: 180.
111 Machiavelli, *Lettere*: 297 (Letter to Vettori of 19 December 1513). This, and not 'politics' or 'science' (*scienza*), is the term that Machiavelli himself used to denote what he was concerned with. To him, the appropriate metaphor is in the work of a physician or an architect (Bondanella/Musa 1979: 27f.).

changing situations can be determined [...]; one can obtain this knowledge only by empirical observation.[112]

Based on the assumption that there is no such thing as coincidence in history, Machiavelli makes a methodical attempt to discover history's concealed and yet intelligible laws (*nomos*) of change and development.[113] His empiricism is thus not free from presuppositions.

This brings us to the end or purpose (*fine*),[114] for which Machiavelli developed an exceptionally sophisticated (at least for his day) method. The end he had in view was efficient and functional politics, a successful commonwealth.[115] But what did 'success' mean under these conditions?

In Machiavelli, we encounter a form of science that is not only a tool for analysis and description, but that also signifies a form of rule – a science that is conceived as the medium of the prince's dominion over his subjects. It is by no means a science *about* rule, but a science for the exercise *of* rule according to set principles. It stated purpose is to rule over human beings in a functioning political commonwealth. The legitimacy of such rule is no longer derived from such transcendent instances as God, Christ or salvation, but rather by its immanent success.[116] Success, to Machiavelli, is ultimately all that constituted the historical greatness of the Athenian *polis* or the Roman state and which the Florentine state as he knew it sadly lacked: the ability successfully to repel enemy attacks, to safeguard peace at home as well as harmony and security in the lives of citizens, and of course power and prestige with regard to other nations.[117] The political form, be it republic or despotism, is ultimately of secondary importance. Though Machiavelli's own sympathies may lie with a republican constitution, he has no objection to the state's goals being achieved by a charismatic (even despotic) prince.[118]

---

112 Berlin 1997: 41.
113 Kluxen 1967: 106.
114 It has been shown that, compared to the *Discourses*, the usage of the term '*fine*' in *The Prince* is less semantically fixed (Diesner 1987: 163).
115 Gaille-Nikodimov 2007: 29; Tarlton 2007: 46f.
116 Gaille-Nikodimov 2007: 29; Tarlton 2007: 46f.
117 Berlin 1997: 43; Walsh 2007: 274.
118 Voigt 2004.

In pursuing and attaining the end or *fine*, civic good is safeguarded and thereby freed from the yoke of historical accident, of the vagaries of fortune. Without wanting to reopen a case that has already been amply discussed,[119] I would like to underscore just how great the hopes are that Machiavelli's method places in suppressing fortune. Like any science, this method is built on the rational, logical and causal understanding of events, by which surprises can be avoided.[120] Methodical procedures can indeed see into the future – by prognostication, that is, and not mantically, by means of fortune-telling, though Machiavelli was a keen and frequent patron of fortune-tellers.[121] Fortune, in *The Prince*, is a political category by whose workings peoples, states and rulers rise and fall.

Though Machiavelli discusses fortune extensively, this should not be mistaken for an indication of fatalism on his part. Instead he demonstrates its immense power in order to make vivid to the reader the advantages of a methodical approach.

> Besides subjective reason, then, there is to Machiavelli a concept of 'objective reason' or a concept of the objective – that is, not or only partly accessible to the subjective capacity for action – determination of political action which, though it can be understood by the rationality of cognition, by its nature [...] constitutes the polar opposite to subjective reason. In other words, anybody acting politically is subject to the constant danger of being challenged and destroyed [...] by objective rules. [...] Yet it is these that must be put to use [...] if the roaring tide of fortune is to be resisted.[122]

Machiavelli indeed tries to place in our hands a powerful weapon against fortune, and that weapon is virtue (*virtù*).[123] Stripped of any moral values,

119   On fortune, see Diesner 1993: 179f.; Kocìs 1998: 46ff.
120   Viroli 2008: 53.
121   King 2007: 60f., 101.
122   Deppe 1987: 296. See also Münkler 1990: 302ff. 'Rationality' remains a tricky concept. Machiavelli's rationality may be said to accord with the following definition: 'By rationalisation, we mean the ordering and systematisation of reality with the purpose of making it calculable and controllable' (Van der Loo/ Reijen 1992: 118). This is most probably just one of many possible approaches. Unfortunately, it considers rationalisation, as an effect of rationality, only in its effects, but not in its origins and functioning. With this caveat in mind, this definition nonetheless offers a useful perspective.
123   On this, see Mayer 1912; Diesner 1993: 178f.; Kocìs 1998: 52f.; Kim 2004.

virtù to Machiavelli denotes above all the capacity to act with intelligence, judgment and foresight.[124] Understood thus, *virtù* is less a concept than a semantics of political ability.[125] Numerous translations of the term '*virtù*' have been suggested,[126] and Machiavelli himself rather progressively gives his readers the opportunity to form their own sense of its meaning from the examples and contexts provided.[127] Strikingly, the *segredario* himself often uses it synonymously with *prudenza* or prudence (which entails caution, foresight, shrewdness, judgement, etc.), in a sense resembling the *pronoia* of Thucydides.[128]

> For men almost always follow in the footsteps of others, imitation being a leading principle of human behaviour. Since it is not always possible to follow in the footsteps of others, or to equal the ability [*virtù*] of those whom you imitate, a shrewd man [*uomo prudente*] will always follow the methods of remarkable men, and imitate those who have been outstanding, so that, even if he does not succeed in matching their ability [*virtù*], at least he will get within sniffing distance of it. He should act as skilful [*prudenti*] archers do [...].[129]

Here, we are witnesses to the semantic unfolding of *virtù* as skilfulness, as ability. *Virtù* is ascribed to the man who is shrewd (*prudente*) or, conversely, able men (*virtuosi*) are described as shrewd (*prudenti*). *Prudenza* is the attitude to cultivate if one is looking to avoid being taken by surprise

---

124 Rippel 2007: 248.
125 Nitschke 2000: 42; Kim 2004: 104ff.; Skinner 2009: 165.
126 Russell Price gives an overview of the term's senses in the notes to his translation of *The Prince*, 103f. Machiavelli uses *virtù* in a variety of meanings, allowing it to be understood as resolve, energy and derring-do as well as *prudenza* (Ottmann 2006: 21f.). Klaudia Knauer has produced a list of no fewer than thirty-nine possible (German) translations of *virtù* (Knauer 1990: 116).
127 Zăgrean 2002: 49.
128 Belliotti 2009: 3; Stockhammer 2009: 54, 57f.
129 *Prince* 19. Original: '[P]erché, camminando gli uomini quasi sempre per le vie battute da altri, e procedendo nelle azioni loro con le imitazioni, né si potendo le vie di altri al tutto tenere, né alla virtù di quelli che tu imiti aggiugnere, debbe uno uomo prudente intrare sempre per vie battute da uomini grandi, e quelli che sono stati eccellentissimi imitare, acciò che, se la sua virtù non vi arriva, almeno ne renda qualche odore; e fare come gli arcieri prudenti [...]' (Machiavelli, *Principe*: 40–41).

or wrong-footed. It entails weighing advantages and disadvantages prior to making the right decision.[130] Machiavelli's *virtù* is less of a 'something' than a 'how'. A prince is not a *virtuoso* simply by dint of being a prince, but in his conduct: '*virtù come virtuosità*'.[131] This form of virtue is not a property inherent to human nature, but one that can and must be learned. It is a matter neither of intuition nor of divine grace. Instead, *prudenza* consists in the painstaking work of gathering data and weighing evidence, of comparison, examination and application.[132] It is a virtue of (intellectual) diligence or industry (*industria*).[133]

The wise ruler always knows when there is an opportunity to be seized ('e la eccellente virtù loro fece quella occasione essere conosciuta').[134] And those possessed of *virtù* have little to fear from fortune.[135] *Prudenza*, being a manifestation of *virtù*, is to Machiavelli the enactment of the entire intellectual process, from obtaining information to political action. In the epistemic rhythm of scientific steps, there is little scope for accident: God's will comes to be replaced by the free will of man. *Homo mensura*, man as the measure, is the subject of the *virtù* that Machiavelli pits against fortune.[136] Man is now able to help himself and to that end has discovered the benefits of

130   'But prudence consists in knowing how to assess the dangers, and to choose the least bad curse of action as being the right one to follow' (*Prince* 79). Original: 'Ma la prudenza consiste in sapere conoscere le qualità degli inconvenienti e pigliare il meno tristo per buono' (Machiavelli, *Principe*: 178–179).

131   Frosini 2006: 51.

132   Münkler 1985: 25, 38.

133   Machiavelli, *Principe*: 14–15.

134   Machiavelli, *Principe*: 42–43.

135   Fortune, to Machiavelli, remains an extraneous instance that statecraft may tame by methodical rule, though never quite banish (Tarlton 2007: 59). The case in point, according Machiavelli, was that of Cesare Borgia, who had done everything right as far as human reason could tell, and yet was laid low by fortune. Borgia, however, was an exception and 'should not be blamed', having suffered 'extraordinarily bad luck' (*Prince* 23; original: *una estraordinaria ed estrema malignità di fortuna*, Machiavelli, *Principe*: 50–51). By doing everything right, the prince might at least reduce the likelihood of such ill fortune.

136   Schröder 2004: 107; Dreier 2005: 318ff., 323 n. 165; Kersting 2006: 113; Vilches 2007: 2.

science.[137]

'Machiavelli's work was situated at the beginning of science.'[138] Though the scientific study of Creation was not altogether new in Europe, it certainly intensified at the threshold of the sixteenth century. This was accompanied but the increasing adoption of methods from the natural sciences in areas of study that had previously been the domain of metaphysics, theology and philosophy. Nature now came to be understood as not sustained by the workings of God, but governed by natural laws and forces of its own, and even by logic.[139] This new awareness was also brought to bear on political theory, in which – and Machiavelli was among the first to do so[140] – rule and the ruler were uncoupled from the ideality of *Christianitas* and of Christian moral values and faith.[141]

According to the immanent logic of the natural sciences, only that can be reflected and referred to, which has been perceived, seen, experienced, measured, tried, tested, compared and generalised. Knowledge begins with the isolated uniqueness of the individual case and from there ascends to the understanding of the order and regularity underlying phenomena. This allows human beings to tame nature, which hitherto had been 'inestimable' or 'incalculable'.[142] From physics derives the habit of thinking in constants and the idea of those constants' variability. Both are reflected in *The Prince*: structurally, human nature is always corrupt,[143] though it is

---

137 Deppe 1987: 293.

138 Gaetano Mosca apud Walsh 2007: 287.

139 Münkler 1990: 101.

140 Francis Bacon (d. 1626) considered Machiavelli to have been one of the first exponents of the scientific-empirical method and an example of analytical procedure (Prezzolini 2004: 91).

141 This immanentisation of the image of the world and of political power is already discernible in the high Middle Ages (Jeremias 2005: 153), for example, in the *Policraticus* of John of Salisbury (John of Salisbury, *Policraticus* 1990; Nederman 1990: xxiii; Grigore 2010: 139, 155, 166).

142 Horkheimer 1930: 7; Schölderle 2002: 84; Rippel 2007: 240.

143 Diesner 1994: 68; Prezzolini 2004: 82; Gaille-Nikodimov 2007: 28; Stockhammer 2009: 53. John Chrysostom or Augustine also held human nature to be corrupt, though they found the cause to reside in original sin (Grigore 2010: 132; Grigore 2012: 333ff., with references). Machiavelli attempts no such explanation, offering

subject to the historical variability of becoming: 'For this may said of men generally: they are ungrateful, fickle, feigners and dissemblers, avoiders of danger, eager for gain.'[144] Hence man is able to be calculated and the variability of his actions to be methodically circumscribed: human beings can thus be influenced and ruled.[145]

It is not without reason that the method of Machiavelli is often mentioned in the same breath as those of Giordano Bruno or of Galileo, for all three accord the central roles in episteme to experiment (*experimentum*) and observation (*consideratio*).[146] The experimental aspect of Machiavelli's thought lies in his observant 'dissection' of history and in the quasi-critical manner in which he scrutinises it, looking for guidelines for action. A new method here enters into political thought: a new appreciation of cause and effect, of comparison and analogy, the testing of theories by experience, and the consideration of historical context and the scope for generalisation.[147]

Another parallel that has often been invoked is that between Machiavelli and his contemporary, Leonardo da Vinci. Leonardo made a point of putting the discoveries of the natural sciences to use in his art. His paintings and drawings testify to Leonardo's engagement with the laws of optics, three-dimensional perspective, physics, anatomy and physiology.[148] For his part, Machiavelli can be seen to set great store by the perspective from which events are considered and the distance at which the observer

---

only the conclusion based on an observation of human actions throughout history (Prezzolini 2004: 92ff.).

144 *Prince* 59. Original: 'Perché degli uomini si può dire questo generalmente: che sieno ingrati, volubili, simulatori e dissimulatori, fuggitori de' pericoli, cupidi di guadagno' (Machiavelli, *Principe*: 128–129).

145 Horkheimer 1930: 10; Klein 1984: 69; Kluxen 1986: 571; Münkler 1990: 254; Van der Loo/Reijen 1992: 122; Kondylis 2007: 9.

146 De Pace 2002; Keßler 2002: 65; Rohls 2002: 291ff., 296ff.

147 Borelli 2009: 189ff. The epistemic processes of observation, quantification, inference and linking effects to causes can already be found in the work of Duns Scotus (d. 1308) (Decorte 2006: 275). Machiavelli makes observation dependent on the experience of the observer: the less experienced the eye, the more rudimentary the observation. This assumption continues to underpin modern scientific observation (Daston 2008: 99).

148 Flasch 1986: 569; Körber 2002: 2f.

stands to events and which determines his own position with regard to them.[149] The times, in which Machiavelli was writing, emphasised pragmatic considerations, a concern with matters of immediate utility and open to technical or methodical approaches. The guiding motto might have been that 'secular necessity demands secular solutions'. With their focus on eternity, afterlife and transcendence, God and Christianity had not enough to contribute to immediate necessities.

Europe witnessed pragmatism and science – in the sense of knowledge obtained and applied by the natural sciences – make inroads into new realms, those of art and philosophy, and even theology and history. Interest was now directed at that which *is* rather than that which *might* be. Knowledge and life were no longer to be founded on the uncertainties of faith and revelation. A rift now opened between things that had to be believed because they could not be proved by logic and reason, and things that no longer had to be believed because they were accessible to rational explanation and hence could be considered certain.[150]

It is difficult, however, to set a precise date for this sea-change in intellectual history. Such processes take a long time to ripen, as it were, and this is certain to have begun earlier than the fifteenth or sixteenth centuries. High medieval nominalism – which of course had antecedents of its own – in the thirteenth century[151] broke with the dominant scholastic theology of its day and rethought metaphysics.[152] Faced with the ancient problem of universals, nominalist scholars denied any reality of the *universalia* in the things themselves, which were real only in thought and thus in a mental process on the part of the human subject. The reality of things *extra nos* was repudiated.[153] William of Occam (d.

---

149   Jeremias 2005: 237. The principles of perspective were introduced into Florentine painting and sculpture as central tenets in the fifteenth century. The viewer's own angle and imagination were part of the artist's calculation and could be played with accordingly. To Machiavelli, it was 'politics that had to follow ever-shifting perspectives' (Schölderle 2002: 105).

150   Decorte 2006: 275.

151   Klein 1984: 134ff.

152   Keßler 2002: 76. 'Yet this also means that the scholastic understanding of immanence as an interpretation of transcendence is invalidated' (Münkler 1985: 24f.).

153   Paqué 1970: 270.

1349)[154] maintained that the possibilities of being were not anchored in reality (essence, existence, act, potentiality). To him, they were but *modi* of the subjective predication of being.

Being was thus removed from the sphere of medieval realism and introduced into that of linguistic and conceptual possibilities, that of terms' (*termini*) referential dimension.[155] This further means that that which is must not only be capable of being stated explicitly to have any presence for us in the first place, but it must also be comprehensible to our minds.[156] The path was thus cleared for knowledge and science to be premised on individual experience, both actual and potential, both intellectual and sensory, of *res*.

Some scholars hence consider Occam an 'empiricist'.[157] All we have are individual things, which are referred to in our thinking by general concepts. General concepts are 'produced' by our mind, which generalises from the intuitive knowledge of existing things. Generalisation is made possible by comparison, from which similarity may be concluded. Generalisation is thus the result of scientific processes.[158]

Attention must be drawn, however, to the reverse of this argument. Taken to its ultimate conclusion, a particular current of radical nominalist logic, in its aversion to the objectively general, turns into an argument directed against science itself. 'In a nominalist universe marked by atom-like kernels of being and a network of accidental relationships of causality, both of which are contingent, science is obviously a precarious business.'[159] This,

---

154   On Occam as political theorist, see Hirsch McIntyre 1972.

155   The *terminus* is three-dimensional, being *terminus mentalis*, *terminus prolatus* and *terminus scriptus*. These acquire meaning not by being unique words, but by association with a proposition. *Termini* are *actus intelligendi* (acts of understanding) and hence of grasping something. To Occam, only language is universal. Occam ties ontology to language; the *termini* or *nomina* he takes to be immutable forms of referring to extraneous objects (Schulthess 1998: 411; Wolter 2003: 311; Panaccio 2004: 182f.).

156   Rohls 2002: 232; Kenny 2005: 173f.; Decorte 2006: 293f. Occam can thus be considered a pioneer of cognitive philosophy (Perler 2008).

157   Colish 1997: 312. On this, see also 1970: 264; Goldstein 1998: 268; Keßler 2002: 61.

158   Rohls 2002: 229.

159   Decorte 2006: 295.

however, was only one current, and it was largely without consequence for Machiavelli and early modern natural science.[160]

The elevation of personal experience to the benchmark of episteme features strongly in Machiavelli's method. Nominalist insights can thus be seen to permeate not only the history of natural science in the Renaissance, but also political thought up to and indeed beyond Hobbes.[161] Machiavelli's concept of 'experience' is the same that, in political thought, leads to the departure from the humanist ideal of *humanitas* and the freedom of man self-developing towards the good. It was experience that taught Machiavelli that human beings were subject to urges and drives as well as to the eternal laws of nature, and that these urges themselves were immutable. The ability to see through these structures was thus an efficient means to gaining and securing political power.

But how does Machiavelli see through and decode structures? He does so by means of particular methodical steps that still find application in certain areas of the humanities.[162]

The first step from perception to knowledge of general valid truths is the *observation* of particular cases, persons and actions. This is accomplished above all by methodical *distancing*. Considering situations from an appropriate distance is a major step both of method and of rule. Such observation is *targeted* (one hopes to see something) and *perspectival* (one hopes to see something from various angles, better to appreciate the whole).[163]

Machiavelli's preferred metaphor is that of the landscape artist, whose gaze, from a distance, encompasses both the hills, seen from the plain, and the extent of the plain itself, seen from on high.[164] Perspectival observation thus allows the observer to perceive what is observed as a whole, thereby raising neutral distance to a higher power: only by distance and perspectives (plural) does what is observed truly become an object, and the observer minimises the risk of identifying with the object and thereby compromising

160   Rohls 2002: 290ff.
161   Regli 1921: 76.
162   Jeremias 2005: 243.
163   Schölderle 2002: 104.
164   Machiavelli, Principe: 6–7; Berlin 1997: 33.

his own 'objectivity'.[165] In a sense, the freedom of the observer is a function of his distance from the observed.

Machiavelli makes much use of *examples*, which serve him methodically as case studies by which a claim is substantiated or a hypothesis tested.[166] Examples are given both positively and negatively, as demanded by perspective.[167] This use of examples gives the Florentine free movement across time and space, history and the world, and allows him to invoke *analogies* in order to frame advice for action.[168] Yet this advice must not be reduced to a mere reproduction or copy[169] of what others have done, but rather its creative interpretation, a hermeneutics making use of new contexts:[170]

> From this, again, arise changes in prosperity; because if a man acts cautiously and patiently, and the times and circumstances change in ways for which *his methods* are appropriate, he will be successful. But if the times and circumstances change again, he will come to grief, because he does not change *his methods*.[171]

One must first enquire into the consequences or effects of events; the findings must then be causally situated in context.[172]

165 Gaille-Nikodimov 2007: 25.
166 Burnham 1943: 45.
167 Gaille-Nikodimov 2007: 25.
168 Machiavelli held that analogies were to be drawn not only from history, from temporally remote contexts, but also from topography. In order to prepare for war, the prince 'should very frequently engage in hunting', thereby 'becoming familiar with the terrain'; this knowledge of the characteristics of certain kinds of countryside would then redound to his advantage when fighting on similar terrain even without any prior experience of the country itself (*Prince* 52f.).
169 Greene 1984: 62f.; Keßler 2002: 216. 'Because prudence consists in a reflective and problematic relation between rules and causes, Machiavelli must not just tell the Prince "Be wise, avoid imitating too mechanically and stupidly [...]"' (Garver 1987: 50).
170 Kersting 2006: 60 and 113. Consider the archery metaphor in chapter six of *The Prince* (on which, see Gaille-Nikodimov 2007: 28; Benner 2009: 109).
171 *Prince* 86, emphasis added.
172 'Da questo ancora depende la variazione del bene: perché, se uno che si governa con respetti e pazienzia, e' tempi e le cose girono in modo che il governo suo sia buono, e' viene felicitando; ma se li tempi, e le cose si mutano, e' rovina, perché non muta modo di procedere' (Machiavelli, *Principe*: 194–195). Compare Machiavelli's view as expressed in the *Discourses*: 'I have considered on many occasions that the

From the multitude of images, events, actions and persons, Machiavelli 'extracts' typologies and *leitmotifs*. This occurs not least by *reduction* and *naming*, for instance by reducing the typology of principalities to the opposition of hereditary (*ereditarii*) and new (*nuovi*) or naming the ruler's principal operations, for example, to acquire (*acquistare*) or maintain (*mantenere*) a principality.[173] Reduction also occurs when only that which is 'utilisable' is extracted from a train of events.[174]

Machiavelli gathers data, reduces them to structures, applies them to historical contexts by means of analogy and *generalises* them by induction to frame general rules (*regole generali*).[175] As an aspect of Machiavelli's 'scientificity', this act of generalisation and rule-setting by no means entails relinquishing distance, perspective and context. It is rather a case of being aware that true generalisation can only occur when general rules are applied in the appropriate context.[176]

With Philipp Rippel, we can only conclude that in Machiavelli, the entire process from observation to knowledge and thence to action informed by that knowledge is a chain of 'experiences condensed to theory'.[177]

---

cause of the bad and good fortune of man lies in how well their mode of conduct fits the times. Because it is evident that in their works some men proceed with impetuosity, others with care and caution; and because either of these methods may exceed the proper limits, being unable to follow the true path, one may err in following either one' (*Discourses* 281) ('Io ho considerato più volte come la cagione della trista e della buona fortuna degli uomini è riscontrare il modo del procedere suo coi tempi: perchè e' si vede che gli uomini nelle opere loro procedono alcuni con impeto, alcuni con rispetto e con cauzione. E perchè nell'uno e nell'altro si era. Ma quello viene ad err meno, et avere la fortuna prospera, che riscontra, come io ho detto, con il suo modo il tempo, e sempre mai si procede [...]') (Machiavelli, *Discorsi* [orig.]: 255).

173 Schölderle 2002: 83.
174 Machiavelli, *Principe*: chs. 1ff. and Machiavelli, *Lettere*: 296.
175 Machiavelli, Principe: 24–25, 28–29; Burnham 1943: 40ff.; Deppe 1987: 202; Femia 2004: 44; Jeremias 2005: 284f.
176 To Machiavelli, truth is a methodical process for arriving at political decisions and hence not an object in itself. The method can be widely applied in order to obtain such knowledge as is necessary in a particular situation. The singularity of contexts confirms the necessity of treating them in general terms methodically, that is, applied (Gaille-Nikodimov 2007: 29; Viroli 2008: 36).
177 Rippel 2007: 230.

This manner of putting political and historical knowledge to use met with criticism even among Machiavelli's contemporaries. His friend Francesco Guicciardini[178] objected to the giant historical leaps the *Segredario* was wont to make:

> I do not agree with him in what he says, that there was always as much good in one age as in another although it varied from place to place [...]. The world has seen some ages full of wars, in others has known and enjoyed peace. As a result of changes in arts and religion and the movements of human affairs it is not surprising that men's customs too should vary [...]. It is therefore a true conclusion that ancient times are not always to be preferred to the present.[179]

To Guicciardini's mind, Machiavelli's assumption that the historical could yield guidelines for present action if examined methodically was indefensible. Such were the spatial, temporal and cultural differences that they could but thwart any 'phenomenological', trans-contextual and generalising deductions.[180] History did not repeat itself, and generalisations – like the claim that humans were weak and inclined to evil – were mere constructs that, far from providing 'objective' knowledge, were cases

178   On Guicciardini's approach: Guicciardini, *Das politische Erbe*; Rubinstein 1989; Sumberg 1993: 72; Moulakis 1998. Francesco Guicciardini's political career was longer and more distinguished than that of his friend, Niccolò Machiavelli. He had already been dispatched on a mission to Spain in 1512, was appointed to the Florentine *Signoria* in 1515 and papal governor in Modena in 1516. From 1525 to 1526 he was president of the Romagna, then a papal state, and represented Pope Clement VII at the signing of the so-called League of Cognac (see Münkler 1985: 40; Rubinstein 1989: 146ff.; Reinhardt 2004). Machiavelli's correspondence with Guicciardini began much later than that with Vettori and was less confidential (see Gilbert 1965: 241).

179   Guicciardini, *Considerations*: II, introduction, p. 107f. 'Non concordo giá seco in quello che dice, che sempre nel mondo fu tanto del buono in una etá quanto in una altra, benché si variino e' luoghi [...]. Ha visto qualche etá el mondo pieno di guerre, un'altra ha sentito e goduto la pace; dalle quale variazione delle arte, della religione, de' movimenti delle cose umane, non è maraviglia siano anche variati e' costumi degli uomini [...]. è adunche vera conclusione che non sempre e' tempi antichi sono da essere preferiti a' presenti [...]' (Guicciardini, *Considerazioni*: II, p. 49f.).

180   Rahe 2000: 305.

of *petitio principii*.[181] The postulates of genuine historical scholarship, to Guicciardini, were much rather satisfied by restriction to the singular historical case, the circumstances (*circonstanze*) of the limited context of its singularity and to its exceptions (*eccezioni*).[182] This approach, too, seems 'modern' in its way and is to this day enshrined in the methodology of historical research.

Yet as I hope to have shown above, it would be wrong to accuse Machiavelli of disregarding context and circumstances. Far from merely adopting or 'copying' rules from the past, he proceeds in the manner of a physician, prognosticating, diagnosing and formulating knowledge on a case-by-case basis:[183]

> [B]ut if one lets trouble develop, the medicine will be too late, because the malady will have become incurable. And what physicians say about consumptive diseases is also true of this matter, namely, that at the beginning of the illness, it is easy to treat but difficult to diagnose but, if it has been treated at an early stage, as time passes it becomes easy to diagnose but difficult to treat. This also happens in affairs of state; for if one recognises political problems early (which only a shrewd and far-seeing man [*uno prudente*] can do), they may be resolved quickly, but if they are not recognised, and left to develop so that everyone recognises them, there is no longer any remedy.[184]

Machiavelli follows no one slavishly, not even his historical sources (e.g., Polybius).[185] His method is not mathematical and mechanical, but nor is

---

181   Stockhammer 2009: 128ff.

182   Gilbert 1965: 279.

183   Buck 1985: 157, 159; Campagna 2003: 152; Jeremias 2005: 285; Zwierlein 2007: 95.

184   *Prince* 11. Original: 'Ma, aspettando che ti si appressino, la medicina non è a tempo, perché la malattia è divenuta incurabile. E interviene di questa, come dicono e' fisici dello etico, che, nel principio del suo male, è facile a curare e difficile a conoscere, ma, nel progresso del tempo, non l'avendo in principio conosciuta né medicata, diventa facile a conoscere e difficile a curare. Cosí interviene nelle cose di stato; perché, conoscendo discosto (il che non è dato se non a uno prudente) e' mali che nascono in quello, si guariscono presto; ma quando, per non li avere conosciuti, si lasciano crescere in modo che ognuno li conosce, non vi è piú remedio' (Machiavelli, *Principe*: 20–21).

185   On Machiavelli's rather casual treatment of Polybius or Thucydides, see Ellinger 1888: 4, 35.

it 'dogmatic',[186] for the same data may often produce different guidelines for action. The method under examination here is one that is hermeneutical, interpretive, prognosticating, descriptive and understanding, in a sense also phenomenological, and concerned with taking broader contexts into consideration.[187]

Questions of contextual differentiation play the key part here. We may observe the emergence, in the early modern age, of competing scientific paradigms, which make different decisions concerning their basic premises and methods in their quest for knowledge.[188] On the one hand, we have a paradigm that, following the natural sciences, restricts itself to 'pure' observation and description, forgoing any interpretation and 'metahistory'. On the other, there stands a method of deduction proceeding from the general to the particular. We would do well to avoid setting one above the other in terms of their quality.[189]

More recent scholarship in particular, however, has tended to disregard this advice.[190] It is probably fair to say that, by modern standards of

---

186   In the historicism debate of the nineteenth and early twentieth centuries, the term 'dogmatic' denotes the counter-position to 'historicism', the shorthand for the historical method. This polarity was discussed in an essay by Ernst Troeltsch, which has since become classical (Troeltsch 1913). On the historicism debate and its significance for historical scholarship, see Oexle 2007. 'Dogmatism' as the deductive procedure by which a priori truths are confirmed by history is essentially the charge that Guicciardini brought against Machiavelli. Restriction to a pure description of individual cases and forgoing the construction of trans-historical 'constants' are the hallmarks of a particular branch of historical scholarship which, in the nineteenth century, often professed its adherence to the principles of observation identified with the natural sciences (Oexle 2007: 11). The debate over historicism shows to what extent distancing and the constant deconstruction of phenomena can lead to relativism or contingency. On this, see Meinecke 1965; Rüsen 1993; Troeltsch 2002.

187   Kersting 2006: 50.

188   Kondylis 2007: 109.

189   Guicciardini's method, for instance, was described as 'genuine realism' (Gil 1994: 196). To attempts at making the debate between the two a battleground in modern arguments over scientific truth, I would object that they are both inappropriate and anachronistic.

190   Wolin 1960: 211; Greene 1984: 70; Berlin 1997: 67f. '[H]e was an especially sloppy researcher' (Belliotti 2009: 69). Machiavelli was supposedly an illusionist of the

scientific procedure, Machiavelli frequently deviates from his own method. In the *Discourses* as well as in *Dell'arte della guerra* (1521) he opposes the new artillery weapons of his day in spite of their proven efficiency.[191] He is also in the habit of setting too much store by the argument from antiquity (Guicciardini's criticism is apt in this respect), making something of a golden age of classical antiquity and using history as a 'quarry'.[192] Worse still, his fondness for generalisation led him to a severe misjudgement: an expert opinion he issued in 1527 underestimated the strength of the Duke of Bourbon's forces (22,000 Spanish soldiers and German *landsknechts*) and told the *Signoria* that, barring unforeseen circumstances, the army would be easy to beat, being starving and undisciplined. But Machiavelli seems to have forgotten that a similar force had conquered Florence in 1512. These 'easily defeated' troops captured Rome on 6 May 1527 and sacked it dreadfully (*Sacco di Roma*).[193]

Other examples might be given of style as well as of substance. The question nonetheless remains whether modern criteria for and understandings of 'science' or 'scientificity' can be applied one-to-one – that is, without conceptual and historical clarifications – to someone writing in the sixteenth century. These criteria remain, it must be remembered, highly controversial today. The point of scientific procedure is not necessarily to produce perfectly 'finished' knowledge, but rather to expand it while subjecting it to reflection and scrutiny. Machiavelli thus emerges as a pioneer of methodical procedure in dealing with the 'reality' of the factual. We are now able to appreciate that he stands at the beginning of a tradition rather than at its centre. Machiavelli's achievement is not to have set the standard of faultless scientificity by modern standards, but rather

---

state, a utopian, etc. (Wolin 1960: 212; Diesner 1994: 76ff.). The central category of fortune was the prime example of this tendency of Machiavelli's to hide the inadequacies of his method behind the vagaries of fortune (Deppe 1987: 203).

191   Machiavelli thereby diverged from the admiration and enthusiasm with which the new technical achievement of artillery was commonly greeted. The serious and systematic study of the uses of artillery and warfare had begun in the fifteenth century (Leng 2002).

192   The term 'quarry' (*Steinbruch*) can be found in Deppe 1987: 203, 293; see also Diesner 1994: 67.

193   King 2007: 199f., 225ff.

to have made the first decisive steps in that direction.[194] He ought to be considered the originator not so much of political 'products' – that is, universally applicable solutions – as of a method.[195] He is also remarkable for having accomplished, against Christian cultural norms and Christian (discourses of) power, a new coherence of argument and meaning without recourse to the ubiquitous semantics of *Christianitas*. Machiavelli held up an alternative. If that seems unexceptional today, it was certainly far from it in the sixteenth century.

An Example

To consider Machiavelli in the context of the modern theory of science by virtue of a method that was highly progressive is hardly a new approach. He has, for instance, been portrayed as an ancestor of Max Weber's concept of charismatic rule[196] or of Emile Durkheim's sociology of religion.[197] Above, I tried to show that his method in many respects anticipates today's phenomenological criteria and also that many of the epistemic processes used (not only) by Machiavelli can also be observed in the historicism debate spanning the nineteenth and twentieth centuries. Not without reason did Friedrich Meinecke celebrate Machiavelli as the founder of modern historicism.[198]

For my part I am struck by the parallels between Machiavelli's method and that of the phenomenologist of religion, Gerardus (Gerhard) van der Leeuw. In his *Religion as Essence and Manifestation* (1938; original: *Phänomenologie der Religion*, 1933), van der Leeuw proposes seven methodical steps for a scientific approach to religious phenomena: (1)

---

194 Burnham 1943: 40; Buck 1985: 156; Berlin 1994: 111; Femia 2004: ch. 4, 'The Empirical Method'. Machiavelli has been credited, for example, with establishing Italian as a scientific language (Buck 1985: 162f.).

195 Benner 2009: 126.

196 Jeremias 2005: 284; Stockhammer 2009: 166ff.

197 Preus 1979: 188f.

198 Deppe 1987: 33.

naming that which we perceive; (2) *inserting* it into our own lives, that is, asking why we are even approaching a phenomenon; (3) *epoché* (suspense), that is to say, to retreat into a contemplative distance, to address the phenomenon alone without asking (in the manner of Rudolf Otto) 'what' is thereby revealed, 'what' is behind the phenomena; (4) *clarification*, that is, seeking to categorise the phenomenon by means of comparison; (5) *understanding*, that is, interpreting the phenomenon and placing it in a context with analogous phenomena; (6) *correction*, testing one's own interpretation against archaeological or other evidence; (7) *bearing witness* by announcing the finding of one's investigations.[199]

Keeping in mind that these methodical steps are not consistently and cleanly delineated by van der Leeuw – which may not even be achievable – I would argue that they can be found in a similar form and even in the same sequence in *The Prince* of Machiavelli: (1) *naming* the perceived historical phenomenon; (2) asking *why* this phenomenon is to be discussed; (3) considering it from a distance, putting it into *perspective*; (4) *comparing* it; (5) *generalisation*, that is, inferring the general rule from particular cases; (6) *confirmation* or verification by other historical situations; (7) *presenting* one's conclusions, delivering an overview of them. Although Machiavelli does not describe each of these steps as such, they are nonetheless performed in *The Prince*. Machiavelli either begins each chapter by setting up a hypothesis that is then tested by examples and comparisons or, conversely, a series of examples is given, from which a general rule is then inferred by means of the above-mentioned epistemic processes.

Let us turn to chapter 13 of *The Prince* – 'Auxiliaries, mixed troops and native troops' (*De militibus auxiliariis, mixtis et propriis*) – to illustrate this procedure. The chapter begins (Step 1) with a definition: 'Auxiliaries [...] are troops that are sent to you to aid and defend you, when you call on a powerful ruler for help.'[200]

199   Van der Leeuw 1933: 638ff.
200   *Prince* 48. Original: 'L'armi ausiliarie [...] sono quando si chiama uno potente che con le armi sue ti venga ad aiutare e defendere [...]' (Machiavelli, *Principe*: 104–105).

Step 2: 'In themselves, these auxiliaries can be capable and effective but they are almost always harmful to those who use them; for if they lose you will be ruined, and if they win you will be at their mercy.'[201]

There follows Step 3, considering the problem from a variety of angles and by a number of examples: Pope Julius II, the city of Florence, the Emperor of Constantinople.[202]

Step 4 is then the comparison:

> Therefore, anyone who wants to be unable to conquer should use such troops, because they are much more dangerous than mercenaries: for with them ruin is complete. They form a united force, and are used to obeying others. But when mercenaries conquer, more time and greater opportunities are required before they will be in a position to do you harm. They do not form a united body, since they have been engaged and paid by you. And an outsider whom you appoint as their leader cannot at once assume such authority over them that harm to you will result.[203]

Step 5, the generalisation, follows without further ado: 'In short, with mercenaries, their cowardice or reluctance to fight is more dangerous; with auxiliaries, their skill and courage.'[204] This generalisation is then tested in Step 6 by the recurrent example of Cesare Borgia who, having been burned by his experiences with French auxiliaries and mercenaries led by the *condottieri* Orsini and Vitellozzo Vitelli, raised troops of his own in the Romagna and was triumphant.[205] Further evidence is adduced

---

201   *Prince* 48. 'Queste arme possono essere utile e buone per loro medesime, ma sono, per chi le chiama, quasi sempre dannose; perché, perdendo, rimani disfatto: vincendo, resti loro prigione' (Machiavelli, *Principe*: 104–105).

202   *Prince* 48f.

203   *Prince* 49. Original: 'Colui, adunque, che vuole non potere vincere, si vaglia di queste armi; perché sono molto più pericolose che le mercenarie. Perché in queste è la ruina fatta: sono tutte unite, tutte volte alla obedienzia di altri; ma nelle mercenarie, a offenderti, vinto che le hanno, bisogna più tempo e maggiore occasione, non sendo tutto uno corpo, ed essendo trovate e pagate da te; nelle quali uno terzo che tu facci capo, non può pigliare subito tanta autorità che ti offenda' (Machiavelli, *Principe*: 106–107).

204   *Prince* 49. Original: 'In somma, nelle mercenarie è più pericolosa la ignavia, nelle ausiliarie, la virtù' (Machiavelli, *Principe*: 106–107).

205   *Prince* 49.

and a summary of findings (Step 7) given at the chapter's conclusion (*concludo*, as Machiavelli himself says).[206]

To conclude this example, I would like to emphasise once more that Machiavelli's procedure stands only at the beginning of a tradition of scientific method and is thus not scrupulously adhered to. Though this approach may be considered rudimentary in the eyes of modern science, it is striking just how much more systematic Machiavelli's account is than those of Neagoe Basarab, Erasmus or even Luther.

Principe savio, Not *Principe Cristiano*: Dispensing with *Christianitas*

The Prince is not a work of reference in which the ruler can look up solutions tailored to specific situations. What Machiavelli intended was to offer rulers a manual or textbook for the development and application of methodical *procedere*:[207] a textbook for self-learning.

The treatise appears foremost not as a political analysis or expertise, but rather as an account of how rule can be methodically designed. Since its intended designer is the prince himself, one might say that Machiavelli regarded the ruler as a scientist in his own right. Rather than a passive consumer of political advice, Machiavelli imagines the prince as the agent of methodical policy. In Machiavelli's mind, the *arte dello state* is an 'art' in the traditional sense of the *artes liberales*, which in many respects corresponds to modern definitions of 'science', understood in the broader sense of *Wissenschaft*.[208]

It seems inaccurate, then, to claim that Machiavelli had sought to create the new prince,[209] for in Machiavelli's vision it is the prince himself

---

206 *Prince* 51. See also the summary Machiavelli gives of his methodical procedure in *Prince* 53f.
207 Vacano 2007: 4
208 Klein 1984: 133.
209 Vilches 2007: 5.

who appears as the creator, as the powerful and ever vigilant force able to outwit fortune and imprint his will upon history.[210] The greatest distinction a prince can aspire to is to be a 'wise ruler' (*principe savio*); it is this wisdom that sets him, that qualifies him for his task, not his faith in – or faithfulness to the example of – Christ. Compared to other authors' accounts, Machiavelli's prince acts methodically and in accordance with the 'objective' possibilities presented to him by the world. In a world that neither is moral nor permits moral action, it is impossible for a prince to be morally good in the Christian sense, and it would be misleading to claim otherwise.[211]

Machiavelli can be understood as attempting to answer the question of how successful rule might be organised or how a prince might rule successfully. His answers are not of the kind that would tell a prince what to do in a given situation. Instead, Machiavelli shows the prince how he might *himself* come to understand what is to be done.[212] The prince is exhorted to use his freedom to gather relevant material for himself, to structure, evaluate, abstract from and apply it.[213] Machiavelli's aim is not to make princes, but to establish a new form of applied science or indeed of applied rule. One notable achievement of Machiavelli's work in that respect is to have established, by the end of the sixteenth century, *prudenza* as a *terminus technicus* of politics, neutral and stripped of any moral or ethical connotations.[214]

Even *before* Machiavelli's time we encounter rulers who acted pragmatically and were branded demagogues or even 'diabolical'. Yet before Machiavelli, morally questionable actions were usually justified in religious terms. It was important to invoke religious support of some kind for the most despicable policies, for it was in the material and spiritual interest of mediaeval man to see his actions as morally justified.[215] With Machiavelli, it became possible to imagine the immanence of politics and to conceive of earthly success and prosperity as ends in themselves.[216] An idea of reason

210   Tarlton 2007: 58.
211   Machiavelli, *Principe*: 118–119, 134–135.
212   Garver 1987: 28; Dreier 2005: 379.
213   Berlin 1997: 38; Benner 2009: 125.
214   Zwierlein 2007: 96.
215   Rahe 2000: 253.
216   Deppe 1987: 35, 287.

of state rooted in the transience of secular affairs came to replace an earlier one rooted in the timeless transcendence of Christian certainties. To dress earthly ambitions in higher, transcendent motivations gradually falls out of fashion.

'Cassirer's and others' analysis overlooks Machiavelli's intentions: he composed all these political and historical works, not only to describe and explain facts, as scientists do, but above all to persuade his readers [i.e. the princes] to act, as orators do.'[217] Although Machiavelli was not an academic (unlike, say, Luther), he was a 'cool' observer. Yet he was also a passionate writer and an advocate of certain political actions and an active stance.[218] These two qualities need not be seen as incompatible. Interpreters of *The Prince* often fall into the trap of reading it either as a scholarly, scientific analysis *or* as an *oratio*, a rhetorical exercise.[219] The treatise is in fact both. It is a work laden with intentions, an exhortation to the prince to think independently, to cultivate 'scientificity' and thereby to rule 'well' – successfully, gloriously, patriotically.[220] Machiavelli does not cut the notion of the 'good' out of politics, but he removes it from the realm of ethics and (religious) normativity and recasts it as a process or method: a 'method of exploring the truth'.[221] '[The prince] will recognise that some [rulers] acted in one way and others in the opposite way, and that one ruler in each group was successful and the others ended badly.'[222]

In all this methodical reconstruction of facticity, there is no longer a place for the post-rational normativity of *Christianitas*. The ruler's *Christomimesis*, enacted mystically (Neagoe Basarab), ethically (Erasmus) or practically (Luther) and thereby constantly bringing the concrete world into contact with transcendence, is far removed from the notion of the *realia* that underpins methodical rule as envisaged by Machiavelli.[223] Since

---

217 Viroli 2008: 4.
218 Vacano 2007: 46.
219 Viroli 2008: 5.
220 Campagna 2003: 111; Benner 2009: 43.
221 Klein 1984: 75.
222 *Prince* 71. Original: 'E conoscerà ancora donde nacque che parte di loro procedendo in uno modo e parte al contrario, in qualunque di quelli, uno di loro ebbe felice e gli altri infelice fine' (Machiavelli, *Principe*: 162–163).
223 Flasch 1986: 583.

the valuations that constitute the normativity of *Christianitas* can factually be neither measured nor experienced in political immanence, the entire semantics is set aside as methodically inadequate. To situate oneself ethically in the semantics of *Christianitas* would be, for example, incompatible with the epistemic act of contextualisation and the acceptance it entails of the contingency and relativity of trans-historic 'truth'.[224]

Generalities, to Machiavelli, existed only in their contextual concretisations and on the basis of tangible knowledge. He no longer considers a revealed transcendent and generally valid truth that might be legible in or inferred from the world to be a sound methodical foundation. The semantics of *Christianitas* has lost its epistemic value to Machiavelli,[225] who will accept it at best as a stabilising factor in political communities, as a form of 'opiate for the people'.[226] Even fortune is of more 'use' to Machiavelli's method than *Christianitas*. Since he was himself of the opinion that human beings, by their own will and reason, could neither explore nor alter God's foresight and plans with the world,[227] he replaced the transcendence of *Christianitas* with the indeterminacy of fortune. Yet there is methodical value to this 'indeterminacy': from accident and arbitrariness, Machiavelli transforms fortune into a variable which, for all its indeterminacy, nonetheless can be used in calculations and is thus amenable to methodical application. This was not true of Christian ideals, which according to Machiavelli's method could be neither deduced nor induced.[228] Machiavelli expresses no opinion of their truth, but simply avoids and ignores them.[229]

---

224   Walsh 2007: 291.
225   Kocís 1998: 43; Ottmann 2006: 23.
226   Meinecke 1929: 44; Gilbert 1939: 464; Nitschke 2000: 44; Kondylis 2007: 11. It has been claimed that *The Prince* was an explicit and programmatic attack on Christianity (see Berlin 1997: 28). This, however, is a misunderstanding based on the application of modern categories. The absence of *Christianitas* from Machiavelli's methodological approach does not itself constitute a rejection of Christianity and the Church. Had it done so, Pope Clement VII would scarcely have given the book his blessing.
227   Jeremias 2005: 242.
228   Preus 1979: 188.
229   Berlin 1997: 37; Fontana 1999: 641.

This demystification of *Christianitas* in political thought entails the rejection of divine omnipotence. In traditional, pre-modern societies, in which the dominant framework of meaning was religion, people simply could not imagine there not being a meaning to political events and activity. And if no human meaning offered itself, there were always the mysterious ways of God to impart a meaning above and beyond the merely human. Divine meaning usually was invoked where human understanding ended or as its decisive complement. This allowed meaning to be found even in incomprehensible or unexpected events.

By imagining, in the early modern age, the arbitrary power of fortune, Machiavelli inaugurated the 'de-divinification' of the political discourse of rule, for a God who is not omnipotent might as well not *exist*. Machiavelli himself does not yet take that radical step, imagining as he does fortune as a quasi-divine entity with reason, sentiments and a will of its own. Indeed, the wilful and inscrutable fortune of Machiavelli seems congruent in many respects with the ineffable God of Christian mysticism. But the arbitrary power that Machiavelli still associated with fortune took on an independent existence, over the course of the early modern age, as 'chance' and hence as a simply factual precondition of human activity.

Chance is no longer a person, entity or deity, but merely that variable which *must* be taken into consideration in all spheres of life. Unlike the Christian God, it can be neither determined nor influenced. Determinative logic (e.g. the idea that God can be propitiated by moral conduct) is obviated by the immanent contingency of factual chance, which cannot be predicted or calculated. To put it another way, once 'chance' was no longer just another word for God's involvement or intervention in history, (political) knowledge became uncoupled from its normative association with transhistorical moral valuations (such as *Christianitas*) and instead assumed the character of knowledge of facticity, of which chance was an aspect. And while there was no longer a cause or meaning to be found in chance, it certainly had consequences. To this day chance remains a category in the (human) sciences to be reckoned with methodically in the epistemic process of obtaining knowledge. It is a 'motivational trace' (*Motivationsrest*), an aid to understanding circumstances for which there is apparently no logical explanation.[230]

Machiavelli performs the break with what I referred to above as 'dogmatism' not least in bidding farewell to general or universal concepts, norms and commitments.[231] It is because Machiavelli was a man of action – as his correspondence shows – that he developed an '*éthique de l'action*',[232] an activist ethic and an ethic of action, to replace Christian ethics. In the eyes of the Florentine, Christian ethics were the exact opposite of activism; they constituted – and Machiavelli seems to anticipate Nietzsche here – an ethic of weakness and passivity.[233] This logic is consistent with Machiavelli's admiration for Moses, whom he admired not so much for his piety as for his decisive and successful political action.[234]

There can be no doubt that the natural-scientific mode of observation and the empirical quest for knowledge in Italy and Europe at large did not begin in the sixteenth century, but look back to a far longer tradition. We need only to recall the enlightened rule of Frederick II (d. 1250),[235] who made his court a centre of science and scholarship. Yet what made Machiavelli the pioneer of a tradition was the manner in which he completely uncoupled the discourse of rule, which encompassed so many complex lines of argument and logic, from that of *Christianitas*. He did so, moreover, without compromising its plausibility, and that was truly an innovation in a deeply religious era.

---

230   Jordan 2005: 122. *Motivationsrest* originarily in Koselleck 2004: chapter 8.
231   Jeremias 2005: 285.
232   Sfez 1998: 279. See also Garver 1987: 59.
233   Machiavelli, *Discourses*, 16.
234   Machiavelli, *Principe*: 42–43; Geerken 1999: 594f.
235   On this, see Stürner 2009.

CHAPTER 6

Conclusion: Beyond Concepts, in the Thick of Semantics

The present analysis of the concept *Princeps Christianus* was intended to open up a variety of perspectives from which the history of religion might reflect on the manner in which religion, the political public sphere and historical reality are connected. At issue, in other words, are the links between key norms and valuations, and between political action and religious commitments in the early sixteenth century, as they found discursive formulation in the literary genre of the mirror for princes.

To this end, I consulted four authors – Neagoe Basarab, Erasmus of Rotterdam, Martin Luther and Niccolò Machiavelli – each of whom stands for a different stage along the path of the so-called 'secularisation' of the discourse of rule in early modern Europe. Paradoxically – and I tried to suggest as much by adopting a comparative and contextualising approach – these 'stages' do not combine to form a linear historical development, but each represents a dimension of meaning, standing beside one another in simultaneous complexity. Within the space of ten years, four approaches were formulated and created discourses of their own:

The political theory – or political theology – of Neagoe Basarab is consistently oriented towards the hereafter and conceives of the world as the antechamber and image of the heavenly realm. To Basarab, the Christian ruler is an image of Christ, Himself the epitome of the ruler, on whom, amidst the angelic choirs, the world is centred in praise as a doxological whole. Basarab's *mystical Christianitas* is subject to otherworldly preconditions. Erasmus and Luther give a distinctly practical and immanent flavouring to the Christian element of rule, of a kind that is completely absent in the work of Basarab. Whereas Basarab takes the political to a mystical extreme – his affinity for 'political hesychasm' is a case in point – Erasmus and Luther stand for the gradual discovery of Christianity's immanence in the world.

Needless to say, Erasmus and Luther continue to refer to the hereafter, but they clearly place the practical implementation of the Christian faith on earth in the foreground. Luther, for instance, finds the kingdom of Christ wherever the gift of faith leads to services being rendered to neighbours. The *Reich Christi* thus exists in the world and for the benefit of the world. Yet the 'final stage' of this process – which, chronologically speaking, stands at its beginning – consists in the complete occlusion of any Christian relevance and validity from the world's political relevance and validity in the work of Machiavelli.

To describe in this manner the various stages of the de-Christianisation of political discourse should not, however, mislead readers into a simplified, schematic understanding of political rule amid its complex position in *Christian* early modern Europe. Neither can Basarab be considered a purely theocratic thinker, nor can Erasmus and Luther be regarded as having resolved to introduce secularism into Christian discourse. Even the 'facticity' of Machiavelli displays theoretical fault lines that prohibit it from being treated as having inaugurated complete, immanent secularism.

We are faced here with a complex spectrum, with a discourse unfolding and manifesting its socio-political effects at three levels. First, there is the *gulf* separating ideal conceptions, be they religious and normative or social and political in nature, from historical reality. Then there is the 'resolution' of this apparent contradiction, the *semanticisation* of concepts in history, practices and founding discourses. Finally, there comes reflection on the *concretisation* of semantics, in other words, the manner in which it informs and becomes political action, attitudes, expectations, desires, language and purpose.

It has been shown that all four authors examined here are aware of the gulf between the ideal (Christ, conformity to Christ, a Christian lifestyle, Christian valuations, etc.) and reality.[1] Against this backdrop, it

---

1   Following Samuel Eisenstadt, this is the perception, typical of the axial age, of the hiatus between matter and spirit, secular and transcendent (Eisenstadt 2003: 265).

seems plausible to argue that Machiavelli's departure from the semantics of *Christianitas* is due to a different handling or consciousness of it.

Basarab is as well aware of human frailties as are Erasmus and Luther; none of them can be accused of denying reality. Nobody was better informed of the political state of Europe than Erasmus.[2] Yet the only author under consideration actually to have had experience of rule was Prince Neagoe Basarab. All three, however, are united in their pursuit of the ideal. Rulers were to strive for a higher state of being, to remain steadfast in their attempts at overcoming the merely human in favour of being a Christian and indeed (like) Christ and not to cease from their efforts to bring about the Christianisation of the political. Machiavelli, on the other hand, all but abandons such claims, insisting instead on 'reality' as the only valid point of reference for a discussion of rule and the ruler.

The question arising here concerns the relation between theory and praxis or, specifically, whether the idealism of the first three authors found practical expression. Did they make reality to be better in Christian terms? In answering this question, we ought to bear in mind that even setting down opinions or writing political treatises may be considered a form of political action and participation. By means of their thought and writings, authors intervene in political praxis, thereby actively shaping it. Ideas, theories, concepts and 'political language' in general serve not only to depict and reflect upon history, but can themselves shape historical events.[3] That is why the present study devotes such attention to the reception and influence of the four authors it discusses.

Basarab, Erasmus and Luther all remember frequently to appeal and refer to the ideal, using it as their lodestar and being convinced of the possibility of it being fulfilled. Ideals, they assume, may be made real, whereas Machiavelli gives them up as impossible. Instead of concerning himself with what might and ought to be – or with what is found desirable – Machiavelli restricts himself to talking about that which is. We are dealing with four constructs here, three of which describe their own ideal version of the *Princeps Christianus*. Machiavelli, by contrast, develops his own vision of

2   Fricke 1967: 25.
3   Kosuch 2011: 32.

'reality'. Basarab, Erasmus and Luther derive the power of their ideal from its ahistorical validity, from the ideal's replicability and constant presence in human affairs. The ideals they imagine are founded on the paradigm of Christian values and their atemporality, on the eternity of the Christian scheme of which Christ is the palpable historical manifestation.[4] This idea found numerous expressions over the course of Christian history, and the first three authors accordingly invoke Christian rulers from the past – for example, Constantine or Theodosius I – as examples.

Whereas Basarab, Erasmus and Luther all situate the ideal in the overall meta-history of the Christian God's relations with man and thence try to establish general norms, applicable irrespective of context, the Florentine assumes the opposite pole. Machiavelli postulates history as the immanent dimension of the real, which can be observed and described in the facts that constitute it. To him, history and its contextual manifestations are 'real' in that they have logical consequences that can be interpreted, from which the truth may be deduced, and which are even susceptible to calculation. Doing so, Machiavelli promises, is the key to success, which was more than could be hoped from the ideals of the Christian authors, as history proved. The fact that his goal of postulating general rules of political procedure, valid across historical situations, leads him to produce a generalising, sweeping method, seems to trouble Machiavelli but little.

We are thus confronted with a rift in the dialectic of the 'ideal': Basarab, Erasmus and Luther maintain the ideal as the normative lodestar from which all action takes its bearings. It is from this fixed orientation that the ideal derived its ability to act upon reality. These three authors are hence able to view transcendent and trans-factual commitments (such as *Christianitas*) as real – as demonstrated by Christ the God-man. To Machiavelli, by contrast, the ideal is not real, since it does not accord with the factual as vouchsafed by history. Of the commitments, Machiavelli makes 'objectified commitments' of the kind that are simply historically given. Basarab, Erasmus and Luther meanwhile consider *Christianitas* in light of the *homoiosis,* mimesis or *imitatio* of a trans-historical example, that is, Jesus. Christomimesis is represented as the mode in which Christ

4   Fricke 1967: 25.

is re-actualised and made present in acting and being like Christ, which is expected of every subject and more still of the ruler.

In the case of Machiavelli, it can be clearly seen how science or scientificity – the methodical extraction of knowledge from facts – generates rule or power. Lucid calculation, the weighing of advantages against disadvantages, and the morally neutral, mechanical application of rules and regularities together constitute the soundest foundation for rulers. In light of such a view, it is surely no coincidence that so many modern dictators have taken *The Prince* as their manual. There is no denying that dictatorship is built on knowledge, on gathering, cataloguing and archiving 'facts' (i.e., information), which dictators put to the end of exercising dominance over people. Dictatorship is a political form that relies on the efficiency of informers and media of information. In post-Machiavellian modernity, a ruler's pre-eminence accordingly no longer derives from values and morally performative 'achievements', but rather on facticity, on the information it yields and on its methodical extraction and processing.[5] On the other hand, the failure of dictatorships and the crises of modernity give rise to doubts as to the predictability of history, or rather, doubts as to the reality of the factual.

Hence, in the view of Basarab, Erasmus and Luther as well as of Machiavelli, the perfect *Christianitas* of the ruler has never been attained in the history of Christian powers. Yet Basarab, Erasmus and Luther do hold the ideal of *Christianitas* in the political realm to be attainable and therefore real since, from a dialectical perspective, all that can be thought is also (at least potentially) real. Machiavelli, on the other hand, finds it to be non-real, for *his* own observations led him to conclude that the semantics of *Christianitas* had been (and continued to be) unable to impose any factual commitments. At best, it made supra-factual postulates ('the way things ought to be') with scant connection to reality. *Christianitas* lacked any historical relevance to Machiavelli. The ahistorical perspective taken by a discourse of timeless *realia* – God, Christ, the kingdom of God, asceticism, *illuminatio*, morality, Christian love, etc. – which intend to provide a

---

5   See Henning Ottmann's account of modernity as paving the way for dictatorship (Ottmann 2004a: 74).

normative and universally valid means of overcoming human temporality, contingency and transience, thus finds itself displaced. The novelty that comes in its stead is the programmatic reflection on what was to be done in the midst of a history that was 'factually' God-free. Actors pursuing their worldly interests would not, Machiavelli implies, be content with otherworldly solutions. To put it another way, transcendent logic is not the obvious key to secular immanence.

We encounter all four authors as they try to develop a method for coming to terms with accident or coincidence in history[6] by assuming that everything that happens does so for a reason and is not in vain. Basarab, Erasmus and Machiavelli tie rule and the ruler to Christ, who as both God and man in Himself creates the possibility of stabilising history. Machiavelli, on the other hand, virtually 'discovers' the facticity of history, with the facts yielding up to him legible *realia* that are supposedly capable of being quantified, interconnected and interpreted. Historical accident – 'fortune' to Machiavelli – is tamed by general rules of reality being deduced from the facts. A new myth thereby arises, which maintains that the world, by means of its history, can be brought under human control.

The above-mentioned gulf between ideal and reality (or praxis) is filled semantically. 'Semantics' here does not signify a conscious, rational and poietic (in the sense of Aristotelian *poiesis*) mode of substantiation by an individual or collective. As Niklas Luhmann has shown, semantics is not the product of a society, but rather its life. In other words, social structures are semantic, they are communication, interests, actions, expectations, desires and concepts. A society produces knowledge about itself and about structures of meaning that go beyond it in a twofold manner. First, as elementary or assumed knowledge, which can be built on in the ultimate assurance of one's own present existence not being cast into uncertainty. At the same time as the historical perspective, the functional

---

6   'The core of this program [the cultural and political program of modernity] has been that the premises and legitimation of the social, ontological and political were *no longer taken for granted*' (Eisenstadt 2003: 104f., emphasis added). Modern historical scholarship refers to the accidents of history as 'events', meaning at one level the unexpected challenge to a given order, at another a category for understanding what would otherwise be beyond historical comprehension (Blänkner 2005: 96).

perspective entered onto the scene with the attempt to question reality as it is presented itself directly to the senses and instead to transpose it into the form of relations by which possibilities of substitution are regulated.[7]

A semantics (first) has the function of illustrating or mapping historical events and the social life shaped by them. In the symbolism of its working-through of history, it enacts a semanticisation of its life. Conversely (second), semantics is the enactment of life in a social context. Semantics (third) generates social systems and allows them constantly to refresh themselves, keeping them 'alive'.[8]

Since *Christianitas* offered no foundation for a political ethic or praxis of resolving antagonisms, Machiavelli sought this foundation elsewhere, in the facticity of immanent (economic, social, political) interests at work in what had already occurred, that 'which is', rather than acting according to what was ethically and morally permissible. In Machiavelli's view, such antagonisms are factual and determined by material or symbolic interests (e.g. prestige). In *Christianitas*, all are guided by the *one single* 'good', which must accordingly reflect the interest of all.

Erasmus, for instance, had proposed *Christianitas*, with its ability to promote concord, as the practical and ethical field in which antagonism might be overcome. Like all members of a common species, human beings were created, Erasmus thought, in order that they might live in concord and harmony. It was education that paved the way to a new *humanitas* as a form of social solidarity, a solidarity that was to prove itself in action – just as Christ Himself had practised it as the epitome of divine solicitude and philanthropy.

Basarab, by contrast, proposes an anthropological and mystical *Christianitas* as the foundation for society. Because human beings, in the act of Creation, had been designed and created as doxological creatures – from whom a doxological presence is hence to be expected – sociability and political community emerge as the simultaneous and shared 'concentration'[9] of many upon the same point – on God, that is, in the act of praising Him. Basarab finds the political significance of this doxological

---

7   Luhmann 1980: 9.
8   Luhmann 1980: 17ff.; Grigore 2009: 12.
9   From *centrum* or *concentra*.

orientation in the equal standing of those united in praise in the world, cosmos and Creation. They are all as one in that they all were made to give praise as soon as they come to life. If not, they are not only sinners from a soteriological perspective, but are politically excluded from the Christian 'state' under the Christian rule of the *Princeps Christianus*. In postlapsarian history the doxological community is restored in the mystical act of illumination, in which is secured the individual's immediacy to and simultaneity with God, his Creator. In illumination, man becomes God and God the creator glorifies Himself in man. This is *homoiosis*, an intensified form of *theomimesis*. It is from this personal relationship that the Christian ruler derives his public, political qualification to exercise leadership over human beings, that is, Christians. The ruler's illumination represents an intensification of Christian existence, which as such is within reach of all believers. This is the meaning of so-called 'political hesychasm'.

In contrast to Luther's view, Basarab finds the Christian state where God is praised – where the Christian, indeed the *Orthodox* God is praised. To Luther, the ruler's *Christianitas* found its concrete form in his being called by God to serve his fellow human beings. The Christian ruler, according to Luther, is Christ in His humble servitude, stripped of all His glory. Luther held rule and authority to be aspects of service, tasks set by God to select human beings. Rulers were passive beneficiaries of the grace by which God had chosen princes, kings and emperors for a purpose. To Luther, rule was less of a promise (as it was to Erasmus), but rather a profession or vocation. God acts in the world through the Christian prince. The ruler himself, in this scheme, is a passive *cooperator* rather than the active *co-regent* as which he appears in Basarab's political thought.

Unlike the other three authors, Machiavelli conceives of the prince as a self-made politician and autonomous actor. In Machiavelli's vision, rule lacks any supra-factual point of reference (such as Christ), instead creating such references for itself in ancient history as well as in recent events. By dispensing with *Christianitas* as an idea or even a criterion of rule, Machiavelli hopes that political life can be made more efficient and effective. A shift is thus discernible from a vertical semantics of *Christianitas*, pointing towards God (as in Basarab, Erasmus and Luther), to a horizontal methodology (in Machiavelli's case) of a 'professionalised' approach to historical events – ultimately, however, to history being made absolute by means of a consciousness of the past that is interpreted in the present in order to shape the future.

In all four authors, we encounter a process by which the key concept of the *Princeps (Christianus)* becomes semanticised and seeming contradictions are bridged semantically. An example is the 'political hesychasm' of Neagoe Basarab, which referred to a mystical, individual and ascetic experience before becoming established as a political discourse. Semanticisation takes place when concepts, in their somewhat inflexible essentialism, impose limits on human action. Beneath concepts lie entire semantic spheres, and it is within these spheres that concepts encounter practices. Concepts are interpreted through practices. Such incompatibilities as may arise between the 'one-sided', 'limited' and 'essentialist' aspect of concepts are resolved semantically. Through semantics, praxis is made compatible with concepts, it is centred, reflected and 'named' or designated by concepts. In other words, the realisation of concepts takes place semantically. The example of the *Princeps Christianus* is an instance of such a semantics developing and designating its concepts. The praxis and the discourse of coming to resemble Christ, and the practical consequences for the Christian state that follow therefrom, precede the designation of *Princeps Christianus*. A process of semanticisation is less about a 'what' than a 'how': how concepts are made useful or applicable in practice, or how dimensions of human action and socio-political action are invested with meaning and encapsulated in plausible terms. This definition of semanticisation presupposes such key aspects of political ethics as procedure, praxis, utility, *telos* and tradition.

In a context such as that of the early sixteenth century, when European states were still overwhelmingly religious in character, it comes as no surprise to find that both the central concepts and the semantics centred upon them were religiously coloured. These are semantics of religious lives lived in the public sphere, in culture and society, semantics of religious hopes and expectations. To be more precise, in considering the process of the semanticisation of *Christianitas* in the sixteenth century, we are faced not with a concept that might as such be considered neutral, but with one that contains a valuation – the *Princeps Christianus*. Semantics can thus be understood as a means of creating, applying and realising valuations.

We are faced, as it were, with an attempted routinisation of valuations and norms, if I may be forgiven this appropriation of Weber's concept. All this can be accomplished only semantically.

Although Basarab, like Erasmus and Luther, speaks of the 'Christian prince', the concept's underpinning differs in each case. These differences are the result of a multitude of factors, one of which is of course historical context. Yet we should bear in mind that all three are still talking about the same thing, the 'Christian prince'. What is at stake here is the semantic concretisation of the relation between concept and practice.

Hence it is interesting that in the case of all three authors who write on the *Princeps Christianus* with an orientation towards Christ it is perfectly clear what they are talking about. We have at our disposal a single hermeneutical key: we know that they each aim to describe the Christian prince. Yet paradoxically, in the case of Machiavelli, whose stated aim is the pursuit of reality and facticity, of the facts and lessons of history, the discourse seems increasingly elusive. Accordingly, his ultimate purpose remains contested: does he imagine a ruler who is moral (Maurizio Viroli) or diabolical (Leo Strauss); is he concerned with the prince himself or rather with the advantages of democracy (Isaiah Berlin)? There is unlikely to be a more vivid example of the difference between 'centred' semantic spheres on the one hand and 'free' ones on the other, between those that form around clear concepts and those that require a conceptual framework to create meaning in the first place. That is the understanding of 'semantics' that underpins the present analysis.

This understanding resembles that of Niklas Luhmann, to whom semantics was not merely a process by which society communicates with and within itself. Luhmann's view was that society objectified and historically concretised itself in concepts:

> This version of the theory leads to the insight that the conceptual dichotomies of stability and change on the one hand and structure and process on the other must be distinguished. The emergence of a difference between structure and process can then in turn be understood as an institution on the part of the system to resolve difficulties of time. It helps the system simultaneously to stay constant and to change.[10]

10   Luhmann 1980: 235.

At this level of concretisation, semantics can be observed and described. It *makes* sense. In contradistinction to Luhmann, however, it must be noted that a semantics charges words with value, and hence one is more likely to encounter value or valuations in a semantics than simple concepts, that is, value-free neutral concepts. That is certainly the case with the concept of *Princeps Christianus*, which becomes a valuation, an ideal and a norm within the semantics of *Christianitas*.

The mirrors for princes of Basarab, Erasmus and Luther illustrate a tendency that I find to be typical of the religious landscape of sixteenth-century Europe, namely the centrality of the political concept of the *Princeps Christianus*. With regard to all three of these authors, it furthermore is interesting to observe that they argue not to make an outward distinction or to demarcate a boundary – for example, with (Ottoman) Islam – but instead unfold a discourse that is situated entirely within Christianity and requires no external referent. They assume Christianity as given and have no concerns beyond it.

This is a phenomenon of 'normative centring', the name given by Berndt Hamm to such processes of concentric orientation towards central religious values, symbols, persons, objects and texts.[11] From the vantage point of political theory, in each of the three authors we encounter a doctrine of 'internalised rule', according to which the consensual obedience of subjects, which may or may not be reinforced by oaths of allegiance, relies on the observation and evaluation of rule according to inward norms on the part of the political subjects.[12]

As soon as Europe was fully Christianised and the status of the Christian religion beyond question, the semantics of *Christianitas* underwent a shift in emphasis: the desideratum that the ruler should be a Christian was supplanted by the postulate that he must be a *good* Christian. When Ambrose of Milan, for example, addressed Emperor Theodosius I (379–394) as *Christian(issim)us princeps*, his purpose is likely to have been above all to emphasise the mere fact that the emperor was a Christian. That the emperor was a true believer was probably implied by the word *Christian(issim)us*, but

---

11   Hamm 1993.
12   Holenstein 1991: 495f.

was secondary to the phrase's primary use of indicating the ruler's Christian allegiance.[13] The use and the understanding of the epithet *Christianus* were completely different in the sixteenth century, now implying above all that the ruler was a *genuine* Christian.

In other words, in the Christian Europe of the early sixteenth century, it was no longer merely to be desired that the ruler and his subjects were believing Christians. At stake now were the authenticity, validity and viability of socio-political models, of the realisation of a true *Christianitas* according to criteria that were conceived of variously. The guiding question was clearly who was to be considered a truly Christian ruler – the question of genuine 'Christian-ness' being to some extent typical of the modern age.[14]

To Neagoe Basarab – as for Erasmus, and in contradistinction to Luther, let alone Machiavelli – politics, the state, etc., are not political products to which, by reason of existing for a purpose, can be ascribed a beginning, finality and end. In a pure Aristotelian line of thought, and against the Platonic utilitarianism of the likes of John Chrysostom, he regards politics as beginning not with the Fall, but with Creation. Politics, in the Aristotelian view (*Nicomachean Ethics* I), stems from a natural human inclination to sociability. Basarab responds to this tradition by reformulating it in the terms of Christian anthropology: politics had emerged with the creation of man, and the Fall represented merely a minor, nearly insignificant impairment of this status. Basarab does not accord the Fall any world-changing significance.

Human beings, in Basarab's view, were created as doxological creatures – created, that is, that they might communally and liturgically praise God in faith and action, and to be united with Him in Creation. God had created for Himself not a slave or an instrument, but rather a 'friend', a 'brother' and an 'heir', His co-regent in heaven and on earth. That was the status of humanity before as after the Fall, with only *minor* qualifications such as death. That is why he frames politics – as the community and doxological presence of all Christians – as neither becoming (i.e., no pedagogical approach, as in Aristotle or Erasmus) nor as coercion (as partly

13   Groß-Albenhausen 1999: 134, 136, 140f.
14   Rendtorff 1969: 222.

in Luther and completely in Machiavelli). The political is instead the permanent and consistent presence of humanity in glory – beside God, with God, for God, as God, and this moreover in active, creative partnership, not passively, as with Luther. In this wholeness, the illumined Christian ruler is revealed as a Christian who by illumination exists in an intensified relation to God and the world. The ruler centres the Christian community of subjects and orients it towards God.

The Christian ruler is, to Basarab as well as to Erasmus and Luther, the *conditio sine qua non* of the Christian state and thus ultimately of politics. For without the Christian ruler's function as centre and example, Christ's flock would be dispersed and the kingdom of God on earth dissolved. Whether his presence was conceived of as ethically imitative (Erasmus), kenotically serving (Luther) or mystically illumined (Basarab), the Christian ruler makes present Christ Himself amid the earthly society of the faithful.

This is why it is appropriate to speak, in the discourses of Basarab, Erasmus and Luther, of a view that is more pragmatic than its apparent preoccupation with ideals might at first suggest. In the historical contexts with which they were familiar, and in light of the challenges and social tensions these contexts entailed, they tried to impart semantic force to the concept of the *Princeps Christianus*, to make it relevant for public, personal and everyday life, to establish it as a framework for faith, action and thought. Machiavelli, on the other hand, found the political use of Christian valuations to decrease with distance from reality, though he did grant one important political function to the Christian religion: to entice and pacify the masses, to make them docile.[15] Though it had no political content as such, Machiavelli found Christianity to be useful for the power it exercised over the masses, making them open to manipulation. And though the Florentine situated his own discourse beyond the semantics of *Christianitas* associated with the *Princeps Christianus*, he was too astute an observer to overlook the political advantages to be derived from the ruler's nominal profession of Christianity.

From the perspective of the study of religion, we are faced here with an important phenomenon observable in all religious societies: the transition

---

15   Ottmann 2004a: 75.

from a religious persuasion, experience and engagement that is individual and personal to generally relevant statements on which communities are founded.[16] At issue here is religious individualisation in its historical projection, a process that invariably creates publicity in that it is perceived and discussed publicly. In the semantics surrounding the core concept of the *Princeps Christianus*, we encounter first of all a tension between the ruler's individual achievement and performance qua Christian and his presence as a centre for or creator of a public sphere as an imitator of Christ or a Christ-like one. The question that arises here concerns the suitability of such individual examples as given by Christ and His successors for the agora. This transition, and how appropriate a given model might be to the public sphere, is most probably effected by the semantics of the ruler's *Christianitas*, which adapts to its various historical and cultural contexts and shapes them in its turn.

History interprets core concepts like *Princeps Christianus* in various ways – it semanticises them. Concepts unfold as semantics, while practices are summed up in concepts.

16 Of relevance here is the work of the research group 'Religious individualisation in historical perspective' at the Max-Weber-Kolleg for Advanced Cultural and Social Studies at the University of Erfurt: <https://www.uni-erfurt.de/index.php?id=6702&L=1> (accessed 27.03.2020).

Appendices

Illustrations

Figure 1: Neagoe Basarab with his wife Despina and their six children. The tallest of the three figures in the foreground on the left is their son, Theodosius (fresco by Dobromir Zugravul in the cathedral of Curtea de Argeş, first half of the sixteenth century).

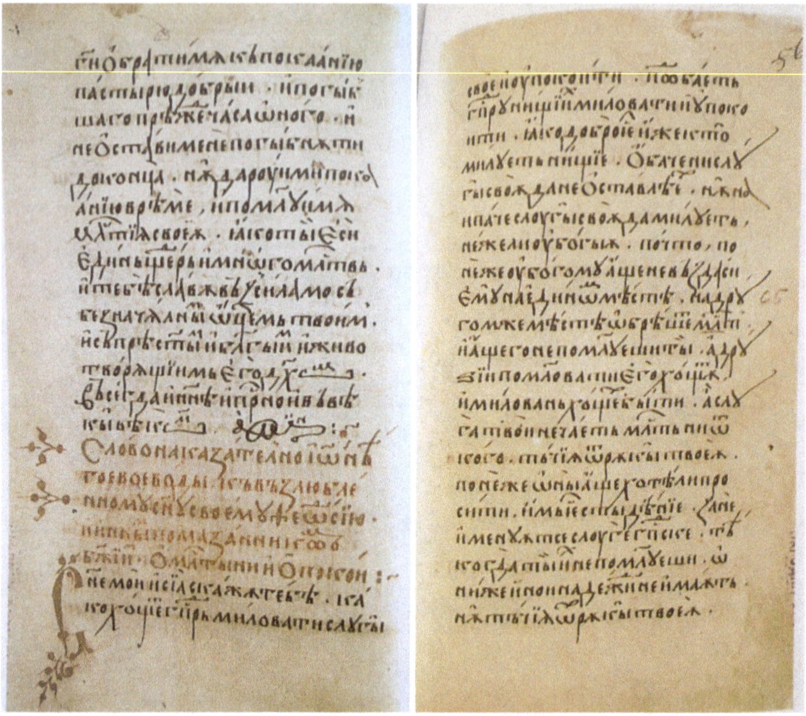

Figure 2: Pages from the Church Slavonic original of the *Teachings*, the beginning of chapter ten (sixteenth century, MS 313, SS. Cyril and Methodius National Library, Sofia. Scan of a facsimile, see Neagoe Basarab 1996).

Figure 3: Frontispiece and title page of the first edition of the *Teachings*, ed. Ioan Eclisiarhul, Bucharest, at the Printing Press of St Sava's College.

Figure 4: Neagoe Basarab and Niphon II (painting on the reliquary of St Niphon donated by Basarab at Dionysiou monastery, Mount Athos).

Maps

Map 1: South-eastern Europe c. 1475. Modified version of the map no. 5 in Clewing/
Schmitt 2011.

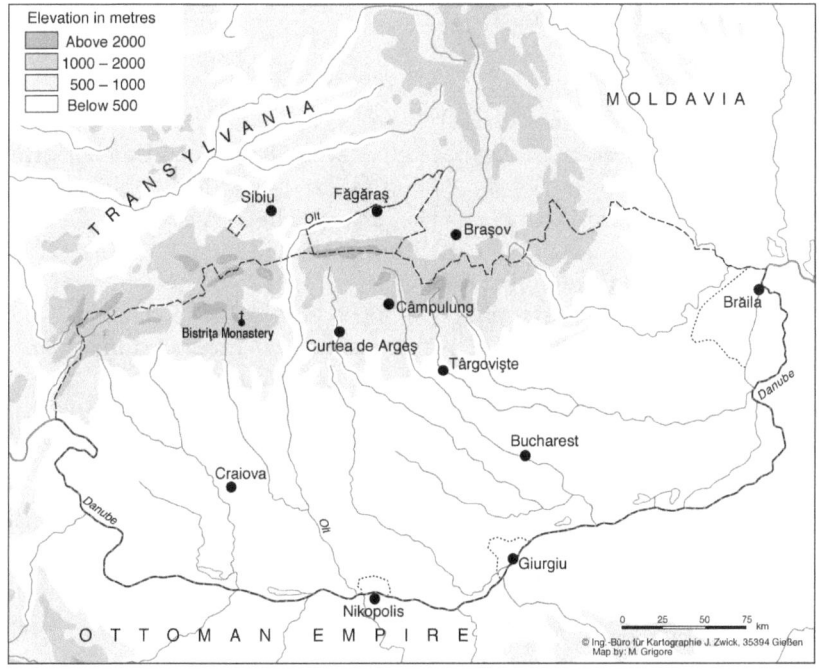

Map 2: The Principality of Wallachia c. 1520.

Rulers of Wallachia, 1290–1522[1]

1. Thochomerius (c. 1290–c. 1310)
2. Basarab I the Founder (*Întemeietorul*) (c. 1310–1352), son of Thochomerius
3. Nicholas Alexander (*Nicolae Alexandru*) (1352–1364), son of Basarab I
4. Vladislav I (*Vlaicu*) (1364–c. 1377), son of Nicholas Alexander
5. Radu I (c. 1377–c. 1383), son of Nicholas Alexander
6. Dan I (c. 1383–1386), son of Radu I
7. Mircea the Elder (*cel Bătrân*) (1386–1418), son of Radu I
8. Vlad I (1394–1397), son of Dan I, anti-prince to Mircea the Elder
9. Michael I (Mihail) (1418–1420), son of Mircea the Elder
10. Dan II (1420–1421), son of Dan I
11. Radu II the Bald (*Prasnaglava*) (1421), son of Mircea the Elder
12. Dan II (1421–1423)
13. Radu II the Bald (1423)
14. Dan II (1423–1424)
15. Radu II the Bald (1424–1426)
16. Dan II (1426–1427)
17. Radu II the Bald (1427)
18. Dan II (1427–1431)
19. Alexander I Aldea (1431–1436), son of Mircea the Elder
20. Vlad II the Dragon (*Dracul*) (1436–1442), son of Mircea the Elder
21. Mircea II (1442), son of Vlad II
22. Basarab II (1442–1443), son of Dan II
23. Vlad II the Dragon (1443–1447)
24. Vladislav II (1447), son of Dan II
25. Vlad II the Impaler (or Little Dragon; *Țepeș* or *Drăculea*) (1448), son of Vlad II.
26. Vladislav II (1448–1456)
27. Vlad III the Impaler (1456–1462)
28. Radu III the Fair (*cel Frumos*) (1462–1473), son of Vlad II
29. Basarab III the Elder (*Bătrânul* or *Laiotă*) (1473), son of Dan II
30. Radu III the Fair (1473–1474)
31. Basarab III the Elder (1474)

---

1   This list is compiled from information in Oțetea 1972: 567f. and URL: <http://ro.wikipedia.org/wiki/Lista_domnilor_%C8%9A%C4%83rii_Rom%C3%A2ne%C8%99ti> (accessed 26.06.2020)

32. Radu III the Fair (1474)
33. Basarab III the Elder (1474)
34. Radu III the Fair (1474)
35. Basarab II the Elder (1475–1476)
36. Vlad III the Impaler (1476–1477)
37. Basarab III the Elder (1476–1477)
38. Basarab IV the Younger (*cel Tânăr* but also *Țepeluș*) (1477–1481), son of Basarab II
39. Mircea II (1481), son of Vlad II (rule uncertain)
40. Vlad IV the Monk (*Călugărul*) (1481), son of Vlad II
41. Basarab IV the Younger (1481–1482)
42. Vlad IV the Monk (*Călugărul*) (1482–1482)
43. Radu IV the Great (*cel Mare*) (1495–1508), son of Vlad IV
44. Mihnea I the Evil (*cel Rău*) (1508–1509), son of Vlad III
45. Mircea III (*Miloș*) (1509–1510), son of Mihnea I
46. Vlad V the Younger (*Vlăduț*) (1510–1512), son of Vlad IV
47. Neagoe Basarab (1512–1521), son of Pârvu Craiovescu
48. Theodosius (September 1521–October 1521), son of Neagoe Basarab
49. Vlad VI Dragomir the Monk (*Călugărul*) (1521), of unknown dynasty
50. Theodosius (November 1521–December 1522)

Bibliography

Abbreviations

ABR   American Benedictine Review

ARG   Archiv für Reformationsgeschichte

ASP   Archiv für slavische Philologie

BbFb   Nicolae Iorga (ed.), *Scrisori de boieri, scrisori de domni* [letters of princes and boyars], Vălenii-de-Munte 1931

BMGS   Byzantine and Modern Greek Studies

BZ   Byzantinische Zeitschrift

CIC   *Corpus iuris civilis, vol. I. Institutiones/Digesta*, ed. P. Krueger/Th. Mommsen, Hildesheim ²⁵1993; vol. 3, Novellae, ed. R. Schöll/G. Knoll, Berlin ⁶1954

DGR II/3   *Documente privitoare la Istoria Românilor. 1510–1530* [documents concerning the history of the Romanians. 1510-1530], vol. II, partea 3, ed. Eudoxiu Hurmuzaki/Nic. Densuşianu, Bucureşti 1892

DGR IX/1   *Documente privitoare la Istoria Românilor. 1650–1747* [documents concerning the history of the Romanians. 1650-1747], vol. IX, partea 1, ed. Eudoxiu Hurmuzaki/Nic. Densuşianu, Bucureşti 1897

DOP   Dumbarton Oaks Papers

DRG I   Academia Republicii Populare Române (ed.), *Documente privind istoria României, veacul XVI, B. Ţara Românească* [documents concerning Romanian history, 16th c., B. Wallachia], vol. I (1501–1525), Bucureşti 1951

DRG V   Academia Republicii Populare Române (ed.), *Documente privind istoria României, veacul XVI, B. Ţara Românească* [documents concerning Romanian history, 16th c., B. Wallachia], vol. V (1581–1590), Bucureşti 1952

DZP	Deutsche Zeitschrift für Philosophie
EVKOC	Erfurter Vorträge zur Kulturgeschichte des Orthodoxen Christentums
GRBS	Greek, Roman, and Byzantine Studies
HJ	Historisches Jahrbuch
HZ	Historische Zeitschrift
IRK	Nicolae Iorga (ed.), *Inscripţii din bisericile României* [inscriptions in Romanian churches], number I, Bucureşti 1905
JAC	Jahrbuch für Antike und Christentum
JBTh	Jahrbuch für Biblische Theologie
JHI	Journal of the History of Ideas
JHP	Journal of the History of Philosophy
JMH	Journal of Modern History
JÖBG	Jahrbuch der Österreichischen Byzantinischen Gesellschaft
JRH	Journal of Religious History
MGH	Monumenta Germaniae Historica
NJKAGDLP	Neue Jahrbücher für klassisches Altertum, Geschichte und deutsche Literatur und für Pädagogik
NZSTR	Neue Zeitschrift für systematische Theologie und Religionsphilosophie
PSBA	Proceedings of the Society of Biblical Archaeology
RBS	Roman and Byzantine Studies
RESEE	Revue des études sud-est européennes
SBAW	Sitzungsberichte der Bayerischen Akademie der Wissenschaften
SHAW	Sitzungsberichte der Heidelberger Akademie der Wissenschaften
SMIM	Studii şi materiale de istorie medie
SRD	Stoica Nicolaescu (ed.), *Documente slavo-române cu privire la relaţiile Ţării Româneşti şi Moldovei cu Ardealul în sec. XV şi XVI* [Slavo-Romanian documents concerning the relations of Wallachia

	and Moldavia with Transsylvania in the 15th and 16th centuries], Bucureşti 1905
SSAWL	Sitzungsberichte der Sächsischen Akademie der Wissenschaften zu Leipzig
TRE	*Theologische Realenzyklopädie*, 36 vols, Berlin/New York, 1993–2006
VD	*Verzeichnis der im deutschen Sprachbereich erschienenen Drucke des XVI. Jahrhunderts*, herausgegeben von der Bayerischen Staatsbibliothek in München in Verbindung mit der Herzog August Bibliothek in Wolfenbüttel, 1. Abteilung, vol. 12, Stuttgart 1988
VWO	Luther, Martin: Von weltlicher Obrigkeit, in Hans-Ulrich Delius (ed.), *Martin Luther Studienausgabe*, vol. 3, Berlin 1983, S. 27–71
WA Br.	D. Martin Luthers Werke. *Briefwechsel*. Kritische Gesamtausgabe, vols 1–18, Weimar 1930–1947
WA TR	D. Martin Luthers Werke. *Tischreden*. Kritische Gesamtausgabe, vols 1–6, Weimar 1912–1921
WA	D. Martin Luthers Werke. *Schriften*. Kritische Gesamtausgabe, vols 1–73, Weimar 1883–2009
WJT	Wiener Jahrbuch für Theologie
ZAG (KLK)	Zeitschrift für allgemeine Geschichte, Kultur-, Literatur- und Kunstgeschichte
ZfB	Zentralblatt für Bibliothekswesen
ZKG	Zeitschrift für Kirchengeschichte

Principal Sources

Acta Patriarchatus Constantinopolitani (1315–1402), ed. Fr. Milosisch/I. Müller, Wien 1862.

Agapetus: Die Ekthesis des Diakons Agapetos, in W. Blum (ed.), *Byzantinische Fürstenspiegel: Agapetos, Theophylakt von Ochrid, Thomas Magister*, Stuttgart 1981, pp. 59–80.

Akropolites, George: *Georgii Acropolitae Opera*, vol. I, ed. A. Heisenberg, Leipzig 1903.

Anonymus Hanivaldanus: *Der fromme Sultan Bayezid. Die Geschichte seiner Herrschaft (1481–1512) nach den altosmanischen Chroniken des Oruç und des Anonymus Hanivaldanus*, ed. Richard F. Kreutel, Graz. 1978.

Aristotle: Aristoteles, *Nikomachische Ethik*, ed. G. Bien, Hamburg ^{4}1985.

—— *Politik*, ed. O. Gigon, Zürich/München ^{2}1971.

—— *Politics*, tr. H. Rackham, Cambridge, MA 1932.

Atkinson, James B./David Sices (eds): *Machiavelli and His Friends. Their Personal Correspondence*, DeKalb 1996.

Augustine: Augustinus, *Vom Gottesstaat*, ed. W. Thimme, 2 vols, Zürich 1955.

Augustine: The City of God, in *A Select Library of the Nicene and Post-Nicene Fathers of the Christian Church*, vol. II, ed. Philip Schaff, Buffalo 1887.

—— *On Christian Doctrine*, tr. J. F. Shaw, URL: <https://faculty.georgetown.edu/jod/augustine/ddc1.html> (accessed 08.04.2020).

Barsanuphius and John: *Letters from the Desert. A Selection of Questions and Responses*, ed. John Chryssavgis, New York 2003.

Basil the Great: Basilius der Große, *Ausgewählte Schriften*, vol. 2, Bibliothek der Kirchenväter, 1. Reihe, vol. 47, Kempten/München 1925, URL: <http://www.unifr.ch/bkv/kapitel2129.htm> (accessed 26.01.2012).

Basil of Caesarea: Basilius von Caesarea, *Briefe*, Erster Teil, ed. W.-D. Hauschild, Stuttgart 1990.

—— *Address to Young Men on the Right Use of Greek Literature*, ed. Frederick Morgan Padelford. URL: <https://www.ccel.org/ccel/pearse/morefathers/files/basil_litterature01.htm> (accessed 05.05.2020).

Bernard of Clairvaux – De laude: Bernhard von Clairvaux, Ad milites Templi. De laude novae militiae, in Bernhard von Clairvaux, *Sämtliche Werke I*, ed. G. B. Winkler, Innsbruck 1990, pp. 257–326.

—— Rückkehr zu Gott: Bernhard von Clairvaux, *Rückkehr zu Gott*, ed. B. Schellenberger, Düsseldorf 2001.

—— Sermones CC: Sermones super Canticum Canticorum, in Bernhard von Clairvaux, *Sämtliche Werke 6*, ed. G. B. Winkler, Innsbruck 1995.

—— SS II: *On the Song of Songs II*, ed. Kilian Walsh, Kalamazoo 1976.

—— *Selected Works*, ed. G. R. Evans, New York 1987.

Bolocan, Gheorghe (ed.) 1981: *Dicționarul elementelor românești din documentele slavo-române 1374–1600* [Dictionary of Romanian elements in Slavo-Romanian documents 1374–1600], București.

Cantacuzinischer Anonymus A: Grecescu, Constantin/D. Simonescu (eds), *Istoria Țării Românești 1290–1690. Letopisețul Cantacuzinesc* [History of Wallachia 1290–1690. The Cantacuzène Letopiset], București 1960.

Cantacuzinischer Anonymus B: *Istoriia Țării Românești de când au descălecat pravoslavnicii creștini* [History of Wallachia since its foundation by the true-believing Christians], in M. Gregorian (ed.), *Cronicari munteni*, București 1961, pp. 81–224.

Chițimia, Ion C. (ed.) 1963: *Varlaam și Ioasaf* [Barlaam and Josaphat], in I. C. Chițimia/D. Simonescu (eds), *Cărțile populare în literatura românească*, vol. I, București, pp. 289–302.

Cicero: *Der Staat/De re publica*, ed. H. Merklin, Düsseldorf/Zürich 1999.

Clement of Rome: Clemens von Rom, *Epistola ad Corinthios/Brief an die Korinther*, ed. G. Schneider, Fontes Christiani 15, Freiburg 1994.

Constantine Cantacuzino: Stolnicul Constantin Cantacuzino, *Istoria Țării Românești* [History of Wallachia], ed. M. Gregorian, Chișinău 1984.

Constantine Porphyrogenitus – De administrando imperio: Constantinus Porphyrogennitus, *De administrando imperio*, ed. G. Moravcsik/R. J. H. Jenkins, Budapest 1949.

German translation: Klaus Belke/Peter Soustal (eds): *Die Byzantiner und ihre Nachbarn. Die De administrando imperio genannte Lehrschrift des Kaisers Konstantinos Porphyrogennetos für seinen Sohn Romanos*, Wien 1995.

Romanian translation: Vasile Grecu (ed.): *Constantin Porfirogenetul, Carte de învățătură către fiul său Romanos*, București 1971.

—— De ceremoniis: *Constantini Porphyrogeniti De ceremoniis aulae byzantinae*, vol. 2, ed. J. J. Reiske, Bonn 1829.

French translation: Constantin VII Porphyrogénète, *Le livre des cérémonies*, vol. II, ed. Albert Vogt, Paris, 1935.

—— Konstantin Porphyrogennetos, *Vom Bauernhof auf den Kaiserthron. Leben des Kaisers Basileios I., des Begründers der Makedonischen Dynastie, beschrieben von seinem Enkel, dem Kaiser Konstantinos VII. Porphyrogennetos*, ed. L. Breyer, Graz 1981.

Decretum Gratiani: *Corpus Juris Canonici*, Pars I. Decretum Gratiani, ed. E. L. Richter, Leipzig 1839.

Dietrich, Karl (ed.) 1912: *Hofleben in Byzanz. Zum ersten Male aus den Quellen übersetzt*, Leipzig.

Edgerton, Franklin (ed.) 1924: *The Pantchatantra Reconstructed*, 2 vols, New Haven.

Ephrem the Syrian: Ephräm der Syrer, *Ausgewählte Schriften*, vol. 1, Bibliothek der Kirchenväter, 1. Reihe, vol. 37, Kempten/München 1919, URL: <http://www.unifr.ch/bkv/kapitel2451.htm> (accessed 26.01.2012).

—— *Ephraemus Hymnes über das Paradies*, ed. Edmund Beck O. S. B., Rom 1951.

—— *Rede über die Verklärung Christi*, Bibliothek der Kirchenväter, URL: <http://unifr.ch/bkv/kapitel2451.htm> (accessed 30.04.2015).

Erasmus – IPC: Institutio Principis Christiani, ed. O. Herding, in *Opera Omnia Desiderii Erasmi Roterodami*. Ordinis qvarti, Tomus primvs, Amsterdam 1974.

—— *Teachings: The Education of a Christian Prince with the Panegyric for Archduke Philip of Austria*, ed. Lisa Jardine, Cambridge 1997.

—— OE: *Opus Epistolarum Desiderii Erasmi Roterodami*, 12 vols, ed. P. S. Allen, Oxford 1906–1958.

—— Briefe: Erasmus von Rotterdam, *Briefe*, ed. W. Köhler, Bremen 1956.

—— *The Correspondence of Erasmus*, ed. R. A. B. Mynors et al., Toronto 1974ff.

—— Querela: Erasmus von Rotterdam, Querela pacis, in Erasmus von Rotterdam, *Ausgewählte Schriften*, vol. 5, ed. W. Welzig, Darmstadt 1968, pp. 359–451.

—— *Complaint*: The Complaint of Peace, Chicago 1917.

—— Enchiridion: Erasmus von Rotterdam. *Ausgewählte Schriften*, vol. 1, ed. W. Welzig, Darmstadt ⁴2006, pp. 56–375.

Eusebius of Caesarea: Eusebius von Caesarea – Das Leben Constantins: *Eusebius Werke*, 1. vol., ed. I. A. Heikel, Leipzig 1902.

—— *Life of Constantine*, ed. Averil Cameron and Stuart G. Hall, Oxford 1999.

—— *De vita Constantini/über das Leben Konstantins*, ed. Bruno Bleckmann, Fontes Christiani 83, Turnhout 2007.

—— *Kirchengeschichte*, ed. H. Kraft/H. A. Gärtner, München 1967.

—— Kirchengeschichte: *Eusebius Werke*, vols 2/1. and 2/2, ed. E. Schwartz, Leipzig 1903.

Euthymius von Bulgarien: *Werke des Patriarchen von Bulgarien Euthymius (1375–1393)*, ed. Emil Kaluzniacki, Wien 1901.

Fennell, J. L. I. (ed.): *The Correspondence Between Prince A. M. Kurbsky and Tsar Ivan IV of Russia 1564–1579*, Cambridge 1955.

Gabriel Protos: Gavriil Protul, *Viaţa Sfântului Nifon* [The life of Saint Niphon], ed. Vasile Grecu, 2 vols (Greem/Romanian/German), Bucureşti 1944.

Ghazali: *Counsel for Kings*, ed. F. R. C. Bagley, London 1964.

Giraldus Cambrensis: *Giraldi Cambrensis Opera*, vol. 3: De principis instructione liber, ed. G. F. Warner, London 1891.

Gregory Nazianzus: Gregor von Nazianz: *Briefe*, ed. M. Witting, Stuttgart 1981.

——— *Gregory of Nazianzus's Letter Collection: The Complete Translation*, ed. Bradley K. Storin, Berkeley 2019.

Gregory of Sinai: Gregory the Sinaite, *Discourse on the Transfiguration*, ed. David Balfour, San Bernardino 1986.

Guicciardini – Considerations: Francesco Guicciardini, Considerations on the 'Discourses' of Machiavelli, in idem, *Selected Writings*, ed. C. Grayson, London 1965, pp. 57–124.

——— Considerazioni: Francesco Guicciardini, Considerazioni intorno ai Discorsi del Machiavelli, in idem, *Scritti politici e ricordi*, ed. R. Palmarocchi, Bari 1933.

——— Das politische Erbe: Francesco Guicciardini, *Das politische Erbe der Renaissance* ['Ricordi'], ed. E. Grassi, Bern 1946.

——— Ricordi: Francesco Guicciardini, *Das politische Erbe der Renaissance* ['Ricordi'], ed. E. Grassi, Bern 1966.

Hans Schiltberger: *Hans Schiltbergers Reisebuch*. Faksimiledruck nach Originalausgabe von Anton Sorg (Augsburg 1476), Wiesbaden 1969.

Haşdeu, Bogdan-P. (ed.) 1865: *Arhiva istorică a României* [Historical archive of Romania], vol. I/1, Bucureşti.

Hertel, Johannes (ed.) 1908: *The Pantchatantra. A Collection of Ancient Hindu Tales. Critical Edited in the Original Sanscrit*, Cambridge, MA.

Holban, Maria (ed.) (1968–2001): *Călători străini despre Ţările Române* [Foreign travellers' accounts of the Danubian Principalities], vol. 1–10/2, Bucureşti.

Ioannes Saresberiensis: *Ioannis Saresberiensis Episcopi Carnotensis Policratici sive De Nugis Curialium et Vestigiis Philosophorum Libri VIII*, 2 vols, ed. C. C. I. Webb, London 1909.

Ioannes Viterbiensis: *Iohannis Viterbiensis liber de regimine civitatum*, ed. C. Salvemini, in Bibliotheca iuridica medii aevi 3, Bononiae 1901, pp. 217–280.

John Chrysostom: *A Comparison Between a King and a Monk/Against the Opponents of the Monastic Life. Two Treatises by John Chrysostom*, Lewiston/Queenston 1988, pp. 69–76.

——— Johannes Chrysostomus, *Kommentar zum Evangelium des Hl. Matthäus*, vol. 3, Bibliothek der Kirchenväter 26, Kempten/München 1916.

——— Johannes Chrysostomus. *Homilien über die Genesis oder das erste Buch Moses*, vol. 2, ed. Max, Herzog zu Sachsen, Paderborn 1914.

——— *Homilies on Genesis*, 1–17, ed. R.C. Hill, Washington, DC 1999.

——— *Commentary on the Psalms*, vol. 1, ed. R. C. Hill, Brookline 1998.

——— *Old Testament Homilies. vol. 1: Homilies on Hannah, David and Saul*, ed. R. C. Hill, Brookline 2003.

—— über das Priestertum: *Des heiligen Kirchenlehrers Johannes Chrysostomus Erzbischofs von Konstantinopel Kommentar zum Evangelium des hl. Matthäus*, ed. J. C. Baur (Bibliothek der Kirchenväter, 1. Reihe, Band 27/4), Kempten/ München 1916.

St. John Climacus: *The Ladder of Divine Ascent*, ed. Lazarus Moore, Willits 1959.

John of Salisbury: *Policraticus*, ed. C. J. Nederman, Cambridge 1990.

Kekaumenos: *Vademecum des byzantinischen Aristokraten. Das sogenannte Strategikon des Kekaumenos*, ed. H.-G. Beck, Graz 1956.

Krabinger, Johannes G. (ed.) 1850: *Synesii Cyrenaei orationes et homiliarum fragmenta*, Landshut.

Kyminitis, Sevastos: *Metafrasi del* De regno *di Sinesio di Cirene*, ed. Adriana Pignani, Napoli 1967.

Lavrov, Piotr A. (П. А. Лавровь) (ed.) 1904: *Слова наказательныя воеводы валашскаго Іоанна Нѣгоя* [Slova nakazatelnija voevodi valatschskazo Ioana Njagoja], St Petersburg.

Leon Diakonos: *Nikephoros Phokas 'Der bleiche Tod der Sarazenen' und Johannes Tzimiskes*, ed. F. Loretto, Graz 1961.

Liutprand von Cremona: *Die Werke Liutprand von Cremona*, ed. J. Becker, Leipzig ³1915.

Liutprandi Legatio: Liutprand Gesandtschaft an den Kaiser Nikephoros Phokas in Konstantinopel, in R. Buchner (ed.): *Ausgewählte Quellen zur deutschen Geschichte des Mittelalters*, Darmstadt 1971, pp. 524, 525–588, 589.

Lucianus: De Saltatione, in *Lucianus*, vol. 5, ed. A. M. Harmon, Cambridge 1936.

Luther – Freiheitsschrift: Martin Luther, *Von der Freiheit eines Christenmenschen*, Stuttgart ²2000.

—— OSA: *On Secular Authority*, in Harro Höpfl (ed.), *Luther and Calvin on secular authority*, Cambridge 1991, pp. 1–43.

—— LW: *Luther's Works*, ed. Jaroslav Pelikan and Helmut Lehmann, 55 vols, Philadelphia/ St. Louis.

—— Briefe an Freunde u. Familie: Martin Luther, *Briefe an Freunde und an die Familie*, ed. Albrecht Beutel, München 1987.

—— *Luther on education; including a historical introduction, and a translation of the reformer's two most important educational treatises*, ed. F. V. N. Painter, Philadelphia, 1889.

—— *The Christmas Postil of 1522*, ed. Finn B. Andersen. URL: <http:// www.lutherdansk.dk/Web-Julepostillen%20AM/Jule.htm> (accessed 08.04.2020).

—— *On the Freedom of a Christian.* Text from Henry Wace and C. A. Buchheim, *First Principles of the Reformation*, London1883. URL: <https://sourcebooks. fordham.edu/mod/luther-freedomchristian.asp> (accessed 08.04.2020).

—— *The German Mass and Order of Divine Service, January 1526*, ed. B. J. Kidd, in idem, *Documents Illustrative of the Continental Reformation*, Oxford 1911, pp. 193–202. URL: <https://history.hanover.edu/texts/luthserv.html> (accessed 08.04.2020).

—— *A Treatise on Good Works together with the Letter of Dedication* (1520). URL: <https://www.gutenberg.org/files/418/418-h/418-h.htm> (accessed 08.04.2020).

—— *On the Bondage of the Will: To the Venerable Mister Erasmus of Rotterdam* (1525), tr. E. T. Vaughan, London 1823.

Machiavelli: Discorsi (G), in Machiavelli, *Discorsi. Staat und Politik*, ed. H. Günther, Frankfurt a. M. 2000.

—— *Discourses: Discourses on Livy*, ed. Julia Conaway Bondanella and Peter Bondanella, Oxford 1997.

—— Discorsi (M): Niccolò Machiavelli, Discorsi, in idem, *Politische Schriften*, ed. H. Münkler, Frankfurt a. M., pp. 125–269.

—— Discorsi (Orig.): *Discorsi die Niccolò Machiavelli*, Milano 1874.

—— GF: Niccolò Machiavelli, Geschichte von Florenz, in idem, *Politische Schriften*, ed. H. Münkler, Frankfurt a. M., pp. 273–340.

—— Florentine histories, ed. Laura F. Banfield and Harvey C. Mansfield, Jr., Princeton 1988.

—— Lettere: Niccolò Machiavelli, *Opere II. Lettere. Legazioni e commissarie*, ed. C. Vivanti, Torino 1999.

—— Principe: Niccolò Machiavelli, *Il Principe/Der Fürst*, ed. P. Rippel, Stuttgart 2007 (see also Niccolò Machiavelli, *Il Principe*, ed. M. Martelli, Roma 2006).

—— *Prince: The Prince*, ed. Quentin Skinner and Russell Price, Cambridge 1988.

Macarius: Ion Bogdan/P. P. Panaitescu (eds) 1959, *Cronicile slavo-române din sec. XV–XVI. Cronica lui Macarie* [The Slavo-Romanian chronicles of the 15th and 16th centuries. The chronicle of Macarius], Bucureşti, pp. 74–105.

Mardarie Cozianul: *Lexicon slavo-românesc şi tâlcuirea numelor din 1649* [Slavo-Romanian lexicon and the translation of names of 1649], ed. G. Creţu, Bucureşti 1900.

Marsilius von Padua: *Der Verteidiger des Friedens/Defensor pacis*, 2 vols, ed. H. Kusch, Berlin 1958.

Martyrium des Polykarp [Martyrdom of Polycarp], in Rudolph Knopf (ed.), *Ausgewählte Märtyreracten*, Tübingen/Leipzig 1901, pp. 1–10.

Mihăilă, Gheorghe (ed.) 1974: *Dicţionar al limbii române vechi* [Old Romanian dictionary], Bucureşti.

Miklosich, Fr.: *Lexicon paleoslovenico-graeco-latinum*, Wien 1862–1865.

Millet, Gabriel (ed.): *Broderies religieuses de style byzantine*, Paris 1947.

Mirandola, Giovanni Pico della: *De hominis dignitate/über die Würde des Menschen*, ed. A. Buck, Hamburg 1990.

Müller, Ludolf (ed.) 1962: *Des Metropoliten Ilarion Lobrede auf Vladimir den Heiligen und Glaubensbekenntnis*, Wiesbaden (introduction pp. 1–54).

Neagoe Basarab: *Come vivere e praticare l'esichia. Libro di insegnamento del principe romeno Neagoe Basarab per suo figlio Teodosio*, ed. Adriana Mitescu, Rom 1993.

—— *Învăţăturile bunului şi credinciosului Domn al Ţării Româneşti Neagoe Basarab Vvd către fiul său Teodosie Vvd* [The teachings of the good and faithful Lord of Wallachia, Neagoe Basarab Voivode, to his son Theodosius Voivode], ed. Ioan Eclisiarhul Curţii, Bucureşti 1843.

—— *Învăţăturile lui Neagoe Basarab către fiul său Theodosie* [The teachings of Neagoe Basarab to his son Theodosius], critical edition of the Old Romanian version, ed. F. Moisil/D. Zamfirescu, Bucureşti ³1984.

—— *Învăţăturile lui Neagoe Basarab către fiul său Theodosie. Versiunea originală* [The teachings of Neagoe Basarab to his son Theodosius. Original version], bilingual edition in Romanian and Church Slavonic, ed. G. Mihăilă, Bucureşti 1996.

—— *Învăţăturile lui Neagoe Basarab domnul Ţării Româneşti. Versiunea greceasca editată şi însoţită de o traducere în româneşte de Vasile Grecu* [The teachings of Neagoe Basarab, prince of Wallachia. The Greek version edited and translated into Romanian by Vasile Grecu], Bucureşti 1942.

—— Învăţăturile lui Neagoe Vodă Basarab către fiul său, Teodosie [The teachings of Neagoe Basarab to his son Theodosius], in P. P. Panaitescu (ed.), *Cronicile slavo-române din sec. XV–XVI publicate de Ion Bogdan*, Bucureşti 1959, pp. 218–316.

—— *Învăţăturile lui Neagoe Basarab domnul Ţării Româneşti. Versiunea românească de la Curtea de Argeş* [The teachings of Neagoe Basarab to his son Theodosius. The Romanian version of Curtea de Argeş], ed. D. Zamfirescu, Bucureşti 2010.

Nestor: *Die Nestor-Chronik ins Deutsche übersetzt von Ludolf Müller*, München 2001.

Nizam al-Mulk: *The Book of Government or Rules for Kings. The Siyásat-náma or Siyar al Mulúk of Nizám al-Mulk*, ed. Hubert Darke, London 1960.

Pitra, B. P. (ed.): Physiologus, in B. P. Pitra (ed.), *Spicilegium solesmonense complectens Sanctorum Patrum scriptorumque ecclesiasticorum*, vol. 3, Paris 1855, pp. 338–373.

Plato: Platon, Politeia, in Platon, *Sämtliche Werke in drei Bänden*, vol. II, ed. E. Loewenthal, Darmstadt ⁸2004, pp. 5–407.

—— *Der Staat*, ed. K. Vretska, Stuttgart 1982.

—— *Republic*, vol. I, ed. and tr. Christopher Emlyn-Jones and William Preddy, Cambridge, MA 2013.

Plethon: Georgios Gemistos Plethon, *Politik, Philosophie und Rhetorik im spätbyzantinischen Reich (1355–1452)*, ed. W. Blum, Stuttgart 1988.

Polybius: Polybios, *Geschichte I*, ed. H. Drexler, Zürich/Stuttgart 1961.

—— *The Histories*, ed. Robin Waterfield, Oxford 2010.

Popa-Lisseanu, G. (ed.): *Izvoarele istoriei românilor VII. Cronica lui Nestor* [Sources of the history of the Romanians VII. The Nestor chronicle], Bucureşti 1935.

Priskos: Aus der Gotengeschichte des Rhetors und Sophisten Priskos, in E. Doblhofer (ed.), *Byzantninische Diplomaten und östliche Barbaren*, Graz 1955, pp. 13–82.

Pseudo-Augustine: *Pseudo-Augustini Quaestiones veteris et novis testamenti CXXVII*, ed. A. Souter, Corpus scriptorum ecclesiasticorum Latinorum 50, Leipzig 1908.

Radu Popescu Vornicul B: Radu Popescu, Istoriile Domnilor Ţărâi Rumâneşti, in M. Gregorian (ed.), *Cronicari munteni* [Histories of the Wallachian princes], Bucureşti 1961, pp. 225–577.

Radu Popescu Vornicul: Radu Popescu Vornicul, *Istoriile domnilor Ţării Româneşti* [Histories of the Wallachian princes], ed. C. Grecescu, Bucureşti 1963.

Sacerdoţeanu, Aurelian: Pomelnicul Mănăstirii Argeşului [Die Gedenkliste des Klosters Argeş], in *Biserica Ortodoxă Română* 83/1965, no. 3–4, pp. 297–330.

Simonescu, Dan (ed.) 1963: Istoriia a Alexandrului celui Mare din Machedoniia şi a lui Darie din Persida Împăraţilor [Histories of Alexander the Great and of Darius of imperial Persia], in I. C. Chiţimia/D. Simonescu (eds), *Cărţile populare în literatura românească*, vol. 1, Bucureşti, pp. 5–84.

Smil Flaška z Pardubic: *Nová rada*, ed. J. Daňhelka, Praha 1950.

Symeon the New Theologian: *The Epistles of St. Symeon the New Theologian*, ed. H. J. M. Turner, Oxford 2009.

Symeon Monachos: Simeon Monahul, *Cuvinte pentru străpungerea inimii* [Words to awaken the heart], ed. Ioan I. Jr., Sibiu 2009.

Tanaşoca, Nicolae-Ş. (ed.) 2011: *Scrisoarea marelui ritor al Patriarhiei Ecumenice Manuil din Corint către Neagoe Basarab* [The letter of the grand rhetor Manuel of Corinth to Neagoe Basarab], in Tabor 8, pp. 5–15.

Tertullian: *Apologeticum/Verteidigung des Christentums*, ed. C. Becker, München 1952.

—— *The Apology of Tertullian for the Christians*, ed. by T. Herbert Bindley, Oxford 1890.

Theophylakt von Ochrid: Der Fürstenspiegel des Theophylakt von Ochrid, in W. Blum (ed.), *Byzantinische Fürstenspiegel: Agapetos, Theophylakt von Ochrid, Thomas Magister*, Bibliothek der griechischen Literatur 14, Stuttgart 1981, pp. 81–98.

Thomas Magistros: Der Fürstenspiegel des Thomas Magister, in W. Blum (ed.), *Byzantinische Fürstenspiegel: Agapetos, Theophylakt von Ochrid, Thomas Magister*, Bibliothek der griechischen Literatur 14, Stuttgart 1981, pp. 99–145.

Thomas Aquinas: *De regimine principum. Divi Thomae Aquinatis opuscula philosophica*, ed. P. F. Raymund/M. Spiazzi, Turin/Rom 1954.

—— Thomas von Aquin, *Summa Theologiae*. Die deutsche Thomas-Ausgabe 18: Recht und Gerechtigkeit, Heidelberg 1953.

—— *The Summa Theologiæ of St. Thomas Aquinas*, 5 vol. translated by the Fathers of the English Dominican Province, New York 1911.

—— Thomas von Aquin, *über die Herrschaft des Fürsten*, Stuttgart 1990.

Tschižewskij, Dmitrij (ed.) 1969: *Die Nestor-Chronik*, Wiesbaden.

Veress, Endre (ed.) 1914: *Acta et epistolae relationum Transylvaniae Hungariaeque cum Moldavia et Valachia. 1468–1540*, Budapest.

Wipo: Tetralogus, in *Scriptores in usum scholarum*, vol. 12, ed. Breslau, Leipzig ³1915.

—— Gesta Chuonradi: *Wiponis Opera*, MGH, Scriptores rerum Germanicarum in usum scholarum, vol. 61, ed. Bresslau, Leipzig ³1915.

Xanthopoulos, Kallistos and Ignatios: Richtschnur und Regel, ed. A. M. Ammann S. J., in *Die Gottesschau im palamitischen Hesychasmus*, Würzburg 1948, pp. 51–192.

Other Sources and Literature

Aalders, Gerald Jean D. H. Wzn 1969: ΝΟΜΟΣ ΕΜΨΥΧΟΣ, in P. Steinmetz (ed.), *Politeia und Res Publica. Beiträge zum Verständnis von Politik, Recht und Staat in der Antike*, Wiesbaden, pp. 314–329.

Abmeier, Karlies/Michael Borchard/Matthias Riemenschneider (eds) 2013: *Religion im öffentlichen Raum*, Paderborn.

Adontz, Nicolas 1933: La portée historique de l'oraison funèbre de Basile I par son fils Léon VI le Sage, in *Byzantion* 8, no. 2, pp. 501–513.

Afentoulidou-Leitgeb, Eirini 2007: Die Dioptra des Philippos Monotropos und ihr Kontext. Ein Beitrag zur Rezeptionsgeschichte, in *Byzantion* 77, pp. 9–31.

Ahrweiler, Hélène 1975: *L'idéologie politique de l'Empire byzantin*, Paris.

Albu, Remus-D. 2008: Încercare asupra mimesis-ului sec. IV–VI, temelie a culturii şi spiritualităţii bizantine [Essay on Mimesis in the 4th to 6th centuries, the foundation of Byzantine culture ans spirituality], in *Studii Teologice* 2, pp. 129–175.

Alexander, Paul J. 1978: Religious Persecution and Resistance in the Byzantine Empire of the Eight and Ninth Centuries: Methods and Justifications, in P. J. Alexander (ed.), *Religious and Political History and Thought in the Byzantine Empire*, London, pp. 238–264.

Alföldi, Andreas 1935: Insignien und Tracht der römischen Kaiser, in *Mitteilungen des deutschen Archäologischen Instituts*, Römische Abteilung, 50, no. 1–2, pp. 3–171.

Allen, Percy S. 1914: *The Age of Erasmus*, Oxford.

Althusser, Louis 2000: *Machiavelli and Us*, London/New York.

Ammann, Albert M. 1948: Darstellung, in idem, *Die Gottesschau im palamitischen Hesychasmus*, Würzburg, pp. 8–50.

Amsdorff, Nikolaus von, 1550: *Bekentnis Unterricht und vermanung der Pfarrhern und Prediger der Christlichen Kirchen zu Magdeburg*, Magdeburg.

Anca, Alexandru Ş. 2005: Ehrerweisung durch Geschenke in der Komnenzeit. Gewohnheiten und Regel des herrscherlichen Schenkens, in *Mitteilungen zur spätantiken Archäologie und byzantinischen Kunstgeschichte* 4, pp. 185–194.

—— 2010: *Herrschaftliche Repräsentation und kaiserliches Selbstverständnis. Berührung der westlichen mit der byzantinischen Welt in der Zeit der ersten Kreuzzüge*, Münster.

Andreopoulos, Andreas 2005: *Metamorphosis. The Transfiguration in Byzantine Theology and Iconography*, New York.

Andresen, Carl 1971: *Die Kirchen der alten Christenheit*, Stuttgart.

Angelov, Dimităr 1989: Hesychasm in Medieval Bulgaria, in *Bulgarian Historical Review* 17, no. 3, pp. 41–61.

Angelov, Dimiter 2007: *Imperial Ideology and Political Thought in Byzantium. 1204–1330*, Cambridge.

Anghel, Paul 1972: Colaj și elaborare originală la Neagoe Basarab [Literary collage and the original in Neagoe Basarab], in Societatea culturală *Neagoe Basarab* din Curtea de Argeș (ed.), *Neagoe Basarab 1512–1521. La 460 de ani de la urcarea sa pe tronul Țării Românești*, București, pp. 76–88.

Anglo, Sidney 2005: *Machiavelli – The First Century. Studies in Enthusiasm, Hostility and Irrelevance*, Oxford.

Anton, Hans H. 1968: *Fürstenspiegel und Herrscherethos in der Karolingerzeit*, Bonn.

—— 2006: Einleitung, in H. H. Anton (ed.), *Fürstenspiegel des frühen und hohen Mittelalters*, Darmstadt, pp. 3–44.

Antonopoulou, Theodora (ed.) 1997: *The Homilies of the Emperor Leo VI*, Leiden.

Arendt, Hannah ²2006: *Der Liebesbegriff bei Augustin. Versuch einer philosophischen Interpretation*, Hildesheim et al.

Argegni, Corrado 1936–1937: *Condottieri, capitani, tribuni*, Milano.

Armstrong, Arthur H. 1983: The Negative Theology of Nous in Later Neoplatonism, in H.-D. Blume/F. Mann (eds), *Platonismus und Christentum, JAC, Ergänzungsband* 10, pp. 31–37.

Arnakis, George G. 1963: The Role of Religion in the Development of Balkan Naionalism, in C. Jelavich/B. Jelavich (eds), *The Balkans in Transition*, Berkeley/Los Angeles, pp. 115–144.

Arquillière, Henri-X. ²1955: L'Augustinisme politique. Essai sur la formation des théories politiques du Moyen-Age, Paris.

Auer, Alfons 1954: *Die vollkommene Frömmigkeit des Christen. Nach dem Echiridion militis Christiani des Erasmus von Rotterdam*, Düsseldorf.

Augustijn, Cornelis 1969: The Ecclesiology of Erasmus, in J. Coppens (ed.), *Scrinium Erasmianum*, I, Leiden, pp. 135–155.

—— 1991: *Erasmus. His Life, Works, and Influence*, Toronto.

—— 1992: Hieronymus in Luthers 'De servo arbitrio'. Eine Teiluntersuchung zu Luthers Väterverständnis, in W.-D. Hauschild/W. H. Neuser/C. Peters (eds), *Luthers Wirkung*, Stuttgart, pp. 193–208.

—— 1993: 'Erasmus', in TRE 10, pp. 1–18.

Aulotte, Robert 1965: *Amyot et Plutarque. La tradition des Moralia au XVIe siècle*, Genève.

Avram, Mircea 1970: *Cartea românească manuscrisă* [Romanian manuscript literature], Sibiu.

Bachmann, Max 1935: *Die Rede des Johannes Syropulos an den Kaiser Isaak II. Angelos (1185–1195) (Text und Kommentar)*, München.

Bădiliță, Cristian 1997: Studiu introductiv, in idem (ed.), *Evagrie Ponticul. Tratatul Practic. Gnosticul*, Iași.

Bak, János M. 2010–2011: Ikonoklastische Gedankenfragmente zu den Begriffen 'Südosteuropa' und 'Ostmitteleuropa', in *Südost-Forschungen* 69–70, pp. 389–396.

Balas, David L. 1966: *Metousia Theou. Man's Participation in God's Perfections accordign to Saint Gregory of Nyssa*, Roma.

Ballor, Jordan J. 2013: State, Church, and the Reformational Roots of Subsidiarity, in P. Opitz (ed.), *The Myth of the Reformation*, Göttingen, pp. 148–175.

Bagley, Frank R. C. 1964: Introduction, in idem (ed.), *Ghazali. Counsel for Kings*, London, pp. ix–lxxiv.

Bahner, Werner 1974: *Ein bedeutender Gelehrter an der Schwelle zur Frühaufklärung. Dimitri Cantemir (1673–1723)*, Berlin.

Bainton, Roland H. 1951: The Querela Pacis of Erasmus, Classical and Christian Sources, in *ARG* 42, no. 1–2, pp. 32–48.

Baldini, Artemio E. (ed.) 2010: *L'educazione di un principe luterano. Il 'Furschlag' di Johann Eberlin tra Erasmo, Lutero e la sconfitta dei Contadini. Edizione critica in 'Neuhochdeutsch' e versione italiana del testo manoscritto inedito*, Milano.

Baldwin, John W. 1982: Masters at Paris from 1179 to 1215. A Social Perspective, in R. L. Benson/G. Constable (eds), *Renaissance and Renewal in the Twelfth Century*, Oxford, pp. 138–172.

Balotă, Anton 1969: Autenticitatea Învățăturilor lui Neagoe Basarab [The authenticty of the teachings of Neagoe Basarab], in *Studii, revistă de istorie* 22, no. 2, pp. 271–280.

Barber, Charles 2007: *Contesting the Logic of Painting. Art and Understanding in Eleventh-Century Byzantium*, Leiden/Boston.

Barbu, Daniel 1998: *Byzance, Rome et les Roumains. Essais sur la production politique de la foi au Moyen Âge*, Bucarest.

—— 2001: *Bizanț contra Bizanț. Explorări în cultura politică românească* [Byzanz gegen Byzanz. Untersuchungen in rumänischer politischer Kultur], București.

Bărbulescu, Ilie 1928: *Curentele literare la români în perioada slavonismului cultural* [The literary currents among the Romanians in the period of cultural Slavonicism], București.

Barincou, Edmond 1958: *Niccolò Machiavelli in Selbstzeugnissen und Bilddokumenten*, Hamburg.

Barker, Ernest (ed.) 1957: *Social and Political Thought in Byzantium. From Justinian to the Last Paleologus. Passages from Byzantine Writers and Documents*, Oxford.

Baron, Hans 1932: Das Erwachen des historischen Denkens im Humanismus des Quattrocento, in *HZ* 147, no. 1, pp. 5–20.

Bartlett, Kenneth (ed.) 1992: *The Civilization of the Italian Renaissance. A Sourcebook*, Lexington/Toronto.

Bartos, Emil 1999: *Deification in Eastern Orthodox Theology. An Evaluation and Critique of the Theology of Dumitru Stăniloae*, Carlisle.

Baumann, Zygmunt 2003: The Great Separation Mark Two or Politics in the Globalizing and Individualizing Society, in A. Nassehi/M. Schroeder (eds), *Der Begriff des Politischen*, Baden-Baden, pp. 17–43.

Bäumer, Remigius (ed.) 1972: *Lutherprozess und Lutherbann. Vorgeschichte, Ergebnis, Nachwirkung*, Münster.

Baur, Chrysostomus 1930: *Der Heilige Johannes Chrysostomus und seine Zeit*, München.

Bausi, Francesco 2005: *Machiavelli*, Roma.

Bauve Hébert, Maurice la, 1992: *Hesychasm, Word-Weaving, and Slavic Hagiography. The Literary School of Patriarch Euthymius*, München.

Bayer, Oswald 1995: *Freiheit als Antwort. Zur theologischen Ethik*, Tübingen.

—— 2003: *Martin Luthers Theologie. Eine Vergegenwärtigung*, Tübingen.

—— 2007: Das Wort ward Fleisch. Luthers Christologie als Lehre von der Idiomenkommunikation, in O. Bayer/B. Gleede (eds), *Creator est creatura. Luthers Christologie als Lehre von der Idiomenkommunikation*, Berlin/New York, pp. 5–34.

Bazilescu, Ştefan 1971: Relaţiile lui Neagoe Basarab cu lumea ortodoxă din afara graniţelor Ţării Româneşti [The relations of Neagoe Basarabs with the Orthodox world beyond the Wallachian frontier], in *Mitropolia Olteniei* 23, no. 9–10, pp. 676–690.

Becher, Matthias 2009: *Merowinger und Karolinger*, Darmstadt.

Becht, Michael 2000: *Pium consensum tueri. Studien zum Begriff* consensus *im Werk von Erasmus von Rotterdam, Philipp Melanchthon und Johannes Calvin*, Münster.

Beck, Hans-G. 1960: Reichsidee und nationale Politik im spätbyzantinischen Staat, in *Byzantinische Zeitschrift* 53, pp. 86–94.

—— 1963: Humanismus und Palamismus, in *Actes du XIIe congrès internaional d'études byzantines*, vol. 1, Belgrad, pp. 63–82.

—— 1970: Res Publica Romana. Vom Staatsdenken der Byzantiner, in *SBAW*, Philos.-Hist. Kl., 2.

—— 1975: Der Leserkreis der byzantinischen 'Volksliteratur' im Licht der handschriftlichen überlieferung, in *Byzantine Books and Bookmen*, ed. Dumbarton Oaks Center for Byzantine Studies, Washington, DC, pp. 47–67.

—— 1980: *Geschichte der orthodoxen Kirche im byzantinischen Reich*, Göttingen.

Becke, Ulrich 1970: Eine hinterlassene psychiatrische Studie Paul Johann Reiters über Luther, in *ZKG* 90, pp. 85–95.

Beckmann, Jan P. 1995: *Wilhelm von Ockham*, München.

Beierwaltes, Werner 1997: Dionysios Areopagites – Ein christlicher Proklos, in T. Kobusch/B. Mojsisch (eds), *Platon in der abendländischen Geistesgeschichte*, Darmstadt, pp. 71–100.

Bell, Peter N. 2009: Introduction, in idem (ed.), *Three Political Voices from the Age of Justinian. Agapetus, Advice to the Emperor, Dialogue on Political Science, Paul the Silentiary, Description of Hagia Sophia*, Liverpool, pp. 1–97.

Bell, Theo M. M. A. C. 1999: Die Rezeption Bernhard von Clairvaux bei Luther, in *ARG* 90, pp. 72–102.

—— 1993: *Divus Bernhardus. Bernhard von Clairvaux in Martin Luthers Schriften*, Mainz.

Belliotti, Raymond A. 2009: *Niccolò Machiavelli. The Laughing Lion and the Stutting Fox*, Lanham.

Bellomo, Antonio 1906: *Agapeto Diacono e la sua Scheda Regia*, Bari.

Béné, Charles 1969: *Érasme et Saint Augustin ou Influence de Saint Augustin sur l'humanisme d'Érasme*, Genève.

Benfey, Theodor (ed.) 1859: *Pantschatantra. Fünf Bücher indischer Fabeln, Märchen und Erzählungen*, 2 Teile, Leipzig.

Benner, Erica 2009: *Machiavelli's Ethics*, Princeton/Oxford.

Benson, Robert L. 1982: Political Renovation. Two Models from Roman Antiquity, in R. L. Benson/G. Constable (eds), *Renaissance and Renewal in the Twelfth Century*, Oxford, pp. 68–87.

Benzing, Josef 1965: *Lutherbibliographie, 1. Lieferung*, Baden-Baden.

Berend, Nora 2007: Introduction, in N. Berend (ed.), *Christianization and the Rise of Christian Monarchy*, Cambridge, pp. 1–46.

Berges, Wilhelm 1938: *Fürstenspiegel des hohen und späten Mittelalters*, Leipzig.

Berlin, Isaiah 1972: The Originality of Machiavelli, in M. P. Gilmore (ed.), *Studies on Machiavelli*, Florenz, pp. 147–206.

—— The Originality of Machiavelli, in *Against the Current: Essays in the History of Ideas,* London 1997, pp. 25–79.

—— 1994: Die Originalität Machiavellis, in idem, *Wider das Geläufige. Aufsätze zur Ideengeschichte*, Frankfurt a. M., pp. 93–157.

Bertelli, Sergio/P. Innocenti 1979: *Bibliographia machaivelliana*, Verona. Bertelli, Sergio 1975: Machiavelli and Soderini, in *Renaissance Quarterly* 28, pp. 1–16.

Beurlier, E. 1891: *Le culte impérial, son histoire et son organisation depuis Auguste jusqu'à Justinien*, Paris.

Beutel, Albrecht [2]2006: *Martin Luther. Eine Einführung in Leben, Werk und Wirkung*, Leipzig.

Bianu, Ioan/Nerva Hodoş (eds) 1903: *Bibliografia românească veche 1508–1830* [Old Romanian bibliography], vol. 1, Bucureşti.

Biesen, Kees den, 2002: *Bibliography on Ephrem the Syrian*, Giove in Umbria.

Binder Iijima, Edda/Vasile Dumbravă (eds) 2005: *Stefan der Große – Fürst der Moldau. Symbolfunktion und Bedeutungswandel eines mittelalterlichen Herrschers*, Leipzig.

Biondo, Biondi 1951: Humanitas nelle leggi degli imperatori romano-cristiani, in *Miscellanea Giovanni Galbiati* 2, pp. 81–94.

Bîrsan, Cristina 2004: *Dimitrie Cantemir and the Islamic World*, Istanbul.

Black, Robert 1986: The Political Thought of the Florentine Chancellors, in *The Historical Journal* 29, pp. 991–1003.

Blänkner, Reinhard 2005: Historizität, Institutionalität, Symbolizität. Grundbegriffliche Aspekte einer Kulturgeschichte des Politischen, in B. Stollberg-Rilinger (ed.), *Was heißt Kulturgeschichte des Politischen?*, Zeitschrift f. Hist. Forschung, Beiheft 35, Berlin, pp. 71–96.

Bleicken, Jochen 2007: Constantin der Große und die Christen. überlegungen zur konstantinischen Wende, in H. Schlange-Schöningen (ed.), *Konstantin und das Christentum*, Darmstadt, pp. 64–108.

Blickle, Peter 2004: *Die Revolution von 1525*, München.

Bloch, Marc 1998: *Die wundertätigen Könige*, München.

Bloomfield, Paul 2008: Why It's Bad to be Bad?, in idem (ed.), *Morality and Self-Interest*, Oxford, pp. 251–271.

Blum, Georg G. 2009: *Byzantinische Mystik. Ihre Praxis und Theologie vom 7. Jahrhundert bis zum Beginn der Turkokratie, ihre Fortdauer in der Neuzeit*, Berlin.

Blum, Wilhelm 1974: Justinian I. – Die philosophische und christologische Fundierung kaiserlicher Herrschaft, in pp. Otto (ed.), *Die Antike im Umbruch. Politisches Denken zwischen hellenistischer Tradition und christlicher Offenbarung bis zur Reichstheologie Justinians*, München, pp. 109–125.

—— 1981: Einleitung, in idem (ed.), *Byzantinische Fürstenspiegel: Agapetos, Theophylakt von Ochrid, Thomas Magister*, Stuttgart, pp. 1–58.

Bobzin, Hartmut 1985: Martin Luthers Beitrag zur Kenntnis und Kritik des Islam, in *NZSTR* 27, pp. 262–289.

Bochmann, Klaus 2008: *Dimitrie Cantemir. Fürst der Moldau, Gelehrter, Akteur der europäischen Kulturgeschichte*, Leipzig.

Bochmann, Klaus/Heinrich Stiehler 2010: *Einführung in die rumänische Sprach- und Literaturgeschichte*, Bonn.

Boer, Wietse de/Christiane Göttler (eds) 2013: *Religion and the Senses in Early Modern Europe*, Leiden/Boston.

Bogdan, Damian I. 1968: 13 file inedite din cel de-al doilea arhetip al Învățăturilor lui Neagoe Basarab [13 new sheets from the second archetype of the teachings of Neagoe Basarab], in *Revista de istorie și teorie literară* 17, pp. 487–497.

Bogdan, Ioan 1902: *Originea voevodatului la români* [On the origins of the institution of voivode among the Romanians], București.

——— 1903 und 1904: *über die rumänischen Knesen*, 2 Teile, Sonderdruck aus: Archiv für slavische Philologie 25, pp. 522–543 und 26, pp. 100–114.

Bogner, Daniel 2011: Säkularisierung als Programmierungswechsel: Der frühneuzeitliche Rollentausch von Religion und Politik, in M. Hildebrandt/ M. Brocker/H. Behr (eds), *Säkularisierung und Resakralisierung in westlichen Gesellschaften*, Wiesbaden, pp. 43–55.

Boia, Lucian 2003: *Geschichte und Mythos: über die Gegenwart des Vergangenen in der rumänischen Gesellschaft*, Köln.

Bojović, Boško I. 2008: *Chilandar et les Pays Roumains (Xve–XVIIe siècles)*, Paris.

Boldur, Alexandru von 2001: *Adunările de stări sociale în istoria Moldovei și a Țării Românești. Sfatul mare de obște* [The assemblies of the estates in the history of Moldavia and Wallachia. The great general council], București.

Bolgar, Robert 1981: The Classical Tradition. Legend and Reality, in M. Mullett/R. Scott (eds), *Byzantium and the Classical Tradition*, Birmingham, pp. 7–19.

Bondanella, Peter/Mark Musa 1979: Introduction, in eidem (eds), *The Portable Machiavelli*, Middlesex.

Borelli, Gianfranco 2009: *Il lato oscuro del Leviathan. Hobbes contro Machiavelli*, Napoli.

Borgolte, Michael 2001: *Perspektiven europäischer Mittelalterhistorie an der Schwelle zum 21. Jahrhundert*, in idem (ed.), Das europäische Mittelalter im Spannungsbogen des Vergleichs, Berlin, pp. 13–27.

Born, Lester K. 1968: Introduction, in idem (ed.), *The Education of a Christian Prince*, New York, pp. 3–130.

Bornkamm, Heinrich 1960: *Luthers Lehre von den zwei Reichen im Zusammenhang seiner Theologie*, Gütersloh.

——— 1975a: Luther und sein Vater, in idem, *Luther. Gestalt und Wirkungen. Gesammelte Aufsätze*, Gütersloh, pp. 11–32.

——— 1975b: Der Christ und die zwei Reiche, in idem, *Luther. Gestalt und Wirkungen. Gesammelte Aufsätze*, Gütersloh, pp. 255–266.

Boshof, Egon 1993: *Königtum und Königsherrschaft im 10. und 11. Jahrhundert*, München.

Bosl, Karl 1988: Der theologisch-theozentrische Grund des mittelalterlichen Weltbildes und seiner Ordnungsidee, in I. Fetscher/H. Münkler (eds), *Pipers Handbuch der politischen Ideen*, vol. 2, München/Zürich, pp. 175–188.

Bott, Gerhard/Gerhard Ebeling/Bernd Moeller (eds) 1983: *Martin Luther. Sein Leben in Bildern und Texten*, Frankfurt a. M.

Bradford, Sarah 1979: *Cesare Borgia. Ein Leben in der Renaissance*, Hamburg.

Brady Jr., Thomas A. 2009: *German Histories in the Age of Reformations, 1400–1650*, Cambridge.

Brändle, Rudolf 1999: *Johannes Chrysostomus. Bischof – Reformer – Märtyrer*, Stuttgart.

Brătianu, Gheorghe I. 1996: *Adunările de stări în Europa și în Țările Române* [Assemblies of estates in Europe and the Danubian Principalities], București.

Brecht, Martin 1981–1987: *Martin Luther*, 3 vols, Stuttgart.

Bréhier, Louis 1975: ΙΕΡΕΥΣ ΚΑΙ ΒΑΣΙΛΕΥΣ, in H. Hunger (ed.): *Das byzantinische Herrscherbild*, Darmstadt, pp. 86–93.

Brennecke, Hans G. 2007: Ecclesia est in re publica, id est in imperio Romano (Optatus III). Das Christentum in der Gesellschaft an der Wende zum konstantinischen Zeitalter, in idem, *Ecclesia est in re publica*, Berlin/New York, pp. 69–102.

Brezeanu, Stelian 1999: *Romanitatea orientală în Evul Mediu* [Oriental Romanity in the middle ages], București.

Brezoianu, Ioan 1882: *Vechile instituțiuni ale României (1327–1866)* [The old institutions of Romania (1327–1866)], București.

Brincken, Anne-D. von den, 2000: *Historische Chronologie des Abendlandes*, Stuttgart.

Bringmann, Klaus 2007: Die konstantinische Wende. Zum Verhältnis von politischer und religiöser Motivation, in H. Schlange-Schöningen (ed.), *Konstantin und das Christentum*, Darmstadt, pp. 109–132.

Brinkhus, Gerd 1978: *Eine bayerische Fürstenspiegelkompilation des 16. Jahrhunderts*, München.

Briquet, Charles M. 1968: *Les filigranes*, vol. 1, Amsterdam.

Brissaud, Jean 1898: *Un libéral au XVIIe siècle: Claude Joly (1607–1700)*, Paris.

Brock, Sebastian ²1992: *The Luminous Eye. The Spiritual World Vision of Saint Ephrem*, Kalamazoo.

Brooke, Christopher 1969: *The Twelfth Century Renaissance*, London.

Brosch, Moritz 1903: Machiavelli am Hofe und im Kriegslager Maximilians I., in *Mitteilungen des Instituts für österreichische Geschichtsforschung* 24, pp. 87–110.

Brown, Peter 1981: Sozialpolitische Anschauungen Augustins, in C. Andresen (ed.), *Zum Augustin-Gespräch der Gegenwart II*, Darmstadt, pp. 179–204.

Browning, Robert 1963: Byzantinische Schulen und Schulmeister, in *Das Altertum* 9, no. 2, pp. 105–118.

Brunnbauer, Ulf 2011: Der Balkan als translokaler Raum. Verflechtung, Bewegung und Geschichte, in *Südosteuropa Mitteilungen* 51, no. 3, pp. 78–93.

Bryer, Anthony 2008: Chronology and Dating, in E. Jeffreys/J. Haldon/R. Cormack (eds), *The Oxford Handbook of Byzantine Studies*, Oxford, pp. 31–37.

Buck, August 1985: *Machiavelli*, Darmstadt.

—— 1986: Machiavellis Dialog über die Kriegskunst, in F. J. Worstbrock (ed.), *Krieg und Frieden im Horizont der Renaissancehumanismus*, Weinheim, pp. 1–12.

—— 1987: *Humanismus. Seine europäische Entwicklung in Dokumenten und Darstellungen*, Freiburg/München.

—— 1996: Der italienische Humanismus, in N. Hammerstein (ed.), *Handbuch der deutschen Bildungsgeschichte*, vol. 1, München, pp. 1–56.

Bulat, Toma G. (o. J.): *Personalitatea religioasă a Voevodului Neagoe Basarab al IV-lea* [The religious personality of Voivode Neagoe Basarab IV], Craiova.

Bultot, R. 1969: Érasme, Épicure et le *De contemptu mundi*, in J. Coppens (ed.), *Scrinium Erasmianum II*, Leiden, pp. 205–238.

Burger, Christoph 1993: Erasmus' Auseinandersetzung mit Augustin im Streit mit Luther, in L. Grane/A. Schindler/M. Wriedt (eds), *Auctoritas Patrum. Zur Rezeption der Kichernväter im 15. und 16. Jahrhundert*, vol. 1, Mainz, pp. 1–13.

—— 1999: Luthers Gebetsvorschlag für Herzog Johann Friedrich von Sachsen, in E. Campi/L. Grane/A. M. Ritter (eds), *Oratio. Das Gebet in patristischer und reformatorischer Sicht*, Göttingen, pp. 185–196.

—— 2014: *Tradition und Neubeginn. Martin Luther in seinen frühen Jahren*, Tübingen.

Burkard, Dominik 2011: Die politische Dimension kirchlichen Handelns. Historische Zugänge, in I. Dingel/C. Tietz (eds), *Die politische Aufgabe von Religion. Perspektiven der drei monotheistischen Religionen*, Göttingen, pp. 143–177.

Burkhardt, Johannes 2002: *Das Reformationsjahrhundert. Deutsche Geschichte zwischen Medienrevolution und Institutionenbildung (1517–1617)*, Stuttgart.

Burnham, James 1943: *The Machiavellians. Defenders of Freedom*, New York.

Buschmann, Gerd (ed.) 1998: *Das Martyrium des Heiligen Polycarp*, Göttingen.

Butterworth, Charles E. 1988: Die politischen Lehren von Avicenna und Averroes, in I. Fetscher/H. Münkler, *Pipers Handbuch der politischen Ideen*, vol. 2, München/Zürich, pp. 141–173.

Buzescu, Alexandru I. 1943: *Domnia în Ţările Române până la 1866* [The institution of princes in the Danubian Principalities until 1866], Bucureşti.

Câdă, Nicolae-C. (ed.) 2012: *Sfântul Voievod Neagoe Basarab – ctitor de biserici şi cultură românească* [Saint Voivode Neagoe Basarab – fiunder of churches and Romanian culture], Bucureşti.

Calhoun, Craig 2012: Nachwort. Die Vielen Mächte der Religion, in E. Mendieta/J. Van Antwerpen (eds), *Religion und Öffentlichkeit*, Frankfurt a. M., pp. 170–195.

Callahan, John F. 1958: Greek Philosophy and the Cappadocian Cosmology, in *DOP* 121, pp. 29–57.

Camarino-Cioran, Ariadna 1979: Parénèses byzantines dans les Pays Roumains, in E. Stănescu/N.-Ş. Tanaşoca (eds), *Études byzantines et post-byzantines*, vol. 1, Bucureşti, pp. 117–133.

Cameron, Alan 1982: The Empress and the Poet. Paganism and Politics at the Court of Theodosius II, in *Yale Classical Studies* 27, pp. 217–289.

Cameron, Averil 1981: Images of Authority. Elites and Icons in late Sixth-Century Byzantium, in M. Mullet/R. Scott (eds), *Byzantium and the Classical Tradition*, Birmingham, pp. 205–234.

Campagna, Norbert 2003: *Niccolò Machiavelli. Eine Einführung*, Berlin.

Cândea, Virgil et al. 1966: *Pagini din trecutul diplomaţiei româneşti* [Pages from the past of Romanian diplomacy], Bucureşti.

—— 1968: L'humanisme d'Udrişte Năsturel et l'agonie des lettres slavonnes en Valachie, in *RESEE* 6, no. 2, pp. 239–287.

—— 1998: *Mărturii româneşti peste hotare* [Romanian testimonies beyond her frontiers], vol. 2, Bucureşti.

Carabă, Adrian V. 2012: Ausdrucksformen der byzantinischen *Symphonia* am Beispiel des Hofzeremoniells, in M.-D. Grigore/R. H. Dinu/M. Zivojinovic (eds), *Herrschaft in Südosteuropa. Kultur- und sozialwissenschaftliche Perspektiven*, Göttingen, pp. 135–154.

Carile, Antonio 2008: *Teologia politica bizantina*, Spoleto.

Carlyle, Robert W./A. J. Carlyle 1903/1909: *A History of Mediaeval Political Theory in the West*, 2 vols, Edinburgh.

Cartojan, Nicolae 1922: *Alexandria în literatura românească. Noi contribuţii* [The Alexander Romance in Romanian literature. New aporoaches], Bucureşti.

—— 1974: *Cărţile populare în literatura românească. Epoca influenţei sud-slave* [Die Volksbücher der rumänischen Literatur. Die Zeit des südslavischen Einflusses], Bucureşti.

—— 1980: *Istoria literaturii române vechi* [Geschichte der altrumänischen Literatur], Bucureşti.

Casiday, Augustine 2012: Neagoe Basarab, in idem (ed.), *The Orthodox Christian World*, London/New York, pp. 310–317.

Caspari, Fritz 1947: Erasmus on the Social Functions of Christian Humanism, in *JHI* 8, no. 1, pp. 78–106.

Cavalo, Jo A. 2007: Machiavelli and Women, in P. Vilches/G. Seaman (eds), *Seeking Real Truths. Multidisciplinary Perspectives on Machiavelli*, Leiden/ Boston, pp. 123–148.

Cazacu, Matei 1967: De ce a clădit Neagoe Basarab biserica Mănăstirii Argeşului? [Why did Neagoe Basarab found the monastery church of Argeş?], in *Glasul Bisericii* 26, no. 7–8.

—— 1989: Les *Enseignements du Prince Neagoe Basarab à son fils Théodose* dans l'histoire des idées politiques, in *Buletinul bibliotecii române. Studii şi documente româneşti* 15(19), Neue Folge, pp. 106–121.

Cazacu, Matei/Dan I. Mureşan 2013: *Ioan Basarab, un domn român la începuturile Ţării Româneşti* [John Basaraba lord of the early years of Wallachia], Bucureşti.

Charlier, Gustave 1912: Jean le Blond et son apologie de la langue française (1546), in *Revue de l'instruction publique en Belgique*, Bruxelles, pp. 331–344.

Cherel, Albert 1935: *La pensée de Machiavel en France*, Paris.

Chester, Stephen 2009: Who is Freedom for? Martin Luther and Alain Badiou on Paul and Politics, in P. Middleton/A. Paddison/K. Wenell (eds), *Paul, Grace and Freedom*, New York, pp. 97–118.

Chesterton, Gilbert K. 1960: *Der stumme Ochse. über Thomas von Aquin*, Freiburg.

Chihaia, Pavel 1964: Deux armoiries sculptées appartenant aux voïvodes Vlad Dracul et Neagoe Basarab, in *Revue roumaine d'histoire de l'art*, I, no. I, pp. 151–167.

—— 1971a: Învăţăturile lui Neagoe Basarab [Die Lehrworte des Neagoe Basarabs], in *Luceafărul*, Nr. 3 vom 6. Febr.

—— 1971b: Tot despre Învăţăturile lui Neagoe [Once more on the teachings of Neagoe], in *Luceafărul*, no. 11 (13 March), pp. 3 und 5.

—— 1972: Cu privire la Învăţături si la câteva monumente din vremea lui Neagoe Basarab [Regarding the teachings of Neagoe Basarab and several monuments of his time], in *Neagoe Basarab 1512–1521. La 460 de ani de la urcarea sa pe tronul Ţării Româneşti*, Bucureşti, pp. 130–202.

—— 1976: *De la 'Negru-Vodă' la Neagoe Basarab* [Von 'Negru-Vodă' bis zu Neagoe Basarab], Bucureşti.

—— 1995a: Două fiale în Ţara Românească construite de voievodul Neagoe Basarab [On two filial churches in Romania founded by Neagoe Basarab], in idem, *Ţara Românească între Bizanţ şi Occident*, Iaşi, pp. 70–100.

—— 1995b: Portrete de voievozi din Ţara Românească (sec. XIV–XVI) [Voivodes of Wallachia (14th–16th c.)], in idem, *Ţara Românească între Bizanţ şi Occident*, Iaşi, pp. 151–195.

Chiţimia, Ion C. 1963: Consideraţii despre *Învăţăturile lui Neagoe Basarab* [Consideration on the *Teachings of Neagoe Basarab*], in *Romanoslavica* 8, pp. 309–339.

—— 1972: Învăţăturile lui Neagoe Basarab [The teachings of Neagoe Basarab], in idem, *Probleme de bază ale literaturii române vechi*, Bucureşti, pp. 109–144.

Christian, Gertraud (ed.) 1968: Erasmus von Rotterdam. Institutio Principis christiani/Die Erziehung des christlichen Fürsten, in *Erasmus von Rotterdam. Ausgewählte Schriften*, vol. 5, ed. W. Welzig, Darmstadt.

Christou, Panayiotis 1971: The Missionary Task of the Byzantine Emperor, in *Byzantina* 3, pp. 277–286.

Chrysos, Evangelos K. 1978: The Title βασιλεύς in the Early Byzantine International Relations, in *DOP* 32, pp. 29–75.

Chryssavgis, John 2004: *John Climacus. From the Egyptian Desert to the Sinaite Mountain*, Burlington.

Ciobanu, Ştefan (Étienne) 1942: Informations sur l'histoire de la Valachie au XVIe siècle dans un œuvre hagiographique bulgare, in *Balcania* 7, pp. 121–151.

—— 1989: *Istoria literaturii române vechi* [History of Old Romanian Literature], Bucureşti.

Ciobanu, Veniamin 1995: *Ţările Române şi Polonia. Secolele XIV–XVI* [The Danubian Principalities and Poland, 14th–16th centuries], Bucureşti.

Clark, Richard G. 1970: Machiavelli: Bibliographical Spectrum, in *Review of National Literatures* 1, 93–135.

Classen, Peter 1974: Burgundio von Pisa. Richter-Gesandter-übersetzer, in *SHAW*, Philos.-Hist. Kl., no. 4.

—— 1985: *Karl der Große, das Papsttum und Byzanz. Die Begründung des karolingischen Kaisertums*, Sigmaringen.

Clewing, Konrad/Oliver J. Schmitt 2011: Südosteuropa: Raum und Geschichte, in eidem (eds), *Geschichte Südosteuropas. Vom frühen Mittelalter bis zur Gegenwart*, Regensburg, pp. 1–16.

Cochrane, Eric W. 1961: Machiavelli 1940–1960, in *JMH* 33, no. 2, pp. 113–136.

Cohn, Samuel K. 1999: *Creating the Florentine State. Peasants and Rebellion 1348–1434*, Cambridge.

Coleman, Janet 1995: Machiavelli's *via moderna*: medieval and Renaissance attitudes to history, in M. Coyle (ed.), *Niccolò Machiavelli's the Prince. New Interdisciplinary Essays*, Manchester/New York, pp. 40–64.

—— 2000: *A History of Political Thought. From the Middle Ages to the Renaissance*, Oxford.

Colish, Marcia L. 1997: *Medieval Foundations of the Western Intellectual Tradition, 400–1400*, New Haven/London.

—— 1999: Republicanism, Religion, and Machiavelli's Savonarolan Moment, in *Journal of the History of Ideas* 60, no. 4, pp. 597–616.

Conaway Bondanella, Julia 2007: The Discourses on Livy. Preserving a Free Way of Life, in P. Vilches/G. Seaman (eds), *Seeking Real Truths. Multidisciplinary Perspectives on Machiavelli*, Leiden/Boston, pp. 69–102.

Conea, Ion/I. Donat 1958: Contribution à l'étude de la toponymie pétchénègue-comane de la plaine roumaine du Bas-Danube, in Académie de la République Populaire Roumaine (ed.), *Contributions onomastiques*, Bucarest, pp. 139–169.

Conea, Ion 1935: *Basarabii din Argeş. Despre originea lor teritorială şi etnică* [The Basarabs of *Argeş*. On their geographical and ethnic roots], Bucureşti.

Coniaris, Anthony 1998: *Philokalia. The Bible of Orthodox Spirituality*, Minneapolis.

Constantelos, Demetrios J. 1962: Philanthropia as an Imperial Virtue in the Byzantine Empire of the Tenth Century, in *Anglican Theological Review* 44, no. 4, pp. 351–365.

Constantinescu, Nicolae A. 1921: *Neagoe-Vodă Basarab şi Sfântul Nifon* [Neagoe Voivode Basarab and Saint Niphon], Bucureşti.

Constantinides, Constantine N. 1982: *Higher Education in Byzantium in the Thirteenth and Early Fourteenth Centuries (1204–ca. 1310)*, Nicosia.

Costăchel, Valeria et al. 1957: *Viaţa feudală în Ţara Românească şi Moldova (sec. XIV–XVII)* [Feudal life in Wallachia and Moldavia between the 14th and 17th centuries], Bucureşti.

Courtenay, William J. 2008: *Ockham and Ockhamism. Studies in the Dissemination and Impact of His Thought*, Leiden/Boston.

Crăciun, Ioachim/A. Ilieş 1963: *Repertoriul manuscriselor de cronici interne, sec. XV–XVIII privind istoria României* [An inventory of domestic manuscript chronucles relating to the history of Romania, 15th–18th c.], Bucureşti.

Creţu, Grigore 1900: Studiu introductiv [Introductory study], in Mardarie Cozianul, *Lexicon slavo-românesc şi tâlcuirea numelor din 1649*, ed. G. Creţu, Bucureşti.

Crum, Roger/J. T. Paoletti (eds) 2006: *Renaissance Florence. A Social History*, Cambridge.

Cumont, Franz 1910: *Die orientalischen Religionen im römischen Heidentum*, Leipzig/Berlin.

Cutinelli-Rèndina, Emanuele 1987: Machiavelli storico: rassegna di studi 1965–1985, in *Rivista di Storia della Storiografia Moderna* 8, pp. 57–72.

—— 1994: Rassegna di studi sulle opere politiche e storiche di Niccolò Machiavelli (1969–1992), in *Lettere Italiane* 46, pp. 123–172.

D'Alverny, Marie-T. 1982: Translations and Translators, in R. L. Benson/G. Constable, *Renaissance and Renewal in the Twelfth century*, Oxford, pp. 421–462.

Daly, Lawrence J. 1975: Themistius' Concept of Philanthropia, in *Byzantion* 45, no. 1, pp. 22–40.

Dandelet, Thomas 2007: Creating a Protestant Constantine. Martin Bucer's *De regno Christi* and the Foundations of English Imperial Political Theology, in C. Ocker et al. (eds), *Politics and Reformations. Communities, Polities, Nations, and Empires*, Leiden/Boston, pp. 539–550.

Daničić, Gjuro 1872: Tri stare priče, in *Sterine* 4, pp. 63–80.

Davie, Grace 2002: *Europe. The Exceptional Case*, London.

Danz, Christian 2006: Wort Gottes, Kirche, Organisation. Zur evangelischen Ekklesiologie im Anschluss an Martin Luther, in *WJT* 6, pp. 155–172.

Dapontés, Constantin 1880: *Éphémérides daces on Chronique de la guerre de quatre ans (1736–1739)*, vol. 1, Paris.

Daston, Lorraine 2008: On Scientific Observation, in *Focus-Isis* 99, no. 1, pp. 97–110.

De Pace, Anna 2002: Copernicus Against a Rhetorical Approach to the Beauty of the Universe. The Influence of the *Phaedo* on the *De revolutionibus*, in E. Kessler/J. Maclean (eds), *Res et verba in der Renaissance*, Wiesbaden, pp. 77–115.

Decorte, Jos 2006: *Eine kurze Geschichte der mittelalterlichen Philosophie*, Paderborn.

Decot, Rolf 2007: *Luthers Reformation zwischen Theologie und Reichspolitik*, Frankfurt a. M.

Deér, Josef 1977a: Der Ursprung der Kaiserkrone, in P. Classen (ed.), *Byzanz und das abendländische Herrschertum. Ausgewählte Aufsätze von Josef Deér*, Sigmaringen, pp. 11–41.

—— 1977b: Byzanz und die Herrschaftszeichen des Abendlandes, in P. Classen (ed.), *Byzanz und das abendländische Herrschertum. Ausgewählte Aufsätze von Josef Deér*, Sigmaringen, pp. 42–69.

—— 1977c: Das Kaiserbild im Kreuz. Ein Beitrag zur politischen Theologie des früheren Mittelalters, in P. Classen (ed.), *Byzanz und das abendländische Herrschertum. Ausgewählte Aufsätze von Josef Deér*, Sigmaringen, pp. 125–177.

Degele, Nina/Christian Dries 2005: *Modernisierungstheorie. Eine Einführung*, München.

Del Treppo, Mario 2002: *Condottieri e uomini d'arme nell'Italia del Rinascimento*, Napoli.

Delatte, Louis (ed.) 1942: *Les traités de la Royauté d'Ecphante, Diotogène et Sthénidas*, Paris.

Delumeau, Jean 1985: *Angst im Abendland*, 2 vols, Reinbek b. Hamburg.

Demetracopoulos, John A. 2011: Palamas transformed. Palamite Interpretation of the Distinction Between God's 'Essence' and 'Energies' in Late Byzantium, in M. Hinterberger/C. Schabel (eds), *Greeks, Latins and Intellectual History 1204–1500*, Leuven, pp. 263–372.

DeMolen, Richard L. 1987: Erasmus as Adolescent. 'Shipwrecked am I, and Lost, 'Mid Water Chill'', in idem, *The Spirituality of Erasmus of Rotterdam*, Nieukoop, pp. 15–34.

—— 1987b: First Fruits. The Place of *Antibarbarorum Liber* and *De Contemptu Mundi* in the Formulation of Erasmus' Philosophia Christi, in idem, *The Spirituality of Erasmus of Rotterdam*, Nieukoop, pp. 125–142.

Dempf, Alois 1973: *Sacrum Imperium*, Darmstadt.

Demus, Otto 1975: The Style of the Kaiye Djami and Its Place in the Development of Palaeologan Art, in P. A. Underwood (ed.), *The Kariye Djami*, vol. 4, Princeton, pp. 107–160.

Denize, Eugen 1995: *Ţările Române şi Veneţia. Relaţiile politice (1441–1541)* [The Danubian Principalities and Venice. Political Relations (1441–1541)], Bucureşti.

Depietri, Marco 2010: *Der jüngere Physiologus. Eine sprachwissenschaftliche Untersuchung*, Hamburg.

Deppe, Frank 1987: *Niccolò Machiavelli. Zur Kritik der reinen Politik*, Köln.

Di Maria, Salvatore 1992: Machiavelli's Ironic View of History, in *Renaissance Quarterly* 45, no. 2, pp. 248–270.

Dickinson, John C. 1950: *The Origins of the Austin Canons and Their Introduction into England*, London.

Diesner, Hans-J. 1987: Fine als Staatszweck/Staatsräson bei Machiavelli, in *Antike und Abendland* 33, no. 2, pp. 163–171.

—— 1992: Die politische Welt des Niccolò Machiavelli, in *SSAWL*, Phil.-hist. Kl., 132, no. 3.

—— 1993: *Virtù, Fortuna und das Prinzip Hoffnung bei Machiavelli*, Göttingen.

—— 1994: *Machiavellis Illusion eines perfekten Staates*, Göttingen.

Dieten, Jan-L. Van, 1979: Politische Ideologie und Niedergang in Byzanz der Palaiologen, in *Zeitschrift für historische Forschungen* 6, pp. 1–35.

Dieter, Theodor 2001: *Der junge Luther und Aristoteles. Eine historisch-systematische Untersuchung zum Verhältnis von Theologie und Philosophie*, Berlin/New York.

Dietz, Mary G./John Langton 1987: Machiavelli's Paradox. Trapping or Teching the Prince, in *American Political Science Review* 81, no. 4, pp. 1277–1288.

Dilger, Konrad 1967: *Untersuchungen zur Geschichte des Osmanischen Hofzeremoniells im 15. und 16. Jahrhundert*, München.

Dillon, John M. 1997: Die Entwicklung des Mittelplatonismus, in T. Kobusch/ B. Mojsisch (eds), *Platon in der abendländischen Geistesgeschichte*, Darmstadt, pp. 15–32.

Dilthey, Wilhelm 1914: *Gesammelte Schriften 2. Weltanschauung und Analyse des Menschen seit Renaissance und Reformation*, Leipzig/Berlin.

Dingel, Irene/Christiane Tietz 2011: Vorwort, in eaedem (eds), *Die politische Aufgabe von Religion. Perspektiven der drei monotheistischen Religionen*, Göttingen, pp. 9–10.

Dingel, Irene/Günther Wartenberg (eds) 2002: *Die theologische Fakultät Wittenberg 1502 bis 1602*, Leipzig.

Dinzelbacher, Peter 2009: *Unglaube im 'Zeitalter des Glaubens'. Atheismus und Skeptizismus im Mittelalter*, Badenweiler.

Djamo-Diaconiţă, Lucia 1965: Contribuţii la studiul terminologiei social-politice a slavonei româneşti [A contribution to the study of socio-political terminolgy in Romanian Church Slavonic], in *Romanoslavica* 12, pp. 93–108.

—— 1977: Contribuţii la cunoaşterea slavonei româneşti. Elemente româneşti în varianta slavonă a Învăţăturilor lui Neagoe Basarab [A contribution to Romanian Church Slavonic. Romanian elements in the Slavonic version of the teachings of Neagoe Basarab], in *Studii şi cercetări lingvistice* 28, pp. 295–302.

Djuvara, Neagu 2000: Iarăşi despre Negru Vodă şi 'Descălecătoare', in *Magazin istoric* 34, no. 7–8, pp. 28–31 und 53–57.

Döhle, Hans-Jürgen 2007: Schwein, Geflügel und Fisch – Bei Luthers zu Tisch, in H. Meller (ed.), *Luther in Mansfeld. Forschungen am Elternhaus des Reformators*, Halle/Saale, pp. 169–186.

Dohrn-Van Rossum, Gerhard 2007: Staatsformen im Mittelalter, in A. Gallus/E. Jesse (eds), *Staatsformen. Von der Antike bis zur Gegenwart*, Bonn, pp. 91–122.

Dolfen, Christian 1936: *Die Stellung des Erasmus von Rotterdam zur scholastischen Methode*, Osnabrück.

Dölger, Franz 1937: Rom in der Gedankenwelt der Byzantiner, in *ZKG* 56, no. 1, pp. 1–42.

—— 1940: Das Sonnengleichnis in einer Weihnachtspredigt des Bischofs Zeno von Verona, in *Antike und Christentum. Kultur- und religionsgeschichtliche Studien* 6, no. 1, pp. 1–58.

—— 1953: *Der griechische Barlaam-Roman. Ein Werk des H. Johannes von Damaskos*, Ettal.

—— 1956: Die Entwicklung der byzantinischen Kaisertitulatur und die Datierung von Kaiserdarstellungen in der byzantinischen Kleinkunst, in idem, *Byzantinische Diplomatik*, Speyer am Rhein, pp. 130–151.

—— 1976: Die 'Familie der Könige' im Mittelalter, in idem, *Byzanz und die europäische Staatenwelt. Ausgewählte Vorträge und Aufsätze*, Darmstadt, pp. 34–69.

Donat, Ion 1934: Toponimie turanică şi vechiu-germană în Dolj [Turanic and Old German toponymy in Dolj], in *Arhivele Olteniei* 13, no. 71–73, pp. 198.

Dotti, Ugo 2003: *Machiavelli rivoluzionario. Vita e opera*, Roma.

Downey, Glanville 1955: Philanthropia in Religion and Statecraft in the Fourth Century after Christ, in *Historia* 4, pp. 199–208.

Dreier, Volker 2005: *Die Architektur politischen Handelns. Machiavelli's Il Principe im Kontext der modernen Wissenschaftstheorie*, Freiburg/München.

Dresden, Sem 1969: Érasme et la notion de humanitas, in J. Coppens (ed.), *Scrinium Erasmianum I*, Leiden, pp. 527–545.

Drömann, Hans-Christian 2007: Bernahrd von Clairvaux. Spuren seiner Frömmigkeit in der Kirche der Reformation, in *Cistercienserchronik* 114, pp. 329–336.

Duchhardt, Heinz 2000: Zwischen Friedensvision und Konturierung des 'modernen' Völkerrechts. Die Epoche Karls V., in C. Strosetzki (ed.), *Aspectos históricos y culturales bajo Carlos V*, Madrid, pp. 138–145.

Duchrow, Ulrich 1981: Ergebnisse und offene Fragen zur 'Civitas'-Lehre Augustins, in C. Andresen (ed.), *Zum Augustin-Gespräch der Gegenwart II*, Darmstadt, pp. 205–226.

—— ²1983: *Christenheit und Weltverantwortung. Traditionsgeschichte und systematische Struktur der Zweireichelehre*, Stuttgart.

Dülmen, Andrea van, 1983: *Luther-Chronik. Daten zu Leben und Werk*, München.

Dumitriu-Snagov, I. 1996: *Monumenta Romaniae Vaticana*, Rom.

Durandin, Catherine 1995: *Histoire des Roumains*, Paris.

Duțu, Alexandru 1968: Le miroir des princes dans la culture roumaine, in *RESEE* 6, pp. 439–479.

—— 1984: *Humanisme, Baroque, Lumières. L'exemple roumain*, Bucarest.

Dvornik, Francis 1966: *Early Christian and Byzantine Political Philosophy. Origins and Background*, 2 vols, Washington, DC.

Dyckhoff, Peter 2006: *Das Gebet als Quelle des Lebens. Systematisch-theologische Untersuchungen des Ruhegebetes ausgehend von Johannes Cassian*, München.

Dykema, Peter A./H. A. Oberman (eds) 1993: *Anticlericalism in Late Medieval and Early Modern Europe*, Leiden.

Eberhardt Bate, Heidi 2007: Portrait and Pageantry. New Idioms in the Interaction Between City and Empire in the Sixteenth-Century Nuremberg, in C. Ocker et al. (eds), *Politics and Reformations. Communities, Polities, Nations, and Empires*, Leiden/Boston, pp. 121–141.

Eberhardt, Otto 1977: *Via regia. Der Fürstenspiegel Smaragds von St. Mihiel und seine literarische Gattung*, München.

Eberle, Christian G. (ed.) 1873: *Luthers Psalmen-Auslegung. Ein Kommentar zu den poetischen oder Lehrbüchern des Alten Testaments*, Stuttgart.

Edsman, Carl-M. 1959: *The Sacral Kingship*, Leiden.

Edwards Jr., Mark U. 1988: Statistics on Sixteenth-Century Printing, in P. N. Bebb/pp. Marshall (eds), *The Process of Change in Early Modern Europe*, Athen, pp. 149–163.

Ehmann, Johannes 2008: *Luther, Türken und Islam. Eine Untersuchung zum Türken- und Islambild Martin Luthers (1515–1546)*, Heidelberg.

Ehrenpreis, Stefan/Ute-L. Heumann ²2008: *Reformation und Konfessionelles Zeitalter*, Darmstadt.

Eisenstadt, Shmuel N. 2003: *Comparative Civilizations and Multiple Modernities,* Part I, Leiden/Boston.

—— ²2005: Die Achsenzeit in der Weltgeschichte, in H. Joas/K. Wiegandt (eds), *Die kulturellen Werte Europas,* Frankfurt a. M., pp. 40–68.

El-Khoury, Nabil 1976: *Die Interpretation der Welt bei Ephraem dem Syrer (4. Jahrhundert),* Tübingen.

Elian, Alexandre 1967: Byzance et les Roumains à la fin du Moyen Age, in J. M. Hussey/D. Obolensky/pp. Runciman (eds), *Proceedings of the XIIIth International Congress of Byzantine Studies Oxford 5–10 September 1966,* London, pp. 195–203.

Ellinger, Georg 1888: Die antiken Quellen der Staatslehre Machiavellis, in *Zeitschrift für die gesamte Staatswissenschaft* 44, pp. 1–58.

Emme, Dietrich 1983: *Martin Luther. Seine Jugend- und Studentenzeit 1483–1505,* Bonn.

Emminger, Kurt 1913: *Studien zu den griechischen Fürstenspiegeln,* München.

Engel, Josef ⁴1994: Von der spätmittelalterlichen *republica Christiana* zum Mächte-Europa der Neuzeit, in T. Schieder (ed.), *Handbuch der europäischen Geschichte 3; Die Entstehung des neuzeitlichen Europa,* Stuttgart, pp. 1–448.

Enßlin, Wilhelm 1975: Gottkaiser und Kaiser von Gottes Gnade, *SBAW,* Phil.-Hist. Kl., no. 6, 1943. Reprinted in H. Hunger (ed.), *Das byzantinische Herrscherbild,* Darmstadt, pp. 54–85.

Ensslin, Wilhelm 1975: Staat und Kirche von Konstantin d. Gr. bis Theodosius d. Gr. Ein Beitrag zur Frage nach dem 'Cäsaropapismus', in H. Hunger (ed.): *Das byzantinische Herrscherbild,* Darmstadt, pp. 193–205.

Enthoven, Ludwig 1909: über die *Institutio Principis Christiani* des Erasmus: Ein Beitrag zur Theorie der Fürstenerziehung, in *NJKAGDLP* 24, pp. 313–329.

Erikson, Erik H. 1975: *Der junge Mann Luther. Eine psychoanalytische und historische Studie,* Frankfurt a. M.

Escribano-Alberca, Ignacio 1972: Zum zyklischen Zeitbegriff der alexandrinischen und kappadokischen Theologie, in *Studia Patristica* 11, pp. 42–51.

Espagne, Michel 2013: Comparison and Transfer. A Question of Method, in M. Middell/L. Roura (eds), *Transnational Challenges to National History Writing,* New York, pp. 36–53.

Estes, James M. 1992: Officium principis christiani. Erasmus and the Origins of the Protestant State Church, in *ARG* 83, pp. 49–72.

—— 2003: Luther and the Role of Secular Authority in the Reformation, in *Lutheran Quarterly* 17, pp. 199–225.

Etzioni, Amitai 2003: What Is Political?, in A. Nassehi/M. Schroeder (eds), *Der Begriff des Politischen,* Baden-Baden, pp. 89–99.

Ewig, Eugen 1975: Das Bild Constantins des Großen in den ersten Jahrhunderten des abendländischen Mittelalters, in H. Hunger (ed.), *Das byzantinische Herrscherbild*, Darmstadt, pp. 133–192.

Fabisch, Peter 2008: *Julius exclusus e coelis. Motive und Tendenzen gallikanischer und bibelhumanistischer Papstkritik im Umfeld des Erasmus*, Münster.

Fairman, H. F. 1958: The Kingship Rituals of Egypt, in pp. H. Hooke (ed.), *Myth, Ritual and Kingship. Essays on the Theory and Practice of Kingship in the Ancient Near East and Israel*, Oxford, pp. 74–104.

Falco, Marian J. (ed.) 2004: *Feminist Interpretation of Machiavelli*, Pennsylvania.

Farina, Raffaele 1966: *L'impero e l'imperatore cristiano in Eusebio di Cesarea*, Zürich.

Faroqhi, Suraiya 2008: *Another Mirror for Princes. The Public Image of the Ottoman Sultans and Its Reception*, Istanbul.

Felmy, Karl Ch. 2003: Warum und zu welchem Behufe treiben wir Ostkirchenkunde?, in *EVKOC* 3, pp. 5–16.

Femia, Joseph V. 2004: *Machiavelli Revisited*, Cardiff.

Fidora, Alexander 2007: Politik, Religion und Philosophie in den Wissenschaftseinteilungen der Artisten im 13. Jahrhundert, in idem et al. (eds), *Politischer Aristotelismus und Religion in Mittelalter und Früher Neuzeit*, Berlin, pp. 27–36.

Filitti, Ioan C. 1922a: Craioveştii, in *Convorbiri literare* 54, no. 3, pp. 193–228.

—— 1922b: Craioveştii, 2. Teil, in *Convorbiri literare* 54, no. 4, pp. 292–320.

—— 1931: Despina, princesse de Valachie, fille présumée de Jean Brankovitch, in *Revista istorică română* 1, pp. 241–250.

Finnis, John 2008: The Ethics of War and Peace in the Catholic Natural Law Tradition, in J. A. Coleman (ed.), *Christian Political Ethics*, Princeton/Oxford, pp. 191–216.

Fiore, Silvia R. 1990: *Niccolò Machiavelli. An Annotated Bibliography of Modern Criticism and Scholarship*, New York.

Fischer-Galati, Stephen 1959: *Ottoman Imperialism and German Protestantism (1521–1555)*, Cambridge.

Fischer, Markus 2000: *Well-Ordered License. On the Unity of Machiavelli's Thought*, Lanham.

Fischer, William 1887: Eine Kaiserkrönung in Byzantion, in *ZAG (KLK)* 4, pp. 81–102.

Flasch, Kurt 1986: *Das philosophische Denken im Mittelalter. Von Augustin zu Machiavelli*, Stuttgart.

Flogaus, Reinhard 2000: Luther versus Melanchthon? Zur Frage der Einheit der Wittenberger Reformation in der Rechtfertigungslehre, in *ARG* 91, pp. 6–46.

Fögen, Marie T. 1993: Das politische Denken der Byzantiner, in I. Fetscher/H. Münkler (eds), *Pipers Handbuch der politischen Ideen*, vol. 2, München/Zürich, pp. 41–85.

Fontana, Bendetto 1999: Love of Country and Love of God. The Political Uses of Religion in Machiavelli, in *Journal of the History of Ideas* 60, no. 4, pp. 639–658.

Förstemann, Carl E. (ed.) 1842: *Neues Urkundenbuch zur Geschichte der evangelischen Kirchen-Reformation*, vol. 1, Hamburg.

Förster, Stig 2010: *Rückkehr der Condottieri? Krieg und Militär zwischen staatlichem Monopol und Privatisierung; von der Antike bis zur Gegenwart*, München.

Fortin, Ernest L. 1959: *Christianisme et culture philosophique au cinquième siècle*, Paris.

Foucault, Michel 1999: Pastoral Power and Political Reason (1979), in idem, *Religion and Culture*, ed. J. R. Carrette, New York, pp. 135–154.

Frank, Erich 1962: Augustin und das griechische Denken, in C. Andresen (ed.), *Zum Augustinus-Gespräch der Gegenwart*, vol. 1, Darmstadt, pp. 182–197.

Frank, Günter (ed.) 2009: *Humanismus und Europäische Identität*, Ubstadt-Weiher.

Fricke, Dietmar 1967: *Die französischen Fassungen der* Institutio Principis Christiani *des Erasmus von Rotterdam*, Kölner romanistische Arbeiten 39, Genève/Paris.

Frieß, Peer/Rolf Kießling (eds) 1999: *Konfessionalisierung und Region*, Konstanz.

Frohne, Renate 1985: *Agapetus Diaconus. Untersuchungen zu den Quellen und zur Wirkungsgeschichte des ersten byzantinischen Fürstenspiegels*, PhD thesis, University of Tübingen.

Frosini, Fabio 2006: L'ambiguità del vero il rischio della virtù. Una lettura del *Principe*, in F. Del Luchese/L. Sartorello/pp. Visentin (eds), *Machiavelli. Immaginazione e contingenza*, Pisa, pp. 31–66.

Fryde, Edmund 2000: *The Early Palaeologan Renaissance (1261–ca. 1360)*, Leiden.

Frygos, Antonis 2005: *Della controversia palamitica alla polemica esicastica (con un'edizione critica delle Epistole greche di Barlaam)*, Rom.

Fuchs, Franz (ed.) 2006: *Die Pirckheimer. Humanismus in einer Nürnberger Patrizierfamilie*, Wiesbaden.

Fuchs, Thomas/Sven Trakulhun 2003: Kulturtransfer in der Frühen Neuzeit. Europa und die Welt, in eidem (eds), *Das eine Europa und die Vielfalt der Kulturen*, Berlin, pp. 7–24.

Fusero, Clemente 1966: *I Borgia*, Mailand.

Gail, Anton J. (ed.) 1968: *Erasmus von Rotterdam. Fürstenerziehung/Institutio Principis Christiani*, Paderborn.

Gaille-Nikodimov, Marie 2007: An Introduction to *The Prince* Edited and Translated from the French by Gerald Seaman, in P. Vilches/G. Seaman (eds), *Seeking Real Truths. Multidisciplinary Perspectives on Machiavelli*, Leiden/ Boston, pp. 21–42.

Gänssler, Hans-J. 1983: *Evangelium und weltliches Schwert. Hintergrund, Entstehungsgeschichte und Anlass von Luthers Scheidung zweier Reiche oder Regimente*, Wiesbaden.

Garin, Eugenio 1947: *Der italienische Humanismus*, Bern.

Garver, Eugene 1987: *Machiavelli and the History of Prudence*, Madison/London.

Garzaniti, Marcello 2001: *Die altslavische Version der Evangelien. Forschungsgeschichte und zeitgenössische Forschung*, Köln.

Gaster, Moses 1883: *Literatura populară română* [Die rumänische Volksliteratur], Bucureşti.

—— 1886–1888: Il Physiologus rumeno, in *Archivio glottologico italiano* 10, pp. 273–304.

—— 1891: *Chrestomaţie română. Texte tipărite şi manuscrise (sec. XVI–XIX). Dialectale şi populare* [Romanian chrestomathy. Manuscript and printed texts (16th–19th c.). Dialect and vernacular], Bucureşti.

—— 1901: Geschichte der rumänischen Literatur, in G. Gröber (ed.), *Grundriss der romanischen Philologie*, vol. 2/3, Straßburg, pp. 262–428.

Gaude, Werner 1979–1983: Zur Krankengeschichte Martin Luthers, in *Beiträge zur Geschichte der Universität Erfurt (1392–1816)* 19, pp. 53–112.

Gäumann, Andreas 2001: *Reich Christi und Obrigkeit. Eine Studie zum reformatorischen Denken und Handeln Martin Bucers*, Bern.

Geary, Patrick 2001: Vergleichende Geschichte und sozialwissenschaftliche Theorie, in M. Borgolte (ed.), *Das europäische Mittelalter im Spannungsbogen des Vergleichs*, Berlin, pp. 29–38.

Geerken, John H. 1976: Machiavelli Studies since 1969, in *Journal of the History of Ideas* 37, pp. 351–368.

—— 1999: Machiavelli's Moses and Reanissance Politics, in *Journal of the History of Ideas* 60, no. 4, pp. 579–595.

Geerlings, Wilhelm 1997: Libri platonicorum. Die philosophische Bildung Augustins, in T. Kobusch/B. Mojsisch (ed.), *Platon in der abendländischen Geistesgeschichte*, Darmstadt, pp. 60–70.

Gelderen, Martin van, 2005: Wie die Universalmonarchie der Volkssouveränität weichen musste, in B. Jussen (ed.), *Die Macht des Königs. Herrschaft in Europa vom Frühmittelalter bis in die Neuzeit*, München, pp. 299–318.

Georgescu, Constantin 1963: Introducere [Introduction], in Radu Popescu Vornicul, *Istoriile domnilor Ţării Româneşti*, ed. C. Grecescu, Bucureşti, pp. LI–CVI.

Georgescu, Valentin Al. 1969: Continuitate elenistico-romană şi inovaţie în doctrina bizantină a filantropiei şi indulgenţei imperiale [Hellenistic and Roman conituity in the Byzantine doctrine of philantrophy and the emperor's charity], in *Studii clasice* 11, pp. 187–219.

Georgescu, Valentin Al. 1971: L'idée impériale byzantine et les réactions des réalités roumaines (XIVe–XVIIIe siècle), in *Byzantina* 3, pp. 313–339.

Gerber, Adolf 1912a/b und 1913: *Niccolò Machiavelli. 147 Faksimiles zur Illustration der Handschriften, Ausgaben und übersetzungen seiner Werke im 16. und 17. Jahrhundert*, Teil 1: Handschriften, Gotha, Teil 3: Übersetzungen, Gotha und Teil 4: Tafeln, München.

Germanisches Nationalmuseum Nürnberg (ed.) 1983: *Martin Luther und die Reformation in Deutschland*, Frankfurt a. M.

Gerstel, Sharon E. J./Alice-Mary Talbot 2006: The Culture of the Lay Piety in Medieval Byzantium 1054–1453, in M. Angold (ed.), *The Cambridge History of Christianity*, vol. 5: Eastern Christianity, Cambridge, pp. 79–100.

Gerstenkorn, Eugen 1956: *Weltlich Regiment zwischen Gottesreich und Teufelsmacht. Die Staatstheoretischen Auffassung Martin Luthers und ihre politische Bedeutung*, Bonn.

Gerstner, Ruth 1941: *Die Geschichte der lothringischen und rheinischen Pfalzgrafschaft*, Bonn.

Ghika-Budeşti, Nicolae 1927: *Evoluţia arhitecturii în Muntenia*, Partea I: Înrâuririle străine de la origină până la Neagoe Basarab [The development of architecture in Wallachia. Part I: Foreign influence from the beginnings to Neagoe Basarab], Bucureşt.

Gil, Christiane 1994: *Machiavelli. Eine Biographie*, Solothurn/Düsseldorf.

Gilbert, Allan H. 1938: *Machiavelli's Prince and Its Forerunners*, Durham.

Gilbert, Allan (ed.) ⁴1965: *Machiavelli. The Chief Works and Others*, 3 vols, Durham, NC.

Gilbert, Felix 1939: The Humanist Concept of the Prince and The Prince of Machiavelli, in *JMH* 11, no. 4, pp. 449–483.

—— 1965: *Machiavelli and Guicciardini. Politics and History in Sixteenth-Century Florence*, Princeton.

—— 1991: *Guicciardini, Machiavelli und die Geschichtsschreibung der italienischen Renaissance*, Berlin.

Gillet, Lev 1997: *The Jesus Prayer*, New York.

Gindele, Egon 1977: *Bibliographie zur Geschichte und Theologie des Augustiner-Eremitenordens bis zum Beginn der Reformation*, Berlin/New York.

Girardet, Klaus M. 2007: Der Vorsitzende des Konzils von Nicaea (325) – Kaiser Konstantin d. Gr., in H. Schlange-Schöningen (ed.), *Konstantin und das Christentum*, Darmstadt, pp. 171–203.

Giurescu, Constantin C. 1926: *Contribuţiuni la studiul marilor dregătorii în sec. XIV şi XV* [Contributions to the study of high offices in the 14th and 15th centuries], Vălenii de Munte.

—— 1980: *Geschichte der Rumänen*, Bukarest.

—— 2003: *Istoria românilor* [History of the Romanians], Bucureşti.

Glixelli, Stefan 1933: Regulile de purtare la masă în românește [Table manners in Romanian], in *Revista istorică română* 3, pp. 327–333.

—— 1936–1937: Neagoe Basarab écrivain, in *Bulletin international de l'Académie polonaise des sciences et des lettres. Classe de philologie. Classe d'histoire et de philosophie*, no. 7–10, pp. 112–114.

Godin, André 1982: *Érasme lecteur d'Origène*, Genève.

Goez, Elke 2010: *Geschichte Italiens im Mittelalter*, Darmstadt.

Goldstaub, Max 1905: Physiologus-Fabeleien über das Brüten des Vogels Strauß, in *Festschrift für Adolf Tobler zum siebzigsten Geburtstage*, Braunschweig, pp. 153–190.

Goldstein, Jürgen 1998: *Nominalismus und Moderne*, Freiburg/München. Göllner, Carl 1961: *Turcica. Die europäischen Türkendrucke des XVI. Jahrhunderts*, vol. 1, București/Berlin.

Görz, Michael 1990: Gottes Wort als Einleitung zum Handeln für den lutherischen Fürsten, in H.-O. Mühleinsen/T. Stammen (eds), *Politische Tugendlehre und Regierungskunst*, Tübingen, pp. 117–139.

Gosewinkel, Dieter/Gunnar F. Schuppert 2008: Politische Kultur. Auf der Suche nach Konturen eines schillernden Begriffs, in eidem (eds), *Politische Kultur im Wandel von Staatlichkeit*, Berlin, pp. 11–40.

Grabar, André 1971: *L'empereur dans l'art byzantin*, London.

Grabmann, Martin 1934: Studien über den Einfluss der aristotelischen Philosophie auf die mittelalterlichen Theorien über das Verhältnis von Kirche und Staat, in *SBAW*, Phil.-Hist. Abt., 2.

—— [17]1946: *Thomas von Aquin*, München/Kempten.

Graf, Friedrich W. 2004: *Die Wiederkehr der Götter. Religion in der modernen Kultur*, Bonn.

Gräf, Holger Th. 2005: 'Erbfeind der Christenheit' oder potentieller Bündnispartner? Das Osmanenreich im europäischen Mächtesystem des 16. und 17. Jahrhunderts–gegenwartspolitisch betrachtet, in M. Kurz et al. (eds), *Das Osmanische Reich und die Habsburgermonarchie*, Wien/München, pp. 37–51.

Grane, Leif 1975: *Modus loquendi theologicus. Luthers Kampf um die Erneuerung der Theologie*, Leiden.

Graupner, Silke 2009: *Zar Nikolaj II. und seine Familie – Heilige der Russisch-Orthodoxen Kirche: Die Kanonisierung aus religions- und kulturgeschichtlicher Perspektive*, Berlin.

Grecescu, Constantin/Dan Simonescu: Introducere, in eidem (eds), *Istoria Țării Românești 1290–1690. Letopisețul Cantacuzinesc*, București 1960, pp. V–LXII.

Grecu, Vasile 1924: *Darstellungen altheidnischer Denker und Schriftsteller in der Kirchenmalerei des Morgenlandes*, Bukarest.

―― 1933: *Influența bizantină în literatura românească* [The Byzantine influence in Romanian literature], Cernăuți.

―― 1939: *Manuscrisul din '1654' pretins pierdut al Învățăturilor lui Neagoe Basarab* [The supposedly lost manuscript of the teachings of Neagoes Basarabs dated to '1654'], Sonderdruck aus: Convorbiri literare, 10–11–12, pp. 1851–1865.

―― 1943a: Izvor sau prelucrare a uneia din Învățăturile lui Neagoe Voevod? [Original source or reworking of one of teachings of Neagoe Voivode?], in *Omagiu lui Ioan Lupaș la împlinirea vârstei de 60 de ani. August 1940*, București, pp. 295–315.

―― 1943b: *O versiune nouă a unei Învățături a lui Neagoe Basarab* [A new version of one of the teachings of Neagoe Basarab], București 1941 (reprinted from: *Omagiul lui Ioan Lupaș la împlinirea vârstei de 60 de ani în 1940*, București, pp. 295–315).

―― 1944: Introducere, in *Gavriil Protul. Viața Sfântului Nifon* [The life of Saint Niphon], ed. V. Grecu, vol. 1, București, pp. 5–23.

―― 1950: Bulgaria în nordul Dunării în veacurile al IX–X-lea [Bulgaria north of the Danube in the 9th and 10th centuries], in *Studii și cercetări de istorie medie*, 1, pp. 223–236.

Green, Lowell C. 2000: The Question of Theosis in the Perspective of Lutheran Christology, in D. O. Wenthe et al. (eds), *All Theology is Christology*, Indiana, pp. 163–180.

Greene, Thomas M. 1984: The End of Discourse in Machiavelli's *Prince*, in *Yale French Studies* 67, pp. 57–71.

Greschat, Martin 2010: *Philipp Melanchthon. Theologe, Pädagoge und Humanist*, Gütersloh.

Grigore, Mihai-D./Radu H. Dinu/Marc Zivojinovic 2012: Herrschaft (nicht) beherrschen. Zentrale Begriffe und Area Studies. Eine Einleitung, in eidem (eds), *Herrschaft in Südosteuropa. Kultur- und sozialwissenschaftliche Studien*, Göttingen, pp. 7–20.

Grigore, Mihai-D. 2008: Die ethische Handlungsgemeinschaft als Voraussetzung der Hermeneutik. Zur Dialektik des Handelns und Verstehens, in C. Ernst/W. Sparn/H. Wagner (eds), *Kulturhermeneutik. Interdisziplinäre Beiträge zum Umgang mit kultureller Differenz*, München, pp. 455–472.

―― 2009: *Ehre und Gesellschaft. Ehrkonstrukte und soziale Ordnungsvorstellungen am Beispiel des Gottesfriedens (10. bis 11. Jahrhundert)*, Darmstadt.

―― 2010: Der Mensch zwischen Gott und Staat. Überlegungen zu politischen Formen im Christentum, in *Studii Teologie. Revista Facultăților de Teologie din Patriarhia Română* 1, pp. 105–175.

―― 2012a: Das Unbehagen des Politischen zwischen Sündhaftigkeit und Natürlichkeit. Anmerkung anhand des byzantinischen Kaiserbildes, in

G. Krieger (ed.), *Herausforderung durch Religion? Begegnungen der Philosophie mit Religionen in Mittelalter und Renaissance*, Würzbürg, pp. 343–356.

—— 2012b: Legitimation von Herrschaft zwischen Verfahren und Tradition am Beispiel Neagoe Basarabs (1512–1521), in M.-D. Grigore/R. H. Dinu/M. Zivojinovic (eds), *Herrschaft in Südosteuropa. Kultur- und sozialwissenschaftliche Perspektiven*, Göttingen, pp. 79–96.

—— 2012c: Ruling Christian. Neagoe Basarab and the Beginning of 'Political Proto-Modernity' in the 16th Century Wallachia. A Case Study, in *Religion, State, and Society* 40, no. 3–4, pp. 286–300.

—— 2017: Space of Power. State Consolidation by Means of Religious Policy in the Danube Principalities in the Fourteenth to Sixteenth Centuries, in *Acta Poloniae Historica* 116, pp. 35–56.

—— 2019a: Europa – Christianitas – Europa Christiana. Zur Geschichte eines umstrittenen Narratives anhand mittelalterlicher Quellen, in M. Meyer-Blanck (ed.), *Christentum und Europa*, Leipzig, pp. 457–473.

—— 2019b: Long Story: Barlaam and Josaphat, Physiologus, and Their Influence on a Wallachian Speculum Principis from the 16th Century, in: A. Cuffel, N. Jaspert (eds), Entangled Hagiographies of the Religious Other, Cambridge, pp. 173–199.

Grimmelshausen, Johann 1999: *Simplicissimus*, tr. Mike Mitchell, Sawtry, Cambs.

Grobien, Gifford 2009: A Lutheran Understanding of Natural Law in the Three Estates, in *Concordia Theological Quarterly*, 73, pp. 211–229.

Groß-Albenhausen, Kirsten 1999: *Imperator christianissimus. Der christliche Kaiser bei Ambrosius und Johannes Chrisostomus*, Frankfurt am Main.

Grumel, Venance 1951: Remarques sur la Dioptra de Philippe le Solitaire, in *BZ* 44, no. 1–2, pp. 198–211.

Grundmann, Siegfried 1972: Kirche und Staat nach der Zwei-Reiche-Lehre Luthers, in G. Wolf (ed.), *Luther und die Obrigkeit*, Darmstadt, pp. 341–369.

Guggisberg, Hans R./Gottfried G. Krodel (eds) 1993: *Die Reformation in Deutschland und Europa: Interpretationen und Debatten*, Sonderband d. ARG, Gütersloh.

Gundert, Hermann 1969: ΘΕΙΟΣ im politischen Denken Platons, in P. Steinmetz (ed.), *Politeia und Res Publica. Beiträge zum Verständnis von Politik, Recht und Staat in der Antike*, Wiesbaden, pp. 91–107.

Günsberg, Maggie 1995: The End Justifies the Means: End-Orientation and the Discourses of Power, in M. Coyle (ed.), *Niccolò Machiavelli's the Prince. New Interdisciplinary Essays*, Manchester/New York, pp. 115–150.

Günter, Wolfgang 1976: *Martin Luthers Vorstellung von der Reichsverfassung*, Münster.

Guran, Petre 2001: Jean VI Cantacuzène, l'hésychasme et l'empire. Les miniatures du codex Parisinus graecus, in idem (ed.): *L'empereur hagiographe*, Bucarest, pp. 73–121.

—— 2001: Patriarche hésychaste et empereur latinophrone. L'accord de 1380 sur les droits impériaux en matière ecclésiastique, in *RESEE* 39, pp. 53–63.

—— 2002: Nouvelles définitions du pouvoir patriarcal à la fin du XIVe siècle, in *RESEE* 40, pp. 109–124.

—— 2007: L'origine et la fonction théologico-politique de la couronne patriarcale, in *Dossiers byzantins 7. Le Patriarcat Œcuménique de Constantinople aux XIVe–XVIe siècles: rupture et continuité. Actes du colloque international Rome, 5–6–7 décembre 2005*, Paris, pp. 407–427.

Gurney, Oliver R. 1958: Hittite Kingship, in pp. H. Hooke (ed.), *Myth, Ritual and Kingship. Essays on the Theory and Practice of Kingship in the Ancient Near East and Israel*, Oxford, pp. 104–112.

Gutierrez, David (ed.) 1975–1988: *Geschichte des Augustinerordens*, 4 vols, Rom.

Haberland, Detlef (ed.) 2007: *Buch- und Wissenstransfer in Ostmittel- und Südosteuropa in der Frühen Neuzeit*, München.

Habermas, Jürgen ³2005: *Zwischen Naturalismus und Religion. Philosophische Aufsätze*, Frankfurt a. M.

—— 2012: 'Das Politische'. Der vernünftige Sinn eines zweifelhaften Erbstücks der Politischen Theologie, in E. Mendieta/J. VanAntwerpen (eds), *Religion und Öffentlichkeit*, Frankfurt a. M., pp. 28–52.

Hagen, Kenneth et al. 1991: *Annotated Bibliography of Luther Studies (1984–1989)*, Saint Louis.

Halkin, Léon E. 1986: Érasme, la guerre et la paix, in F. J. Worstbrock (ed.), *Krieg und Frieden im Horizont des Renaissancehumanismus*, Weinheim, pp. 13–44.

—— 1989: *Erasmus von Rotterdam. Eine Biographie*, Zürich.

Hamel, Adolf 1934: *Der junge Luther und Augustin*, Gütersloh.

Hamm, Berndt 1977: *Promissio, Pactum, Ordinatio. Freiheit und Selbstbindung Gottes in der scholastischen Gnadenlehre*, Tübingen.

—— 1986: Was ist reformatorische Rechtfertigungslehre?, in *Zeitschrift für Theologie und Kirche* 83, pp. 1–38.

—— 1990: Hieronymus-Begeisterung und Augustinismus in der Reformation, in K. Hagen (ed.), *Augustine, the Harvest and Theology (1300–1650)*, Leiden, pp. 127–235.

—— 1993: Von der spätmittelalterlichen *reformatio* zur Reformation: der Prozess normativer Zentrierung von Religion und Gesellschaft in Deutschland, in *ARG* 84, pp. 7–82.

—— 1995: Einheit und Vielfalt der Reformation – oder: Was die Reformation zur Reformation machte, in B. Hamm/B. Moeller/D. Wendenbourg (eds), *Reformations-Theorien*, Göttingen, pp. 57–127.

—— 2007: Wie mystisch war der Glaube Luthers?, in B. Hamm/V. Leppin (eds), *Gottes Nähe unmittelbar erfahren*, Tübingen, pp. 237–287.

—— 2008a: Die Einheit der Reformation in ihrer Vielfalt. Das Freiheitspotenzial der 95 Thesen vom 31. Oktober 1517, in B. Hamm/M. Welker, *Die Reformation. Potentiale der Freiheit*, Tübingen, pp. 29–66.

—— 2008b: Die Emergenz der Reformation, in B. Hamm/M. Welker, *Die Reformation. Potentiale der Freiheit*, Tübingen, pp. 1–27.

—— 2008c: Naher Zorn und nahe Gnade. Luthers frohe Klosterjahre als Beginn seiner reformatorischen Umorientierung, in A. Lexutt/V. Mantey/V. Ortmann (eds), *Reformation und Mönchtum. Aspekte eines Verhältnisses über Luther hinaus*, Tübingen, pp. 103–143.

—— 2012: Pure Gabe ohne Gegengabe – die religionsgeschichtliche Revolution der Reformation, in *JBTh* 27, 241–276.

Hammerstein, Notker 1981: Humanismus und Universitäten, in A. Buck (ed.), *Die Rezeption der Antike. Zum Problem der Kontinuität zwischen Mittelalter und Renaissance*, Hamburg, pp. 23–39.

—— 2003: *Bildung und Wissenschaft vom 15. bis zum 17. Jahrhundert*, München.

Häring, Nikolaus M. 1982: Commentary and Hermeneutics, in R. L. Benson/G. Constable (eds), *Renaissance and Renewal in the Twelfth Century*, Oxford, pp. 173–200.

Harkianakis, Stylianos 1971: Die Stellung des Kaisers in der byzantinischen Geistigkeit, dogmatisch gesehen, in *Byzantina* 3, pp. 45–50.

Härle, Wilfried 1987: Luthers Zwei-Regimenten-Lehre als Lehre vom Handeln Gottes, in *Marburger Jahrbuch Theologie* 1, pp. 12–32.

Harmening, Dieter 1983: *Der Anfang von Dracula zur Geschichte von Geschichten*, Würzburg.

Harmless, William 2004: *Desert Christians. An Introduction to the Literature of Early Monasticism*, Oxford.

Haşdeu, Bogdan-P. (ed.) 1865a: *Arhiva istorică a României* [The historical archive of Romania], vol. I/2, Bucureşti.

—— 1865b: *Arhiva istorică a României* [The historical archive of Romania], vol. II/1, Bucureşti.

—— 1865–1866: Tractatulu lui Negoia Basaraba despre arta militară [The treatise of Neagoe Basarab on the art of warfare], in *Buletinul instrucţiunei publice* 1, pp. 76–77.

—— ²1984: *Cuvente din bătrâni. Cărţile poporane ale românilor în secolul XVI* [Words handed down through the ages. The vernacular literature of the Romanians in the 16th century], Bucureşti.

Hatcher, Brian A. 1999: *Eclecticism and Modern Hindu Discourse*, New York/ Oxford.

Haug-Moritz, Gabriele 2007: Zwischen Spätmittelalter und Reformation – Politischer Föderalismus im Reich der Reformationszeit, in C. Ocker et al. (eds), *Politics and Reformations. Communities, Polities, Nations, and Empires*, Leiden/Boston, pp. 513–537.

Haupt, Heinz-G./Jürgen Kocka 1996: Historischer Vergleich. Methoden, Aufgaben, Probleme. Eine Einleitung, in eidem (eds), *Geschichte und Vergleich. Ansätze und Ergebnisse international vergleichender Geschichtsschreibung*, Frankfurt a. M., pp. 9–45.

Hausherr, Irenée 1978: *The Name of Jesus*, Kalamazoo.

Heckel, Johannes 1938: Cura religionis. Jus in sacra, in *Festschrift Ulrich Stutz*, Stuttgart, pp. 224–298.

Helmrath, Johannes 2013: *Wege des Humanismus*, Tübingen.

Hendrix, Scott H. 1990: Luther's Loyalties and the Augustinian Order, in K. Hagen (ed.), *Augustine, the Harvest, and Theology (1300–1650)*, Leiden, pp. 236–258.

Henkel, Nikolaus 1976: *Studien zum Physiologus im Mittelalter*, Tübingen.

Hennings, Ralph 1998: Hieronymus zum Bischofsamt und seine Autorität in dieser Frage bei Luther, Melanchthon und Zwingli, in L. Grane/A. Schindler/ M. Wriedt (eds), *Auctoritas Patrum II. Neue Beiträge zur Rezeption der Kirchenväter im 15. und 16. Jahrhundert*, vol. 1, Mainz, pp. 85–104.

Henry III, Patrick 1967: A Mirror for Justinian. The Ekthesis of Agapetus Diaconus, in *GRBS* 8, pp. 281–308.

Herding, Otto 1966: Isokrates, Erasmus und die Institutio Principis Chistiani, in R. Vierhaus/M. Botzenhart (eds), *Dauer und Wandel der Geschichte. Aspekte europäischer Vergangenheit*, Münster, pp. 101–142.

—— 1968: Die deutsche Gestalt der *Institutio Principis Christiani* des Erasmus. Leo Jud und Spalatin, in J. Fleckenstein (ed.), *Adel und Kirche. Gerd Tellenbach zum 65. Geburtstag dargebracht von Freunden und Schülern*, Freiburg, pp. 534–551.

—— 1974: Institutio Principis Christiani. Einleitung, in *Opera omnia Desiderii Erasmi Roterodami, Ordinis qvarti, Tomus primvs*, Amsterdam, pp. 95–130.

Hergenröther, Joseph 1867: *Photius. Patriarch von Konstantinopel*, vol. 1, Regensburg.

Hering, Gunnar 1989: Die Osmanenzeit im Selbstverständnis der Völker Südosteuropas, in H. G. Majer (ed.), *Die Staaten Südosteuropas und die Osmanen*, München, pp. 355–380.

Hermann-Otto, Elisabeth 2007: *Konstantin der Große*, Darmstadt.

Hermann, Rudolf 1961: Zur Kontroverse zwischen Luther und Latomus, in V. Vajta (ed.), *Luther und Melanchthon*, Göttingen, pp. 104–118.

Herrmann, Peter 1968: *Der römische Kaisereid, Untersuchungen zu seiner Herkunft und Entwicklung*, Göttingen.

Hertel, Johannes 1914: *Das Pancatantra. Seine Geschichte und seine Verbreitung*, Berlin.

Hiestand, Rudolf 1990: Eirene basileus – Die Frau als Herrscherin, in H. Hecker (ed.), *Der Herrscher. Leitbild und Abbild in Mittelalter und Renaissance*, Düsseldorf, pp. 253–284.

Hill, Robert C. 1998: Introduction, in *St. John Chrysostom. Commentary on the Psalms*, vol. 1, Brookline, pp. 1–44.

—— 2005: *Reading the Old Testament in Antioch*, Leiden/Boston.

Hinsley, Francis H. 1966: *Sovereignty*, London.

Hirsch McIntyre, Kevin-J. 1972: *Nominalism and the Theory of Political Obligation. Ockham and Hobbes*, Diss. Syracuse University.

Höchli, Daniel 2005: *Der Florentiner Republikanismus. Verfassungswirklichkeit und Verfassungsdenken zur Zeit der Renaissance*, Bern.

Hock, Wolfgang ⁴2003: Das Altkirchenslavische, in P. Rehder (ed.), *Einführung in die slavischen Sprachen (mit einer Einführung in die Balkanphilologie)*, Darmstadt, pp. 35–48.

Hoffmann, Lars 1992: *Die* Dioptra *des Philippos Monotropos. Eine Studie zu Verfasser, Werk und dessen Quellen, Diplom* thesis, University of Vienna.

Hoffmann, Manfred 1986: Erasmus on Church and Ministry, in *Yearbook* 6, pp. 1–30.

Hofmann, Hasso ⁴2008: *Einführung in die Rechts- und Staatsphilosophie*, Darmstadt.

Hofmeister, Adolf 1915: Das Wormser Konkordat. Zum Streit um seine Bedeutung, mit einer textkritischen Beilage, in *Forschungen und versuche zur Geschichte des Mittelalters und der Neuzeit. Festschrift für Dietrich Schäfer zum siebzigsten Geburtstag*, dargebracht von seinen Schülern, Jena, pp. 64–148.

Holenstein, André 1991: *Die Huldigung der Untertanen. Rechtskultur und Herrschaftsordnung (800–1800)*, Stuttgart/New York.

Holl, Karl 1921: Luther und das landeskirchliche Regiment, in idem, *Gesammelte Aufsätze zur Kirchengeschichte*, vol. 1: Luther, Tübingen, pp. 279–325.

Holzberg, Niklas 1981: *Willibald Pirckheimer. Griechischer Humanismus in Deutschland*, München.

Honecker, Martin 1978: Zur gegenwärtigen Interpretation der Zweireichelehre, in *ZKG* 89, no. 1–2, pp. 150–162.

Horkheimer, Max 1930: *Anfänge der bürgerlichen Geschichtsphilosophie*, Stuttgart.

Hort, Bernard 2000: Prélude à une théologie protestante de la mondialisation, in *Analecta Bruxellensia* 5, pp. 204–213.

Hösch, Edgar 2004: *Geschichte des Balkans*, München.

Höß, Irmgard 1984: *Georg Spalatin (1484–1545)*, Spalt.

Hoyer, Siegfried 1986: Luther und die Obrigkeit, in H. Bartel et al. (eds), *Martin Luther. Leistung und Erbe*, Berlin, pp. 126–131.

Huber, Manfred 1973: *Grundzüge der Geschichte Rumäniens*, Darmstadt.

Hübner, Kurt 1983: Der Begriff des Naturgesetzes in der Antike und in der Renaissance, in A. Buck/K. Heitmann (eds), *Die Antike-Rezeption in den Wissenschaften während der Renaissance*, Weinheim, pp. 7–27.

Hunger, Herbert 1963: Φιλανθρωπία. Eine griechische Wortprägung auf ihrem Wege von Aischylos bis Theodor Metochites, in *Anzeiger. Österreichische Akademie der Wissenschaften, Philosophisch.-historische Klasse* 100, pp. 1–20.

——— 1964: *Prooimion. Elemente der byzantinischen Kaiseridee in den Arengen der Urkunden*, Wien.

——— 1978: *Die hochsprachliche profane Literatur der Byzantiner*, vol. 1, München.

——— 1981: The Classical Tradition in Byzantine Literature. The Importance of Rhetoric, in M. Mullet/R. Scott (eds), *Byzantium and the Classical Tradition*, Birmingham, pp. 35–47.

Hunter, David G. 1988: Introduction, in *John Chrysostom, A Comparison Between a King and a Monk/Against the Opponents of the Monastic Life. Two Treatises by John Chrysostom*, Lewiston/Queenston, pp. 1–66.

Hyma, Albert ²1965: *The Christian Renaissance: A History of the Devotio Moderna*, Hamden.

——— 1972: *The Life of Desiderius Erasmus*, Assen.

Ierodiakonou, Katerina (ed.) 2002: *Byzantine Philosophy and its Ancient Sources*, Oxford.

Ijsewijn, Joseph 1969: Erasmus ex poeta theologus sive De litterarum instauratarum apud Hollandos incunabulis, in J. Coppens (ed.), *Scrinium Erasmianum I*, Leiden, pp. 375–389.

Iliescu, Octavian 1967: Când au fost traduse în românește Învățăturile lui Neagoe Basarab? [When were the *Teachings* translated into Romanian?], in *Argeș* 10, pp. 6–7.

Ilmer, Detlef 1986: Die Rezeption der spätantiken Mathematik im frühen Mittelalter, in L. Kriss-Rettenbeck/M. Liedtke (eds), *Erziehungs- und Unterrichtsmethoden im historischen Wandel*, Bad Heilbrunn, pp. 92–102.

Ionașcu, Iuvenalie 2005: *Neagoe Basarab, principe isihast* [Neagoe Basarab, a hesychast prince], Curtea de Argeș.

Ionescu-Gion, G. I. 1902: Boierii Craiovești [The Craiovescu boyars], in *Revista pentru Istorie, Arheologie și Filologie* 8, pp. 74–79.

Ionescu, Ioan 1971: Neagoe Basarab și ctitoriile sale [Neagoe Basarab and his foundations], in *Mitropolia Olteniei* 23, no. 9–10, pp. 653–675.

Iorga, Nicolae 1894: *Basarabii. Cine? – De unde? – De când?* [The Basarabs. Who? – From where? – Since when?], Bucureşti.

—— 1904: *Istoria literaturii religioase a românilor până la 1688* [History of the religious literature of the Romanians to 1688], Bucureşti.

—— 1925: *Istoria literaturii româneşti* [History of Romanian literature], vol. 1, Bucureşti.

—— 1972: *Bizanţ după Bizanţ*, Bucureşti (Original: Byzance après Byzance. Continuation de L'histoire de la vie byzantine, Bucarest: Inst. d'Études Byzantines 1935).

—— ²1985: *Istoria literaturii româneşti. Introducere sintetică* [History of Romanian literature. Synthetic introduction], Bucureşti.

—— 1989: Două documente din arhivele ragusane relative la un sol trimis la Veneţia de Basarab al III-lea (Neagoe) [Two documents from the archives of Ragusa relating to an envoy of Basarab III (Neagoe) to the republic of Venice], in *Arhiva societăţii ştiinţifice şi literare din Iaşi* 9, pp. 66–69.

Irigoin, Jean 1975: Centres de copie et bibliothèques, in *Byzantine Books and Bookmen*, ed. Dumbarton Oaks Center for Byzantine Studies, Washington, DC, pp. 17–27.

Iserloh, Erwin 1966: *Luther zwischen Reform und Reformation. Der Thesenanschlag fand nicht statt*, Münster.

Isnardi-Parente, Margherita 1988: Érasme, la République de Platon et la communauté de biens, in J. Sperna Weiland/W. T. M. Frijhoff (eds), *Erasmus of Rotterdam. The Man and the Scholar*, Leiden, pp. 40–45.

Ivanka, Endré von, 1952: Hesychasmus und Palamismus. Ihr gegenseitiges Verhältnis und ihre geistesgeschichtliche Bedeutung, in *JÖBG* 2, pp. 23–34.

—— 1954: Der Fall Konstantinopels und das byzantinische Geschichtsdenken, in *JÖBG* 3, pp. 19–35.

—— 1964: *Plato Christianus. übernahme und Umgestaltung des Platonismus durch die Väter, Einsiedeln.*

Jardine, Lisa 1997: Introduction, in eadem (ed.), Erasmus, *The Education of a Christian Prince*, Cambridge, pp. vi–xxvi.

Jenkins, David 2006: Psellos' Conceptual Precision, in C. Barber/D. Jenkins (eds), *Reading Michael Psellos*, Leiden/Boston, pp. 131–151.

Jeremias, Ralf 2005: *Vernunft und Charisma. Die Begründung der politischen Theorie bei Dante und Machiavelli im Blick Max Webers*, Konstanz.

Joannou, Perikles 1956: *Christliche Metaphysik in Byzanz: Die Illuminationslehre des Michael Psellos und Joannes Italos*, Ettal.

Joantă, Seraphim 1992: *Romania. Its Hesychast Tradition and Culture*, St. Xenia Skete.

Joas, Hans/Klaus Wiegandt (ed.) ²2005: *Die kulturellen Werte Europas*, Frankfurt a. M.

Johnson, Christopher D. L. 2010: *The Globalization of Hesychasm and the Jesus Prayer. Contesting Contemplation*, London/New York.

Jones, Arnold H. M. 1964: *The Later Roman Empire 284–602*, vol. 1, Oxford. Jordan, Stefan 2005: *Einführung in das Geschichtsstudium*, Stuttgart.

Junghans, Helmar 1985: *Der junge Luther und die Humanisten*, Göttinge

—— 2008: Elemente der Zweireichenlehre und der Zweiregimentenlehre Martin Luthers. Eine Einführung, in M. Beyer/J. Flöter/M. Hein (eds), *Christlicher Glaube und weltlicher Herrschaft*, Leipzig, pp. 23–40.

Jürgensmeier, Friedhelm (ed.) 1991: *Erzbischof Albrecht von Brandenburg (1490–1545). Ein Kirchen- und Reichsfürst der Frühen Neuzeit*, Frankfurt a. M.

Kaelble, Hartmut 2003: Die interdisziplinären Debatten über Vergleich und Transfer, in H. Kaelble/J. Schriewer (eds), *Vergleich und Transfer. Komparatistik in den Sozial-, Geschichts- und Kulturwissenschaften*, Frankfurt a. M., pp. 469–493.

Kahl, Thede/Michael Metzeltin/Mihai-R. Ungureanu (eds) 2006: *Rumänien*, Wien/New York.

Kaldellis, Anthony 2011: Aristotle's *Politics* in Byzantium, in V. Syros (ed.), *Well begun is Only Half Done*, Tempe, pp. 121–143.

Kaluzniacki, Emil 1901: Einleitung, in idem (ed.), *Werke des Patriarchen Euthymius von Bulgarien (1375–1393)*, Wien, pp. XIII–CXXVIII.

Kamlah, Wilhelm 1951: *Christentum und Geschichtlichkeit*, Stuttgart/Köln.

Kampmann, Christoph 2001: *Arbiter und Friedensstiftung. Die Auseinandersetzung um den politischen Schiedsrichter im Europa der Frühen Neuzeit*, Paderborn.

Kant, Immanuel 1995: *Kritik der reinen Vernunft*, ed. R. Toman, Köln.

—— 1998: *Critique of Pure Reason*, ed. Paul Guyer and Allen W. Wood, Cambridge.

Kantorowicz, Ernst H. 1946: *Laudes regiae. A Study in Liturgical Acclamations and Medieval Ruler Worship*, Berkeley.

—— 1957: *The King's Two Bodies. A Study in Mediaeval Political Theology*, Princeton, NJ.

Kapriev, Georgi 2011: Lateinische Einflüsse auf die Antilateiner. Philosophie versus Kirchenpolitik?, in M. Hinterberger/C. Schabel (eds), *Greeks, Latins and Intellectual History 1204–1500*, Leuven, pp. 385–395.

Karanasios, Charitonas 2001: *Sebastos Trapezuntios Kyminetes (1632–1702)*, Wiesbaden.

Karant-Nunn, Susan C. 2004: 'Fast wäre mir ein weibliches Gemüt verblieben.' Martin Luthers Männlichkeit, in H. Merdick/P. Schmidt (eds), *Luther zwischen den Kulturen*, Göttingen, pp. 49–65.

Karnejev, A. 1894: Der Physiologus der Moskauer Synodalbibliothek, in *BZ* 31, pp. 26–63.

Karrer, Leo 2009: Wieviel Öffentlichkeit vertragen die Religionen?, in M. Delgado/A. Jödicke/G. Vergauwen (eds), *Religion und Öffentlichkeit. Probleme und Perspektiven*, Stuttgart, pp. 79–98.

Kaser, Karl ²2002: *Südosteuropäische Geschichte und Geschichtswissenschaft*, Wien.

Kaufmann, Thomas 2006: *Martin Luther*, München.

—— 2007: Der 'alte' und der 'junge' Luther als theologisches Problem, in C. Bultmann/V. Leppin/A. Lindner (eds), *Luther und das monastische Erbe*, Tübingen, pp. 187–205.

—— 2008: *'Türckenbüchlein'. Zur christlichen Wahrnehmung 'türkischer Religion' in Spätmittelalter und Reformation*, Göttingen.

—— 2009: *Geschichte der Reformation*, Frankfurt a. M./Leipzig.

Keipert, Helmut 1988: Die slavische übersetzung des Photius-Briefs an Boris-Michael von Bulgarien, in H.-B. Harder/H. Rothe (eds), *Gattungen in den slavischen Literaturen*, Köln/Wien, pp. 89–113.

Kennedy, George 1981: The Classical Tradition in Rethoric, in M. Mullet/R. Scott (eds), *Byzantium and the Classical Tradition*, Birmingham, pp. 20–34.

Kenny, Anthony 2005: *Medieval Philosophy*, Oxford.

Kent, D. 2000: *Cosimo de' Medici and the Florentine Renaissance. The Patron's Oeuvre*, New Haven/London.

Kern, Fritz 1954: *Gottesgnadentum und Widerstandsrecht im frühen Mittelalter*, Münster/Köln.

Kersting, Wolfgang ³2006: *Niccolò Machiavelli*, München.

Kessler, Eckhard 1968: *Das Problem des frühen Humanismus. Seine philosophische Bedeutung bei Coluccio Salutati*, München.

Keßler, Eckhard 1998: *Der Humanismus und die Entstehung der modernen Wissenschaft*, Pforzheim.

—— 2002: Die verborgene Gegenwart und Funktion des Nominalismus in der Renaissance-Philosophie. Das Problem der Universalien, in E. Kessler/J. Maclean (eds), *Res et verba in der Renaissance*, Wiesbaden, pp. 53–76.

—— 2008: *Die Philosophie der Renaissance. Das 15. Jahrhundert*, München.Kim, Yong J. 2008: *'Crux sola est nostra theologia'. Das Kreuz Christi als Schlüsselbegriff der Theologia Crucis Luthers*, Frankfurt a. M.

King, Ross 2007: *Machiavelli. Philosopher of Power*, New York.

Kisch, Guido 1960: *Erasmus und die Jurisprudenz seiner Zeit. Studien zum humanistischen Rechtsdenken*, Basel.

Klein, Jürgen 1984: *Denkstrukturen der Renaissance. Ficino-Bruno-Machiavelli und die Selbstbehauptung der Vernunft*, Essen.

Klein, Richard 1988: Das politische Denken des Christentums, in I. Fetscher/H. Münkler (eds), *Pipers Handbuch der politischen Ideen*, vol. 1, München/Zürich, pp. 595–634.

Kleineidam, Erich 1969: *Universitas studii Erfordensis. überblick über die Geschichte der Universität Erfurt im Mittelalter (1392–1521)*, Teil II (1460–1521), Leipzig.

Klinge, Gerhard 1937: Die Beziehungen zwischen christlicher und islamischer Theologie im Anfang des Mittelalters, in *ZKG*, 56, no. 1, pp. 43–58.

Klueting, Harm 2007: *Das konfessionelle Zeitalter. Europa zwischen Mittelalter und Moderne*, Darmstadt.

Kluxen, Kurt 1967: *Politik und menschliche Existenz bei Machiavelli. Dargestellt am Begriff der Necessità*, Stuttgart.

——— 1986: Nachwort, in *Niccolò Machiavelli. Geschichte von Florenz*, Zürich, pp. 566–590.

Knauer, Klaudia 1990: *Das 'magische Viereck' bei Machiavelli – fortuna, virtù, occasione, necessità*, Würzburg.

Kobusch, Theo 2006: *Christliche Philosophie. Die Entdeckung der Subjektivität*, Darmstadt.

Kochanek, Piotr 2004: *Die Vorstellung vom Norden und der Eurozentrismus*, Mainz.

Kocîs, Robert A. 1998: *Machiavelli Redeemed. Retrieving His Humanist Perspectives on Equality, Power and Glory*, Cranbury.

Koder, Johannes 2003: Griechische Identitäten im Mittelalter. Aspekte einer Entwicklung, in A. Avramea/A. Laiou/E. Xrysos (eds), Βυζάντιο. Κράτος καὶ κοινωνία, Athen, pp. 297–319.

Kogălniceanu, Constantin 1908: Basarab I zis Negru-Vodă [Basarab I, known as Negru-Vodă], in idem, *Cercetări critice cu privire la istoria românilor*, Bucureşti.

Kohler, Alfred 1990: Karl V. (1519–1556), in A. Schindling/W. Ziegler (eds), *Die Kaiser der Neuzeit (1519–1918)*, München, pp. 33–54.

Kohnle, Armin 2001: *Reichstag und Reformation. Kaiserliche und ständische Religionspolitik von den Anfängen der Causa Lutheri bis zum Nürnberger Religionsfrieden*, Heidelberg.

Kolb, Robert 2008: Die Josef-Geschichten als Fürstenspiegel in der Wittenberger Auslegungstradition, in M. Beyer/J. Flöter/M. Hein (eds), *Christlicher Glaube und weltliche Herrschaft*, Leipzig, pp. 41–55.

——— 2009: Luther on Peasants and Princes, in *Lutheran Quarterly* 23, pp. 125–146.

Kolb, Robert, Irene Dingel, L'ubomir Batka 2014 (eds): *The Oxford Handbook of Martin Luther's Theology*, Oxford.

Kondylis, Panajotis 2007: *Machiavelli*, Berlin.

Köpf, Ulrich 2008: Wurzeln reformatorischen Denkens in der monastischen Theologie Bernhards von Clairvaux, in A. Lexutt/V. Mantey/V. Ortmann (eds), *Reformation und Mönchtum. Aspekte eines Verhältnisses über Luther hinaus*, Tübingen, pp. 29–56.

Körber, Esther-B. 2002: *Habsburgs europäische Herrschaft. Von Karl V. bis zum Ende des 16. Jahrhunderts*, Darmstadt.

Koselleck, Reinhart 2004: *Futures Past. On the Semantics of Historical Time*, ed. Keith Tribe, New York.

Kosuch, Andreas 2011: *Abbild und Stellvertreter Gottes. Der König in herrschaftstheoretischen Schriften des Späten Mittelalters*, Köln.

Kraml, Hans/Gerhard Leibold 2003: *Wilhelm von Ockham*, Münster.

Krämpf, Helmut 1935: *Pierre Dubois und die geistigen Grundlagen des französischen Nationalbewusstseins um 1300*, Leipzig/Berlin.

Krausmüller, Dirk 2006: The Rise of Hesychasm, in M. Angold (ed.), *The Cambridge History of Christianity*, vol. 5: Eastern Christianity, Cambridge, pp. 101–126.

—— 2007: Religious Instruction for Laypeople in Byzantium: Stephen of Nicomedia, Nicephorus Ouranos, and the Pseudo-Athansasian *Syntagma ad quendam politicum*, in *Byzantion* 77, pp. 239–250.

Kreeft, Peter 2003: *Socrates Meets Machiavelli. The Father of Philosophy Cross-Examines the Author of* The Prince, San Francisco.

Kresten, Otto 2000: *'Staatsempfänge' im Kaiserpalast von Konstantinopel um die Mitte des 10. Jahrhunderts*, Wien.

Kristeller, Paul O. 1974: *Humanismus und Renaissance I. Die antiken und mittelalterlichen Quellen*, München.

—— 1976a: Die platonische Akademie von Florenz, in idem, *Humanismus und Renaissance II*, München, pp. 101–114.

—— 1976b: Die Verbreitung des italienischen Humanismus, in idem, *Humanismus und Renaissance II*, München, pp. 85–100.

Kristophson, Jürgen 2013: Zu den übersetzungen des Alexanderromans in Südosteuropa, in H. Schaller/R. Zlatanova (eds), *Kontinuität gegen Widerwärtigkeit*, München, pp. 73–87.

Kritzl, Johannes 2008: *Adversus turcas et Turcarum Deum. Beurteilungskriterien der Türkenkriegs und des Islam in den Werken Martin Luthers*, Bonn.

Kroker, Ernst 1906: *Katharina von Bora. Martin Luthers Frau*, Leipzig.

Kroner, Michael 2005: *Dracula. Wahrheit, Mythos und Vampirgeschäft*, Heilbronn.

Krumbacher, Karl 1897a: *Geschichte der byzantinischen Literatur*, vol. 1, München.

—— 1897b: *Geschichte der byzantinischen Literatur. Von Justinian bis zum Ende des Oströmischen Reiches (527–1453)*, München.

Kuchenbuch, Ludolf 1991: *Grundherrschaft im früheren Mittelalter*, Idstein.

Kuckenburg, Martin 2007: *Kultstätten und Opferplätze in Deutschland von der Steinzeit bis zum Mittelalter*, Stuttgart.

Kührer, Florian 2011: Die Pforte der Christenheit. Der Fall Konstantinopels und der Kampf gegen die Osmanen in den rumänischen Geschichtsbüchern 1942–2006, in C. Gastgeber et al. (eds), *Matthias Corvinus und seine Zeit. Europa am übergang vom Mittelalter zur Neuzeit zwischen Wien und Konstantinopel*, Wien, pp. 247–260.

Kunst, Hermann 1976: *Evangelischer Glaube und politische Verantwortung. Martin Luther als politischer Berater seiner Landesherren und seine Teilnahme an den Fragen des öffentlichen Lebens*, Stuttgart.

Kunstmann, Friedrich 1855: Studien über Marino Sanudo den Älteren mit einem Anhang seiner ungedruckten Briefen, in *Abhandlungen der hist. Kl. königl. Bay. Akademie der Wissenschaften* 7, pp. 697–819.

Kunzelmann, Adalbero 1969–1976: *Geschichte der deutschen Augustiner-Eremiten*, 7 vols, Würzburg.

Kurz, Marlene et al. (eds) 2005: *Das Osmanische Reich und die Habsburger-monarchie*, Wien/München.

Kusch, Horst 1955: Friede als Ausgangspunkt der Staatstheorie des Marsilius von Padua, in *Das Altertum* 1, no. 2, pp. 116–125.

Kyung-Hee, Kim 2004: *Virtù bei Machiavelli. Die materialistische Begründung der Machtpolitik*, Diss. Berlin.

Labat, René 1939: *Le caractère religieux de la royauté assyro-babylonienne*, Paris.

Lacombrade, Christian 1951: *Le discours sur la Raoyauté de Synésios de Cyrène à l'empereur Arcadios*, Paris.

Lampros, Spyridonos P. 1895: *Catalogue of the Greek Manuscripts on Mount Athos*, vol. 1, Cambridge.

Lang, David M. 1983: Introduction, in *St. John Damascene. Barlaam and Joasaph*, ed. G. R. Woodward/H. Mattingly, Cambridge, MA, pp. ix–xxxv.

Lang, Heinrich 2009: *Cosimo de' Medici, die Gesandten und die Condottieri. Diplomatie und Kriege der Republik Florenz im 15. Jahrhundert*, München.

Laube, Adolf 1984: Martin Luther und die frühbürgerliche Revolution, in *Sitzungsber. d. Akad. d. Wiss. d. DDR. Gesellschaftswissenschaften*, 12G, pp. 32–42.

Lăzărescu, Emil 1967: O icoană puțin cunoscută din secolul al XVI-lea și problema pronaosului bisericii mănăstirii Argeșului [A little-known 16th century icon and the problem of the narthex of the Argeș church building], in *Studii și cercetări de istoria artei: artă plastică*, 14, no. 2, pp. 187–199.

Lăzărescu, George/Nicolae Stoicescu 1972: *Țările Române și Italia până la 1600* [The Danubian principalities and Italy up to the year 1600], București.

Leclerc, Jean 1982: The Renewal of Theology, in R. L. Benson/G. Constable (eds), *Renaissance and Renewal in the Twelfth Century*, Oxford, pp. 68–87.

Leemans, Johann/Brian J. Matz/Johan Verstraeten (eds) 2011: *Reading Patristic Texts on Social Ethics*, Washington, DC.

Leger, Louis 1884: *Chronique dite de Nestor*, Paris.

Lehmann, Hartmut 2004: Das marxistische Lutherbild von Engels bis Honecker, in H. Medick/P. Schmidt (eds), *Luther zwischen den Kulturen*, Göttingen, pp. 500–514.

Lehmeier, Eva/Gunther Gottlieb 2007: Kaiser Konstantin und die Kirche. Zur Anfänglichkeit eines Verhältnisses, in H. Schlange-Schöningen (ed.), *Konstantin und das Christentum*, Darmstadt, pp. 150–170.

Lehmkuhl, Josef 2008: *Erasmus–Machiavelli. Zweieinig gegen die Dummheit*, Würzburg.

Leidhold, Wolfgang 2000: Aristoteles. Politikwissenschaft und praktische Philosophie, in idem (ed.), *Politik und Politeia. Formen und Probleme politischer Ordnung*, Würzburg, pp. 423–444.

Leng, Rainer 2002: *Ars belli. Deutsche taktische und kriegstechnische Bilderhandschriften und Traktate im 15. und 16. Jahrhundert*, 2 vols, Wiesbaden.

Leppin, Volker 1995: *Geglaubte Wahrheit. Das Theologieverständnis Wilhelms von Ockham*, Göttingen.

—— 2005a: Kirchenväter, in A. Beutel (ed.), *Luther-Handbuch*, Tübingen, pp. 45–49.

—— 2005b: Von der Polarität zur Vereindeutigung. Zu den Wandlungen in Kirche und Frömmigkeit zwischen Spätem Mittelalter und Reformation, in G. Litz/H. Munzert/R. Liebenberg (eds), *Frömmigkeit–Theologie–Frömmigkeitstheologie. Festschrift für Berndt Hamm*, Leiden/Boston, pp. 299–315.

—— 2005c: Von Sturm, Gewittern, Turmstuben und der Nuss der Theologie. Martin Luther (1483–1546) zwischen Legende und Wirklichkeit, in *Wittenberger Lebensläufe im Umbruch der Reformation*, Wittenberg, pp. 11–27.

—— 2006: *Martin Luther*, Darmstadt.

—— 2008a: Aristotelisierung, Immediatisierung und Radikalisierung. Transformationen der Sündenlehre von Thomas von Aquin bis Martin Luther, in W. Härle/R. Preul (eds), *Sünde*, Leipzig, pp. 45–73.

—— 2008b: Humanismus und Mönchtum. überlegungen zu ihrer Bedeutung für ein Verständnis der Wittenberger Reformation, in A. Lexutt/V. Mantey/V. Ortmann (eds), *Reformation und Mönchtum. Aspekte eines Verhältnisses über Luther hinaus*, Tübingen, pp. 79–101.

—— 2008c: Tradition und Traditionskritik bei Luther, in P. Gemeinhardt/B. Oberdorfer (eds), *Gebundene Freiheit? Bekenntnistradition und theologische Lehre im Luthertum*, Gütersloh, 15–30.

—— 2011: Grenzen und Möglichkeiten der Obrigkeit – Zu Entstehung und Kontext von Luthers Zwei-Reiche-Lehre, in I. Dingel/C. Tietz (eds), *Die politische Aufgabe von Religion. Perspektiven der drei monotheistischen Religionen*, Göttingen, pp. 247–258.

Lepsius, M. Rainer 2004: Prozesse der europäischen Identitätsstiftung, in *Aus Politik und Zeitgeschichte* 38, pp. 3–5.

Levi, Anthony H. T. 1986: Introduction, in A. H. T. Levi (ed.), *Collected Works of Erasmus, vol. 27: Panegyricus, Moria, Julius Exclusus, Institutio Principis Christiani, Querela Pacis*, Toronto, pp. ix–xxx.

Lexutt, Athina 2005: Die Rede vom verborgenen Gott. Eine Untersuchung zu Nikolaus von Kues mit einem Blick auf Martin Luther, in *NZSTR* 47, no. 4, pp. 372–391.

—— 2008: Unica regula et norma. Zum Verhältnis von Schrift und Tradition im reformatorischen Verständnis, in P. Gemeinhardt/B. Oberdorfer (eds), *Gebundene Freiheit? Bekenntnistradition und theologische Lehre im Luthertum*, Gütersloh, pp. 143–165.

Liakos, Antonis 2013: The Canon of European History and the Conceptual Framework of National Historiographies, in M. Middell/L. Roura (eds), *Transnational Challenges to National History Writing*, New York, pp. 314–342.

Liebeschütz, Hans 1950: *Mediaeval Humanism in the Life and Writings of John of Salisbury*, London.

Lienert, Elisabeth 2001: *Deutsche Antikenromane des Mittelalters*, Berlin.

Lienhard, Marc 2007: Guerre et paix dans les écrits de Zwingli et de Luther. Une comparaison, in C. Ocker et al. (eds), *Politics and Reformations. Histories and Reformations*, Leiden/Boston, pp. 217–240.

Lilienfeld, Fairy von, 1986: 'Hesychasmus', in *TRE* 15, pp. 282–289.

Lloyd, A. C. 1967: The Early Neoplatonists, in A. H. Armstrong (ed.), *The Cambridge History of Later Greek and Early Medieval Philosophy*, Cambridge, pp. 272–325.

Loewenich, Walther von, 1989: Zur Diskussion über theologia crucis – Versuch einer Bilanz, in R. Decot/R. Vinke (eds), *Zum Gedenken an Joseph Lortz (1887–1975)*, Stuttgart, pp. 323–336.

Lohse, Bernhard 1981: *Martin Luther. Eine Einführung in sein Leben und sein Werk*, München.

—— 1983: Philipp Melanchthon in seinen Beziehungen zu Luther, in H. Junghans (ed.), *Leben und Werk Martin Luthers von 1526 bis 1546*, vol. 1, Göttingen, pp. 403–418.

—— 1995: *Luthers Theologie in ihrer historischen Entwicklung und in ihrem systematischen Zusammenhang*, Göttingen.

Lohse, Eduard 2006: Martin Luther und der Römerbrief des Apostel Paulus, in *Kerygma und Dogma* 52, no. 2, pp. 106–125.

Looß, Sigrid 1986: Eine Sicht der lutherischen Obrigkeitsauffassung, in G. Vogler (ed.), *Martin Luther. Leben. Werk. Wirkung*, Berlin, pp. 105–119.

Lossky, Vladimir ²1973: *The Vision of God*, Leighton Buzzard.

—— 1974: *In the Image and Likeness of God*, New York.

Lössl, Josef 2009: Martin Luther's Jerome. New Evidence for a Changing Attitude, in A. Cain/J. Lössl (eds), *Jerome of Stridon. His Life, Writings, and Legacy*, Fornham/Burlington, pp. 237–251.

Louth, Andrew 1981: *The Origins of the Christian Mystical Tradition. From Plato to Denys*, Oxford.

—— 2003: The Theology of Philokalia, in J. Behr/A. Louth/D. Conomos (eds), *Abba. The Tradition of Orthodoxy in the West*, New York, pp. 351–361.

Luburici, Momcilo (ed.) 2003: *330 de ani de la naşterea lui Dimitrie Cantemir, personalitate marcantă a culturii europene* [330 years since the birth of Dimitrie Cantemir, a defining personality of European culture], Bucureşti.

Luca, Cristian 2008: Documentary notes relative to the kinship of Levantines and Venetians with the princely families from Wallachia and Moldavia, 16th–17th centuries, in Ţeicu/I. Cândea (eds), *Românii în Europa medievală (între Orientul bizantin şi Occidentul latin)*, Brăila, pp. 653–676.

Luca, Santo 1988: Manoscritti greci dimenticati della Biblioteca Vallicelliana, in *Augustinianum* 28, no. 3, pp. 661–702.

Ludolphy, Ingetraut ²2006: *Friedrich der Weise, Kurfürst von Sachsen (1463–1525)*, Leipzig.

Lüdtke, Alf 1991: Herrschaft als soziale Praxis, in idem (ed.), *Herrschaft als soziale Praxis. Historische und sozialanthropologische Studien*, Göttingen, pp. 9–63.

Luhmann, Niklas 1980: *Gesellschaftsstruktur und Semantik. Studien zur Wissenssoziologie der modernen Gesellschaft*, vol. 1, Frankfurt a. M.

Lundt, Bea 2009: *Europas Aufbruch in die Neuzeit (1500–1800). Eine Kultur und Mentalitätsgeschichte*, Darmstadt.

Lutz, Heinrich 1974: Das Reich, Karl V. und der Beginn der Reformation, in H. Fichtenau/E. Zöllner (eds), *Beiträge zur neueren Geschichte Österreichs*, Wien, pp. 47–70.

Maas, Paul 1913: Die Musen des Kaisers Alexios I., in *BZ* 22, no. 3–4, pp. 348–369.

MacKenzie, Cameron A. 2007: The Challenge of History. Luther's Two Kingdoms Theology as a Test Case, in *Concordia Theological Quarterly* 71, pp. 3–28.

Magdalino, Paul/Robert Nelson 1982: The Emperor in Byzantine Art of the Twelfth Century, in *Byzantinsche Forschungen* 8, pp. 123–183.

Maier, Hans/Johannes J. Meister 1966: Augustinus, in H. V. Rausch (ed.), *Politische Denker I*, München, pp. 41–52.

Maier, Hans 1969: 'Politische Theologie'? Einwände eines Laien, in H. Peukert (ed.), *Diskussion zur politischen Theologie*, Mainz/München, pp. 1–25.

—— 1970: *Kritik der politischen Theologie*, Einsiedeln.

Maier, Mischa 2003: Göttlicher Kaiser und christlicher Herrscher? Die christlichen Kaiser der Spätantike und ihre Stellung zu Gott, in *Das Altertum* 48, pp. 129–160.

Major, Rafael 2007: A New Argument for Morality. Machiavelli and the Ancients, in *Political Science Quarterly* 60, pp. 171–179.

Majoros, Ferenc/Bernd Rill 2004: *Das Osmanische Reich*, 1300–1922, Wiesbaden.

Makk, Ferenc 1975: *Traduction et commentaire de l'homélie écrite probablement par Théodore le Syncelle sur le siège de Constantinople en 626*, Szeged.

Makrides, Vasilios N. 2005: Orthodox Christianity, Rationalization, Modernization. A Reassessment, in V. Roudometof/A. Agadjanian/J. Pankhurst (eds), *Eastern Orthodoxy in a Global Age*, Walnut Creek, pp. 179–209.

—— 2010: Orthodox Eastern and South Eastern Europe. Exception or Special Case?, in W. Eberhard/C. Lübke (eds), *The Plurality of Europe. Identities and Spaces*, Leipzig, pp. 189–202.

—— 2011: Orthodoxes Christentum und Moderne. Inkompatibilität oder langfristige Anpassung?, in *Una Sancta* 66, pp. 15–30.

Malysz, Piotr J. 2008: Luther and Dionysius. Beyond Mere Negations, in *Modern Theology* 24, no. 4, pp. 679–692.

Manemann, Jürgen 2002: *Carl Schmitt und die Politische Theologie. Politischer Anti-Monotheismus*, Münster.

Mango, Cyril 1975: The Availibility of Books in the Byzantine Empire. AD 750–850, in Dumbarton Oaks Center for Byzantine Studies (ed.), *Byzantine Books and Bookmen*, Washington, DC, pp. 29–45.

—— 1981: Discontinuity with the Classical Past in Byzantium, in M. Mullet/R. Scott (eds), *Byzantium and the Classical Tradition*, Birmingham, pp. 48–57.

Manns, Peter: 1982: *Martin Luther*, Freiburg i. Br.

—— 1984: Luthers Zwei-Reiche- und Drei-Stände-Lehre, in E. Iserloh/G. Müller (eds), *Luther und die politische Welt*, Stuttgart, pp. 3–26.

Manole, Gheorghe ²2010: *Creştinism şi cultură la Neagoe Vodă Basarab (1512–1521)* [Christian faith and culture in Neagoe Basarab (1512–1521)], Târgovişte.

Margolin, Jean-C. 1963: *Douze années de bibliographie érasmienne (1950–1961)*, Paris.

—— 1969: *Quatorze années de bibliographie érasmienne (1936–1949)*, Paris.

—— 1977: *Neuf anées de bibliographie érasmienne (1962–1970)*, Paris.

—— 2007: *Érasme et la Devotio Moderna*, Bruxelles.

Marin, Maxim 1988: *L'Institution du Prince* d'Érasme et de Guillaume Budé, in J. Sperna Weiland/W. T. M. Frijhoff (eds), *Erasmus of Rotterdam. The Man and the Scholar*, Leiden, pp. 117–122.

Marinescu, Florin 2012: Sfântul Neagoe Basarab şi ajutorul său către Biserici din Răsăritul Ortodox [Saint Neagoe Basarab and his support of the Churches in the Orthodox East], in N.-C. Câdă (ed.), *Sfântul Voievod Neagoe Basarabctitor de biserici și cultură românească*, București, pp. 81–91.

Markus, Robert A. 1967: Marius Victorinus and Augustine, in A. H. Armstrong (ed.), *The Cambridge History of Later Greek and Early Medieval Philosophy*, Cambridge, pp. 329–419.

Marrou, Henri-Irénée 1981: *Histoire de l'éducation dans l'Antiquité*, 2 vols, Paris.

Martelli, Mario 1998: *Machiavelli e gli storici antichi. Osservazioni su alcuni luoghi dei Discorsi sopra la prima deca di Tito Livio*, Roma.

—— 2006: Introduzione, in idem (ed.), *Niccolò Machiavelli. Il Principe*, Roma, pp. 9–49.

Martens, John W. 2003: *One God, One Law. Philo of Alexandria on the Mosaic and Greco-Roman Law*, Leiden.

Marx, Harald/Cecilie Hollberg (eds) 2004: *Glaube und Macht. Sachsen im Europa der Reformationszeit*, 2 vols, Dresden.

Marx, Karl / Friedrich Engels [8]1982: *Werke*, vol. 19 (März 1875 bis Mai 1883), Berlin.

Masters, Roger E. 1999: *Fortuna ist ein reißender Fluss. Wie Leonardo da Vinci und Niccolò Machiavelli die Geschichte verändern wollten*, München.

Matheeussen, Constant 1969: Religio und Litterae im Menschenideal des Erasmus, in J. Coppens (ed.), *Scrinium Erasmianum I*, Leiden, pp. 351–374.

Matschke, Klaus-P. 2002: Sakralität und Priestertum des byzantinschen Kaisers, in F.-R. Erkens (ed.), *Die Sakralität von Herrschaft. Herrschaftslegitimierung im Wechsel der Zeiten und Räume*, Berlin, pp. 143–163.

Mattingly, Garrett 1957–1958: Machiavelli's Prince. Political Science or Political Satire, in *American Scholar* 27, pp. 482–491.

Matuz, Josef [3]1994: *Das Osmanische Reich. Grundlinien seiner Geschichte*, Darmstadt.

Matz, Ulrich 1966: Thomas von Aquino, in H. V. Rausch (ed.), *Politische Denker I*, München, pp. 53–62.

Mau, Rudolf 1983: Luthers Stellung zu den Türken, in H. Junghans (ed.), *Leben und Werk Martin Luthers von 1526 bis 1546*, vol. 1, Göttingen, pp. 646–662.

Maxim, Mihai 1993: *Țările Române și Înalta Poartă. Cadrul juridic al relațiilor româno-otomane în Evul Mediu* [The Danubian Principalities and the Sublime Porte. The legal framework of Romanian-Ottoman relations in the Middle Ages], București.

Mayer, Eduard W. 1912: *Machiavellis Geschichtsauffassung und sein Begriff virtù. Studien zu seiner Historik*, München/Berlin.

Mayer, Thomas F. 2000: *Reginald Pole. Prince and Prophet*, Cambridge.

Mayer, Wendy/Pauline Allen 2000: *John Chrysostom*, London/New York.

Mazilu, Dan H. 2002: Despre *Viața Sfinților Varlaam și Ioasaf* [On the life of Saints Barlaam and Josaphat], in P. H. Stahl (ed.), *Omagiu lui Virgil Cândea la 75 de ani*, vol. 1, București, pp. 391–395.

—— 1981: *Varlaam şi Ioasaf. Istoria unei cărţi* [Barlaam and Josaphat. The history of a book], Bucureşti.

McCanles, Michael 1983: *The Discourse of Il Principe*, Malibu.

McGuckin, John 2001: *Standing in God's Holy Fire. The Byzantine Tradition*, New York.

McQueen, Graeme 2011: Rejecting enlightenment? The Medieval Christian Transformation of the Buddha-legend in Jacobus de Voragine's Barlaam and Josaphat, in *Studies in Religion* 30, no. 2, pp. 151–165.

Mehmet, Mustafa A. 1968: Două documente turceşti despre Neagoe Basarab [Zwei osmanische Dokumente betreffend Neagoe Basarab], in *Revista de istorie*, 21, no. 5, pp. 921–930.

Meier, Christian ²2005: Die griechisch-römische Tradition, in H. Joas/K. Wiegandt (ed.), *Die kulturellen Werte Europas*, Frankfurt a. M., pp. 93–116.

Meier, Heinrich ²2004: *Die Lehre Carl Schmitts. Vier Kapitel zur Unterscheidung Politischer Theologie und Politischer Philosophie*, Stuttgart/Weimar.

Meinecke, Friedrich ³1929: *Die Idee der Staatsräson in der neueren Geschichte*, München/Berlin.

—— 1965: *Die Entstehung des Historismus*, München.

Meister, Johannes J. 1966: Aristoteles, in H. V. Rausch (ed.), *Politische Denker I*, München.

Merki, Hubert 1952: *ΌΜΟΙΩΣΙΣ ΘΕΩ. Von der platonischen Angleichung an Gott zur Gottähnlichkeit bei Gregor von Nyssa*, Freiburg i. d. Schweiz.

Merlan, Philip 1967: Greek Philosophy from Plato to Plotinus, in A. H. Armstrong (ed.), *The Cambridge History of Later Greek and Early Medieval Philosophy*, Cambridge, pp. 14–132.

Mertens, Dieter ²1987: Geschichte der politischen Ideen im Mittelalter, in H. Fenske et al. (eds), *Geschichte der politischen Ideen*, Frankfurt a. M, pp. 143–238.

—— 1992: Mittelalterbilder in der Frühen Neuzeit, in G. Althoff (ed.), *Die Deutschen und ihr Mittelalter*, Darmstadt, pp. 29–54.

—— 1997: Die Rede als institutionalisierte Kommunikation im Zeitalter des Humanismus, in H. Duchhardt/G. Melville (eds), *Im Spannungsfeld von Recht und Ritual. Soziale Kommunikation in Mittelalter und Früher Neuzeit*, Köln, pp. 401–422.

Mestwerdt, Paul 1917: *Die Anfänge des Erasmus. Humanismus und Devotio Moderna*, Leipzig.

Meyendorff, John 1974: *Byzantine Hesychasm. Historical, Theological and Social Problems. Collected Studies*, London.

—— 1982: *The Byzantine Legacy in the Orthodox Church*, New York.

—— 1983: Is 'Hesychasm' the Right Word? Remarks on Religious Ideology in the Fourteenth Century, in C. Mango/O. Pritsak (eds), *Okeanos 7*, Cambridge Massachusetts, pp. 447–457.

Meyer, Ernst ³1976: *Einführung in die antike Staatskunde*, Darmstadt.

Meyer, Otto 1983: Der Privatlehrer des frühen Mittelalters. Eine Studie zur Entstehung und kulturellen Wirkung des Lehrberufs, in L. Kriss-Rettenback/M. Liedtke (eds), *Schulgeschichte im Zusammenhang der Kulturentwicklung*, Bad Heilbrunn, pp. 119–142.

Michel, Anton 1975: Die Kaisermacht in der Ostkirche, in H. Hunger (ed.), *Das byzantinische Herrscherbild*, Darmstadt, pp. 206–234.

Miethke, Jürgen 2008: *Politiktheorie im Mittelalter. Von Thomas von Aquin bis Wilhelm von Ockham*, Tübingen.

Mihăilă, Gheorghe/Dan Zamfirescu 1969: *Literatura română veche (1402–1647)* [Old Romanian Literature (1402–1647)], Bucureşti.

Mihăilă, Gheorghe 1967: Două fragmente inedite din textul slavon al Învăţăturilor lui Neagoe Basarab către fiul său Teodosie [Two newly discovered fragments of the Church Slavonic text of the teachings of Neagoe Basarab to his son Theodosius], in *Romanoslavica* 14, pp. 359–375.

—— 1973: Date noi despre originalul slavon al Învăţăturilor lui Neagoe Basarab şi critica unei ipoteze neîntemeiate [New data on the Church Slavonic original of the *Teachings of Neagoe Basarab* and criticism of an unfounded hypothesis], in idem, *Contribuţii la istoria culturii şi literaturii române vechi*, Bucureşti, pp. 327–383.

—— 1979: *Cultură şi literatură română veche în context european* [Altrumänische Kultur und Literatur in europäischem Kontext], Bucureşti.

—— 1996: Originalul slavon al Învăţăturilor lui Neagoe Basarab către fiul său Theodosie [The Church Slavonic original of the *Teachings* of Neagoe Basarab to his son Theodosius], in idem (ed.), *Învăţăturile lui Neagoe Basarab către fiul său Theodosie*, Bucureşti, pp. XLVI–CXVIII.

Miklas, Heinz 1975: *Die Dioptra des Philippos Monotropos im Slavischen. Allgemeine Untersuchung und Text des ersten Buches*, PhD thesis, University of. Graz.

—— 2008: Die Textologie der Dioptra des Philippos Monotropos. Stand der gegenwärtigen und Aufgaben der künftigen Erforschung, in *Диоптра Филиппа Монотропа* [Dyoptra Philippa Monotropa], Moskau, pp. 52–74.

Minea, Ilie 1934: Începuturile marei bănii de la Craiova [On the origin of the institution of the grand banate of Craiova], in *Arhivele Olteniei* 13, no. 71–73, pp. 1–12.

Mishkova, Diana/Bo Stråth/Balász Trencsényi 2013: Regional History as a 'Challenge' to National Frameworks of Historiography. The Case of Central,

Southeast, and Northern Europe, in M. Middell/L. Roura (eds), *Transnational Challenges to National History Writing*, New York, pp. 257–314.

Mitescu, Adriana 1993: L'impero e l'imperatore cristiano bizantino: la visione teologico-politica del principe Neagoe Basarab, in eadem (ed.), *Come vivere e praticare l'esichia. Libro di insegnamento del principe romeno Neagoe Basarab per suo figlio Teodosio*, Rom, pp. I–CXIII.

Mitteis, Heinrich 1933: *Lehnrecht und Staatsgewalt*, Weimar.

Mitterauer, Michael [3]2004: *Warum Europa? Mittelalterliche Grundlagen eines Sonderwegs*, München.

Mittermaier, Karl 1990: *Machiavelli: Moral und Politik zu Beginn der Neuzeit*, Gernsbach.

Moeller, Bernd/K. Stackmann 1981: *Luder-Luther-Eleutherius. Erwägungen zu Luthers Namen*, Göttingen.

Moeller, Bernd 1991a: Die deutschen Humanisten und die Anfänge der Reformation, in idem, *Die Reformation und das Mittelalter. Kirchenhistorische Aufsätze*, Göttingen, pp. 98–110.

—— 1991b: Das Reich und die Kirche in der frühen Reformationszeit, in idem, *Die Reformation und das Mittelalter. Kirchenhistorische Aufsätze*, Göttingen, pp. 125–137.

—— 1995: Die Rezeption Luthers in der frühen Reformation, in B. Hamm/B. Moeller/D. Wendenbourg (eds), *Reformations-Theorien*, Göttingen, pp. 9–29.

—— [7]2000: *Geschichte des Christentums in Grundzügen*, Göttingen.

—— 2001a: Das Berühmtwerden Luthers, in idem, *Luther-Rezeption. Kirchenhistorische Aufsätze zur Reformationsgeschichte*, Göttingen, pp. 15–41.

—— 2001b: Luther in Europa. Die übersetzung seiner Schriften in nichtdeutschen Sprachen 1520–1546, in idem, *Luther-Rezeption. Kirchenhistorische Aufsätze zur Reformationsgeschichte*, Göttingen, pp. 42–56.

Moldoveanu, Ioan 2007: Aspects of the Relations of the Romanian Principalities with Mount Athos in Light of Recent Research Findings, in E. Băbuş/I. Moldoveanu/A. Marinescu (eds), *The Romanian Principalities and the Holy Places along the Centuries*, Bucureşti, pp. 53–68.

Molitor, Hansgeorg/Heribert Smolinsky (eds) 1994: *Volksfrömmigkeit in der Frühen Neuzeit*, Münster.

Moraw, Peter 1993: Das spätmittelalterliche Universitätssystem in Europa – sozialgeschichtlich betrachtet, in H. Brauner/N. R. Wolf (eds), *Wissensliteratur im Mittelalter und in der Frühen Neuzeit*, Wiesbaden, pp. 9–25.

Mörke, Olaf 2005: *Die Reformation. Voraussetzungen und Durchsetzung*, München.

Morris, Rosemary 1994: Succession and Usurpation: Politics and Rhetoric in the Late Tenth Century, in P. Magdalino (ed.), *New Constantines. Rhythm of Imperial Renewal in Byzantium. 4th–13th Centuries*, Belfast, pp. 199–214.

Moulakis, Athanasios 1998: *Republican Realism in Renaissance Florence. Francesco Guicciardinis Discorso di Logrogno*, Lanham.

Mühlen, Karl-H. zur, 1998: Die auctoritas patrum in Martin Luthers Schrift 'Von den Konzilen und Kirchen' (1539), in L. Grane/A. Schindler/M. Wriedt (eds), *Auctoritas Patrum II. Neue Beiträge zur Rezeption der Kirchenväter im 15. und 16. Jahrhundert*, Mainz, pp. 141–152.

———— 2002: On the Critical Reception of the Thought of Thomas Aquinas in the Theology of Martin Luther, in P. Van Geest/H. Goris/C. Leget (eds), *Aquinas as Authority*, Leiden.

———— 2003: Mystische Erfahrung und Wort Gottes bei Luther, in J. Schilling (ed.), *Mystik. Religion der Zukunft – Zukunft der Religion*, Leipzig, pp. 45–66.

Mühlenberg, Ekkehard 1998: Das Argument: 'Die Wahrheit erweist sich in übereinstimmung mit den Vätern'. Entstehung und Schlagkraft, in L. Grane/A. Schindler/M. Wriedt (eds), *Auctoritas Patrum II. Neue Beiträge zur Rezeption der Kirchenväter im 15. und 16. Jahrhundert*, Mainz, pp. 153–169.

Mühlmann, Sieghard 1983: Einführung zur 'Von weltlicher Obrigkeit …', in H.-U. Delius (ed.), *Martin Luther Studienausgabe 3*, Berlin, pp. 27–29.

Mülhaupt, Erwin 1972: Luther und der politische Auftrag eines Christen, in G. Wolf (ed.), *Luther und die Obrigkeit*, Darmstadt, pp. 443–461.

Müller-Schauenburg, Britta 2011: *Religiöse Erfahrung, Spiritualität und theologische Argumentation. Gotteslehre und Gottesebenbildlichkeit bei Gregorios Palamas*, Stuttgart.

Müller, Albert 1910: Studentenleben im 4. Jahrhundert, in *Philologus*, 69, pp. 292–317.

Müller, Gerhard 1981: Die Aristoteles-Rezeption im deutschen Protestantismus, in A. Buck (ed.), *Die Rezeption der Antike. Zum Problem der Kontinuität zwischen Mittelalter und Renaissance*, Hamburg, pp. 55–70.

———— 1984: Luther und die evangelischen Fürsten, in E. Iserloh/G. Müller (eds), *Luther und die politische Welt,* Stuttgart, pp. 65–83.

———— 1989: Bündnis und Bekenntnis. Zum Verhältnis von Glauben und Politik im deutschen Luthertum des 16. Jahrhunderts, in idem, *Causa Reformationis. Beiträge zur Reformationsgeschichte und zur Theologie Martin Luthers*, Gütersloh, pp. 25–45.

Müller, Harald 2006: *Habit und Habitus. Mönche und Humanisten im Dialog*, Tübingen.

Mullett, Margaret 1981: The Classical Tradition in the Byzantine Letter, in M. Mullet/R. Scott (eds), *Byzantium and the Classical Tradition*, Birmingham, pp. 75–93.

Mullett, Michael A. ²2005: *Martin Luther*, London/New York.

Munier, Charles 1979: *L'Église dans l'Empire Romain (IIe-IIIe siècles)*, Paris.

Münkler, Herfried 1985: Staatsraison und politische Klugheitslehre, in J. Fetscher/H. Münkler (eds), *Pipers Handbuch der politischen Ideen*, vol. 5, München/Zürich, pp. 23–72.

—— 1990: Machiavelli: *Die Begründung des politischen Denkens der Neuzeit aus der Krise der Republik Florenz*, Frankfurt a. M.

—— 1993: Die politischen Ideen des Humanismus, in I. Fetscher/H. Münkler (eds), *Pipers Handbuch der politischen Ideen*, vol. 2, München/Zürich, pp. 553–613.

Mureşan, Dan I./Petre Năsturel 2011: Du καθολικὸς βασιλεὺς à l'αυθέντης καθολικός. Notes sur les avatars d'une idée politique, in E. Popescu/T. Teoteoi/M. O. Căţoi (eds), *Études Byzantines et Post-Byzantines VI*, Bucureşti, pp. 251–281.

Mureşan, Dan I. 2003: Et Theodose dans tout cela? Sur l'élaboration des Enseignements de Neagoe Basarab, in I. Cândea/P. Cernovodeanu/G. Lazăr (eds), *Închinare lui Petre Ş. Năsturel la 80 de ani*, Brăila, pp. 299–320.

—— 2007: Le Mont Athos aux XVe-XVIe siècles. Autour de quelques descriptions d'époque, in E. Băbuş/I. Moldoveanu/A. Marinescu (eds), *The Romanian Principalities and the Holy Places along the Centuries*, Bucureşti, pp. 81–122.

—— 2008: De la nouvelle Rome à la troisième la part des Principautés Roumaines dans la transmission de l'idée impériale, in A. Castaldini (ed.), *L'eredita di Traiano. La tradizione istituzionale romano-imperiale nella storia dello spazio romeno*, Bucarest, pp. 123–166.

—— 2012: The Hesychasts. 'Political Photianism' and the public sphere in the fourteenth century, in A. Casiday (ed.), *The Orthodox Christian World*, London/New York, pp. 294–302.

Murko, Matthias 1971: *Geschichte der älteren südslawischen Litteraturen* [sic], Leipzig 1908. Reprinted München.

Musolff, Hans-U. 2003: Pädagogik in Renaissance und Reformation. Piero Paulo Vergerio, Desiderius Erasmus, Philipp Melanchthon, Johannes Sturm, Juan de la Maldonado, Michel de Montaigne, in H.-E. Tenorth (ed.), *Klassiker der Pädagogik*, vol. 1, München, pp. 21–44.

Muthu, Mircea 1976: *Literatura română şi spiritul sud-est European* [Romanian literature and the south-east European mind], Bucureşti.

Mynors, Roger A. B./D. F. S. Thomson/J. K. McConica (eds) 1974–2003: *The Correspondence of Erasmus*, 12 vols, Toronto/Buffalo.

Najemy, John M. 1993: *Between Friends. Discourses of Power and Desire in the Machiavelli-Vettori Letters of 1513–1515*, Princeton.

—— 2000: Civic Humanism and Florentine Politics, in J. Hankins (ed.), *Renaissance Civic Humanism*, Cambridge, pp. 75–104.

Nandriş, Grigore 1946: The Beginnings of Slavonic Culture in the Roumainian Countries, in *The Slavonic and East European Review* 63, pp. 160–171.

Năsturel, Petre Ş. 1960: Învăţăturile lui Neagoe Basarab în lumina pisaniilor de pe biserica mănăstirii de la Argeş [The *Teachings* of Neagoe Basarab in light of the epitaph tablets in the monastery church of Argeş], în: *Mitropolita Olteniei* 1–2, pp. 12–23.

—— 1971: Remarques sur les versions grecque, slave et roumaine des Enseignements du Prince de Valachie Neagoe Basarab à son fils Théodose, in *Byzantinisch-neugriechische Jahrbücher* 21, pp. 249–271.

—— 2002: Radu Vodă cel Mare şi Patriarhul de Constatinopol Ioachim I-ul [Radu Voivode the Great and Joachim I, patriarch of Constantinople], in *SMIM* 20, pp. 23–32.

Neagoe, Manole 1966: Politica externă a lui Neagoe Basarab [The foreign policy of Neagoe Basarab], in *Studii. Revistă de istorie*, 19, no. 4, pp. 745–764.

—— 1971: *Neagoe Basarab*, Bucureşti.

—— 1972: Concepţia lui Neagoe Basarab despre domnie [Neagoe Basarab's concept of rule], in Societatea culturală *Neagoe Basarab* din Curtea de Argeş (ed.), *Neagoe Basarab 1512–1521. La 460 de ani de la urcarea sa pe tronul Ţării Româneşti*, Bucureşti, pp. 44–50.

Neamţiu, Alexandru 1945: Un capitol din relaţiile Ţării Româneşti cu Transilvania în veacul al XVI-lea. Relaţiile lui Neagoe Basarab cu Sibiul (1512–1521) [A chapter in the relations between Wallachia and Transylvania. Neagoe Basarab's relations with Sibiu (1512–1521)], in *Anuarul Institutului de Istorie Naţională* 10, pp. 350–376.

Nederman, Cary J./J. Bruckmann 1983: Aristotelianism in John of Salisbury's Policraticus, in *JHP* 21, pp. 203–229.

Nederman, Cary J. 1986: The Aristotelian Concept of the Mean and John of Salisbury's Concept of Liberty, in *Vivarium* 24, no. 2, pp. 128–142.

—— 1990: Editor's introduction, in idem (ed.), *John of Salisbury. Policraticus*, Cambridge, pp. xv–xxvi.

Nelson, Eric 2004: *The Greek Tradition in Republican Thought*, Cambridge.

Neumahr, Uwe 2007: *Cesare Borgia. Der Fürst und die italienische Renaissance*, München/Zürich.

Neuser, Wilhelm H. 1992: Luther und Melanchthon – Ein Herr, verschiedene Gaben, in W.-D. Hauschild/W. H. Neuser/C. Peters (eds), *Luthers Wirkung*, Stuttgart, pp. 47–59.

Newman, John K. 1995: Humanitas Christiana, in *Acta selecta Octavi Conventus Academiae Latinitati Fovendae*, vol. 2, Rom, pp. 139–149.

Niarchos, Constantine 1981: The Philosophical Background of the Eleventh-Century Revival of Learning, in M. Mullet/R. Scott (eds), *Byzantium and the Classical Tradition*, Birmingham, pp. 127–135.

Nicol, Donald. M. 1967: The Byzantine View of the West, in *Greek, Roman, and Byzantine Studies* 8, no. 4, pp. 315–339.

—— 1976: The Unction of Emperors in Late Byzantine Coronation Ritual, in *BMGS*, 2, pp. 37–52.

—— 1988: Byzantine Political Thought, in J. Burns (ed.), *The Cambridge History of Political Thought c. 350–c. 1450*, Cambridge, pp. 51–79.

Nicolaescu, Stoica 1924: *Domnia lui Neagoe Basarab Voevod 1512–1521. O danie la Mănăstirea Hilandarul* [The reign of Neagoe Basarab Voivode 1512–1521. A donation to the monastery of Chilandar], Reprint from: *Noua Revistă Bisericească*, Jhg. V, pp. 13–16.

—— 1933: *Un prețios chivot de la Neagoe Basarab Voevod (1512–1521) în mănăstirea Dionisiu din Sfântul Munte Athos* [A valuable reliquary from Neagoe Basarab Voivode (1512–1521) on holy Mount Athos], Reprint from: *Viața literară*, București, pp. 1–8.

Nicolescu, Corina 1968: *Argintăria laică și religioasă în Țările Române (sec. XIV–XIX)* [Silver plate profane and religious in in the Danubian Principalities (14th–19th c.)], București.

—— 1970: *Costumul de curte Țările Române (sec. XIV–XVIII)* [Court costume in the Danubian Principalities (14th–18th c)], București.

Nicolescu, Ilie 1903: Din descendența Craioveștilor [On the origin of the Craiovești], in *Revista pentru Istorie, Arheologie și Filologie* 9, no. 2, pp. 200–212.

Niederberger, Antje 2005: Das Bild der Türken im deutschen Humanismus am Beispiel der Werke Sebastian Brants (1456–1521), in M. Kurz et al. (eds), *Das Osmanische Reich und die Habsburgermonarchie*, Wien/München, pp. 181–204.

Nikolau, Theodor 1981: Der Mensch als politisches Lebewesen bei Basilios dem Großen, in *Vigiliae Christianae* 35, pp. 24–31.

Nitschke, Peter 2000: *Einführung in die politische Theorie der Prämoderne (1500–1800)*, Darmstadt.

Nițulescu, Gabriela 2009: *Cartea tipărită la Târgoviște și Renașterea Românească* [Printing in Târgoviște and the Romanian renaissance], Târgoviște.

Noica, Constantin 1991: *Pagini despre sufletul românesc* [Pages on the Romanian soul], București.

Nouzille, Jean 2005: *Moldova. Istoria tragică a unei regiuni europene* [Moldova. The tragic history of a European region], Chișinău.

O'Donovan, Oliver 2005: *The Ways of Judgment*, Michigan/Cambridge.

O'Meara, Dominic 2002: The Justinianic Dialogue On Political Science and Its Neoplatonic Sources, in K. Ierodiakonou (ed.), *Byzantine Philosophy and Its Ancient Sources*, Oxford, pp. 49–62.

Oberman, Heiko A. 1981: *Luther. Mensch zwischen Gott und Teufel*, Berlin.

—— 1984: Thesen zur Zwei-Reiche-Lehre, in E. Iserloh/G. Müller (eds), *Luther und die politische Welt*, Stuttgart, pp. 27–34.

—— 1986: *Die Reformation. Von Wittenberg nach Genf*, Göttingen.

—— ⁴1994: *Die Kirche im Zeitalter der Reformation, Kirchen- und Theologiegeschichte in Quellen III*, Neunkirchen-Vluyn.

Obolensky, Dimitri 1971: *The Byzantine Commonwealth. Eastern Europe (500–1453)*, London.

Ocoleanu, Picu 2007: *Minima moralia eucharistica. Eine theologische Pathologie der Öffentlichkeit*, Berlin.

Oexle, Otto G. 2007: Krise des Historismus – Krise der Wirklichkeit. Eine Problemgeschichte der Moderne, in idem (ed.), *Krise des Historismus – Krise der Wirklichkeit*, Göttingen, pp. 11–115.

Ohme, Heinz 2007: Das ökumenische Patriarchat von Konstantinopel und die türkische Religionspolitik, in *EVKOC* 6, pp. 7–21.

Ohnsorge, Werner 1947: *Das Zweikaiserproblem im früheren Mittelalter. Die Bedeutung des byzantinischen Reiches für die Entwicklung der Staatsidee in Europa*, Hildesheim.

—— 1958: Byzanz und das Abendland im 9. und 10. Jahrhundert. Zur Entwicklung des Kaiserbegriffes und der Staatsideologie, in idem, *Abendland und Byzanz*, Darmstadt, pp. 1–49.

Oikonomou, Maria/Maria A. Stassinopoulou/Ioannis Zelepos (eds) 2011: *Griechische Dimensionen südosteuropäischer Kultur seit dem 18. Jahrhundert*, Frankfurt a. M.

Olin, John C. 1988: Erasmus and Saint Jerome. An Appraisal of the Bond, in J. Sperna Weiland/W. T. M. Frijhoff (eds), *Erasmus of Rotterdam. The Man and the Scholar*, Leiden, pp. 182–186.

Olster, Michael 1993: *The Politics of Usurpation in the Seventh Century. Rhetoric and Revolution in Byzantium*, Amsterdam.

Olteanu, Pandele et al. (eds) 1975: *Slava veche şi slavona românească* [Old Slavonic and Romanian Church Slavonic], Bucureşti.

—— 1967: Contribuţii la studiul literaturii omiletice în vechile literaturi bulgară şi română [A contribution to the study of homiletic literature in the Church Slavonic and Old Romanian literatures], in *Romanoslavica* 14, pp. 305–357.

Onu, Liviu 1984: Referinţe critice [Critical observations], in M. Gregorian (ed.), *Stolnicul Constantin Cantacuzino. Istoria Ţării Româneşti* [History of Wallachia], Chişinău, pp. 256–257.

Opfermann, Bernhard 1953: *Die liturgischen Herrscherakklamationen im Sacrum Imperium des Mittelalters*, Weimar.

Opgenrooth, Ernst/Günther Schultz ⁶2001: *Einführung in das Studium der neueren Geschichte*, Paderborn.

Ostrogorsky, Georg ³1963: *Geschichte des byzantinischen Staates*, München.

—— 1975: Zur Kaisersalbung und Schilderhebung im spätbyzantinischen Krönungszeremoniell, in H. Hunger (ed.), *Das byzantinische Herrscherbild*, Darmstadt, pp. 94–108.

Oţetea, Andrei (ed.) 1972: *Istoria lumii în date* [Weltgeschichte in Daten], Bucureşti.

Otis, Brooks 1976: Gregory of Nyssa and the Cappadocian Conception of Time, in *Studia Patristica* 14, pp. 327–357.

Ott, Joachim/Martin Treu (eds) 2008: *Luthers Thesenanschlag – Faktum oder Fiktion*, Leipzig.

Ottmann, Henning 2004a: Was ist neu im Denken Machiavellis?, in H. Münkler/R. Voigt/R. Walkenhaus (eds), *Demaskierung der Macht. Niccolò Machiavellis Staats- und Politikverständnis*, Baden-Baden, pp. 145–154.

—— 2004b: Politische Theologie als Herrschaftskritik und Herrschaftsrelativierung, in M. Walther (ed.), *Religion und Politik. Zu Theorie und Praxis des theologisch-politischen Komplexes*, Baden-Baden, pp. 73–83.

—— 2006: *Geschichte des politischen Denkens. Die Neuzeit: Von Machiavelli bis zu den großen Revolutionen*, vol. 3.1, Stuttgart/Weimar.

Otto, Stephan 1974a: Der hierarchische Platonismus des Ps.-Dionysios Areopagites, in pp. Otto (ed.), *Die Antike im Umbruch. Politisches Denken zwischen hellenistischer Tradition und christlicher Offenbarung bis zur Reichstheologie Justinians*, München, pp. 83–107.

—— 1974b: Esoterik und individualistische Gnosis. Der mönchische Platonismus des Euagrios Pontikos, in pp. Otto (ed.), *Die Antike im Umbruch. Politisches Denken zwischen hellenistischer Tradition und christlicher Offenbarung bis zur Reichstheologie Justinians,* München, pp. 65–81.

Padberg, Rudolf 1969: Pax Erasmiana. Das politische Engagement und die 'politische Theologie' des Erasmus von Rotterdam, in J. Coppens (ed.), *Scrinium Erasmianum I*, Leiden, pp. 301–312.

Panaccio, Claude 2004: *Ockham on Concepts*, Hampshire/Burlington.

Panaite, Viorel 1997: *Pace, război şi comerţ în Islam. Ţările Române şi dreptul otoman al popoarelor* [Peace, war and trade in Islam. The Danubian Principalities and the Ottoman law of peoples], Bucureşti.

Panaitescu, Petre P. 1959: Introducere, in idem (ed.), *Cronicile slavo-române din sec. XV–XVI publicate de Ion Bogdan*, Bucureşti, pp. 215–218.

—— 1971a: Autenticitatea Învăţăturilor lui Neagoe Basarab [The authenticity of the teachings of Neagoe Basarab], in idem, *Contribuţii la istoria culturii româneşti*, Bucureşti, pp. 154–162.

—— 1971b: Caracterele specifice ale literaturii slavo-române [The specific traits of Slavo-Romanian literature], in idem, *Contribuţii la istoria culturii româneşti*, Bucureşti, pp. 94–124.

—— 1971c: Învățăturile atribuite lui Neagoe Basarab. O reconsiderare [The teachings ascribed to Neagoe Basarab. A refutation], in *Romanoslavica* 8/1963, pp. 403–424. Reprinted in idem, *Contribuții la istoria culturii românești*, București, pp. 242–273.

—— 1971d: Învățăturile lui Neagoe Basarab. Problema autenticității [The teachings of Neagoe Basarab. The question of their authenticity], in idem, *Contribuții la istoria culturii românești, București*, pp. 163–231.

Panou, Nikos 2006 und 2007: Greek-Romanian Symbiotic Patterns in the Early Modern Period: History, Mentalities, Institutions, Part I and II in *The Historical Review/La Revue Historique* 3, pp. 71–110 bzw. 4, pp. 59–104.

Papacostea, Șerban 1965: Les Roumains et la conscience de leur romanité au Moyen Âge, in *Revue roumaine d'histoire* 4, no. 1, pp. 15–24.

—— 2008: Cruciadă și djihad în spațiul egeano-pontic la mijlocul secolului al XIVlea [Crusades and jihad in the Aegean-Pontic region in the mid–14th century], in D. Țeicu/I. Cândea (eds), *Românii în Europa medievală (între Orientul bizantin și Occidentul latin)*, Brăila, pp. 507–522.

Papadakis, Aristeides/John Meyendorff 1994: *The Christian East and the Rise of the Papacy. The Church 1071–1453 A. D.*, New York.

Papadopoullos, Theodore H. ²1990: *Studies and Documents Relating to the History of the Greek Church and People under Turkish Domination*, Nicosia.

Papu, Edgar 1977a: *Barocul ca tip de existență* [Baroque as a way of life], vol. II, București.

—— 1977b: *Din clasicii noștri. Contribuții la ideea unui protocronism românesc* [From our classics. Contributions to the concept of a Romanian protochronism], București.

Paqué, Ruprecht 1970: *Der Pariser Nominalistenstatut. Zur Entstehung des Realitätsbegriffs der neuzeitlichen Naturwissenschaft*, Berlin.

Păun, Radu G. 2001: 'La couronne est à Dieu'. Neagoe Basarab (1512–1521) et l'image du pouvoir pénitent, in P. Guran (ed.), *L'empereur hagiographe*, Bucarest, pp. 186–223.

Payne, Daniel P. 2011: *The Revival of Political Hesychasm in Contemporary Orthodox Thought*, Lanham.

Payne, John B. 1970: *Erasmus. His Theology of the Sacraments*, Richmond, VA.

Pekáry, Thomas 1985: *Das römische Kaiserbildnis in Staat, Kult und Gesellschaft*, Berlin.

Perler, Dominik 2008: Seeing and Judging. Ockham and Wodeham on Sensory Cognition, in S. Knuutilla/P. Kärkkäinen (eds), *Theories of Perception in Medieval and Early Modern Philosophy*, Berlin, pp. 151–169.

Perthes, Friedrich M. 1853: *Des Bischofs Johannes Chrysostomus Leben*, Hamburg.

Peters, Christian 2005: 'Luther und Melanchthon', in A. Beutel (ed.), Luther-Handbuch, Tübingen, pp. 161–168.

Pfeiffer, Rudolf 1936: Die Wandlungen der Antibarbari, in *Gedenkschrift zum 400. Geburtstag des Erasmus von Rotterdam*, Basel, pp. 50–68.

—— 1955: Erasmus und die Einheit der klassischen und der christlichen Renaissance, *HJ* 74, pp. 174–188.

Pfister, Friedrich (ed.) 1978: *Der Alexanderroman mit einer Auswahl aus den verwandten Texten*, Meisenheim am Glan.

Piepenbrink, Karen ³2010: *Konstantin der Große und seine Zeit*, Darmstadt.

Pilvousek, Josef 2008: Bildung als Weg zu grenzüberschreitender Kommunikation. Kirchen und Klöster als Orte interdisziplinärer Bildung im Mittelalter, in B. Kranemann/V. N. Makrides/A. Schulte (eds), *Religion – Kultur – Bildung. Religiöse Kulturen im Spannungsfeld von Ideen und Prozessen der Bildung*, Münster, pp. 29–44.

Pinches, Theophilus G. 1915: Notes on the Deification of Kings, and Ancestor-Worship, in Babylonia, in *PSBA* 37, pp. 87–95.

Pippidi, Andrei 2001: Βασιλεία και [sic] αυθεντια [sic]. Quelques considérations à propos des Enseignements de Neagoe Basarab, in I. Biliarsky (ed.), *Studia Pontica. Méditerranées. Revue de l'association Méditerranées*, No. 26–27, pp. 151–173.

—— 2012: *Visions of the Ottoman World in Renaissance Europe*, London.

Piru, Alexandru 1961: *Literatura română veche* [Old Romanian Literature], București.

Piscupescu, Ecaterina Şt. 1939: *Literatura slavă din principatele române în veacul al XV-lea* [Slavic literature in the Danubian Principalities in the 15th century], București.

Pitkin, Hanna F. 1984: *Fortune is a Woman. Gender and Politics in the Thought of Niccolò Machiavelli*, Berkeley.

Pitsakis, Constantin G. 2007: De la fin des temps à la continuité impériale. Constructions idéologiques post-byzantines au sein du Patriarcat de Constantinople, in *Le Patriarcat Œcuménique de Constantinople aux XIVe-XVIe siècles. Rupture et continuité. Actes du colloque international Rome. 5–6–7 décembre 2005*, Dossiers Byzantines 7, Paris, pp. 213–239.

Plămădeală, Antonie 1969: Cuprinsul teologic al *Învățăturilor* lui Neagoe Basarab [The theological context of the *Teachings* of Neagoe Basarab], *in Studii Teologice* 20, no. 3–4, pp. 245–262.

Platon, Ioan 1992: *Domnia în Ţările Române până la instaurarea regimului fanariot (sec. XIV–XVII* [sic]) [Princely rule in the Danubian Principalities up the beginning of the Phanariot regime (14th–17th c.)], PhD thesis, University of Bucharest.

Podskalsky, Gerhard 1966: Gott ist Licht – Zur Gotteserfahrung in der griechischen Theologie und Mystik, in *Geist und Leben. Zeitschrift für Aszese und Mystik* 39, pp. 201–214.

—— 1967: Zur Gestalt und Geschichte des Hesychasmus, in *Ostkirchliche Studien* 16, no. 1, pp. 15–32.

—— 1972: *Byzantinische Reichseschatologie*, München.

—— 2000: *Theologische Literatur des Mittelalters in Bulgarien und Serbien 865–1459*, München.

—— 2002: Zur Hermeneutik des theologischen Ost-West-Gesprächs in historischer Perspektive, in *EVKOC* 2, pp. 5–17.

Pöhlmann, Egert 1989: Der Schreiber als Lehrer in der klassischen Zeit Griechenlands, in J. G. Prinz von Hohenzollern (ed.), *Schreiber, Magister, Lehrer. Zur Geschichte und Funktion eines Berufsstandes*, Bad Heilbrunn, pp. 73–82.

Polcar, Aleš 2002: *Machiavelli-Rezeption in Deutschland von 1792 bis 1858*, Bonn.

Polívka, Georg 1892: Zur Geschichte des Physiologus in den slavischen Literaturen, in *ASP* 14, pp. 374–404.

—— 1896: Zur Geschichte des Physiologus in den slavischen Literaturen, in *ASP* 18, pp. 523–540.

Pop, Ioan-Aurel 2011: *Din mâinile valahilor schismatici. Românii și puterea în regatul Ungariei medievale (secolele XIII–XIV)* [From the hands of the schismatic Wallachians. The Romanians and political power in the mediaeval kingdom of Hungary (13th–14th c.)], București.

Popa-Lisseanu, G. 1935: Introducere, in *Izvoarele istoriei românilor VII. Cronica lui Nestor*, București, pp. 9–29.

Popovici, Dimitrie 1945: *La littérature roumaine a l'époque des lumières*, Sibiu.

Post, Regnerus R. 1968: *The Modern Devotion*, Leiden.

Poumarède, Géraud 2004: *Pour en finir avec la Croisade. Mythes et réalités de la lutte contre les Turcs aux XVIe et XVIIe siècles*, Paris.

Praechter, Karl 1893: Der Roman Barlaam und Joasaph in seinem Verhältnis zu Agapets Königsspiegel, in *BZ* 2, pp. 444–460.

—— 1908: Rezension zu Antonio Bellomo, in *BZ* 17, pp. 152–164.

Preus, J. Samuel 1979: Machiavelli's Funtional Analysis of Religion. Context and Object, in *Journal of the History of Ideas* 40, no. 2, pp. 171–190.

Prezzolini, Giuseppe 2004: *Cristo e/o Machiavelli. Assaggi sopra il pessimismo cristiano di sant' Agostino e il pessimismo naturalistico di Machiavelli*, Palermo.

Procacci, Guiliano 1995: *Machiavelli nella cultura europea dell' età moderna*, Bari.

Prunduş, Augustin S. 2001: *Leon al X-lea şi Neagoe Basarab* [Leo X and Neagoe Basarab], Cluj-Napoca.

Puşcariu, Sextil 1921: *Istoria literaturii române. Epoca veche* [History of Romanian literature. The early period], vol. 1, Sibiu.

Rädle, Fidel 1989: Erasmus als Lehrer, in H. Boockmann/B. Moeller/K. Stackmann (eds), *Lebenslehren und Weltentwürfe im Übergang vom Mittelalter zur Neuzeit*, Göttingen, pp. 214–232.

Raeder, Siegfried 1961: *Das Hebräische bei Luther untersucht bis zum Ende der ersten Psalmenvorlesung*, Tübingen.

Raeder, Sigfried 2005: Luther und die Türken, in A. Beutel (ed.), *Luther-Handbuch*, Tübingen, pp. 224–231.

Rahe, Paul A. 2000: Situating Machiavelli, in J. Hankins (ed.), *Renaissance Civic Humanism*, Cambridge, pp. 270–308.

Rahner, Hugo 1961: *Kirche und Staat im frühen Christentum. Dokumente aus acht Jahrhunderten und ihre Deutung*, München.

Ramsay, Maureen 2002: Machiavelli (1469–1527), in A. Edwards/J. Townshend (eds), *Interpreting Modern Political Philosophy. From Machiavelli to Marx*, Basingstoke/New York, pp. 21–40.

Raspa, Venanzio 2006: Della 'verità effettuale della cosa' e del riscontrare le cose. Riflessioni intorno al XV capitolo del *Principe*, in F. Del Luchese/L. Sartorello/ pp. Visentin (eds), *Machiavelli. Immaginazione e contingenza*, Pisa, pp. 150–184.

Rathé, C. Edward 1965: Innocent Gentillet and the first Antimachiavel, in *Bibliothèque d'humanisme et renaissance* 27, pp. 186–225.

Raunio, Antti 2004: Luthers politische Ethik, in R. Vinke (ed.), *Lutherforschung im 20. Jahrhundert*, Mainz, pp. 151–170.

—— 2006: Divine and Natural Law in Luther and Melanchthon, in V. Mäkinen (ed.), *Lutheran Reformation and the Law*, Leiden/Boston, pp. 21–61.

Rausch, Heinz 1966: *Marsilius von Padua*, in idem (ed.), *Politische Denker I*, München, pp. 79–89.

Reale, Giovanni 2004: *Kulturelle und geistige Wurzeln Europas*, Paderborn.

Rebenich, Stefan 2007: Vom dreizehnten Gott zum dreizehnten Apostel? Der tote Kaiser in der Spätantike, in H. Schlange-Schöningen (ed.), *Konstantin und das Christentum*, Darmstadt, pp. 216–244.

Regli, Sebastian 1921: *Die Staatsgewalt bei Thomas Hobbes im Lichte seines Nominalismus*, Diss. Freiburg (CH).

Reinhard, Wolfgang 1999: *Geschichte der Staatsgewalt. Eine vergleichende Verfassungsgeschichte Europas von den Anfängen bis zur Gegenwart*, München.

—— [10]2001: *Probleme deutscher Geschichte (1495–1806). Reichsreform und Reformation (1495–1555), Handbuch der deutschen Geschichte 9*, Stuttgart.

—— 2005: Vom Schedario zur Datenbank. Wege mikropolitischer Forschung, in B. Flug/M. Matheus/A., Rehberg (eds), *Kurie und Region. Festschrift für Brigide Schwarz zum 65. Geburtstag*, Stuttgart, pp. 151–166.

—— 2007: *Geschichte des modernen Staates*, München.

—— 2009: *Paul V. Borghese (1605–1621). Mikropolitische Papstgeschichte*, Stuttgart.

Reinhardt, Karl 1962: Thukydides und Machiavelli, in idem, *Die Krise des Helden. Beiträge zur Literatur- und Geistesgeschichte*, München, pp. 52–88.

Reinhardt, Volker 1998: *Die Medici. Florenz im Zeitalter der Renaissance*, München.

—— 2003: *Geschichte Italiens. Von der Spätantike bis zur Gegenwart*, München.

—— 2004: *Francesco Guicciardini (1483–1540). Die Entdeckung des Widerspruchs*, Göttingen/Bern.

—— 2007: *Francesco Vettori (1474–1539). Das Spiel der Macht*, Göttingen/Bern.

—— 2009: *Geld und Freunde. Wie die Medici die Macht in Florenz eroberten*, Darmstadt.

Reinsch, Diether 2005: Die Kultur des Schenkens in den Texten der Historiker der Komnenzeit, in *Mitteilungen zur spätantiken Archäologie und byzantinischen Kunstgeschichte* 4, pp. 173–183.

Reinsch, Robert 1892: *Le bestiaire. Das Thierbuch des normannischen Dichters Guillaume le Clerc*, Leipzig.

Reiter, Paul J. 1937–1941: *Martin Luthers Umwelt, Charakter und Psychose*, 2 vols, Kopenhagen.

Rendtorff, Trutz 1969: Politische Ethik oder 'Politische Theologie'?, in H. Peukert (ed.), *Diskussion zur 'Politischen Theologie'*, Mainz/München, pp. 217–230.

Reventlow, Henning Graf von, 1997: *Epochen der Bibelauslegung, vol. III: Renaissance, Reformation, Humanismus*, München.

Ribhegge, Wilhelm 2000: Erasmus und Karl V. – Der Intellektuelle und die Politik, in C. Strosetzki (ed.), *Aspectos históricos y culturales bajo Carlos V*, Madrid, pp. 159–187.

Rice, Eugene F., Jr. 1988: *Saint Jerome in the Renaissance*, Baltimore/London.

Richardson, Brian 1995: The Prince and Its Early Italian Readers, in M. Coyle (ed.), *Niccolò Machiavelli's the Prince. New Interdisciplinary Essays*, Manchester/ New York, pp. 18–39.

Richter, Vladimir/Gerhard Leibold 1998: *Unterwegs zum historischen Ockham*, Innsbruck.

Rieger, Fritz 1966: Platon, in H. V. Rausch (ed.), *Politische Denker I*, München, pp. 21–29.

Rigo, Antonio 1993: *L'amore della quiete (ho tes hesychias eros). L'esicasmo bizantino tra il XIII e il XV secolo*, Magnano.

Rippel, Philipp 2007: Nachwort, in idem (ed.), *Niccolò Machiavelli. Il Principe – Der Fürst*, Stuttgart, pp. 225–249.

Ritter, Adolf M. 1993: Dionysius Areopagita im 15. und 16. Jahrhundert, in L. Grane/A. Schindler/M. Wriedt (eds), *Auctoritas Patrum. Zur Rezeption der Kirchenväter im 15. und 16. Jahrhundert I*, Mainz, pp. 143–158.

Ritter, Gerhard [6]1948: *Die Dämonie der Macht. Betrachtungen über Geschichte und Wesen des Machtproblems im politischen Denken der Neuzeit*, München.

Rochler, Wolfgang 1973: *Luther und die mittelalterlichen Mystiker. Ein forschungsgeschichtlicher überblick von Ulmann bis zum Dritten Internationalen Kongress für Lutherforschung 1966*, Diss. Leipzig.

Roe, John 2002: *Shakespeare and Machiavelli*, Cambridge.

Rogge, Joachim 1983: Innerlutherische Streitigkeiten um Gesetz und Evangelium, Rechtfertigung und Heiligung, in H. Junghans (ed.), *Leben und Werk Martin Luthers von 1526 bis 1546*, vol. 1, Göttingen, pp. 187–204.

Rohlmann, Michael 2002: Gemalte Prophetie. Papstpolitik und Familienpropaganda im Bildsystem Rafaels *Stanza dell'Incendio*, in G.-R. Tewes/M. Rohlmann (eds), *Der Medici-Papst Leo X. und Frankreich*, Tübingen, pp. 241–370.

Rohls, Jan 2002: *Philosophie und Theologie in Geschichte und Gegenwart*, Tübingen.

Romanski, Stojan 1908: *Mahnreden des walachischen Wojwoden Nĕgoe Basarab an seinen Sohn Theodosius*, Leipzig.

Rorem, Paul 1997: Martin Luther's Christocentric Critique of Pseudo-Dionysian spirituality, in *Lutheran Quarterly* 11, pp. 291–307.

Rösch, Gerhard 1978: *ONOMA BAΣIΛEIAΣ. Studien zum offiziellen Gebrauch der Kaisertitel in spätantiker und frühbyzantinischer Zeit*, Wien.

Rösener, Werner 2008: Fürstenhof und Sakralkultur im Kontext spätmittelalterlicher Fürstenspiegel, in W. Rösener/C. Fey (eds), *Fürstenhof und Sakralkultur im Spätmittelalter*, Göttingen, pp. 21–40.

Rosen, Klaus [2]1987: Griechenland und Rom, in H. Fenske et al. (ed.), *Geschichte der politischen Ideen*, Frankfurt a. M., pp. 19–39.

Rosetti, Alexandru et al. (eds) 1964: *Istoria literaturii rommâne I: Folclorul. Literatura română în perioada feudală (1400–1780)* [History of Romanian Literature I: folklore. Romanian literature in the feudal age (1400–1780)], București.

Rösger, Alfons 1986: Der gebildete Kaiser. Zum Problem der Herrschererziehung in Rom, in L. Kriss-Rettenbeck/M. Liedtke (eds), *Erziehungs- und Unterrichtsmethoden im historischen Wandel*, Bad Heilbrunn, pp. 65–73.

——— 1989: Lehrer und Lehrerbildung im Imperium Romanum, in Johann G. Prinz von Hohenzollern (ed.), *Schreiber, Magister, Lehrer. Zur Geschichte und Funktion eines Berufsstandes*, Bad Heilbrunn, pp. 119–130.

Rossi, Vincent 2002: Presence, Participation, Performance. The Remembrance of God in the Early Hesychast Fathers, in J. S. Cutsinger (ed.), *Paths to the Heart. Sufism and Christian East*, Bloomington, pp. 64–111.

Rouse, Richard H./Mary A. Rouse 1967: John of Salisbury and the Doctrine of Tyrannicide, in *Speculum* 42, no. 4, pp. 693–709.

Rubin, Berthold 1953: Zur Kaiserkritik Ostroms, in *Studi bizantini e neoellenici* 7, pp. 453–462.

Rubinstein, Nicolai 1972: Machiavelli and the World of Florentine Politics, in M. P. Gilmore (ed.), *Studies on Machiavelli*, Florenz, pp. 3–28.

—— 1989: Francesco Guicciardini, in H. Boockmann/B. Moeller/K. Stackmann (eds), *Lebenslehren und Weltentwürfe im Übergang vom Mittelalter zur Neuzeit*, Göttingen, pp. 141–159.

Rudolph, Günther 1969: Das sozialökonomische Denken des Erasmus von Rotterdam, in *DZP* 9, pp. 1076–1092.

Rudow, Wilhelm 1892: *Geschichte des rumänischen Schrifttums*, Wernigerode.

Rummel, Erika 1985: *Erasmus as a Translator of the Classics*, Toronto.

Rump, Hans-U. 1989: Magister und Scholasticus. Das neue Ansehen des Lehrers in der christlichen Zeit, in Johann G. Prinz von Hohenzollern (ed.), *Schreiber, Magister, Lehrer. Zur Geschichte und Funktion eines Berufsstandes*, Bad Heilbrunn, pp. 133–143.

Runciman, Steven 1971: *The Orthodox Churches and the Secular State*, Oxford.

Rüpke, Jörg 2008: Transformation von Religion in Wissen im alten Rom, in B. Kranemann/V. N. Makrides/A. Schulte (eds), *Religion–Kultur–Bildung. Religiöse Kulturen im Spannungsfeld von Ideen und Prozessen der Bildung*, Münster, pp. 13–27.

—— 2009: Europa und die Europäische Religionsgeschichte, in H. G. Kippenberg/J. Rüpke/K. von Stuckrad (eds), *Europäische Religionsgeschichte*, vol. 1, Göttingen, pp. 3–14.

Rüsen, Jörg 1993: *Konfigurationen des Historismus. Studien zur deutschen Wissenschaftskultur*, Frankfurt a. M.

—— 1998: Theoretische Zugänge zum interkulturellen Vergleich historischen Denkens, in J. Rüsen/M. Gottlob/A. Mittag (eds), *Die Vielfalt der Kulturen*, Frankfurt a. M., pp. 37–73.

Russel, Norman 2004: *The Doctrine of Deification in the Greek Patristic Tradition*, Oxford.

Russo, Demosthene 1939: *Studii istorice greco-române. Opere postume* [Graeco-Romanian studies in history. Posthumous works], ed. C. G. Giurescu/A. Camariano/N. Camariano, vol. 1, Bucureşti.

—— 1910: *Studii şi critice. O carte asupra Învăţăturilor lui Pseudo-Neagoe. Răspuns unui critic. Cărţi de bună cuviinţă. Un catalog de ms. greceşti* [*Studia et critica*. A book on the teachings of Pseudo-Neagoe. Answer to a critic. Books of etiquette. A catalogue of Greek Mss.], Bucureşti.

—— 1982: *Elenizmul în România. Epoca bizantină şi fanariotă* [Hellenism in Romania. The Byzantine and Phanariot age], Bucureşti.

Saak, Eric L. 2002: *High Way to Heaven. The Augustinian Platform Between Reform and Reformation*, 1292–1524, Leiden.

Sacerdoţeanu, Aurelian 1941: *Liste de suverani* [Lists of rulers], Bucureşti.

—— 1964: Contribuții la studiul diplomaticii slavo-române. Sfatul domnesc și sigiliile din timpul lui Neagoe Basarab (1512–1521) [Contributions to the Study of Slavo-Romanian Documents. The council of princes and seals in the age of Neagoe Basarab], in *Romanoslavica* 10, pp. 405–434.

Sandu, Ion D. 1938: *Neagoe Basarab apărător și sprijinitor al ortodoxiei* [Neagoe Basarab: Protector and patron of Orthodoxy], Sibiu/Hermannstadt.

Săsăujan, Mihail-pp. 2012: Actul de ctitorie al Domnului Neagoe Basarab [The foundations of Prnce Neagoe Basarab], in N.-C. Câdă (ed.), *Sfântul Voievod Neagoe Basarab – ctitor de biserici și cultură românească*, București, pp. 63–80.

Sasso, Genaro 1966: *Machiavelli e Cesare Borgia. Storia di un giudizio*, Roma.

Sčepkin, Eugen 1897: Zur Nestorfrage, in *ASP* 19, pp. 498–554.

Schäbler, Birgit 2007: Das Studium der Weltregionen (Area Studies) zwischen Fachdisziplinen und der Öffnung zum Globalen. Eine wissenschaftsgeschichtliche Annäherung, in idem (ed.), *Area Studies und die Welt, Weltregionen und Globalgeschichte*, Wien, pp. 11–45.

Schar, Kurt/R. Gräf 2008: *Rumänien. Geschichte und Geographie*, Wien.

Scheible, Heinz 2010: *Aufsätze zu Melanchthon*, Tübingen.

Schemmel, Fritz 1983: Der Sophist Libanios als Schüler und Lehrer, in G. Fatouros/T. Krischer (eds), *Libanios*, Darmstadt, pp. 3–25.

Schilling, Heinz 1995: Die Konfessionalisierung von Kirchen, Stadt und Gesellschaft – Profil, Leistung, Defizite und Perspektiven eines geschichtswissenschaftlichen Paradigmas, in W. Reinhard/H. Schilling (eds), *Die katholische Konfessionalisierung*, Heidelberg, pp. 1–49.

Schmelz, Lothar/Michael Ludscheidt (eds) 2005: *Luthers Erfurter Kloster. Das Augustinerkloster im Spannungsfeld von monastischer Tradition und protestantischem Geist*, Erfurt.

Schmidt, Kurt D. 1972: Luthers Staatsauffassung, in G. Wolf (ed.), *Luther und die Obrigkeit*, Darmstadt, pp. 181–195.

Schmidt, Richard H. 2008: *God Seekers. Twenty Centuries of Christian Spiritualities*, Grand Rapids.

Schnapp, Joël E. 2010: Antichrist e Antichrists turcs au XVe siècle, in F. Meier (ed.), *Italien und das Osmanische Reich*, Herne, pp. 141–168.

Schneider, Gerhard 1994: Einleitung, in Clemens von Rom, *Epistola ad Corinthios/Brief an die Korinther*, Fontes Christiani 15, Freiburg, pp. 7–61.

Schoek, Richard J. 1988: Erasmus as Latin Secretary to the Bishop of Cambrai. Erasmus Introduction to the Burgundian Court, in J. Sperna Weiland/W. T. M. Frijhoff (eds), *Erasmus of Rotterdam. The Man and the Scholar*, Leiden, pp. 7–14.

Schölderle, Thomas 2002: *Das Prinzip der Macht. Neuzeitliches Politik- und Staatsdenken bei Thomas Hobbes und Niccolò Machiavelli*, Glienicke (Berlin).

Schorn-Schütte, Luise/Sven Tode 2006: Debatten über die Legitimation von Herrschaft. Politische Sprachen in der Frühen Neuzeit. Einleitende Bemerkungen, in eidem (eds), *Debatten über die Legitimation von Herrschaft. Politische Sprachen in der Frühen Neuzeit*, Berlin, pp. 9–15.

Schorn-Schütte, Luise 1996: *Die Reformation. Vorgeschichte-Verlauf-Wirkung*, München.

—— 2004a: Glaube und Obrigkeit bei Luther und im Luthertum, in M. Walther (ed.), *Religion und Politik*, Baden-Baden, pp. 87–103.

—— 2004b: Obrigkeitskritik und Widerstandsrecht. Die *politica christiana* als Legitimitätsgrundlage, in eadem (ed.), *Aspekte der politischen Kommunikation im Europa des 16. und 17. Jahrhunderts*, München, pp. 195–232.

Schottenloher, Karl (ed.) 1940: *Bibliographie zur deutschen Geschichte im Zeitalter der Glaubensspaltung (1517–1585)*, vol. 6, Leipzig.

Schottenloher, Otto 1969: Lex naturae und Lex Christi bei Erasmus, in J. Coppens (ed.), *Scrinium Erasmianum I*, Leiden, pp. 253–300.

—— 1970: Erasmus und die Respublica Christiana, in *HZ* 210, no. 2, pp. 295–323.

—— 1971: Zur *legum humanitas* bei Erasmus, in *Festschrift für Hermann Heimpel zum 70. Geburtstag*, 1. Band, Göttingen, pp. 667–683.

Schrader, Ludwig 1990: Der Herrscher nach Erasmus von Rotterdam, in H. Hecker (ed.), *Der Herrscher. Leitbild und Abbild in Mittelalter und Renaissance*, Düsseldorf, pp. 179–201.

Schramm, Percy E. 1955: *Herrschaftszeichen und Staatssymbolik*, vol. 2, Stuttgart.

—— 1966: 'Mitherrschaft im Himmel'. Ein Topos des Herrschekults in christlicher Einkleidung, in P. Wirth (ed.), *Polychronion*, Heidelberg, pp. 480–485.

—— 1969: *Kaiser, Könige und Päpste*, vol. 3, Stuttgart.

Schreiner, Klaus 2004: 'sygzeichen'. Symbolische Kommunikationsmedien in kriegerischen Konflikten des späten Mittelalters und der frühen Neuzeit, in U. Frevert/W. Braungart (eds), *Sprachen des Politischen. Medien und Medialität in der Geschichte*, Göttingen, pp. 20–94.

Schreiner, Peter 1971: Zur Bezeichnung 'Megas' und 'Megas Basileus' in der byzantinischen Kaisertitulatur, in *Byzantina* 3, pp. 173–192.

Schröder, Peter 2004: *Niccolò Machiavelli*, Frankfurt a. M./New York.

Schubart, Christof 1917: *Die Berichte über die Luthers Tod und Begräbnis*, Weimar.

Schubert, Ernst 1996: *Fürstliche Herrschaft und Territorium im Späten Mittelalter*, München.

Schuder, Gerhard 2004: *Martin Luther – Wechselbalg des Teufels und Vorreiter des Antichrists?*, Traunstein.

Schulte, J. Manuel 2001: *Speculum Regis. Studien zur Fürstenspiegel-Literatur in der griechisch-römischen Antike*, Münster.

Schulthess, Peter 1998: Wilhelm von Ockham. Summa logicae, in K. Flasch (ed.), *Hauptwerke der Philosophie. Mittelalter*, Stuttgart, pp. 402–446.

Schulze, Manfred 1996: Johannes Eck im Kampf gegen Martin Luther, in *Lutherjahrbuch* 63, pp. 39–68.

―――― 2001: Martin Luther and the Church Fathers, in I. Backus (ed.), *The Reception of the Church Fathers in the West*, vol. 2, Boston/Leiden, pp. 572–626.

Schwarcz, Andreas 1993: Die politische Vorstellungswelt der Germanen, in I. Fetscher/H. Münkler, *Pipers Handbuch der politischen Ideen*, vol. 2, München/ Zürich, pp. 17–40.

Schwarz, Reinhard ³2004: *Luther*, Göttingen.

Scott, Roger 1981: The Classical Tradition in Byzantine Historiography, in M. Mullet/R. Scott (eds), *Byzantium and the Classical Tradition*, Birmingham, pp. 61–74.

Scribner, Robert W. 1970: The Social Thought of Erasmus, in *JRH*, 6, pp. 3–26.

Seeber, David A. 1969: Was will die 'politische Theologie'?, in H. Peukert (ed.), *Diskussion zur politischen Theologie*, Mainz/München, pp. 26–37.

Segall, Hermann 1959: *Der* Defensor Pacis *des Marsilius von Padua*, Wiesbaden.

Seibt, Ferdinand 1990: *Karl V. Der Kaiser und die Reformation*, Berlin.

―――― 2005: *Die Begründung Europas. Ein Zwischenbericht über die letzten tausend Jahre*, Bonn.

Seidler, Gregorz L. 1960: *Soziale Ideen in Byzanz*, Berlin.

Selge, Kurt-V. 1976: Die Autoritätengefüge der westlichen Christenheit im Lutherkonflikt (1517–1521), in *HZ* 223, no. 3, pp. 591–617.

Şerban, Constantin 1971: La conception impériale byzantine dans le protocole et le cérémonial diplomatique roumain du Moyen Age, in *Byzantina* 3, pp. 299–309.

―――― 1972: Protocolul şi ceremonialul diplomatic la curtea lui Neagoe Basarab [Diplomatisches Zeremoniell und Protokoll am Hofe des Neagoe Basarabs], in Societatea culturală *Neagoe Basarab* din Curtea de Argeş (ed.), *Neagoe Basarab 1512–1521. La 460 de ani de la urcarea sa pe tronul Ţării Româneşti*, Bucureşti, pp. 51–61.

Sevčenko, Ihor 1954: A Neglected Byzantine Source of Muscovite Political Ideology, in *Harvard Slavic Studies* 2, pp. 141–179.

―――― 1997: On the Greek Poetic Output of Maksim Greek, in *Byzantinoslavica* 58, no. 1, pp. 1–70.

Sfez, Gérald 1998: *Machiavel, le prince sans qualités*, Paris.

Sheldon-Williams, Inglis P. 1967: The Greek Christian Platonist Tradition from the Cappadocians to Maximus and Eriugena, in A. H. Armstrong (ed.), *The Cambridge History of Later Greek and Early Medieval Philosophy*, Cambridge, pp. 423–533.

Sicken, Bernhard 1990: Ferdinand I. (1556–1564), in A. Schindling/W. Ziegler (eds), *Die Kaiser der Neuzeit (1519–1918)*, München, pp. 55–77.

Siegmund, Albert 1943: *Die überlieferung der griechischen christlichen Literatur in der lateinischen Kirche bis zum zwölften Jahrhundert*, München.

Silvestri, Artur 2006: *Bizanţ înainte de Bizanţ* [Byzantium before Byzantium], Bucureşti.

Singleton, Charles pp. 1953: The Perspective of Art, in *Kenyon Review* 15, pp. 169–189.

Siniossoglou, Niktes 2011: *Radical Palamism in Byzantium. Illumination and Utopia in Gemistos Plethon*, Cambridge.

Skinner, Quentin 1978: *The Foundations of Modern Political Thought*, vol. 2, Cambridge.

—— 2008: *Machiavelli zur Einführung*, Hamburg.

—— ⁶2009: *Visions of Politics*, vol. I: Regarding Method, Cambridge.

Smolinsky, Heribert ²2006: *Kirchengeschichte der Neuzeit I*, Düsseldorf.

Soll, Jacob 2005: *Publishing The Prince. History, Reading & the Birth of Political Criticism*, Ann Arbor.

Spade, Paul V. (ed.) 1999: *The Cambridge Companion to Ockham*, Cambridge.

Speake, Graham 2018: *A History of the Athonite Commonwealth. The Spiritual and Cultural Diaspora of Mount Athos*, Cambridge.

Spieß, Karl-H. ²2009: *Lehnsrecht, Lehnspolitik und Lehnsverwaltung der Pfalzgrafen bei Rhein im Spätmittelalter*, Stuttgart.

Spiteris, Yannis 2002: Nicola Cabasila Chamaetos, in C. G. Conticello/V. Conticello (eds), *La théologie byzantine et sa tradition*, vol. 2, Turnhout, pp. 315–410.

Spitz, Lewis W. 1953: Luther's Ecclesiology and His Concept of the Prince as Notbischof, in *Church History* 22, pp. 113–141.

Stahl, Andreas 2007: Die Grafschaft und die Stadt Mansfeld in der Lutherzeit, in H. Meller (ed.), *Luther in Mansfeld. Forschungen am Elternhaus des Reformators*, Halle, pp. 7–16.

—— 2007b: Luther in Mansfeld. Das Elternhaus, in H. Meller (ed.), *Luther in Mansfeld. Forschungen am Elternhaus des Reformators*, Halle/Saale, pp. 113–138.

Stănescu, Eugen 1961: Valoarea istorică şi literară a cronicilor muntene. Studiu introductiv [The historical and literary values of the chronicles of Wallachia], in M. Gregorian (ed.), *Cronicari munteni*, Bucureşti, pp. V–CXXVI.

—— 1963: Cronica 'Istoriile domnilor Ţării Româneşti' şi locul ei în istoria medievală românească [The chronicle 'Histories of the Wallachian princes' and its position in mediaeval Romanian historiography], in C. Grecescu (ed.), *Radu Popescu Vornicul. Istoriile domnilor Ţării Româneşti*, pp. V–L.

Stăniloae, Dumitru 1980: Introducere, in *Filocalia 19: Scara Sfântului Ioan Scărarul şi Învăţăturile lui Ava Doroftei*, Bucureşti, pp. 5–30.

Stark, Rodney 2005: *The Victory of Reason. How Christianity led to Freedom, Capitalism, and Western Success*, New York.

Ştefănescu, Ioan D. 1981: *Arta feudală în Ţările Române. Pictura murală şi icoanele de la origini până în secolul al XIX-lea* [Mediaeval art in the Danuabian Principalities. Murals and icons up to the early 19th century], Timişoara.

Ştefănescu, Iulian 1931: Legende despre Sf. Constantin în literatura română [Legends of St Constantine in Romanian literature], in *Revista Istorică Română* 1, pp. 251–297.

Ştefănescu, Ştefan 1964: Cu privire la oglindirea răscoalei conduse de Gheorghe Doja şi a urmărilor ei în gândirea social-politică a vremii [Concerning the influence of the peasants' revolt led by Gheorghe Doja on contemporary political thought], in *Studii. Revista de istorie* 17, no. 5, pp. 1117–1128.

—— 1965: *Bănia în Ţara Românească* [The institution of the banate in Wallachia], Bucureşti.

Steinlein, Hermann 1912: *Luthers Doktorat. Zum 400jährigen Jubiläum desselben (18. und 19. Oktober 1912)*, Leipzig.

Steinmetz, Fritz 1969: Staatengründung – Aus Schwäche oder natürlichem Geselligkeitsdrang?, in P. Steinmetz (ed.), *Politeia und Res Publica. Beiträge zum Verständnis von Politik, Recht und Staat in der Antike*, Wiesbaden, pp. 181–199.

Sternberger, Dolf 1974: *Machiavellis Principe und der Begriff des Politischen*, Wiesbaden.

Stewart, Columba OSB 2003: Evagrius Ponticus on Monastic Pedagogy, in J. Behr/A. Louth/D. Conomos (eds), *Abba. The Tradition of Orthodoxy in the West*, New York, pp. 241–271.

Stiglmayr, Joseph 1913: *Kirchenväter und Klassizismus*, Freiburg i. Br.

Stockhammer, Nicolas 2009: *Das Prinzip Macht. Die Rationalität politischer Macht bei Thukydides, Machiavelli und Michel Foucault*, Baden-Baden.

Stoicescu, Nicolae 1970: La politique de Neagoe Basarab et ses *Préceptes* pour son fils Teodosie, in *Revue Roumaine d'Histoire* 9, no. 1, pp. 18–42.

Stollberg-Rilinger, Barbara 2005: Was heißt Kulturgeschichte des Politischen?, in eadem (ed.), *Was heißt Kulturgeschichte des Politischen?*, Zeitschrift für Historische Forschung, Beiheft 35, Berlin, pp. 9–24.

Strauss, Leo 1958: *Thoughts on Machiavelli*, Chicago.

Struve, Tillman 1993: Regnum und Sacerdotium, in I. Fetscher/H. Münkler, *Pipers Handbuch der politischen Ideen*, vol. 2, München/Zürich, pp. 189–242.

Stümke, Volker 2007: *Das Friedensverständnis Martin Luthers*, Stuttgart.

Stürner, Wolfgang 1987: Peccatum und Potestas. *Der Sündenfall und die Entstehung der herrscherlichen Gewalt im mittelalterlichen Staatsdenken*, Sigmaringen.

—— 2009: *Friedrich II.*, Darmstadt.

Sumberg, Theodore A. 1993: *Political Literature of Europa Before and After Machiavelli*, Lanham.

Sutton, Jonathan/Wil van den Bercken (eds) 2003: *Orthodox Christianity and Contemporary Europe*, Leuven.

Tanaşoca, Nicolae-Ş. 2012: Din nou despre scrisoarea lui Manuil din Corint către Neagoe Basarab [Once more on the letter of Manuel of Corinth to Neagoe Basarab], in N.-C. Câdă (ed.), *Sfântul Voievod Neagoe Basarab – ctitor de biserici şi cultură românească*, Bucureşti, pp. 350–429.

Tapkova-Zaimova, Vasilka 2010a: Constantin le Grand et les idées étatiques en Bulgarie, in eadem, *Byzance, la Bulgarie, les Balkans*, Plovdiv, pp. 471–478.

—— 2010b: Les monuments de migration dans les Balkans jusqu'à l'époque ottomane, in eadem, *Byzance, la Bulgarie, les Balkans*, Plovdiv, pp. 3–175.

Tappe, Eric D. (ed.) 1964: *Documents concerning Romanian History (1427–1601)*, The Hague.

Tarlton, Charles D. 2007: Machiavelli's Burden: The Prince as Literary Text, in P. Vilches/G. Seaman (eds), *Seeking Real Truths. Multidisciplinary Perspectives on Machiavelli*, Leiden/Boston, pp. 43–67.

Tatakis, Basil 1985: On the Methodology of Gregory Palamas, in *ABR* 36, no. 2, pp. 215–227.

—— 2003: *Byzantine Philosophy*, Indianapolis/Cambridge.

—— 2007: *Christian Philosophy in the Patristic and Byzantine Tradition*, Rollinsford.

Taube, Otto Freiherr von (ed.) 1948: *Von Kreuzzug, Krieg und den Juden. Zwei Briefe des Bernhards von Clairvaux*, München.

Tenace, Michelina 2005: *Creştinismul bizantin. Istorie, teologie, tradiţii monastice*, aus dem Italienischen, Bucureşti (Original: *Il cristianesimo bizantino. Storia, teologia, tradizione monastica*, Roma 2000).

Teodor, Pompiliu 1962: Două manuscrise copiate pentru biblioteca lui Ştefan Cantacuzino [Two manuscripts produced for the library of Ştefan Cantacuzino], in *Anuarul Institutului de Istorie din Cluj* 5, pp. 229–232.

Theißen, Gerd 2007: *Erleben und Verhalten der ersten Christen. Eine Psychologie des Urchristentums*, Gütersloh.

Theodor, Dan G. 2008: Realităţi etnice, demografice şi culturale la Est de Carpaţi în Evul Mediu Timpuriu (secolele VIII–XII) [Ethnic, demographic and cultural realities in the early Middle Ages east of the Carpathian mountains (8th–12th c.)], in D. Ţeicu/I. Cândea (eds), *Românii în Europa medievală (între Orientul bizantin şi Occidentul latin)*, Brăila, pp. 161–174.

Theodorescu, Răzvan 1972: Locul curţii de Argeş la începuturile artei şi culturii medievale româneşti [The relevance of the princely court of Argeş for the beginnings of mediaeval Romanian art and culture], in Societatea culturală

Neagoe Basarab din Curtea de Argeş (ed.), *Neagoe Basarab 1512–1521. La 460 de ani de la urcarea sa pe tronul Ţării Româneşti, Bucureşti*, pp. 94–101.

—— 1974: *Bizanţ, Balcani, Occident la începuturile culturii medievale româneşti (sec. X–XIV)* [Byzantium, Balkans, Occident at the beginning of Romanian culture in the middle ages (10th–14th c.)], Bucureşti.

Thesleff, Holger (ed.) 1968: The Pythagorean Texts of the Hellenistic Period, in *Acta Academiae Aboensis*, Ser. A, Humaniora, vol. 30, pp. 1–266.

Thielicke, Helmut ⁵1981: *Theologische Ethik*, vol. 1: Prinzipienlehre, Tübingen.

Thompson, C. R. 1955: Erasmus as Internationalist and Cosmopolitan, in *ARG* 46, no. 2, pp. 167–195.

Tiersch, Claudia 2002: *Johannes Chrysostomus in Konstantinopel*, Tübingen.

Tinnefeld, Franz H. 1971: *Kategorien der Kaiserkritik in der byzantinischen Historiografie*, München.

—— 1986: Faktoren des Aufstieges zur Patriarchenwürde im späten Byzanz, in *Jahrbuch der österreichischen Byzantinistik* 36, pp. 89–115.

Tiţa, Claudia 2009: Neagoe Basarab 'Ctitor mare a toată Sfetagora'. Icoanele şi avatarurile lor sau despre un tezaur în mişcare [Neagoe Basarab 'great Ktetor of all Sfetagora'. The icons and their avatars or on a movable treasure], in D. Gligore (ed.), *Sfântul Voievod Neagoe Basarab, Domnul Ţării Româneşti*, Curtea de Argeş, pp. 127–170.

Todoran, Isidor/Ioan Zăgrean 1991: *Teologia dogmatică* [Dogmatics], Bucureşti.

Toma, Iancu St. 1943: *Domnia în concepţia Învăţăturilor lui Neagoe Basarab* [The idea of rule in the teachings of Neagoe Basarab], reprint from: *Revista de drept public* 3–4, pp. 3–49.

Tommasini, Oreste 1883–1911: *La vita e gli scritti di Niccolò Machiavelli*, 3 vols, Torino/Roma.

Tracy, James D. 1978: *The Politics of Erasmus. A Pacifist Intellectual and his Political Milieu*, Toronto.

Trautmann, Rudolf 1931: Einleitung, in idem (ed.), *Die altrussische Nestor-Chronik Povest' vremennych let*, Leipzig, pp. VII–XXII.

Trease, Geoffrey 1974: *Die Condottieri. Söldnerführer, Glücksritter und Fürsten der Renaissance*, München.

Treatgold, Warren 1981: Photios and the Reading Public for Classical Philology in Byzantium, in M. Mullet/R. Scott (eds), *Byzantium and the Classical Tradition*, Birmingham, pp. 123–126.

Treptow, Kurt W. 2000: *Vlad III Dracula. The Life and Times of the Historical Dracula*, Iaşi.

Treu, Ursula ³1998: Nachwort, in eadem (ed.), *Physiologus*, Hanau, pp. 111–132.

Triwunatz, Milosch 1903: *Guillaume Budés De l'institution du Prince*, Erlangen.

Troeltsch, Ernst 1913: Historische und dogmatische Methode in der Theologie, in idem, *Zur religiösen Lage, Religionsphilosophie und Ethik*, Tübingen, pp. 729–753.

—— 1915: *Augustinus, die christliche Antike und das Mittelalter*, München/Berlin.

—— 2002: Die Krisis des Historismus, in idem, *Schriften zur Politik und Kulturphilosophie (1918–1923)*, ed. G. Hübinger, Berlin/New York, pp. 437–455.

Trow, Meirion J. 2003: *Vlad the Impaler. In Search of the Real Dracula*, London.

Turdeanu, Emil 1939: *Din vechile schimburi culturale dintre români şi jugoslavi* [On historic cultural exchanges between Romanians and Yugoslavs], reprinted from: N. Cartojan (ed.), *Cercetări literare III*, Bucureşti.

—— 1947: *La littérature bulgare du XIVe siècle et sa diffusion dans les Pays Roumains*, Paris.

—— 1985a: Les Principautés Roumaines et les Slaves du Sud. Rapports littéraires et religieux, in idem, *Études de littérature roumaine et d'écrits slaves et grecs des Principautés Roumaines*, Leiden, pp. 1–14.

—— 1985b: Le roman de Barlaam et Joasaph en roumain. Les versions d'Udrişte Năsturel, de Vlad Boţulescu et des Vies des Saints, in idem, *Études de littérature roumaine et d'écrits slaves et grecs des Principautés Roumaines*, Leiden, pp. 329–380.

Ueberweg, Friedrich [11]1928: *Die patristische und scholastische Philosophie*, Berlin.

Ulrich, Hans G. [2]2007: *Wie Geschöpfe leben. Konturen evangelischer Ethik*, Berlin.

Unger, Miles J. 2008: *Machiavelli. A Biography*, New York.

Unruh, Georg-C. von, 1975: Obrigkeit und Amt bei Luther und das von ihm beeinflusste Staatsverständnis, in R. Schnur (ed.), *Staatsräson. Studien zur Geschichte eines politischen Begriffs*, Berlin, pp. 339–361.

Vacano, Diego A. von, 2007: *The Art of Power. Machiavelli, Nietzsche and the Making of Aesthetic Political Theory*, Lanham.

Văetişi, Atanasia 2012: Portretistica votivă a lui Neagoe Basarab [The epitaph portraits of Neagoe Basarab], in N.-C. Câdă (ed.), *Sfântul Voievod Neagoe Basarab – ctitor de biserici şi cultură românească*, Bucureşti, pp. 185–228.

Vainio, Olli-P. 2008: *Justification and Participation in Christ. The Development of the Lutheran Doctrine of Justification from Luther to the Formula of Concord (1580)*, Leiden/Boston.

Van der Leeuw, Gerhard 1933: *Phänomenologie der Religion*, Tübingen.

Van der Loo, Hans/Wilem van Reijen 1992: *Modernisierung. Projekt und Paradox*, München.

Variot, Estelle 2005: Le message humaniste des Enseignements de Neagoe Basarab à son fils Theodosie, in *Cahiers d'études romanes* 14, pp. 203–222.

Vârtosu, Emil 1960: *Titulatura domnilor și asocierea la domnie în Țara Românească și Moldova până în secolul al XVI-lea* [The titles of the princes and co-regency in Wallachia and Moldavia up to the 16th c.], București.

Vasoli, Cesare 2006: *Ficino, Savonarola, Machiavelli. Studi di storia della cultura*, Torino.

Vătășianu, Virgil 1959: *Istoria artei feudale în Țările Române* [History of feudal art in the Danubian Principalities], vol. 1, București.

Vergatti, Radu Ș. [2]2009: *Neagoe Basarab. Viața, opera, domnia* [Neagoe Basarab. Life, works, reign], Curtea de Argeș.

Verosta, Stephan 1960: *Johannes Chrysostomus. Staatsphilosoph und Geschichtstheologe*, Graz.

Verspohl, Franz-J. 2001: *Michelangelo Buonaroti und Niccolò Machiavelli. Der David, die Piazza, die Republik*, Wien.

Vilches, Patricia/G. Seaman (eds) 2007: *Seeking Real Truths. Multidisciplinary Perspectives on Machiavelli*, Leiden/Boston.

Vilches, Patricia 2007: The Enduring Power of Niccolò Machiavelli. An Overview of His Life and Times, in P. Vilches/G. Seaman (eds), *Seeking Real Truths. Multidisciplinary Perspectives on Machiavelli*, Leiden/Boston, pp. 1–17.

Villari, Pasquale 1882: *Niccolò Machiavelli und seine Zeit. Durch neue Dokumente beleuchtet*, 2 vols, Rudolstadt.

Vincent, Auguste 1937: Les premières editions de l'Institutio Principis Christiani d'Érasme, in *Mélanges offerts a M. Marcel Godet*, Neuchatel, pp. 91–96.

Vind, Anna 2007: 'Christus factus est peccatum metaphorice'. über die theologische Verwendung rhetorischer Figuren bei Luther unter Einbeziehung Quintilians, in O. Bayer/B. Gleede (eds), *Creator est creatura. Luthers Christologie als Lehre von der Idiomenkommunikation*, Berlin/New York, pp. 95–124.

Viroli, Maurizio 2000: *Niccolò's Smile. A Biography of Machiavelli*, New York.

—— 2008: *How to Read Machiavelli*, London.

Voegelin, Eric 1951: Machiavelli's *Prince*: Background and Formation, in *The Review of Politics* 13, no. 2, pp. 142–168.

—— 1957: *Order and History III*, Baton Rouge.

Voet, Leon 1988: Erasmus and His Correspondents, in J. Sperna Weiland/W. T. M. Frijhoff (eds), *Erasmus of Rotterdam. The Man and the Scholar*, Leiden, pp. 195–202.

Vogelstein, Max 1930: *Kaiseridee-Romidee und das Verhältnis von Staat und Kirche*, Breslau.

Vogt, Albert/J. Hausherr (eds) 1932: Oraison funèbre de Basile I par son fils Léon VI le Sage, in *Orientalia Christiana* 26, no. 1, Rom.

Voigt-Goy, Christopher 2008: Die gesellschaftlichen Stände, die Schöpfung und der Fall. Zur Ständelehre in Luthers Genesisvorlesung (1535), in T. Wagner/D.

Vieweger/K. Erlemann (eds), *Kontexte. Festschrift für Hans Jochen Boecker*, Neunkirchen-Vluyn, pp. 65–80.

—— 2014: *Potestas und ministerium publicum. Eine Studie zur Amtstheologie im Mittelalter und bei Martin Luther*, Tübingen.

Voigt, Rüdiger 2004: Im Zeichen des Staates. Niccolò Machiavelli und die Staatsräson, in H. Münkler/R. Voigt/R. Walkenhaus (eds), *Demaskierung der Macht. Niccolò Machiavellis Staats- und Politikverständnis*, Baden-Baden, pp. 33–60.

Völkl, Ekkehard 1979: Neagoe Basarab IV, in *Biographisches Lexikon zur Geschichte Südosteuropas*, vol. 3, München, pp. 296–297.

Volz, Hanz 1967: Die Urfassung von Luthers 95 Thesen, in *ZKG* 78, no. 1–2, pp. 67–93.

Vranoussis, Leandros 1972: Texte şi documente româneşti inedite din Grecia. Gândul şi fapta marelui domn al Ţării Româneşti [New Romanian documents and texts from Greece. Thoughts and deeds of the grand lord of Wallachia], in *Magazin istoric* 6, no. 2, pp. 6–10.

—— 1978: Les *Conseils* attribués au prince Neagoe (1512–1521) et le manuscrit autographe de leur auteur grec, in *Actes du IIe congrès international des études du sud-est européen (Athènes 7–13 mai 1970)*, vol. 4, Athènes, pp. 377–383.

Wadell, Chrysogonus 1982: The Reform of the Liturgy from a Renaissance Perspective, in R. L. Benson/G. Constable, *Renaissance and Renewal in the Twelfth Century*, Oxford, pp. 88–109.

Wagner, Hartmut 2006: *Bezugspunkte europäischer Identität. Territorium, Geschichte, Sprache, Werte, Symbole, Öffentlichkeit – Worauf kann sich das Wir-Gefühl der Europäer beziehen?*, Münster.

Wallace, Peter G. 2004: *The Long European Reformation. Religion, Political Conflict, and the Search for Conformity (1350–1750)*, Hampshire/New York.

Walser, Fritz 1959: *Die spanischen Zentralbehörden und der Staatsrat Karls V.*, Göttingen.

Walsh, Mary 2007: Historical Reception of Machiavelli, in P. Vilches/G. Seaman (eds), *Seeking Real Truths. Multidisciplinary Perspectives on Machiavelli*, Leiden/Boston, pp. 273–301.

Walter, Peter 1991: *Theologie aus dem Geist der Rhetorik. Zur Schriftauslegung des Erasmus von Rotterdam*, Mainz.

Walther, Andreas 1911: *Die Anfänge Karls V.*, Leipzig.

Walther, Manfred 2004: Luthers dualistische politische Theologie der zwei Reiche und Regimente – Das Problem der Lokalisierung der sichtbaren Kirche, in M. Walther (ed.), *Religion und Politik*, Baden-Baden, pp. 105–112.

Ware, Kallistos 1986: The Origins of the Jesus Prayer. Diadochus, Gaza, Sinai, in C. Jones/G. Wainwright/E. Yarnold SJ (eds), *The Study of Spirituality*, New York/Oxford, pp. 175–184.

—— 1987: *The Jesus Prayer*, New York.

—— ⁷1996: *The Orthodox Way*, New York.

—— 2000: *The Inner Kingdom*, New York.

—— 2002: How Do We Enter the Heart?, in J. S. Cutsinger (ed.), *Paths to the Heart. Sufism and Christian East*, Bloomington, pp. 2–23.

Warkotsch, Albert 1973: *Antike Philosophie im Urteil der Kirchenväter*, Paderborn.

Weier, Reinhold 1967: *Das Thema vom verborgenen Gott von Nikolaus von Kues zu Martin Luther*, Münster.

Wellesz, Egon 1949: *A History of Byzantine Music and Hymnography*, Oxford.

Wels, Henrik 2004: *Aristotelisches Wissen und Glauben im 15. Jahrhundert*, Amsterdam/Philadelphia.

Wendel, Carl 1942: Die erste kaiserliche Bibliothek in Konstantinopel, in *ZfB* 59, no. 5–6, pp. 193–209.

Wendelborn, Gert 1983: *Martin Luther. Leben und reformatorisches Werk*, Wien.

Wendenbourg, Dorothea 1980: *Geist oder Energie? Zur Frage der innergöttlichen Verankerung des christlichen Lebens in der byzantinischen Theologie*, München.

—— 1995: Die Einheit der Reformation als historisches Problem, in B. Hamm/B. Moeller/D. Wendenbourg (eds), *Reformations-Theorien*, Göttingen, pp. 31–51.

Wenzig, Joseph (ed.) 1855: *Der neue Rath des Herrn Smil von Pardubic*, Leipzig.

Werner, Ferdinand 1908: Königtum und Lehnswesen im französischen Nationalepos, in *Romanische Forschungen* 25, no. 2, pp. 321–443.

Werner, Michael/Bénédicte Zimmermann 2002: Vergleich, Transfer, Verflechtung. Der Einsatz der histoire croisee und die Herausforderung des Transnationalen, in *Geschichte und Gesellschaft* 28, no. 4, pp. 607–636.

Wicks, Jared 1983: *Cajetan und die Anfänge der Reformation*, Münster. Williams, Anna N. 1999: *The Ground of Union. Deification in Aquinas and Palamas*, New York/Oxford.

Wilson, Nigel G. 1967: The Libraries of the Byzantine World, in *RBS* 8, no. 1, pp. 53–80.

—— 1975: Books and Readers in Byzantium, in *Byzantine Books and Bookmen*, ed. Dumbarton Oaks Center for Byzantine Studies, Washington, DC, pp. 1–15.

Winterhager, Wilhelm E. 1999: Ablaßkritik als Indikator historischen Wandels vor 1517. Ein Beitrag zu Voraussetzungen und Einordnung der Reformation, in *ARG* 90, pp. 6–71.

Wirth, Gerhard 1986: Die leidige Schule. Zum Problem von Schul- und Bildungsreform in der ausgehenden Antike, in L. Kriss-Rettenbeck/M.

Liedtke (eds), *Erziehungs- und Unterrichtsmethoden im historischen Wandel*, Bad Heilbrunn, pp. 74–91.

—— 1989: Lehrer, Kirche, Kaiser. Zum literarischen Bild am Ende der Antike, in J. G. Prinz von Hohenzollern (ed.), *Schreiber, Magister, Lehrer. Zur Geschichte und Funktion eines Berufsstandes*, Bad Heilbrunn, pp. 83–118.

Witt, Christian Volkmar 2011: *Protestanten. Das Werden eines Integrationsbegriffs in der Frühen Neuzeit*, Tübingen.

Wohlfeil, Reiner 1973: Reformation als frühbürgerliche Revolution, in F. Reuter (ed.), *Luther in Worms (1521–1971)*, Worms, pp. 44–59.

Wolf, Ernst 1965: Königsherrschaft Christi und lutherische Zwei-Reiche-Lehre, in idem, *Peregrinatio II*, München, pp. 207–229.

Wolf, Gunther (ed.) 1972: *Luther und die Obrigkeit*, Darmstadt.

Wolf, Peter 1983: Libanios und sein Kampf um die hellenische Bildung, in G. Fatouros/T. Krischer (eds), *Libanios*, Darmstadt, pp. 68–83.

Wolgast, Eike 1970: Die Wittenberger Luther-Ausgabe, in *Archiv f. Geschichte d. Buchwesens* 11, no. 1–2, pp. 1–335.

—— 1977: *Die Wittenberger Theologie und die Politik der evangelischen Stände*, Gütersloh.

Wolin, Sheldon S. [6]1960: *Politics and Visions. Continuity and Innovation in Western Political Thought*, Boston.

Wolter, Allan B. 2003: *Scotus and Ockham. Selected Essays*, New York.

Wolter-von dem Knesebeck, Harald 2013: Der Kontinent der Städte und Wege. Europa und seine Stellung in Welt und Weltgeschichte auf der Ebstorfer Weltkarte, in M. Bernsen/M. Becher/E. Brüggen (eds), *Gründungsmythen Europas im Mittelalter*, Göttingen, pp. 105–123.

Wriedt, Markus 1991: *Gnade und Erwählung. Eine Untersuchung zu Johann von Staupitz und Martin Luther*, Mainz.

—— 2007: Via Augustini – Ausprägungen des spätmittelalterlichen Augustinismus in der observanten Kongregation der Augustinereremiten, in C. Bultmann/V. Leppin/A. Lindner (eds), *Luther und das monastische Erbe*, Tübingen, pp. 9–38.

Xenopol, Alexandru D. [2]1953: *Istoria românilor din Dacia Traiană* [History of the Romanians in *Dacia Traiana*], vol. 2, Madrid.

—— 1889: *Istoria românilor din Dacia Traiană* [History of the Romanians in the Dacia of Trajan], vol. II/1, Iași.

Zacher, Angelika 2009: *Grenzwissen-Wissensgrenzen. Raumstruktur und Wissensorganisation im Alexanderroman Ulrichs von Etzenbach*, Stuttgart.

Zăgrean, Radu 2002: *Der Begriff der* virtù *bei Machiavelli*, München.

Zahariuc, Petronel (ed.) 2010: Câteva documente de la Neagoe Basarab [Some documents of Neagoe Basarab], in *Studii și materiale de istorie medie* 28, pp. 193–213.

Zamfirescu, Dan 1963: Învățăturile lui Neagoe Basarab. Problema autenticității [The teachings of Neagoe Basarab. The question of authenticity], in *Romanoslavica* 8, pp. 341–401. Reprinted in idem, *Studii și articole de literatură română veche*, București 1967, pp. 69–83.

—— 1971: În legătură cu structura Învățăturilor lui Neagoe Basarab [On the structure of the teachings of Neagoe Basarab], in *Luceafărul*, Nr. 7 vom 13. Febr.

—— 1973: *Neagoe Basarab și Învățăturile către fiul său Theodosie. Problemele controversate* [Neagoe Basarab and the teachings to his son Theodosius. Controversial questions], București.

—— 1996: Marea carte a identității românești în Europa Renașterii și în cultura universală [The great book of Romanian identity in the Renaissance and in world culture], in G. Mihăilă (ed.), *Învățăturile lui Neagoe Basarab către fiul său Theodosie*, București, pp. V–XXIV.

—— 2009: O creație singulară a Răsăritului ortodox și valorficare ei în cultura română [A singular creation of the Orthodox East and its uses in Romanian culture], in I. Ică Jr. (ed.), *Simeon Monahul. Cuvinte pentru străpungerea inimii*, Sibiu, pp. 5–16.

Zecherle, Andreas 2012: Die Verantwortung der Obrigkeit für die Kommunikation des Evangeliums aus der Sicht Luthers und seiner Anhänger, in J. Haberer/B. Hamm (eds), *Medialität, Unmittelbarkeit, Präsenz. Die Nähe des Heils im Verständnis der Reformation*, Tübingen, pp. 341–358.

Zelepos, Ioannis 2011: 'Unser orientalisch-christliches Geschlecht' – Zur Formierung eines osmanisch-orthodoxen Identitätzkonzept in der zweiten Hälfte des 18. Jahrhunderts, in M. Oikonomou/M. A. Stassinopoulou/I. Zelepos (eds), *Griechische Dimensionen südosteuropäischer Kultur seit dem 18. Jahrhundert*, Frankfurt a. M., pp. 111–124.

Zibleius-Chen, Karola 1988: Das alte Ägypten, in I. Fetscher/H. Münkler (eds), *Pipers Handbuch der politischen Ideen*, vol. 1, München/Zürich, pp. 113–134.

Ziegler, Walter 2008: *Die Entscheidung deutscher Länder für oder gegen Luther. Studien zu Reformation und Konfessionalisierung im 16. und 17. Jahrhundert*, Münster.

Zingerle, Pius 1870: Einleitung, in idem (ed.), *Ausgewählte Schriften des Hl. Ephräm von Syrien*, vol. 1, Kempten, pp. 231–234.

Zorzi, Andrea 2011: The 'Material Constitution' of the Florentine Dominion, in W. J. Connell/A. Zorzi (eds), *Florentine Tuscany. Structures and Practices of Power*, Cambridge, pp. 6–31.

Zumkeller, Adelar 1979: 'Augustiner-Eremiten', in *TRE* 4, pp. 728–739.

Zwierlein, Cornel 2006: *Discorso und Lex Dei. Die Entstehung neuer Denkformen im 16. Jahrhundert und die Wahrnehmung der französischen Religionskriege in Italien und Deutschland*, Göttingen.

—— 2007: 'Convertire tutta l'Alemagna'. Fürstenkonversionen in den Strategierahmen der römischen Europapolitik um 1600. Zum Verhältnis von 'Machiavellismus' und *'Konfessionalismus'*, in H. Lotz-Heumann/J. F. Missfelder/M. Pohlig (eds), *Konversion und Konfession in der Frühen Neuzeit*, Gütersloh, pp. 63–105.

Index

Studies in Eastern Orthodoxy

Edited by René Gothóni and Graham Speake

This series is concerned with Eastern Orthodox Christianity in its various manifestations. Originating as the church of the East Roman or Byzantine empire, Eastern Orthodoxy comprises the group of churches that have traditionally owed allegiance to the Ecumenical Patriarchate in Constantinople. The Orthodox Church has exercised unparalleled influence over the history, thought, and culture of the region and remains one of the most dynamic and creative forces in Christendom today. The series will publish studies in English, both monographs and edited collections, in all areas of social, cultural, and political activity in which the Orthodox Church can be seen to have played a major role.

Vol. 6   Mihai-D. Grigore
         Neagoe Basarab – Princeps Christianus. The Semantics of
         Christianitas in Comparison with Erasmus, Luther and Machiavelli
         (1513–1523).
         2021. ISBN 978-1-80079-060-5